BARRON'S

MAT™

MILLER ANALOGIES TEST™

11TH EDITION

Robert J. Sternberg, Ph.D.
Professor of Psychology and Education, University of Wyoming

Karin Sternberg, Ph.D.
Sternberg Consulting, LLC

BARRON'S

All inquiries should be addressed to:
Barron's Educational Series, Inc.
250 Wireless Boulevard
Hauppauge, New York 11788
www.barronseduc.com

ISBN: 978-1-4380-0226-2

International Standard Serial No. 1533-7715

Printed in the United States of America

9 8 7 6 5 4 3

10%
POST-CONSUMER
WASTE
Paper contains a minimum
of 10% post-consumer
waste (PCW). Paper used
in this book was derived
from certified, sustainable
forestlands.

Contents

Part 6   *MAT* Practice Tests / 145

Introduction

WHAT THIS BOOK CAN DO FOR YOU

This book is designed to help bring you to the point where your performance on the *Miller Analogies Test (MAT)* is the best of which you are capable. If the book succeeds in doing so, it has succeeded admirably, and so have you.

Many individuals do not reveal their true abilities on the *MAT* and other standardized tests. There are several reasons why this is so:

1. *The mystique of standardized tests.* One reason for underperformance stems from the aura of mystery that surrounds standardized tests. The mystique of standardized tests evolves from three common misconceptions. The first misconception is that the tests evaluate the whole person. In fact, the tests evaluate just a small segment of the person's behavior, and their evaluation of this small segment of behavior is, as we shall soon see, highly fallible. A second misconception is that there is nothing one can do to improve one's test performance, since the tests measure something that is innate rather than something that is learned. In fact, there is a great deal you can do to improve your test score, and in reading this book and in working on the practice tests, you are already doing it. The third misconception is an emotional one—it is the feeling of awe that people often have when faced with something they don't understand. By the time you are done with this book, however, you will understand the *Miller Analogies Test* very well, and what once seemed mysterious to you will be quite familiar.

   There are certain basic facts about the *MAT* that anyone who is to take the test ought to know. Some of these facts are readily available to the public through various pamphlets provided by the test publisher, but others are not. Many of the most important facts are among the least well known. Parts Two and Four of this book contain the basic facts that you ought to know about the *MAT*.

2. *Unfamiliarity with test-taking strategies and skills.* Many individuals never acquire the test-taking strategies and skills that would enable them to optimize their performance on the *MAT*. As a result, they make blunders that reflect their deficiencies in test-taking rather than in intellectual ability. Part Three of this book shows you just what an analogy is, the types of analogies that appear on the *MAT*, and the strategies you can employ to systematically

TIP

Although there are 120 items, only 100 are scored. The other 20 are experimental items. It is not possible to tell which items are scored and which are experimental.

approach *MAT* problems. Included are helpful hints that will prove useful to you in preparing for and then taking the actual test.

Part Five will help you in learning the words commonly used on the *MAT* and in reviewing some of the basic facts from the content areas used in the test. As you will see, the number of questions from each content area is small, and an extensive review of all possible areas is simply unfeasible.

3. *Lack of practice in taking MAT-type tests.* It is one thing to have developed a repertoire of test-taking strategies and skills, but it is another to readily apply them. Part Six of this book contains ten practice tests that are similar in difficulty, content, and form to the actual *MAT.* Like the actual test, each practice test has 120 items, is timed for 60 minutes, and requires a multiple-choice answer selection process from among four possible alternatives. As in the real test, answers are recorded on a separate answer sheet. By taking these tests, you will have an opportunity to utilize the test-taking strategies that you will acquire. You will build up a facility with *MAT*-type questions so that when you take the actual test, you will not have to waste time and points warming up to the types of questions that appear.

Before reading about the *MAT* and how to improve your performance on it, take the pretest in Part One to give yourself a sense of what the *MAT* is like. You will then stand to profit more from the suggestions that follow.

Answer Sheet
PRETEST

1 Ⓐ Ⓑ Ⓒ Ⓓ	31 Ⓐ Ⓑ Ⓒ Ⓓ	61 Ⓐ Ⓑ Ⓒ Ⓓ	91 Ⓐ Ⓑ Ⓒ Ⓓ
2 Ⓐ Ⓑ Ⓒ Ⓓ	32 Ⓐ Ⓑ Ⓒ Ⓓ	62 Ⓐ Ⓑ Ⓒ Ⓓ	92 Ⓐ Ⓑ Ⓒ Ⓓ
3 Ⓐ Ⓑ Ⓒ Ⓓ	33 Ⓐ Ⓑ Ⓒ Ⓓ	63 Ⓐ Ⓑ Ⓒ Ⓓ	93 Ⓐ Ⓑ Ⓒ Ⓓ
4 Ⓐ Ⓑ Ⓒ Ⓓ	34 Ⓐ Ⓑ Ⓒ Ⓓ	64 Ⓐ Ⓑ Ⓒ Ⓓ	94 Ⓐ Ⓑ Ⓒ Ⓓ
5 Ⓐ Ⓑ Ⓒ Ⓓ	35 Ⓐ Ⓑ Ⓒ Ⓓ	65 Ⓐ Ⓑ Ⓒ Ⓓ	95 Ⓐ Ⓑ Ⓒ Ⓓ
6 Ⓐ Ⓑ Ⓒ Ⓓ	36 Ⓐ Ⓑ Ⓒ Ⓓ	66 Ⓐ Ⓑ Ⓒ Ⓓ	96 Ⓐ Ⓑ Ⓒ Ⓓ
7 Ⓐ Ⓑ Ⓒ Ⓓ	37 Ⓐ Ⓑ Ⓒ Ⓓ	67 Ⓐ Ⓑ Ⓒ Ⓓ	97 Ⓐ Ⓑ Ⓒ Ⓓ
8 Ⓐ Ⓑ Ⓒ Ⓓ	38 Ⓐ Ⓑ Ⓒ Ⓓ	68 Ⓐ Ⓑ Ⓒ Ⓓ	98 Ⓐ Ⓑ Ⓒ Ⓓ
9 Ⓐ Ⓑ Ⓒ Ⓓ	39 Ⓐ Ⓑ Ⓒ Ⓓ	69 Ⓐ Ⓑ Ⓒ Ⓓ	99 Ⓐ Ⓑ Ⓒ Ⓓ
10 Ⓐ Ⓑ Ⓒ Ⓓ	40 Ⓐ Ⓑ Ⓒ Ⓓ	70 Ⓐ Ⓑ Ⓒ Ⓓ	100 Ⓐ Ⓑ Ⓒ Ⓓ
11 Ⓐ Ⓑ Ⓒ Ⓓ	41 Ⓐ Ⓑ Ⓒ Ⓓ	71 Ⓐ Ⓑ Ⓒ Ⓓ	101 Ⓐ Ⓑ Ⓒ Ⓓ
12 Ⓐ Ⓑ Ⓒ Ⓓ	42 Ⓐ Ⓑ Ⓒ Ⓓ	72 Ⓐ Ⓑ Ⓒ Ⓓ	102 Ⓐ Ⓑ Ⓒ Ⓓ
13 Ⓐ Ⓑ Ⓒ Ⓓ	43 Ⓐ Ⓑ Ⓒ Ⓓ	73 Ⓐ Ⓑ Ⓒ Ⓓ	103 Ⓐ Ⓑ Ⓒ Ⓓ
14 Ⓐ Ⓑ Ⓒ Ⓓ	44 Ⓐ Ⓑ Ⓒ Ⓓ	74 Ⓐ Ⓑ Ⓒ Ⓓ	104 Ⓐ Ⓑ Ⓒ Ⓓ
15 Ⓐ Ⓑ Ⓒ Ⓓ	45 Ⓐ Ⓑ Ⓒ Ⓓ	75 Ⓐ Ⓑ Ⓒ Ⓓ	105 Ⓐ Ⓑ Ⓒ Ⓓ
16 Ⓐ Ⓑ Ⓒ Ⓓ	46 Ⓐ Ⓑ Ⓒ Ⓓ	76 Ⓐ Ⓑ Ⓒ Ⓓ	106 Ⓐ Ⓑ Ⓒ Ⓓ
17 Ⓐ Ⓑ Ⓒ Ⓓ	47 Ⓐ Ⓑ Ⓒ Ⓓ	77 Ⓐ Ⓑ Ⓒ Ⓓ	107 Ⓐ Ⓑ Ⓒ Ⓓ
18 Ⓐ Ⓑ Ⓒ Ⓓ	48 Ⓐ Ⓑ Ⓒ Ⓓ	78 Ⓐ Ⓑ Ⓒ Ⓓ	108 Ⓐ Ⓑ Ⓒ Ⓓ
19 Ⓐ Ⓑ Ⓒ Ⓓ	49 Ⓐ Ⓑ Ⓒ Ⓓ	79 Ⓐ Ⓑ Ⓒ Ⓓ	109 Ⓐ Ⓑ Ⓒ Ⓓ
20 Ⓐ Ⓑ Ⓒ Ⓓ	50 Ⓐ Ⓑ Ⓒ Ⓓ	80 Ⓐ Ⓑ Ⓒ Ⓓ	110 Ⓐ Ⓑ Ⓒ Ⓓ
21 Ⓐ Ⓑ Ⓒ Ⓓ	51 Ⓐ Ⓑ Ⓒ Ⓓ	81 Ⓐ Ⓑ Ⓒ Ⓓ	111 Ⓐ Ⓑ Ⓒ Ⓓ
22 Ⓐ Ⓑ Ⓒ Ⓓ	52 Ⓐ Ⓑ Ⓒ Ⓓ	82 Ⓐ Ⓑ Ⓒ Ⓓ	112 Ⓐ Ⓑ Ⓒ Ⓓ
23 Ⓐ Ⓑ Ⓒ Ⓓ	53 Ⓐ Ⓑ Ⓒ Ⓓ	83 Ⓐ Ⓑ Ⓒ Ⓓ	113 Ⓐ Ⓑ Ⓒ Ⓓ
24 Ⓐ Ⓑ Ⓒ Ⓓ	54 Ⓐ Ⓑ Ⓒ Ⓓ	84 Ⓐ Ⓑ Ⓒ Ⓓ	114 Ⓐ Ⓑ Ⓒ Ⓓ
25 Ⓐ Ⓑ Ⓒ Ⓓ	55 Ⓐ Ⓑ Ⓒ Ⓓ	85 Ⓐ Ⓑ Ⓒ Ⓓ	115 Ⓐ Ⓑ Ⓒ Ⓓ
26 Ⓐ Ⓑ Ⓒ Ⓓ	56 Ⓐ Ⓑ Ⓒ Ⓓ	86 Ⓐ Ⓑ Ⓒ Ⓓ	116 Ⓐ Ⓑ Ⓒ Ⓓ
27 Ⓐ Ⓑ Ⓒ Ⓓ	57 Ⓐ Ⓑ Ⓒ Ⓓ	87 Ⓐ Ⓑ Ⓒ Ⓓ	117 Ⓐ Ⓑ Ⓒ Ⓓ
28 Ⓐ Ⓑ Ⓒ Ⓓ	58 Ⓐ Ⓑ Ⓒ Ⓓ	88 Ⓐ Ⓑ Ⓒ Ⓓ	118 Ⓐ Ⓑ Ⓒ Ⓓ
29 Ⓐ Ⓑ Ⓒ Ⓓ	59 Ⓐ Ⓑ Ⓒ Ⓓ	89 Ⓐ Ⓑ Ⓒ Ⓓ	119 Ⓐ Ⓑ Ⓒ Ⓓ
30 Ⓐ Ⓑ Ⓒ Ⓓ	60 Ⓐ Ⓑ Ⓒ Ⓓ	90 Ⓐ Ⓑ Ⓒ Ⓓ	120 Ⓐ Ⓑ Ⓒ Ⓓ

Pretest

Directions: In each of the following questions, you will find three initial terms and, in parentheses, four answer options designated *a*, *b*, *c*, and *d*. You are to select from the four answer options the one that best completes the analogy with the three initial terms. To record your answers, use the answer sheet provided.

Time: 60 minutes

1. GRAY : ELEPHANT :: (*a*. white, *b*. brown, *c*. green, *d*. gray) : GRIZZLY BEAR

2. (*a*. ratatouille, *b*. vermouth, *c*. lemonade, *d*. gin) : EAT :: MANHATTAN : DRINK

3. EARTH : PLANET :: (*a*. asteroid, *b*. sun, *c*. comet, *d*. Orion) : CONSTELLATION

4. JOHN : (*a*. Jackson, *b*. Adams, *c*. Pierce, *d*. Garfield) :: ANDREW : JOHNSON

5. 1 + 2 : MARCH :: 12 − 3 : (*a*. September, *b*. October, *c*. November, *d*. December)

6. CANNON : CANNON :: STIMULI : (*a*. stimulation, *b*. stimuluses, *c*. stimulate, *d*. stimulus)

7. GRAPES : WINE :: (*a*. alcohol, *b*. hops, *c*. alfalfa, *d*. kemp) : BEER

8. SCROOGE : GREEDY :: (*a*. Antony, *b*. Portia, *c*. Cassius, *d*. Macduff) : TREACHEROUS

9. (*a*. hurricane, *b*. hail, *c*. sleet, *d*. thunder) : RAIN :: BLIZZARD : SNOW

10. BLANC : ALPS :: EVEREST : (*a*. Andes, *b*. Himalayas, *c*. Jungfrau, *d*. Caucasus)

11. i : e :: (*a*.$-\infty$, *b*. π, *c*. 1, *d*. $\sqrt{-1}$) : 2.71828

12. (*a.* Na, *b.* Al, *c.* O_2, *d.* N) : SALT :: H : HYDROCHLORIC ACID

13. UROLOGIST : (*a.* bladder, *b.* urine, *c.* heart, *d.* ears) :: OPHTHALMOLOGIST : EYES

14. A : C :: ALPHA : (*a.* lambda, *b.* kappa, *c.* omicron, *d.* gamma)

15. (*a.* coin, *b.* bullion, *c.* currency, *d.* check) : CASH :: PROBABLE : CERTAIN

16. SKINNER : ENVIRONMENT :: (*a.* Galton, *b.* Locke, *c.* Watson, *d.* Spence) : HEREDITY

17. DOG : NOUN :: (*a.* newspaper, *b.* at, *c.* the, *d.* is) : ARTICLE

18. IRISH : (*a.* setter, *b.* Guernsey, *c.* mutt, *d.* St. Bernard) :: LABRADOR : RETRIEVER

19. PERSHING : (*a.* French, *b.* U.S., *c.* English, *d.* Canadian) :: WELLINGTON : ENGLISH

20. MORNING STAR : EVENING STAR :: VENUS : (*a.* Mercury, *b.* Mars, *c.* Jupiter, *d.* Venus)

21. HYPERBOLE : HYPERBOLA :: STATEMENT : (*a.* statements, *b.* curve, *c.* exaggeration, *d.* ellipse)

22. $\bar{X}$: SAMPLE :: (*a.* μ, *b.* σ, *c.* λ, *d.* ρ) : POPULATION

23. METHYL : ETHYL :: GRAIN : (*a.* turpentine, *b.* alcohol, *c.* rain, *d.* wood)

24. SHORTEST : (*a.* February, *b.* August, *c.* April, *d.* December) :: LONGEST : JUNE

25. (*a.* nadir, *b.* zenith, *c.* summit, *d.* hilt) : BOTTOM :: APEX : TOP

26. PERCENT : 100 :: PROPORTION : (*a.* 0, *b.* 1, *c.* 0.1, *d.* 0.01)

27. RATIONAL : $\sqrt{100}$ :: IRRATIONAL : (*a.* $\sqrt{1}$, *b.* $\sqrt{-4}$, *c.* $\sqrt{50}$, *d.* $\sqrt{0}$)

28. ENORMITY : (*a.* great wickedness, *b.* great largess, *c.* great goodness, *d.* great passion) :: VILIFICATION : SLANDER

29. VANILLA : TEA :: (*a.* stem, *b.* root, *c.* flower, *d.* bean) : LEAF

30. NOON : EVE :: 12:21 : (*a.* 8:34, *b.* 10:01, *c.* 7:54, *d.* 11:29)

31. (*a.* soap, *b.* aspirin, *c.* base, *d.* litmus) : ACID :: LYE : ALKALINE

32. SAM : AIR :: ABM : (*a.* sea, *b.* land, *c.* ballistic, *d.* missile)

33. STEP : STAIRCASE :: (*a.* notch, *b.* support, *c.* poles, *d.* rung) : LADDER

34. OCHER : (*a.* yellow, *b.* green, *c.* blue, *d.* gray) :: LAVENDER : PURPLE

35. MARE : EWE :: HORSE : (*a.* goat, *b.* sheep, *c.* pig, *d.* deer)

36. RAVIOLI : (*a.* spaghetti, *b.* linguine, *c.* cannelloni, *d.* enchilada) ::
    MANICOTTI : TORTELLINI

37. (*a.* bacteria, *b.* viruses, *c.* fungi, *d.* rickettsiae) : TYPHUS ::
    MYCOBACTERIA : TUBERCULOSIS

38. TWO : IMPEACH :: (*a.* zero, *b.* one, *c.* three, *d.* four) : CONVICT

39. 0 PROOF : 0% :: 50 PROOF : (*a.* 10%, *b.* 25%, *c.* 75%, *d.* 100%)

40. BENEDICT : ALFREDO :: EGGS : (*a.* oeufs, *b.* clams, *c.* ziti, *d.* fettuccini)

41. INDUCE : INDUCT :: (*a.* adduce, *b.* reason, *c.* persuade, *d.* deduct) :
    INSTALL

42. (*a.* maroon, *b.* crimson, *c.* pink, *d.* scarlet) : RED :: GRAY : BLACK

43. STOP : POT :: STOOL : (*a.* feces, *b.* toilet, *c.* chair, *d.* loot)

44. PICASSO : (*a.* Bosch, *b.* Daumier, *c.* Tintoretto, *d.* Dali) :: GUERNICA :
    GARDEN OF EARTHLY DELIGHTS

45. $3x^2$: $6x$ :: $5y$: (*a.* 5, *b.* 10, *c.* $5y^{1/2}$, *d.* $10y^{1/2}$)

46. UNICORN : (*a.* mythical beast, *b.* duet, *c.* zebra, *d.* union) ::
    SINGLETON : BICYCLE

47. (*a.* Holland, *b.* Yugoslavia, *c.* Denmark, *d.* Switzerland) : ALPINE ::
    GREECE : MEDITERRANEAN

48. M.D. : EARNED : (*a.* D.D., *b.* Ph.D., *c.* D.D.S., *d.* O.D.) : HONORARY

49. (*a.* Don Juan, *b.* Pablo, *c.* Sancho, *d.* Dulcinea) : DON QUIXOTE ::
    WATSON : HOLMES

50. SONATA : (*a.* movement, *b.* sonatina, *c.* coda, *d.* solo) :: NOVEL :
    NOVELLA

51. NOVICE : EXPERT :: (*a.* teacher, *b.* apprentice, *c.* journeyman, *d.* layman) : MASTER

52. CLUB : (*a.* diamond, *b.* heart, *c.* spade, *d.* ace) :: LOWEST : HIGHEST

53. GOSLING : GOOSE :: SHOAT : (*a.* goat, *b.* sheep, *c.* horse, *d.* hog)

54. C : LEMON :: A : (*a.* liver, *b.* lettuce, *c.* orange, *d.* cake)

55. PACIFIC : OCEAN :: (*a.* Mercury, *b.* Jupiter, *c.* Uranus, *d.* Neptune) : PLANET

56. ICHTHYOLOGIST : (*a.* sentences, *b.* algae, *c.* insects, *d.* fish) :: ZOOLOGIST : ANIMALS

57. ELECT : SELECT :: TIE : (*a.* lose, *b.* win, *c.* sty, *d.* rope)

58. MALLET : (*a.* hunting, *b.* rugby, *c.* cricket, *d.* croquet) :: BAT : BASEBALL

59. BAROMETER : AIR PRESSURE :: TACHOMETER : (*a.* speed of descent, *b.* speed of rotation, *c.* acceleration, *d.* inertia)

60. EMERALD : GRUE :: (*a.* ruby, *b.* sapphire, *c.* amethyst, *d.* diamond) : BLEEN

61. MARTIN : DAVID :: (*a.* Dombey, *b.* Micawber, *c.* Magoun, *d.* Chuzzlewit) : COPPERFIELD

62. (*a.* 2:00, *b.* 3:00, *c.* 5:00, *d.* 6:00) : SEATTLE :: 4:00 : CHICAGO

63. VENUS : (*a.* Uranus, *b.* Mars, *c.* Saturn, *d.* Pluto) :: LOVE : THE DEAD

64. SUBORN : (*a.* give birth to, *b.* prove, *c.* bribe, *d.* demand) :: SUBORDINATE : INFERIOR

65. A : O :: (*a.* E, *b.* OA, *c.* B, *d.* RH) : AB

66. (*a.* coal, *b.* petroleum, *c.* black opal, *d.* uranium) : BLACK GOLD :: PYRITE : FOOL'S GOLD

67. MALACHITE : GREEN :: LAPIS LAZULI : (*a.* blue, *b.* red, *c.* yellow, *d.* amber)

68. LONGITUDE : LATITUDE :: (*a.* 110°, *b.* 90°, *c.* 70°, *d.* 50°) : 20°

69. VALENTINE : SECOND :: NICHOLAS : (*a.* first, *b.* sixth, *c.* tenth, *d.* twelfth)

70. MARK : (*a.* Munich, *b.* Berlin, *c.* Zurich, *d.* Basel) :: FRANC : PARIS

71. (*a.* biology, *b.* chemistry, *c.* physics, *d.* astronomy) : HERSCHEL :: SURGERY : LISTER

72. METER : KILOMETER :: LOG 10 : (*a.* e, *b.* 10, *c.* 10^3, *d.* $\sqrt{10{,}000}$)

73. (*a.* Ash Wednesday, *b.* St. Bartholomew's Day, *c.* Maundy Thursday, *d.* All Saints' Day) : EASTER :: FIRST : LAST

74. GHOST : SPIRIT :: GHOUL : (*a.* body, *b.* vampire, *c.* nightmare, *d.* grave robber)

75. GERUND : (*a.* adverb, *b.* pronoun, *c.* conjunction, *d.* noun) :: PARTICIPLE : ADJECTIVE

76. N.Y. : N.J. :: N.H. : (*a.* N.D., *b.* N.C., *c.* N.M., *d.* N.W.)

77. (*a.* Abelard, *b.* Aquinas, *c.* Erasmus, *d.* Eusebius) : HELOÏSE :: TRISTAN : ISOLDE

78. GOBI : (*a.* Africa, *b.* Asia, *c.* South America, *d.* Central America) :: SAHARA : AFRICA

79. X : X^2 :: STANDARD DEVIATION : (*a.* mode, *b.* median, *c.* variance, *d.* chi square)

80. LEONINE : (*a.* vulpine, *b.* porcine, *c.* supine, *d.* bovine) :: LION : FOX

81. AUGUST 8 : LEO :: (*a.* January 8, *b.* April 8, *c.* October 8, *d.* December 8) : SAGITTARIUS

82. CHESS : CHESSMEN :: GO : (*a.* cards, *b.* stones, *c.* pegs, *d.* balls)

83. CIPHER : NAUGHT :: (*a.* zero, *b.* all, *c.* most, *d.* one) : NONE

84. SEVENTH-DAY ADVENTIST : (*a.* Friday, *b.* Saturday, *c.* Sunday, *d.* Monday) :: MUSLIM : FRIDAY

85. (*a.* 10, *b.* 11, *c.* 12, *d.* 13) : DUODECIMAL :: 13 : DECIMAL

86. (*a.* shawl, *b.* belt, *c.* cloak, *d.* sash) : BURNOOSE :: CAP : BUSBY

87. LEGHORN : (*a.* cattle, *b.* goat, *c.* sheep, *d.* fowl) :: ANGORA : GOAT

88. LISZT : HUNGARY :: MENOTTI : (*a.* U.S.A., *b.* Greece, *c.* Spain, *d.* England)

89. MELODY : (*a.* immediate, *b.* successive, *c.* retrogressive, *d.* momentary) :: HARMONY : SIMULTANEOUS

90. SINUSITIS : SINUS :: MENINGITIS : (*a.* liver, *b.* heart, *c.* artery, *d.* membrane)

91. APPROXIMATE : EXACT :: (*a.* analog, *b.* analogous, *c.* analogical, *d.* analogy) : DIGITAL

92. (*a.* is as, *b.* is almost, *c.* is virtually, *d.* is) : IS LIKE :: METAPHOR : SIMILE

93. CONGRESS : U.S.A. :: DIET : (*a.* Germany, *b.* Turkey, *c.* Japan, *d.* China)

94. MAYOR : (*a.* Montevideo, *b.* Sussex, *c.* Casterbridge, *d.* Marseilles) :: HUNCHBACK : NOTRE DAME

95. INDUCTION : DEDUCTION :: HUME : (*a.* Locke, *b.* Leibniz, *c.* Berkeley, *d.* Mill)

96. STOP : (*a.* h, *b.* j, *c.* t, *d.* v) :: FRICATIVE : F

97. (*a.* $\frac{1}{2}gt^2$, *b.* ra, *c.* $\frac{1}{4}g^2k$, *d.* pc) : D :: MA : F

98. FIDELIO : BORIS GODUNOV :: BEETHOVEN : (*a.* Rimski-Korsakov, *b.* Shostakovich, *c.* Prokofiev, *d.* Mussorgsky)

99. MISER : AVARICIOUS :: SYCOPHANT : (*a.* plutonic, *b.* veracious, *c.* unctuous, *d.* sybaritic)

100. (*a.* genitive, *b.* dative, *c.* ablative, *d.* vocative) : ACCUSATIVE :: INDIRECT : DIRECT

101. (*a.* wheat, *b.* barley, *c.* oats, *d.* rice) : SAKE :: JUNIPER BERRIES : GIN

102. A RAISIN IN THE SUN : THE GRAPES OF WRATH :: (*a.* Morrison, *b.* Hansberry, *c.* Miller, *d.* Hare) : STEINBECK

103. SHARP : TACK :: COOL : (*a.* cucumber, *b.* stone, *c.* stream, *d.* milk)

104. SASQUATCH : NORTH AMERICA :: YETI : (*a.* South America, *b.* Europe, *c.* Australia, *d.* Asia)

105. CRETE : (*a.* Turkey, *b.* Syria, *c.* Greece, *d.* Albania) :: SICILY : ITALY

106. $a^2 + b^2$: (*a.* hypotenuse squared, *b.* rectangular area, *c.* circumference cubed, *d.* spherical volume) :: $(y - y_1) / (x - x_1)$: SLOPE

107. (*a.* tomato, *b.* peanut, *c.* chestnut, *d.* ginger) : PARSNIP :: TURNIP : POTATO

108. KEEL : FRAMES :: BREASTBONE : (*a.* human, *b.* ribs, *c.* pectorals, *d.* backbone)

109. PUSILLANIMOUS : (*a.* brave, *b.* hungry, *c.* joyful, *d.* jealous) : PERFIDIOUS : LOYAL

110. MARS : VENUS :: EARTH : (*a.* Jupiter, *b.* Saturn, *c.* Mercury, *d.* Neptune)

111. CACOPHONOUS : NOISOME :: SOUND : (*a.* sight, *b.* feel, *c.* smell, *d.* taste)

112. CAT : MOUSE :: (*a.* squirrel, *b.* bandicoot, *c.* lemur, *d.* mongoose) : SNAKE

113. ELEPHANT : (*a.* piano, *b.* tusk, *c.* table, *d.* hoof) :: WHALE : LAMP

114. (*a.* Padua, *b.* Siberia, *c.* Verona, *d.* Narnia) : OZ :: SHANGRI-LA : ATLANTIS

115. AURORA BOREALIS : (*a.* Northern Lights, *b.* Gulf Stream, *c.* Black Forest, *d.* El Niño) :: CRANIUM : SKULL

116. PUMMELO : CITRUS FRUIT :: (*a.* rutabaga, *b.* grain, *c.* lentil, *d.* artichoke) : LEGUME

117. KENNEDY : (*a.* House Representative, *b.* Senator, *c.* Mayor, *d.* Governor) :: CLINTON : GOVERNOR

118. ARGES : CYCLOPS :: MEDUSA : (*a.* gorgon, *b.* minotaur, *c.* siren, *d.* hydra)

119. I.E. : (*a.* English, *b.* Italian, *c.* Latin, *d.* Greek) :: RSVP : French

120. (*a.* weary, *b.* tenacious, *c.* harmonious, *d.* sprightly) : JOCUND :: VERITABLE : AUTHENTIC

Answer Key

PRETEST

1. **B**	31. **B**	61. **D**	91. **A**
2. **A**	32. **C**	62. **A**	92. **D**
3. **C**	33. **D**	63. **D**	93. **C**
4. **B**	34. **A**	64. **C**	94. **C**
5. **A**	35. **B**	65. **C**	95. **B**
6. **D**	36. **C**	66. **B**	96. **C**
7. **B**	37. **D**	67. **A**	97. **A**
8. **C**	38. **A**	68. **A**	98. **D**
9. **A**	39. **B**	69. **D**	99. **C**
10. **B**	40. **D**	70. **B**	100. **B**
11. **D**	41. **C**	71. **D**	101. **D**
12. **A**	42. **C**	72. **C**	102. **B**
13. **A**	43. **D**	73. **A**	103. **A**
14. **D**	44. **A**	74. **D**	104. **D**
15. **D**	45. **A**	75. **D**	105. **C**
16. **A**	46. **B**	76. **C**	106. **A**
17. **C**	47. **D**	77. **A**	107. **D**
18. **A**	48. **A**	78. **B**	108. **B**
19. **B**	49. **C**	79. **C**	109. **A**
20. **D**	50. **B**	80. **A**	110. **C**
21. **B**	51. **B**	81. **D**	111. **C**
22. **A**	52. **C**	82. **B**	112. **D**
23. **C**	53. **D**	83. **A**	113. **A**
24. **D**	54. **A**	84. **B**	114. **D**
25. **A**	55. **B**	85. **B**	115. **A**
26. **B**	56. **D**	86. **C**	116. **C**
27. **C**	57. **C**	87. **D**	117. **B**
28. **A**	58. **D**	88. **A**	118. **A**
29. **D**	59. **B**	89. **B**	119. **C**
30. **B**	60. **B**	90. **D**	120. **D**

ANSWER EXPLANATIONS FOR PRETEST

In the following, explanations concerning the correct response are in a large font. Explanations regarding distracters (incorrect responses) that are not self-explaining or could be misinterpreted are in a smaller font in order to highlight the explanations of the answers that are correct.

1. GRAY : ELEPHANT :: (*a.* white, ***b.* brown**, *c.* green, *d.* gray) : GRIZZLY BEAR

   (**b**) An elephant is gray; a grizzly bear is brown.
   General Information—Description

2. (***a.* ratatouille**, *b.* vermouth, *c.* lemonade, *d.* gin) : EAT :: MANHATTAN : DRINK

   (**a**) Ratatouille is something one eats; a Manhattan is something one drinks.
   General Information—Description

3. EARTH : PLANET :: (*a.* asteroid, *b.* sun, *c.* comet, ***d.* Orion**) : CONSTELLATION

   (**c**) Earth is a planet. Orion is a constellation of stars in the sky.
   None of the other choices are constellations.
   Natural Science—Description

4. JOHN : (*a.* Jackson, ***b.* Adams**, *c.* Pierce, *d.* Garfield) :: ANDREW : JOHNSON

   (**b**) John Adams and Andrew Johnson were both U.S. presidents.
   The names of the other presidents were Andrew Jackson, Franklin Pierce, and James Garfield.
   Humanities—Completion

5. 1 + 2 : MARCH :: 12 − 3 : (***a.* September**, *b.* October, *c.* November, *d.* December)

   (**a**) March is the third (1 + 2) month of the year; September is the ninth (12 − 3) month.
   General Information—Description

6. CANNON : CANNON :: STIMULI : (*a.* stimulation, *b.* stimuluses, *c.* stimulate, ***d.* stimulus**)

   (**d**) *Cannon* is the plural form of *cannon*. *Stimuli* is the plural form of *stimulus*.
   General Information—Class

7. GRAPES : WINE :: (*a.* alcohol, ***b.* hops**, *c.* alfalfa, *d.* kemp) : BEER

(**b**) Wine is made from grapes; beer is made from hops.
General Information—Description

8. SCROOGE : GREEDY :: (*a.* Antony, *b.* Portia, ***c.* Cassius**, *d.* Macduff) : TREACHEROUS

(**c**) Scrooge (in *A Christmas Carol*) was greedy; Cassius (in *Julius Caesar*) was treacherous. Macduff is a character in Shakespeare's *Macbeth* who kills Macbeth in the final act. Portia is the wife of Brutus (Julius Caesar's famous assassin) in Shakespeare's *Julius Caesar*. Antony is a soldier and ruler of the Roman Empire in Shakespeare's *Antony and Cleopatra*.
Humanities—Description

9. (***a.* hurricane**, *b.* hail, *c.* sleet, *d.* thunder) : RAIN :: BLIZZARD : SNOW

(**a**) A hurricane is characterized by strong wind and heavy rain; a blizzard is characterized by strong wind and heavy snow.
General Information—Description

10. BLANC : ALPS :: EVEREST : (*a.* Andes, ***b.* Himalayas**, *c.* Jungfrau, *d.* Caucasus)

(**b**) Mont Blanc is the highest mountain peak in the Alps; Mount Everest is the highest mountain peak in the Himalayas. The Alps are a mountain range in Europe. The Andes are a mountain range in South America. The Himalayas are a mountain range in Asia. The Jungfrau is a mountain in the Swiss Alps and the Caucasus is the mountain range that separates the continents of Asia and Europe.
General Information—Description

11. i : e :: (*a.* $-\infty$, *b.* π, *c.* 1, ***d.* $\sqrt{-1}$**) : 2.71828

(**d**) The quantity i is equal to $\sqrt{-1}$; the quantity e is (approximately) equal to 2.71828. The quantity of π is approximately equal to 3.14159. The symbol ∞ represents infinity.
Mathematics—Equality/Negation

12. (***a.* Na**, *b.* Al, *c.* O_2, *d.* N) : SALT :: H : HYDROCHLORIC ACID

(**a**) Salt is a compound containing sodium (Na); hydrochloric acid is a compound containing hydrogen (H). O_2 stands for oxygen, N stands for nitrogen, and Al stands for aluminum.
Natural Science—Part/Whole

13. UROLOGIST : (***a. bladder***, *b.* urine, *c.* heart, *d.* ears) ::
OPHTHALMOLOGIST : EYES

(**a**) A urologist treats the bladder; an ophthalmologist treats the eyes.
General Information—Description

14. A : C :: ALPHA : (*a.* lambda, *b.* kappa, *c.* omicron, ***d. gamma***)

(**d**) *A* is the first letter and *c* is the third letter of the Roman alphabet;
alpha is the first letter and gamma is the third letter of the Greek alphabet.
Lambda is the 11th letter of the Greek alphabet, kappa the 10th letter, and omicron is the
15th letter.
Humanities—Class

15. (*a.* coin, *b.* bullion, *c.* currency, ***d. check***) : CASH :: PROBABLE :
CERTAIN

(**d**) A check has probable value in a financial transaction (it is not certain to
clear). Cash has certain value. A bullion is a pure form of a precious metal and
therefore has a certain value. A coin is a metal disc usually issued by a government that is
used as money. A currency is the form of money used in a country.
General Information—Description

16. SKINNER : ENVIRONMENT :: (***a. Galton***, *b.* Locke, *c.* Watson,
d. Spence) : HEREDITY

(**a**) Skinner is known for his belief that environment largely shapes behavior;
Galton believed that heredity largely shapes behavior. John Locke was an English
philosopher and empiricist. John Watson was an American psychologist who established the
school of behaviorism. Kenneth Spence was an American psychologist who developed the
theory of Stimulus Control.
Social Science—Description

17. DOG : NOUN :: (*a.* newspaper, *b.* at, ***c. the***, *d.* is) : ARTICLE

(**c**) *Dog* is a noun; *the* is an article. *Humanities—Description*

18. IRISH : (***a. setter***, *b.* Guernsey, *c.* mutt, *d.* St. Bernard) :: LABRADOR :
RETRIEVER

(**a**) An Irish setter and a Labrador retriever are both kinds of dogs.
General Information—Completion

19. PERSHING : (*a.* French, **b. U.S.**, *c.* English, *d.* Canadian) ::
WELLINGTON : ENGLISH

    (**b**) Pershing was a U.S. general who led the American Expeditionary Force
    in World War I; Wellington was an English general who served in the
    Napoleonic wars.
    Humanities—Description

20. MORNING STAR : EVENING STAR :: VENUS : (*a.* Mercury, *b.* Mars,
c. Jupiter, **d. Venus**)

    (**d**) Venus is known both as the morning star and as the evening star.
    General Information—Similarity/Contrast

21. HYPERBOLE : HYPERBOLA :: STATEMENT : (*a.* statements, **b. curve**,
c. exaggeration, *d.* ellipse)

    (**b**) A hyperbole is a type of statement; a hyperbola is a type of curve.
    Mathematics—Description

22. $\bar{X}$: SAMPLE :: (**a.** μ, *b.* σ, *c.* λ, *d.* ρ) : POPULATION

    (**a**) $\bar{X}$ is a symbol for a sample mean; μ is a symbol for a population mean.
    σ stands for the standard deviation of a population. λ stands for eigenvalues and Lagrange
    multipliers. ρ stands for a correlation coefficient in statistics. Note that these Greek letters
    have additional meanings in other sciences.
    Mathematics—Description

23. METHYL : ETHYL :: GRAIN : (*a.* turpentine, *b.* alcohol, **c. rain**, *d.* wood)

    (**c**) *Ethyl* is *methyl* without the initial *m*; *rain* is *grain* without the initial *g*.
    Nonsemantic

24. SHORTEST : (*a.* February, *b.* August, *c.* April, **d. December**) ::
LONGEST : JUNE

    (**d**) The shortest day of the year occurs in December. The longest day
    of the year occurs in June.
    General Information—Description

25. (**a. nadir**, *b.* zenith, *c.* summit, *d.* hilt) : BOTTOM :: APEX : TOP

    (**a**) The nadir is the lowest point, or bottom of something; the apex is the
    highest point, or top. A zenith is the direction pointing directly above a particular
    location. A summit is the highest point of a mountain. A hilt is the handle of a sword.
    Vocabulary—Similarity/Contrast

26. PERCENT : 100 :: PROPORTION : (*a.* 0, ***b.* 1**, *c.* 0.1, *d.* 0.01)

(**b**) The highest possible percent is 100; the highest possible proportion is 1.
Mathematics—Description

27. RATIONAL : $\sqrt{100}$ :: IRRATIONAL : (*a.* $\sqrt{1}$, *b.* $\sqrt{-4}$, ***c.* $\sqrt{50}$**, *d.* $\sqrt{0}$)

(**c**) $\sqrt{100}$ is a rational number; $\sqrt{50}$ is an irrational number. A rational number can be expressed as a ratio of two integers (which are natural numbers like 1, 2, 3, and their negatives). An irrational number is a real number that cannot be expressed as a fraction and therefore is not a rational number.
Mathematics—Description

28. ENORMITY : (***a.* great wickedness**, *b.* great largess, *c.* great goodness, *d.* great passion) :: VILIFICATION : SLANDER

(**a**) Enormity is great wickedness; vilification is slander.
Vocabulary—Similarity/Contrast

29. VANILLA : TEA :: (*a.* stem, *b.* root, *c.* flower, ***d.* bean**) : LEAF

(**d**) Vanilla is from a bean, tea from a leaf. *General Information—Description*

30. NOON : EVE :: 12:21 : (*a.* 8:34, ***b.* 10:01**, *c.* 7:54, *d.* 11:29)

(**b**) *Noon* and *eve* are both palindromes (they read the same spelled backward and forward), as are 12:21 and 10:01.
Nonsemantic

31. (*a.* soap, ***b.* aspirin**, *c.* base, *d.* litmus) : ACID :: LYE : ALKALINE

(**b**) Aspirin is acid; lye is alkaline.
General Information—Description

32. SAM : AIR :: ABM : (*a.* sea, *b.* land, ***c.* ballistic**, *d.* missile)

(**c**) The second letter in the acronym *SAM* (surface-to-air missile) stands for air; the second letter in the *ABM* (anti-ballistic missile) stands for ballistic.
General Information—Part/Whole

33. STEP : STAIRCASE :: (*a.* notch, *b.* support, *c.* poles, ***d.* rung**) : LADDER

(**d**) A staircase has steps; a ladder has rungs.
General Information—Part/Whole

34. OCHER : (***a.* yellow**, *b.* green, *c.* blue, *d.* gray) :: LAVENDER : PURPLE

(**a**) Ocher is a shade of yellow; lavender is a shade of purple.
Vocabulary—Description

Answer Explanations

35. MARE : EWE :: HORSE : (*a*. goat, ***b*. sheep**, *c*. pig, *d*. deer)

    (**b**) A mare is a female horse; a ewe is a female sheep.
    Vocabulary—Description

36. RAVIOLI : (*a*. spaghetti, *b*. linguine, ***c*. cannelloni**, *d*. enchilada) ::
    MANICOTTI : TORTELLINI

    (**c**) Ravioli, cannelloni, manicotti, and tortellini are all stuffed pasta dishes.
    General Information—Class

37. (*a*. bacteria, *b*. viruses, *c*. fungi, ***d*. rickettsiae**) TYPHUS ::
    MYCOBACTERIA : TUBERCULOSIS

    (**d**) Typhus is caused by rickettsiae (parasitic bacteria), tuberculosis
    by mycobacteria.
    Natural Science—Description

38. TWO : IMPEACH :: (***a*. zero**, *b*. one, *c*. three, *d*. four) : CONVICT

    (**a**) Two presidents of the United States have been impeached
    (Andrew Johnson and Bill Clinton); no president has been convicted.
    Humanities—Description

39. 0 PROOF : 0% :: 50 PROOF : (*a*. 10%, ***b*. 25%**, *c*. 75%, *d*. 100%)

    (**b**) Something that is 0 proof has a 0% concentration of alcohol;
    something that is 50 proof has a 25% concentration of alcohol.
    General Information—Description

40. BENEDICT : ALFREDO :: EGGS : (*a*. oeufs, *b*. clams, *c*. ziti, ***d*. fettuccini**)

    (**d**) Eggs Benedict and fettuccini Alfredo are both food dishes.
    General Information—Completion

41. INDUCE : INDUCT :: (*a*. adduce, *b*. reason, ***c*. persuade**, *d*. deduct) :
    INSTALL

    (**c**) To induce is to persuade; to induct is to install. To adduce means to cite
    or to allege in order to support an argument; to deduct is to take away, as from an
    amount; to reason means to think logically.
    Vocabulary—Similarity/Contrast

42. (*a*. maroon, *b*. crimson, ***c*. pink**, *d*. scarlet) : RED :: GRAY : BLACK

    (**c**) Pink is red mixed with white; gray is black mixed with white.
    General Information—Description

43. STOP : POT :: STOOL : (*a*. feces, *b*. toilet, *c*. chair, ***d*. loot**)

    (**d**) *Pot* is all but the first letter of *stop* reversed; *loot* is all but the first letter of *stool* reversed.
    Nonsemantic

44. PICASSO : (***a*. Bosch**, *b*. Daumier, *c*. Tintoretto, *d*. Dali) :: GUERNICA : GARDEN OF EARTHLY DELIGHTS

    (**a**) Picasso painted *Guernica*. Bosch painted *The Garden of Earthly Delights*. Daumier is famous for his works depicting the life of Don Quixote; Tintoretto is known for his painting of the last supper (and da Vinci created a painting with the same title!); Dali is famous for his bizarre, surreal images, often of soft watches like in *The Persistence of Memory*.
    Humanities—Description

45. $3x^2$: $6x$ :: $5y$: (***a*. 5**, *b*. 10, *c*. $5y^{1/2}$, *d*. $10y^{1/2}$)

    (**a**) The expression $6x$ is the first derivative of $3x^2$; 5 is the first derivative of $5y$.
    Mathematics—Description

46. UNICORN : (*a*. mythical beast, ***b*. duet**, *c*. zebra, *d*. union) :: SINGLETON : BICYCLE

    (**b**) A unicorn and a singleton both refer to one of something; a duet and a bicycle both refer to two of something.
    General Information—Equality/Negation

47. (*a*. Holland, *b*. Croatia, *c*. Denmark, ***d*. Switzerland**) : ALPINE :: GREECE : MEDITERRANEAN

    (**d**) Switzerland is an Alpine country; Greece is a Mediterranean country. Croatia is an eastern European country. Denmark is located in northern Europe and Holland is located in western Europe.
    General Information—Description

48. M.D. : EARNED :: (***a*. D.D.**, *b*. Ph.D., *c*. D.D.S., *d*. O.D.) : HONORARY

    (**a**) An M.D. (Doctor of Medicine) degree is earned; a D.D. (Doctor of Divinity) degree is honorary. A Ph.D. is a Doctor of Philosophy, a D.D.S. is a Doctor of Dental Surgery, and an O.D. is a Doctor of Optometry.
    General Information—Description

49. (*a.* Don Juan, *b.* Pablo, **c. Sancho**, *d.* Dulcinea) : DON QUIXOTE :: WATSON : HOLMES

    (**c**) Sancho was the sidekick of Don Quixote; Watson was the sidekick of Holmes. Don Juan, the protagonist of a legend, is a rogue and likes to seduce women. Pablo is a character from John Steinbeck's novel *Tortilla Flat*. Dulcinea is a character who is referred to in *Don Quixote* but does not actually appear.
    Humanities—Description

50. SONATA : (*a.* movement, **b. sonatina**, *c.* coda, *d.* solo) :: NOVEL : NOVELLA

    (**b**) A sonatina is a short sonata; a novella is a short novel. A movement is a self-contained part of a larger composition. A coda is a musical passage that brings a piece to a conclusion. A solo is a (part of a) piece played or sung by one artist alone.
    Humanities—Description

51. NOVICE : EXPERT :: (*a.* teacher, **b. apprentice**, *c.* journeyman, *d.* layman) : MASTER

    (**b**) An apprentice is a novice; a master is an expert.
    Vocabulary—Similarity/Contrast

52. CLUB : (*a.* diamond, *b.* heart, **c. spade**, *d.* ace) :: LOWEST : HIGHEST

    (**c**) In bridge, the club represents the lowest suit and the spade represents the highest suit.
    General Information—Description

53. GOSLING : GOOSE :: SHOAT : (*a.* goat, *b.* sheep, *c.* horse, **d. hog**)

    (**d**) A gosling is a young goose; a shoat is a young hog.
    Vocabulary—Description

54. C : LEMON :: A : (**a. liver**, *b.* lettuce, *c.* orange, *d.* cake)

    (**a**) A lemon is a very good source of vitamin C; liver is a very good source of vitamin A.
    General Information—Description

55. PACIFIC : OCEAN :: (*a.* Mercury, **b. Jupiter**, *c.* Uranus, *d.* Neptune) : PLANET

    (**b**) The Pacific Ocean is the largest of the oceans; Jupiter is the largest of the planets.
    General Information—Description

56. ICHTHYOLOGIST : (*a.* sentences, *b.* algae, *c.* insects, ***d.* fish**) ::
ZOOLOGIST : ANIMALS

   (**d**) An ichthyologist studies fish; a zoologist studies animals of all types.
   Natural Science—Description

57. ELECT : SELECT :: TIE : (*a.* lose, *b.* win, ***c.* sty**, *d.* rope)

   (**c**) *Elect* is pronounced like *select*, minus the initial *s* consonant sound;
   tie is pronounced like *sty*, minus the initial *s* consonant sound.
   Nonsemantic

58. MALLET : (*a.* hunting, *b.* rugby, *c.* cricket, ***d.* croquet**) :: BAT : BASEBALL

   (**d**) Croquet is played with a mallet, baseball with a bat.
   General Information—Description

59. BAROMETER : AIR PRESSURE :: TACHOMETER : (*a.* speed of descent,
***b.* speed of rotation**, *c.* acceleration, *d.* inertia)

   (**b**) A barometer measures air pressure; a tachometer measures speed
   of rotation.
   General Information—Description

60. EMERALD : GRUE :: (*a.* ruby, ***b.* sapphire**, *c.* amethyst, *d.* diamond) :
BLEEN

   (**b**) In Nelson Goodman's famous paradox, an emerald can now be
   construed as grue (green until the year 2000 and blue thereafter),
   whereas a sapphire can be construed as bleen (blue until the year 2000
   and green thereafter).
   Humanities—Description

61. MARTIN : DAVID :: (*a.* Dombey, *b.* Micawber, *c.* Magoun,
***d.* Chuzzlewit**) : COPPERFIELD

   (**d**) *Martin Chuzzlewit* and *David Copperfield* are both titles of novels by
   Charles Dickens. *Dombey and Son* is a novel by Charles Dickens; Wilkins Micawber is a
   character in *David Copperfield*, and Francis Magoun was a writer and professor at Harvard.
   Humanities—Completion

62. (***a.* 2:00**, *b.* 3:00, *c.* 5:00, *d.* 6:00) : SEATTLE :: 4:00 : CHICAGO

   (**a**) When it is 2:00 in Seattle, it is 4:00 in Chicago.
   General Information—Description

63. VENUS : (*a.* Uranus, *b.* Mars, *c.* Saturn, **d. Pluto**) :: LOVE : THE DEAD

    (**d**) In Roman mythology, Venus was the goddess of love; Pluto was alleged to be the god of the dead. Saturn was the god of agriculture and harvest, Uranus was the god of the sky, and Mars was the god of war.
    Humanities—Description

64. SUBORN : (*a.* give birth to, *b.* prove, **c. bribe**, *d.* demand) :: SUBORDINATE : INFERIOR

    (**c**) *Suborn* and *bribe* are synonyms, as are *subordinate* and *inferior.*
    Vocabulary—Similarity/Contrast

65. A : O :: (*a.* E, *b.* OA, **c. B**, *d.* RH) : AB

    (**c**) A, O, B, and AB are all blood types.
    Natural Science—Class

66. (*a.* coal, **b. petroleum**, *c.* black opal, *d.* uranium) : BLACK GOLD :: PYRITE : FOOL'S GOLD

    (**b**) Petroleum is black gold; pyrite fool's gold.
    General Information—Similarity/Contrast

67. MALACHITE : GREEN :: LAPIS LAZULI : (***a.* blue**, *b.* red, *c.* yellow, *d.* amber)

    (**a**) Malachite is green in color; lapis lazuli is blue.
    General Information—Description

68. LONGITUDE : LATITUDE :: (***a.* 110°**, *b.* 90°, *c.* 70°, *d.* 50°) : 20°

    (**a**) Lines of longitude and latitude are at right (90°) angles to each other, as are lines at 110° and 20°.
    Mathematics—Description

69. VALENTINE : SECOND :: NICHOLAS : (*a.* first, *b.* sixth, *c.* tenth, **d. twelfth**)

    (**d**) St. Valentine's Day occurs during the second month of the year; St. Nicholas Day occurs during the twelfth month.
    General Information–Description

70. MARK : (*a.* Munich, **b. Berlin**, *c.* Zurich, *d.* Basel) :: FRANC : PARIS

    (**b**) The mark was the unit of currency in Germany, of which Berlin is the capital; the franc was the unit of currency in France, of which Paris is the capital.
    General Information—Description

71. (*a.* biology, *b.* chemistry, *c.* physics, ***d.* astronomy**) : HERSCHEL :: SURGERY : LISTER

    (**d**) Herschel is famous in the field of astronomy; Lister is famous in the field of surgery.
    Natural Science—Description

72. METER : KILOMETER :: LOG 10 : (*a.* e, *b.* 10, ***c.* 10^3**, *d.* $\sqrt{10,000}$)

    (**c**) A kilometer is 1000 meters; 10^3 is 1000 times log 10.
    Mathematics—Equality/Negation

73. (***a.* Ash Wednesday**, *b.* St. Bartholomew's Day, *c.* Maundy Thursday, *d.* All Saints' Day) : EASTER :: FIRST : LAST

    (**a**) Ash Wednesday is the first day of Lent; Easter is the last day.
    General Information—Description

74. GHOST : SPIRIT :: GHOUL : (*a.* body, *b.* vampire, *c.* nightmare, ***d.* grave robber**)

    (**d**) A ghost is a spirit; a ghoul is a grave robber.
    Vocabulary—Similarity/Contrast

75. GERUND : (*a.* adverb, *b.* pronoun, *c.* conjunction, ***d.* noun**) :: PARTICIPLE : ADJECTIVE

    (**d**) A gerund is a verb form that can act like a noun; a participle is a verb form that can act like an adjective.
    General Information—Description

76. N.Y. : N.J. :: N.H. : (*a.* N.D., *b.* N.C., ***c.* N.M.**, *d.* N.W.)

    (**c**) N.Y., N.J., N.H., and N.M. are all abbreviations for two-word states of which the first word is *New*.
    General Information—Class

77. (***a.* Abelard**, *b.* Aquinas, *c.* Erasmus, *d.* Eusebius) : HELOÏSE :: TRISTAN : ISOLDE

    (**a**) Abelard and Heloïse were lovers, as were Tristan and Isolde. Abelard was a medieval philosopher and theologian. Tristan and Isolde are characters in a legend. Desiderius Erasmus was a Dutch Renaissance humanist and Catholic theologian. Eusebius Caesarea was the bishop of Caesarea Palestine and through his work provided a basis for Church History. Saint Thomas Aquinas was an Italian Catholic priest and proponent of natural theology.
    Humanities—Class

78. GOBI : (*a.* Africa, ***b.* Asia**, *c.* South America, *d.* Central America) ::
SAHARA : AFRICA

    (**b**) The Gobi Desert is in Asia; the Sahara Desert in Africa.
    General Information—Description

79. X : X² :: STANDARD DEVIATION : (*a.* mode, *b.* median, ***c.* variance**,
d. chi square)

    (**c**) A variance is a standard deviation squared.
    Mathematics—Description

80. LEONINE : (***a.* vulpine**, *b.* porcine, *c.* supine, *d.* bovine) :: LION : FOX

    (**a**) *Leonine* means "like a lion"; *vulpine* means "like a fox." *Porcine* means
    "like a pig," *supine* means "lying on the back," and *bovine* means "like a cow."
    Vocabulary—Description

81. AUGUST 8 : LEO :: (*a.* January 8, *b.* April 8, *c.* October 8,
***d.* December 8**) : SAGITTARIUS

    (**d**) Someone born on August 8 is born under the sign of Leo; someone
    born on December 8 is born under the sign of Sagittarius. Aries (March
    21–April 20); Taurus (April 21–May 21); Gemini (May 22–June 21); Cancer (June 22–
    July 22); Leo (July 23–August 21); Virgo (August 22–September 23); Libra (September
    24–October 23); Scorpio (October 24–November 22); Sagittarius (November
    23–December 22); Capricorn (December 23–January 20); Aquarius (January 21–February
    19); Pisces (February 20–March 20).
    General Information—Description

82. CHESS : CHESSMEN :: GO : (*a.* cards, ***b.* stones**, *c.* pegs, *d.* balls)

    (**b**) The game of chess is played with chessmen; the game of go is played
    with stones. *General Information—Description*

83. CIPHER : NAUGHT :: (***a.* zero**, *b.* all, *c.* most, *d.* one) : NONE

    (**a**) *Cipher, naught, zero,* and *none* all refer to nullity.
    Vocabulary—Class

84. SEVENTH-DAY ADVENTIST : (*a.* Friday, ***b.* Saturday**, *c.* Sunday,
d. Monday) : MUSLIM :: FRIDAY

    (**b**) Sabbath occurs on Saturday for a Seventh-Day Adventist and on Friday
    for a Muslim.
    General Information—Description

85. (*a.* 10, ***b.* 11**, *c.* 12, *d.* 13) : DUODECIMAL :: 13 : DECIMAL

    (**b**) The number 11 in duodecimal (base 12) notation equals the number 13 in decimal (base 10) notation.
    Mathematics—Equality/Negation

86. (*a.* shawl, *b.* belt, ***c.* cloak**, *d.* sash) : BURNOOSE :: CAP : BUSBY

    (**c**) A burnoose is a type of cloak; a busby is a type of cap.
    General Information—Description

87. LEGHORN : (*a.* cattle, *b.* goat, *c.* sheep, ***d.* fowl**) :: ANGORA : GOAT

    (**d**) A leghorn is a type of fowl; an angora is a type of goat.
    General Information—Description

88. LISZT : HUNGARY :: MENOTTI : (***a.* U.S.A.**, *b.* Greece, *c.* Spain, *d.* England)

    (**a**) Liszt was a noted composer from Hungary; Menotti is a noted composer from the United States.
    Humanities—Description

89. MELODY : (*a.* immediate, ***b.* successive**, *c.* retrogressive, *d.* momentary) :: HARMONY : SIMULTANEOUS

    (**b**) Melody is successive; harmony is simultaneous.
    Humanities—Description

90. SINUSITIS : SINUS :: MENINGITIS : (*a.* liver, *b.* heart, *c.* artery, ***d.* membrane**)

    (**d**) Sinusitis is an inflammation of the sinus; meningitis is an inflammation of a membrane.
    Natural Science—Description

91. APPROXIMATE : EXACT :: (***a.* analog**, *b.* analogous, *c.* analogical, *d.* analogy) : DIGITAL

    (**a**) An analog computer yields approximate results; a digital computer yields exact results.
    Natural Science—Description

92. (*a.* is as, *b.* is almost, *c.* is virtually, ***d.* is**) : IS LIKE :: METAPHOR : SIMILE

    (**d**) A metaphor often uses the linking verb *is*; a simile links two concepts by *is like*. A metaphor compares seemingly unrelated subjects. A simile compares two unlike things as well, but similes do not equate the subjects as metaphors do.
    Humanities—Description

93. CONGRESS : U.S.A. :: DIET : (*a.* Germany, *b.* Turkey, **c. Japan**, *d.* China)

(**c**) The main legislative body of the United States is the Congress; the main legislative body of Japan is the Diet.
General Information—Description

94. MAYOR : (*a.* Montevideo, *b.* Sussex, **c. Casterbridge**, *d.* Marseille) :: HUNCHBACK : NOTRE DAME

(**c**) *The Mayor of Casterbridge* and *The Hunchback of Notre Dame* are both titles of books.
Humanities—Completion

95. INDUCTION : DEDUCTION :: HUME : (*a.* Locke, **b. Leibniz**, *c.* Berkeley, *d.* Mill)

(**b**) Hume, an empiricist, used induction as his major mode of reasoning. Leibniz, a rationalist, used deduction as his major mode of reasoning.
Humanities—Description

96. STOP : (*a.* h, *b.* j, **c. t**, *d.* v) :: FRICATIVE : F

(**c**) The sound of *t* is a stop; the source of *f* is a fricative. A fricative is a sound that is produced by forcing air through a narrow passage. A stop is a consonant produced by stopping the flow of air at some point.
Social Science—Description

97. (**a. $\frac{1}{2}$ gt²**, *b.* ra, *c.* $\frac{1}{4}$ g²k, *d.* pc) : D :: MA : F

(**a**) Distance fallen by an object equals one-half the force of gravity times the amount of time squared; force equals mass times acceleration.
Natural Science—Equality/Negation

98. FIDELIO : BORIS GODUNOV :: BEETHOVEN : (*a.* Rimski-Korsakov, *b.* Shostakovich, *c.* Prokofiev, ***d.* Mussorgsky**)

(**d**) *Fidelio* is an opera by Beethoven; *Boris Godunov* is an opera by Mussorgsky.
Humanities—Description

99. MISER : AVARICIOUS :: SYCOPHANT : (*a.* plutonic, *b.* veracious, ***c.* unctuous**, *d.* sybaritic)

(**c**) A miser is avaricious; a sycophant is unctuous.
Vocabulary—Description

100. (*a.* genitive, ***b.* dative**, *c.* ablative, *d.* vocative) : ACCUSATIVE ::
INDIRECT : DIRECT

    (**b**) In Latin, the dative case is used for indirect objects; the accusative case
    is used for direct objects.
    Humanities—Description

101. (*a.* wheat, *b.* barley, *c.* oats, ***d.* rice**) : SAKE :: JUNIPER BERRIES : GIN

    (**d**) Just as the beverage gin is made from juniper berries, so is the beverage
    sake made from rice.
    General Information—Part/Whole

102. A RAISIN IN THE SUN : THE GRAPES OF WRATH :: (*a.* Morrison,
***b.* Hansberry**, *c.* Miller, *d.* Hare) : STEINBECK

    (**b**) Lorraine Hansberry wrote *A Raisin in the Sun* and John Steinbeck wrote
    The Grapes of Wrath.
    Humanities—Description

103. SHARP : TACK :: COOL : (***a.* cucumber**, *b.* stone, *c.* stream, *d.* milk)

    (**a**) The phrases "sharp as a tack" and "cool as a cucumber" can both be used
    to describe people.
    General Information—Completion

104. SASQUATCH : NORTH AMERICA :: YETI : (*a.* South America,
b. Europe, *c.* Australia, ***d.* Asia**)

    (**d**) The myth of the existence of a hairy hominid called sasquatch
    originated in North America just as the myth of the existence of a
    hairy hominid called yeti originated in Asia.
    General Information—Description

105. CRETE : (*a.* Turkey, *b.* Syria, ***c.* Greece**, *d.* Albania) :: SICILY : ITALY

    (**c**) Crete is a large island that is part of Greece and Sicily is a large island
    that is part of Italy.
    General Information—Description

106. $a^2 + b^2$: (***a.* hypotenuse squared**, *b.* rectangular area, *c.* circumference
cubed, *d.* spherical volume) :: $(y - y_1) / (x - x_1)$: SLOPE

    (**a**) The expression $a^2 + b^2$ is equal to hypotenuse squared just as
    $(y - y_1)/(x - x_1)$ is equal to slope.
    Mathematics—Equality/Negation

107. (*a.* tomato, *b.* peanut, *c.* chestnut, ***d.* ginger**) : PARSNIP :: TURNIP : POTATO

    (**d**) Ginger, parsnips, turnips, and potatoes are all edible root vegetables.
    General Information—Class

108. KEEL : FRAMES :: BREASTBONE : (*a.* human, ***b.* ribs**, *c.* pectorals, *d.* backbone)

    (**b**) The keel is the structural centerline of a ship, to which the frames are attached. The breastbone is a structural midline of the body, to which the ribs are attached.
    General Information—Part/Whole

109. PUSILLANIMOUS : (***a.* brave**, *b.* hungry, *c.* joyful, *d.* jealous) : PERFIDIOUS : LOYAL

    (**a**) Pusillanimous means the opposite of brave, just as perfidious is the opposite of loyal.
    Vocabulary—Similarity/Contrast

110. MARS : VENUS :: EARTH : (*a.* Jupiter, *b.* Saturn, ***c.* Mercury**, *d.* Neptune)

    (**c**) Mars, Venus, Earth, and Mercury are all terrestrial or "rocky" planets. Jupiter, Saturn, and Neptune are gas planets.
    Natural Science—Class

111. CACOPHONOUS : NOISOME :: SOUND : (*a.* sight, *b.* feel, ***c.* smell**, *d.* taste)

    (**c**) Something cacophonous is an unpleasant sound. Something noisome is an unpleasant smell.
    Vocabulary—Description

112. CAT : MOUSE :: (*a.* squirrel, *b.* bandicoot, *c.* lemur, ***d.* mongoose**) : SNAKE

    (**d**) Cats are frequently kept to ward off mice just as mongooses are kept to ward off snakes.
    General Information—Description

113. ELEPHANT : (***a.* piano**, *b.* tusk, *c.* table, *d.* hoof) :: WHALE : LAMP

    (**a**) The elephant was once poached so that its ivory could be used for keys on pianos. The whale was once poached so that its oil could be used to burn in lamps.
    General Information—Description

114. (*a.* Padua, *b.* Siberia, *c.* Verona, ***d.* Narnia**) : OZ :: SHANGRI-LA : ATLANTIS

(**d**) Narnia, Oz, Shangri-La, and Atlantis are all fictitious places of literature. Padua and Verona are cities in Italy. Siberia is a part of Northern Asia located in Russia.
Humanities—Class

115. AURORA BOREALIS : (***a.* Northern Lights**, *b.* Gulf Stream, *c.* Black Forest, *d.* El Niño) :: CRANIUM : SKULL

(**a**) Aurora Borealis is the term of Latin origin used for the Northern Lights. Cranium is the term of Latin origin used for the skull.
Natural Science—Similarity/Contrast

116. PUMMELO : CITRUS FRUIT :: (*a.* rutabaga, *b.* grain, ***c.* lentil**, *d.* artichoke) : LEGUME

(**c**) A pummelo is a citrus fruit just as a lentil is a legume.
General Information—Class

117. KENNEDY : (*a.* House Representative, ***b.* Senator**, *c.* Mayor, *d.* Governor) :: CLINTON : GOVERNOR

(**b**) Before becoming president, Kennedy and Clinton were a senator and a governor, respectively.
General Information—Description

118. ARGES : CYCLOPS :: MEDUSA : (***a.* gorgon**, *b.* minotaur, *c.* siren, *d.* hydra)

(**a**) Arges was a cyclops just as Medusa was a gorgon. The Minotaur is a mythical creature with the head of a bull and the body of a man. A siren is a mythical sea nymph that lures sailors to their demise. Hydra is a mythical monster with nine heads; when one head is struck off it is replaced by two new ones.
Humanities—Class

119. I.E. : (*a.* English, *b.* Italian, ***c.* Latin**, *d.* Greek) :: RSVP : French

(**c**) The commonly used acronym "i.e." is derived from Latin just as the commonly used acronym "rsvp" is derived from French.
Nonsemantic—Nonsemantic

120. (*a.* weary, *b.* tenacious, *c.* harmonious, ***d.* sprightly**) : JOCUND :: VERITABLE : AUTHENTIC

(**d**) Jocund means sprightly just as veritable means authentic.
Vocabulary—Similarity/Contrast

PRETEST

Item Classification Chart

	RELATIONSHIP						
	Similarity/ Contrast	Description	Class	Completion	Part/ Whole	Equality/ Negation	Nonsemantic
Vocabulary	25, 28, 41, 51, 64, 74, 109, 120	34, 35, 53, 80, 99, 111	83				
General Information	20, 66	1, 2, 5, 7, 9, 10, 13, 15, 24, 29, 31, 39, 42, 47, 48, 52, 54, 55, 58, 59, 62, 67, 69, 70, 73, 75, 78, 81, 82, 84, 86, 87, 93, 104, 105, 112, 113, 117	6, 36, 76, 107, 116	18, 40, 103	32, 33, 101, 108	46	
Humanities		8, 17, 19, 38, 44, 49, 50, 60, 63, 88, 89, 92, 95, 98, 100, 102	14, 77, 114, 118	4, 61, 94			
Social Science		16, 96					
Natural Science	115	3, 37, 56, 71, 90, 91	65, 110		12	97	
Mathematics		21, 22, 26, 27, 45, 68, 79				11, 72, 85, 106	
Nonsemantic							23, 30, 43, 57, 119

C O N T E N T

Item Classifications

Achieving Success on the *Miller Analogies Test*

PART 2

- Facts about the *MAT*
- A word on computer-based tests
- How to solve analogies
- Practice in analogical thinking
- 30 helpful hints

- The 12 biggest mistakes test-takers make
- Advice on preparing for the *MAT*
- Improving your intellectual skills

FACTS ABOUT THE *MAT*

History of the *MAT*

The *MAT* was developed for use at the University of Minnesota, where it was first administered in 1926. At the time, its use was restricted to this university. However, the test received a great deal of attention from psychologists and educators, and it was subsequently made more widely available on a restricted basis. Today, it may be administered only at licensed centers, and distribution of the test booklets is carefully regulated. New forms of the test have been issued periodically over the years, each of which has test items of equal average difficulty and of similar content.

Description of the Test

The *MAT* is a 120-item, 60-minute verbal analogies test. All questions are in the form A : B :: C : D (A is to B as C is to D), with one of the four terms missing. Four possible options are given for the missing term. Of the 120 items, 100 count toward your score and 20 are experimental and do not count.

Your task is to select the option that best completes the analogy. Answers are recorded on a separate answer sheet. You are not allowed to make any marks in the test booklet. The answer sheet is later scored either by hand or by machine.

What the *MAT* Measures

According to the *Miller Analogies Test Manual* (1970), the "*Miller Analogies Test* (*MAT*) was developed to measure the scholastic aptitude at the graduate school level . . . The test items require the recognition of relationships rather than the display of enormous erudition [p.3]."

As is often the case with standardized tests, theory is rosier than practice. While there is no question but that the "recognition of relationships" is required, its importance relative to that of plain (and some not so plain) knowledge (or "enormous erudition," if you prefer) is probably overstated in the Manual.

Meer, Stein, and Geertsma (1955) investigated the relationship of *MAT* scores to scores on each subtest of the *Wechsler-Bellevue Intelligence Scale* (Wechsler, 1944), a former version of what has been among the most popular and highly respected intelligence tests (yes, some people actually do respect such things). These authors found by far the strongest relationship between scores on the *MAT* and scores on the Vocabulary subtest of the Wechsler-Bellevue. The second strongest relationship was with the scores on the Information subtest. The correlation between scores on the *MAT* and those on the verbal reasoning (Similarities) subtest of the Wechsler-Bellevue was not statistically significant!

Although this study was conducted on a restricted population, and therefore must be interpreted with caution, it points out something you will soon discover on your own: Vocabulary and, to a lesser extent, general information play an important role in determining *MAT* scores. No matter how good you are at reasoning, you first have to recognize and comprehend the concepts with which you are supposed to reason. You will probably find some (if not many) items on which your difficulty does not involve reasoning with the concepts, but of understanding them in the first place.

In one respect, all of this is not as bad as it sounds. Numerous studies have found that vocabulary is the best single predictor both of general intelligence and of performance in a fairly wide variety of tasks. This fact will probably be of more comfort to those who view themselves as walking dictionaries (or even better, walking encyclopedias) than to those whose vocabularies haven't kept up with their razor-sharp reasoning abilities.

Reasons for Taking the *MAT*

Most people who take the *MAT* do so for one of four reasons:

1. **Graduate Study.** The most common reason for taking the *MAT* is to support an application for admission to a graduate level academic program at either the masters' or doctoral level.

2. **Scholarship Aid.** A second common reason for taking the *MAT* is to support an application for financial aid in pursuing a graduate program.

3. **Business.** A third use of the *MAT* is as a selection or placement device in a business firm or agency. For example, an industrial organization may require the test of applicants to their management traineeship program.

4. **Guidance.** A fourth use of the *MAT* is for personal guidance by a college adviser or placement office.

If a school to which you are applying requires the *MAT*, you have no choice but to take it. But some schools offer you a choice of either the *GRE* or the *MAT*. In that case, you can take one or both. If you have the choice, here are the considerations that might incline you toward the *MAT*.

1. If you are weak in mathematics, the *MAT* is the preferred choice. One of three tests of the *GRE* is *Quantitative Reasoning*, whereas the *MAT* has just a few mathematically oriented items.
2. If you are particularly strong in vocabulary and general knowledge of the world, the *MAT* is the way to go. Although it is billed as a test of reasoning, vocabulary and general knowledge weigh heavily in the score, probably even more than does reasoning.
3. If you have difficulty taking tests that are long and grueling, the *MAT* is probably the better option. It is only 1 hour, versus 2½ hours of testing time for the *GRE*.
4. If you have found analogies to be a particular strength of yours, the *MAT* is also the way to go, as it is all analogies.
5. If you are weak in writing skills, you may wish to choose the *MAT* because, unlike the *GRE*, it does not require writing an essay.

More schools require the *GRE* than the *MAT,* so if you have the time or money only for one test, you may want to choose the *GRE*.

No matter what the reason for taking the test, it is usually not taken before the senior year in college unless it is administered through special programs.

About the *MAT*

The following information is a summary of information contained in the Candidate Information Booklet, 2013, for the *Miller Analogies Test* (2013).

THE TEST

The test is administered in a computer-based format. It is usually administered through Controlled Testing Centers (CTC). Each CTC formulates its own schedule for testing, its own application process, and its own fee structure. Applications to take the test are made to the CTCs rather than to Pearson, except in rare cases described below. Today, there are more than 500 CTCs in the United States, Canada, and overseas. Locations of CTCs can be found in the Candidate Information Booklet, which can be downloaded from the Web.

There are different versions of the *MAT* to make sure that you won't be presented with the same items again if you take the test more than once.

A WORD ON COMPUTER-BASED TESTS

These days you do not have a choice between paper-and-pencil testing and computer-based testing anymore—when you take the *MAT,* you will need to do so at a computer terminal. The experience of taking a test on a computer may feel quite different from that of taking the same test in a paper-and-pencil version. But remember that it feels different for everyone else as well, so this does not put you at any disadvantage. And like most people today, you probably are also used to doing a lot of things on a computer. By the way, many studies show that even when people have a choice of how to take a test, their chosen medium does not have an impact on their performance: Scores from computer-based tests and their paper-and-pencil equivalents are usually comparable to each other (Karkee, Kim, & Fatica, 2010; Tsai & Shin, 2012; Wang et al., 2008).

The major difference between computer-based tests and paper-and-pencil tests is that you cannot get a grand overview of the test on the computer screen as conveniently as you can by skimming through paper pages. Going back to an item left unanswered is also different and may be a bit more time-consuming or difficult on the computer than with a paper test, but this is again true for anyone taking the test. So from our perspective, it is not worth worrying about the fact that the *MAT* now can be taken only by computer.

THE PUBLISHER

The publisher of the test is NCS Pearson, Inc. The company was founded in 1921 and is the oldest publisher of commercial tests in the United States. Pearson develops many of the tests used in the testing industry today, such as the *Wechsler Adult Intelligence Scales* and the *Metropolitan Achievement Tests*. It has a reputation for creating sound tests that are carefully researched and validated. However, like most testing companies, it tends to be rather conservative in the kinds of tests it publishes. The *Miller Analogies Test*, for example, is a very old test. It was already an old test when the first author worked at The Psychological Corporation (then the publisher of the *MAT*) during the summers of 1968 and 1969!

Testing Centers

At present, there are more than 500 testing centers in 50 states and in several foreign countries. Special arrangements can be made in foreign countries where there are no regular centers, but you should allow at least a month for arrangements of this kind to be made. If you reside more than 100 miles from a test center, or if you are not able to reach such a center within a month, special arrangements may also be made, but again you should allow ample time for these to be completed.

A complete list of testing centers may be obtained at *www.milleranalogies.com*, by calling 1-800-622-3231, or by writing to *MATscoring.services@pearson.com*. You should also contact them if you have made arrangements to take the *MAT* but have not received the bulletin of information regarding the test. The website for the test, which contains comprehensive information, is *www.milleranalogies.com*

Alternative Testing Site

If you reside more than 100 miles from a CTC, you have the option of requesting an alternative testing site. In this case, you may actually find an individual to administer the test to you. The individual must be cleared by the company. It might be, for example, a faculty member at your college or university, an administrator at the school, or a U.S. Embassy administrator or consulate. The fee for such a testing is a stiff $149. The procedure for setting up such an alternative testing site is rather elaborate and is described in the Candidate Information Booklet.

SERVICE AND FEES

Normal Fees

Fees are set by each CTC. Generally, today they are around $65 to $90, on average. However, there are additional fees that can quickly add to the cost of taking the test.

Accommodations

Special accommodations can be made at most CTCs if you need them. Such accommodations include a Braille, large-print edition, or audio edition for the visually impaired. It is even possible to arrange for a reader. Other accommodations can be made as well for those with specific disabilities or disorders.

No Score Option

If you should decide during the test that you don't want the test scored, you can request this by clicking the Do Not Process This Score button. Once you click this option, your test will not be scored and consequently no scores will be reported to any score recipients. You will be sent a blank Official Score Report. Be aware, however, that once you click the Do Not Process This Score button, you cannot change your mind anymore—your fees will not be refunded, and you cannot request to have your test scored at a later time.

Retesting

You can repeat the *MAT* by applying for another test date at your testing center of choice. Of course, you also will have to pay the test fee again. It also may be worthwhile checking with the schools to which you plan to apply to learn whether they have a policy concerning scores from repeat exams.

Information for the Handicapped

Nonstandard administrations can be arranged for the handicapped, but the testing center must be notified well in advance so that appropriate preparations can be made. Both Braille and enlarged-print editions of the *MAT* are available. If you are unable to mark your answer sheet yourself, you may make oral responses to an examiner, who will then mark the answer sheet for you. Oral administration of the *MAT* by a reader provided by the testing center is permitted.

Information for Those Who Speak English as a Second Language

You will not be permitted to use a dictionary or any other aids while taking the *MAT*. Although scores obtained by an individual for whom English is not a first language are always difficult to interpret, these scores would be completely uninterpretable if the test-takers were allowed to use English-language aids. If your command of the English language does not reflect your true verbal abilities, you will obviously be at a competitive disadvantage in taking the test, although you will very likely find yourself at a similar disadvantage when entering the academic or employment situation for which the *MAT* is required.

Since there are no foreign-language editions of the *MAT*, you must take the test in English. However, any competent interpreter aware of your linguistic background will take into account the fact that English is not your native language when interpreting your score. It would be to your advantage to make this fact known to the appropriate official at any institution to which your score is sent.

Test Dates

The *MAT* is administered throughout the year by appointment. Since testing dates and times vary from one center to another, you will have to consult a local center for this information.

Score Reports

When you report for the test, you will be given an *Examinee's Report* to address to yourself. It will be returned to you with your score recorded on it in a few days after you take the test.

Scoring

NORMAL SCORING

Scoring is done electronically. You will receive a Preliminary Score Report when you have completed the test. Those scores still need to be verified by Pearson, however. It normally takes 10–15 days from the time you take the test until you receive your Official Score Report.

The following information is contained in the score report.

Scale Scores

On the *MAT*, scaled scores range from 200 to 600. The average score is 400. Percentile ranks from 1 to 99.

Percentile for Intended Major

This tells you the percentage of people who scored below you in the major field in which you plan to concentrate.

Percentile for Total Group

This percentile is relative to all examinees who have taken the test, regardless of major.

The average score is 400 (cf. with the average on the GRE, which is 500). The theoretical range is 200 to 600, but extreme scores are very rare because the standard deviation is only 25 points, meaning that roughly two-thirds of all scores fall between 375 and 425, and roughly 95% of all scores fall between 350 and 450. Scores over 475 or under 325 will be extremely rare, each achieved by only a fraction of 1% of test-takers. According to Meagher and Perez (2008), in the

2001–2003 normative sample (i.e., the sample on the basis of which raw scores were converted to standard scores), the range of scores was 231 to 563. However, the bottom and top scores were the extremes—no one scored lower than 231 or higher than 563 of more than 126,000 candidates.

NORMATIVE DATA

As noted above, scores on the *MAT* show a theoretical range of 200 to 600, but very few people score under 325 or over 475. Meagher and Perez (2008) have provided means (average scores) for different fields. They found averages of 397 for business applicants, 400 for education applicants, 414 for humanities applicants, 403 for applicants in the natural sciences, and 399 for applicants in the social sciences. In 2013 Pearson is introducing new norms that better reflect the current candidate population. The range of 200 to 600 stays the same.

VERIFYING YOUR SCORE

If when you receive your score you believe there is a mistake, you can write to Pearson within 60 days of your test date and request that your test be rescored manually. There is a $35 fee for this service. For the most part, such requests are not worth the bother. Machine scoring is typically accurate. But if your score appears totally off to you, it is probably worth the money, if only for the peace of mind.

REPLACEMENT SCORE REPORTS

If after four weeks from the date of testing you have still not received your score report, or if you receive a score report in a timely fashion but it is damaged, you can request a replacement at no charge if you send your request within six weeks of taking the test. Otherwise, there is a charge of $25. You can find the request form for your Score Report at *www.milleranalogies.com*

SCORE RECIPIENTS AND TRANSCRIPTS

The fee for the test includes a score report to you as well as to as many as three institutions. However, for the institutions to be included in your official score report, they must be specified at the time you take the test. If you request them later, you will have to pay a fee of $25 per score report. Only accredited institutions of higher education and approved scholarship and fellowship organizations are entitled to receive score reports.

At the time of testing, you may list up to three addresses to which you want official score reports sent. It is essential that you know at this time the correct and complete address of any institutions to which you want the score sent. You cannot expect the testing center to supply this information. The charge for reporting scores at the time of testing to as many as three institutions is included in the test fee.

Should you later decide that you wish additional score reports sent out, you will have to mail a request to Pearson. You can find the request form at *www.milleranalogies.com*.

The fee is $25 for each report. Money orders are required.

Scores of tests taken more than 5 years ago will not be reported, since these scores may not be accurate reflections of current ability. You must therefore take the test again if you need a score reported but have not taken the test during the preceding 5 years. If you took the test more than 2 years but less than 5 years ago, the old score will be reported, but you are strongly urged to retake the test nevertheless. If you take the test twice within 2 years, both scores will be reported.

CANCELLATION OF SCORES

Pearson reserves the right to cancel scores. Scores may be cancelled for a variety of reasons. They include (a) repeating the same form of the *MAT* within a 1-year period, (b) the occurrence of an irregularity in the administration of the test, (c) questionable item responses or unusual answer patterns, or (d) a score gain that seems questionable. A questionable score gain is one that is 50 points or greater than the previous score. If your score is invalidated for reasons of questionable gain, you may take a third test at no charge. If your third score is within 25 points of the second one, the second score is validated. If it is not, no scores will be released. Exceptions can be made in special cases.

Practice Tests

You can take three practice tests offered by the publisher. At the time we are writing this book, the cost for each test is $30.00. The website to access for more information is *http://tpc-etesting.com/matopt/*. The tests will be scored for you by the test publisher.

What to Bring to the Test Center

Bring all necessary forms and identifications. You will receive the necessary forms in the mail. Don't forget to bring them to the test, as well as other information you may want to supply, such as addresses of the universities to which you want the scores sent. Do not bring notes, dictionaries, or the like; they are not permitted.

Bring *two* forms of identification with you, at least one of which has a photo and your signature. The best forms of identification are government-issued ones, such as a driver's license or passport. Credit-card photos are not accepted as a form of photo identification. You will not be admitted to the testing until you show the two forms of identification.

Bring a watch. There may not be a clock in the room, or it may not be easily visible. Having your own watch ensures that you will be able to check the time easily. A watch will also help you to pace yourself as you work on the test and will enable you to fill in any unanswered questions before the end of the testing period.

Bring one or two pencils with good erasers. The testing center will provide scratch paper so you can write down any items you want to return to later on. Note that no writing instruments other than pencils are allowed.

Bring your Retest Admission Ticket. If you are retaking the test, be sure to bring your Retest Admission Ticket. This is extremely important so that you do not risk the test score being invalidated.

What Not to Bring

Do not bring calculators, books, papers, notes of any kind, cell phones, digital personal assistants, cameras, pagers, or any other similar kinds of materials into the testing room. Also, do not bring food or beverages into the room where you will be tested. Visitors are not permitted in the testing room either, so leave your friends, loved ones, and chauffeurs outside!

When You Are at the Test Center

GUIDELINES FOR BEING AT THE CTC

When you go to the CTC, you should observe certain guidelines. First you should arrive on time. If you arrive late, the policy is to not admit you. Thus, if you are traveling from a distance, be sure to leave more than enough time for your arrival.

Listen carefully to all the instructions you are given. You will be asked to provide various kinds of information, and it is important that you are prepared to provide it in order to ensure that your score is properly reported and validated. You will need to know your social security number, if you have one.

You must sign your name by clicking a signature box. If you do not sign, your scores will be held up.

Make sure that you ask any questions you have before the test begins, because you will not be allowed to ask questions after it has begun. Also you cannot leave the testing room until after the test is over. So please—if you need to go to the bathroom, go before the testing starts. Do not plan to wait until afterward. You do not want to be spending the testing session thinking about these kinds of needs.

At the risk of stating the obvious, you are forbidden to give or receive aid during the test. If you do either, you will be required to terminate the testing session, your test will not be scored, and you will not receive a refund.

HOW TO SOLVE ANALOGIES

What Is an Analogy?

An analogy is a problem of the form A is to B as C is to D. For notational convenience, the problem is often written as

$$A : B :: C : D.$$

This is the way problems are presented on the *MAT*.

Processes Involved in Solving Analogies

Some years ago, the senior author did a detailed analysis of the mental processes people use to solve analogies (Sternberg, 1977). He found that, overwhelmingly, people use a common and fairly straightforward strategy.

Consider the analogy **Washington : 1 :: Lincoln : (a) 5, (b) 10, (c) 15, (d) 23** as an example.

Step 1. *Encode the first analogy term.* You see the term "Washington," so you access meanings available to you in long-term memory, such as that Washington is the name of the first president, the name of a city, and the name of a state.

Step 2. *Encode the second analogy term.* You see the term "1," and you access meanings available to you in long-term memory, such as that 1 is the first whole number, that it can be a unitary quantity of things, and that it is also often used to refer to something that is the best of a bunch.

Step 3. *Infer the relation between the first and second analogy terms.* You try to figure out how Washington might be related to 1. You might now think of two possible relations, given your encoding: that Washington was the first (#1) president and that a bust of Washington appears on a $1 bill.

Step 4. *Encode the third term of the analogy.* You see that the third term is "Lincoln."

Step 5. *Map the relation between the first and second halves of the analogy.* You now can begin to relate the concept of *Lincoln* to the various relations between *Washington* and *1*. Of the inferred relations, both are still viable. Lincoln was also a president and also appears on a bill.

Step 6. *Encode the answer options.* You see the terms "5," "10," "15," and "23," and know what each of the numbers is.

Step 7. *Apply the relation you inferred between Washington and 1 in the second half of the analogy.* You now can try out the mapped version of the inferred relations on each of the options.

Note at this point the importance of knowledge to success on the *MAT*. To get this item correct, you had to know something about *Washington*. Now you have to know something about *Lincoln*. If you know that Lincoln is on the $5 bill, you have a possible answer, namely, (a). But unless you know that Lincoln was the 16th president, you may wonder whether one of the other options represents the ordinal position of his presidency. And if you do not know that Lincoln is on the $5 bill and you do not know that he was the 16th president, you may find any of the options potentially attractive. So in this item as in all *MAT* items, knowledge as well as reasoning is needed for a correct response.

Step 8. *Discriminate among the answer options.* At this point, you decide which option best satisfies the constraints of the inferred relation. If you know both that Lincoln is on the $5 bill and that he was the 16th president, you can select (a) with confidence.

Sometimes there is an (optional) additional step after 7 and before 8. If you solve an analogy and believe that none of the answer options is correct, then you do that additional step.

Step 8a. *Justify one option as best although not optimal.* In this case, you choose the best answer, even if you believe it is not a perfect answer.

Step 9. *Respond.* Mark "(a)" or whatever your preferred answer is on the answer sheet.

Four Ways of Presenting Analogies

On *MAT* analogies, one of the four terms, A, B, C, or D, will be missing. In its place will be four options. Your task will be to select the option that best fits the analogy. The following analogy might be presented in any of four ways.

EXAMPLE

BLACK : WHITE :: DARK : LIGHT
1. BLACK : WHITE :: DARK : (*a.* gray, *b.* shaded, *c.* light, *d.* heavy)
2. BLACK : WHITE :: (*a.* somber, *b.* blue, *c.* gray, *d.* dark) : LIGHT
3. BLACK : (*a.* color, *b.* white, *c.* gray, *d.* coal) :: DARK : LIGHT
4. (*a.* gray, *b.* black, *c.* heavy, *d.* somber) : WHITE :: DARK : LIGHT

The correct options, of course, are *c, d, b,* and *b,* respectively.

Ways of Perceiving Relationships

You may conceive of the relationship between the terms of the above analogy in two ways. First, you may say to yourself something like "White is the opposite of black, and light is the opposite of dark." Instead, you may say "Black is dark and white is light." Either way you will arrive at the same answer.

The first way looks at the two terms on the left (A : B) as one unit and the two terms on the right as a unit (C : D). The second way looks at the first and third terms as a unit (A : C) and the second and fourth terms as another unit (B : D). The important thing is to discover a relationship that is the same between the two terms in each unit.

Sometimes it is more convenient to solve an analogy in one way, and sometimes in the other.

EXAMPLE

1. DOCTOR : PATIENT :: LAWYER (*a.* judge, *b.* jury, *c.* district attorney, *d.* client)

If the analogy is presented in this form, it is easier to consider the first and third terms as one unit, and the second and fourth terms as another.

A Common Mistake

A common mistake made by those who are relatively unfamiliar with analogies is to try to find a relationship between the first and fourth or the second and third terms. Don't do this. Often an incorrect answer option is waiting to be picked by those who use this kind of faulty reasoning.

In solving analogies, keep the following diagram in mind:

A : B :: C : D   This is OK.

A : B :: C : D   This is OK.

A : B :: C : D   This is NOT OK!

The analogy DOCTOR : PATIENT :: LAWYER : CLIENT is acceptable. The analogy DOCTOR : LAWYER :: PATIENT : CLIENT is acceptable. The analogy DOCTOR : PATIENT :: CLIENT : LAWYER is *not* acceptable. The third and fourth terms of an analogy may not be reversed, nor may the first and second terms. You can look for relations between A and B, C and D, A and C, and B and D in an analogy. You should **not** look for relationships between A and D or between B and C.

Errors Stemming from Reversals

Errors stemming from reversals are frequent.

EXAMPLE

BIRD : SPARROW :: (*a.* boy, *b.* species, *c.* mammal, *d.* phylum) : HUMAN BEING

The relationship is that a sparrow is a type of bird, and a human being is a type of mammal.

Someone might carelessly interpret the analogy as requiring him or her to infer that a sparrow is a type of bird and a boy is a type of human being. This relationship is correct, but it is not the one posed by the analogy.

Examples

It is important to realize that an analogy cannot be inverted. That is, in the analogy A : B :: C : D, the relationship of A to B must be the same as that of C to D. Or the relationship of A to C can be the same as that of B to D.

But the relationship CANNOT BE that A is to B as D is to C, or A is to D as B is to C. Inversions are not allowed. Consider some examples:

EXAMPLE

CAT : SIAMESE :: (*a.* animal, *b.* boxer, *c.* angorra, *d.* pedigree) : DOG

The correct answer is *a.* The reason is that a Siamese is a kind of cat and a dog is a kind of animal. The tempting distracter is *b.* But note that if you were to choose *b,* you would be committing an inversion. View the analogy as taking the form A : B :: C : D. The relationship cannot be A (CAT) is related to B (SIAMESE) in the same way that D (DOG) is related to C (BOXER). Rather, it must be that A (CAT) is related to B (SIAMESE) in the same way that C (ANIMAL) is related to D (DOG). It cannot be that A is related to B as D is related to C.

EXAMPLE

PROTON : ATOM :: DIAL : (*a.* numeral, *b.* watch, *c.* band, *d.* time)

The correct answer is *b.* A proton is part of an atom and a dial is part of a watch. Note that the inverted form—PROTON is to ATOM as DIAL is to NUMERAL— does not work, because the analogy does not permit A to be related to B in the same way as D is related to C.

EXAMPLE

(*a.* tree, *b.* hemlock, *c.* maple, *d.* trunk) : DECIDUOUS :: SPRUCE : EVERGREEN

The correct answer is *c* because a maple is a kind of deciduous tree and a spruce is a kind of evergreen. Note that *a* does not work because it inverts the analogy. It would make a tree a superset of deciduous trees, but a spruce is not a superset but rather a subset of evergreen trees.

EXAMPLE

STREPTOCOCCUS : BACTERIUM :: HERPES : (*a.* type I, *b.* virus, *c.* bacteria, *d.* simplex)

The correct answer is *b* because streptococcus is a type of bacterium and herpes a type of virus. Note that one cannot invert the analogy. Thus, Type I is a type of herpes virus, but one is not allowed to have an analogy where A relates to B and D relates to C. Hence, the correct answer must be *b*.

What Makes an Analogy Difficult?

Miller analogies differ widely in difficulty. In general, one analogy may be more or less difficult than another analogy for any one or more of five reasons.*

1. Difficulty of Words—You may simply be unfamiliar with the meanings of some or all of the words in the analogy. In this case, you may be stumped by vocabulary limitations before you even begin to figure out relationships. For example, the analogy IDOLATRY : IDOLS :: OPHIOLATRY : (*a.* icons, *b.* fire, *c.* serpents, *d.* darkness) would be easy for most people to solve if they knew that *ophiolatry* is serpent worship. The difficulty of the analogy resides in the unfamiliarity of a single word.

2. Difficulty of Relation between *A* and *B*—You may know the meanings of the *A* and *B* (first two) terms of the analogy, but be unable to figure out the relationship between them. Consider, for example, the analogy TRAP : PART :: TEN : (*a.* net, *b.* twenty, *c.* whole, *d.* lost). The terms are all easily recognizable. The difficulty of the analogy is in recognizing that the relationship between the first two terms is that the second is the first spelled backward.

3. Difficulty of Relation between *A* and *C*—An analogy may be difficult because it is not immediately obvious how the *A* and *C* (first and third) terms match up. Consider, for example, the analogy GARMENT : WEAR :: POTION : (*a.* clothing, *b.* liquid, *c.* drink, *d.* magic). The terms *garment* and *potion* have little in common. Recognizing that one wears a garment does not immediately help you to decide what to do with *potion*. You must recognize that the rule that relates the first half of the analogy to the second half is that "*B* is what one does with *A*." One wears a garment, and drinks a potion.

4. Difficulty of Relation between *C* and *D*—Sometimes you may be able to infer the relation between *A* and *B*, but have difficulty applying the analogous relation from *C* to *D*. Consider, for example, the analogy GOVERNOR : PRESIDENT :: LEGISLATURE : (*a.* Capitol, *b.* Congress, *c.* House, *d.* Speaker). The terms of the analogy are all familiar ones, and the relations between *A* and *B* and between *A* and *C* are straightforward. The difficulty of

---

*Sternberg, R.J. Component processes in analogies reasoning. *Psychological Review*, 1977, 84, 353–378.
Sternberg, R.J. *Intelligence, Information Processing, and Analogical Reasoning: The Componential Analysis of Human Abilities*. Hillsdale, N.J.: Lawrence Erlbaum Associates, 1977.

this analogy is in applying the analogy rule from *legislature* to the best answer. Options *a*, *b*, and *c* are all fairly plausible, but reflection will reveal that *b* is the best answer. Option *a*, *Capitol*, refers to a specific building; option *c*, *House*, refers to only one of two congressional bodies. *Congress* (option *b*) is the national legislative body, however, and a legislature is a state legislative body.

5. Difficulty of Relation between D and Ideal Answer—Occasionally, you may come upon an analogy that for one reason or another seems to have no "perfect" answer. Consider, for example, the analogy MINUTE : HOUR :: FOOT : (*a*. yard, *b*. day, *c*. inch, *d*. length). The best answer is option *a*, although one could argue that this answer is far from perfect, since there are 60 minutes in an hour, but 3 feet in a yard. When none of the answer options seems quite right, you must either reconsider the way you have interpreted the analogy or else simply pick the answer that seems closest to the ideal one.

How to Select the Correct Answer

1. **Read all the options.** You must choose the best of the four alternative options presented. Keep in mind that item-writers make a deliberate (and usually successful) effort to make the incorrect options as plausible as possible. This fact has an important implication: *Read all the possible answer choices before selecting one.* Ace and Dawis (1973) found that analogies in which the last option is the correct one tend to be most difficult. A likely reason is that people sometimes don't bother to read through all the answers; they pick a plausible but incorrect option before they ever get to the last and correct option.

2. **Check the parts of speech.** In selecting an option, be systematic. When you don't know what all the terms mean, or when the relationship between them is not obvious to you, try to use context cues to figure things out. Remember that while not all terms of the analogy have to be of the same part of speech, they can be of no more than two parts of speech (except for nonsemantic analogies). Therefore, if an option you are considering introduces a third part of speech, it is probably incorrect.

3. **Infer the type of analogy.**

EXAMPLE

THRIFTY : (*a*. wasteful, *b*. economical, *c*. cheerful, *d*. wealthy) ::
SLATTERNLY : UNTIDY

Suppose that you don't know what the word *slatternly* means. You need not give up on the analogy either by skipping it or by answering randomly. The first inference you can make is that it is probably a Vocabulary item (see Content Category I, page 67). As you will soon learn by taking the practice tests, Vocabulary items frequently turn out to be Similarity or Contrast items (see Relationship Categories I-1 and I-2, page 75), and they are more likely to be items of the former kind (synonyms) than of the latter kind (antonyms). So a reasonable inference to make would be that *slatternly* means untidy, and that therefore option *b* is the correct answer, since *thrifty* means economical. Of course, you might not want to rule out the possibility of an antonym.

4. **Consider the sounds of words.** One thing you can do (and this really works on many occasions) is simply to look at the word *slatternly* and decide whether it *sounds* more like a word meaning tidy or one meaning untidy. Most people will choose *untidy*, and they will be correct. The answer to this problem is option *b*.

5. **Guess intelligently.** Suppose the item had been presented in this form:

EXAMPLE

THRIFTY : ECONOMICAL :: SLATTERNLY : (*a.* cheerful, *b.* quickly, *c.* circular, *d.* untidy).

The problem is now more difficult, with fewer context cues available. However, you can still approach the item systematically. First, you can reasonably eliminate option *b*. You know that *thrifty* and *economical* are adjectives, and three of the four answer options are also adjectives. *Quickly*, however, is an adverb, probably included as an incorrect option because it ends in *-ly*, as does *slatternly*. Next, you can reasonably eliminate option *c*. Although it is an *adjective*, it describes a property of an object, whereas *thrifty* almost always describes a characteristic of a person. You are now left with two options and have to make a choice, based on your past experience with words. When you finally choose an answer, you will still be guessing, but you will be guessing intelligently rather than blindly. Guessing can improve your score if you do it intelligently. Because there is no penalty for guessing, make an educated guess on any item when you are unsure of the correct answer. Try not to leave any items unanswered. Guessing intelligently can only improve your score.

6. **Use word association.** You will probably encounter some analogies on the *MAT* in which you find yourself simply unable to infer the relationship between the given terms. When all else fails, a strategy that is slightly better than wild guessing is to try word association. In using this strategy, you attempt to select the option that seems most closely related (in whatever way) to the given terms of the analogy.

The psychologist A. Willner had individuals take a form of the *MAT* as a word association test. Rather than try to solve the analogies, subjects were instructed to pick the answer option that seemed most highly associated to the given element. Willner found that on one of every four items, the correct answer (as keyed for the analogies test) was picked with greater than chance frequency. The indication is that, at least on some items, the word association technique will help you to do better than would random guessing. It is by no means a powerful strategy, however, and should be used only when your attempts to discover any kind of relationship have failed.

For example, consider the very first item of the Pretest. Suppose you were not sure of the exact relation being sought. If you selected option *b* because the color brown has the highest association with bears, in general, or grizzly bears, in particular, you would get the item correct, as brown is the color of the grizzly bear as well as being more highly associated with bears than are the other colors.

Allocating Your Time

A common problem in taking a test such as the *MAT* is one of time allocation. In particular, how much time do you allocate per item? You have 60 minutes for 120 items, meaning that you have to complete two analogies per minute in order to finish. And you really want to finish because items not answered are items lost. Moreover, looking at an item and getting an idea of what is on it provides a much better basis for taking a chance on an item than just answering at random!

First, always go in order because items are in order of difficulty. Your chances of getting items right are better on earlier than on later items. If you see an analogy and cannot answer it rather quickly—in 20 seconds or so—then make a notation somewhere of the item number. We recommend you use two different types of notations. One is for items for which you have an idea of what the correct answer is. The other is for items where you believe you pretty much have no idea of the correct answer. Then, when you go back, start with the items for which you have some idea of the correct answer. Do the items for which you have little idea last. But always answer the item once you have looked at it because you may not have time to go back. If you do have time, you can change your answer later. It is best to answer all items because it is the rare item for which you have absolutely no idea whatsoever of what the correct answer is.

A big mistake is to get hung up on a hard item. Sometimes, when taking a test, we lose track of the time. Losing track of time can be disastrous on a test such as the *MAT*. Each item counts the same, so it is absolutely not worth your time to spend a great deal of time on an item at the expense of other items. This is doubly true because, for all you know, the item may be one of the 20 experimental ones that do not count in any case. If you have answered all the other items, it is fine to spend that extra time. But if you haven't, be sure you answer all items to the best of your ability before you linger over any one item.

Sometimes, when people go back, they come up with a different answer than their initial one. A question they sometimes ask is whether to change the answer. We recommend you change the answer only if you are confident that the second answer is better than the first. There is some research to suggest that initial answers are better than redo answers.

Practice in Analogical Thinking

Directions: In each of the following the first two terms are related, sometimes in multiple ways. The third term is like the first two terms in some way but different from them in another. See how the third term is (a) like the first two terms and (b) different from them.

1. LEMON : TANGERINE :: PEACH

2. JUICE : MILK :: PANCAKES

3. DANCE : LEAP :: TURNED

4. PLANETS : ASTEROIDS :: SUN

5. ¾ : 0.75 :: 0.25

6. CENTIMETER : MILLIMETER :: INCH

7. DEGAS : MONET :: COURBET

8. SATURN : MERCURY :: PLANETS

9. BRASS : TUBA :: PERCUSSION

10. MISSISSIPPI : HUDSON :: HURON

11. MORGAN : MUSTANG :: MALTESE

12. WHELK : LIMPET :: KELP

13. STAMP : PHILATELIST :: NUMISMATIST

14. PURPLE : GREEN :: RED

15. DISCOVERY : ATLANTIS :: VIKING

16. CALDECOTT : NEWBERY :: PULITZER

17. LIMESTONE : SANDSTONE :: MARBLE

18. PHALANGES : METATARSALS :: FEMUR

19. MILK : CHEESE :: WHEAT

20. VITAMIN A : VITAMIN D :: VITAMIN C

21. ARTERIOSCLEROSIS : MYOCARDIAL INFARCTION :: CARDIOVASCULAR DISEASE

22. CARBON MONOXIDE : NITROGEN OXIDE :: ASBESTOS

23. MONOPHONIC : HOMOPHONIC :: DUPLE METER

24. INCUS : STAPES :: PINA

25. PRESIDENT'S DAY : VALENTINE'S DAY :: MARTIN LUTHER KING, JR., DAY

26. WOOD-CARVED RELIEF : CORK INLAY :: TEXTURE DRAWING

27. WATERCOLOR : TEMPERA :: CHARCOAL

28. EQUILATERAL TRIANGLE : SQUARE :: RHOMBUS

29. SPAN : CUBIT :: STONE

30. PHAEDO : REPUBLIC :: POETICS

31. SOPHOCLES : ARISTOPHANES :: HIPPOCRATES

32. TUNDRA : TAIGA :: TROPICAL RAIN FOREST

33. DONATELLO : MASACCIO :: RAPHAEL

34. DADA : SURREALISM :: SOCIAL REALISM

35. LYMPHOCYTES : MONOCYTES :: ERYTHROCYTES

36. SPRUCE : PONDEROSA :: HICKORY

37. PECK : BUSHEL :: FLUIDRAM

38. TROPIC OF CANCER : ARCTIC CIRCLE :: INTERNATIONAL DATE LINE

39. STARS AND STRIPES : OLD GLORY :: STARS AND BARS

40. FLINT : MATCHES :: LIGHTNING

41. DOMINICAN REPUBLIC : CUBA :: CHAD

42. OFFSIDE : CLIPPING :: GOALTENDING

43. KENYA : BRAZIL :: AUSTRALIA

44. FILMORE : VAN BUREN :: MARSHALL

45. TALLAHASSEE : COLUMBUS :: HOUSTON

46. IONESCO : BECKETT :: IBSEN

47. STIGMA : STYLE :: ANTHERS

48. CIRRUS : CIRROCUMULUS :: NIMBOSTRATUS

49. ORTHOCLASE : QUARTZ :: CALCITE

50. ST. PETER'S : SISTINE CHAPEL :: SANTA MARIA DELLA SALUTE

ANSWER EXPLANATIONS

1. A lemon, tangerine, and peach are fruits. Lemons and tangerines are citrus fruits, but peaches are not.

2. Juice, milk, and pancakes are foods. Juice and milk are liquid; pancakes are solid.

3. *Dance*, *leap*, and *turned* are verbs. *Dance* and *leap* are present tense; *turned* is past tense.

4. Planets, asteroids, and the sun are heavenly bodies. Planets and asteroids revolve around a star (the sun), whereas the sun is a star.

5. $\frac{3}{4}$, 0.75, and 0.25 are numbers less than 1. $\frac{3}{4}$ equals 0.75, whereas 0.25 does not.

6. Centimeter, millimeter, and inch are units of measure. Centimeter and millimeter are units in the metric system; inch is a unit in the English system.

7. Degas, Monet, and Courbet were painters. Degas and Monet are considered impressionists; Courbet, a realist.

8. Saturn and Mercury are planets; planet is the superordinate category.

9. A tuba is an instrument in the superordinate category "brass." Percussion is a different category of musical instruments.

10. The Mississippi, Hudson, and Huron are all bodies of water. The Mississippi and Hudson are rivers; Huron is a lake.

11. Morgan, Mustang, and Maltese are all breeds. Morgan and Mustang are breeds of horses. Maltese is a breed of dog or cat.

12. Whelk, limpet, and kelp are found in the ocean. Whelk and limpet are marine gastropods that live in shells. Kelp is seaweed.

13. A philatelist and a numismatist are collectors. A philatelist collects or studies stamps; a numismatist, coins.

14. Purple, green, and red are colors. Purple and green are secondary colors; red is primary.

15. Discovery, Atlantis, and Viking are space vehicles. Discovery and Atlantis are space shuttles; Viking is a planetary probe.

16. The Caldecott, Newbery, and Pulitzer are awards given to literature. The Caldecott and Newbery are given specifically to children's books, whereas the Pulitzer is not.

17. Limestone, sandstone, and marble are rocks. Limestone and sandstone are sedimentary rocks; marble is a metamorphic rock.

18. The phalanges, metatarsals, and femur are bones. The phalanges and metatarsals are bones in the foot; the femur is a bone in the leg.

19. Milk, cheese, and wheat are foods. Milk and cheese are members of the dairy nutritional group; wheat is not.

20. A, D, and C are vitamins. Vitamins A and D are fat-soluble; C is a water-soluble vitamin.

21. Arteriosclerosis and myocardial infarction are examples of the superordinate category "cardiovascular disease"—a disease of the heart and blood vessels.

22. Carbon monoxide, nitrogen oxide, and asbestos are air pollutants. Carbon monoxide and nitrogen oxide are gases that contribute to outdoor air pollution. Asbestos is usually an indoor air pollutant; also, asbestos is not a gas.

23. Monophonic, homophonic, and duple meter are examples of basic musical elements. Monophonic and homophonic are examples of musical texture; duple meter is an example of musical rhythm.

24. The incus, stapes, and pina are parts of the ear. The incus and stapes are parts of the inner ear; the pina is part of the outer ear.

25. President's Day, Valentine's Day, and Martin Luther King, Jr., Day are observed as special days in the United States. President's Day and Valentine's Day are in February; Martin Luther King, Jr., Day is in January.

26. Wood-carved relief, cork inlay, and texture drawing are art techniques. Wood-carved relief and cork inlay are three-dimensional; a texture drawing is two-dimensional.

27. Watercolor, tempera, and charcoal are media of artwork. Watercolor and tempera are types of paints, but charcoal is not.

28. An equilateral triangle, a square, and a rhombus are polygons. An equilateral triangle and a square are regular polygons; a rhombus is not a regular polygon because its angles do not have the same number of degrees.

29. Span, cubit, and stone have been used as units of measure. Span and cubit are measures of length; stone is a measure of weight.

30. The *Phaedo*, the *Republic*, and the *Poetics* are literary works associated with Greek philosophy. The *Phaedo* and the *Republic* are Platonic dialogues, whereas the *Poetics* was written by Aristotle.

31. Sophocles, Aristophanes, and Hippocrates were Greek. Sophocles and Aristophanes were masters of dramatic art; Hippocrates is identified with science and medicine.

32. Tundra, taiga, and tropical rain forest are examples of biomes. Tundra and taiga are cold-climate biomes; tropical rain forests are warm-climate biomes.

33. Donatello, Masaccio, and Raphael were Italian painters. Donatello and Masaccio are associated with 15th century Italian art and are considered painters of the "Proto-Renaissance." Raphael's work is classified as 16th century, High Renaissance.

34. Dada, surrealism, and social realism are 20th century art movements. Dadaists and surrealists fought against conventional, accepted meanings in their art. Social realists believed that art has a social purpose and meaning.

35. Lymphocytes, monocytes, and erythrocytes are blood cells. Lymphocytes and monocytes are white blood cells; erythrocytes are red blood cells.

36. Spruce, ponderosa, and hickory are trees. Spruce and ponderosa are pines; hickory is a broad-leaf tree.

37. Peck, bushel, and fluidram are all units of measure. Peck and bushel are units of capacity (dry measure); fluidram is a unit of liquid measure.

38. The Tropic of Cancer, the Arctic Circle, and the International Date Line are divisions of the earth. The Tropic of Cancer and the Arctic Circle divide the earth horizontally; the International Date Line divides the earth vertically.

39. Stars and Stripes, Old Glory, and Stars and Bars are names given to American flags. Stars and Stripes and Old Glory denote the flag; Stars and Bars was a name for the Confederate flag.

40. Flint, matches, and lightning can start fires. Flint and matches are human means of starting a fire; lightning is a natural means.

41. The Dominican Republic, Cuba, and Chad are countries. The Dominican Republic and Cuba are in the Western Hemisphere; Chad is in Africa.

42. Offside, clipping, and goaltending are penalties imposed in sports. Offside and clipping are used in football; goaltending, in basketball.

43. Kenya, Brazil, and Australia are countries. Kenya and Brazil are located on the equator. Australia is in the Southern Hemisphere.

44. Filmore, Van Buren, and Marshall have served as high officials of the U.S. government. Filmore and Van Buren were presidents. Marshall was a Supreme Court judge.

45. Tallahassee, Columbus, and Houston are cities in the United States. Tallahassee and Columbus are capital cities; Houston is not.

46. Ionesco, Beckett, and Ibsen are playwrights. Ionesco and Beckett are considered modern playwrights (1944–1975). Ibsen preceded Ionesco and Beckett but is considered the "father of modern drama" because he introduced social problems into his plays.

47. Stigma, style, and anthers are all parts of a flower. Stigma and style are considered parts of the "female" flower (carpel); the "male" plant structure (stamen) is tipped with anthers that produce pollen.

48. Cirrus, cirrocumulus, and nimbostratus are clouds. Cirrus and cirrocumulus are high-altitude clouds; nimbostratus clouds often occur at low altitude.

49. Orthoclase, quartz, and calcite are minerals. Orthoclase and quartz are silicate minerals; calcite is a carbonate mineral.

50. St. Peter's, the Sistine Chapel, and Santa Maria Della Salute are cathedrals. St. Peter's and the Sistine Chapel are in Rome; Santa Maria Della Salute is in Venice.

30 HELPFUL HINTS —— STRATEGY

Certain strategies are effective for raising scores on the *Miller Analogies Test*. Here are 30 of the most important ones.

HINT 1. *Don't wait until the last minute to prepare for the test.*
Research shows that you will do better if you spread your studying a little at a time over a longer period, rather than cramming all your studying into a shorter time right before the test. Therefore, start preparing at the earliest possible date!

HINT 2. *When you take practice tests, duplicate actual testing conditions as closely as possible.*
You best prepare yourself for the actual test if you take the practice tests under realistic conditions. Taking a standardized test means more than just answering a set of questions. It means you will be in an unusually stark testing room and will have to answer questions under time pressure. Actual testing conditions typically produce some degree of anxiety. Too much anxiety can hurt test scores, but so can too little anxiety. If you are too relaxed, you may find yourself not putting in maximal effort. Therefore, it is to your advantage to replicate actual testing conditions as closely as possible. When you take the practice tests, it is important that you strictly observe the time limit. Simulate all aspects of the testing situation as closely as possible and don't allow distractions (such as phone calls or errands).

HINT 3. *Realize that you can improve your score.*
One of the greatest sources of defeat is the belief that intellectual skills are fixed and hence unmodifiable. Once you believe that, it becomes true for you, because you make no effort to improve your intellectual performance.

Carol Dweck (1999) has studied thousands of students and found that they can be placed into two groups with respect to their beliefs about their abilities. One group believes that abilities are fixed; the other group believes that abilities are modifiable. When tasks are easy, the two groups of students do about equally well. But when tasks are difficult, the group that believes in the modifiability of abilities outperforms the group that believes that abilities are fixed. The reason is that the group that believes in the modifiability of abilities is willing to take on difficult challenges, whereas the group that believes in the fixedness of abilities is afraid to undertake tough challenges. People in this group are afraid they will look stupid if they try something hard. Believing that you can improve your intellectual skills is the first step toward improving them.

In fact, there is good evidence that intellectual abilities are modifiable (Grotzer & Perkins, 2000; Perkins & Grotzer, 1997; Sternberg, 1997; Ramey, 1994). It is to your advantage to act on this evidence.

HINT 4. *Be mindful when you take the test.*

How many times have you gone over the results of a test and felt like kicking yourself because you missed easy questions—questions to which you knew the answer? People often find that a major proportion of the test items they answer incorrectly are answered incorrectly not because they did not know the answer, but because their attention slipped or they got careless. Ellen Langer (1989, 1997) has referred to such behavior as *mindless*.

When we behave mindlessly, we act as though we are on automatic pilot—doing things without thinking. Have you ever been driving for a while and then discovered that you missed making a turn, or that you have lost track of what you are doing? Or have you ever been reading and gotten to the end of a page or even a book chapter, only to realize that you have only the foggiest idea of what you have just read? These are examples of mindless behavior.

You might think that people would not show such behavior during tests, but they do. Sometimes people let their minds stray even when the potential stakes in the situation are very high. Think about the catastrophes that can result from being mindless when driving! Make the decision that for the 60 minutes you take the test, you will be completely *mindful* and will concentrate fully on the test.

HINT 5. *Take responsibility for your test score.*

Julian Rotter (1990) has found that some people tend to be what he refers to as *internals*, whereas others tend to be *externals*. Internals take responsibility for their own successes and failures, whereas externals tend to blame other people or circumstances for their successes and failures. Research has consistently shown that *internals* tend to outperform externals in a variety of kinds of life tasks.

First, you need to take responsibility for your test preparation. There are always factors that will get in the way. You will have other things to do; perhaps you will have started preparing later than you should have; perhaps some catastrophic event has recently happened in your life or the life of a loved one. Whatever problems may emerge, it is essential that you take responsibility for preparing. This is the only way you can become truly prepared.

Second, you need to take responsibility for what happens the day of the test. The first author remembers that when he took the *Miller Analogies Test* some years ago, he was seated at a desk that was too small for him. It was uncomfortable, and he cursed his luck for getting stuck with such a small desk, not to mention the occasional noises of construction that came from outside. But then he realized that he had to take responsibility for his own performance. In many testing situations, *something* goes wrong. It may be different things on different days. Maybe you didn't sleep enough, or maybe the desk is too small, or the room too noisy, or the illumination less than adequate. For the 60 minutes you take the test, put all of this stuff out of your mind. Just focus on the test. The mark of the expert test-taker is deciding that, for the time that the test is in progress, he will focus on the test and put other things out of his mind.

HINT 6. *Be motivated, regardless of the stakes.*

Several years ago, the undergraduates in the first author's department at the time (the Psychology Department at Yale) invited him to give a talk to a group of them. He was honored to have been asked to speak and showed up at the appointed time. Unfortunately, no one else showed up except the woman who had organized the talk. She was extremely apologetic and started to give him a number of possible explanations for why no one else showed up.

At first, the first author felt hurt, but then he started to laugh. He said that he was actually very grateful that only she had shown up. The reason was that he could expect (or, at least, hope) that any talk he ever gave in the future would have at least as good and probably a better turnout. He now would be able to motivate himself to give his best possible talk, if at least two people (the organizer plus one other person) showed up! If at least two people turned out, it would be better than the turnout that ill-fated day. And sure enough, whether he gets two people or two thousand, he gives it his best shot regardless of the stakes, remembering the time that only the organizer showed up.

Some of you will be taking the *Miller Analogies Test* for extremely high stakes. The test may play a pivotal role in your being admitted or not admitted to the graduate school of your choice, or it may determine whether or not you get financial aid. Others of you will be taking the test for lower stakes. Perhaps only schools you do not care so much about require this particular test, or perhaps you are not even sure you want to go to graduate school in the first place, so a low score will not bother you so much.

Remember the lesson from the speaking engagement, though. If it is worth your time to take the test, it is worth your time to give the test your best shot. You should prepare for the experience with whatever resources you can bring to bear. Too often, people sabotage themselves, telling themselves that something is not important. This way, if they do not do well on it, they do not feel so bad. Don't fall into self-sabotage. Give the *MAT* your best shot, regardless of the stakes.

HINT 7. *Combat test anxiety with visualization and relaxation.*

If you tend to be test anxious, there are steps you can take to help yourself combat your test anxiety. Spend some time each day imagining yourself in the actual testing situation, and try to relax while you visualize yourself actually taking the test.

If that image is too stressful, start with less threatening images and build up to the image of yourself taking the test. For example, you might first imagine yourself three weeks before the test, preparing for the test. That image should be less threatening. So try to relax. Then imagine yourself two weeks before, then one week before, then right at the test. In each case, try to relax as you construct your image.

This description is a simplification of a psychotherapeutic technique called *systematic desensitization*. If you find that this self-help technique does not enable you to relax, you might seriously consider going for a few sessions of therapy to a behavior therapist or a cognitive-behavioral therapist. These therapists can help you alleviate your anxiety.

HINT 8. *Eat something light before the test, avoiding large amounts of sugar.*

Taking a standardized test consumes a great deal of your energy. The day of the test is not the day to fast or to skip breakfast. You need the energy you get from the meal. But don't eat a heavy meal right before a test. You want your energy going to the test, not to digestion. Also, avoid large quantities of sugar. Sugar can give you an immediate high after you consume it, but often leads to a slump somewhat later. You cannot risk feeling the slump while you are taking the test.

HINT 9. *Go to the restroom before you start the MAT.*

You also do not want to waste time getting up and going to the restroom—or needing to go! Make every effort to take care of your restroom needs before the test begins.

HINT 10. *Keep in mind that early items will tend to be easy and later items, difficult.*

You should answer test items in the order that they are presented because they are in average order of difficulty. Thus, for the hypothetical "average" person, the items will be in exact order of difficulty. But because there really is no completely average person, each person will find the order of difficulty a bit different.

An important implication of the principle that items are in order of difficulty is that, if you find an early item to be very hard or a late item to be very easy, you may be misperceiving the point of the question. If you perceive an early item as very difficult, you may be reading things into the item that simply are not there. Ask yourself whether there might be some easier way to see the problem. If you see a later item as very easy, you may be failing to appreciate whatever it is that makes the item difficult, and you may choose a sucker response as your answer choice. Ask yourself whether you might be missing something important in the question. So keep in mind that early items ought to be, on average, relatively easy, and later items, on average, relatively difficult.

Consider two examples. Suppose the following analogy occurs relatively early in the test.

HIT : HIT :: TALK : (*a.* speak, *b.* lecture, *c.* talked, *d.* silent)

This analogy is a straightforward one but not a totally obvious one. At first glance, it might look like it is unbelievably simple, representing simply a repetition of a word. But it becomes obvious quickly that it does not involve merely a repetition, because none of the answer options is *talk*. It is not a synonym analogy either, because HIT is not a synonym for HIT, but, at first glance, the same word.

Option *c* should give the answer away. TALKED is the past tense of TALK, just as HIT is the past tense of HIT. That's all there is to the analogy. There is nothing more, nothing deep. Select option *c* and move on.

Now suppose the following analogy comes rather late in the test:

(*a.* France, *b.* Russia, *c.* Italy, *d.* St. Helena) : NAPOLEON BONAPARTE :: ENGLAND : SIGMUND FREUD

The analogy at first appears to be straightforward. Napoleon was from France. But wait a minute. Sigmund Freud was not originally from England. He was from Austria. So the analogy is not about where a person was from, at least, not originally. The analogy requires you to know that Sigmund Freud, although he was born in Austria, died in England. Napoleon Bonaparte died on the island of St. Helena. The analogy, then, is quite difficult.

HINT 11. *Read every question completely*.

Look at *all* the answer options presented for each question. Remember, distracters (wrong answers) are there, literally, to distract you. Sometimes, the first option (or the second or the third) may look good and you may be inclined to save yourself time by selecting it. *Don't do it*. The distracter may be a near miss. Consider an example:

PEN : INK :: PENCIL : (*a.* lead, *b.* eraser, *c.* paper, *d.* graphite)

A test-taker in a hurry might quickly select option *a* because at first glance, it looks right. But in analogies, you are looking for the *best* answer, and you cannot know what the best answer is until you have read *all* the answer options. If you take the little additional time it requires to read *all* the options, you will discover that option *d* is graphite, which is a good competitor for being correct.

So which is the better option, "lead" or "graphite"? Well, in this case, ink is the substance contained inside the pen. The substance inside a pencil is graphite, not lead. The "lead" of a pencil is made of graphite. Thus, a pen uses (writes with) ink in the same way that a pencil uses (writes with) graphite, not lead. But if you do not read the whole test item, you may never get to choose the better answer.

HINT 12. *Read every question carefully*.

You need to read every question not only completely, but carefully. Consider an example.

TERRIBLE : HORRIBLE :: INGENUOUS : (*a.* clever, *b.* sophisticated, *c.* naïve, *d.* foolish)

If you read this item carelessly, you may quickly choose *clever* as the correct answer, and end up getting it wrong. *Clever* would have been the best response had the third word in the stem of the analogy been INGENIOUS, but the word is INGENUOUS, not INGENIOUS. The best answer is thus the synonym for INGENUOUS, namely, NAÏVE. You need to read the words carefully.

Suppose you do not know what INGENUOUS means. In this case, you will have to guess. Use the process of elimination. If, at least, you read the question carefully, you will know that the word for which you need a synonym is *not* INGENIOUS, so that *clever* probably is *not* the best answer, but rather, a distracter. At least you have eliminated one distracter and can choose from among the remaining three. It is also a good guess that *foolish* is wrong, because *foolish* is the opposite of *ingenious*; but we have now determined that the item most likely has nothing to do with being ingenious. Hence, your best bet is either option *b* or option *c*. As it turns out, option *c* is the best answer.

Here is another example:

FROWARD : (*a.* obedient, *b.* backward, *c.* disobedient, *d.* frontward) :: AHEAD : BEHIND

If read carelessly, the whole analogy appears to be about antonyms with respect to directions of movement. But that is not what the analogy is about. The first word is FROWARD, not FORWARD. And FROWARD means not easily controlled or contrary. The best answer is therefore *a*, because *obedient* is an antonym to FROWARD. Again, you must read each word carefully.

You may not know what FROWARD means. In this case, though, you can guess by using the process of elimination. Because you know that FROWARD is *not* FORWARD, it is a safe guess that you can eliminate the options pertaining to direction, namely, *b* and *d*. So *a* or *c* is probably the best answer. In fact, *a* is correct.

HINT 13. ***Don't avoid questions just because they initially look difficult.***
Sometimes, a question that looks difficult when you first glance at it proves not to be very hard at all. Therefore, before deciding to skip a question and come back to it, make sure that the question actually is difficult. Consider an example:

VENUS : BEAUTY :: PLUTO : (*a*. prosperity, *b*. underworld, *c*. war, *d*. hearth)

Maybe your first reaction is that you just don't remember all those Greek and Roman gods. But wait a minute. Look at the item. You may find that you remember a few of them, and the one you remember is that Pluto was supposed to be the god of the underworld.

HINT 14. ***Watch out for reversals.***
Remember that the direction of the relationship must be the same on both sides of the analogy. Do not trip yourself up by reversing directions. Consider an example:

METER : (*a*. millimeter, *b*. centimeter, *c*. decimeter, *d*. kilometer) ::
YEAR : MILLENNIUM

It is very easy to trip yourself up on this analogy, because option *a*, *millimeter*, has the same initial letters, *mill*, as has the stem term MILLENNIUM. The option therefore sounds right if one is not sensitive to reversals. But a millennium is one thousand years. Because order counts, the second term must represent a thousand of the first term (METER), just as the fourth term (MILLENNIUM) represents a thousand of the third term (YEAR). The correct option thus must represent one thousand meters, not one-thousandth of a meter. The correct option therefore is *d*.

HINT 15. ***Look for all valid relationships but only for valid relationships.***
Remember that you can look for relationships either between the first and second and then the third and fourth terms, or between the first and third and then the second and fourth terms. All these relationships are *valid* for solving an analogy. But you *cannot* look for relationships between the first and fourth or between the second and third terms. These relationships are *invalid* for solving an analogy.
Consider the following analogy:

FOUR : 120/15 :: 32 : (*a*. 2^6, *b*. One hundred twenty-eight, *c*. Twenty-four, *d*. LXIV)

The basic analogy here is one of doubling. The second term is double the first and the correct option for the fourth term is double the third. Thus, removing differences of notation, 4 : 8 :: 16 : 32. But there is an option designed to trick test-takers who might look for a relationship between the first and fourth or between the second and third terms. This option is *b*. The third term (32) is four times the second term (120/15), and option *b*, one hundred twenty-eight, is four times the third term (32). Note also that the second and third terms are in Arabic numerals, and that if one selects option *b* (One hundred twenty-eight) or even option *c* (Twenty-four), one will have the first and fourth as well as the second and third terms in the same system of notation. But these relations are irrelevant. The only relations that matter are between the first and second terms and the third and fourth terms, on the one hand, and the first and third terms and the second and fourth terms, on the other. The correct answer is *d*.

HINT 16. *Analyze item contents and relations carefully.*
Remember that not all terms of the analogy have to be from the same content area. Do not be fooled by clang associations just because they seem to be from the right content area. Also, analyze the relations carefully. Consider an example:

ANNA KARENINA : LEO TOLSTOY :: (*a.* Scarlett O'Hara, *b.* Melanie Wilkes, *c. Gone with the Wind, d. War and Peace*) : MARGARET MITCHELL

The analogy starts off with a name that is both the name of a character and the name of a book by Leo Tolstoy. At this point, one cannot tell whether the correct relation is about being a character in a book or about being the name of the book. The second half of the analogy clarifies the issue. The options contain two names of characters that are from *Gone with the Wind*, as well as the title of the book by Margaret Mitchell. Because options *a* and *b* cannot both be correct, the analogy must be about titles of books, so the correct option is *c, Gone with the Wind*.

This analogy can be confusing. First, Scarlett O'Hara is so highly associated with *Gone with the Wind* that she can quickly appear to provide an attractive answer option. Moreover, it is quite possible that the correct relationship is one of characters in a novel. But the appearance of the name Melanie Wilkes, who is less closely associated with the novel, renders Scarlett O'Hara a less plausible option. The analogy thus appears to be about book titles, not about characters. Unless one carefully considers both the contents and the relations in the analogy, however, it is easy to get the analogy wrong.

HINT 17. *Examine parts of speech.*
Remember that many words can serve as multiple parts of speech, and that you need to check the various meanings of a word to ensure that you are using the word in its proper meaning and part of speech. Check that parts of speech match properly. An option is wrong if it does not correctly match the needed part of speech, even though the option may be otherwise plausible. Consider an example:

WAG : (*a.* tail, *b.* rattle, *c.* roll, *d.* joker) :: HARM : INJURE

This is quite a difficult analogy that easily confuses the test-taker. The most frequent use of the term WAG is as a verb, and the second half of the analogy contains two verbs, reinforcing the notion that, apparently, the entire analogy involves verbs.

Because HARM and INJURE are synonyms, the relation must be one of synonymy. But the problem is that neither *rattle* nor *roll* is a good synonym for WAG. Both are somewhat related, but neither really comes anywhere close to being a synonym. So there is no option that fits WAG as a verb. The test-taker must realize that WAG is being used as a noun and therefore that the synonym must also be a noun. A WAG is a joker.

HINT 18. *Be systematic.*
Try to be systematic in selecting the correct option. Use word association only if all else fails.

Consider an example:

LIBERATE : FREEDOM :: LIAISE : (*a.* connection, *b.* captivity, *c.* limit, *d.* destine)

This analogy is difficult in part because many test-takers will never have used or perhaps even seen the word LIAISE. It is an uncommon word, used primarily in Great Britain, and hence one can be forgiven for not knowing it. But you can be systematic and use your prior knowledge to try to solve the analogy.

First of all, LIAISE sounds like a verb, like LIBERATE. Because FREEDOM, the pair of LIBERATE, is a noun, you will want an option that is a noun. That removes option *d*, which is a verb. Because you know that liberating an individual or groups establishes a kind of freedom for that individual or group, you want to figure out what you would establish when you liaise. You probably know that a liaison is a person who establishes a connection. Therefore your best bet is to infer that to liaise is to establish a liaison, or a connection. You choose option *a*, which is the correct option.

HINT 19. *Pace yourself.*
Because you will have 60 minutes to answer 120 items, you should average no more than 30 seconds per analogy. Some items will take more time, some less. Do not get bogged down on a few difficult items. This can be a tremendous waste of time. If an answer just does not come to you, come back to the particular question when (or if) you have time.

For example, suppose you come across the analogy:

K : POTASSIUM :: (*a.* So, *b.* Sd, *c.* Na, *d.* Hg) : SODIUM

You took chemistry and you are pretty sure that, if you really set your mind to it, you can retrieve the chemical symbol for sodium. The problem is that it just isn't coming to you. So you stare at the item and stare some more, and try to think of everything you learned in chemistry, hoping that the association will come to you.

You're wasting your time. You might wish to pick whatever answer looks the best to you, flag the item, and move on. You are much better off going on to other items, and coming back to this one if you have time. You could stare at the item for five minutes, and still not remember that the chemical symbol for sodium is Na.

HINT 20. *Use all the time you are allotted.*
Never leave the test early. If you have time at the end of the test, review your answers, particularly to questions that you found to be difficult.

HINT 21. *Forget about other problems in your life.*
If, while you are taking the test, you start thinking about anything but the test (e.g., a misunderstanding with a friend or a money problem), STOP! You can think about these other things later. Give the test 100% concentration.

HINT 22. *Answer every question.*
If you have only a couple of minutes left and have not reached questions near the end, then fill in answers to these items anyway. If you left any items unanswered that you already looked at, fill in answers to those items too. There is no penalty for incorrect answers, and by leaving items unanswered you are wasting possible points.

HINT 23. *Wear a watch.*
It is amazing how people can fail to take even the simplest steps to help them improve their score. They may spend hours studying for the test and even taking sample tests, and then neglect to wear a watch when they are tested. You must wear a watch or bring a pocket watch or other clock. There may not be a clock in the testing room, or it may not be easily visible. If the clock is not easily visible, do you really want to waste time trying to decipher the time from it? It is the watch that enables you both to pace yourself and then to fill in at the end answers to questions you may not have reached. Remember that to fill in these answers a minute or two before time is up is called *test-wiseness*, but to do so at any time after time is up is called *cheating*. Therefore, make sure you're test-wise.

Hint 24. *Write down the number of the items you need to go back to.*
You may not be able to figure out the correct solution to every item right away. Remember you have only 30 seconds for each item. Move on to work on other items, but write down the items you thought are difficult so you can return to them once you have finished the test.

HINT 25. *Don't panic.*
If you find you don't know the answer to the first question, or to the second, or to the third, don't worry. Although items are arranged in order of difficulty, this ordering is of *average* difficulty. What is difficult for one person may be easy for another, and vice versa. The test is tough to begin with, so you can expect to find questions you can't answer scattered throughout the test.

HINT 26. *Be self-confident.*
Even if you're a notoriously poor test-taker, after working through this book, you will have done pretty much all you can to ensure that you perform up to your full potential. That's the most you can ask of yourself.

HINT 27. *If you don't do as well as you had hoped, retake the test.*
If things do not go as well as you had hoped, you can always retake the test. People typically do substantially better the second time they take a test. These "practice effects" are particularly notable on the *Miller Analogies Test*. Thus if things do not go as you had hoped, try again. Chances are you will do better the second time around.

HINT 28. *Remember that the test score is only one factor that is considered in admissions and financial aid decisions.*
Decisions about admissions and financial aid are almost always based on many factors. Thus, you should not believe that your whole future will hinge on how you do on the *MAT*. After making your best effort, keep in mind that in most cases the test score is not a decisive factor in admissions and financial aid decisions.

HINT 29. *Don't confuse test scores with measures of intelligence.*
Tests such as the *Miller Analogies Test* measure only a part—and arguably a relatively small part—of intelligence. These tests do not measure creative abilities or common-sense abilities, for example. These test scores account for only a relatively small proportion of the sources of individual differences that determine who succeeds to a greater or lesser extent in life (Gardner, 1983, 1999; Sternberg, 1997, 2000). Indeed, these tests account for only about 10% of the variation among individuals in their success. If you do well on the *MAT*, congratulations. If you don't, remember that there is much more to intelligence than what this or other similar tests measure.

HINT 30. *If you bought this book, then you have the right attitude toward life.*
If you bought this book, then your attitude toward life is that you can do better if you work at it. Ultimately, that will probably count for a lot more than a test score. Albert Bandura (1997) has shown that one of the best predictors of success in life is a sense of *self-efficacy*, the belief that one can do what one needs to get done. Your buying this book shows that you believe that, with hard work, you can do better. And that is the attitude that will help you succeed in life.

References

Bandura, A. *Self-efficacy: The Exercise of Control*. New York: W. H. Freeman and Company, 1997.

Dweck, C. S. *Self-theories: Their Role in Motivation, Personality, and Development*. Philadelphia: Psychology Press, 1999.

Gardner, H. *Frames of Mind: The Theory of Multiple Intelligences*. New York: Basic, 1983.

Gardner, H. *Intelligence Reframed: Multiple Intelligences for the 21st Century*. New York: Basicbooks, 1999.

Grotzer, T. A., & Perkins, D. A. Teaching of intelligence: A performance conception. In R. J. Sternberg (Ed.), *Handbook of Intelligence* (pp. 492–515). New York: Cambridge University Press, 2000.

Karkee, T., Kim, D., & Fatica, K. *Comparability study of online and paper and pencil tests using modified internally and externally matched criteria*. Paper presented at the annual meeting of the American Educational Research Association, Denver, CO, April 2010.

Langer, E. J. *Mindfulness*. New York: Addison-Wesley, 1989.

Langer, E. J. *The Power of Mindful Learning.* Needham Heights, MA: Addison-Wesley, 1997.

Perkins, D. N., & Grotzer, T. A. Teaching intelligence. *American Psychologist,* Vol. 52, 1125–1133, 1997.

Ramey, C. T. Abecedarian Project. In R. J. Sternberg (Ed.), *Encyclopedia of Human Intelligence* (Vol. 1, pp. 1–2). New York: Macmillan, 1994.

Rotter, J. B. Internal versus external control of reinforcement: A case history of a variable. *American Psychologist,* Vol. 45, 489–493, 1990.

Sternberg, R. J. *Successful Intelligence.* New York: Plume, 1997.

Sternberg, R. J. Successful intelligence: A unified view of giftedness. In C. F. M. van Lieshout & P. G. Heymans (Ed.), *Developing Talent, Across the Life Span* (pp. 43–65). Hove, UK: Psychology Press, 2000.

Tsai, T. & Shin, C. D. A score compatibility study for the NBDHE: Paper-pencil versus computer versions. *Evaluation and the Health Professions* (published online before print; doi: 10.1177/0163278712445203), 2012.

Wang, S., Jiao, H., Young, M. J., Brooks, T., & Olson, J. Comparability of computer-based and paper-and-pencil testing in K-12 Reading Assessments: A meta-analysis of testing mode effects. *Educational and Psychological Measurement,* Vol. 68(1), 5–24, 2008.

THE 12 BIGGEST MISTAKES TEST-TAKERS MAKE

1. **Believing that test scores are the measure of a man or woman.** All societies share certain "conventional wisdom." Some of it is true; some of it is not. For example, in 1787, a "three-fifths compromise" was enacted that, for determining political representation in the House of Representatives, would count each slave as three-fifths of a person. This was silly, and yet it was actually written into law. Societies do things at times that later seem odd. Our society believes, properly, we think, that tests have a useful role in high-stakes educational decisions, but some people start to view tests as measuring the worth of a person. Is the score of someone, which is three-fifths of someone else's worth only three-fifths as much? The answer, of course, is no. But you need not only to know that, but to feel it. Your worth as a person is *not* determined by your test scores. Many people with lower test scores go on to do great things. Some with higher test scores go on to do little.

2. **Believing the hype that the tests measure all they are supposed to measure.** Don't believe the hype. People are either analytical thinkers or not analytical thinkers. And can't someone be a good analytical thinker without having the vocabulary and general information to do well on this particular test? Certainly. It will not identify analytical thinkers who do not speak English. And how about those for whom English is a second language? Our society hypes various products, including tests. Don't get sucked in. No test

is perfect. No test identifies analytical or any other kinds of thinkers in a fool-proof way. The test is a means to help you get into graduate school or to help you get a scholarship or fellowship. It's not a whole lot more than that.

3. **Believing that test scores are immutable.** Many students believe the statements that test publishers sometimes make that using books or taking courses to improve scores really cannot make much of a difference in test scores. Not so. Test-taking is a learnable skill, just as is riding a bicycle or using a word-processing program on a computer. Almost every skill is learnable and modifiable. Test-taking is no exception. At the same time, it is better to expect reasonable gains than unreasonable ones. If your goal is to increase your score 10 or 15 points out of 100, that is quite reasonable, and you may attain this goal. If your goal is to increase your score 30 or 40 points, for most people, that will not be a realistic goal.

4. **Being overconfident or underconfident.** People who are overconfident set themselves up for a fall. They do not take the challenge of the test seriously enough, thinking that without hard work and preparation they will ace the test. Often, they end up being disappointed. People who are underconfident often choke when they take this test or any other. They become so nervous that they cannot perform at their optimum level. So they create for themselves a self-fulfilling prophecy.

5. **Taking the test close to the deadline for which the score must be submitted.** All tests have a standard error of measurement. That means that sometimes you will do better than you could have expected to do, and other times you will do worse. If you do worse, you can always retake the test. But you cut off your chance of doing that if you take the test too close to when the score is due. In that case, if you get a score that is lower than you had hoped for, you do not allow yourself the option to take it again. Don't wait until the last minute. Take the test early so that if you need to take it again, you will have time.

6. **Drinking a lot of coffee or tea before taking the test.** Research shows that caffeine can help mental performance. So a little coffee or tea before the test may actually help your score. But do not consume too much caffeine. First, it may make you jumpy and actually hurt your performance. Second, it may leave you wanting to go the bathroom, and you will not be permitted to go during the testing session. Third, if you are not used to it, you may have side effects such as feeling restless, irritable, or trembling of the hands—the last thing you need when you take a test.

7. **Cramming at the last moment.** Just don't. Research shows that last-minute cramming is not helpful and can actually hurt you. Don't study in the last 24 hours before the test. Just get plenty of rest and go to the test refreshed. You need to have a study plan that starts you early and not at the last moment.

8. **Spending too much time on hard items.** If you get stuck on an item, move on. You then can later return to it. There are 120 items to be completed in

60 minutes. That is two per minute. You cannot afford to waste lots of time on hard items.

9. **Not reading items carefully.** Don't waste points on sloppy reading of items. Many people, on later finding out the answers to a test, feel like kicking themselves for getting items wrong for which they knew the answer, because they did not read the item carefully. You cannot afford to waste points on sloppy reading of items.

10. **Leaving items blank.** There is *no* penalty for wrong answers. Do *not* leave any blanks. When time is soon going to be up, make sure you answer every question, even if you answer at random.

11. **Not budgeting time.** You have 30 seconds per item. That's it. So you have to keep budgeting your time so as not to waste time. Don't let yourself get behind. If an item is too hard, move on. Near the end, fill in an answer at random if you cannot get back to it.

12. **Eliminating answer options that are correct.** Distracters—wrong answers—are chosen on the Miller Analogies Test to be attractive. That means it may be tempting to eliminate as incorrect an answer option that is actually correct. Unless you are confident that an option is wrong, do not eliminate it. If you cannot eliminate even one answer option *for sure,* guess at random. You will have a 1 out of 5 chance of getting the item right.

References

www.MillerAnalogies.com.
http://harcourtassessment.com/haiweb/Cultures/en-US/dotCom/milleranalogies.com.htm

ADVICE ON PREPARING FOR THE *MAT*

That the *MAT* is not just a test of your reasoning abilities is probably evident to you from doing the Pretest in this book. The *MAT* also assesses your vocabulary and your store of general information, as well as specific information in diverse areas. A person whose native language is not English and whose culture is not mainstream will find the *MAT* extremely difficult, even if the aid of a dictionary were allowed. The level of vocabulary on the test is high; in addition, the definition used for a particular word is not always the most salient or obvious.

In using this book, you are strongly advised to keep a notebook of words you don't know along with their definitions. Use a dictionary to look up words you're not sure of. Study these words regularly, and use them as much as possible, in order to add them to your vocabulary. Also study the vocabulary given in this book as well as the words in the practice tests. The vocabulary on pages 87–104 contains words often used in graduate-level tests and, in addition, provides you with useful synonyms and antonyms.

Five other techniques are also useful in learning new words:

1. Use mnemonics as much as possible, visualizing the words and their meanings as vividly as you can.

2. Group together similar words to study. Also, put together words with similar roots and related meanings.
3. Make flashcards with words on one side, definitions on the other. Study the cards during any free time you have.
4. Whenever possible, study the words with their antonyms and synonyms.
5. Read a good newspaper regularly, such as *The New York Times* or *The Wall Street Journal*, to reinforce the vocabulary you have learned.

Not all these techniques work for everyone; some are better than others for different people. But the benefits of increasing your vocabulary are enormous—you will raise not only your *MAT* scores but other test scores as well.

Fighting Test Anxiety

Almost everyone is familiar with test anxiety. You walk into the examination room and your heart starts beating rapidly, you start sweating, and you start thinking about how poorly you are about to do on the exam. This is detrimental to your test-taking. You may know all there is to know, but if you go into the exam overly anxious, you will not do as well as you should. It is normal for a test-taker to have a mild amount of anxiety; it's what gets a person through an exam. However, too much anxiety can have a crippling effect when a person focuses on negative thoughts and ignores positive ones.

Causes of an individual's test anxiety may be one's exaggeration of the consequences of the exam, the demands one has placed on oneself, or the evaluation of oneself in terms of one's performance on the exam. The most effective way to handle test anxiety is with professional help (e.g., a clinical psychologist). Psychologists have found several techniques, most of which are based on relaxation, to be effective in battling test anxiety. One such technique is systematic desensitization.

Systematic desensitization teaches an individual to be able to relax in the presence of whatever causes the anxiety—in this case, an exam. The individual seeking this therapy is initially taught to relax while imagining anxiety-producing scenarios. The scenarios are graded. Some produce mild amounts of anxiety, whereas others produce extreme amounts of anxiety. Individuals work their way up from the least to the most anxiety-producing scenarios. The client begins by imagining the scenario that produces the least amount of anxiety while relaxing, and if that does not cause anxiety, the person imagines the next scenario on the scale. If it does cause anxiety, the client repeats imagining scenarios until he or she can do so without experiencing anxiety. The client gradually works through all of the scenarios until all of them can be imagined without a great deal of anxiety. It typically takes weeks or even a few months to get through all of them.

For example, a woman seeking treatment for test anxiety may first be told to imagine herself driving to the test center. If she does not feel anxiety while imagining this, she may then imagine getting out of the car, then imagine walking to the building, then imagine walking to the examination room, etc. She will go through this progression of scenarios until she can imagine herself picking up her pencil and taking the test without too much anxiety. At this point, her anxiety about taking tests should diminish.

Although this process works best when it is done with professional help over many sessions, you can learn from it. Its greatest lessons are that you should acquaint yourself with the testing process, and you should relax before an exam, not just a few minutes before sitting down to take it, but weeks in advance. Imagine all the details about the examination day that you can think of. For example, picture how you will get ready to go to the testing center, how you will get there, and how you will get through the paperwork. You should also take the practice tests in this book very seriously; they are very comparable to the real *MAT*. Take the practice tests under real test-taking conditions. For instance, find a quiet place, do not allow any distractions, set a time limit, and pretend you are in the examination room taking the real test. If you take all the practice tests in this book in that manner, when it comes time to take the real one, you will feel more comfortable with the test and the procedures.

Other recommendations that you may want to consider are:

1. Do not wait until the last minute to study. If you wait, you will get flustered by all the studying there is to do, and you will not be able to study as effectively. Study with a positive attitude. Of course there will be information you don't know—no one knows everything—but learn as much as you can, and remember that there is a lot that you do know.

2. As you go to the test center, keep a positive attitude. Do not panic. You have done all the preparing you could do. Remember, the *MAT* is only one part of your entire portfolio. You have accomplished a great deal to get to where you are today, including higher education or employment. Those taking your *MAT* score into consideration will also take into consideration everything else you have accomplished. Think ahead to after the exam. When the exam is over, and it is no longer looming over your head, you will still be the same person. This exam will not drastically change your life.

3. When you take the *MAT*, try to put aside other problems in your life. Give this exam your full concentration. Continue to relax. Have self-confidence. Answering a question you know should fuel your confidence. When you come to a question you don't know, as everyone does, do not let it discourage you. Make an educated guess and then move on.

IMPROVING YOUR INTELLECTUAL SKILLS

Recommended Reading

Most people read this book in order to attain as high a score as possible on the *Miller Analogies Test*. Many readers are also interested in improving the general level of their intellectual skills. Whereas the material in this book is aimed primarily at raising your score on the *MAT*, and only secondarily at improving your general intellectual skills, other books with the primary aim of improving your general intellectual skills are available. Although such books are not intended to improve your score on any one particular test, sharpening your intellectual skills can help you on a large variety of tests, including the *MAT*.

SUCCESSFUL INTELLIGENCE

By Robert J. Sternberg, published as a paperback by Plume, 1997. This book contains further ideas about mind improvement based on the author's triarchic theory of human intelligence.

Other Test Preparation Books

Numerous other books containing problems of various kinds, including other test preparation books, can be quite helpful in improving general thinking skills. Thus, for the person whose goal is general improvement in thinking, Barron's other test preparation books, such as *How to Prepare for the Graduate Record Examination*, are recommended as supplements.

Kinds of Analogies Found on the Miller Analogies Test

- Content of *MAT* analogies
- Practice in recognizing content areas
- Relationships used in *MAT* analogies
- Practice in using and recognizing relationships
- Distribution of categories

CONTENT OF *MAT* ANALOGIES

Success on the *MAT* requires familiarity with a broad range of subjects. There are different ways of classifying the subject areas. The following list of the general content areas covered by the *MAT* shows just one way to group these areas conveniently.

I Vocabulary

II General Information

III Humanities

    A. History
    B. Literature
    C. Mythology
    D. Philosophy
    E. Religion
    F. Art
    G. Music
    H. Grammar

IV Social Sciences

A. Psychology
B. Sociology
C. Economics
D. Linguistics
E. Anthropology
F. Political Science

V Natural Sciences

A. Biology
B. Physics
C. Chemistry

VI Mathematics

VII Nonsemantic

The following examples will give you an idea of what each area covers:

1. *Vocabulary:*

   STRIDENT : (*a.* wide, *b.* shrill, *c.* confident, *d.* rigid) :: TURBULENT : AGITATED
   Answer: (**b**). This analogy deals with similarities in meaning. *Strident* and *shrill* are synonyms, as are *turbulent* and *agitated.*

2. *General Information:*

   JAPAN : ORIENT :: FRANCE : (*a.* Europe, *b.* Continent, *c.* Paris, *d.* Occident)
   Answer: (**d**). This analogy concerns locations of countries. Japan is a country in the Orient. France is a country in the Occident.

3. *History:*

   (*a.* T. Roosevelt, *b.* F. Roosevelt, *c.* Wilson, *d.* Eisenhower) : SQUARE DEAL :: TRUMAN : FAIR DEAL
   Answer: (**a**). This analogy involves presidential programs. T. Roosevelt introduced what he called the Square Deal. Truman introduced what he called the Fair Deal.

4. *Literature:*

NAPOLEON : FRENCH ARMY :: MAJOR BARBARA : (*a.* Salvation
Army, *b.* English Army, *c.* American Army, *d.* Children's Army)
Answer: (**a**). This analogy is about army affiliations of officers. Napoleon
was an officer in the French Army. Major Barbara, in Shaw's play by the
same name, was an officer in the Salvation Army.

5. *Mythology:*

ZEUS : HERA :: JUPITER : (*a.* Venus, *b.* Minerva, *c.* Juno, *d.* Diana)
Answer: (**c**). This analogy requires recognition of two different names for
the same god. Zeus was the Greek name and Jupiter the Roman name for
the king of the gods. Hera was the Greek name and Juno the Roman name
for his wife.

6. *Philosophy:*

LOCKE : INDUCTION :: (*a.* Berkeley, *b.* Bentham, *c.* Hume, *d.* Spinoza) :
DEDUCTION
Answer: (**d**). This analogy deals with methodologies used by major
philosophers. Locke was an empiricist philosopher and hence his mode of
reasoning was primarily inductive. Spinoza, a rationalist philosopher, relied
primarily on deductive reasoning in order to draw conclusions.

7. *Religion:*

ADAM : (*a.* Eve, *b.* Eden, *c.* Heaven, *d.* Israel) :: OEDIPUS : THEBES
Answer: (**b**). This analogy concerns places from which people were expelled.
Adam was expelled from Eden. Oedipus was expelled from Thebes.

8. *Art:*

RENOIR : IMPRESSIONIST :: (*a.* Monet, *b.* Bosch, *c.* Van Gogh,
d. Munch) : EXPRESSIONIST
Answer: (**d**). This analogy involves schools of famous painters. Renoir was
an impressionist painter. Munch was an expressionist painter.

9. *Music:*

(*a.* coda, *b.* aria, *c.* overture, *d.* coloratura) : OPERA :: PREFACE : BOOK
Answer: (**c**). This analogy is about introductions to works of art. An
overture introduces an opera. A preface introduces a book.

10. *Social Sciences:*

FREUD : OEDIPUS COMPLEX :: (*a.* Jung, *b.* Horney, *c.* Adler,
d. Allport) : INFERIORITY COMPLEX
Answer: (**c**). This analogy requires recognition of originators of terms
describing psychological complexes. Freud coined the expression *Oedipus
complex*; Adler coined the expression *inferiority complex*.

11. *Biology:*

(*a.* stomach, *b.* throat, *c.* lung, *d.* gullet) : PHARYNX :: WINDPIPE :
TRACHEA
Answer: (**b**). This analogy deals with organs in the body. The pharynx is
the throat. The trachea is the windpipe.

12. *Physics:*

MECHANICAL ADVANTAGE : RESISTANCE :: (*a.* distance, *b.* rate,
c. effort, *d.* seconds) : TIME
Answer: (**a**). This analogy concerns variation between physical concepts.
Mechanical advantage varies directly with resistance (when effort is held
constant). Distance varies directly with time (when rate is held constant).

13. *Chemistry:*

HCl : HYDROCHLORIC :: H_2SO_4 : (*a.* hydrofluoric, *b.* hydrocyanic, *c.*
sulfuric, *d.* nitric)
Answer: (**c**). This analogy involves chemical symbols for acids. HCl is the
chemical formula for hydrochloric acid. H_2SO_4 is the chemical formula for
sulfuric acid.

14. *Mathematics:*

$2^1 : 2^3 :: 1^2 :$ (*a.* 0, *b.* 1, *c.* 2, *d.* 4)
Answer: (**d**). This analogy is about equivalent ratios. 2 is to 8 as 1 is to 4.

15. *Nonsemantic:*

DEER : DEER :: OX : (*a.* oxen, *b.* oxes, *c.* oxae, *d.* oxena)
Answer: (**a**). This analogy requires recognition of plurals of words. The
plural of deer is deer. The plural of ox is oxen.

NOTE

One thing to keep in mind while solving analogies is that the two relationships that comprise
the analogy need not come from the same content domain. In the analogy presented as an
example of literary content, NAPOLEON : FRENCH ARMY :: MAJOR BARBARA :
SALVATION ARMY, the left side of the analogy is taken from the content domain of history,
while the right side, the one requiring selection of a correct answer, comes from the content
category of literature.

PRACTICE IN RECOGNIZING CONTENT AREAS

Directions: The following quiz consists of 30 pairs of words. Your task is to write next to each pair of words the relationship between the words and then to classify the pair of words in terms of the 15 content categories just described. The purpose of the quiz is to get you thinking actively about the different content areas from which *MAT* items are drawn. There are two examples of each content area. An answer key is given at the end of the quiz.

Word Pair	*Relationship*	*Content Area*
1. PIAGET : STAGE THEORY	_____	_____
2. NEON : INERT	_____	_____
3. MARS : WAR	_____	_____
4. DESCARTES : RATIONALIST	_____	_____
5. ANDES : SOUTH AMERICA	_____	_____
6. RESISTANCE : OHMS	_____	_____
7. SKIN : ORGAN	_____	_____
8. MITIGATE : ASSUAGE	_____	_____
9. EROICA : BEETHOVEN	_____	_____
10. SAWYER : FINN	_____	_____
11. PETER : THE GREAT	_____	_____
12. KORAN : ISLAM	_____	_____
13. IMAGINARY : COMPLEX	_____	_____

Word Pair	Relationship	Content Area
14. PERSONA : PERSONAE	_____	_____
15. MUNCH : EXPRESSIONIST	_____	_____
16. LINCOLN : REPUBLICAN	_____	_____
17. STEP : PETS	_____	_____
18. PATON : SOUTH AFRICA	_____	_____
19. DURKHEIM : SUICIDE	_____	_____
20. TRENCHANT : INCISIVE	_____	_____
21. AORTA : ARTERY	_____	_____
22. MICHELANGELO : DAVID	_____	_____
23. TREBLE : BASS	_____	_____
24. BASE : EXPONENT	_____	_____
25. HOLLANDAISE : CREAM	_____	_____
26. MONK : MONASTERY	_____	_____
27. CAMUS : EXISTENTIALIST	_____	_____
28. FORCE : MASS × ACCELERATION	_____	_____
29. PLUTO : HADES	_____	_____
30. WATER : HYDROGEN	_____	_____

ANSWER EXPLANATIONS

Relationship	*Content Area*
1. Piaget's theory of intellectual development is a stage theory.	SOCIAL SCIENCES (10)
2. Neon is an inert gas.	CHEMISTRY (13)
3. Mars was the god of war in Roman mythology.	MYTHOLOGY (5)
4. Descartes was a rationalist philosopher.	PHILOSOPHY (6)
5. The Andes Mountains are in South America.	GENERAL INFORMATION (2)
6. Resistance is measured in ohms.	PHYSICS (12)
7. The skin is an organ.	BIOLOGY (11)
8. *Mitigate* and *assuage* are synonyms (meaning "to make less severe or to improve").	VOCABULARY (1)
9. Beethoven wrote the Eroica Symphony.	MUSIC (9)
10. Tom Sawyer and Huck Finn are characters in novels by Mark Twain (named after these characters).	LITERATURE (4)
11. Peter the Great was a Russian czar.	HISTORY (3)
12. The Koran is the holy book of Islam.	RELIGION (7)
13. *Imaginary* and *complex* are two kinds of numbers.	MATHEMATICS (14)
14. *Personae* is the plural form of *persona*.	NONSEMANTIC (15)
15. Munch was an expressionist painter.	ART (8)
16. President Lincoln was a member of the Republican Party.	HISTORY (3)
17. *Pets* is *Step* spelled backwards.	NONSEMANTIC (15)

Relationship	*Content Area*
18. Paton is a famous South African author.	LITERATURE (4)
19. Durkheim is the author of *Suicide*.	SOCIAL SCIENCES (10)
20. *Trenchant* and *incisive*, both of which mean "penetrating," are synonyms.	VOCABULARY (1)
21. The aorta is an artery in the body.	BIOLOGY (11)
22. Michelangelo was the sculptor of *David*. (Alternatively, David was an artist, as was Michelangelo.)	ART (8)
23. Treble and bass are musical clefs.	MUSIC (9)
24. In the numerical expression x^y, x is the base and y the exponent.	MATHEMATICS (14)
25. Hollandaise is a cream sauce.	GENERAL INFORMATION (2)
26. A monk lives in a monastery.	RELIGION (7)
27. Camus was an existentialist philosopher.	PHILOSOPHY (6)
28. In physics, force = mass × acceleration.	PHYSICS (12)
29. Pluto (the Roman name) and Hades (the Greek name) were the god of the underworld.	MYTHOLOGY (5)
30. Water is composed in part of hydrogen gas.	CHEMISTRY (13)

NOTE

In some cases, more than one content area could be justified. For example, Camus was also an existentialist writer, and hence item 27 could have been classified under LITERATURE. Also, multiple relationships are sometimes possible, meaning that you may have discovered a relationship other than or in addition to the one mentioned in each item.

RELATIONSHIPS USED IN *MAT* ANALOGIES

Analogical reasoning requires you to recognize many possible relationships between pairs of concepts. Unfortunately, classification of relationships is not nearly so straightforward as classification of content areas. There have been numerous attempts to classify the possible ways in which words can be related, but none of the systems is completely successful. To quote George Miller, "Words are related to one another in an amazing number of ways."

The classification system outlined on the following pages, similar to one proposed by George Miller, comprises 14 specific categories, which are organized into 7 general groups. Such a scheme, which makes use of a relatively small number of categories, strikes a balance between being too general and being too particular in describing a relationship.

I Similarity/Contrast

1. Similarity
2. Contrast

II Description

3. Predication

III Class

4. Subordination
5. Coordination
6. Superordination

IV Completion

7. Completion

V Part/Whole

8. Part–Whole
9. Whole–Part

VI Equality/Negation

10. Equality (equivalence)
11. Negation

VII Nonsemantic

12. Sound Relationships
13. Letter Relationships
14. Word Relationships

The following examples will give you an idea of what each relationship means.

1. *Similarity*

Relationships are between synonyms or words that are nearly the same in meaning.

HAPPY : GLAD :: DULL : (*a.* razor, *b.* blunt, *c.* sharp, *d.* bright)
Answer: (**b**). This analogy deals with similarities in meaning. *Happy* and *glad* are synonyms, as are *dull* and *blunt*.

2. *Contrast*

Relationships are between antonyms or words that are nearly the opposite in meaning.

WET : (*a.* dry, *b.* moist, *c.* towel, *d.* water) :: STOP : GO
Answer: (**a**). This analogy concerns contrasts in meaning. *Wet* and *dry* are opposites, as are *stop* and *go*.

3. *Predication*

Terms of the analogy are related by a verb or verb relationship. One term *describes* something about the other term. Most analogies fall in this category. Some of the variations are as follows: A is caused by B; A makes B; A rides on B; A eats B; A is a source of B; A induces B; A studies B; A is made of B; A uses B.

AUTOMOBILE : ROAD :: TRAIN : (*a.* conductor, *b.* track, *c.* engine, *d.* ticket)
Answer (**b**). This analogy involves surfaces on which vehicles travel. An automobile travels on a road, and a train travels on a track. The implicit verb is *travels*.

DOG : BARK :: (*a.* cat, *b.* giraffe, *c.* frog, *d.* rabbit) : MEOW
Answer: (**a**). This analogy involves sounds made by animals. A dog barks. A cat meows.

4. *Subordination*

Relationships are those in which an object A is a type of B.

(*a.* lizard, *b.* toad, *c.* sponge, *d.* trout) : FISH :: FROG : AMPHIBIAN
Answer: (**d**). This analogy is about types of animals. A trout is a type of fish and a frog is a type of amphibian.

5. *Coordination*

The first two terms are one type of thing and the last two are another.

LETTUCE : CABBAGE :: PEAR : (*a.* fruit, *b.* peach, *c.* radish, *d.* carrot)
Answer: (**b**). This analogy requires recognition of members of classes. Lettuce and cabbage are both types of vegetables, while a pear and a peach are both types of fruit.

6. *Superordination*

Relationships are those in which A is a category into which B falls.

BIRD : ROBIN :: MOLLUSK : (*a.* fish, *b.* water, *c.* sponge, *d.* snail)
Answer: (**d**). This analogy deals with category membership. Bird is a category that includes the robin; mollusk is a category that includes the snail.

7. *Completion*

Each term of this kind of analogy is part of a complete expression.

SAN : FRANCISCO :: (*a.* San, *b.* Santa, *c.* La, *d.* Los) : ANGELES
Answer: (**d**). This analogy concerns full names of cites. *San* and *Los* complete the names of two cities, San Francisco and Los Angeles, respectively.

8. *Part–Whole*

Relationships are those in which A is a part of B.

DAY : WEEK :: MONTH : (*a.* hour, *b.* minute, *c.* year, *d.* time)
Answer: (**c**). This analogy involves parts of larger amounts of time. A day is part of a week, and a month is part of a year.

9. *Whole–Part*

Relationships are those in which B is a part of A.

(*a.* hour, *b.* minute, *c.* year, *d.* time) : MONTH :: WEEK : DAY
Answer: (**c**). This analogy is about parts of the calendar. A month is part of a year. A day is part of a week.

10. *Equality*

Relationships involve mathematical or logical equivalence.

$\frac{1}{2}$: $\frac{1}{4}$ :: 0.26 : (*a.* 0.52, *b.* 0.18, *c.* 0.13, *d.* 0.11)
Answer: (**c**). This analogy requires recognition of mathematical equalities. Whereas $\frac{1}{4}$ is equal to one-half of $\frac{1}{2}$, 0.13 is equal to one-half of 0.26.

11. *Negation*

Relationships involve logical or mathematical negation.

EQUAL : UNEQUAL :: GREATER THAN : (*a.* less than, *b.* equal to,
c. greater than or equal to, *d.* less than or equal to)
Answer: (**d**). This analogy deals with possible relationships between pairs of numbers. Any number is either *equal* to or *unequal* to another number. Any number is either *greater than* or *less than or equal to* another number.

12. *Sound Relationships*

Two words are related because they sound similar in some way. The relationship is nonsemantic in that it has nothing to do with the meanings of the words.

TOE : ROW :: LO : (*a.* now, *b.* crow, *c.* boy, *d.* you)
Answer: (**b**). This analogy concerns vowel sounds in words. All the terms have a long ō vowel sound.

13. *Letter Relationships*

The letters of one term are permuted or in some other way transformed to form the letters of another term.

PAT : TAP :: RAT : (*a*. trap, *b*. skunk, *c*. tar, *d*. eat)
Answer: (**c**). This analogy involves backward spelling of words. *Tap* is obtained by spelling *pat* backwards, *tar*, by spelling *rat* backwards.

14. *Word Relationships*

These usually express grammatical relationships between words.

EAT : ATE :: MEET : (*a*. meat, *b*. meet, *c*. met, *d*. meets)
Answer: (**c**). This analogy involves past tenses of verbs. *Ate* is the past tense of *eat* and *met* is the past tense of *meet*.

NOTE

You will need to recognize much more specific relationships than those described above. However, if you understand the preceding relationships, you will have a general framework into which you can fit specific relationships.

PRACTICE IN USING AND RECOGNIZING RELATIONSHIPS

Directions: The following quiz consists of 28 pairs of words. Your task is to write next to each pair of words the relationship between the words and then to classify the pair of words in terms of the 14 relationship categories just described. The purpose of the quiz is to get you thinking actively about the different ways in which pairs of words on the *MAT* can be related. There are two examples of each relationship. An answer key is given at the end of the quiz.

Word Pair	*Relationship*	*Classification*
1. COVER : BOOK	_____	_____
2. RUE : CHEW	_____	_____
3. AIRPLANE : FLIES	_____	_____
4. DAFFODIL : LILAC	_____	_____
5. EMPTY SET : NULL SET	_____	_____
6. CLUE : HINT	_____	_____

Word Pair	Relationship	Classification
7. LAID : DIAL	_____	_____
8. EARLY : LATE	_____	_____
9. LADDER : RUNG	_____	_____
10. NEGATIVE : NONNEGATIVE	_____	_____
11. BETTER : BEST	_____	_____
12. HUMAN : MAMMAL	_____	_____
13. NEW : ORLEANS	_____	_____
14. STAR : DWARF	_____	_____
15. CARPENTER : HAMMER	_____	_____
16. X or Y : Not X and Not Y	_____	_____
17. CIRCLE : SEMICIRCLE	_____	_____
18. CRATE : FREIGHT	_____	_____
19. FURNITURE : CHAIR	_____	_____
20. MELIORATE : IMPROVE	_____	_____
21. STICK : STUCK	_____	_____
22. HEAVENLY : HELLISH	_____	_____
23. FINGER : HAND	_____	_____
24. TAP : PAT	_____	_____
25. ABRAHAM : LINCOLN	_____	_____
26. $\sqrt{64} : 2^3$	_____	_____

Word Pair	Relationship	Classification
27. CLUB : WEAPON	_____	_____
28. POLLACK : COD	_____	_____

ANSWER EXPLANATIONS

Relationship	*Classification*
1. A cover is a part of a book.	PART–WHOLE (8)
2. *Rue* and *chew* rhyme.	SOUND (12)
3. An airplane flies for its locomotion.	PREDICATION (3)
4. A daffodil and a lilac are both kinds of flowers.	COORDINATION (5)
5. The empty set and the null set are mathematically equivalent.	EQUALITY (10)
6. *Clue* and *hint* are synonymous.	SIMILARITY (1)
7. *Dial* is *laid* spelled backwards.	LETTER (13)
8. *Early* and *late* are antonyms.	CONTRAST (2)
9. A ladder is composed in part of rungs.	WHOLE–PART (9)
10. All real numbers that are not negative are nonnegative.	NEGATION (11)
11. *Better* is the comparative form and *best* the superlative form of *good*.	WORD (14)
12. A human is a kind of mammal.	SUBORDINATION (4)
13. New Orleans is a city.	COMPLETION (7)
14. A dwarf is a kind of star.	SUPERORDINATION (6)

> **NOTE**
>
> In some cases, more than one classification can be justified. For example, an empty set and a null set (item 5) can be viewed as synonymous, and hence as related via category 1 (Similarity). Also, multiple relationships are possible in some cases, meaning that you may have discovered a relationship other than the one mentioned in the explanation.

Relationship	*Classification*
15. A carpenter uses a hammer.	PREDICATION (3)
16. The logical negation of "X or Y" is "Not X and Not Y."	NEGATION (11)
17. A circle can be divided into two semicircles.	WHOLE–PART (9)
18. *Crate* and *freight* rhyme.	SOUND (12)
19. One kind of furniture is a chair.	SUPERORDINATION (6)
20. *Meliorate* and *improve* are synonyms.	SIMILARITY (1)
21. *Stuck* is the past tense of *stick*.	WORD (14)
22. *Heavenly* and *hellish* are antonyms.	CONTRAST (2)
23. A finger is part of a hand.	PART–WHOLE (8)
24. *Pat* is *tap* spelled backward.	LETTER (13)
25. Abraham Lincoln was a president of the United States.	COMPLETION (7)
26. $\sqrt{64}$ and 2^3 both equal 8.	EQUALITY (10)
27. A club is a kind of weapon.	SUBORDINATION (4)
28. Pollack and cod are both kinds of fish.	COORDINATION (5)

DISTRIBUTION OF CATEGORIES

All *MAT* items are classified both by content and relationship. The items on the *MAT* practice tests in this book are also classified in this way. A content/relationship item categorization is included in the explanatory answer for each question. Following each practice test is an Item Classification Chart that shows the breakdown of item categories.

Each content/relationship item categorization grid consists of a matrix of the 7 major content areas and 7 major relationship categories described in the preceding sections. Because there are 7 content areas and 7 relationship areas, there are 49 cells in the overall matrix. However, you will notice that some cells in the charts are empty, while others contain many entries. This occurs because content and relationship areas are not "independent." Certain types of item content and relationship never go together, and hence no items fall in the corresponding cells. Other types of item content and relationship are frequently associated, and hence the corresponding cells are filled with entries. For example, Mathematics items frequently fall into the Equality/Negation relationship category, but never into the Sound/Letter/Word category.

As a rule, more items fall into the General Information content category than into any other content category. With respect to content, General Information and Humanities (including history, literature, mythology, philosophy, religion, art, and music) are usually the largest categories, and Nonsemantic is the smallest. On the most recent forms of the *MAT*, there are no Nonsemantic items at all. However, older forms of the *MAT* are still in use, and hence such items are included in the practice tests. With respect to relationship, Description is usually the largest category and Sound/Letter/Word the smallest. Again, the latter category does not appear on the most recent forms of the *MAT*.

For several reasons, there is always a certain amount of ambiguity in the assignment of items to categories. One reason is that different individuals may arrive at the correct answer to a given item via alternative routes, and thus use different relationships to reach the same conclusion. A second reason for the ambiguity is that there is not always a clear line of demarcation between different categories. What is General Information to one person may appear to be Humanities, for example, to another. Hence, item classification is a useful tool in understanding the "anatomy" of an item, but only up to a certain point.

It is not recommended that you make extensive use of the Item Classification Charts during your preparation for the *MAT*. The primary purpose of these charts is to give you an idea of the breakdown of items on typical forms of the *MAT*, not to assist you in pinpointing your strengths and weaknesses. There are two reasons why you should not use the charts for diagnostic purposes. First, on the *MAT* (and on the practice tests) items within the various categories are not of equal difficulty, so that part scores on various categories are not directly comparable. For example, Mathematics items tend to be the most difficult ones, and hence more errors are to be expected on them. Second, it would not be worth your time to study a textbook or other aid in an area in which, if you used the charts diagnostically, you perceived yourself as weak. On a typical form of the *MAT*, there will be only a few items from any one specific content area, and so the probability of your learning from a textbook skimmed a few days before the test exactly what is covered on the particular form of the *MAT* you will take is exceedingly small.

The best way to prepare for the various types of content and relationship that will appear on the *MAT* is to take as many of the practice tests as you have time for, preferably all of them, and to make sure that you understand each error you have made. The Answer Explanations following each Answer Key will help you to understand your errors. Once you have taken the tests and studied the kinds of items that give you difficulty, you can be confident that you will do your best on the *MAT*.

References

Kuncel, N. R., Hezlett, S. A., & Ones, D. S. (2004). Academic performance, career potential, creativity, and job performance: Can one construct predict them all? *Journal of Personality and Social Psychology*, Vol. 86(1), 148–161.

Meagher, D., & Perez, C. *An introduction to the MAT*. Presentation at the Annual Meeting of the National Association of Graduate Admissions Professionals, May 2, 2008.

The *Miller Analogies Test*

PART **4**

- Validity
- Stability of *MAT* scores
- What *MAT* scores mean
- A word of caution
- A note to be reread when you get your score

SUCCESS OF THE *MAT* AS A MEASURING INSTRUMENT

Many studies have looked at how well the *MAT* predicts graduate school performance. A much smaller number have looked at the test as a predictor of success in occupational settings. Since the number of such studies is limited, we shall be concerned only with research of the former kind.

A review of the literature on the validity of the *MAT* (how well it measures what it is supposed to measure) safely permits one uninformative generalization about the usefulness of the *MAT* in various types of situations: About the only way to find out how valid the *MAT* will be in a given situation is to try it and find out. There are no stunning and clear-cut patterns in the results, perhaps in part because what one school calls basket weaving another calls textile engineering. While situational generalizations are not possible, however, more global statements can be made.

Validity

On the average, the *MAT* accounts for slightly more than 5% of the variance in various types of graduate school performance. In the large majority of studies, it accounts for more than 1%, but less than 15%, of this variance. This means that the *MAT* generally affords a low level of predictive accuracy to those who use it.

The best predictive scholastic aptitude tests account for up to 20% or even 25% of the variance in school performance, so that on this basis the *MAT* does not rank with the best tests as a predictor. However, these "best tests" tend to be predictors of high school and sometimes undergraduate grades. At this level, straightforward verbal ability tends to be as good a predictor as anything else. In graduate school, however, professors look for such exotic traits as creativity in designing experiments (in science) and level of rapport achieved with patients (in medicine). Even straightforward course work requires more complex combinations of abilities than are usually needed in high school and undergraduate programs. As a result, graduate school performance is harder to predict in part because all students who go on to graduate school tend to be high in ability, so there is not so much range in performance to predict!

It may surprise you to learn that, on the whole, the *MAT* is about as good a predictor of graduate school performance as any other test around, and that even undergraduate grades usually provide only a little better prediction. The simple fact is that *nothing* provides consistently good prediction of performance in graduate-level programs, and educators resort to the *MAT* and similar tests on the assumption that some prediction is better than none at all. This is true as long as the test results are not misused. If the test scores are considered in conjunction with various other sources of information, if they are interpreted as indicating a range rather than a specific level of ability, and if the limitations on their validity are fully appreciated, then they can be somewhat helpful in spite of their usually low predictive power. If the scores are misused, usually by their being overinterpreted, then they certainly illustrate an application of the maxim that "A little knowledge is a dangerous thing." Fortunately, gross misinterpretation is becoming increasingly rare as educators become more sophisticated in the use of standardized tests.

Now that you have become aware of some limitations surrounding *MAT* and other test scores, you won't feel it necessary to hide in a dark corner if your test score isn't what you'd hoped for, and you won't sell autographs (not quite yet, anyway) if your score is much better than you'd imagined possible. Your score can give you and others who interpret it properly some guidance as to how you might perform in graduate work or employment. Many other factors—motivation, study habits, intellectual curiosity, personal sense of well-being, and the like, as well as abilities not tapped by the *MAT*—will also enter into your future success in whatever program you enter.

Meagher and Perez (2008) have reported relatively recent validity data for the *MAT*. The validity data are reported on a scale of 0 to 1, where 0 indicates no relationship between two variables and 1 indicates a perfect relationship. In 2005–2006, across studies, the average correlation between *MAT* scores and graduate school GPA was 0.27, compared with 0.21 for the Graduate Record Examination (*GRE*) verbal, 0.27 for the *GRE* quantitative, and 0.11 for the *GRE* analytical-writing scores. The correlation for previous graduate GPA was 0.30. These correlations indicate somewhat modest but statistically significant relationships between the test scores and graduate GPA. Available data suggest that the *MAT* and the *GRE* verbal section measure very similar but not identical psychological constructs. The *MAT* puts more emphasis on general knowledge, the *GRE* verbal on in-depth reading skills.

A detailed study on the validity of the *MAT* was conducted by Kuncel, Hezlett, and Ones (2004). They found a correlation of 0.70 between the *MAT* and the *GRE* verbal test, which is a relatively strong relationship. When they corrected for various statistical factors, the correlation went up to 0.88, suggesting that the two tests measure almost the same construct. The *MAT* also correlates moderately to highly with other tests of verbal ability. The correlation with the *GRE* quantitative test was 0.42, which is moderate and indicates some but far from complete overlap. Correlations with measures of graduate school performance were generally in the high 0.20s. The *MAT* also showed modest but significant correlations with work performance, ranging from 0.15 to 0.33. A curious finding of this study was that higher *MAT* scores were associated with *longer* times to degree completion (with a correlation of 0.35). It is unclear what this means, other than that people who scored higher took longer to finish their degrees!

Stability of *MAT* Scores

As the preceding section states, scores on a given form of the *MAT* usually account for only 1% to 15% of the variance in diverse criteria of performance in graduate school. However, there is something for which such scores usually account for 85% to 90% of the variance, and that is scores on another form of the *MAT*. There you have it. Scores on one form of the *MAT* are excellent predictors of scores on another form of the *MAT*. But you should realize just what this tidbit means. It means that, when a group of people take the test twice (a different form each time), their ranks within the group will probably not change much. However, even if their *ranks* in relation to each other remain stable, their scores may not. Most people gain around 5 points on a second administration. Does this mean you should take the test twice? Probably not. First, you will have capitalized on much of this *practice effect* by reading this book and working at the practice tests it contains. Second, educators and administrators using the test realize that people tend to gain in score from one testing to the next, and they are therefore likely to discount small gains. Large gains, however, are another story and often indicate that for one reason or another, one of the scores is not representative of the candidate's true ability. In such cases, the higher score almost always counts as much as or more than the lower score. For this reason, if you feel reasonably confident that you were at some sort of disadvantage during the first administration, you may want to consider taking the test again. However, such retesting will be a waste of time and money unless the disadvantage was genuine. You should remember that, even if your score was not quite what you'd hoped for, it is only one of many factors considered in making most admissions, financial aid, and employment decisions.

What *MAT* Scores Mean

Your score on the *MAT* will be reported to you as a *raw score*—you are informed of the number of questions you answered correctly, which may range anywhere from zero to one hundred. Before learning what the score means, you should learn what it does *not* mean.

The first thing for you to do is to rid yourself of any preconceptions you may have about percentage scores. A frequent one is that 90—100% = A, 80—89% = B, 70—79% = C, 60—69% = D, and anything below that is failing. Unfortunately, some *MAT* preparation books foster rather than dispel such erroneous notions. For example, one such book provides five practice tests, and suggests that a score of 475 (95%) is excellent, 425 (85%) is good, 350 (70%) is passing, and anything less is failing. Forget it! These standards may or may not be appropriate for the practice tests in that particular book, but they have no conceivable relation to the *MAT*.

In the first place, there is no such thing as a failing score on the *MAT*. Although a very few institutions may establish cut-off scores (a practice of dubious merit), almost none rely on the *MAT* to the exclusion of other sources of information. Such total reliance would be irresponsible and counterproductive. Second, what is an excellent score in one program may be just average in another, and quite low in a third. *MAT* scores simply cannot be interpreted in absolute terms. They can be interpreted only in relation to those of other individuals applying to programs similar or identical to your own.

Because raw scores are virtually uninterpretable taken by themselves, the test publisher provides percentile equivalents for various groups of individuals who have taken the *MAT*. What is a percentile equivalent? It is the number of people out of 100 whose scores your own score exceeds. Thus, if your score places you in the 56th percentile, this means that your score was higher than those of 56% of the people who were in the particular reference group for which the percentiles were computed. In general terms, the middle score in a group is the 50th percentile, and the highest score is the 100th percentile.

A Word of Caution

A final word of caution is in order with regard to the prediction of your *MAT* score. Obviously, one way to make this prediction is to average your scores on the practice tests in this book, but such a procedure is risky. Items on actual editions of the *MAT* are pretested by giving them as experimental items to large numbers of individuals who take the *MAT*. Only experimental items that precisely match older items are used on new forms of the test. The various forms of the *MAT* are thus referred to as *equated*.

Since the *MAT* is a restricted test, it was of course not possible to equate the practice tests in this book to actual *MAT* forms, and hence estimates of *MAT* scores obtained by averaging scores on these practice tests will be imprecise. Experience indicates that scores on the practice tests tend to run slightly lower than actual *MAT* scores. You might therefore look at your scores on these tests as conservative estimates of what you can expect your *MAT* score to be. Of course, in some cases, individuals may do worse on the actual test; the prediction game, as you know by now, is a very uncertain one. The important thing, however, is not that you go into the test knowing what your score will be (you'll find out just a few days after you take the test), but that you go in knowing that you will get a score that reflects your intellectual ability and not an inability to take tests. After working through this book, you can be confident that you will do your very best on the actual test.

A Note to Be Reread When You Get Your Score

If you did well, congratulations. You have good reason to be proud of yourself. The *MAT* is one of the most difficult ability tests around, and a high score is a genuine accomplishment.

If you didn't do as well as you'd hoped, don't despair. Follow the simple steps below:

STEP 1: Look back and observe how well the *MAT* predicts (or, rather, doesn't predict) graduate school performance. It's not that the *MAT* is worse than other similar tests. It's just that all of these tests don't predict that well. You should be feeling a little better already.

STEP 2: Ask your friendly local librarian for a copy of the January 1973 issue of *The American Psychologist*, and check out the article by David McClelland, "Testing for Competence Rather Than for 'Intelligence.'" McClelland's main point is simple. While aptitude tests provide some (but not much) prediction of performance in school, their ability to predict success in life (as measured by virtually any criterion except test scores and grades) is practically zero. So keep your test score in perspective. In the long run, it isn't that important.

Review for the
Miller Analogies Test

PART 5

- What this review contains
- Vocabulary
- Special collective nouns
- *-ology* words
- Word demons
- Selected foreign words and phrases used in English
- Alphabets and their characteristics

- Geography
- History
- Social sciences
- Art and architecture
- Literary forms and figures
- Music
- Science
- Mythology

WHAT THIS REVIEW CONTAINS

As stated earlier in this book, the *MAT* is a test of vocabulary and general information as well as specific information in diverse areas. It is not possible to review the content of all the subjects that may be included in a *MAT* exam. The reviews provided in this chapter are intended as brief refreshers. They may help you recall important names, events, and terms in different areas of study.

VOCABULARY

The vocabulary list below consists of words often used in graduate tests. For some entries, synonyms, antonyms, or other related words are provided as an added help in handling analogy questions.

abdicate   to denounce; to discard; to abandon
aberration   something not typical; a deviation
abhorrence   repugnance; detestation
abjure   to renounce upon oath
abnegation   self-denial
abrogate   to break, as a treaty or law
abscond   to depart secretly; to hide (oneself)
absolve   to set free from an obligation or the consequences of guilt
abstain   to refrain deliberately from an action or practice, usu. as a form of self-denial
abstemious   sparing or moderate, especially in eating or drinking (antonym: **gluttonous**)
abstruse   hard to understand or grasp; esoteric
abut   to border on; to terminate at the boundary or point of contact

abysmal   immeasurable; bottomless

accolade   an award or honor; high praise

acquiesce   to agree silently; to accept tacitly

acrid   unpleasantly pungent in odor or taste

acrimonious   caustic, biting in feeling or manner

acrophobia   the fear of heights

acumen   keenness

adamant   unyielding; stubborn

addle   to throw into confusion; to confound

adduce   to offer as example or proof

adjure   to command solemnly; to advise earnestly; to beg

admonition   warning against oversight

adroit   showing skill, cleverness, or resourcefulness

adulation   excessive praise

adumbrate   to intimate or foreshadow; to obscure

aestivate (estivate)   to spend the summer in an inactive state

affable   being pleasant and friendly with others

agglomeration   a collection in a mass, heap, or cluster; aggrandizement

agoraphobia   the fear of open spaces

alacrity   liveliness or eagerness; readiness (antonym: **lassitude**)

allegory   a symbolic expression or description

allusion   an indirect reference to something else; a hint

alms   charity; something given to the poor (usu. refers to small change)

alpinism   mountain climbing

altruistic   unselfish; concerned with the welfare of others

ambergris   a product of sperm whales used in the manufacture of perfume

amphora   an ancient two-handled Greek jar

anathema   a ban or curse; a denunciation accompanied by excommunication

andiron   a metal support used for holding logs in a hearth

androphobia   the fear of men

anneal   to toughen or to strengthen

anodyne   a pain reliever

anomaly   an aberration; a deviation; an irregularity

antipathy   firm dislike; hatred (antonym: **sympathy**)

antiseptic   free from germs, exceptionally clean

antithesis   the direct opposite

aphelion   the point in a planet's orbit that is farthest from the sun

apocalyptic   of, or relating to, a revelation or discovery

apocryphal   of doubtful authenticity; spurious

apogee   the point in a satellite's orbit that is farthest from the center
   of the earth

apothegm   a short, instructive pithy saying

aquiline   hooked; like an eagle

arachnophobia   the fear of spiders

archon   the chief magistrate in ancient Athens; any ruler

arid   dull; unimaginative; extremely dry

arrogate   to claim or seize without justification; to usurp

artifice   cleverness; ingenuity

assiduous   diligent

assuage   to ease the intensity of; to appease; to pacify (antonym: **exacerbate**)

astraphobia   the fear of lightning

atrophy   a wasting away; degeneration

attenuate   to lessen in amount, force, or value; to weaken

audacity   daring spirit

austral   southern (antonym: **boreal**)

axiom   a self-evident rule or truth; a widely accepted saying

azure   sky blue

baleful   menacing; harmful

balmy   soothing; mild

banal   trite; commonplace

bellicose   inclined to start wars or fights (antonym: **pacific**)

beneficent   beneficial (antonym: **deleterious**)

benign   gracious; favorable; not threatening to health (antonym: **malignant**)

benison   spoken blessing

bibliophile   one who loves books

biennial   occurring every two years

bifurcate   divided in two branches; forked

biped   having two feet

blighted   withered or rotten; destroyed; frustrated

blithe   happy; merry; cheerful

bombastic   pompous; overblown; turgid

boreal   northern (antonym: **austral**)

boycott   to engage in a concerted refusal to have dealings with (a person, store, organization) as a sign of disapproval [derived from Charles C. Boycott, an English land agent who was ostracized in Ireland because of his refusal to lower rents]

broach   to make known for the first time; to open up (a subject) for discussion

bromidic   lacking originality; trite

brontophobia   the fear of thunder

brook   to bear or tolerate; to put up with

brusque   abrupt or short in manner or speech

buccal   pertaining to the cheeks or side of the mouth

bucolic   pastoral; relating to rural life

buffoon   a clown or ludicrous figure; someone who amuses with jokes or tricks

bulbous   rotund; round like a bulb

bumptious   aggressive and assertive in an offensive way (antonym: **shy; self-effacing**)

buoyant   (1) having the ability to float; (2) cheerful; gay

burgeon   to grow and flourish

burnish   to make shiny or lustrous; to polish

burnoose   a hooded Arabic cloak

  cassock   a loose robe worn by priests

cabal   group united to plot, esp. the overthrow of authority

cache   (1) a hiding place; (2) something hidden in a secure place

cacophony   a harsh-sounding mixture of words, voices, or sounds

caduceus the emblem of the medical profession (a staff with intertwined snakes and wings at the top)

cajole to persuade a reluctant person to do something; to coax

caliber the diameter of the bore of a gun

    gauge the size of a shotgun; measure of the interior diameter of the barrel

calumny a lie told to damage another's reputation; slander

candid frank

canonical orthodox; authoritative

capitulate to cease resisting; to surrender (often after negotiations)

capricious unpredictable; governed by a whim

captious critical; fault-finding

carp to complain

cashmere a fine wool from a cashmere goat [derived from Kashmir, India]

catharsis purification of emotions, esp. through art

    bathos sentimentalism; overdone pathos; triteness; anticlimax

    pathos something that evokes pity, compassion, or sorrow

catholic universal (antonym: **provincial; parochial**)

caustic acrid; biting

cavil to raise trivial objections; to nitpick

cerulean resembling the blue of the sky

chaff waste material from the threshing of wheat

    dross waste material from molten metal

    slag scoria; refuse from the melting of metals or reduction of ore

    tailings waste material from the preparation of ores or grains

chalice a bowl-shaped drinking cup

chartreuse yellow-green

chastise to criticize harshly; to castigate

chauvinism excessive or blind patriotism [derived from Nicholas Chauvin, a character in a French play]

chicanery trickery; artful deception

chimerical fantastically visionary; wildly fanciful

choleric easily angered or irritated

Cimmerian (1) *adj.* shrouded in gloom and darkness; (2) *n.* a mythical people described by Homer as dwelling in gloom

    stygian (1) dark and gloomy; (2) relating to the Styx (in Greek mythology, the river of the underworld)

circumlocution an indirect expression; wordy or evasive language

circumspect considering all options; cautious

clandestine surreptitious; secret

claustrophobia the fear of closed places

clemency an act of leniency; mercy

cloy to satiate

    glut to oversupply; to satiate

coalesce to grow together; to unite into a whole

coda a passage that concludes a musical or literary work

cogent pertinent; compelling; convincing

cognizant perceptive; observant

colloquial of or relating to conversation; characteristic of informal speech

collusion   a secret agreement, esp. for an illegal purpose

compulsion   an impulse to perform an irrational act

   phobia   an inexplicable fear of something

conjoin   to join or act together

contentious   argumentative; quarrelsome

contumacious   rebellious; stubbornly disobedient; renegade

conundrum   a puzzle; a riddle

cooper   a maker of casks or barrels

corroborate   to confirm; to back up with evidence

cowl   (1) a hood; (2) a cover for an engine

croupier   a collector and payer of bets at a casino

culinary   having to do with the kitchen or cooking

cynophobia   the fear of dogs

cynosure   the center of interest

dauntless   fearless

dearth   severe shortage

debacle   a violent breakdown; a sudden overthrow

debauchery   wild living; corruption by sensuality

debilitate   to weaken (antonym: **invigorate**)

debonair   suave; courteous; sophisticated

deciduous   falling off or shedding at a certain season; ephemeral; not
   permanent

declaim   to make a bombastic speech

decorous   proper; in good taste; correct

defalcate   to embezzle; to abscond with money

deleterious   harmful (antonym: **beneficial; salubrious; salutary**)

delineate   to describe; to portray; to sketch

deliquesce   to melt away or dissolve; to become soft, esp. with age

delusion   a deception; a false psychotic belief regarding oneself or others

demur   to object; to take exception

denim   a durable, twilled, usually cotton fabric woven with white filling thread
   [derived from *serge de Nime* (Nîmes, France)]

denouement   the unfolding or outcome of a series of events

denounce   to express strong disapproval, esp. publicly

depraved   morally corrupt or evil

deprecate   to play down; to belittle

depredate   to lay waste; to plunder

desiccate   to dry out

despot   a ruler with absolute power

desultory   lacking plan, regularity, or purpose; random

dexterous   mentally skillful; artful; clever

dialectic   logical argumentation

diametric   completely opposed; at opposite extremes

diaphanous   sheer; extremely delicate

diatribe   a bitter denunciation (antonym: **panegyric**)

dichotomy   division, esp. into two contradictory groups

didactic   intended to teach, moralize, or preach

diffident   shy; lacking in self-confidence

dilatory tending to cause delay (antonym: **expeditious**)

dilettante one who is involved in a variety of things, none of them seriously; dabbler

diminution a decrease; a lessening

dint a force; a power

disavow to deny

discomfit to confuse, to deject; to frustrate; to deceive

discourse to converse; to discuss formally

disingenuous lacking in candor

disinterested unbiased

dissemble to feign or pretend

dissenter one who goes against an opinion; nonconformist

dissuade to persuade someone not to do something

djellabah a loose-fitting gown worn in North Africa (see also **burnoose**)

doctrinaire dogmatic

doggerel comic, loose verse

dolt a stupid person

doughty fearless; valiant

dour stubbornly unyielding; uninviting

draconian severe (as a code of laws); cruel

dray a vehicle used to haul goods

    teamster a person who drives a truck as an occupation

ductile malleable

dunce a dull-witted or stupid person [derived from John Duns Scotus, whose writings were ridiculed in the 16th century]

duplicity concealment of one's true intentions by misleading words or actions; deception

ebullient lively; enthusiastic; boiling up

eclectic selecting from many sources what seems to be the best; catholic

ecumenical (1) having to do with a body of churches; (2) worldwide or general in extent or application

edification instruction; improvement; enlightenment

efface to make indistinct by wearing away; to erase or remove

effervescent lively; bubbly (antonym: **effete**)

effete exhausted; worn-out (antonym: **effervescent**)

effluvium a disagreeable or noxious vapor; escaping gas

effusive overflowing; very demonstrative

egregious conspicuously bad; flagrant

egress (1) *n.* exit; (2) *v.* to go out from

elan dash; vigorous spirit

elegy a lament for the dead

elucidate to shed light upon; to make clear

emanate to send out; to emit

eminent prominent; famous; standing above others in some quality or position

encomium formal expression of praise

endue to provide; to endow

enervate to exhaust, weaken, or unnerve (antonym: **invigorate**)

engender to bring into being; to produce

enigma   a baffling situation; something that is hard to explain or solve

entreat   to request earnestly

ephemeral   lasting a short time; transient

epiphany   a sudden, and often divine, enlightenment or realization

epitome   a typical or ideal example

equivocal   ambiguous; deliberately confusing; able to be interpreted in more than one way

erratic   unpredictable; wandering; arbitrary (antonym: **static; stable**)

eschew   to avoid; to shun

eulogy   formal expression of praise

euphemism   (1) the substitution of a positive expression for something that may be interpreted as negative or distasteful; (2) the expression that is substituted

evanescent   fleeting; hardly visible; ephemeral

exacerbate   to make more violent or more severe (antonym: **assuage; appease**)

excoriate   to wear off the skin

exculpate   to exonerate; to clear of guilt or blame

exegesis   an interpretation of a text

exigent   urgent; requiring prompt action; taxing

expedite   to speed up; to hasten

expiate   to make amends for

expletive   a syllable or word that fills a vacancy but does not add to the sense of what was said

explicate   to explain

expunge   to strike out; to obliterate or erase

extemporaneous   with little preparation

extirpate   to destroy completely

facetious   humorous; not serious

factitious   artificial; sham (antonym: **authentic**)

fagoting   a type of embroidery

fallacious   erroneous; deceiving; misleading

fallible   capable of making a mistake or error

fastidious   hard to please; fickle

fatuous   silly; inane

fealty   allegiance

feasible   practical; workable

feckless   worthless; feeble

fecund   fruitful; fertile

fervid   very hot; intense in feeling or emotion; impassioned

fetid   having an offensive odor

  vapid   flat; uninteresting; insipid

fetish   (1) a charm; a talisman; an amulet; an object thought to deflect evil or bring luck; (2) a fixation; an object of obsessive desire; a preoccupation

fiduciary   a trustee

fitful   irregular; spasmodic

flaccid   limp; flabby (antonym: **resilient**)

flag   to weaken; to slow down

flagon   a flask with a handle and lid
   tureen   a casserole or bowl usually used to serve soup
flibbertigibbet   female fool
foible   a minor flaw or shortcoming in character; a weakness
foment   to instigate, incite, or arouse
foray   (1) *v.* to ravage for spoils; to pillage; (2) *n.* sudden, sometimes brief, invasion
forbear   an ancestor or forefather
fortuitous   happening by chance; unplanned
fractious   unruly; quarrelsome
franchise   the right to vote; a special privilege granted to a few; the right to market certain goods in a particular region
fraught   laden; charged
frenetic   frantic; frenzied
fricative   produced by forcing air through a constricted passage
froward   habitually disobedient; not willing to compromise
frugal   economical; thrifty; sparing
fuchsia   vivid reddish purple
fugacious   disappearing after a short time; short-lived; evanescent
fulminate   to denounce; to send forth invectives; to explode
fulsome   (1) abundant; copious; (2) morally offensive; disgusting
furtive   sly; shifty
gainsay   to deny; to contradict
galvanize   (1) to stimulate or excite; (2) to coat with zinc
gamut   the entire range
garner   to collect; to accumulate
garrote   to strangle and rob
garrulous   wordy; extremely talkative; gabby (antonym: **taciturn**)
gauche   lacking social grace; crude; awkward
gaunt   excessively thin; lean
gelding   a castrated male horse
genre   an artistic category or type
genuflect   to go down on one's knee; to kneel, usu. in obedience or respect
germane   closely related; relevant; fitting
glabrous   smooth; referring to a surface without hair or projections
   hirsute   roughly hairy
goad   to urge, egg on, or incite to do something (antonym: **curb**)
gorgon   one of three snake-haired sisters whose glance turned the beholder into stone
gourmand   one who eats and drinks excessively; glutton
gratuitous   not required by the circumstances; unwarranted; unnecessary
gregarious   liking companionship; sociable
griffin   a mythical animal having the head and wings of an eagle and the body and legs of a lion
   chimera   (1) a fire-breathing monster with the head of a lion, the body of a goat, and the tail of a serpent; (2) illusion or mental fabrication.
   minotaur   a monster, half man and half bull, confined in a labyrinth
guffaw   a loud, boisterous burst of laughter

guile   deceitful cunning; cleverness

gulch   a deep pit; a ravine

hackneyed   overused; trite; commonplace

haiku   a type of unrhymed Japanese poem consisting of three lines

halcyon   peaceful; tranquil

harangue   a ranting speech without much real meaning

harbinger   someone or something that foreshadows what is to come

Hellene   a native or inhabitant of Greece

heretic   one who goes against an established religion or belief; nonconformist

hermeneutics   the study of principles of interpretation (e.g., of the Bible)

hermetic   sealed off from external influence; airtight; abstruse or occult

herpetophobia   the fear of snakes

hiatus   a gap or interruption in time or in a continuum

hibernate   to spend the winter in a dormant, inactive state

hierarchy   a graded or ranked classification determined on the basis of age, economic status, or class

hirsute   hairy (antonym: **glabrous**)

hoary   gray or white with age

homily   an inspirational discourse; a sermon

homogeneous   of uniform structure or composition

homophobia   the fear of homosexuals

homophones   words that sound alike but have different meanings

  homonyms   homophones; also, words that are spelled the same but have different meanings (e.g., *cleave, quail, bear*)

hone   to sharpen

hyaline   transparent or almost so; glassy

hybrid   anything that is the product of at least two different sources

hydroponics   cultivation of plants in liquid nutrients

hyperbole   an exaggeration

hypertrophy   an exaggerated increase or complexity

hypocritical   pretending to have qualities or virtues that are not possessed; dissembling

hypothetical   based on conjecture; conditional

  empirical   based on expertise, observation, or experimental evidence

iconoclast   one who destroys religious images or attacks established beliefs

  vandal   one who destroys property

idyllic   carefree and lighthearted; peaceful

igneous   referring to rock formed from molten magma; volcanic

  metamorphic   referring to rock formed from sedimentary rock and changed through pressure or heat

ignominious   infamous; despicable

imbue   to permeate or influence

imminent   about to happen (usu. referring to something threatening)

immiscible   incapable of being mixed

immutable   not susceptible to change

impassive   apathetic; expressionless

impecunious   having little or no money

impermeable   impervious; not permitting passage through

impolitic   unwise; injudicious

imprecate   to curse

improvident   not providing for the future; careless

  prescient   having foresight or foreknowledge of the future

impugn   to attack, esp. as false or lacking integrity

inanition   a loss of vitality from lack of food and water

incarnadine   blood red

inchoate   beginning; insipient; only imperfectly formed

incipient   just beginning; in the early stages; commencing

incisive   keen; direct; decisive

incommodious   troublesome; inconvenient

incongruous   not like the others in a group; out of place; incompatible

incontrovertible   unquestionable; indisputable

incorrigible   unruly; delinquent

inculcate   to teach and impress by repetition

indemnify   (1) to secure against loss; (2) to compensate for hurt or loss

indigenous   having originated naturally in a particular environment

indigent   impoverished

induction   (1) an initiation into military service; (2) reasoning from parts to whole

  ordination   an initiation into religious service

ineluctable   inescapable; inevitable

inimical   hostile; unfriendly (antonym: **amicable**)

iniquitous   vicious; wicked

innuendo   a veiled allusion; insinuation

insurgent   a person who revolts against established authority

intractable   hard to manage; unruly; obstinate

intransigent   stubborn; uncompromising

intrepid   fearless (antonym: **timorous**)

inure   to accustom to accept something undesirable; to habituate

invective   insulting or abusive language

invidious   offensive; envious; obnoxious

irascible   easily angered; choleric; malevolent

jalousie   a type of blind or shutter having adjustable slats or louvers and usu. made of glass

jargon   specialized terminology of a certain group; a lingo

jejune   immature; juvenile

jenny   a female donkey

jettison   to sacrifice cargo to lighten a ship or vehicle

jetty   a projection or structure extending into a body of water

jezebel   a shameless, brazen woman

jocose   humorous; witty

jocular   habitually happy or cheerful

jocund   gay; cheerful

judicious   wise; sagacious; prudent

junk   (1) trash; something that is not worth saving; (2) a type of Chinese ship

junta   a political group or committee, esp. after a revolution

juxtapose   to place right next to something

kaleidoscope   (1) a succession of changing patterns or scenes; (2) a changing pattern or scene

kindle   to activate or inspire; to arouse

kindred   (1) *n.* relatives; kinship; (2) *adj.* similar in nature; like

kinetic   related to motion

knave   a sly, deceitful man or boy

kudos   praise; compliments

labyrinth   a place full of intricate passageways; something extremely complex or intricate

laconic   concise (antonym: **verbose; redundant**)

lambent   flickering; softly bright or radiant, as a candle

lampoon   harsh, satirical writing, usu. attacking an individual

lascivious   lewd; lustful; wanton

lassitude   fatigue; weariness (antonym: **alacrity**)

laudable   worthy of praise

lethargic   slow moving; sluggish

levity   lightness; lack of seriousness; frivolity

libertine   a person who is not restrained by convention or morality

licentious   lacking moral restraints, esp. sexual ones; lustful

ligneous   woodlike

limpid   clear and simple in style; transparent; serene and untroubled

  lucid   clear; sane; translucent; luminous

  pellucid   reflecting light evenly; easy to understand

litigate   to try in court; to contest in law

littoral   relating to the shore or coastal region

loggia   a roofed, open gallery, like a porch

loquacious   talkative

lucre   monetary gain; profit

ludicrous   laughable; ridiculous

lugubrious   gloomy; sorrowful

lurid   (1) gruesome; shocking; (2) ghastly pale

magenta   deep purplish red

malefactor   an evil-doer; a criminal

malfeasance   wrongdoing; official misconduct

malignant   evil; injurious; tending to produce death (antonym: **benign**)

mandatory   necessary; obligatory

marred   injured; blemished; damaged

martinet   a strict disciplinarian

masticate   to chew

maudlin   foolishly sentimental or morose

maverick   a rebel; a nonconformist

megalomaniac   one who exhibits delusions of omnipotence or grandeur

mercurial   quickly changing; inconstant

meretricious   attractive only on the surface; superficial; pretentious

meticulous   extremely concerned with details; well organized

miasma   a depleting or corrupting influence or atmosphere

millennium   a thousand years

miscreant   a heretic; a villain; one who commits illegal acts

misogynistic   characterized by hatred of women

mitigate   to soften; to lessen the severity of

moot   questionable; debatable

mordant   biting in manner or style; incisive

motility   movement

munificent   lavish; generous; liberal

nadir   (1) the lowest point; (2) a point in the sky opposite the zenith

naiad   a water nymph

napery   table linens

necromancy   magic; witchcraft

  chiromancy   palmistry

necrophobia   the fear of death

necropolis   a cemetery

nefarious   wicked; vile

neophyte   a novice

nexus   a connection or link

niggardly   stingy

noisome   offensive; harmful

nomenclature   a standardized system of symbols for a particular subject, usu. art or science

nonfeasance   failure to perform an act that should have been completed

notorious   widely and unfavorably known

nuance   a subtle distinction, variation, or quality

nugatory   inconsequential; trifling

nullify   to void legally; to make of no consequence

numismatist   one who studies and collects coins and tokens

nuncupative   not written; oral

nyctophobia   the fear of darkness

obdurate   persistent; unyielding

obfuscate   to confuse (antonym: **clarify**)

objurgate   to denounce harshly; to declaim; to castigate

obliterate   to destroy completely; to cause to disappear

obloquy   (1) abusive language; (2) bad repute

obscurant   tending to make obscure

obsequious   obedient; subservient

  sycophant   a servile, self-seeking flatterer

obtrude   to force, usu. oneself or one's ideas on another without request

obviate   to make unnecessary

ocher   earthy yellow or red

ochlophobia   the fear of crowds

officious   meddling; interfering

olfactory   relating to the sense of smell

oligarchy   form of government in which control is placed in the hands of a few, esp. associated with corruption

omnipotent   all-powerful

omnipresent   being all places at once

omniscient   knowing everything

omnivore   one who eats both animals and vegetables

onerous   burdensome; oppressive

onomatopoeia   the use of words whose sounds convey their meanings (e.g., *buzz, hiss*)

ontogeny   the development of an organism

onus   a burden; an obligation

ophidiophobia   the fear of snakes

opprobrium   disgrace due to a shameful act

opus   a major work, esp. a set of musical compositions

ornithophobia   the fear of birds

oscillate   to swing back and forth; to vary

osmosis   diffusion through a membrane

ossify   to become hard as a bone

ostentatious   showy; pretentious

oviparous   producing eggs that hatch outside the maternal body

palindrome   a word, sentence, or number that reads the same backward and forward (e.g., *mom*)

palliate   to cover up with excuses; to extenuate

panegyric   high praise; a tribute; an encomium (antonym: **diatribe**)

paradigm   an example; a pattern; an archetype

paradox   (1) something true that appears to be false; (2) something false that appears to be logical

pariah   an outcast

parry   (1) to ward off; (2) to escape by dodging

parsimony   the quality of being careful with money; thrift (antonym: **extravagance**)

partisan   one who is committed to a particular person, cause, or idea

parvenu   one recently risen to an unaccustomed position and not yet possessing the requisite dignity or characteristics; upstart

paucity   a small amount; a scarcity

pecuniary   having to do with money

pedantic   characterized by an ostentatious display of learning

pedometer   an instrument used to measure the distance walked

penultimate   next to last

peremptory   precluding a right of action, delay, or debate; admitting of no contradiction

perfidious   faithless; disloyal; treacherous

peripatetic   wandering; itinerant

peruse   to read carefully; to study

pervade   to spread throughout

petulant   ill-tempered; irritable; fractious

philatelist   one who studies and collects stamps

  -phile   a love of or affinity for (e.g., *philogyny*: love of women)

  -phobe   a fear of or aversion to

philistine (1) characterized by material rather than spiritual or artistic values; (2) narrow-minded or uninformed with respect to a specific topic area

piscatorial of or relating to fish

platen (1) a roller on a typewriter; (2) a flat plate

platitude the state of being dull, banal, or trite

plethora a superfluity; an excess

plumb (1) *n.* a lead weight used to find the true vertical; (2) *v.* to measure the depth of; to fathom

polemic strong argument in refutation of another; disputation; practice of engaging in controversy

poltroon a coward

potlatch (1) a ceremonial feast, with gifts, of northwest coast Indians; (2) a festival or celebration

precipitous steep

precocious exhibiting maturity at an early age

prescience the anticipation of upcoming events; foresight

prevaricate to deviate from the truth; to lie

probity honesty; uprightness; rectitude

prodigal recklessly wasteful; very generous

profusion a great amount; an abundance

prognosticate to forecast; to prophesy

propinquity closeness; proximity

proxy a person authorized to act for another (e.g., to vote corporate stock)

pseudonym a fictitious or pen name

surname (1) a family name; (2) an added name or nickname

puce dark red

puerile childish; juvenile

pundit an expert; an authority; a critic; a savant

purloin to steal

purview a range of authority, competence, or responsibility; scope

pusillanimous cowardly; fearful

Pyrrhic usu. referring to a victory won at excessively high cost

quaff to drink heartily

quagmire a bog; a difficult or entrapping situation; a predicament

qualm (1) a sudden onset of illness, esp. of nausea; (2) a feeling of unease about a point of conscience

quandary a state of confusion or doubt

quell to suppress

querulous complaining; whining

quintessence the essence of something in its most concentrated form; the purest representative from a certain category

quisling a traitor [derived from Vidkum Quisling, a Norwegian who collaborated with the Nazis during World War II]

quittance a release from debt or obligation

quixotic foolishly impractical and idealistic; capricious

quizzical (1) eccentric; odd; (2) inquisitive; questioning

quondam former; sometime

quorum   the minimum number of a group that must be present to conduct business legally

quotidian   daily

rancorous   with ill-will; with enmity (antonym: **benevolent**)

raze   to demolish completely; to destroy

recalcitrant   obstinately defiant of authority; resistant

recidivism   repeated relapse, as in tendency to repeat criminal activity

reciprocal   (1) mutual; shared; common; (2) inversely related

recondite   obscure; concealed; incomprehensible; esoteric

recumbent   lying down; leaning; resting

recusant   marked by refusal to obey authority

redolent   having a pleasing scent; fragrant

refurbish   to freshen or make new; to renovate

relegate   to assign to a place of insignificance; to banish

relume   to light or light again; to rekindle; to reestablish

remonstrate   to object; to protest

reprehend   to voice disapproval of

reprobate   a villain; an immoral person

repugnant   distasteful; abhorrent; obnoxious (antonym: **congenial**)

rescind   to take away; to remove

resilient   able to recover easily from hardship or misfortune; flexible

restive   tense

revile   to use abusive speech; to rail; to scold

ribald   rude or offensive; indecent

risible   capable of laughing or provoking laughter

rookery   a breeding place among rocks for mammals (e.g., seals) or birds

roseate   overoptimistic; cheerful

rotund   round; plump; chubby

ruminate   to reflect on something; to ponder

saboteur   one who willfully hinders, through destruction or obstruction, industrial production or a nation's war effort

   fifth column   supporters of an enemy that engage in sabotage within defense lines or national boundaries

sagacious   wise; astute; perspicacious

salubrious   healthy; promoting well-being; salutary (antonym: **deleterious**)

sanctimonious   (1) devout; holy; (2) hypocritically devout or holy

sanction   to authorize or approve

sanguine   hopeful

sardonic   disdainful; sarcastic

satiric   using ridicule or sarcasm to convey criticism; lampooning

saturnine   gloomy; sullen; morose

savant   one with detailed knowledge in a specialized field

   prodigy   highly talented child

   virtuoso   one who is highly skilled in the practice of an art, esp. music

scintilla   a minute trace or jot; an iota

   tittle   a particle

sectarian   of or relating to a sect or a smaller group within a larger group that adopts only certain beliefs; narrow-minded

sequester   (1) to set apart from others; to segregate; (2) to confiscate

sidereal   related to the stars; astral

sophomoric   (literally "wise fool") believing one's level of knowledge and maturity to be higher than it actually is

soporific   marked by, or causing, sleepiness or lethargy; drowsy

sordid   wretched; vile; foul

spelunker   one who studies and explores caves as a hobby

splenetic   hot-tempered; easily angered

spurious   false; forged; counterfeit

staid   sedate; serious; grave

sterile   unimaginative; unfruitful; bare (antonym: **fecund; fertile**)

stolid   dull; unemotional; immovable

stoma, stomata   a minute opening in outside surface of a plant (e.g., a leaf) for the passage of gases

striated   referring to muscle with alternate light and dark bands, as opposed to smooth muscle

strident   loud; harsh; grating

stygian   hellish

superfluous   more than necessary; extra

surfeit   overabundant supply; immoderate indulgence

surmise   to imagine; to make inferences based on insufficient evidence

surreptitious   secret; covert (antonym: **brazen; overt**)

sybaritic   voluptuous; sensual

sycophant   servile flatterer; parasite

synthesis   the combination of parts to form a whole, or of thesis and antithesis to form a higher truth

tacit   unspoken; implied (antonym: **explicit**)

taciturn   silent; having little inclination to talk (antonym: **garrulous**)

tactile   perceptible by touch; tangible

tangential   touching only the edge; marginally relevant

tangerine   a deep orange to almost scarlet mandarin orange [derived from Tangiers, Morocco]

tawdry   appearing gaudy or cheap

temerity   audacity; effrontery; boldness (antonym: **caution**)

tempest   storm

temporal   referring to time, as opposed to eternity; secular

tenet   a doctrine upheld by members of an organization

tepid   moderately warm; lukewarm

termagant   a shrew; a nagging woman, as Xanthippe (Socrates' wife); a virago; an ogress; a harpy

terrestrial   having to do with the earth

terse   (1) polished; refined; (2) short and to the point; concise

therapeutic   used in the treatment of diseases or disorders; curative

timbre   the quality of a sound or tone, distinctive of a particular voice or instrument

timorous   fearful; timid (antonym: **intrepid**)

tirade   a long, intemperate speech; diatribe

torpid   dormant; lacking energy; lethargic; apathetic; dull

   vapid   lacking vitality; flat; uninteresting

torque   (1) *n.* a twisting or turning force; (2) *v.* to cause to rotate or twist

torrid   oppressively hot

tort   a civil wrong for which the injured party is entitled to compensation

tractable   docile; malleable; obedient (antonym: **unruly**)

transient   lasting only a short time; changing; ephemeral; transitory

trenchant   (1) caustic; penetrating; (2) separate; distinct

triskaidekaphobia   the fear of the number 13

troglodyte   someone who lives in solitude

truculent   cruel; brutal; belligerent

turbid   muddy

turpitude   baseness; corruption; depravity

umbrage   (1) a feeling of offense or annoyance; (2) a shadow; a hint; a suspicion

unctuous   oily; smug; suave

undulate   to move in wavelike motions; to fluctuate

unduly   excessively

unequivocal   clear; obvious; certain

ungainly   hard to handle; unwieldy; clumsy

ungulate   hooflike; referring to hoofed animals

urbane   polished; polite or finished in manner

utopian   referring to paradise or an impossible ideal

uxoricide   the murder of one's wife

vacillate   to waver; to fluctuate; to oscillate

vacuous   stupid; lacking intelligence

vagrancy   the state of being homeless (legally, a misdemeanor)

vapid   insipid; spiritless

venal   corruptible

venerate   to honor

venial   forgivable

verbose   wordy (antonym: **laconic**)

vernal   suggestive of youth

viable   (1) capable of living; (2) able to stand or develop independently

vicarious   experienced through another medium; experienced through imaginary participation in the events of another's life

vilify   to slander; to verbally abuse; to defame

virago   a loud, overbearing woman; a termagant

viscous   thick; having a gummy consistency

vitriolic   caustic; biting

viviparous   producing living young, as most mammals, some reptiles, and a few fishes

volatile   easily aroused; explosive

volition   choice or decision; will

voracious   ravenous; gluttonous; insatiable
vulpine   foxlike; crafty
wan   pale; sickly
wanton   flirtatious; lascivious
whet   to stimulate; to incite; to make more intense, esp. an appetite
wizened   shrunken and wrinkled with age
wright   a worker, esp. in wood; used in combination with another word
   (e.g., *wheelwright, playwright*)
wroth   intensely angry; incensed
xanthic   yellowish
xenophobia   the fear of strangers
yean   to give birth, used of sheep or goats
yore   time long past
yowl   to cry out loudly; to wail
zealot   one who is enthusiastic, sometimes fanatical, about a cause
zenith   (1) the highest point; (2) the highest point reached by a celestial body
   (antonym: **nadir**)

SPECIAL COLLECTIVE NOUNS

bed of roses
bevy of beauties
cache of jewels
clew of worms
clutch of eggs
coven of witches
covey of quails
drift of swans
gaggle of geese
kindle of kittens
leap of leopards

litter of puppies
lock of hair
muster of peacocks
parcel of penguins
pod or **gam** of whales
pride of lions
rafter of turkeys
shoal or **school** of fish
string of pearls
swarm of bees
walk of snails

-OLOGY WORDS

The suffix *-ology* means the study of or the science of. The root of the word gives you the key to the field of study. The suffix *-ist* added to the name of the field of study refers to someone who works in that area. For example, the root *herpe* means reptile. Herpetology is the study of reptiles, and a herpetologist is one who studies snakes.
   In the following definitions, "the study of" or "the science of" is understood.

alalogy   algae
anthropology   human beings—their distributions, origins, classifications,
   physical characteristics, environmental and social relations, and cultures
archaeology   remains of past human life and activities
axiology   values and value judgments (e.g., in ethics)
bacteriology   bacteria
biology   living organisms and vital processes

cosmology nature, origin, structure, and space-time relationships of the universe

cryptology codes and ciphers

cytology cell and its functions

deontology ethics

enology wines and wine making

entomology insects

epistemology the nature, grounds, and limits of knowledge

eschatology end of the world

ethology animal behavior under natural conditions

etiology causes of phenomena

geology earth and its history

gerontology aging and the problems of the aged

hagiology saints and other revered persons

herpetology reptiles and amphibians

histology living tissue

homology similarity in structure (thought to be due to common origin)

horology measurement of time

ichthyology fishes

kinesiology principles of mechanics and anatomy in relation to human movement

limnology fresh waters

mammalogy mammals

morphology structures and forms of plants and animals; word formation in a language

mycology fungi

numismatology coins

oncology tumors

ontology nature and relations of being

ophthalmology structure, function, and diseases of the eye

ornithology birds

paleontology fossils

parasitology parasites and parasitism

pathology diseases

philology language, speech, linguistics, and literature

physiology functions and activities of living organisms

primatology primates, especially other than recent humans

radiology use of radiant energy (X rays, radium, etc.) in the diagnosis and treatment of disease

teleology final causes or purpose in nature

thanatology death and dying

toxicology poisons, their effects, and the problems involved

urology urinary system

virology structure and function of viruses

zoology animals

WORD DEMONS

Some words are frequently misused because they sound alike, are spelled almost the same, or are very close in meaning. The following is a list of such words. You should be familiar with the correct spelling, meaning, and use of each word.

adapt   to change or adjust
  When she moved to the foreign country, she had to adapt to new customs.
adept   skilled
  He was adept in all aspects of carpentry.
adopt   to accept or embrace, to accept formally
  The couple hopes to adopt several children.
  The council voted to adopt the new amendment.

adverse   unfavorable, unfriendly, opposing
  She overcame several adverse conditions to win the race.
averse   opposed
  The councilwoman was averse to the new proposal.

advice   suggestion
  The best advice I can give you is to read as much as you can.
advise   to counsel, to give suggestions
  We advise you to start studying for the test as soon as possible.

affect   influence, be of importance to, produce an effect on
  The rain will affect the picnic plans.
affect   to make a pretense of, to fake, to feign
  She affects a British accent.
effect   result, consequence; to bring about, to produce
  The farmers felt the effect of the drought.
  The drought effected a major change in the farmers' life.

affront   insult, offense
  His comment was an affront to the speaker.
confront   to face
  He will confront the student with the evidence.

allusion   reference to
  The author uses several allusions to Greek mythology in his story.
illusion   unreal image
  She has the illusion that I like jazz; I don't.

apprise   to let know, to inform
  The judge will apprise the jury of the pertinent statutes.
appraise   to estimate the value of
  The painting was appraised at two million dollars.

chronic   constant, long-lasting
  Parking is a chronic problem in the inner city.
acute   short-lived, perhaps severe
  He had acute appendicitis.

coherent   intelligible, meaningful, logical
  The newscaster gave a coherent report of the accident.
inherent   innate, essential, intrinsic
  Freedom of speech is an inherent part of the Bill of Rights.

complacent   contented
  The students were complacent about their grades.
complaisant   willing, obliging
  All day long the complaisant horse pulled the vegetable cart.

complement   to complete, to go well with
  Two angles complement each other when they add up to 180 degrees.
  Cranberries complement a turkey dinner.
compliment   a remark of courtesy or respect, praise
  I'd like to compliment you on the excellent job that you did.

continual   repeated, happening often
  His continual absence from classes resulted in his suspension.
continuous   uninterrupted, ceaseless
  The continuous hum of the machine gave her a headache.

credible   believable, plausible
  The child's story simply was not credible.
creditable   worthy of credit or praise, commendable
  The teacher did a creditable job in preparing the students for the test.
credulous   ready to believe, gullible, easily convinced
  The credulous woman accepted the neighbor's story without question.

denote   to refer to explicitly
  The word *black* denotes the characteristic of an object that reflects no color.
connote   to suggest
  The word *black* has been taken to connote wickedness or evil.

depredation   sack, plunder, robbing
  The effects of the Huns' depredation of the villages were obvious.
deprecation   disapproval, disparagement
  The deprecation of the new exhibit hall by all of the townspeople was
  disheartening to the architect.

detract   to take away from, to diminish
  The cracked sidewalks detract from the appearance of the house.
distract   to divert, to turn away from
  The student was unable to concentrate because the loud noises from the street
  distracted him.

discreet   prudent, careful, tactful
The attorney was discreet in his questioning of the young girl.
discrete   separate, distinct, separate
The party was composed of two discrete groups—the progressives and the conservatives.

disinterested   impartial, having nothing to gain
The chairperson was completely disinterested in the outcome of the committee vote.
uninterested   not interested in, unconcerned, incurious
The boy was completedly uninterested in the subjects he had to study.

elicit   to draw out
She questioned him for an hour but was unable to elicit any information.
illicit   unlawful, illegal
The police will crack down on all illicit parking.

eminent   prominent, illustrious, preeminent
Gandhi was an eminent statesman.
imminent   close at hand, impending
The jury's verdict is imminent.
immanent   inherent, innate, intrinsic
Psychologists are studying behavior patterns to determine which are immanent and which are acquired.

farther   to a greater distance
The runway was only one-half mile farther than the site of the plane crash.
further   more, additionally (in time or degree)
The council will discuss the budget further in the next meeting.

fewer   smaller in number
There are fewer students in school now than 10 years ago.
less   more limited in amount
Inflation is less now than in the late 1970s.

flammable   combustible, able to burn
inflammable   combustible, able to burn
You must be careful when storing flammable material.
(The antonym of *flammable* and *inflammable* is *unflammable*.)

flout   to scorn, to treat with disdain
Her unconventional dress flouted the guests' sensibilities.
flaunt   to show off, to exhibit
The boy flaunted his new scout badge.

homogeneous of the same kind, uniform, unmixed, similar in structure
It was a homogeneous class, all the students having basically the same socioeconomic and educational background.
The classes were homogeneously grouped according to abilities.

heterogeneous mixed or varied in composition
The class was heterogeneous, with students from different economic and educational backgrounds.
The crowd outside the theater was a heterogeneous group of students and townspeople.

imply to hint, to suggest, to indicate
The teacher's frown implied that the girl's answer was wrong.

infer to conclude from known facts or premises
From the evidence presented, the judge inferred that the defendant was guilty.

ingenious clever
The ingenious monkey figured out how to reach the bananas by constructing a platform.

ingenuous frank, artless, naive
The ingenuous child told his grandmother that he didn't like her dress.

ludicrous ridiculous
Italian western movies may seem ludicrous to an American.

lugubrious gloomy
The music was lugubrious, suitable for a funeral.

perquisite privilege that comes with a job
Members of Congress receive mailing privileges as a perquisite.

prerequisite necessity, something required beforehand
Mathematics is a prerequisite for most physics courses.

precipitate to bring on, to hasten, to quicken
The Great Depression precipitated the rise of fascism in Germany.

precipitous steep
Prices during the inflation period rose precipitously.

persecute to harass, to badger, to victimize
The Puritans came to America after they were persecuted for their religious beliefs.

prosecute to put on trial, to indict, to bring legal action against
The state will prosecute him for drug trafficking.

perspective viewpoint
From the perspective of the Native American, land is sacred.

prospective future, expected
The prospective merger of the two companies caused a flurry of activity on the stock market.

precede   to go in front of
   An incubation period usually precedes the onset of the disease.
proceed   to go ahead
   After you reach the center of town, proceed three more blocks to the hotel.

prescribe   to order or advise (as in medicine)
   The physician will prescribe a drug to combat the infection.
proscribe   to condemn, to disapprove, to outlaw
   During the Middle Ages, the Catholic Church proscribed certain books by
   scientists.

supplement   to add to something
   He will supplement his regular school work with night and summer courses.
supplant   to replace, to usurp the place of
   Robots will supplant workers in some factories.

venal   capable of being bribed, corrupt
   The judge was accused of being venal and accepting large sums of money.
venial   forgivable
   His continual tardiness was often annoying but venial.

SELECTED FOREIGN WORDS AND PHRASES USED IN ENGLISH

addenda   a list of additions (Latin)
ad hoc   for a particular purpose (Latin)
aficionado   an ardent devotee (Spanish)
agent provocateur   one who incites another person or an organization (French)
alfresco   outdoors (Italian)
alter ego   a second self; a trusted friend (Latin)
amour-propre   self-esteem (French)
angst   dread, anxiety (German)
a priori   based on theory rather than observation (Latin)
au courant   informed of the latest (French)
baksheesh   tip, gratuity (Persian)
bête noire   a strongly detested person or thing (French)
bildungsroman   personal development novel (German)
bona fide   in good faith (Latin)
bon vivant   an epicure; a lover of good living (French)
bravura   a display of spirit and dash (Italian)
casus belli   a pretext or reason that justifies or allegedly justifies an attack
   of war (Latin)
caveat emptor   let the buyer beware (Latin)
chef d'oeuvre   chief work; masterpiece (French)
chutzpah   gall, arrogance, audacity (Yiddish)
comme il faut   as it ought to be; proper (French)
contretemps   an inopportune or embarrassing situation (French)

corpus delicti   the evidence necessary to prove that a crime has been committed (Latin)

coup de grâce   a final, decisive blow or event (French)

cul-de-sac   a dead end (French)

de facto   actual (Latin)

déjà vu   illusion of having experienced something already (French)

de jure   technically (Latin)

de rigueur   necessary, obligatory (French)

dernier cri   the last word; the newest fashion (French)

déshabillé   undressed or partially undressed (French)

doppelgänger   a counterpart of a living person (German)

enfant terrible   a bad child; one whose behavior is embarrassing (French)

errata   a list of errors (Latin)

ex cathedra   by virtue of one's position or office (Latin)

faux pas   a social blunder (French)

fiasco   disaster (Italian)

idée fixe   an idea that dominates one's mind, especially for a long time (French)

in extenso   at full length (Latin)

in extremis   near death (Latin)

ingenue   the stage role of an ingenuous girl; a naive girl (French)

in loco parentis   in the place of a parent; acting as a guardian (Latin)

in medias res   in the middle of things (Latin)

in re   in reference to (Latin)

insouciance   indifference; lack of concern (French)

in vacuo   in a vacuum (Latin)

junta   group (usually military) that assumes leadership after a coup or overthrow of a government (Spanish)

laissez-faire   a policy of free trade or noninterference (French)

leitmotif   recurring theme (German)

mélange   a mixture or medley, often of incongruous elements (French)

ménage   a household (French)

mirabilis dictu   wonderful to relate (Latin)

modus operandi   a method of procedure, working, or operating (Latin)

ne plus ultra   the highest point that can be attained; the acme (Latin)

noblesse oblige   nobility obligates; the behavior and graciousness of the nobility (French)

nolo contendere   no contest; legally, not contesting a charge against one, but without pleading guilty (Latin)

nom de plume   a pen name (French)

non sequitur   something that does not logically follow (Latin)

nuance   a subtle distinction (French)

pax vobiscum   peace be with you; peace (Latin)

persona non grata   an unacceptable or unwelcome person (Latin)

pièce de resistance   the main course or dish; the most valuable object (French)

presto   rapidly, quickly (Italian)

prima facie   on the face of; at first view (Latin)

pro bono publico   for the public good (Latin)

pro forma   done as a matter of form (Latin)

pro rata   proportionally according to a factor (Latin)

pro tempore (pro tem)   for the time being; temporarily (Latin)

punctilio   a fine point; a minute detail of conduct (Italian)

quid pro quo   something given or received for something else; substitute (Latin)

raison d'être   reason for being (French)

rapprochement   establishing a cordial relationship; developing mutual understanding (French)

rara avis   an unusual specimen (Latin)

rendezvous   an appointment for two or more people to meet at a particular place (French)

riposte   a retort; a retaliatory verbal sally (French)

safari   a trip or journey (Swahili)

salaam   peace (as a salutation) (Arabic)

sanctum sanctorum   the holy of holies; the office of an awesome person (Latin)

sang froid   cold blood; self-possession, composure (French)

schadenfreude   pleasure at someone else's misfortunes (German)

sine qua non   indispensable (Latin)

soupçon   suspicion; a little bit or trace, as in a recipe (French)

sui genera   one of a kind (Latin)

tour de force   a feat of strength, skill, or ingenuity (French)

vendetta   a blood feud (Italian)

vis-à-vis   face to face with; in relation to; as compared with (French)

weltschmerz   sorrow over the evils of the world (German)

zeitgeist   the spirit of the times (German)

ALPHABETS AND THEIR CHARACTERISTICS

Alphabet	Characteristics/Comments
Cyrillic	Slavic and Russian languages
Cuneiform	Ancient Egyptian iconographic writing
Hieroglyphic	Ancient Egyptian ideographic writing
Devanagari	Indian writing with syllabic features
Greek	Ancient or modern; Greek alphabet
Hebrew	written right to left, no vowels
Arabic	written right to left, no vowels
Roman	used in Romance languages and English
ogham	Old Irish, 5th and 6th century, notches
rune	Germanic, from 3rd to 13th centuries

GEOGRAPHY

It is not possible to provide a review of basic geography here. Since questions involving name changes of countries and cities have appeared on some *MAT* exams, a table of such changes is given below.

Current Name	Previous Names
Angola	Portuguese West Africa
Bangladesh	East Pakistan
Belize	British Honduras
Cambodia	French Indo-China
Chad	French Equatorial Africa
Ethiopia	Abyssinia
Ghana	Gold Coast
Guyana	British Guiana
Ho Chi Minh City	Saigon
Indonesia	Netherlands East Indies
Iran	Persia
Iraq	Mesopotamia, Babylon, Assyria
Istanbul	Constantinople
Laos	French Indo-China
Madagascar	Malagasy
Namibia	South West Africa
Niger	French West Africa
Petrograd	Leningrad, Petrograd
Santo Domingo	Trujillo
Sri Lanka	Ceylon
Surinam	Dutch Guiana
Thailand	Siam
Volgograd	Stalingrad; Tsaritsyn
Zaire	Congo
Zambia	Northern Rhodesia
Zimbabwe	Rhodesia

HISTORY

MAT analogies may include the names of people, events, wars, treaties, conferences, and documents important in U.S. and world history. The following may serve as a quick review.

Explorers

Amundsen, Roald (1872–1928)   (Norwegian) was first to reach South Pole and to fly over North Pole

Balboa, Vasco Núñez de (1475–1517)   (Spanish) Pacific Ocean

Cabot, John (1450–1498)   (English) explored North America

Cartier, Jacques (1491–1557)   (French) St. Lawrence river region

Columbus, Christopher (1451–1506)   (Italian/Spanish) discovery of the New World

Coronado, Francisco Vásquez de (1510–1554)   (Spanish) mythical city of Cibola, SW region of the U.S.

Cortes, Hernando (1485–1547)   (Spanish) Mexico, Aztec nation

de Soto, Hernando (1500–1542)   (Spanish) Cuba, Florida, SE region of U.S.

Diaz, Bartolomeu (1450–1500)   (Portuguese) Cape of Good Hope

Drake, Sir Francis (1540–1596)   (British) circumnavigated the globe; helped defeat Spanish Armada

Hudson, Henry (d. 1611)   (British) Hudson River, Hudson Bay area

Magellan, Ferdinand (1480–1521)   (Portuguese) the first to sail around the world

Marquette, Jacques (1637–1675)   (French) discovered the Mississippi

Peary, Robert E. (1856–1920)   (American) North Pole (disputed claim; prior claim of Fred Cook)

Pizarro, Francisco (1470–1541)   (Spanish) Peru, Inca empire

Polo, Marco (1254–1324)   (Italian) explored China and Asia

Ponce de Leon, Juan (1460–1521)   (Spanish) first European explorer in Florida

Raleigh, Sir Walter (1552–1618)   (British) eastern coast of U.S.

Scott, Robert (1868–1912)   (British) Antarctica, South Pole (prior claim of Amundsen)

Vasquez de Coronado, Francisco (1510–1554)   (Spanish) first European to explore Arizona and New Mexico

Vespucci, Amerigo (1454–1521)   (Italian) America was named after him; first to realize that the Americas were a different continent than Asia

Inventors

Beaufort, Francis (1774–1854)   (French) Beaufort Scale: wind force scale named after him

Bell, Alexander Graham (1847–1922)   (American) telephone

Benz, Karl (1844–1929)   (German) the petrol-powered automobile

Berners-Lee, Tim (b. 1955)   (English) with Robert Cailliau, the World Wide Web

Braille, Louis (1809–1852)   (French) the Braille writing system

Daimler, Gottlieb (1834–1900)   (German) first high-speed internal-combustion engine

Da Vinci, Leonardo (1452–1519)   (Italian) conceptualized a helicopter, painted the Mona Lisa, advanced anatomy, etc.

Diesel, Rudolf (1853–1913)   (German) first internal-combustion engine using fuel oil instead of gasoline

Drais, Karl (1785–1851)   (German) bicycle (Draisine)

Edison, Thomas Alva (1847–1931)   (American) lightbulb, phonograph

Einstein, Albert (1879–1955)   (German) theory of relativity

Engelbart, Douglas (b. 1925) (American) the computer mouse

Fermi, Enrico (1901–1954)   (Italian) one of the first developers of the nuclear reactor

Fleming, Alexander (1881–1955)   (English) penicillin

Ford, Henry (1863–1947)   (American) developed modern assembly lines for mass production

Franklin, Benjamin (1706–1790)   (American) lightning rod

Galilei, Galileo (1564–1642)   (Italian) improved the telescope, physicist

Gutenberg, Johannes (1400–1468)   (German) movable type, printing press

Marconi, Guglielmo (1874–1937)   (Italian) wireless radio

Montgolfier, Joseph-Michel (1740–1810)   (French) hot-air balloon

Newton, Isaac (1642–1727)   (English) reflecting telescope (reduces chromatic aberration)

Nobel, Alfred (1833–1896)   (Swedish) dynamite

Roentgen, Wilhelm Conrad (1845–1923)   (German) the X-ray machine

Stephenson, George (1781–1848)   (English) first steam locomotive

Whitney, Eli (1765–1825)   (American) interchangeable parts, cotton gin

Liberators or Unifiers

Bismarck, Otto von (1815–1898)   Germany

Bolívar, Simón (1783–1830)   Venezuela, Peru, Bolivia

Garibaldi, Giuseppe (1807–1882)   Italy

O'Higgins, Bernardo (1778–1842)   Chile

San Martin, José de (1778–1850)   Peru, Chile (march across the Andes)

Major Wars

Knowledge of the most important events and treaties associated with major wars will help in taking the *MAT*. Below is a list of some major items that may be found in analogies.

THE AMERICAN REVOLUTION

first battles—Lexington and Concord (1775)
major battles—Bunker Hill (1775), Fort Ticonderoga (1775), Saratoga (1777), Valley Forge (1777)

Declaration of Independence—declared that colonies were free from England, 1776

Continental Congress—federal legislature of the 13 colonies under the Articles of Confederation (1774, 1775)

Constitution—replaced Articles of Confederation in 1789

end of war—surrender of British General Cornwallis to George Washington at Yorktown (1781); treaty recognizing the United States as a separate nation signed in Paris (1782)

AMERICAN CIVIL WAR

start of war—Harper's Ferry (1859)

first battles—Fort Sumter (1861) and Bull Run (1861) (both Confederate victories)

major battles—Antietam (1862), Fredericksburg (1862), Gettysburg (1863), Shiloh (1862) (the Union named battles after towns; the Confederates named battles after streams), Sherman's March to the Sea (1864), Vicksburg (1863) (great victory for Grant)

end of war—surrender of General Lee to General Grant at Appomatox (1865)

FRENCH REVOLUTION

start of war—storming of the Bastille (1789)

important events/documents—Declaration of the Rights of Man and Citizen (Preamble to the Constitution), 1791; Reign of Terror, which ended 9 Thermidor (July 27, 1794) with the execution of Robespierre; coup d'etat of 18 Brumaire (November 9–10, 1799) whereby Napoleon I becomes consul

end of war—treaty of Amiens, France (1802)

RUSSIAN CIVIL WAR

conflicting sides—Bolsheviks (majority) vs. Mensheviks (minority)

leaders of opposing sides—Lenin and Trotsky (Reds) vs. Kerensky and Plekanov (Whites)

WORLD WAR I

start of war—assassination of Archduke Ferdinand (1914); sinking of *Lusitania* (British ship with American passengers) by the Germans led to U.S. entry into the war (1915)

major battles—Ypres (1917), Marne (1914), Verdun (1916), Somme (1916)

offensive characteristics—trench warfare, use of poison gas

end of war—Treaty of Versailles (1918); attempt to divide nations on basis of national self-determination; establishment of the League of Nations

WORLD WAR II

major events—Munich Pact (1938), policy of appeasement, associated with British Prime Minister Chamberlain

start of war—blitzkrieg over Poland (1939); sinking of *Arizona* and other ships at Pearl Harbor attack in Honolulu led to U.S. declaration of war against Japan and Germany (1941)

major battles—Dunkirk (1940), Ardennes (1944), Alamein (North Africa 1942), Stalingrad (1942–1943)

characteristics—tank warfare, blitzkrieg, use of massive bombing by air force; development of atomic weapons

end of war—Japan surrenders unconditionally at Potsdam Conference (1945)

OTHER CONFERENCES AND PEACE TREATIES

Ghent, Belgium—end of War of 1812

Vienna, Congress of—end of Napoleonic Wars (1814–1815)

Yalta Conference—meeting of Roosevelt, Churchill, and Stalin during World War II (1945)

Potsdam (German) Conference—meeting of Truman, Churchill (replaced by Atlee), and Stalin during World War II (1945)

Panmunjon, Korea—end of Korean War (1953)

Reykjavik Conference—Reagan-Gorbachev summit meeting (1986)

SOCIAL SCIENCES

The following brief list of people and movements in the social sciences is intended as a quick review only.

Adler, Alfred (1870–1937)   Austrian psychiatrist; inferiority complex

Allison, Graham (b. 1940)   American political scientist, has worked in decision-making and is an important analyst of national security

Barzun, Jacques (b. 1907)   American historian specializing in expressions of culture like music, literature, and education

Behaviorism (Psychology)   School of thought in psychology since the early 1900s. Suggests that behavior can be explained by means of environmental causes. Proponents were John B. Watson, Ivan Pavlov, and B. F. Skinner, for example. Focus on classical and operant conditioning.

Benedict, Ruth (1887–1948)   American anthropologist; author of *Patterns of Culture*

Binet, Alfred (1851–1911) and **Simon, Théodore** (1873–1961)   French psychologists; development of IQ tests

Boas, Franz (1858–1942)   German American anthropologist; known for being the "father" of modern anthropology as he applied the scientific method to his anthropological studies

Cognitive Psychology   Focuses on mental processes including how people think, perceive, remember, and learn. One of the most influential theories was the stages of cognitive development theory proposed by Jean Piaget. Other cognitive psychologists include Albert Bandura, Daniel Kahneman, Steven Pinker, Daniel Schacter, and Robert Sternberg.

Coleman, James (1926–1995)   American sociologist; one of the early users of the term "social capital"

Cultural Materialism (Anthropology)   Attaches special importance to technology and economic factors in the development of a society.

Dewey, John (1859–1952)   American educator/philosopher; pragmatism

DuBois, W. E. B. (1868–1963)   American sociologist and historian; active in the area of racism

Durkheim, Emile (1859–1917)   French sociologist; considered one of the fathers of modern sociology

Erikson, Erik (1902–1994)   American psychologist; stage theory of development

Ferguson, Niall (b. 1964)   Scottish historian specializing in financial and economic history

Freud, Sigmund (1856–1939)   Austrian psychiatrist; sexual drive, Oedipus complex

Friedman, Milton (1912–2006)   American economist, recipient of the Nobel Prize in economics; opposed government regulation

Functionalism (Anthropology, Sociology)   Applies the scientific method to the examination of the social world (e.g., social surveys, interviews) and uses analogies between individual organisms and society. Emphasis is on use. Proponents include Emile Durkheim and Talcott Parsons.

Gall, Franz Joseph (1758–1828)   German anatomist/physiologist; study of nervous system and brain, founded pseudoscience of phrenology

Galton, Sir Francis (1822–1911)   English scientist; belief in heredity as predeterminant force, IQ tests

Geertz, Clifford (1926–2006)   American anthropologist; worked in the field of symbolic anthropology, which attributes special importance to thoughts (symbols)

Gestalt Psychology   Developed in Germany and Austria in the late 19th century. Gestalt psychologists believe that the conscious experience must be considered as a whole, rather than broken down into small elements. The whole is greater than just the sum of its parts. Prononents include Max Wertheimer, Kurt Koffka, Wolfgang Koehler, and Fritz Perls.

Gibbon, Edward (1737–1794)   English historian who wrote *The History of the Decline and Fall of the Roman Empire*

Goffman, Erving (1922–1982)   American sociologist who studied social interaction

Goodall, Jane (b. 1934)   American anthropologist and primatologist; known for her chimpanzee studies in Tanzania

Greenspan, Alan (b. 1926)   American economist; former chairman of the Federal Reserve

Harlow, Harry (1905–1981)   American psychologist; importance of attachment for baby monkeys

Heterodox economics   Economic schools of thought that are outside of mainstream economics. They include the Austrian School, ecological economics, and Post-Keynesian economics.

Horney, Karen (1885–1952)   American psychiatrist; importance of social and cultural influences on behavior

Huizinga, Johan (1872–1945)   Dutch historian, one of the founders of modern cultural history

Humanistic Psychology   Developed in the 1950s in response to both behaviorism and psychoanalysis. Focused on individual free will, personal growth, and self-actualization. Major proponents include Abraham Maslow and Carl Rogers.

Hume, David (1711–1776)   Scottish philosopher; use of induction

Huntington, Samuel (1927–2008)   American political scientist, famous for his theory of the "Clash of Civilizations"

James, William (1842–1910)   American philosopher; pragmatism, functionalism

Jung, Carl (1875–1961)   Swiss psychiatrist; self-realization

Kant, Immanuel (1724–1804)   German philosopher; proposed categorical imperative

Keynes, John Maynard (1883–1946)   British developer of Keynesian economics, founder of modern theoretical macroeconomics

Kohlberg, Lawrence (1927–1987)   American psychologist; moral stages of development

Köhler, Wolfgang (1887–1967)   German-American psychologist; Gestaltist, worked with chimps

Krugman, Paul (b. 1953)   American economist; won the Nobel Memorial Prize in Economic Sciences in 2008 for his work on New Trade Theory

Leibnitz, Gottfried (1646–1716)   German philosopher/mathematician; use of deduction

Malinowski, Bronislaw (1884–1942)   Polish anthropologist, pioneer in ethnographic fieldwork

Malthus, Thomas (1766–1834)   English demographer and political economist; noted the potential for populations to increase rapidly, and more rapidly than the food supply

Mansfield, Harvey (b. 1932)   American political scientist; conservative; author of *Manliness*

Marx, Karl (1818–1883)   German economist; founder of communism

Mill, John Stuart (1806–1873)   English philosopher; used principle of utility

Nye, Joseph (b. 1937)   American political scientist; developed the concepts of asymmetrical and complex interdependence with Robert Keohane

Parsons, Talcott (1902–1979)   American sociologist; developed structural functionalism as a means of analyzing society

Patterson, Orlando (b. 1940)   American sociologist known for his work on race

Pavlov, Ivan (1849–1936)   Russian physiologist/psychologist; conditioning of reflexes, worked with dogs

Peirce, Charles Sanders (1839–1914)   American philosopher; pragmatist

Piaget, Jean (1896–1980)   Swiss psychologist; stage theory of intellectual development

Psychoanalysis (Psychology)   Founded by Sigmund Freud. States that the human mind is composed of three elements: the id, the ego, and the superego. The unconscious plays an important role in the explanation of behavior. Other psychoanalysts include Anna Freud, Carl Jung, and Erik Erikson.

Sachs, Jeffrey (b. 1954)   American economist; author of *The End of Poverty*; Special Advisor to United Nations Secretary-General Ban Ki-Moon

Skinner, B[urrhus] F[rederic] (1904–1990)   American psychologist; behaviorist; studied effects of reinforcement on behavior; worked with rats, pigeons (Skinner box)

Smith, Adam (1723–1790)   English; one of the founders of modern economics, author of *The Wealth of Nations*

Strauss, Claude Levi (1908–2008)   French anthropologist; author of *Structural Anthropology*; viewed culture as a system of symbolic communication

Structuralism (Anthropology, Sociology)   Suggests that meaning is produced through practices and activities. The mind uses binary opposites (like day and night) that differ from culture to culture. Proponents include Claude Levi-Strauss.

Symbolic interactionism (Sociology)   People interact with each other by interpreting each other's actions. Their interactions are therefore based on the meaning they attach to the actions. Proponents include George H. Mead, Herbert Blumer, and Erving Goffman.

Thorndike, Edward (1874–1949)   American educator/psychologist; intelligence, IQ tests, worked with cats

Titchener, Edward (1867–1927)   American psychologist; structuralist

von Ranke, Leopold (1795–1886)   German historian considered one of the founders of modern source-based history

Walzer, Michael (b. 1935)   American political philosopher; known for his work on just and unjust wars, economic justice, and ethnicity

Watson, John (1878–1958)   American psychologist; behaviorist

Weber, Max (1864–1920)   German sociologist; argued in *The Protestant Ethic and the Spirit of Capitalism* that Protestantism influenced the development of capitalism

ART AND ARCHITECTURE

Use the following list of the most important artists and architects and schools and movements in art history as a quick review. The names of artists associated with the movement or school and the works of particular artists are given in parentheses.

Important Artists, Architects, and Schools/Movements

abstract art   art form that assumes that artistic values reside in form and color and are independent of the subject of the art or painting

abstract expressionism   1940s-to-1950s American art movement stressing spontaneous, nonrepresentational creation with emphasis on the paint itself; first truly American school of art (Pollock)

art deco   1920s-to-1930s art movement stressing highly decorative art, utilizing geometric, streamlined forms inspired by industrial design (Chrysler Building in New York City)

art nouveau   1895-to-1905 "new art" movement characterized by motifs of highly stylized flowing plants, curving lines, and fluent forms

ashcan school   early 20th century school of American realist painters who abandoned idealized subjects for more sordid aspects of urban life

Audubon, John James (1785–1851)   early 19th century American artist and illustrator known for his color engravings of birds (*Birds in America*)

Barbizon school   mid-19th century group of landscape artists who rejected the classical and romantic to portray nature as they perceived it; forerunner of impressionism (Rousseau)

baroque   late 16th-to-early 18th century movement, developed in Italy, that stressed grand theatrical effects and elaborate ornamentation (Palace of Versailles)

Bauhaus   most famous school of architecture and design of modern times; founded in Germany in 1919; austere, geometric style (founder: Gropius; teachers: Klee and Kandinsky)

beaux arts   architectural style, popular from 1890 to 1920, using formal and classical techniques

Bosch, Hieronymus (1450–1516)   early 16th century painter considered perhaps the greatest master of fantasy ever (*Garden of Earthly Delights*)

Botticelli, Sandro (1444–1510)   15th century Italian Renaissance artist (*The Birth of Venus, St. Sebastian*)

Brancusi, Constantin (1876–1957)   19th-to-20th century Romanian sculptor known for highly simplified archetypical human and animal forms (*The Kiss, Bird in Space*)

Brueghel, Pieter (the Elder) (1525–1569)   16th century Flemish painter known for peasant scenes and large landscapes; sometimes known as "Peasant Bruegel" (*Hunters in the Snow, The Harvesters*)

Byzantine art   Eastern (Greek) art of the 5th to 15th centuries, characterized by Oriental motifs, formal design, and free use of gilding

Caldecott, Randolph (1864–1886)   19th century English illustrator known for his illustrations of children's books; the prestigious Caldecott Award is given annually for excellence in children's book illustration

Calder, Alexander (1898–1976)   20th century American sculptor and abstract painter best known for mobiles and stabiles (nonmoving sculptures) (*Lobster Trap and Fish Tail, Spiral*)

Cellini, Benvenuto (1500–1571)   16th century Florentine sculptor, goldsmith, and designer of coins and medals (*Perseus* bronze, gold saltcellar)

Cézanne, Paul (1839–1906)   19th century French painter, often considered the forerunner of many 20th century art movements; romantic, impressionist, classical, and naturalistic influences are all condensed in his work (*Grande Baigneuses, Self Portrait, The Black Clock, Card Players*)

Chagall, Marc (1889–1985)   20th century French painter of Russian-Jewish origin, forerunner of surrealism (*The Juggler, The Green Violinist*)

chiaroscuro   the balance of light and shadow in a picture; used to describe works that are predominantly dark, like those of Rembrandt

classicism   art attributed to ancient Greece and Rome, characterized by discipline, harmony, objectivity, and reason

cloisonné   a process of enameling in which a design is displayed in strips of metal on a china or metal background, making channels, or cloisons, to hold the enamel colors

Cole, Thomas (1801–1848)   19th century American landscape painter; member of the Hudson River school of painting

collage   a picture built up wholly or partly from pieces of paper, cloth, or other material stuck on canvas or other surface (early cubists, dadaists, Matisse)

Constable, John (1776–1837)   19th century English landscape painter (*The Holy Wain*)

constructivism   movement, since the 1920s, principally in Russia, involving the creation of three-dimensional art, using iron, glass, plastic, and other materials to express technological society (Calder's mobiles)

Copley, John Singleton (1738–1815)   18th century American protrait painter

cubism   1907-to-1915 art movement, mainly French, characterized by fragmentation of reality; used geometric forms in nature as a departure from representational art; a reaction to impressionism (Picasso)

Currier, Nathaniel T. (1813–1888) and **Ives, James Merrit** (1824-1895)   19th century American lithographers known for prints depicting American life

dada   1915-to-1923 international anti-art movement reflecting cynicism by producing bizarre works that represented the absurd (*Mona Lisa with a Mustache*)

Dali, Salvador (1904–1989)   20th century Spanish painter, considered one of the foremost surrealists (*Premonition of the Civil War, Christ of St. John of the Cross, Persistence of Memory*)

Daumier, Honoré (1808–1879)   19th century French lithographer, cartoonist, and social satirist (*The Print Collector, The People of Justice*)

Degas, Edgar (1834–1917)   late 19th–early 20th century French painter (*Study of a Dancer, Woman on Horseback*)

de Kooning, Willem (1904–1997)   20th century Dutch abstract painter known for distorted shapes and tragic expressions (*Woman, I*)

Delacroix, Eugène (1798–1863)   19th century French painter of the Romantic period (*Liberty at the Barricades*)

Donatello (1386–1466)   15th century Florentine sculptor; one of the founders of Italian Renaissance sculpture (*David, St. George Slaying the Dragon*)

Dürer, Albrecht (1471–1528)   late 15th–early 16th century German artist known for his woodcuts and engravings (*His Mother*, a charcoal drawing; *Adam and Eve*, an engraving; and *The Apocalypse*, a series of woodcuts)

engraving   a method of multiplying prints. See also, **relief**, **intaglio**, and **lithography**

Ernst, Max (1891–1976)   20th century German-born French artist, a leading surrealist and one of the founders of dada; known for his "reveries" (*Europe After the Rain, Mundus est Fabula*)

expressionism   20th century art in which the expression of the artist takes precedence over rational and faithful rendering of the subject matter; stress on emotions and inner visions (van Gogh, El Greco)

fauvism   work of early 20th-century impressionists, characterized by strident color and distortion; first artistic revolution of the 20th century (Matisse, Roualt)

Fayum portrait   realistic form of portraiture found on shrouds and mummy cases from the 1st to 4th centuries

fresco   wall painting; painting on wet plaster

frieze   middle section of a building, where relief sculpture was often executed

Fuller, Buckminster (1895–1983)   20th century American avant-garde architect famous for his geodesic domes

futurism   1910 Italian art movement that stressed motion and sought to glorify the machine by painting and sculpting multitudes of moving parts

Gainsborough, Thomas (1727–1788)   18th century English painter of landscapes and portraits (*Blue Boy*)

gargoyle   in Gothic architecture, a bizarre creature whose open mouth was used as a gutter to carry water away from the walls

Gauguin, Paul (1848–1903)   19th century French painter best known for his depiction of simple life in Tahiti (*Indian Ocean Maiden*)

glazing   a process of applying a transparent layer of oil paint over a solid one so that the color of the first layer is greatly modified

Gothic   12th-to-16th century style of architecture typical of northern Europe (cathedrals with elaborate architecture and stained glass panels)

Goya, Francisco José de (1746–1828)   late 18th–early 19th century Spanish painter and printmaker (*Majas on a Balcony*)

Greco, El (1541–1614)   16th century Greek painter who lived and worked in Spain (*The Annunciation, The Burial of the Count of Orgaz*)

Hogarth, William (1697–1764)   18th century English artist (*Signing the Marriage Contract*)

Holbein, Hans (the Younger) (1497–1543)   16th century German Renaissance painter (*Dance of Death, Dead Christ*)

holograph   an image in three dimensions created by a laser passing through a photographic film or plate without a camera

Homer, Winslow (1836–1910)   late 19th century American painter and illustrator; Civil War illustrations

Hopper, Edward (1882–1967)   20th century American artist known for bleak, surreal scenes depicting city life and the ennui of workers

Hudson River school   mid-19th century American school of landscape painting known for its romantic scenes glorifying nature

impasto   thick application of pigment to canvas

impressionism   late 19th century French school that stressed visual impression; first of the modern art movements (Monet, Renoir, Degas)

intaglio   engraving on stone to achieve a concave effect; opposite of cameo

Johns, Jasper (b. 1930)   20th century American pop artist known for blown-up images (*Flags, Targets*)

Kandinsky, Wassily (1866–1944)   late 19th–early 20th century Russian-born German artist, one of the founders of the abstract movement; known for kinetic lines

Kinetic art   art that moves through magnets, motorized parts, etc.

Klee, Paul (1879–1940)   late 19th–early 20th century Swiss painter and etcher known for his whimsical works that sought to portray reality through its inner nature (*Inventions, Senecio*)

Leonardo da Vinci (1452–1519)   late 15th–early 16th century Italian artist and scientist; most versatile genius of the Renaissance (fresco: *The Last Supper*, painting: *Mona Lisa*; notebook drawings of human anatomy)

lithography   method of printing that uses wax and ink on hard plates

luminism   American art movement associated with impressionism, concerned with the effect of light

Maillol, Aristide (1861–1944)   late 19th–early 20th century French painter and sculptor (*The Three Graces, Seated Woman*)

Manet, Edouard (1832–1883)   19th century French painter who contributed much to the development of impressionism, although he himself was not a member of the group (*The Fifer, Guitarist*)

mannerism   1520s-to-1590s school of art and architecture characterized by the exotic and confusing and the distortion of the human form (El Greco, Vassari)

Matisse, Henri (1869–1954)   late 19th–early 20th century French artist known for his still-life subjects; a member of the fauve group and influenced by impressionism (*Jazz: Icarus, Fruits and Flowers*)

Michelangelo, Bounarotti (1475–1564)   late 15th–early 16th century Italian sculptor, painter, architect, and poet who embodied the Renaissance (*Pieta, David, Madonna and Child*, ceiling of the Sistine Chapel)

Mies van der Rohe, Ludwig (1886–1969)   20th century German-American architect known for clean-line skyscrapers of glass and metal and for steel-framed furniture (Barcelona chair)

minimal art   contemporary art movement that rejects emotional expression and stresses restraint, understatement, and precision

Miró, Joan (1893–1983)   20th century Spanish surrealist painter known for depicting fantasies (*Dutch Interior, Woman and Bird in the Moonlight*)

mobile   a kinetic sculpture consisting of shapes cut from different materials and hung at different levels (Calder)

modern art   art, since the 1850s, that has extricated itself from subject matter and stresses form

Modigliani, Amedeo (1884–1920)   late 19th–early 20th century Italian sculptor and painter known for his sad, elongated faces (*Seated Nude, The Brown Haired Girl*)

Mondrian, Piet (1872–1944)   late 19th–early 20th century Dutch abstract painter known for his geometric shapes (*Composition with Red, Yellow and Blue*)

Monet, Claude (1840–1926) late 19th–early 20th century French painter, a leader of impressionism; known for seeing nature with an "objective eye" (*Water Lily* paintings)

montage sticking one layer over another, especially photographs applied to an unusual background; associated with cubists

Moore, Henry (1898–1986) 20th century British sculptor known for large-scale abstract works and "truth to materials" doctrine (*Family Group*)

Moses, Anna Mary (Grandma) (1860–1961) late 19th–early 20th century American painter known for her simple depictions of New England life and landscapes

Murillo, Bartolomé Estebon (1617–1682) 17th century Spanish painter (*Immaculate Conception, Beggar Boy*)

Nast, Thomas (1840–1902) 19th century American illustrator and cartoonist known for his depictions of Tweed ring and Tammany Hall

naturalism late 19th century art movement that tried to depict humans and society true to life and in precise detail

neoclassicism 1790s-to-1830s rejection of rococo and a return to classical style; characterized by restraint and balance

O'Keeffe, Georgia (1887–1986) 20th century American painter known for her large New Mexican landscapes

op art 1960s American art movement derived from popular culture and commercial art, with art culled from everyday life (Warhol)

pastiche piece of art created in the style of a particular artist or movement but not faked, as in forgery

Picasso, Pablo (1881–1973) 20th century Spanish painter, sculptor, and printmaker considered one of the foremost artists of the 20th century. After his "Blue period" paintings of despairing people and his "Rose period" circus paintings, he turned to cubism and still later to surrealism and collage (*Guernica, Three Musicians, Artists*)

pointillism 1880s art form in which tiny dots of paint, when viewed from a distance, take on the shape of objects (Seurat)

Pollock, Jackson (1912–1956) 20th century American painter of the abstract expressionist school known for his large canvases (later cut up) that aim to create subconscious reality

Raphael (1483–1520) early 16th century Italian painter who, along with Leonardo da Vinci and Michelangelo, is considered a creator of the Renaissance (*Transfiguration, St. Michael, Saint George and the Dragon*)

realism art form that attempts to search for the squalid and depressing with a style of strict attention to detail

relief sculpture that is not free standing; in having a background, the sculpture resembles a painting

Rembrandt, Harmensz (1606–1669) 17th century Dutch painter who is best known for his portraits but who also did landscapes, Biblical subjects, and etchings (*Self Portrait with Sprouting Beard, Night Watch, The Anatomy Lesson of Dr. Nicolaes Tulp*)

Remington, Frederic (1861–1909) 19th century American painter, illustrator, and sculptor known for his romantic scenes of the American Old West

Renoir, Pierre-Auguste (1841–1919)   late 19th–early 20th century French painter; a founder of impressionism (*Moulin de la Galette, Les Grandes Baigneuses*)

Reynolds, Sir Joshua (1723–1792)   18th century British portrait painter

rococo   1730s-to-1780s style of European art that glorified asymmetrical ornamentation on paneling, porcelain, and jewelry to display a love of gaiety and elegance

Rodin, Auguste (1840–1917)   late 19th–early 20th century French sculptor, the most famous sculptor of the late 19th century (*The Thinker, The Kiss*)

romanticism   a current throughout art history that stresses the importance of fantasy and the imagination over reason and order

Rothko, Mark (1903–1970)   20th century Russian-born American abstract expressionist painter known for his canvases of irregular shapes and bands of color

Rouault, Georges (1871–1958)   late 19th–early 20th century French expressionist painter (*The Apprentice, Christian Nocturne, The Holy Face*)

Rousseau, Henri (1844–1910)   19th century French painter, one of the foremost primitive artists of the modern age (*The Sleeping Gypsy, The Dream*)

Rubens, Peter Paul (1577–1640)   late 16th–early 17th century Flemish baroque painter, the most famous artist of northern Europe in his day (*The Judgment of Paris, Portrait of Helene Fourment, The Descent from the Cross*)

Sargent, John Singer (1856–1925)   late 19th–early 20th century American portrait painter (*Lady Hamilton*)

serial art   the repetition, possibly with slight variation, of a particular image in a work of art (*Warhol*)

serigraphy   a type of silk screen painting

Seurat, Georges (1859–1891)   19th century French artist who introduced pointillism (*Sunday Afternoon on the Island of La Grande Jatte*)

sfumato   painting technique in which one tone is blended into another without an abrupt outline

still life   the depiction of inanimate objects

surrealism   art form, since 1924, that seeks to reveal psychological reality behind appearances; subject matter stresses dreams, fantasies, and the subconscious (Magritte, Dali, Miró)

symbolism   1885 movement in art that sought to depict the world through the visionary eye of dreams and illusions

Titian (1488–1576)   16th century Italian artist, one of the greatest masters of the Renaissance (*Assumption, Venus of Urbino, Venus and Adonis*)

Toulouse-Lautrec, Henri de (1864–1901)   19th century French artist influenced by the impressionists (*Jane Avril, The Moulin Rouge*)

triptych   three panels, usually arranged or joined by hinges so that the two wings can be folded over to cover the larger central panel

Turner, Joseph Mallord William (1775–1851)   late 18th–early 19th century British landscape artist (*Fighting Téméraire*)

Utrillo, Maurice (1883–1955)   late 19th–early 20th century French painter (*Sacré Coeur*)

van Dyck, Sir Anthony (1599–1641)   17th century Flemish painter (*Charles I of England in Hunting Dress, Portrait of Charles V*)

van Eyck, Jan (1390–1440)   15th century Flemish painter known for his perfection of the oil medium

van Gogh, Vincent (1853–1890)   19th century Dutch postimpressionist painter (*The Sunflowers, Starry Night, Self-Portrait*)

Velázquez, Diego (1599–1660)   17th century Spanish painter (*The Maids of Honor, Pope Innocent X*)   pg 99

Vermeer, Jan (1632–1675)   17th century Dutch painter known for his domestic scenes (*Woman With a Water Jug, The Lacemaker*)

vignette   decoration, often of leaves, adorning the first letter of a chapter of book section

Vuillard, Edouard (1868–1940)   late 19th–early 20th century French post-impressionist painter (*Under the Trees*)

Warhol, Andy (1928–1987)   20th century American pop artist (*Ten-Foot Flowers*)

Whistler, James Abbott McNeill (1834–1903)   19th century American painter and etcher (*Whistler's Mother*)

Wood, Grant (1892–1942)   20th century American regionalist painter famous for midwestern American themes (*American Gothic*)

Wren, Sir Christopher (1632–1723)   late 17th–early 18th century English architect known for his reconstruction of St. Paul's Cathedral and other parts of London

Wright, Frank Lloyd (1867–1959)   20th century American architect known for "organic architecture" (Taliesin West, Guggenheim Museum in New York City)

Wyeth, Andrew (1917–2009)   20th century American painter known for his depictions of Chadds Ford, Pennsylvania, and Maine fishing village subjects (*Ground Hog Day*)

Famous Art Museums in the World

Guggenheim	New York
Hagia Sophia	Istanbul
Hermitage	Leningrad
Louvre	Paris
Metropolitan	New York
Pergamon	Berlin
Prado	Madrid
Rijks	Amsterdam
Tate	London
Tretyakov	Moscow
Uffizi	Florence

LITERARY FORMS AND FIGURES

The following is a list of many important writers and literary terms. The works of particular authors are given in parentheses.

Aeschylus (525–456 B.C.)   earliest Greek dramatist (*Prometheus Bound, The Oresteia*)

allegory   a narrative poem or prose work in which persons, events, and objects represent or stand for something else, frequently abstract ideas

alliteration   the repetition of consonant sounds in two or more neighboring words or syllables

  assonance   the close repetition of similar vowel sounds

Aristophanes (445–380 B.C.)   Greek playwright, master of Old Comedy (*Lysistrata, The Frogs*)

Austen, Jane (1775–1817)   English novelist (*Pride and Prejudice, Emma*)

Baldwin, James (1924–1987)   American author (*Go Tell It on the Mountain*)

Balzac, Honoré de (1799–1850)   French novelist (*The Human Comedy, Cousin Bette, Pere Goriot*)

Baudelaire, Charles-Pierre (1821–1867)   French symbolist writer (*The Flowers of Evil*)

Beat Movement   American writers of the 1950s who expressed their feelings of alienation from society (Kerouac, Ginsberg, Ferlinghetti)

Beckett, Samuel (1906–1989)   Irish-born novelist, dramatist, and poet; lived in France (*Waiting for Godot, Molloy*)

Bellow, Saul (1915–2005)   American novelist (*Seize the Day, Herzog*)

Beyle, Marie-Henri (pseudonym **Stendhal**) (1783–1842)   one of the leading 19th century French novelists, famous for the psychological and political insight of his works (*The Red and the Black, The Charterhouse of Parma*)

bildungsroman   a novel, usually autobiographical, that covers the principal subject's life from adolescence to maturity

Blair, Eric (pseudonym **George Orwell**) (1903–1950)   British novelist (*Animal Farm, 1984*)

Blake, William (1757–1827)   visionary English poet, engraver, and artist; early Romantic (*Songs of Innocence, Songs of Experience, The Marriage of Heaven and Hell*)

blank verse   poetry in which each line must have 10 syllables and a specific rhythm (iambic pentameter); the lines are unrhymed

  free verse   a verse form without regular meter (Whitman's *Leaves of Grass* is written in free verse)

Boswell, James (1740–1795)   wrote famous biography of Samuel Johnson

Brontë, Charlotte (1816–1855) and **Emily** (1818–1848)   English authors (Charlotte, *Jane Eyre*; Emily, *Wuthering Heights*)

Browning, Elizabeth Barrett (1806–1861)   English poet, married to Robert Browning (*Sonnets from the Portuguese*)

Browning, Robert (1812–1889)   English poet, married to Elizabeth Barrett Browning, known for dramatic monologues (*My Last Duchess*)

Bryant, William Cullen (1794–1878)   American nature poet ("Thanatopsis")

Bunyan, John (1628–1688)   17th century English writer of religious allegories (*Pilgrim's Progress*)

Byron, Lord George Gordon (1788–1824)   English Romantic poet (*Childe Harold's Pilgrimage, Don Juan*)

Camus, Albert (1913–1960)   French existentialist writer (*The Stranger*)

canto   a major division of a long poem

Cather, Willa Sibert (1873–1947)   American author, wrote about 1880s pioneering life in the Midwest (*O Pioneers!, My Antonia*)

Cervantes, Miguel de (1547–1616)   Spanish writer (*Don Quixote de la Mancha*)

Chaucer, Geoffrey (1343–1400)   14th century English author, often called the Father of English Poetry (*The Canterbury Tales*)

Chekhov, Anton Pavlovich (1860–1904)   Russian writer, best known for his plays (*The Cherry Orchard, The Three Sisters*)

Christie, Agatha (1890–1976)   English mystery writer; created the famous detective Hercule Poirot

classicism   literature characterized by balance, restraint, unity, and proportion; epitomized by Virgil, Pope, Homer

Clemens, Samuel (pseudonym **Mark Twain**) (1835–1910)   American author (*Tom Sawyer, Huckleberry Finn, A Connecticut Yankee in King Arthur's Court*)

Coleridge, Samuel Taylor (1772–1834)   English Romantic poet; with Wordsworth, published *Lyrical Ballads*, which inaugurated the romantic movement in England (*The Rime of the Ancient Mariner*, "Kubla Khan," "Christabel")

Conrad, Joseph (1857–1924)   English novelist born in Poland (*Heart of Darkness, Lord Jim*)

Cooper, James Fenimore (1789–1851)   18th century American novelist who wrote about the American frontier (*Leather-Stocking Tales*, which includes *The Last of the Mohicans* and *The Deerslayer*)

couplet   two successive rhyming lines of poetry, usually having the same meter

Dante (1265–1321)   (13th–early 14th century) considered the greatest Italian poet (*The Divine Comedy*, an allegory in verse consisting of 100 cantos)

deconstructionism   contemporary literary criticism

Defoe, Daniel (1660–1731)   early English novelist (*Robinson Crusoe, Moll Flanders*)

Dickens, Charles (1812–1870)   English novelist (*David Copperfield, A Tale of Two Cities, Oliver Twist, Nicholas Nickleby, A Christmas Carol*)

Dickinson, Emily (1830–1886)   one of the great American poets of the 19th century ("Because I Could Not Stop for Death")

Donne, John (1572–1631)   considered the greatest English metaphysical poet ("The Flea," "Death Be Not Proud")

Dos Passos, John (1896–1970)   American author, best known for his trilogy *U.S.A.* about the first 30 years of 20th century America

Dostoyevsky, Fyodor Mikhaylovich (1821–1881)   Russian novelist (*Crime and Punishment, The Brothers Karamazov, The Idiot*)

Doyle, Sir Arthur Conan (1859–1930)   English author, creator of Sherlock Holmes and his aide, Watson

Dreiser, Theodore (1871–1945)   American novelist associated with naturalist movement (*Sister Carrie, An American Tragedy*)

Dumas, Alexandre (1802–1870)   French novelist and dramatist (*The Three Musketeers, The Count of Monte Cristo*)

Eliot, T[homas] S[tearns] (1888–1965)   20th century English (American born) poet, dramatist, and critic (*Prufrock and Other Observations, The Waste Land, Murder in the Cathedral*)

Emerson, Ralph Waldo (1803–1882)   American poet and essayist; central figure in American transcendentalism

epistolary novel   a novel in which the story is carried forward entirely through letters from one or more persons (Richardson's *Pamela*)

epithalamion or **epithalamium**   a song or poem written to celebrate marriage

Euripides (480–406 B.C.)   Greek tragic dramatist (*Medea*)

Evans, Mary Anne (pseudonym **George Eliot**) (1819–1880)   English novelist (*Middlemarch, The Mill on the Floss, Silas Marner*)

existentialism   school of thought based on belief that people have free will and are therefore completely responsible for their actions (Sartre, Camus)

Faulkner, William (1897–1962)   20th century American novelist; wrote about the South; known for his use of stream of consciousness (*The Sound and the Fury, As I Lay Dying, Absalom, Absalom!*)

Fielding, Henry (1707–1754)   early English novelist (*Tom Jones, Joseph Andrews*)

Fitzgerald, F[rancis] Scott (1896–1940)   considered the literary spokesperson for America's "Jazz Age" [the "Lost Generation"] (*This Side of Paradise, The Great Gatsby*)

Flaubert, Gustave (1821–1880)   French novelist (*Madame Bovary*)

Frost, Robert (1874–1963)   most popular 20th century American poet ("Stopping by Woods on a Snowy Evening," "Mending Wall," "After Apple-Picking")

Gardner, Erle Stanley (1889–1970)   American writer, author of Perry Mason mysteries

genre   a type or classification of literary work (e.g., tragedy, comedy, epic, satire, lyric, novel, essay, biography)

Goethe, Johann Wolfgang von (1749–1832)   German poet, playwright, and novelist (*Faust*, a verse play in which the character Mephistopheles is the devil; *The Sorrows of Young Werther*, an epistolary novel)

Golding, William (1911–1993)   20th century English author (*Lord of the Flies*)

Gray, Thomas (1716–1771)   early English Romantic poet ("Elegy Written in a Country Churchyard")

haiku   form of verse or poetry made up of 3 unrhymed lines containing 5, 7, and 5 syllables, respectively

sonnet   14-line poem with rigidly prescribed rhyme scheme

Hardy, Thomas (1840–1928)   the last of England's great Victorian novelists (*Mayor of Casterbridge, Tess of the D'Urbervilles, Jude the Obscure, Far from the Madding Crowd, The Return of the Native*)

Hawthorne, Nathaniel (1804–1864)   19th century American author who set many of his stories against the somber background of Puritan New England (*The Scarlet Letter*, in which Hester Pryne is the adulteress, Arthur Dimmesdale the adulterer, and Roger Chillingworth the husband; *The House of the Seven Gables*)

Hemingway, Ernest (1899–1961)   American author, noted for his crisp, economical, highly charged prose style and his ideals of courage, endurance, and honor (*A Farewell to Arms, For Whom the Bell Tolls, The Old Man and the Sea*)

Hersey, John (1914–1993)   American novelist, known for his works about World War II (*A Bell for Adano*)

Hesse, Hermann (1877–1962)   German author (*Siddhartha, Steppenwolf, Narcissus and Goldmund, Magister Ludi*)

Homer (9th–8th century B.C.)   the earliest Greek writer whose works have survived; his two major epics, *The Iliad* and *The Odyssey*, are both about events connected with the Trojan War

hubris   excessive pride leading to the downfall of the hero in a tragic drama

Hugo, Victor (1802–1885)   French novelist (*The Hunchback of Notre Dame, Les Misérables*)

Huxley, Aldous (1894–1963)   English novelist and critic (*Brave New World*)

hyperbole   bold overstatement or extravagant exaggeration of fact, used for either serious or comic effect

Ibsen, Henrik (1828–1906)   Norwegian playwright; considered the father of modern realistic drama (*A Doll's House, Hedda Gabler*)

irony   a literary device in which the meaning stated is contrary to the one intended

James, Henry (1843–1916)   American author, known for his subtle psychological character studies (*The Turn of the Screw, The Ambassadors, Daisy Miller, Washington Square, The Portrait of a Lady*)

Johnson, Samuel (1709–1784)   18th century English writer, noted for Boswell's famous biography of him, as well as for his *Dictionary of the English Language, The Lives of the English Poets*, and *Rasselas*

Joyce, James (1882–1941)   Irish author, noted for use of interior monologue and stream of consciousness (*Ulysses, Portrait of the Artist as a Young Man, The Dubliners, Finnegan's Wake*)

Keats, John (1795–1821)   English Romantic poet ("Endymion," "Ode to a Nightingale," "Ode on a Grecian Urn," "La Belle Dame sans Merci")

kitsch   a German word that literally means "trash" and frequently is applied to a work of poor quality that appeals to low-brow tastes

Lamb, Charles (1775–1834)   English essayist

lampoon   in prose or poetry, a vicious character sketch or satire of a person

Lawrence, D[avid] H[erbert] (1885–1930)   English novelist, poet, and short-story writer (*Sons and Lovers, Lady Chatterley's Lover*)

Lewis, Sinclair (1885–1951)   early 20th century American novelist and social critic (*Main Street, Babbitt, Arrowsmith, Elmer Gantry*)

London, Jack (1876–1916)   American novelist and short-story writer, whose works deal romantically with elemental struggles for survival (*Call of the Wild*)

Longfellow, Henry Wadsworth (1807–1882)   most popular American poet of the 19th century (*Evangeline, Hiawatha*)

lost generation   term coined by Gertrude Stein, originally referring to the many young American writers who gathered in Paris after World War I (Hemingway, Fitzgerald)

Mailer, Norman (1923–2007)   contemporary American novelist, essayist, and journalist (*The Naked and the Dead*)

Mann, Thomas (1875–1955)   American (German-born) author (*Death in Venice, The Magic Mountain*)

Marlowe, Christopher (1564–1593)   16th century English poet and dramatist; he was the first to use blank verse on the stage, influenced Shakespeare (*Dr. Faustus, The Jew of Malta*)

Melville, Herman (1819–1891)   19th century American novelist (*Moby Dick*, in which Ismael narrates the story of Captain Ahab's search for a white whale; *Billy Budd; Typee*)

Mencken, H[enry] L[ouis] (1880–1956)   the most influential American critic of the 1920s and early 1930s

Miller, Arthur (1915–2005)   contemporary American dramatist (*Death of a Salesman, The Crucible, The Misfits*)

Miller, Henry (1891–1980)   20th century American author (*Tropic of Cancer, Tropic of Capricorn*)

Milne, A[lan] A[lexander] (1882–1956)   English author, creator of *Winnie-the-Pooh*

Milton, John (1608–1674)   17th century English poet (*Paradise Lost, Paradise Regained, Samson Agonistes*, all three written when he was blind)

Molière (1622–1673)   (stage name of **Jean Baptiste Poquelin**) the greatest French writer of comedy (*Tartuffe, The Misanthrope*)

motif   the recurrence of a theme, word pattern, or character in a literary work

Nabokov, Vladimir (1899–1977)   American author (*Lolita, Invitation to a Beheading*)

naturalism   a type of realistic fiction that developed in France, America, and England in the late 19th and early 20th centuries. It presupposes that human beings are like puppets, controlled completely by external and internal forces
  realism   the idea that people have a measure of free will

octave   a poetic stanza with eight lines
  sestet   a poetic stanza with six lines

ode   a sustained lyric poem with a noble theme and intellectual tone

O'Neill, Eugene (1888–1953)   one of the greatest American playwrights (*The Emperor Jones, Desire Under the Elms, Ah! Wilderness, The Iceman Cometh, Long Day's Journey Into Night*)

onomatopoeia   a word whose sound is descriptive of its sense of meaning

Orwell   see **Eric Blair**

Ovid (43 B.C.–17 A.D.)   Roman poet (*Metamorphoses, The Art of Love*)

oxymoron   an expression that employs two opposing terms; for example, "benign neglect"

parable   a story told to illustrate a moral truth or lesson

parody   a humorous literary work that ridicules a serious work by imitating and exaggerating its style

personification   a figure of speech that gives human forms and characteristics to abstractions, objects, animals, etc.

Petrarch (1304–1374)   14th century Italian poet and scholar, known for his love poems and his discovery of classical authors (*Canzoniere* [*Book of Songs*], a collection of 400 of his poems, most of them about a woman named Laura)

Poe, Edgar Allan (1809–1849)   19th century American poet, critic, and short-story writer; the father of modern mystery and detective fiction ("The Murders in the Rue Morgue," "The Fall of the House of Usher," "The Raven")

Pope, Alexander (1688–1744)   the greatest English poet of the early 1700s, brilliant satirist (*The Rape of the Lock, An Essay on Criticism, An Essay on Man*)

potboiler   an inferior literary work written solely to provide the author with money

Pound, Ezra (1885–1972)   American poet and critic, one of the most influential poets and controversial figures of the 20th century (*Cantos*)

Proust, Marcel (1871–1922)   French author (*The Remembrance of Things Past*, the story of his life told as an allegorical search for truth)

Pushkin, Aleksandr Sergeyvich (1799–1837)   Russia's most celebrated poet; also wrote plays and other prose (*Eugene Onegin, The Bronze Horseman*)

Racine, Jean (1639–1699)   17th century French classicist writer of tragic drama (*Phaedra, Andromache*)

roman à clef   a novel based on real persons and events

romantic movement   19th century literary movement that began in England; contrasts with classicism; emphasizes passion rather than reason, and imagination and inspiration rather than logic (Blake, Wordsworth, Coleridge, Shelley, Keats, Byron)

Sandburg, Carl (1878–1967)   major 20th century American poet, also an historian and a biographer (*Abraham Lincoln*, "The Fog," "Chicago")

satire   a type of literary work that uses sarcasm, wit, and irony to ridicule and expose the follies of mankind (*The Rape of the Lock, Gulliver's Travels*)

Scott, Sir Walter (1771–1832)   later 18th–early 19th century Scottish novelist and poet; inventor of the historical novel (*The Lady of the Lake, Waverly, Ivanhoe*)

Shakespeare, William (1564–1616)   the towering figure in English literature, considered both the greatest dramatist and the greatest poet

Shaw, George Bernard (1856–1950)   English (Irish-born) author of satirical plays (*Pygmalion*, used as basis for *My Fair Lady; Man and Superman; Saint Joan*)

Shelley, Percy Bysshe (1792–1822)   early 19th century English Romantic poet (*Prometheus Unbound, Adonais, Ode to the West Wind*)

simile   figure of speech in which a comparison between two distinctly different things is indicated by the word *like* or *as* ("O my love is like a red, red rose")

metaphor   figure of speech in which a statement of identity instead of comparison is made ("O my love is a red, red rose")

sonnet   a poem of 14 iambic pentameter lines and a rigidly prescribed rhyme scheme; two types: Italian or Petrarchan, and English or Shakespearean

Sophocles (496–406 B.C.)   Greek dramatist (*Oedipus the King, Antigone*)

Spenser, Edmund (1552–1599)   great Elizabethan poet (*The Faerie Queene*)

Stein, Gertrude (1874–1946)   American author, central figure in a circle of outstanding artist and writer expatriates in Paris (*The Autobiography of Alice B. Toklas*)

Steinbeck, John (1902–1968)   20th century American author, known for his powerful novels about agricultural workers (*The Grapes of Wrath, Of Mice and Men, East of Eden*)

Stendhal   see **Beyle, Marie-Henri**

Stevenson, Robert Louis (1850–1894)   19th century Scottish novelist, essayist, and poet; known for his adventure stories (*Treasure Island, Kidnapped, A Child's Garden of Verses*)

stream of consciousness   literary style, employed especially by Joyce and Faulkner, that presents the inner thoughts of a character in an uneven, endless stream that simulates the character's consciousness

Swift, Jonathan (1667–1745)   late 17th–18th century English author, great satirist (*Gulliver's Travels*, "A Modest Proposal")

Thoreau, Henry David (1817–1862)   American philosopher and writer; renowned for having lived the doctrines of transcendentalism ("Civil Disobedience," *Walden*)

Tolkien, J. R. R. (1892–1973)   English author (*The Hobbit, The Lord of the Rings*)

Tolstoy, Count Leo (1828–1910)   19th century Russian author, one of the world's greatest novelists (*War and Peace, Anna Karenina*)

transcendentalism   school of thought based on belief in the essential unity of all creation, the innate goodness of human beings, and the supremacy of insight over logic and experience for the revelation of the deepest truths (Thoreau, Emerson)

Twain   see **Clemens, Samuel**

Updike, John (1932–2009)   contemporary American author (*Rabbit* series)

Vergil or **Virgil** (70–19 B.C.)   greatest Roman poet; wrote the *Aeneid*, the epic that tells of the founding of Rome and describes the adventures of Aeneas, the legendary Trojan hero who founded the city

Victorian Age   refers to 19th century England; typified by optimism and conservative ideals

Voltaire (1694–1778)   18th century French author (*Candide*)

Walker, Alice (b. 1944)   20th century American author (*The Color Purple*)

Whitman, Walt (1819–1892)   one of the great American poets; his poems sing the praise of America and democracy (*Leaves of Grass*, "O Captain! My Captain!" a poem on Lincoln's death)

Wilde, Oscar (1854–1900)   late 19th century Irish playwright, poet, and novelist; attacked Victorian narrow-mindedness and complacency (*The Picture of Dorian Gray, The Importance of Being Earnest*)

Wilder, Thornton (1897–1975)   American novelist and playwright (*The Bridge of San Luis Rey, Our Town, Matchmaker,* which was the basis for the Broadway musical *Hello, Dolly*)

Williams, Tennessee (1911–1983)   considered the greatest American playwright (*The Glass Menagerie, A Streetcar Named Desire, Cat on a Hot Tin Roof*)

Wolfe, Thomas (1900–1938)   American author, known for his autobiographical novels (*Look Homeward, Angel; You Can't Go Home Again*)

Woolf, Virginia (1882–1941)   English novelist and critic; with her husband Leonard, provided a center for the Bloomsbury Group, an informal group of famous intellectuals (*Mrs. Dalloway, To the Lighthouse*)

Wordsworth, William (1770–1850)   English romantic poet (*Lyrical Ballads, The Prelude*)

Wright, Richard (1908–1960)   20th century American author, known for his description of black life in America (*Native Son, Black Boy,* his autobiography)

Yeats, William Butler (1865–1939)   Irish poet and dramatist, considered by many the greatest poet of his time; led the Irish Literary Revival; his love for Maud Gonne, a beautiful Irish nationalist leader, influenced many of his plays and love lyrics

Zola, Émile (1840–1902)   leader of the French naturalistic school, which de-emphasized the role of free will in human life (*Nana; J'accuse,* which helped win a new trail for Alfred Dreyfus)

MUSIC ♪

Use the following list of the most important composers and music terms as a quick review. The works of particular composers are given in parentheses.

adagio   slow; a slow movement; slower than andante, faster than largo

allegro   lively; rather fast, but not as fast as presto

alto   a high adult male voice, employing falsetto; a lower female voice

andante   at moderate speed, between allegro and adagio

Argerich, Martha (b. 1941)   Argentinean pianist

aria   air; song, especially a complex one in an opera or oratorio ("Batti, Batti" from Mozart's opera *Don Giovanni*)

arpeggio   chord (e.g., on a piano) performed spread out

Bach, Johann Sebastian (1685–1750)   late 17th–early 18th century German composer of baroque style; organ music and cantatas (*Brandenburg Concertos; St. Matthew Passion*)

bagatelle   short, light piece, often for piano (Beethoven)

ballad   old song, often a folk song, that tells a story, with the music repeated for each verse (Wagner's *The Flying Dutchman*)

ballet   form of dancing, of Italian origin, that usually uses orchestra music, full stage decoration (*The Sleeping Beauty, Giselle, The Nutcracker*)

Barenboim, Daniel (b. 1942)   Israeli conductor and pianist

baroque   1600-to-1750 style of music (Monteverdi, Bach)

Bartók, Béla (1881–1945)   20th century Hungarian composer who developed Hungarian national musical style; known for dissonant, atonal sounds (*Bluebeard's Castle*)

bass   lowest male voice; the lower regions of musical pitch

Beecham, Sir Thomas (1879–1961)   English conductor

Beethoven, Ludwig van (1770–1827)   late 18th–early 19th century German composer, considered one of the greatest composers of all time (9 symphonies, including *Eroica*, *Pastoral*, the *Ninth* or *Choral*; piano concerto *Emperor*; opera *Fidelio*)

Bell, Joshua (b. 1967)   American violinist

Berlioz, Hector (1803–1869)   19th century French composer (*Fantastic Symphony*)

Bernstein, Leonard (1918–1990)   20th century American conductor and composer (*The Age of Anxiety* symphony; *West Side Story* musical)

bolero   Spanish dance

Borodin, Aleksandr Porfiryevich (1833–1887)   19th century Russian composer (opera *Prince Igor*)

Brahms, Johannes (1833–1897)   19th century German composer and pianist known for his symphonies, piano concertos, and chamber music (*First, Second, Third, Fourth symphonies*; song *Lullaby*)

Brandenburg Concertos   six works by J. S. Bach for varying instrumental combinations

Britten, Benjamin (1913–1976)   English conductor and composer (*The Young Person's Guide to the Orchestra*)

Bruch, Max (1838–1920)   German composer and conductor (*Kol Nidrei*)

Bruckner, Anton (1824–1896)   19th century Austrian composer and organist known for his symphonies

buffo (buffa)   comic bass, as in an opera

cadence   a progression of chords giving an effect of closing a sentence

cantata   an extended choral work, with or without solo voices, and usually with orchestral accompaniment

Casals, Pablo (1876–1973)   20th century Spanish cellist

chamber music   music intended for a room as distinct from a large hall or theater

chanson   type of song popular in 14th-to-16th century France

Chopin, Frédéric (1810–1849)   19th century Polish composer known for his piano works

chorale   a type of traditional German hymn-tune for congregational use; an instrumental piece based on a chorale

chord   a blending of two or more notes

classicism   1770s-to-1830s period; opposed to romanticism and folk or popular music (Haydn, Mozart, and Beethoven)

coda   section of movement added as a rounding off rather than a structural necessity

coloratura   agile, florid style of vocal music

concerto   work making contrasted use of solo instruments and orchestra, generally in 3 movements (Beethoven, Mozart)

contralto   lowest female singing range

Copland, Aaron (1900–1990)   20th century American composer and pianist (opera *The Tender Land, Music for the Theater*, many film scores)

counterpart   simultaneous combination of 2 or more melodies to make musical sense

crescendo   music that gradually becomes louder

Debussy, Claude (1862–1918)   late 19th–early 20th century French impressionist-style composer (opera *Pelleas and Melisande, The Afternoon of a Faun, La Mer*)

diminuendo   music that slowly becomes softer

Du Pre, Jacqueline (1945–1987)   English cellist

Dvořák, Antonin (1841–1904)   19th century Czech (Bohemian) composer known for his symphonies (*From the New World*)

étude   an instrumental piece written to demonstrate the facility of the performer

fortissimo   music played very loudly

fugue   a musical composition in which one or two themes are repeated by different interweaving voices (Bach)

Gershwin, George (1898–1937)   20th century American pianist and composer of popular music (*Rhapsody in Blue, An American in Paris*)

Gould, Glenn (1932–1982)   Canadian pianist

Grieg, Edvard (1843–1907)   19th century Norwegian composer and pianist (music for *Peer Gynt*)

Hahn, Hilary (b. 1979)   American violinist

Handel, George Frideric (1685–1759)   late 17th–early 18th century German baroque composer (oratorio *Messiah*, opera *Rinaldo*)

Haydn, Franz Joseph (1732–1809)   18th century Austrian composer (symphonies *The Surprise* and *The Clock*, oratorios *The Creation* and *The Seasons*)

Heifetz, Jascha (1901–1967)   Lithuanian violinist

Horowitz, Vladimir (b. 1937) Russian pianist and conductor

interval   distance between 2 notes insofar as one is higher or lower than the other

Kodaly, Zoltán (1882–1967)   late 19th–20th century Hungarian composer; edited Hungarian folk songs (with Bartók) (*Psalmas Hungaricus*, opera *Háry Janos*)

largo   slow

lento   slow

libretto   text of an opera or oratorio

liederkranz   song-cycle (Schumann's *Liederkreis*)

Liszt, Franz (1811–1886)   19th century Hungarian romantic-style pianist and composer (*Dante Sonata, The Preludes*)

Ma, Yo-Yo (b. 1955) Chinese-American cellist

madrigal   16th–17th century composition for several voices

Mahler, Gustav (1860–1911)   late 19th–early 20th century Austrian composer and conductor (*Symphony of a Thousand*)

Mehta, Zubin (b. 1936)   Indian conductor

Mendelssohn, Felix (1809–1847)   19th century German composer and conductor (operetta *Son and Stranger, Scottish* symphony, *Elijah*, overture to *Midsummer Night's Dream*)

Menotti, Gian Carlo (1911–2007)   20th century Italian-American composer of opera (*Amahl and the Night Visitors*)

Menuhin, Yehudi (1916–1999)   American-born British violinist, violist, and conductor

Milhaud, Darius (1892–1974)   20th century French composer (operas *David* and *Christopher Columbus*, ballets *Jeux de printemps* and *Creation of the World*)

Monteverdi, Claudio (1567–1643)   late 16th–early 17th century Italian composer (opera *La favola d'Orfeo*)

Mozart, Wolfgang Amadeus (1756–1791)   18th century Austrian composer, mainly of operas and piano concertos (*Don Giovanni, The Marriage of Figaro, The Magic Flute, Cosi Fan Tutte*)

Mussorgsky, Modest Petrovich (1839–1881)   19th century Russian composer (operas *Boris Godunov, Pictures at an Exhibition, Night on Bald Mountain*)

Mutter, Anne-Sofie (b. 1963)   German violinist

nocturne   melancholy composition for one or more instruments

opera   drama in which all or most characters sing and music constitutes a principal element

opera buffa   comic opera

oratorio   religious compositions for orchestra, chorus, and soloists

Orff, Carl (1895–1982)   20th century German composer and conductor (operas: *Oedipus the Tyrant*, incidental music and choral works, *Songs of Catullus, Carmina Burana*)

Pachelbel, Johann (1653–1706)   17th century German organist and composer of keyboard music

Paganini, Nicolò (1782–1840)   late 18th–early 19th century Italian violinist and composer (*Bell Rondo, The Carnival of Venice*)

presto   fast

Prokofiev, Sergey Sergeyevich (1891–1953)   20th century Russian composer and pianist (*Peter and the Wolf*)

Puccini, Giacomo (1858–1924)   late 19th–early 20th century Italian composer (operas *Madame Butterfly, La Bohème, Tosca*)

quartet   four musical instruments played together

Rachmaninoff, Sergey Vasilyevich (1873–1943)   late 19th–early 20th century Russian composer and pianist (*Rhapsody on a Theme of Paganini, The Isle of the Dead*)

Rameau, Jean-Philippe (1683–1764)   18th century French composer and organist (*Castor et Pollux*)

Ravel, Maurice Joseph (1875–1937)   late 19th–early 20th century French composer (*Bolero, Gaspard de la Nuit, Spanish Rhapsody*)

Rodgers, Richard (1902–1979)   20th century American composer of light music; worked with writers Hart and Hammerstein (*The Sound of Music, A Connecticut Yankee, Oklahoma!*)

rondo   form of composition in which one section recurs intermittently

Rossini, Gioacchino Antonio (1792–1868)   19th century Italian composer (operas *The Barber of Seville, Othello, William Tell*)

Rubinstein, Anton (1829–1894)   20th century Polish-born American pianist

Scarlatti, Domenico (1685–1757)   late 17th–early 18th century Italian composer, chiefly of opera

Schoenberg, Arnold (1874–1951)   20th century Austrian-American composer (*Ode to Napoleon*, opera *Moses and Aaron*)

Schubert, Franz (1797–1828)   19th century Austrian composer (*Impromptus, Moments Musicaux*)

Schumann, Robert (1810–1856)   19th century German composer and pianist

Scriabin, Aleksandr Nikoloyevich (1872–1915)   late 19th–early 20th century Russian composer and pianist (*Divine Poem*)

Segovia, Andrés (1893–1987)   20th century Spanish classical guitarist

Shostakovich, Dmitry Dmitriyevich (1906–1975)   20th century Russian composer (*Leningrad* symphony, opera *The Golden Age*, ballet *Songs of the Forests*)

Sibelius, Jean (1865–1957)   late 19th–early 20th century Finnish composer (*Finlandia*)

Smetana, Bedřich (1824–1884)   19th century Czech composer and pianist (opera *The Bartered Bride*)

sonata   instrumental musical composition usually of 3 or 4 movements (sonatina–short sonata)

soprano   highest female voice

Sousa, John Philip (1854–1932)   late 19th–early 20th century American band conductor and composer of marches (*Stars and Stripes Forever*)

Stern, Isaac (1920–2001)   20th century Russian-born American violinist

Stradivari   family of renowned violin makers

Strauss, Johann (1825–1899)   19th century Austrian violinist, conductor, and composer of waltzes (*The Blue Danube, Tales from the Vienna Woods*)

Strauss, Richard (1864–1949)   late 19th–early 20th century German composer and conductor (*Symphonic Poem*, operas *Salome, Elektra*)

Stravinsky, Igor (1882–1971)   20th century Russian-born composer, pianist, and conductor (ballets *The Firebird, Petrushka*, and *The Rite of Spring*, opera *The Rake's Progress*)

symphony   grand orchestral work in 4 movements

Tchaikovsky, Pyotr Ilich (1840–1893)   19th century Russian composer (*Pathéthique* symphony, ballets *Swan Lake, The Sleeping Beauty, The Nutcracker*)

tenor   highest normal male voice (apart from alto, which uses falsetto)

Toscanini, Arturo (1867–1957)   Italian conductor

Verdi, Giuseppe (1813–1901)   19th century Italian composer (operas *Rigoletto, il Trovatore, Don Carlos, Falstaff, Aïda, Requiem*)

Vivaldi, Antonio (1678–1741)   late 17th–early 18th century Italian violinist and composer (*The Four Seasons*)

von Karajan, Herbert (1908–1989)   Austrian-born German conductor
Wagner, Richard (1813–1883)   19th century German composer and
  conductor known for cycles of opera and use of leitmotif (operas *The Flying
  Dutchman, Tristan and Isolde, Der Ring*)
Weber, Carl Maria von (1786–1826)   late 18th–early 19th century German
  composer, conductor, and pianist (operas *Der Freischütz, Oberon*)
Weil, Kurt (1900–1950)   20th century German-born American composer
  (opera *The Threepenny Opera*)

SCIENCE

Detailed knowledge of the sciences is not required for the *MAT*. What is necessary
is a general familiarity with the major people, theories, and terms of science. It is
impossible to review biology, physics, chemistry, geology and the other sciences
here. Below are a list of major scientists, a table of animal names that include vocabulary that may appear in an analogy, a brief explanation of classification terms, and
a geologic time scale chart.

Important Scientists

Becquerel, Antoine (1788–1878)   (French) discovered radioactivity
Copernicus, Nicolaus (1473–1543)   (Polish) founded modern astronomy,
  declared that sun is center of solar system
Curie, Marie (1867–1934) and **Pierre** (1859–1906)   (French) discovered
  radium, polonium
Darwin, Charles (1809–1882)   (English) natural selection, theory of evolution
Einstein, Albert (1879–1955)   (German) theory of relativity
Fermi, Enrico (1901–1954)   (Italian-American) radioactivity, chain reactions,
  H-bomb
Fleming, Sir Alexander (1881–1955)   (British) discovered penicillin
Galen (129–199 A.D.)   (ancient Greek) physician, studied personality
Galileo (1564–1642)   (Italian) astronomer and physicist, laws of gravity
Gauss, Carl Friedrich (1777–1855)   (German) mathematician and astronomer,
  invented electric telegraph
Herschel, Sir John Frederick William (1738–1822)   (British) astronomer
Hippocrates (460–377 B.C.)   (ancient Greek) physician, father of medicine (oath)
Jenner, Edward (1749–1823)   (British) physician, cowpox vaccine
Lamarck, Chevalier de (1744–1829)   (French) naturalist, theory of inheritance
  of acquired characteristics
Linnaeus, Carolus (1707–1778)   (Swedish) devised system of classifying living
  organisms
Lister, Joseph (1827–1912)   (British) surgeon, promoted antiseptic methods
Lysenko, Trofim Denisovich (1898–1976)   (Soviet) geneticist, follower of
  Lamarck, led to demise of Soviet biology
Mendel, Gregor (1822–1884)   (Austrian) botanist, transmission of
  characteristics in plants (genetics)

Pasteur, Louis (1822–1895)　(French) chemist, germ theory, use of heat to destroy bacteria

Ptolemy (90–168 A.D.)　(Egyptian) astronomer, geocentric theory of solar system

Rutherford, Ernest (1871–1937)　(British) physicist, radioactivity

Sabin, Albert (1906–1993)　(American) developed oral vaccine against polio

Salk, Jonas (1914–1995)　(American) developed first vaccine against polio

Watson, James (b. 1928)　(American) and **Crick, Francis** (b. 1916–2004) (British) biophysicists, discovered structure of DNA molecule (double helix)

Animal Names

Animal	Male	Female	Offspring	Adjective Form
bear	boar	sow	cub	ursine
cattle	bull steer (castrated)	cow	calf	bovine
chicken	rooster capon (castrated)	hen	chick	
deer	buck	doe	fawn	cervine
fox	fox	vixen	cub/kit	vulpine
goat	billy	nanny	kid	
hog	boar	sow	shoat	
horse	stallion gelding (castrated)	mare	foal, colt (m.) filly (f.)	equine
lion	lion	lioness	cub	leonine
pig	boar	sow	piglet	porcine
sheep	ram	ewe	lamb	ovine
swan	cob	pen	cygnet	

Taxonomy

Taxonomy is the science of classifying living organisms. Each living organism is given a scientific name—for example, *Homo sapiens* for human beings—that consists of a genus name—in our example, *Homo*—and a species name—*sapiens*. Organisms are also grouped into larger taxa (singular, taxon) based on similarities in structure and evolutionary relationships. The following table lists the major taxonomic groups, briefly describes each, and provides an example.

Classification Group	Definition	Example
kingdom	largest classification unit; most scientists agree on a basic 5-kingdom system	Animalia
phylum	major division of a kingdom	Chordata
class	division of a phylum	Vertebrata
order	division of a class; contains one or more related families	Primates
family	division of an order; contains one or more related genera; members often show obvious similarities	Hominidae
genus	division of a family; contains one or more closely related species; part of scientific name (written with initial capital letter and italicized)	*Homo*
species	basic unit of classification; a group of organisms that can mate and produce offspring; second word of scientific name; always lower case and italicized	*sapiens*

Geologic Time Scale

Era	Periods	Life Forms
Azoic era	(earliest period after formation of the earth)	
Precambrian time:		
Archeozoic era (3800–2500 mya)		
Proterozoic era (2500–543 mya)		spores, marine algae

Geologic Time Scale (continued)

Era	Periods	Life Forms
Paleozoic era (543–249 mya)	Cambrian period (543–490 mya)	
	Ordovician (490–443 mya)	fishes
	Silurian (443–417 mya)	
	Devonian (417–354 mya)	amphibians
	Carboniferous (354–290 mya)	insects, reptiles, gymnosperm
	Permian (290–248 mya)	ferns
Mesozoic (248–65 mya)	Triassic (248–206 mya)	first dinosaurs
	Jurassic (206–144 mya)	reptiles dominant, first birds, mammals
	Cretacious (144–65 mya)	dinosaurs climax, disappear; flowering plants
Cenozoic (65 mya–today)	Tertiary	
	Paleocene (65–54.8 mya)	earliest placental mammals
	Eocene (54.8–33.7 mya)	modern mammals
	Oligocene (33.7–23.8 mya)	
	Miocene (23.8–5.3 mya)	
	Pliocene Epochs (5.3–1.8 mya)	
	Quaternary	humankind (glacial)
	Pleistocene epoch (1.8 mya–10,000 years ago)	
	Holocene epoch (10,000 years–today)	

Note: mya is million years ago

MYTHOLOGY

Adonis   Greek god of male beauty

Aphrodite   Greek goddess of love, beauty, and fertility. Roman counterpart: Venus; Norse counterpart: Freyja

Apollo   one of the twin children of Zeus (the other twin is Artemis); Greek god of prophecy, medicine, and music. Norse counterpart: Frey

Ares   Greek god of war; son of Zeus and Hera. Roman counterpart: Mars

Artemis   one of the twin children of Zeus (the other twin is Apollo); Greek goddess of the moon, woods, forest, animals, and the hunt. Roman counterpart: Diana

Asgard   home of the Norse gods

Athena   Greek goddess of wisdom, cities, and handicrafts; "sprung full-blown from the head of Zeus." Roman counterpart: Minerva

Balder   Norse god of the sun. Greek counterpart: Helios

Ceres   Roman god of grain. Greek counterpart: Demeter

Cronus and **Rhea**   Greek gods; parents of the gods. Roman counterparts: Saturn and Ops

Demeter   Greek goddess of harvest and fertility. Roman counterpart: Ceres

Diana   Roman goddess of the moon, forest, animals, and the hunt. Greek counterpart: Artemis

Dionysus   Greek god of wine and joy, son of Zeus. Roman counterpart: Bacchus

Frey   Norse god; twin brother of Freyja. Greek counterpart: Apollo

Freyja   Norse goddess; twin of Frey; goddess of love and fertility. Greek counterpart: Aphrodite

Frigga   Norse goddess of heavens, love, and household; wife of Odin

Hades   Greek ruler of the dead and god of the underworld. Roman counterpart: Pluto

Helios   Greek sun god. Roman counterpart: Sol; Norse counterpart: Balder

Hera   Greek goddess; sister and wife of Zeus and queen of the gods. Roman counterpart: Juno; Norse counterpart: Frigga

Hermes   Greek messenger of the gods; symbol is caduceus. Roman counterpart: Mercury

Ishtar   Babylonian goddess of love and war. Greek counterpart: Aphrodite

Juno   Roman goddess; wife and sister of Jupiter. Greek counterpart: Hera; Norse counterpart: Frigga

Jupiter   Roman king of the gods. Greek counterpart: Zeus; Norse counterpart: Odin

Mercury   Roman messenger and god of commerce. Greek counterpart: Hermes

Minerva   Roman goddess of wisdom, cities, and handicrafts; like Greek Athena, said to have sprung fullblown from king of the gods. Greek counterpart: Athena

Neptune   Roman sea god. Greek counterpart: Poseidon; Norse counterpart: Njord

Njord   Norse god of the sea. Greek counterpart: Poseidon; Roman counterpart: Neptune

Odin   Norse king of the gods. Greek counterpart: Zeus; Roman counterpart: Jupiter

Olympus   Home of the Greek gods

Pluto   Roman ruler of the underworld. Greek counterpart: Hades

Poseidon   Greek god of the sea; symbol is a trident. Roman counterpart: Neptune; Norse counterpart: Njord

Saturn and **Ops**   Roman gods; parents of the gods. Greek counterparts: Cronus and Rhea

Thor   Norse god of thunder

Valhalla   Norse hall of heroes

Venus   Roman goddess of love, good fortune, and vegetation. Greek counterpart: Aphrodite; Norse counterpart: Freyja

Zeus   Greek king of the gods. Roman counterpart: Jupiter; Norse counterpart: Odin

MAT Practice Tests

In the following you will find ten complete Practice Tests. They are preceded by an answer sheet that you can use to mark your responses. Each test consists of 120 items that need to be completed within 60 minutes. At the end of each test you will find an answer key for scoring as well as answer explanations. Good luck!

Answer Sheet
PRACTICE TEST 1

1 Ⓐ Ⓑ Ⓒ Ⓓ	31 Ⓐ Ⓑ Ⓒ Ⓓ	61 Ⓐ Ⓑ Ⓒ Ⓓ	91 Ⓐ Ⓑ Ⓒ Ⓓ
2 Ⓐ Ⓑ Ⓒ Ⓓ	32 Ⓐ Ⓑ Ⓒ Ⓓ	62 Ⓐ Ⓑ Ⓒ Ⓓ	92 Ⓐ Ⓑ Ⓒ Ⓓ
3 Ⓐ Ⓑ Ⓒ Ⓓ	33 Ⓐ Ⓑ Ⓒ Ⓓ	63 Ⓐ Ⓑ Ⓒ Ⓓ	93 Ⓐ Ⓑ Ⓒ Ⓓ
4 Ⓐ Ⓑ Ⓒ Ⓓ	34 Ⓐ Ⓑ Ⓒ Ⓓ	64 Ⓐ Ⓑ Ⓒ Ⓓ	94 Ⓐ Ⓑ Ⓒ Ⓓ
5 Ⓐ Ⓑ Ⓒ Ⓓ	35 Ⓐ Ⓑ Ⓒ Ⓓ	65 Ⓐ Ⓑ Ⓒ Ⓓ	95 Ⓐ Ⓑ Ⓒ Ⓓ
6 Ⓐ Ⓑ Ⓒ Ⓓ	36 Ⓐ Ⓑ Ⓒ Ⓓ	66 Ⓐ Ⓑ Ⓒ Ⓓ	96 Ⓐ Ⓑ Ⓒ Ⓓ
7 Ⓐ Ⓑ Ⓒ Ⓓ	37 Ⓐ Ⓑ Ⓒ Ⓓ	67 Ⓐ Ⓑ Ⓒ Ⓓ	97 Ⓐ Ⓑ Ⓒ Ⓓ
8 Ⓐ Ⓑ Ⓒ Ⓓ	38 Ⓐ Ⓑ Ⓒ Ⓓ	68 Ⓐ Ⓑ Ⓒ Ⓓ	98 Ⓐ Ⓑ Ⓒ Ⓓ
9 Ⓐ Ⓑ Ⓒ Ⓓ	39 Ⓐ Ⓑ Ⓒ Ⓓ	69 Ⓐ Ⓑ Ⓒ Ⓓ	99 Ⓐ Ⓑ Ⓒ Ⓓ
10 Ⓐ Ⓑ Ⓒ Ⓓ	40 Ⓐ Ⓑ Ⓒ Ⓓ	70 Ⓐ Ⓑ Ⓒ Ⓓ	100 Ⓐ Ⓑ Ⓒ Ⓓ
11 Ⓐ Ⓑ Ⓒ Ⓓ	41 Ⓐ Ⓑ Ⓒ Ⓓ	71 Ⓐ Ⓑ Ⓒ Ⓓ	101 Ⓐ Ⓑ Ⓒ Ⓓ
12 Ⓐ Ⓑ Ⓒ Ⓓ	42 Ⓐ Ⓑ Ⓒ Ⓓ	72 Ⓐ Ⓑ Ⓒ Ⓓ	102 Ⓐ Ⓑ Ⓒ Ⓓ
13 Ⓐ Ⓑ Ⓒ Ⓓ	43 Ⓐ Ⓑ Ⓒ Ⓓ	73 Ⓐ Ⓑ Ⓒ Ⓓ	103 Ⓐ Ⓑ Ⓒ Ⓓ
14 Ⓐ Ⓑ Ⓒ Ⓓ	44 Ⓐ Ⓑ Ⓒ Ⓓ	74 Ⓐ Ⓑ Ⓒ Ⓓ	104 Ⓐ Ⓑ Ⓒ Ⓓ
15 Ⓐ Ⓑ Ⓒ Ⓓ	45 Ⓐ Ⓑ Ⓒ Ⓓ	75 Ⓐ Ⓑ Ⓒ Ⓓ	105 Ⓐ Ⓑ Ⓒ Ⓓ
16 Ⓐ Ⓑ Ⓒ Ⓓ	46 Ⓐ Ⓑ Ⓒ Ⓓ	76 Ⓐ Ⓑ Ⓒ Ⓓ	106 Ⓐ Ⓑ Ⓒ Ⓓ
17 Ⓐ Ⓑ Ⓒ Ⓓ	47 Ⓐ Ⓑ Ⓒ Ⓓ	77 Ⓐ Ⓑ Ⓒ Ⓓ	107 Ⓐ Ⓑ Ⓒ Ⓓ
18 Ⓐ Ⓑ Ⓒ Ⓓ	48 Ⓐ Ⓑ Ⓒ Ⓓ	78 Ⓐ Ⓑ Ⓒ Ⓓ	108 Ⓐ Ⓑ Ⓒ Ⓓ
19 Ⓐ Ⓑ Ⓒ Ⓓ	49 Ⓐ Ⓑ Ⓒ Ⓓ	79 Ⓐ Ⓑ Ⓒ Ⓓ	109 Ⓐ Ⓑ Ⓒ Ⓓ
20 Ⓐ Ⓑ Ⓒ Ⓓ	50 Ⓐ Ⓑ Ⓒ Ⓓ	80 Ⓐ Ⓑ Ⓒ Ⓓ	110 Ⓐ Ⓑ Ⓒ Ⓓ
21 Ⓐ Ⓑ Ⓒ Ⓓ	51 Ⓐ Ⓑ Ⓒ Ⓓ	81 Ⓐ Ⓑ Ⓒ Ⓓ	111 Ⓐ Ⓑ Ⓒ Ⓓ
22 Ⓐ Ⓑ Ⓒ Ⓓ	52 Ⓐ Ⓑ Ⓒ Ⓓ	82 Ⓐ Ⓑ Ⓒ Ⓓ	112 Ⓐ Ⓑ Ⓒ Ⓓ
23 Ⓐ Ⓑ Ⓒ Ⓓ	53 Ⓐ Ⓑ Ⓒ Ⓓ	83 Ⓐ Ⓑ Ⓒ Ⓓ	113 Ⓐ Ⓑ Ⓒ Ⓓ
24 Ⓐ Ⓑ Ⓒ Ⓓ	54 Ⓐ Ⓑ Ⓒ Ⓓ	84 Ⓐ Ⓑ Ⓒ Ⓓ	114 Ⓐ Ⓑ Ⓒ Ⓓ
25 Ⓐ Ⓑ Ⓒ Ⓓ	55 Ⓐ Ⓑ Ⓒ Ⓓ	85 Ⓐ Ⓑ Ⓒ Ⓓ	115 Ⓐ Ⓑ Ⓒ Ⓓ
26 Ⓐ Ⓑ Ⓒ Ⓓ	56 Ⓐ Ⓑ Ⓒ Ⓓ	86 Ⓐ Ⓑ Ⓒ Ⓓ	116 Ⓐ Ⓑ Ⓒ Ⓓ
27 Ⓐ Ⓑ Ⓒ Ⓓ	57 Ⓐ Ⓑ Ⓒ Ⓓ	87 Ⓐ Ⓑ Ⓒ Ⓓ	117 Ⓐ Ⓑ Ⓒ Ⓓ
28 Ⓐ Ⓑ Ⓒ Ⓓ	58 Ⓐ Ⓑ Ⓒ Ⓓ	88 Ⓐ Ⓑ Ⓒ Ⓓ	118 Ⓐ Ⓑ Ⓒ Ⓓ
29 Ⓐ Ⓑ Ⓒ Ⓓ	59 Ⓐ Ⓑ Ⓒ Ⓓ	89 Ⓐ Ⓑ Ⓒ Ⓓ	119 Ⓐ Ⓑ Ⓒ Ⓓ
30 Ⓐ Ⓑ Ⓒ Ⓓ	60 Ⓐ Ⓑ Ⓒ Ⓓ	90 Ⓐ Ⓑ Ⓒ Ⓓ	120 Ⓐ Ⓑ Ⓒ Ⓓ

Practice Test 1

Directions: In each of the following questions, you will find three initial terms and, in parentheses, four answer options designated *a*, *b*, *c*, and *d*. You are to select from the four answer options the one that best completes the analogy with the three initial terms. To record your answers, use the answer sheet provided.

Time: 60 minutes

1. CANARY : (*a.* red, *b.* blue, *c.* brown, *d.* yellow) :: POLAR BEAR : WHITE

2. SHIRT : WEAR :: BLOODY MARY : (*a.* kill, *b.* eat, *c.* dress, *d.* drink)

3. DAY : NIGHT :: DIURNAL : (*a.* nocturnal, *b.* eternal, *c.* vernal, *d.* external)

4. (*a.* Howard, *b.* Phineas, *c.* Ernest, *d.* Millard) : FILLMORE :: THOMAS : JEFFERSON

5. APRIL : 2 × 15 :: FEBRUARY : (*a.* 2 × 14, *b.* 2 × 15, *c.* 2 × 16, *d.* 2 × 17)

6. COMPARATIVE : (*a.* good, *b.* better, *c.* best, *d.* great) :: SUPERLATIVE : BEST

7. WINE : FRUIT :: BEER : (*a.* grape, *b.* hay, *c.* grain, *d.* lemon)

8. OTHELLO : JEALOUS :: HAMLET : (*a.* greedy, *b.* reflective, *c.* unintelligent, *d.* joyous)

9. (*a.* skirmish, *b.* war, *c.* disaster, *d.* truce) : BATTLE :: DRIZZLE : RAINFALL

10. SHETLAND : (*a.* monkey, *b.* lion, *c.* chicken, *d.* pony) :: HOLSTEIN : COW

11. (*a.* donkey, *b.* horse, *c.* bulldog, *d.* cougar) : DEMOCRAT :: ELEPHANT : REPUBLICAN

12. (*a.* green, *b.* red, *c.* blue, *d.* yellow) : CARDINAL :: ORANGE : ORIOLE

13. GERIATRICS : (*a.* old age, *b.* childhood, *c.* adolescence, *d.* adulthood) :: PEDIATRICS : CHILDHOOD

14. DOVE : PEACE :: (*a.* falcon, *b.* hawk, *c.* bluejay, *d.* vulture) : WAR

15. CHECK : (*a.* account, *b.* finesse, *c.* no trump, *d.* checkmate) ::
TENTATIVE : FINAL

16. PHENOMENOLOGIST : HUSSERL :: EXISTENTIALIST : (*a.* Camus,
b. Russell, *c.* Ryle, *d.* Quine)

17. GONDOLA : (*a.* canal, *b.* air, *c.* ocean, *d.* hangar) :: TRAIN : TRACK

18. (*a.* Babylonia, *b.* Phoenecia, *c.* Egypt, *d.* India) : PHARAOH :: ROMAN
EMPIRE : EMPEROR

19. ACHILLES : TROJANS :: SAMSON : (*a.* Egyptians, *b.* Canaanites,
c. Philistines, *d.* Moabites)

20. SPUMONI : TORTONI :: PARMESAN : (*a.* amontillado, *b.* mozzarella,
c. manzanilla, *d.* maraschino)

21. HYPERBOLE : (*a.* geometric object, *b.* exaggeration, *c.* understatement,
d. metaphysical object) :: HYPOCRITE : PRETENDER

22. MOOT COURT : HYPOTHETICAL CASES :: (*a.* kangaroo court,
b. monkey court, *c.* cabbage court, *d.* dandelion court) : IRREGULAR
PROCEDURES

23. ETHYL : METHYL :: GRAIN : (*a.* petrol, *b.* alcohol, *c.* sulfur, *d.* wood)

24. NEAPOLITAN : ITALY :: MUSCOVITE : (*a.* U.S.A., *b.* Hungary,
c. Russia, *d.* Turkey)

25. APEX : SUMMIT :: ZENITH : (*a.* nadir, *b.* end, *c.* top, *d.* beginning)

26. (*a.* temporary, *b.* porous, *c.* impenetrable, *d.* permanent) :
IMPERMEABLE :: COMMENCE : COMPLETE

27. PHILE : (*a.* love, *b.* hate, *c.* trust, *d.* distrust) :: PHOBE : FEAR

28. SOCRATES : (*a.* dagger, *b.* suffocation, *c.* noose, *d.* hemlock) ::
GARFIELD : BULLET

29. OCHLOCRACY : MOB :: AUTOCRACY : (*a.* intellectual elite, *b.* rich,
c. dictator, *d.* senate)

30. MOOR : PIN :: ROOM : (*a.* cue, *b.* nip, *c.* swim, *d.* thread)

31. FIREWATER : (*a.* acid, *b.* fire, *c.* liquor, *d.* lye) :: POTLATCH : FESTIVAL

32. (*a.* voluble, *b.* mum, *c.* lively, *d.* deaf) : MUTE :: SILENT : TACITURN

33. ATOM : MOLECULE :: CELL : (*a.* DNA, *b.* cytoplasm, *c.* tissue, *d.* ectoplasm)

34. AZURE : (*a.* blue, *b.* red, *c.* yellow, *d.* brown) :: MAGENTA : PURPLE

35. (*a.* quail, *b.* turkey, *c.* duck, *d.* pheasant) : DRAKE :: CHICKEN : ROOSTER

36. CIRRHOSIS : LIVER :: NEPHROSIS : (*a.* gallbladder, *b.* lung, *c.* pancreas, *d.* kidneys)

37. IMPEACH : HOUSE :: (*a.* protect, *b.* convict, *c.* rebut, *d.* remand) : SENATE

38. (*a.* metabolism, *b.* anabolism, *c.* menabolism, *d.* atabolism) : CONSTRUCTION :: CATABOLISM : DESTRUCTION

39. GALAHAD : (*a.* size, *b.* cowardice, *c.* nobility, *d.* lechery) :: GRISELDA : PATIENCE

40. INDUCTION : DEDUCTION :: (*a.* synthetic, *b.* inferential, *c.* a priori, *d.* a fortiori) : ANALYTIC

41. FLOOZY : DISREPUTABLE :: FLIBBERTIGIBBET : (*a.* immoral, *b.* unintelligent, *c.* mentally unbalanced, *d.* flighty)

42. RED : LONGEST :: (*a.* blue, *b.* yellow, *c.* violet, *d.* green) : SHORTEST

43. STABLE : TABLE :: START : (*a.* motion, *b.* horse, *c.* stop, *d.* tart)

44. IN VIVO : (*a.* in vitro, *b.* in moribus, *c.* in extremis, *d.* in vacuo) :: LIVING ORGANISM : TEST TUBE

45. f'' : f' :: (*a.* speed, *b.* distance, *c.* time, *d.* acceleration) : VELOCITY

46. UNICYCLE : BICYCLE :: BICYCLE : (*a.* locomotive, *b.* dirigible, *c.* motorcycle, *d.* automobile)

47. SPELUNKER : (*a.* deserts, *b.* caves, *c.* glaciers, *d.* forests) :: ALPINIST : MOUNTAINS

48. APOTHECARY : (*a.* doctor, *b.* pharmacist, *c.* drug addict, *d.* patient) :: LAWYER : ATTORNEY

49. (*a.* Daniel Boone, *b.* The Headless Horseman, *c.* Paul Bunyan, *d.* Tonto) : BABE :: LONE RANGER : SILVER

50. SCULPTOR : STATUE :: (*a.* composer, *b.* politician, *c.* psychiatrist, *d.* blacksmith) : FUGUE

51. JOURNEYMAN : APPRENTICE :: ASSOCIATE PROFESSOR : (*a.* professor, *b.* research associate, *c.* assistant professor, *d.* teacher)

52. HOLMES : (*a.* Baker, *b.* Bond, *c.* Watson, *d.* Moriarty) :: CRUSOE : FRIDAY

53. FILLY : MARE :: GIRL : (*a.* adult, *b.* human, *c.* mother, *d.* woman)

54. IMPECUNIOUS : (*a.* generous, *b.* poor, *c.* wealthy, *d.* greedy) :: OBESE : CORPULENT

55. WAR BETWEEN THE STATES : CIVIL WAR :: GREAT WAR : (*a.* American Revolution, *b.* Hundred Years War, *c.* World War I, *d.* World War II)

56. HISTOLOGIST : TISSUE :: GRAPHOLOGIST : (*a.* maps, *b.* weather, *c.* handwriting, *d.* earthquakes)

57. (*a.* to play, *b.* will have played, *c.* playing, *d.* having played) : INFINITIVE :: WAITING : PARTICIPLE

58. PEDOMETER : (*a.* breaths, *b.* steps, *c.* heart beats, *d.* salivations) :: PROTRACTOR : DEGREES

59. ANGLE OF INCIDENCE : 45° :: ANGLE OF REFLECTION : (*a.* 0°, *b.* 22.5°, *c.* 45°, *d.* 90°)

60. (*a.* professional, *b.* hireling, *c.* journeyman, *d.* tyro) : NOVICE :: AMATEUR : BEGINNER

61. (*a.* novella, *b.* trial, *c.* soliloquy, *d.* epic) : POETRY :: NOVEL : PROSE

62. CONGLOMERATION : AGGLOMERATION :: CLUSTER : (*a.* heap, *b.* dispersion, *c.* hierarchy, *d.* aggrandizement)

63. (*a.* Jackson, *b.* Jefferson, *c.* Howe, *d.* Taylor) : DAVIS :: SHERMAN : LINCOLN

64. UMBRAGE : (*a.* offense, *b.* defense, *c.* innocence, *d.* responsibility) :: GUILT : CULPABILITY

65. PERFECT : PREFECT :: FLAWLESS : (*a.* caretaker, *b.* government official, *c.* refectory, *d.* preface)

66. DOZEN : 12 :: BAKER'S DOZEN : (*a.* 8, *b.* 11, *c.* 13, *d.* 16)

67. (*a.* tawdry, *b.* dehiscent, *c.* seraphic, *d.* edacious) : GAUDY :: NADIR : BOTTOM

68. PLUTO : (*a.* Hades, *b.* Thanatos, *c.* heaven, *d.* purgatory) :: SATAN : HELL

69. DEMONSTRATE : SHOW :: FORSWEAR : (*a.* promise, *b.* curse, *c.* renounce, *d.* conceal)

70. SHEEP : SHEEP :: (*a.* rhinocerii, *b.* rhinoceres, *c.* rhinoceroses, *d.* rhinocerae) : RHINOCEROS

71. PRETEND : PORTEND :: FEIGN : (*a.* fain, *b.* act realistically, *c.* presage, *d.* look back on)

72. UNIVERSAL DONOR : (*a.* A, *b.* B, *c.* O, *d.* Rh⁻) :: UNIVERSAL RECIPIENT : AB

73. (*a.* landscape, *b.* portrait, *c.* madonna, *d.* still life) : CLAUDE LORRAIN :: CARICATURE : HONORÉ DAUMIER

74. BRUNET : DARK BROWN :: HOARY : (*a.* red, *b.* white, *c.* black, *d.* blonde)

75. POINT : LINE :: LINE : (*a.* solid, *b.* plane, *c.* hypersphere, *d.* polygon)

76. LA BOHEME : PUCCINI :: LA TRAVIATA : (*a.* Berlioz, *b.* Menotti, *c.* Verdi, *d.* Rossini)

77. PESETA : SPANIARDS :: SHEKEL : (*a.* Chinese, *b.* Israelis, *c.* French, *d.* Indians)

78. (*a.* Declaration of Independence, *b.* Articles of Confederation, *c.* Declaration of Rights and Grievances, *d.* Townshend Acts) : U.S. CONSTITUTION :: LEAGUE OF NATIONS : UNITED NATIONS

79. MILLIMETER : CENTIMETER :: CENTIMETER : (*a.* decimeter, *b.* meter, *c.* decameter, *d.* kilometer)

80. ENSIGN : NAVY :: (*a.* private, *b.* sergeant, *c.* second lieutenant, *d.* colonel) : ARMY

81. COLT : REVOLVER :: NOBEL : (*a.* A-bomb, *b.* tear gas, *c.* rifle, *d.* dynamite)

82. HYDRATED : WATER :: ORGANIC : (*a.* hydrogen, *b.* nitrogen, *c.* oxygen, *d.* carbon)

83. (*a.* doctors, *b.* officers, *c.* clergymen, *d.* saboteurs) : FIFTH COLUMN :: SPIES : INTELLIGENCE

84. PING-PONG : BADMINTON :: TENNIS : (*a.* lacrosse, *b.* football, *c.* handball, *d.* soccer)

85. (*a.* Aegisthus, *b.* Priam, *c.* Agamemnon, *d.* Theseus) : PARIS :: DAEDALUS : ICARUS

86. BLACKSTONE : (*a.* medicine, *b.* politics, *c.* law, *d.* teaching) :: ROBERTS : PARLIAMENTARY PROCEDURE

87. WIFE OF BATH : (*a.* Chaucer, *b.* Milton, *c.* Wordsworth, *d.* Spenser) :: BELINDA : POPE

88. CATTON : CIVIL WAR :: (*a.* Plutarch, *b.* Thucydides, *c.* Herodotus, *d.* Pliny the Elder) : PELOPONNESIAN WAR

89. JEHOVAH'S WITNESSES : RUSSELL :: MORMONS : (*a.* Wesley, *b.* Smith, *c.* Thomas, *d.* Kirby)

90. 10 : OCTAL :: (*a.* 1, *b.* 1000, *c.* 111, *d.* 101) : BINARY

91. NEW JERSEY : THIRD :: (*a.* Virginia, *b.* New York, *c.* Delaware, *d.* New Hampshire) : FIRST

92. URIAH HEEP : HYPOCRITICALLY HUMBLE : WILKINS MICAWBER : (*a.* poor but optimistic, *b.* poor and pessimistic, *c.* rich and optimistic, *d.* rich but pessimistic)

93. ABBOTT : FLATLAND :: DANTE : (*a.* China, *b.* Purgatory, *c.* Never-Never Land, *d.* Moonland)

94. (*a.* catharsis, *b.* tragedy, *c.* bathos, *d.* ethos) UNIVERSAL :: PATHOS : PERSONAL

95. CANTOR : RABBI :: MUEZZIN : (*a.* minaret, *b.* guru, *c.* Brahmin, *d.* imam)

96. ORPHEUS : RETURN OF EURYDICE TO HADES :: WIFE OF LOT : (*a.* transformation into a star, *b.* return to Sodom, *c.* transformation into a pillar of salt, *d.* return to Canaan)

97. CENTIGRADE : 100 :: KELVIN : (*a.* 132, *b.* 100, *c.* 0, *d.* 373)

98. LA GIACONDA : (*a.* Mona Lisa, *b.* Pieta, *c.* Madonna, *d.* Venus de Milo) :: ARRANGEMENT IN BLACK AND GRAY : WHISTLER'S MOTHER

99. EMPIRICIST : UTILITARIAN :: HUME : (*a.* Spinoza, *b.* Leibnitz, *c.* Kant, *d.* Mill)

100. BLOOMFIELD : SURFACE STRUCTURE :: (*a.* Whorf, *b.* Sapir, *c.* Skinner, *d.* Chomsky) : DEEP STRUCTURE

101. GERMANIC : EUROPE :: (*a.* Swahili, *b.* Bantu, *c.* Zulu, *d.* Nigerian) : AFRICA

102. EVAPORATE : (*a.* freeze, *b.* melt, *c.* dehydrate, *d.* condense) :: VAPOR : SOLID

103. POSITION : VELOCITY :: VELOCITY : (*a.* speed, *b.* acceleration, *c.* torque, *d.* jerk)

104. TESTOSTERONE : HORMONE :: NEURON : (*a.* brain, *b.* dendrite, *c.* tissue, *d.* cell)

105. 1066 : BATTLE OF HASTINGS :: 1588 : (*a.* defeat of Napoleon, *b.* King Philip's War, *c.* defeat of the Spanish Armada, *d.* establishment of Jamestown)

106. PSYCHOSOCIAL STAGES : (*a.* Erickson, *b.* Freud, *c.* Chomsky, *d.* Lewin) :: DEVELOPMENTAL STAGES : PIAGET

107. HIP : PELVIS:: (*a.* shoulder blade, *b.* kneecap, *c.* jaw, *d.* cranium) : MANDIBLE

108. TANTALUS : SUSTENANCE :: SISYPHUS : (*a.* food, *b.* mobility, *c.* oxygen, *d.* rest)

109. (*a.* tsetse fly, *b.* snail, *c.* roundworm, *d.* housefly) : SLEEPING SICKNESS :: MOSQUITO : MALARIA

110. RICE : CHRISTOPHER :: (*a.* Kissinger, *b.* Christopher, *c.* Shultz, *d.* Baker III) : EAGLEBURG

111. (*a.* Mussolini, *b.* Carbonari, *c.* Ciampi, *d.* Virgil) : ITALY :: HIROHITO : JAPAN

112. VIRILE : FERAL :: ENERGETIC : (*a.* potent, *b.* tame, *c.* angry, *d.* wild)

113. EVA PERON : ARGENTINA :: IMELDA MARCOS : (*a.* Indonesia, *b.* Portugal, *c.* The Philippines, *d.* Spain)

114. (*a.* Rudyard Kipling, *b.* Salman Rushdie, *c.* Chinua Achebe, *d.* Graham Greene) : INDIA :: JOSEPH CONRAD : THE CONGO

115. MARY ANN CROSS : (*a.* Jane Eyre, *b.* Sense and Sensibility, *c.* Virginia Woolf, *d.* Middlemarch) :: SAMUEL CLEMENS : TOM SAWYER

116. TITANIC : ATLANTIC OCEAN :: EDMUND FITZGERALD : (*a.* Pacific Ocean, *b.* Lake Superior, *c.* Lake Michigan, *d.* Indian Ocean)

117. MURINE : RODENT :: (*a.* ursine, *b.* lupine, *c.* equine, *d.* vulpine) : FOX

118. (*a.* Sancho Panza, *b.* Tuesday, *c.* Don Quixote, *d.* Candide) : CERVANTES :: FRIDAY : DEFOE

119. SAILING: (*a.* trim, *b.* batten, *c.* jibe, *d.* turnbuckle) :: SKIING : SLALOM

120. NaCl : SALT :: NH_3 : (*a.* bleach, *b.* pepper, *c.* baking soda, *d.* ammonia)

Answer Key

PRACTICE TEST 1

1.	D	31.	C	61.	D	91.	C
2.	D	32.	B	62.	A	92.	A
3.	A	33.	C	63.	A	93.	B
4.	D	34.	A	64.	A	94.	D
5.	A	35.	C	65.	B	95.	D
6.	B	36.	D	66.	C	96.	C
7.	C	37.	B	67.	A	97.	D
8.	B	38.	B	68.	A	98.	A
9.	A	39.	C	69.	C	99.	D
10.	D	40.	A	70.	C	100.	D
11.	A	41.	D	71.	C	101.	B
12.	B	42.	C	72.	C	102.	A
13.	A	43.	D	73.	A	103.	B
14.	B	44.	A	74.	B	104.	D
15.	D	45.	D	75.	B	105.	C
16.	A	46.	D	76.	C	106.	A
17.	A	47.	B	77.	B	107.	C
18.	C	48.	B	78.	B	108.	D
19.	C	49.	C	79.	A	109.	A
20.	B	50.	A	80.	C	110.	A
21.	B	51.	C	81.	D	111.	A
22.	A	52.	C	82.	D	112.	D
23.	D	53.	D	83.	D	113.	C
24.	C	54.	B	84.	A	114.	A
25.	C	55.	C	85.	B	115.	D
26.	B	56.	C	86.	C	116.	B
27.	A	57.	A	87.	A	117.	D
28.	D	58.	B	88.	B	118.	A
29.	C	59.	C	89.	B	119.	C
30.	B	60.	D	90.	B	120.	D

ANSWER EXPLANATIONS FOR PRACTICE TEST 1

In the following, explanations concerning the correct response are in a large font. Explanations regarding distracters (incorrect responses) that are not self-explaining or could be misinterpreted are in a smaller font in order to highlight the explanations of the answers that are correct.

1. CANARY : (*a.* red, *b.* blue, *c.* brown, ***d.* yellow**) :: POLAR BEAR : WHITE

   (**d**) A canary is usually yellow; a polar bear is generally white.
   General Information—Description

2. SHIRT : WEAR :: BLOODY MARY : (*a.* kill, *b.* eat, *c.* dress, ***d.* drink**)

   (**d**) One wears a shirt; one drinks a Bloody Mary.
   General Information—Description

3. DAY : NIGHT :: DIURNAL : (***a.* nocturnal**, *b.* eternal, *c.* vernal, *d.* external)

   (**a**) *Diurnal* refers to the daytime, while *nocturnal* refers to the nighttime. *Eternal* means "endless"; *vernal* means "youthful"; *external* means "outward."
   Vocabulary—Similarity/Contrast

4. (*a.* Howard, *b.* Phineas, *c.* Ernest, ***d.* Millard**) : FILLMORE :: THOMAS : JEFFERSON

   (**d**) Millard Fillmore and Thomas Jefferson were both presidents of the United States.
   Humanities—Completion

5. APRIL : 2×15 :: FEBRUARY : (***a.* 2×14**, *b.* 2×15, *c.* 2×16, *d.* 2×17)

   (**a**) April has 2×15, or 30 days; February usually has 2×14, or 28 days.
   General Information—Description

6. COMPARATIVE : (*a.* good, ***b.* better**, *c.* best, *d.* great) :: SUPERLATIVE : BEST

   (**b**) *Better* is the comparative form and *best* the superlative form of the adjective *good*.
   General Information—Description

7. WINE : FRUIT :: BEER : (*a.* grape, *b.* hay, ***c.* grain**, *d.* lemon)

   (**c**) Wine is fermented fruit; beer is fermented grain.
   General Information—Description

8. OTHELLO : JEALOUS :: HAMLET : (*a.* greedy, ***b.* reflective**, *c.* unintelligent, *d.* joyous)

   (**b**) In the respective Shakespearean plays in which they appear, Othello is a jealous character and Hamlet a reflective one.
   Humanities—Description

9. (***a.* skirmish**, *b.* war, *c.* disaster, *d.* truce) : BATTLE :: DRIZZLE : RAINFALL

   (**a**) A skirmish is a minor battle; a drizzle is a minor rainfall.
   Vocabulary—Class

10. SHETLAND : (*a.* monkey, *b.* lion, *c.* chicken, ***d.* pony**) :: HOLSTEIN : COW

    (**d**) A Shetland is a type of pony; a Holstein is a type of cow.
    General Information—Class

11. (***a.* donkey**, *b.* horse, *c.* bulldog, *d.* cougar) : DEMOCRAT :: ELEPHANT : REPUBLICAN

    (**a**) A donkey is the symbol of the Democratic Party, while an elephant is the symbol of the Republican Party.
    General Information—Description

12. (*a.* green, ***b.* red**, *c.* blue, *d.* yellow) : CARDINAL :: ORANGE : ORIOLE

    (**b**) A cardinal is red; an oriole is orange.
    General Information—Description

13. GERIATRICS : (***a.* old age**, *b.* childhood, *c.* adolescence, *d.* adulthood) :: PEDIATRICS : CHILDHOOD

    (**a**) Geriatrics is the branch of medicine dealing with old age; pediatrics is the branch of medicine dealing with childhood.
    Natural Science—Description

14. DOVE : PEACE :: (*a.* falcon, ***b.* hawk**, *c.* bluejay, *d.* vulture) : WAR

    (**b**) A dove is a symbol of peace; a hawk is a symbol of war.
    General Information—Description

15. CHECK : (*a.* account, *b.* finesse, *c.* no trump. ***d.* checkmate**) :: TENTATIVE : FINAL

    (**d**) In the game of chess, a king is in tentative danger when in check, and in final danger when in checkmate.
    General Information—Description

16. PHENOMENOLOGIST : HUSSERL :: EXISTENTIALIST : (***a. Camus***, *b*. Russell, *c*. Ryle, *d*. Quine)

    (**a**) In modern philosophy, Husserl is identified with the phenomenologist movement, Camus with the existentialist movement. Gilbert Ryle is primarily known for his critique of Cartesian Dualism; Bertrand Russell was a founder of Analytic Philosophy; Willard Van Orman Quine was an analytic philosopher.
    Humanities—Description

17. GONDOLA : (***a. canal***, *b*. air, *c*. ocean, *d*. hangar) :: TRAIN : TRACK

    (**a**) A gondola moves along a canal; a train moves along a track.
    General Information—Description

18. (*a*. Babylonia, *b*. Phoenecia, ***c. Egypt***, *d*. India) : PHARAOH :: ROMAN EMPIRE : EMPEROR

    (**c**) In ancient times, Egypt was ruled by a pharaoh and the Roman Empire was ruled by an emperor.
    Humanities—Description

19. ACHILLES : TROJANS :: SAMSON : (*a*. Egyptians, *b*. Canaanites, ***c. Philistines***, *d*. Moabites)

    (**c**) Achilles fought against the Trojans, Samson against the Philistines. Samson is a biblical figure; Achilles is a figure from Greek mythology.
    Humanities—Description

20. SPUMONI : TORTONI :: PARMESAN : (*a*. amontillado, ***b. mozzarella***, *c*. manzanilla, *d*. maraschino)

    (**b**) Spumoni and tortoni are both Italian ice-cream desserts; Parmesan and mozzarella are both Italian cheeses.
    General Information—Class

21. HYPERBOLE : (*a*. geometric object, ***b. exaggeration***, *c*. understatement, *d*. metaphysical object) :: HYPOCRITE : PRETENDER

    (**b**) A hyperbole is an exaggeration; a hypocrite is a pretender.
    Vocabulary—Similarity/Contrast

22. MOOT COURT : HYPOTHETICAL CASES :: (***a. kangaroo court***, *b*. monkey court, *c*. cabbage court, *d*. dandelion court) : IRREGULAR PROCEDURES

    (**a**) A moot court tries hypothetical cases; a kangaroo court exhibits irregular procedures.
    Social Science—Description

23. ETHYL : METHYL :: GRAIN : (*a.* petrol, *b.* alcohol, *c.* sulfur, *d.* **wood**)

    (**d**) Ethyl alcohol is grain alcohol; methyl alcohol is wood alcohol.
    Natural Science—Description

24. NEAPOLITAN : ITALY :: MUSCOVITE : (*a.* U.S.A., *b.* Hungary, *c.* **Russia**, *d.* Turkey)

    (**c**) A Neapolitan is a resident of Naples, and thus lives in Italy. A Muscovite is a resident of Moscow, and therefore lives in Russia.
    General Information—Description

25. APEX : SUMMIT :: ZENITH : (*a.* nadir, *b.* end, *c.* **top**, *d.* beginning)

    (**c**) *Apex, summit, zenith,* and *top* are all synonyms. The nadir is the point directly below the observer directly opposite the zenith.
    Vocabulary—Similarity/Contrast

26. (*a.* temporary, *b.* **porous**, *c.* impenetrable, *d.* permanent) : IMPERMEABLE :: COMMENCE : COMPLETE

    (**b**) *Porous* and *impermeable* are antonyms, as are *commence* and *complete.*
    Vocabulary—Similarity/Contrast

27. PHILE : (*a.* **love**, *b.* hate, *c.* trust, *d.* distrust) :: PHOBE : FEAR

    (**a**) *-phile* is a suffix denoting love for something, while *-phobe* is a suffix denoting fear of something. Both suffixes are derived from the Greek language.
    Vocabulary—Description

28. SOCRATES : (*a.* dagger, *b.* suffocation, *c.* noose, *d.* **hemlock**) :: GARFIELD : BULLET

    (**d**) Socrates died from drinking hemlock, Garfield from being shot with a bullet.
    Humanities—Description

29. OCHLOCRACY : MOB :: AUTOCRACY : (*a.* intellectual elite, *b.* rich, *c.* **dictator**, *d.* senate)

    (**c**) Ochlocracy is rule by a mob; autocracy is rule by a single dictator.
    Social Science—Description

30. MOOR : PIN :: ROOM : (*a.* cue, *b.* **nip**, *c.* swim, *d.* thread)

    (**b**) *Room* is *moor* spelled backwards; *nip* is *pin* spelled backwards.
    Nonsemantic

31. FIREWATER : (*a.* acid, *b.* fire, **c. liquor**, *d.* lye) :: POTLATCH : FESTIVAL

    (**c**) *Potlatch* was an Indian name for a winter festival; *firewater* was an Indian name for liquor.
    General Information—Similarity/Contrast

32. (*a.* voluble, **b. mum**, *c.* lively, *d.* deaf) : MUTE :: SILENT : TACITURN

    (**b**) *Mum* and *mute* are synonyms, as are *silent* and *tactiturn*.
    Vocabulary—Similarity/Contrast

33. ATOM : MOLECULE :: CELL : (*a.* DNA, *b.* cytoplasm, **c. tissue**, *d.* ectoplasm)

    (**c**) Atoms combine to form molecules. Cells combine to form tissue.
    Natural Science—Part/Whole

34. AZURE : (**a. blue**, *b.* red, *c.* yellow, *d.* brown) :: MAGENTA : PURPLE

    (**a**) Azure is a shade of blue; magenta is a shade of purple.
    General Information—Description

35. (*a.* quail, *b.* turkey, **c. duck**, *d.* pheasant) : DRAKE :: CHICKEN : ROOSTER

    (**c**) A drake is a male duck; a rooster is a male chicken.
    General Information—Description

36. CIRRHOSIS : LIVER :: NEPHROSIS : (*a.* gallbladder, *b.* lung, *c.* pancreas, **d. kidneys**)

    (**d**) Cirrhosis is a disease that usually strikes the liver; nephrosis is a disease of the kidneys. In cirrhosis, scar tissue replaces the healthy tissue in the liver impairing normal functioning of the liver. There are many causes, for example, alcoholism or hepatitis. Nephrosis is a non-inflammatory disease that may manifest itself, for example, in low albumin level and high cholesterol level in the blood. A disease of the gallbladder is gallstones; gallstones are crystalline bodies that form when the fluid in the gallbladder hardens. The pancreas stores digestive enzymes; therefore, it may be very difficult if it gets injured or punctured. A disease of the lung is asthma, whereby the airways constrict and become inflamed, leading to wheezing and troubled breathing.
    Natural Science—Description

37. IMPEACH : HOUSE :: (*a.* protect, **b. convict**, *c.* rebut, *d.* remand) : SENATE

    (**b**) The House has the power to impeach the President, while the Senate has the power to convict him or her. Impeachment is the first stage in the

process of removing a government official. It is a legal statement of charges. The second step is conviction, in which the Senate tries the accused. A two-third majority is required for conviction.
Social Science—Description

38. (*a.* metabolism, ***b.* anabolism**, *c.* menabolism, *d.* atabolism) : CONSTRUCTION :: CATABOLISM : DESTRUCTION

(b) Anabolism is constructive metabolism, while catabolism is destructive metabolism. Anabolism constructs molecules from smaller units and requires energy. Catabolism breaks down molecules into smaller units and releases energy. Metabolism is the process by which living cells absorb nutrients and convert them into living substance.
Natural Science—Description

39. GALAHAD : (*a.* size, *b.* cowardice, ***c.* nobility**, *d.* lechery) :: GRISELDA : PATIENCE

(c) Galahad was the most virtuous knight in the Arthurian legend and was distinguished for his nobility. Griselda is a character from folklore who stands for patience.
Humanities—Description

40. INDUCTION : DEDUCTION :: (***a.* synthetic**, *b.* inferential, *c.* a priori, *d.* a fortiori) : ANALYTIC

(a) Induction is a synthetic form of thinking, while deduction is an analytic form of thinking. Synthetic thinking involves the combination of several ideas into one whole. Analytic thinking involves the separation of a whole into its parts. Inferential thinking is reasoning that is based on circumstantial evidence (rather than observations) in order to make a logical judgment. *A priori* means that something is derived by logic without need of observed facts. *A fortiori* means "for a stronger reason."
Humanities—Class

41. FLOOZY : DISREPUTABLE :: FLIBBERTIGIBBET : (*a.* immoral, *b.* unintelligent, *c.* mentally unbalanced, ***d.* flighty**)

(d) A floozy is disreputable, while a flibbertigibbet is flighty.
Vocabulary—Description

42. RED : LONGEST :: (*a.* blue, *b.* yellow, ***c.* violet**, *d.* green) : SHORTEST

(c) Red light waves are the longest in the spectrum; violet waves, the shortest. The order from the shortest to the longest wavelength is violet, blue, green, yellow, orange, and red.
Natural Science—Description

43. STABLE : TABLE :: START : (*a.* motion, *b.* horse, *c.* stop, **d. tart**)

(**d**) The word *table* is the same as the word *stable*, but without the initial *s*. Similarly, the word *tart* is the same as the word *start*, again without the initial *s*.
Nonsemantic

44. IN VIVO : (**a. in vitro**, *b.* in moribus, *c.* in extremis, *d.* in vacuo) :: LIVING ORGANISM : TEST TUBE

(**a**) Something grown *in vivo* is grown inside a living organism. Something grown *in vitro* is grown inside a test tube. *In vacuo* means "in an empty space"; *in moribus* means "in a dead object"; *in extremis* means "to the furthest degree."
Natural Science—Description

45. f'' : f' :: (*a.* speed, *b.* distance, *c.* time, **d. acceleration**) : VELOCITY

(**d**) The second derivative of a function, f'', can be used to determine acceleration. The first derivative, f', can be used to determine velocity.
Natural Science—Description

46. UNICYCLE : BICYCLE :: BICYCLE : (*a.* locomotive, *b.* dirigible, *c.* motorcycle, **d. automobile**)

(**d**) A bicycle has twice as many wheels as a unicycle. An automobile has twice as many wheels as a bicycle.
General Information—Equality/Negation

47. SPELUNKER : (*a.* deserts, **b. caves**, *c.* glaciers, *d.* forests) :: ALPINIST : MOUNTAINS

(**b**) A spelunker explores caves; an alpinist climbs mountains.
General Information—Description

48. APOTHECARY : (*a.* doctor, **b. pharmacist**, *c.* drug addict, *d.* patient) :: LAWYER : ATTORNEY

(**b**) An apothecary is a pharmacist; a lawyer is an attorney.
General Information—Similarity/Contrast

49. (*a.* Daniel Boone, *b.* The Headless Horseman, **c. Paul Bunyan**, *d.* Tonto) : BABE :: LONE RANGER : SILVER

(**c**) Babe was an animal (ox) belonging to Paul Bunyan. Silver was an animal (horse) belonging to the Lone Ranger. Paul Bunyan was a legendary lumberjack who embodied frontier vitality in American folklore. Daniel Boone (1734–1820), a pioneer and hunter, was one of the first American folk heroes. The Headless Horseman is a character from Washington Irving's short story "The Legend of

Sleepy Hollow." Tonto was the Native American assistant of the Lone Ranger, both of whom are fictional characters who were created by George Trendle and Fran Striker.
Humanities—Description

50. SCULPTOR : STATUE :: (***a*. composer**, *b*. politician, *c*. psychiatrist, *d*. blacksmith) : FUGUE

    (**a**) A statue is a work of art created by a sculptor; a fugue is a work of art created by a composer.
    Humanities—Description

51. JOURNEYMAN : APPRENTICE :: ASSOCIATE PROFESSOR : (*a*. professor, *b*. research associate, ***c*. assistant professor**, *d*. teacher)

    (**c**) In craft guilds, a journeyman is one step above an apprentice. In colleges and universities, an associate professor is one step above an assistant professor.
    General Information—Description

52. HOLMES : (*a*. Baker, *b*. Bond, ***c*. Watson**, *d*. Moriarty) :: CRUSOE : FRIDAY

    (**c**) In their respective exploits, Holmes was assisted by Watson, Crusoe by Friday. James Bond is a fictitious British agent in a series of novels (later made into films) by Ian Fleming. 221B Baker Street is the street address at which Holmes' office was located. Moriarty was his mortal enemy, a mathematics professor but also a villain.
    Humanities—Description

53. FILLY : MARE :: GIRL : (*a*. adult, *b*. human, *c*. mother, ***d*. woman**)

    (**d**) A filly grows into a mare; a girl grows into a woman.
    General Information—Description

54. IMPECUNIOUS : (*a*. generous, ***b*. poor**, *c*. wealthy, *d*. greedy) :: OBESE : CORPULENT

    (**b**) *Impecunious* and *poor* are synonyms, as are *obese* and *corpulent*.
    Vocabulary—Similarity/Contrast

55. WAR BETWEEN THE STATES : CIVIL WAR :: GREAT WAR: (*a*. American Revolution, *b*. Hundred Years War, ***c*. World War I**, *d*. World War II)

    (**c**) The Civil War is often called the War Between the States. World War I is often called the Great War.
    Humanities—Similarity/Contrast

56. HISTOLOGIST : TISSUE :: GRAPHOLOGIST : (*a.* maps, *b.* weather, ***c.* handwriting**, *d.* earthquakes)

    (**c**) A histologist studies tissue; a graphologist studies handwriting.
    General Information—Description

57. (***a.* to play**, *b.* will have played, *c.* playing, *d.* having played) : INFINITIVE :: WAITING : PARTICIPLE

    (**a**) *To play* is an infinitive; *waiting* is a participle.
    General Information—Description

58. PEDOMETER : (*a.* breaths, ***b.* steps**, *c.* heart beats, *d.* salivations) :: PROTRACTOR : DEGREES

    (**b**) A pedometer measures numbers of steps; a protractor measures numbers of degrees.
    General Information—Description

59. ANGLE OF INCIDENCE : 45° :: ANGLE OF REFLECTION : (*a.* 0°, *b.* 22.5°, ***c.* 45°**, *d.* 90°)

    (**c**) If the angle of incidence of a light ray is 45°, its angle of reflection is also 45°.
    Natural Science—Equality/Negation

60. (*a.* professional, *b.* hireling, *c.* journeyman, ***d.* tyro**) : NOVICE :: AMATEUR : BEGINNER

    (**d**) *Tyro, novice, amateur,* and *beginner* are all synonymous.
    Vocabulary—Similarity/Contrast

61. (*a.* novella, *b.* trial, *c.* soliloquy, ***d.* epic**) : POETRY :: NOVEL : PROSE

    (**d**) An epic is a form of poetry; a novel is a form of prose. A novella is a form of prose as well, being shorter than a novel but longer than a novelette. A soliloquy is a form of dramatic monologue where the speaker is addressing himself. *The Trial* is a novel by Franz Kafka.
    Humanities—Description

62. CONGLOMERATION : AGGLOMERATION :: CLUSTER : (***a.* heap**, *b.* dispersion, *c.* hierarchy, *d.* aggrandizement)

    (**a**) A conglomeration is a cluster; an agglomeration, a heap.
    Vocabulary—Similarity/Contrast

63. (*a.* **Jackson**, *b.* Jefferson, *c.* Howe, *d.* Taylor) : DAVIS :: SHERMAN : LINCOLN

(**a**) Stonewall Jackson was a Confederate general under Jefferson Davis, while William Sherman was a Union general under Abraham Lincoln. Thomas Jefferson (1743–1826) was the third president of the United States. Both Albion Howe (1818–1897) and George Taylor (1808–1862) were generals in the Union Army.
Humanities—Description

64. UMBRAGE : (*a.* **offense**, *b.* defense, *c.* innocence, *d.* responsibility) :: GUILT : CULPABILITY

(**a**) *Umbrage* and *offense* are synonymous, as are *guilt* and *culpability*.
Vocabulary—Similarity/Contrast

65. PERFECT : PREFECT :: FLAWLESS : (*a.* caretaker, *b.* **government official**, *c.* refectory, *d.* preface)

(**b**) Something that is perfect is flawless. A prefect is a government official.
General Information—Similarity/Contrast

66. DOZEN : 12 :: BAKER'S DOZEN : (*a.* 8, *b.* 11, *c.* **13**, *d.* 16)

(**c**) There are 12 objects in a dozen, and 13 objects in a baker's dozen. The expression of a baker's dozen comes from 13th century England, where bakers could be severely punished if they were found to gyp their customers. Therefore, they often preferred to bake more items to ensure they would not betray their customers.
General Information—Equality/Negation

67. (*a.* **tawdry**, *b.* dehiscent, *c.* seraphic, *d.* edacious) : GAUDY :: NADIR : BOTTOM

(**a**) *Tawdry* and *gaudy* are synonyms, as are *nadir* and *bottom*.
Vocabulary—Similarity/Contrast

68. PLUTO : (*a.* **Hades**, *b.* Thanatos, *c.* heaven, *d.* purgatory) :: SATAN : HELL

(**a**) According to Roman mythology, Pluto resided in Hades. According to certain Christian doctrine, Satan resides in hell. Thanatos was the Greek personification of death. Heaven is the abode of God, angels, and the souls who received salvation. Purgatory is a Roman Catholic concept of a place for those who are ultimately destined to go to heaven but who need to be purged of their imperfections.
Humanities—Description

69. DEMONSTRATE : SHOW :: FORSWEAR : (*a.* promise, *b.* curse, **c. renounce**, *d.* conceal)

    (**c**) *Demonstrate* and *show* are synonyms, as are *forswear* and *renounce*.
    Vocabulary—Similarity/Contrast

70. SHEEP : SHEEP :: (*a.* rhinocerii, *b.* rhinoceres, **c. rhinoceroses**, *d.* rhinocerae) : RHINOCEROS

    (**c**) *Sheep* is the plural form of *sheep*; *rhinoceroses* is the preferred plural form of *rhinoceros*.
    Nonsemantic

71. PRETEND : PORTEND :: FEIGN : (*a.* fain, *b.* act realistically, **c. presage**, *d.* look back on)

    (**c**) *Pretend* and *feign* are synonyms, as are *portend* and *presage*.
    Vocabulary—Similarity/Contrast

72. UNIVERSAL DONOR : (*a.* A, *b.* B, **c. O**, *d.* Rh⁻) :: UNIVERSAL RECIPIENT : AB

    (**c**) People with blood type O are called universal donors because people with all blood types can receive their blood; people with blood type AB are called universal recipients because they can receive every blood type.
    Natural Science—Description

73. (**a. landscape**, *b.* portrait, *c.* madonna, *d.* still life) : CLAUDE LORRAIN :: CARICATURE : HONORÉ DAUMIER

    (**a**) Claude Lorrain (ca. 1602–1682) is best known for his landscapes, Honoré Daumier (1808–1879) for his caricatures.
    Humanities—Description

74. BRUNET : DARK BROWN :: HOARY : (*a.* red, **b. white**, *c.* black, *d.* blonde)

    (**b**) Brunet coloring is dark brown, while hoary coloring is white.
    General Information—Similarity/Contrast

75. POINT : LINE :: LINE : (*a.* solid, **b. plane**, *c.* hypersphere, *d.* polygon)

    (**b**) An infinite collection of consecutive points forms a line. An infinite collection of consecutive lines forms a plane.
    Mathematics—Part/Whole

76. LA BOHEME : PUCCINI :: LA TRAVIATA : (*a*. Berlioz, *b*. Menotti, *c*. **Verdi**, *d*. Rossini)

    (**c**) *La Boheme* is an opera composed by Puccini (1858–1924); *La Traviata* is an opera composed by Verdi (1813–1901).
    Humanities—Description

77. PESETA : SPANIARDS :: SHEKEL : (*a*. Chinese, *b*. **Israelis**, *c*. French, *d*. Indians)

    (**b**) A peseta is a coin that was used by Spaniards; a shekel is a coin used by Israelis. The French used francs as currency; the Indians use rupees as a currency; the Chinese use yuans as a currency.
    Humanities—Description

78. (*a*. Declaration of Independence, *b*. **Articles of Confederation**, *c*. Declaration of Rights and Grievances, *d*. Townshend Acts) : U.S. CONSTITUTION :: LEAGUE OF NATIONS : UNITED NATIONS

    (**b**) The U.S. Constitution replaced the Articles of Confederation. The United Nations replaced the League of Nations. The Townshend Acts were passed by the British Parliament in 1767 to establish that Britain had the right to raise revenue and to tax the colonies. In 1774, the British Parliament passed the Coercive Acts in response to which the First Congress drafted the Declaration of Rights and Grievances, which declared that taxes imposed on British colonists were unconstitutional lest British colonists had consented. The Articles of Confederation (completed in 1781) was the first attempt at establishing a constitution of the alliance of the 13 independent states.
    Humanities—Description

79. MILLIMETER : CENTIMETER :: CENTIMETER : (*a*. **decimeter**, *b*. meter, *c*. decameter, *d*. kilometer)

    (**a**) There are 10 millimeters in a centimeter, and 10 centimeters in a decimeter.
    Mathematics—Part/Whole

80. ENSIGN : NAVY :: (*a*. private, *b*. sergeant, *c*. **second lieutenant**, *d*. colonel) : ARMY

    (**c**) An ensign is the lowest ranking commissioned officer in the Navy; a second lieutenant is the lowest ranking commissioned officer in the Army.
    General Information—Description

81. COLT : REVOLVER :: NOBEL : (*a.* A-bomb, *b.* tear gas, *c.* rifle, *d.* **dynamite**)

    (**d**) Colt invented a type of revolver; Nobel invented dynamite.
    General Information—Description

82. HYDRATED : WATER :: ORGANIC : (*a.* hydrogen, *b.* nitrogen, *c.* oxygen, *d.* **carbon**)

    (**d**) A hydrated substance contains water; an organic substance contains carbon.
    Natural Science—Description

83. (*a.* doctors, *b.* officers, *c.* clergymen, *d.* **saboteurs**) : FIFTH COLUMN :: SPIES : INTELLIGENCE

    (**d**) During a war, saboteurs comprise a network that is often called a fifth column. Spies work in an intelligence network.
    General Information—Description

84. PING-PONG : BADMINTON :: TENNIS : (*a.* **lacrosse**, *b.* football, *c.* handball, *d.* soccer)

    (**a**) The games of Ping-Pong, badminton, tennis, and lacrosse are all played with rackets.
    General Information—Class

85. (*a.* Aegisthus, *b.* **Priam**, *c.* Agamemnon, *d.* Theseus) : PARIS :: DAEDALUS : ICARUS

    (**b**) Priam was the father of Paris; Daedalus was the father of Icarus and tried to escape to Crete by flight. Aegisthus was the son of Thyestes and of his daughter, Pelopia. Agamemnon was the the son of King Atreus of Mycenae and Queen Aerope. He was eventually murdered by his wife Clytemnestra. Theseus was a king of Athens.
    Humanities—Description

86. BLACKSTONE : (*a.* medicine, *b.* politics, *c.* **law**, *d.* teaching) :: ROBERTS : PARLIAMENTARY PROCEDURE

    (**c**) Blackstone is known for his work on law, Roberts for his work on parliamentary procedure.
    Social Science—Description

87. WIFE OF BATH : (*a. Chaucer*, *b.* Milton, *c.* Wordsworth, *d.* Spenser) ::
BELINDA : POPE

(**a**) The Wife of Bath is a literary character created by Geoffrey Chaucer for
The Wife of Bath's Tale. Belinda is the name of a fictional character in
Alexander Pope's *The Rape of the Lock.*
Humanities—Description

88. CATTON : CIVIL WAR :: (*a.* Plutarch, ***b.* Thucydides**, *c.* Herodotus,
d. Pliny the Elder) : PELOPONNESIAN WAR

(**b**) Catton is known for his historical writing on the Civil War
(1861–1865), Thucydides for his historical work on the Peloponnesian War
(431–404 B.C.) Plutarch was a Roman historian and wrote *Parallel Lives* and *Moralia.*
Herodotus was a Greek historian who was the first to have a "scientific" approach to
history. His most famous work is *The Histories.* Pliny the Elder was a Roman writer who
wrote *Naturalis Historia.*
Humanities—Description

89. JEHOVAH'S WITNESSES : RUSSELL :: MORMONS : (*a.* Wesley,
***b.* Smith**, *c.* Thomas, *d.* Kirby)

(**b**) The Jehovah's Witnesses sect was founded by Charles Russell;
the Mormons were founded by Joseph Smith.
Humanities—Description

90. 10 : OCTAL :: (*a.* 1, ***b.* 1000**, *c.* 111, *d.* 101) : BINARY

(**b**) 10 in octal is equal to 1000 in binary; both are equal to 8 in
conventional decimal notation.
Mathematics—Equality/Negation

91. NEW JERSEY : THIRD :: (*a.* Virginia, *b.* New York, *c.* **Delaware**,
d. New Hampshire) : FIRST

(**c**) New Jersey was the third state to join the Union; Delaware was the
first. New Hampshire was the 9th state to join the Union, Virginia was 10th, and
New York 11th.
Humanities—Description

92. URIAH HEEP : HYPOCRITICALLY HUMBLE : WILKINS
MICAWBER :
(*a. poor but optimistic*, *b.* poor and pessimistic, *c.* rich and optimistic,
d. rich but pessimistic)

(**a**) In Charles Dickens' *David Copperfield*, Uriah Heep is a character who is
hypocritically humble, while Wilkins Micawber is poor but optimistic.
Humanities—Description

93. ABBOTT : FLATLAND :: DANTE : (*a.* China, ***b. Purgatory***, *c.* Never-Never Land, *d.* Moonland)

(**b**) Abbott wrote a narrative describing his travels in Flatland; Dante wrote *The Divine Comedy*, describing in the second part of the trilogy his travels in Purgatory.
Humanities—Description

94. (*a.* catharsis, *b.* tragedy, *c.* bathos, ***d. ethos***) : UNIVERSAL :: PATHOS : PERSONAL

(**d**) Ethos describes universal elements in a work of art, while pathos describes personal ones.
Humanities—Description

95. CANTOR : RABBI :: MUEZZIN : (*a.* minaret, *b.* guru, *c.* Brahmin, ***d. imam***)

(**d**) A cantor and a rabbi are both religious functionaries in the Jewish religion, while a muezzin and an imam are both functionaries in Islam. Gurus are commonly found in the religions of Hinduism, Buddhism, and Sikhism. A minaret is the spire of a mosque. Brahmin is the highest of the four traditional social castes in India. The term today is used more broadly to refer to a charismatic leader with many followers.
Humanities—Class

96. ORPHEUS : RETURN OF EURYDICE TO HADES :: WIFE OF LOT : (*a.* transformation into a star, *b.* return to Sodom, ***c. transformation into a pillar of salt***, *d.* return to Canaan)

(**c**) As a result of Orpheus' looking back when he went to fetch her from the underworld, Eurydice was forced to return to Hades (Greek mythology). As a result of Lot's wife's looking back on Sodom, she was transformed into a pillar of salt (Book of Genesis in the Bible).
Humanities—Description

97. CENTIGRADE : 100 :: KELVIN : (*a.* 132, *b.* 100, *c.* 0, ***d. 373***)

(**d**) The boiling point of water is 100° Centigrade, and (to the nearest unit) 373 Kelvin.
Natural Science—Description

98. LA GIACONDA : (***a. Mona Lisa***, *b.* La Pieta, *c.* Madonna, *d.* Venus de Milo) :: ARRANGEMENT IN BLACK AND GRAY : WHISTLER'S MOTHER

(**a**) *La Giaconda* and *Mona Lisa* refer to the same painting by Leonardo da Vinci. *Arrangement in Black and Gray* and *Whistler's Mother* refer to the same painting by Whistler.
Humanities—Similarity/Contrast

99. EMPIRICIST : UTILITARIAN :: HUME : (*a.* Spinoza, *b.* Leibnitz, *c.* Kant, ***d.* Mill**)

   (**d**) Hume was an empiricist philosopher; Mill, a utilitarian philosopher. Spinoza and Leibniz were rationalists. Kant tried with his work to build a bridge between empiricists and rationalists.
   Humanities—Description

100. BLOOMFIELD : SURFACE STRUCTURE :: (*a.* Whorf, *b.* Sapir, *c.* Skinner, ***d.* Chomsky**) : DEEP STRUCTURE

   (**d**) In their respective linguistic analyses, Bloomfield theorized on the basis of surface structure, while Chomsky has theorized primarily on the basis of deep structure. Benjamin Whorf was an American linguist who developed the theory of linguistic relativity. Together with Edward Sapir who was his teacher, he proposed that language affects thoughts (the Sapir-Whorf hypothesis). Burrhus F. Skinner was a psychologist who is known for his work on operant conditioning.
   Social Science—Description

101. GERMANIC : EUROPE :: (*a.* Swahili, ***b.* Bantu**, *c.* Zulu, *d.* Nigerian) : AFRICA

   (**b**) Germanic languages are found throughout Europe. Bantu languages are found throughout Africa.
   General Information—Description

102. EVAPORATE : (***a.* freeze**, *b.* melt, *c.* dehydrate, *d.* condense) :: VAPOR : SOLID

   (**a**) To evaporate is to become vapor. To freeze is to become solid.
   Natural Science—Description

103. POSITION : VELOCITY :: VELOCITY : (*a.* speed, ***b.* acceleration**, *c.* torque, *d.* jerk)

   (**b**) The measure of the rate of change of position is velocity just as the measure of the rate of change of velocity is acceleration.
   Natural Science—Description

104. TESTOSTERONE : HORMONE :: NEURON : (*a.* brain, *b.* dendrite, *c.* tissue, ***d.* cell**)

   (**d**) Testosterone is one of many different types of hormones just as a neuron is one of many different types of cells.
   Natural Science—Class

105. 1066 : BATTLE OF HASTINGS :: 1588 : (*a.* defeat of Napoleon, *b.* King Philip's War, **c. defeat of the Spanish Armada,** *d.* establishment of Jamestown)

(**c**) The year 1066 was when the Battle of Hastings was fought, and 1588 was the year of the defeat of the Spanish Armada. Napoleon's failed invasion of Russia took place in 1812. King Philip's War took place from 1675 to 1676. Jamestown, the first permanent English settlement in North America, was established in 1607.
General Information—Description

106. PSYCHOSOCIAL STAGES : (**a. Erickson**, *b.* Freud, *c.* Chomsky, *d.* Lewin) :: DEVELOPMENTAL STAGES : PIAGET

(**a**) This analogy is about theories of psychological stages. A series of psychosocial stages was proposed by Erickson. A series of developmental stages was proposed by Piaget. Freud is famous for the development of psychoanalysis. Chomsky developed a theory of generative grammar; Lewin is considered one of the founders of social psychology.
Social Science—Description

107. HIP : PELVIS:: (*a.* shoulder blade, *b.* kneecap, **c. jaw**, *d.* cranium) : MANDIBLE

(**c**) The name of the hipbone is the pelvis just as the name of the jawbone is the mandible.
Natural Science—Similarity/Contrast

108. TANTALUS : SUSTENANCE :: SISYPHUS : (*a.* food, *b.* mobility, *c.* oxygen, **d. rest**)

(**d**) In classical mythology, Hades denied Tantalus of sustenance and Sisyphus of rest.
Humanities—Description

109. (**a. tsetse fly**, *b.* snail, *c.* roundworm, *d.* housefly) : SLEEPING SICKNESS :: MOSQUITO : MALARIA

(**a**) The tsetse fly is known to spread sleeping sickness, while the mosquito passes malaria.
General Information—Description

110. RICE : CHRISTOPHER :: (**a. Kissinger**, *b.* Christopher, *c.* Shultz, *d.* Baker III) : EAGLEBURG

(**a**) Rice and Kissinger were both political scientists who became Secretaries of State. Christopher and Eagleburg were both diplomats who became Secretaries of State. Shultz was an economist, and Baker III was a lawyer.
General Information—Similarity/Contrast

111. (*a.* **Mussolini**, *b.* Carbonari, *c.* Ciampi, *d.* Virgil) : ITALY :: HIROHITO : JAPAN

(**a**) During World War II, Mussolini was the leader of Italy while Hirohito was the leader of Japan. The Carbonari were a secret brotherhood founded in the early 19th century in Italy to overthrow the government. Carlo Ciampi was President of Italy from 1999 to 2006. Virgil was a Roman poet (70 B.C.–19 B.C.).
General Information—Description

112. VIRILE : FERAL :: ENERGETIC : (*a.* potent, *b.* tame, *c.* angry, *d.* **wild**)

(**d**) Virile means energetic, while feral means wild and undomesticated.
Vocabulary—Similarity/Contrast

113. EVA PERON : ARGENTINA :: IMELDA MARCOS : (*a.* Indonesia, *b.* Portugal, *c.* **The Philippines**, *d.* Spain)

(**c**) Eva Peron was a world-famous first lady of Argentina, and Imelda Marcos was a world-famous first lady of The Philippines.
General Information—Description

114. (*a.* **Rudyard Kipling**, *b.* Salman Rushdie, *c.* Chinua Achebe, *d.* Graham Greene) : INDIA :: JOSEPH CONRAD : THE CONGO

(**a**) Rudyard Kipling traveled to and wrote fictional literature set in India. Joseph Conrad traveled to and wrote fictional literature set in The Congo. Salman Rushdie is a British-Indian writer who faced death threats by Muslims after the publication of *The Satanic Verses*. Chinua Achebe is a Nigerian writer best known for *Things Fall Apart*. Graham Greene is an English writer whose works often revolved around Catholicism.
Humanities—Description

115. MARY ANN CROSS : (*a.* Jane Eyre, *b.* Sense and Sensibility, *c.* Virginia Woolf, *d.* **Middlemarch**) :: SAMUEL CLEMENS : TOM SAWYER

(**d**) Mary Ann Cross used a pen name (George Eliot) in writing her famous novel, *Middlemarch*. Samuel Clemens used a pen name (Mark Twain) in writing his famous novel, *Tom Sawyer*.
Humanities—Similarity/Contrast

116. TITANIC : ATLANTIC OCEAN :: EDMUND FITZGERALD : (*a.* Pacific Ocean, *b.* **Lake Superior**, *c.* Lake Michigan, *d.* Indian Ocean)

(**b**) The *Titanic* was a ship that sank in the Atlantic Ocean, and the *Edmund Fitzgerald* was a ship that sank in Lake Superior.
General Information—Description

117. MURINE : RODENT :: (*a.* ursine, *b.* lupine, *c.* equine, ***d.* vulpine**) : FOX

(**d**) The word murine describes something that is in some way like or relating to a rodent and the word vulpine describes something that is in some way like or relating to a fox. *Ursine* describes something that is like a bear. *Lupine* describes something that is like a wolf, and *equine* describes something that is like a horse.
Vocabulary—Description

118. (***a.* Sancho Panza**, *b.* Tuesday, *c.* Don Quixote, *d.* Candide) : CERVANTES :: FRIDAY : DEFOE

(**a**) Sancho Panza was the loyal friend of the title character in Cervantes' novel *Don Quixote*. Friday was the loyal friend of the title character in Defoe's *Robinson Crusoe*.
Humanities—Description

119. SAILING: (*a.* trim, *b.* batten, ***c.* jibe**, *d.* turnbuckle) :: SKIING : SLALOM

(**c**) To turn back and forth in a zigzag through the water while sailing is called to jibe. To do the same motion while downhill skiing is called to slalom.
General Information—Description

120. NaCl : SALT :: NH_3 : (*a.* bleach, *b.* pepper, *c.* baking soda, ***d.* ammonia**)

(**d**) NaCl is the chemical formula for household salt, while NH_3 is the chemical formula for household ammonia.
Natural Science—Equality/Negation

PRACTICE TEST 1

Item Classification Chart

| | RELATIONSHIP | | | | | | |
	Similarity/ Contrast	Description	Class	Completion	Part/ Whole	Equality/ Negation	Nonsemantic
Vocabulary	3, 21, 25, 26, 54, 60, 62, 64, 67, 69, 71, 112	27, 41, 117	9				
General Information	31, 32, 48, 65, 74, 107, 110	1, 2, 5, 6, 7, 11, 12, 14, 15, 17, 24, 34, 35, 38, 47, 51, 53, 56, 57, 58, 80, 81, 83, 101, 105, 109, 111, 113, 116, 119	10, 20, 84			46, 66	
Humanities	55, 98	8, 16, 18, 19, 28, 39, 49, 50, 52, 61, 63, 68, 73, 76, 77, 78, 85, 87, 88, 89, 91, 92, 93, 94, 96, 99, 108, 114, 115, 118	40, 95	4			
Social Science		22, 29, 37, 86, 100, 106					
Natural Science		13, 23, 36, 42, 44, 45, 72, 82, 97, 102, 103, 104, 120			33	59	
Mathematics					75, 79	90	
Nonsemantic							30, 43, 70

CONTENT (vertical label on left side)

Answer Sheet
PRACTICE TEST 2

1	Ⓐ Ⓑ Ⓒ Ⓓ	31 Ⓐ Ⓑ Ⓒ Ⓓ	61 Ⓐ Ⓑ Ⓒ Ⓓ	91 Ⓐ Ⓑ Ⓒ Ⓓ
2	Ⓐ Ⓑ Ⓒ Ⓓ	32 Ⓐ Ⓑ Ⓒ Ⓓ	62 Ⓐ Ⓑ Ⓒ Ⓓ	92 Ⓐ Ⓑ Ⓒ Ⓓ
3	Ⓐ Ⓑ Ⓒ Ⓓ	33 Ⓐ Ⓑ Ⓒ Ⓓ	63 Ⓐ Ⓑ Ⓒ Ⓓ	93 Ⓐ Ⓑ Ⓒ Ⓓ
4	Ⓐ Ⓑ Ⓒ Ⓓ	34 Ⓐ Ⓑ Ⓒ Ⓓ	64 Ⓐ Ⓑ Ⓒ Ⓓ	94 Ⓐ Ⓑ Ⓒ Ⓓ
5	Ⓐ Ⓑ Ⓒ Ⓓ	35 Ⓐ Ⓑ Ⓒ Ⓓ	65 Ⓐ Ⓑ Ⓒ Ⓓ	95 Ⓐ Ⓑ Ⓒ Ⓓ
6	Ⓐ Ⓑ Ⓒ Ⓓ	36 Ⓐ Ⓑ Ⓒ Ⓓ	66 Ⓐ Ⓑ Ⓒ Ⓓ	96 Ⓐ Ⓑ Ⓒ Ⓓ
7	Ⓐ Ⓑ Ⓒ Ⓓ	37 Ⓐ Ⓑ Ⓒ Ⓓ	67 Ⓐ Ⓑ Ⓒ Ⓓ	97 Ⓐ Ⓑ Ⓒ Ⓓ
8	Ⓐ Ⓑ Ⓒ Ⓓ	38 Ⓐ Ⓑ Ⓒ Ⓓ	68 Ⓐ Ⓑ Ⓒ Ⓓ	98 Ⓐ Ⓑ Ⓒ Ⓓ
9	Ⓐ Ⓑ Ⓒ Ⓓ	39 Ⓐ Ⓑ Ⓒ Ⓓ	69 Ⓐ Ⓑ Ⓒ Ⓓ	99 Ⓐ Ⓑ Ⓒ Ⓓ
10	Ⓐ Ⓑ Ⓒ Ⓓ	40 Ⓐ Ⓑ Ⓒ Ⓓ	70 Ⓐ Ⓑ Ⓒ Ⓓ	100 Ⓐ Ⓑ Ⓒ Ⓓ
11	Ⓐ Ⓑ Ⓒ Ⓓ	41 Ⓐ Ⓑ Ⓒ Ⓓ	71 Ⓐ Ⓑ Ⓒ Ⓓ	101 Ⓐ Ⓑ Ⓒ Ⓓ
12	Ⓐ Ⓑ Ⓒ Ⓓ	42 Ⓐ Ⓑ Ⓒ Ⓓ	72 Ⓐ Ⓑ Ⓒ Ⓓ	102 Ⓐ Ⓑ Ⓒ Ⓓ
13	Ⓐ Ⓑ Ⓒ Ⓓ	43 Ⓐ Ⓑ Ⓒ Ⓓ	73 Ⓐ Ⓑ Ⓒ Ⓓ	103 Ⓐ Ⓑ Ⓒ Ⓓ
14	Ⓐ Ⓑ Ⓒ Ⓓ	44 Ⓐ Ⓑ Ⓒ Ⓓ	74 Ⓐ Ⓑ Ⓒ Ⓓ	104 Ⓐ Ⓑ Ⓒ Ⓓ
15	Ⓐ Ⓑ Ⓒ Ⓓ	45 Ⓐ Ⓑ Ⓒ Ⓓ	75 Ⓐ Ⓑ Ⓒ Ⓓ	105 Ⓐ Ⓑ Ⓒ Ⓓ
16	Ⓐ Ⓑ Ⓒ Ⓓ	46 Ⓐ Ⓑ Ⓒ Ⓓ	76 Ⓐ Ⓑ Ⓒ Ⓓ	106 Ⓐ Ⓑ Ⓒ Ⓓ
17	Ⓐ Ⓑ Ⓒ Ⓓ	47 Ⓐ Ⓑ Ⓒ Ⓓ	77 Ⓐ Ⓑ Ⓒ Ⓓ	107 Ⓐ Ⓑ Ⓒ Ⓓ
18	Ⓐ Ⓑ Ⓒ Ⓓ	48 Ⓐ Ⓑ Ⓒ Ⓓ	78 Ⓐ Ⓑ Ⓒ Ⓓ	108 Ⓐ Ⓑ Ⓒ Ⓓ
19	Ⓐ Ⓑ Ⓒ Ⓓ	49 Ⓐ Ⓑ Ⓒ Ⓓ	79 Ⓐ Ⓑ Ⓒ Ⓓ	109 Ⓐ Ⓑ Ⓒ Ⓓ
20	Ⓐ Ⓑ Ⓒ Ⓓ	50 Ⓐ Ⓑ Ⓒ Ⓓ	80 Ⓐ Ⓑ Ⓒ Ⓓ	110 Ⓐ Ⓑ Ⓒ Ⓓ
21	Ⓐ Ⓑ Ⓒ Ⓓ	51 Ⓐ Ⓑ Ⓒ Ⓓ	81 Ⓐ Ⓑ Ⓒ Ⓓ	111 Ⓐ Ⓑ Ⓒ Ⓓ
22	Ⓐ Ⓑ Ⓒ Ⓓ	52 Ⓐ Ⓑ Ⓒ Ⓓ	82 Ⓐ Ⓑ Ⓒ Ⓓ	112 Ⓐ Ⓑ Ⓒ Ⓓ
23	Ⓐ Ⓑ Ⓒ Ⓓ	53 Ⓐ Ⓑ Ⓒ Ⓓ	83 Ⓐ Ⓑ Ⓒ Ⓓ	113 Ⓐ Ⓑ Ⓒ Ⓓ
24	Ⓐ Ⓑ Ⓒ Ⓓ	54 Ⓐ Ⓑ Ⓒ Ⓓ	84 Ⓐ Ⓑ Ⓒ Ⓓ	114 Ⓐ Ⓑ Ⓒ Ⓓ
25	Ⓐ Ⓑ Ⓒ Ⓓ	55 Ⓐ Ⓑ Ⓒ Ⓓ	85 Ⓐ Ⓑ Ⓒ Ⓓ	115 Ⓐ Ⓑ Ⓒ Ⓓ
26	Ⓐ Ⓑ Ⓒ Ⓓ	56 Ⓐ Ⓑ Ⓒ Ⓓ	86 Ⓐ Ⓑ Ⓒ Ⓓ	116 Ⓐ Ⓑ Ⓒ Ⓓ
27	Ⓐ Ⓑ Ⓒ Ⓓ	57 Ⓐ Ⓑ Ⓒ Ⓓ	87 Ⓐ Ⓑ Ⓒ Ⓓ	117 Ⓐ Ⓑ Ⓒ Ⓓ
28	Ⓐ Ⓑ Ⓒ Ⓓ	58 Ⓐ Ⓑ Ⓒ Ⓓ	88 Ⓐ Ⓑ Ⓒ Ⓓ	118 Ⓐ Ⓑ Ⓒ Ⓓ
29	Ⓐ Ⓑ Ⓒ Ⓓ	59 Ⓐ Ⓑ Ⓒ Ⓓ	89 Ⓐ Ⓑ Ⓒ Ⓓ	119 Ⓐ Ⓑ Ⓒ Ⓓ
30	Ⓐ Ⓑ Ⓒ Ⓓ	60 Ⓐ Ⓑ Ⓒ Ⓓ	90 Ⓐ Ⓑ Ⓒ Ⓓ	120 Ⓐ Ⓑ Ⓒ Ⓓ

Answer Sheet

Practice Test 2

Directions: In each of the following questions, you will find three initial terms and, in parentheses, four answer options designated *a*, *b*, *c*, and *d*. You are to select from the four answer options the one that best completes the analogy with the three initial terms. To record your answers, use the answer sheet provided.

Time: 60 minutes

1. CANDLE : TALLOW :: TIRE : (*a.* automobile, *b.* round, *c.* rubber, *d.* hollow)

2. TERRESTRIAL : (*a.* palatial, *b.* partial, *c.* martial, *d.* celestial) :: EARTH : HEAVEN

3. (*a.* father, *b.* uncle, *c.* brother, *d.* son) : SIBLING :: HUSBAND : SPOUSE

4. 3.6% : (*a.* 0.0036, *b.* 0.036, *c.* 0.36, *d.* 3.6) :: 480% : 4.8

5. PERIODIC : INTERMITTENT :: CONSTANT : (*a.* incessant, *b.* occasional, *c.* infrequent, *d.* never)

6. DARWIN : (*a.* gravity, *b.* planetary orbits, *c.* evolution, *d.* magnetism) :: EINSTEIN : RELATIVITY

7. COMPOSER : SONATA :: (*a.* physicist, *b.* artist, *c.* sculptor, *d.* author) : LITHOGRAPH

8. HUNGRY : LION :: BUSY : (*a.* squirrel, *b.* beaver, *c.* hare, *d.* chipmunk)

9. MATRICIDE : MOTHER :: FRATRICIDE : (*a.* uncle, *b.* father, *c.* brother, *d.* son)

10. (*a.* United, *b.* League, *c.* National, *d.* NFL) : DODGERS :: AMERICAN : YANKEES

11. KNOCK : PIGEON :: KNEED : (*a.* toed, *b.* waisted, *c.* armed, *d.* headed)

12. (*a.* Memorial Day, *b.* Thanksgiving, *c.* Christmas, *d.* Labor Day) : DECORATION DAY :: VETERANS' DAY : ARMISTICE DAY

13. HANG : NOOSE :: BEHEAD : (*a.* guillotine, *b.* Savonarola, *c.* Robespierre, *d.* ablation)

14. APPROPRIATE : INAPPROPRIATE :: APROPOS : (*a.* inapropos, *b.* misapropos, *c.* anapropos, *d.* malapropos)

15. (*a.* gases, *b.* good eating, *c.* intestinal tract, *d.* gasoline) : GASTRONOMY :: HEAVENLY BODIES : ASTRONOMY

16. CONGRESS : UNITED STATES :: (*a.* UNICEF, *b.* Secretary-General, *c.* Security Council, *d.* General Assembly) : UNITED NATIONS

17. EXECUTOR : (*a.* executriss, *b.* executress, *c.* executrex, *d.* executrix) :: ACTOR : ACTRESS

18. CANCEROUS : NONCANCEROUS :: MALIGNANT : (*a.* benign, *b.* benevolent, *c.* beneficent, *d.* latent)

19. (*a.* syllogism, *b.* intellect, *c.* troop movements, *d.* weapons) : LOGISTICS :: LANGUAGE : LINGUISTICS

20. SUBWAY : NEW YORK :: (*a.* Metro, *b.* monorail, *c.* cable car, *d.* airplane) : PARIS

21. (*a.* velocity, *b.* humidity, *c.* pressure, *d.* THI) : BAROMETER :: MILEAGE : ODOMETER

22. KANSAS : WHEAT :: (*a.* Nebraska, *b.* Arkansas, *c.* Wisconsin, *d.* Idaho) : POTATO

23. HYPO : DERMIC :: UNDER : (*a.* skin, *b.* medicine, *c.* blood, *d.* syringe)

24. PECCADILLO : (*a.* stutter, *b.* pretense, *c.* amnesia, *d.* sin) :: MISDEMEANOR : CRIME

25. MISANTHROPE : (*a.* life, *b.* religion, *c.* women, *d.* people) :: MISOGAMIST : MARRIAGE

26. OSTENTATIOUS : (*a.* showy, *b.* proud, *c.* modest, *d.* fickle) :: ONEROUS : BURDENSOME

27. NATURE : NURTURE :: HEREDITY : (*a.* gene, *b.* progenitor, *c.* evolution, *d.* environment)

28. HURRY : SCURRY :: HURLY : (*a.* burly, *b.* curly, *c.* gurly, *d.* wurly)

29. STEM : METS :: (*a.* tab, *b.* ball, *c.* team, *d.* root) : BAT

30. SATAN : BEELZEBUB :: DEVIL : (*a.* Charon, *b.* Pandemonium, *c.* Lucifer, *d.* Hades)

31. FORT SUMTER : CIVIL WAR :: (*a.* Valley Forge, *b.* Princeton, *c.* Lexington, *d.* Trenton) : AMERICAN REVOLUTION

32. (*a.* chameleon, *b.* salamander, *c.* tadpole, *d.* chamois) : FICKLE :: MULE : STUBBORN

33. NEW AMSTERDAM : NEW YORK :: CONSTANTINOPLE : (*a.* Budapest, *b.* Istanbul, *c.* Cairo, *d.* Baghdad)

34. ANESTHESIA : FEEL :: (*a.* eyeball, *b.* eyes, *c.* glasses, *d.* blindness) : SEE

35. CORPORAL : BEAT :: CAPITAL : (*a.* stun, *b.* spend, *c.* kill, *d.* shock)

36. (*a.* neutron, *b.* electron, *c.* nucleon, *d.* positron) : PROTON :: NEGATIVE : POSITIVE

37. CARPE : DIEM :: CAVEAT : (*a.* corpus, *b.* emptor, *c.* deum, *d.* mandamus)

38. RAIN : (*a.* tempest, *b.* frost, *c.* hail, *d.* dry ice) :: WATER : ICE

39. FEINT : (*a.* fall, *b.* remove, *c.* pretend, *d.* authenticate) :: SEVER : SEPARATE

40. 10 : COMMANDMENTS :: (*a.* 5, *b.* 7, *c.* 10, *d.* 12) : DEADLY SINS

41. DOUBLE ENTENDRE : (*a.* ambiguity, *b.* treachery, *c.* meaninglessness, *d.* misperception) :: DOUBLE TAKE : DELAYED REACTION

42. (*a.* nominalism, *b.* phenomenalism, *c.* determinism, *d.* rationalism) : FATALISM :: EXISTENTIALISM : FREE WILL

43. (*a.* carmine, *b.* yellow, *c.* brown, *d.* orange) : RED :: AZURE : BLUE

44. FRAME : PICTURE :: (*a.* cell wall, *b.* endoplasmic reticulum, *c.* cytoplasm, *d.* nuclear envelope) : CELL

45. (*a.* keno, *b.* kalaha, *c.* wari, *d.* soma) : CRAPS :: ROULETTE : TWENTY-ONE

46. HECTOR : (*a.* Rome, *b.* Carthage, *c.* Sicily, *d.* Troy) :: ACHILLES : GREECE

47. KUNG FU : JUDO :: (*a.* Korean, *b.* Chinese, *c.* Vietnamese, *d.* Japanese) : JAPANESE

48. SWARM : BEES :: (*a.* colony, *b.* covey, *c.* pack, *d.* pride) : QUAIL

49. BITUMINOUS : ANTHRACITE :: (*a.* wood, *b.* lead, *c.* lignite, *d.* oil) : STEEL

50. CARRY NATION : (*a.* women's suffrage, *b.* low-income housing, *c.* temperance, *d.* abolition of child labor) :: MARTIN LUTHER KING, JR. : CIVIL RIGHTS

51. STENCIL : LETTERS :: COMPASS : (*a.* time, *b.* direction, *c.* northwest, *d.* circle)

52. (*a.* proposal, *b.* talk, *c.* dissertation, *d.* dialogue) : ORATION :: QUIZ : EXAMINATION

53. ANTERIOR : POSTERIOR :: (*a.* ventral, *b.* lateral, *c.* external, *d.* internal) : DORSAL

54. IMMIGRATION : EMIGRATION :: ENTRY : (*a.* expulsion, *b.* migration, *c.* egress, *d.* estuary)

55. SATRAP : (*a.* ruler, *b.* bush, *c.* miser, *d.* loner) :: TRAP : AMBUSH

56. ELEGY : LAMENTING :: EPIGRAM : (*a.* inane, *b.* abstruse, *c.* witty, *d.* obtuse)

57. REFORMATION : PROTESTANTS :: COUNTER-REFORMATION : (*a.* Catholics, *b.* Protestants, *c.* Anglicans, *d.* Jews)

58. (*a.* beriberi, *b.* rickets, *c.* anemia, *d.* pellagra) : D :: SCURVY : C

59. GO DUTCH : PAY YOUR OWN EXPENSES :: IN DUTCH : (*a.* in luck, *b.* in trouble, *c.* rich, *d.* poor)

60. FOOL'S GOLD : (*a.* ore, *b.* pyrite, *c.* bauxite, *d.* manganese) :: PENCIL LEAD : GRAPHITE

61. MILL : (*a.* franc, *b.* centime, *c.* shilling, *d.* cent) :: PENNY : DIME

62. (*a.* Spain, *b.* Italy, *c.* Israel, *d.* Lebanon) : RUSSIA :: EL AL : AEROFLOT

63. GAUGUIN : (*a.* England, *b.* U.S.A., *c.* Tahiti, *d.* Madagascar) :: GOYA : SPAIN

64. (*a.* bifteck, *b.* legume, *c.* glace, *d.* poulet) : STEAK :: ESCARGOTS : SNAILS

65. TEMERITY : AUDACITY :: (*a.* softness, *b.* boldness, *c.* shyness, *d.* depravity) : BRAVERY

66. CALORIE : (*a.* weight, *b.* basal metabolism, *c.* fat, *d.* energy) :: DECADE : TIME

67. PETROLOGY : (*a.* sandstone, *b.* brontosaurus, *c.* moth, *d.* nylon) :: BOTANY : ROSE

68. HANSEL : GRETEL :: ORESTES : (*a.* Jocasta, *b.* Electra, *c.* Ophelia, *d.* Alicia)

69. (*a.* rude, *b.* talkative, *c.* immodest, *d.* brash) : GARRULOUS :: PETULANT : PEEVISH

70. PONCE DE LEON : (*a.* Atlantic Ocean, *b.* Mexico, *c.* Georgia, *d.* Florida) :: BALBOA : PACIFIC OCEAN

71. ATTENUATE : (*a.* disprove, *b.* weaken, *c.* prove, *d.* strengthen) :: ATTRACT : REPEL

72. CEREBRUM : THINKING :: CEREBELLUM : (*a.* olfaction, *b.* muscular coordination, *c.* glandular secretion, *d.* audition)

73. BEHAVIORISM : U.S.A. :: GESTALT : (*a.* France, *b.* England, *c.* Switzerland, *d.* Germany)

74. MONROE : (*a.* Treatise, *b.* Edict, *c.* Decree, *d.* Code) :: DOCTRINE : NAPOLEON

75. LXII : CLXXXVI :: D : (*a.* M, *b.* MC, *c.* MD, *d.* MM)

76. (*a.* loudness, *b.* compression, *c.* brightness, *d.* hardness) : MOHS :: TEMPERATURE : KELVIN

77. FOX : OWL :: (*a.* Saul, *b.* David, *c.* Iago, *d.* Lear) : SOLOMON

78. 1 : LINE :: 2 : (*a.* length, *b.* ellipse, *c.* point, *d.* sphere)

79. EXOSKELETON : LOBSTER :: ENDOSKELETON : (*a.* oyster, *b.* tiger, *c.* barnacle, *d.* worm)

80. FEZ : SOMBRERO :: BERET : (*a.* phylactery, *b.* millinery, *c.* muffler, *d.* fedora)

81. (*a.* angry, *b.* sanguine, *c.* dejected, *d.* pale) : PESSIMISTIC :: HOPEFUL : DISPIRITED

82. $4^{1/2} : 9^{1/2} :: 36^{1/2} :$ (*a.* 6, *b.* 9, *c.* 12, *d.* 81)

83. INCUBUS : (*a.* faccubus, *b.* excubus, *c.* succubus, *d.* maccubus) :: WOMEN : MEN

84. HEAD MONEY : (*a.* warn, *b.* punish, *c.* capture, *d.* bribe) :: HUSH MONEY : SILENCE

85. SUSTAIN : OVERRULE :: IN CAMERA : (*a.* in trouble, *b.* in public, *c.* in court, *d.* out of court)

86. CRONUS : SATURN :: (*a.* Poseidon, *b.* Ares, *c.* Zeus, *d.* Hermes) : MARS

87. D MINOR : F MAJOR :: (*a.* E minor, *b.* F minor, *c.* F# minor, *d.* G# minor) : A MAJOR

88. TAME : MATE :: LAME : (*a.* female, *b.* injured, *c.* male, *d.* excuse)

89. (*a.* spinal, *b.* neutral, *c.* temporal, *d.* spatial) : PARIETAL :: OCCIPITAL : FRONTAL

90. PARADISE : LOST :: JERUSALEM : (*a.* Sanctified, *b.* Discovered, *c.* Delivered, *d.* Vanquished)

91. PENN : PENNSYLVANIA :: CALVERT : (*a.* South Carolina, *b.* Vermont, *c.* Maryland, *d.* Rhode Island)

92. ETEOCLES : (*a.* Theseus, *b.* Laius, *c.* Oedipus, *d.* Polynices) :: ANTIGONE : ISMENE

93. DECIMAL : 10 :: DUODECIMAL : (*a.* 2, *b.* 8, *c.* 12, *d.* 16)

94. RATIONALIST : EMPIRICIST :: (*a.* Berkeley, *b.* Hume, *c.* Mill, *d.* Leibniz) : LOCKE

95. (*a.* Ivan Karamazov, *b.* Anna Karenina, *c.* Nicolai Gogol, *d.* Grigory Smirnov) : DOSTOYEVSKY :: THÉRÈSE : MAURIAC

96. PALESTRINA : 16th :: (*a.* Beethoven, *b.* Bach, *c.* Tchaikovsky, *d.* Stravinsky) : 20th

97. NICHOLAS II : RUSSIAN REVOLUTION :: (*a.* Louis XIV, *b.* Louis XV, *c.* Louis XVI, *d.* Louis XVII) : FRENCH REVOLUTION

98. GLENN GOULD : PIANO :: YO-YO MA : (*a.* piano, *b.* violin, *c.* cello, *d.* clarinet)

99. (*a.* Versailles, *b.* Xanadu, *c.* St. Malo, *d.* Rouen) : LOUIS XIV :: AMBOISE : FRANCIS II

100. ISHMAEL : (*a.* Hagar, *b.* Rebeccah, *c.* Esther, *d.* Sophia) :: ISAAC : SARAH

101. COLITIS : COLON :: ENCEPHALITIS : (*a.* brain, *b.* duodenum, *c.* pancreas, *d.* liver)

102. GOLDA MEIR : (*a.* Poland, *b.* Israel, *c.* United States, *d.* Czech Republic) :: MARGARET THATCHER : GREAT BRITAIN

103. PICCOLO : FLUTE :: EUPHONIUM : (*a.* phonograph, *b.* tuba, *c.* organ, *d.* homonym)

104. FORCE : DISTANCE :: (*a.* mass × acceleration, *b.* friction × momentum, *c.* volume / temperature, *d.* mass / energy) : RATE × TIME

105. (*a.* spear, *b.* cupid, *c.* arrow, *d.* wing) : LOVE :: SCYTHE : DEATH

106. CEILING : GLASS :: (*a.* heart, *b.* wall, *c.* side, *d.* curtain) : IRON

107. LEGS : EGGS :: FROG : (*a.* chicken, *b.* dolphin, *c.* sturgeon, *d.* goose)

108. GOAT : (*a.* pan, *b.* faun, *c.* pegasus, *d.* minotaur) :: HORSE : CENTAUR

109. ORCZY : PIMPERNEL :: HAWTHORNE : (*a.* letter, *b.* rose, *c.* wind, *d.* tide)

110. GUSTAV : (*a.* Wolfgang, *b.* Friedrich, *c.* Johann, *d.* Ludwig) :: MAHLER : BEETHOVEN

111. RESTIVE : TRANQUIL :: VERBOSE : (*a.* loquacious, *b.* timorous, *c.* talkative, *d.* taciturn)

112. HOLY SEE : (*a.* Rome, *b.* Hungary, *c.* Italy, *d.* Chad) :: LESOTHO : SOUTH AFRICA

113. LEAGUE OF NATIONS : UNITED NATIONS :: THE ARTICLES OF CONFEDERATION : (*a.* U.S. Constitution, *b.* The Bill of Rights, *c.* Human Rights Treaty, *d.* The Constitution of the Confederate States)

114. AM : AMPLITUDE :: FM : (*a.* force, *b.* frequency, *c.* Fahrenheit, *d.* friction)

115. (*a.* England, *b.* Waterloo, *c.* Russia, *d.* Elba) : NAPOLEON :: LITTLE BIG HORN RIVER : CUSTER

116. ROMEO : JULIET :: PYRAMUS : (*a.* Thisbe, *b.* Titania, *c.* Helen, *d.* Athena)

117. GOAT : WORM :: (*a.* wool, *b.* felt, *c.* cashmere, *d.* chinchilla) : SILK

118. XXIX : 29 :: MDVI : (*a.* 1551, *b.* 1056, *c.* 1061, *d.* 1506)

119. GUANINE : (*a.* cytosine, *b.* purine, *c.* uracil, *d.* pyrimidine) :: ADENINE : THYMINE

120. ESOPHAGUS : SARCOPHAGUS :: GULLET : (*a.* trachea, *b.* monument, *c.* stone coffin, *d.* crystal chandelier)

Answer Key
PRACTICE TEST 2

1. **C**	31. **C**	61. **D**	91. **C**
2. **D**	32. **A**	62. **C**	92. **D**
3. **C**	33. **B**	63. **C**	93. **C**
4. **B**	34. **D**	64. **A**	94. **D**
5. **A**	35. **C**	65. **B**	95. **A**
6. **C**	36. **B**	66. **D**	96. **D**
7. **B**	37. **B**	67. **A**	97. **C**
8. **B**	38. **C**	68. **B**	98. **C**
9. **C**	39. **C**	69. **B**	99. **A**
10. **C**	40. **B**	70. **D**	100. **A**
11. **A**	41. **A**	71. **D**	101. **A**
12. **A**	42. **C**	72. **B**	102. **B**
13. **A**	43. **A**	73. **D**	103. **B**
14. **D**	44. **A**	74. **D**	104. **A**
15. **B**	45. **A**	75. **C**	105. **C**
16. **D**	46. **D**	76. **D**	106. **D**
17. **D**	47. **B**	77. **C**	107. **C**
18. **A**	48. **B**	78. **B**	108. **B**
19. **C**	49. **B**	79. **B**	109. **A**
20. **A**	50. **C**	80. **D**	110. **D**
21. **C**	51. **D**	81. **B**	111. **D**
22. **D**	52. **B**	82. **B**	112. **C**
23. **A**	53. **A**	83. **C**	113. **A**
24. **D**	54. **C**	84. **C**	114. **B**
25. **D**	55. **A**	85. **B**	115. **B**
26. **A**	56. **C**	86. **B**	116. **A**
27. **D**	57. **A**	87. **C**	117. **C**
28. **A**	58. **B**	88. **C**	118. **D**
29. **A**	59. **B**	89. **C**	119. **A**
30. **C**	60. **B**	90. **C**	120. **C**

Answer Key

ANSWER EXPLANATIONS FOR PRACTICE TEST 2

In the following, explanations concerning the correct response are in a large font. Explanations regarding distracters (incorrect responses) that are not self-explaining or could be misinterpreted are in a smaller font in order to highlight the explanations of the answers that are correct.

1. CANDLE : TALLOW :: TIRE : (*a.* automobile, *b.* round, **c. rubber**, *d.* hollow)

   (**c**) A candle is frequently made of tallow. A tire is frequently made of rubber.
   General Information—Description

2. TERRESTRIAL : (*a.* palatial, *b.* partial, *c.* martial, ***d.* celestial**) :: EARTH : HEAVEN

   (**d**) Something that is terrestrial is of the earth. Something that is celestial is of heaven.
   Vocabulary—Description

3. (*a.* father, *b.* uncle, **c. brother**, *d.* son) : SIBLING :: HUSBAND : SPOUSE

   (**c**) A brother is a sibling. A husband is a spouse.
   Vocabulary—Description

4. 3.6% : (*a.* 0.0036, ***b.* 0.036**, *c.* 0.36, *d.* 3.6) :: 480% : 4.8

   (**b**) 3.6% is equal to 0.036. 480% is equal to 4.8.
   Mathematics—Equality/Negation

5. PERIODIC : INTERMITTENT :: CONSTANT : (***a.* incessant**, *b.* occasional, *c.* infrequent, *d.* never)

   (**a**) *Periodic* and *intermittent* are synonyms, as are *constant* and *incessant*.
   Vocabulary—Similarity/Contrast

6. DARWIN : (*a.* gravity, *b.* planetary orbits, **c. evolution**, *d.* magnetism) :: EINSTEIN : RELATIVITY

   (**c**) Charles Darwin is primarily responsible for the theory of evolution, while Albert Einstein is primarily responsible for relativity theory.
   Natural Scicence—Description

7. COMPOSER : SONATA :: (*a.* physicist, ***b.* artist**, *c.* sculptor, *d.* author) : LITHOGRAPH

   (**b**) A sonata is the creation of a composer. A lithograph is the creation of an artist.
   Humanities—Description

8. HUNGRY : LION :: BUSY : (*a.* squirrel, ***b.* beaver**, *c.* hare, *d.* chipmunk)

   (**b**) "Hungry as a lion" and "busy as a beaver" are both common similes used in everyday speech.
   General Information—Description

9. MATRICIDE : MOTHER :: FRATRICIDE : (*a.* uncle, *b.* father, ***c.* brother**, *d.* son)

   (**c**) The act of killing one's mother is called matricide. The act of killing one's brother is called fratricide. The act of killing one's uncle is called avunculicide; the act of killing one's father is called patricide; the act of killing one's son is called filicide.
   Vocabulary—Description

10. (*a.* United, *b.* League, ***c.* National**, *d.* NFL) : DODGERS :: AMERICAN : YANKEES

    (**c**) The Dodgers are a National League baseball team, while the Yankees are an American League team. The American League is the more recent of the two leagues making up American Major League Baseball. The older is the National League.
    General Information—Description

11. KNOCK : PIGEON :: KNEED : (***a.* toed**, *b.* waisted, *c.* armed, *d.* headed)

    (**a**) A person may be referred to as knock-kneed or pigeon-toed. *Knock-kneed* means that a person's knees touch each other when he or she is standing straight. A pigeon-toed person's toes point inward when he or she walks.
    General Information—Completion

12. (***a.* Memorial Day**, *b.* Thanksgiving, *c.* Christmas, *d.* Labor Day) : DECORATION DAY :: VETERANS' DAY : ARMISTICE DAY

    (**a**) Memorial Day and Decoration Day are two names for the same holiday. Veterans' Day and Armistice Day are also two names for the same holiday.
    General Information—Similarity/Contrast

13. HANG : NOOSE :: BEHEAD : (***a.* guillotine**, *b.* Savonarola, *c.* Robespierre, *d.* ablation)

    (**a**) A person is hanged with a noose, but beheaded with a guillotine. Girolamo Savonarola was a religious and political reformer, known for his book burnings and opposition to Pope Alexander VI. Maximilien Robespierre was one of the most famous personalities of the French Revolution and played an important role during what is known as the *Reign of Terror. Ablation* refers to the surgical removal of a body part or tissue.
    General Information—Description

14. APPROPRIATE : INAPPROPRIATE :: APROPOS : (*a.* inapropos, *b.* misapropos, *c.* anapropos, ***d.* malapropos**)

    (**d**) Something that is not appropriate is inappropriate. Something that is not apropos is malapropos.
    Vocabulary—Similarity/Contrast

15. (*a.* gases, ***b.* good eating**, *c.* intestinal tract, *d.* gasoline) : GASTRONOMY :: HEAVENLY BODIES : ASTRONOMY

    (**b**) Gastronomy is the study of good eating. Astronomy is the study of heavenly bodies.
    General Information—Description

16. CONGRESS : UNITED STATES :: (*a.* UNICEF, *b.* Secretary-General, *c.* Security Council, ***d.* General Assembly**) : UNITED NATIONS

    (**d**) The Congress is the main legislative body of the United States. The General Assembly is the main legislative body of the United Nations.
    General Information—Description

17. EXECUTOR : (*a.* executriss, *b.* executress, *c.* executrex, ***d.* executrix**) :: ACTOR : ACTRESS

    (**d**) The feminine form of *executor* is *executrix*. The feminine form of *actor* is *actress*.
    General Information—Class

18. CANCEROUS : NONCANCEROUS :: MALIGNANT : (***a.* benign**, *b.* benevolent, *c.* beneficent, *d.* latent)

    (**a**) A cancerous tumor is called malignant. A noncancerous tumor is called benign.
    General Information—Similarity/Contrast

19. (*a.* syllogism, *b.* intellect, ***c.* troop movements**, *d.* weapons) :
LOGISTICS :: LANGUAGE : LINGUISTICS

(**c**) Logistics is the study of troop movements. Linguistics is the study
of language.
General Information—Description

20. SUBWAY : NEW YORK :: (***a.* Metro**, *b.* monorail, *c.* cable car, *d.* airplane) :
PARIS

(**a**) What is called a subway in New York is called the Metro in Paris.
General Information—Description

21. (*a.* velocity, *b.* humidity, ***c.* pressure**, *d.* THI) : BAROMETER :: MILEAGE
: ODOMETER

(**c**) A barometer measures pressure. An odometer measures mileage.
General Information—Description

22. KANSAS : WHEAT :: (*a.* Nebraska, *b.* Arkansas, *c.* Wisconsin, ***d.* Idaho**) :
POTATO

(**d**) Kansas is known for its wheat fields, Idaho for its potato fields.
General Information—Description

23. HYPO : DERMIC :: UNDER : (***a.* skin**, *b.* medicine, *c.* blood, *d.* syringe)

(**a**) A hypodermic needle goes under (hypo) the skin (dermis).
Vocabulary—Similarity/Contrast

24. PECCADILLO : (*a.* stutter, *b.* pretense, *c.* amnesia, ***d.* sin**) ::
MISDEMEANOR : CRIME

(**d**) A peccadillo is a minor sin. A misdemeanor is a minor crime.
Vocabulary—Description

25. MISANTHROPE : (*a.* life, *b.* religion, *c.* women, ***d.* people**) ::
MISOGAMIST : MARRIAGE

(**d**) A misanthrope detests people. A misogamist detests marriage.
Vocabulary—Description

26. OSTENTATIOUS : (***a.* showy**, *b.* proud, *c.* modest, *d.* fickle) ::
ONEROUS : BURDENSOME

(**a**) *Ostentatious* means showy. *Onerous* means burdensome.
Vocabulary—Similarity/Contrast

27. NATURE : NURTURE :: HEREDITY : (*a.* gene, *b.* progenitor, *c.* evolution, ***d.* environment**)

    (**d**) A "nature—nurture" controversy is one between the effects of heredity and environment.
    General Information—Description

28. HURRY : SCURRY :: HURLY : (***a.* burly**, *b.* curly, *c.* gurly, *d.* wurly)

    (**a**) *Hurry-scurry* and *hurly-burly* both refer to disorder and confusion.
    Vocabulary—Completion

29. STEM : METS :: (***a.* tab**, *b.* ball, *c.* team, *d.* root) : BAT

    (**a**) *Stem* spelled backwards is *mets*. *Tab* spelled backwards is *bat*.
    Nonsemantic

30. SATAN : BEELZEBUB :: DEVIL : (*a.* Charon, *b.* Pandemonium, ***c.* Lucifer**, *d.* Hades)

    (**c**) Satan, Beelzebub, the Devil, and Lucifer are all different names for the same entity. Charon is a figure from Greek mythology. He was a ferryman and carried the dead across the river Styx into the underworld, Hades. Pandemonium commonly refers to a state of wild confusion and is derived from its Greek mythological meaning of "the entirety of all Demons."
    Humanities—Similarity/Contrast

31. FORT SUMTER : CIVIL WAR :: (*a.* Valley Forge, *b.* Princeton, ***c.* Lexington**, *d.* Trenton) : AMERICAN REVOLUTION

    (**c**) Fort Sumter was the scene of the first battle of the Civil War. Lexington was the scene of the first battle of the American Revolution. The Continental Army had its campsite over the winter of 1777–1778 in Valley Forge during the American Revolutionary War. The forces of General Washington defeated the British in the Battle of Princeton in 1777. The Battle of Trenton took place in 1776 after General Washington's crossing of the Delaware.
    Humanities—Description

32. (***a.* chameleon**, *b.* salamander, *c.* tadpole, *d.* chamois) : FICKLE :: MULE : STUBBORN

    (**a**) A chameleon is fickle; a mule, stubborn.
    General Information—Description

33. NEW AMSTERDAM : NEW YORK :: CONSTANTINOPLE : (*a.* Budapest, ***b.* Istanbul**, *c.* Cairo, *d.* Baghdad)

    (**b**) New Amsterdam is a former name of New York City. Constantinople is a former name of Istanbul.
    General Information—Similarity/Contrast

34. ANESTHESIA : FEEL :: (*a.* eyeball, *b.* eyes, *c.* glasses, ***d.* blindness**) : SEE

    (**d**) Anesthesia is a state in which one does not feel. Blindness is a state in which one does not see.
    General Information—Description

35. CORPORAL : BEAT :: CAPITAL : (*a.* stun, *b.* spend, ***c.* kill**, *d.* shock)

    (**c**) In corporal punishment, a person is beaten. In capital punishment, a person is killed.
    General Information—Description

36. (*a.* neutron, ***b.* electron**, *c.* nucleon, *d.* positron) : PROTON ::
    NEGATIVE : POSITIVE

    (**b**) An electron has a negative electrical charge. A proton has a positive electrical charge.
    Natural Science—Description

37. CARPE : DIEM :: CAVEAT : (*a.* corpus, ***b.* emptor**, *c.* deum, *d.* mandamus)

    (**b**) *Carpe diem* (seize the opportunity—literally, the day) and *caveat emptor* (let the buyer beware) are both Latinisms used in English. *Corpus* means "body"; *deum* is the accusative of the Latin word *deus* (God); *mandamus* means "we command."
    Vocabulary—Completion

38. RAIN : (*a.* tempest, *b.* frost, ***c.* hail**, *d.* dry ice) :: WATER : ICE

    (**c**) Hail is frozen rain; ice is frozen water.
    General Information—Class

39. FEINT : (*a.* fall, *b.* remove, ***c.* pretend**, *d.* authenticate) :: SEVER :
    SEPARATE

    (**c**) To feint is to pretend. To sever is to separate.
    Vocabulary—Similarity/Contrast

40. 10 : COMMANDMENTS :: (*a.* 5, ***b.* 7**, *c.* 10, *d.* 12) : DEADLY SINS

    (**b**) There are 10 Commandments and 7 deadly sins. The 10 Commandments are found in the Old Testament of the Bible; the 7 deadly sins originated in early Christian doctrine.
    General Information—Class

41. DOUBLE ENTENDRE : (***a.* ambiguity**, *b.* treachery, *c.* meaninglessness, *d.* misperception) :: DOUBLE TAKE : DELAYED REACTION

    (**a**) A double entendre is characterized by ambiguity. A double take is characterized by a delayed reaction.
    Vocabulary—Similarity/Contrast

Answer Explanations

42. (*a.* nominalism, *b.* phenomenalism, **c. determinism**, *d.* rationalism) :
FATALISM :: EXISTENTIALISM : FREE WILL

(**c**) The philosophical doctrine of determinism argues for fatalism.
The doctrine of existentialism argues for free will. Nominalism refers to a
doctrine stating that various objects that have the same name have nothing in common but
that name. Phenomenalism refers to a theory that limits knowledge to phenomena only.
Rationalism is a theory stating that reason is a source of knowledge superior to the
perceptions of senses.
Humanities—Description

43. (**a. carmine**, *b.* yellow, *c.* brown, *d.* orange) : RED :: AZURE : BLUE

(**a**) Carmine is a shade of red. Azure is a shade of blue.
General Information—Class

44. FRAME : PICTURE :: (**a. cell wall**, *b.* endoplasmic reticulum, *c.* cytoplasm,
d. nuclear envelope) : CELL

(**a**) A frame surrounds a picture. A cell wall surrounds a cell. The endoplasmic
reticulum is a system of interconnected cytoplasmic membranes that functions especially in
the transport of materials within the cell. Cytoplasm is the organized complex of inorganic
and organic substances external to the nuclear membrane of a cell. The nuclear envelope is
a membrane system that surrounds the nucleus of eukaryotic cells.
Natural Science—Description

45. (**a. keno**, *b.* kalaha, *c.* wari, *d.* soma) : CRAPS :: ROULETTE :
TWENTY-ONE

(**a**) Keno, craps, roulette, and twenty-one are all gambling games. Kalaha
is a game in the mancala family (board games mainly played in Africa that have a role
similar to chess in Western culture). Wari is the Malinese name of an adult game often
called Oware, which is played in Africa and the Caribbean. Soma is an intoxicating,
ritual drink used in Ancient India.
General Information—Class

46. HECTOR : (*a.* Rome, *b.* Carthage, *c.* Sicily, **d. Troy**) :: ACHILLES :
GREECE

(**d**) In the Trojan War, Hector fought for Troy and Achilles fought for
Greece.
Humanities—Description

47. KUNG FU : JUDO :: (*a.* Korean, ***b.* Chinese**, *c.* Vietnamese, *d.* Japanese) : JAPANESE

    (**b**) Kung Fu is a Chinese form of martial arts; Judo is a Japanese form of martial arts.
    General Information—Class

48. SWARM : BEES :: (*a.* colony, ***b.* covey**, *c.* pack, *d.* pride) : QUAIL

    (**b**) A group of bees is referred to as a swarm. A group of quail is referred to as a covey.
    General Information—Description

49. BITUMINOUS : ANTHRACITE :: (*a.* wood, ***b.* lead**, *c.* lignite, *d.* oil) : STEEL

    (**b**) Bituminous coal is soft, and anthracite coal is hard. Lead is a soft metal, and steel a hard metal.
    General Information—Class

50. CARRY NATION : (*a.* women's suffrage, *b.* low-income housing, ***c.* temperance**, *d.* abolition of child labor) :: MARTIN LUTHER KING, JR. : CIVIL RIGHTS

    (**c**) Carry Nation fought for temperance, while Martin Luther King, Jr. fought for civil rights.
    Humanities—Description

51. STENCIL : LETTERS :: COMPASS : (*a.* time, *b.* direction, *c.* northwest, ***d.* circle**)

    (**d**) A stencil is used to draw letters. A compass is used to draw a circle.
    Mathematics—Description

52. (*a.* proposal, ***b.* talk**, *c.* dissertation, *d.* dialogue) : ORATION :: QUIZ : EXAMINATION

    (**b**) An oration is a large-scale talk. An examination is a large-scale quiz.
    Vocabulary—Description

53. ANTERIOR : POSTERIOR :: (***a.* ventral**, *b.* lateral, *c.* external, *d.* internal) : DORSAL

    (**a**) In humans, the anterior and ventral sides are the front. The posterior and dorsal sides are the rear.
    Natural Science—Similarity/Contrast

Answer Explanations

54. IMMIGRATION : EMIGRATION :: ENTRY : (*a.* expulsion, *b.* migration, **c. egress**, *d.* estuary)

    (**c**) Immigration is entry into a country, while emigration is egress from a country.
    Vocabulary—Similarity/Contrast

55. SATRAP : (**a. ruler**, *b.* bush, *c.* miser, *d.* loner) :: TRAP : AMBUSH

    (**a**) A satrap is one kind of ruler (a governor of provinces in Ancient Persia). A trap is a kind of ambush.
    Vocabulary—Similarity/Contrast

56. ELEGY : LAMENTING :: EPIGRAM : (*a.* inane, *b.* abstruse, **c. witty**, *d.* obtuse)

    (**c**) An elegy is lamenting. An epigram is witty.
    Vocabulary—Description

57. REFORMATION : PROTESTANTS :: COUNTER-REFORMATION : (**a. Catholics**, *b.* Protestants, *c.* Anglicans, *d.* Jews)

    (**a**) The Reformation was staged by Protestants, while the Counter-Reformation was staged by Catholics.
    Humanities—Description

58. (*a.* beriberi, **b. rickets**, *c.* anemia, *d.* pellagra) : D :: SCURVY : C

    (**b**) Rickets is caused by a deficiency of vitamin D. Scurvy is caused by a deficiency of vitamin C. Beriberi is caused by a lack of thiamine. Anemia can be caused through a decreased production of red blood cells in the bone marrow or heavy blood loss, among other causes. Pellagra is caused by lack of niacin.
    Natural Sciences—Description

59. GO DUTCH : PAY YOUR OWN EXPENSES :: IN DUTCH : (*a.* in luck, **b. in trouble**, *c.* rich, *d.* poor)

    (**b**) To go Dutch is to pay your own expenses. To be in Dutch is to be in trouble.
    Vocabulary—Similarity/Contrast

60. FOOL'S GOLD : (*a.* ore, **b. pyrite**, *c.* bauxite, *d.* manganese) :: PENCIL LEAD : GRAPHITE

    (**b**) Fool's gold is pyrite. Pencil lead is graphite.
    General Information—Similarity/Contrast

61. MILL : (*a.* franc, *b.* centime, *c.* shilling, ***d.* cent**) :: PENNY : DIME

(**d**) A mill is a tenth of a cent. A penny is a tenth of a dime.
General Information—Part/Whole

62. (*a.* Spain, *b.* Italy, ***c.* Israel**, *d.* Lebanon) : RUSSIA :: EL AL : AEROFLOT

(**c**) El Al is an Israeli airline, while Aeroflot is an airline of Russia.
An airline in Spain is Iberia, an airline in Italy is Alitalia, and an airline in Lebanon is Airliban.
General Information—Description

63. GAUGUIN : (*a.* England, *b.* U.S.A., ***c.* Tahiti**, *d.* Madagascar) :: GOYA : SPAIN

(**c**) Gauguin is famous for his paintings relating to Tahiti. Goya is famous for his paintings relating to Spain.
Humanities—Description

64. (***a.* bifteck**, *b.* legume, *c.* glace, *d.* poulet) : STEAK :: ESCARGOTS : SNAILS

(**a**) In France, steak is called bifteck, while snails are called escargots.
General Information—Similarity/Contrast

65. TEMERITY : AUDACITY :: (*a.* softness, ***b.* boldness**, *c.* shyness, *d.* depravity) : BRAVERY

(**b**) *Temerity, audacity, boldness,* and *bravery* are synonyms.
Vocabulary—Similarity/Contrast

66. CALORIE : (*a.* weight, *b.* basal metabolism, *c.* fat, ***d.* energy**) :: DECADE : TIME

(**d**) A calorie is a measure of energy. A decade is a measure of time.
Natural Science—Description

67. PETROLOGY : (***a.* sandstone**, *b.* Brontosaurus, *c.* moth, *d.* nylon) :: BOTANY : ROSE

(**a**) Petrology is the study of rocks, among which is sandstone. Botany is the study of plants, among which is a rose.
Natural Science—Description

Answer Explanations

68. HANSEL : GRETEL :: ORESTES : (*a.* Jocasta, *b.* **Electra**, *c.* Ophelia, *d.* Alicia)

    (**b**) Hansel and Gretel were brother and sister, as were Orestes and Electra. Hansel and Gretel are characters in one of the Brother Grimm's fairytales. Orestes and Electra were son and daughter of Agamemnon. Jocasta was the wife of Laius, mother and wife of Oedipus, and the mother of Antigone. Ophelia is Hamlet's love in Shakespeare's play *Hamlet*. Alicia is a distracter term that has no particular meaning in this context.
    Humanities—Class

69. (*a.* rude, *b.* **talkative**, *c.* immodest, *d.* brash) : GARRULOUS :: PETULANT : PEEVISH

    (**b**) A garrulous person is talkative; a petulant person is peevish.
    Vocabulary—Similarity/Contrast

70. PONCE DE LEON : (*a.* Atlantic Ocean, *b.* Mexico, *c.* Georgia, *d.* **Florida**) :: BALBOA : PACIFIC OCEAN

    (**d**) Ponce de Leon discovered Florida; Balboa discovered the Pacific Ocean.
    Humanities—Description

71. ATTENUATE : (*a.* disprove, *b.* weaken, *c.* prove, *d.* **strengthen**) :: ATTRACT : REPEL

    (**d**) *Attenuate* and *strengthen* are antonyms, as are *attract* and *repel*.
    Vocabulary—Similarity/Contrast

72. CEREBRUM : THINKING :: CEREBELLUM : (*a.* olfaction, *b.* **muscular coordination**, *c.* glandular secretion, *d.* audition)

    (**b**) In the brain, the cerebrum controls thinking, while the cerebellum controls muscular coordination.
    Natural Sciences—Description

73. BEHAVIORISM : U.S.A. :: GESTALT : (*a.* France, *b.* England, *c.* Switzerland, *d.* **Germany**)

    (**d**) In psychology, behaviorism originated in the United States, while the Gestalt movement originated in Germany.
    Social Science—Description

74. MONROE : (*a.* Treatise, *b.* Edict, *c.* Decree, ***d.* Code**) :: DOCTRINE : NAPOLEON

(**d**) The Monroe Doctrine and the Code Napoleon were both policy statements. The Monroe Doctrine (1823) states that the European powers were no longer to regard the countries of the western hemisphere as "subjects for future colonization." The Code Napoleon is a set of civil laws that Napoleon instituted.
Humanities—Completion

75. LXII : CLXXXVI :: D : (*a.* M, *b.* MC, ***c.* MD**, *d.* MM)

(**c**) 62 is to 186 as 500 is to 1,500. In Roman numerals, I = 1, V = 5, X = 10, L = 50, C = 100, D = 500, M = 1,000.
Mathematics—Equality/Negation

76. (*a.* loudness, *b.* compression, *c.* brightness, ***d.* hardness**) : MOHS :: TEMPERATURE : KELVIN

(**d**) The Mohs scale measures hardness, while the Kelvin scale measures temperature.
Natural Science—Description

77. FOX : OWL :: (*a.* Saul, *b.* David, ***c.* Iago**, *d.* Lear) : SOLOMON

(**c**) Iago was cunning, as a fox is supposed to be. Solomon was wise, as an owl is supposed to be. Iago tricked Othello into murdering his wife in Shakespeare's tragedy *Othello*. Solomon was the son of David and also became a king of the Israelites. Saul was the first king of the Israelites. David was the second king of the Israelites and fought the giant Goliath. Lear was betrayed by two of his daughters in Shakespeare's *King Lear*.
Humanities—Description

78. 1 : LINE :: 2 : (*a.* length, ***b.* ellipse**, *c.* point, *d.* sphere)

(**b**) A line is one-dimensional, while an ellipse is two-dimensional.
Mathematics—Description

79. EXOSKELETON : LOBSTER :: ENDOSKELETON : (*a.* oyster, ***b.* tiger**, *c.* barnacle, *d.* worm)

(**b**) A lobster has an exoskeleton; a tiger has an endoskeleton. An exoskeleton is an external supportive covering of an animal. An endoskeleton is an internal skeleton.
Natural Science—Description

Answer Explanations

80. FEZ : SOMBRERO :: BERET : (*a.* phylactery, *b.* millinery, *c.* muffler, ***d.* fedora**)

    (**d**) A fez, a sombrero, a beret, and a fedora are all forms of headgear. A phylactery is an amulet worn by observant Jewish men. Millinery refers to hats for women or the shop that sells them. A muffler is a noise-reducing device in the exhaust system of a car as well as a thick scarf.
    General Information—Class

81. (*a.* angry, ***b.* sanguine**, *c.* dejected, *d.* pale) : PESSIMISTIC :: HOPEFUL : DISPIRITED

    (**b**) *Sanguine* means *hopeful*; *pessimistic* means *dispirited*.
    Vocabulary—Similarity/Contrast

82. $4^{1/2} : 9^{1/2} :: 36^{1/2} :$ (*a.* 6, ***b.* 9**, *c.* 12, *d.* 81)

    (**b**) 2 is to 3 as 6 is to 9.
    Mathematics—Equality/Negation

83. INCUBUS : (*a.* faccubus, *b.* excubus, ***c.* succubus**, *d.* maccubus) :: WOMEN : MEN

    (**c**) An incubus was once thought to be a demon that sought to have intercourse with sleeping women. A succubus sought to have intercourse with sleeping men.
    General Information—Description

84. HEAD MONEY : (*a.* warn, *b.* punish, ***c.* capture**, *d.* bribe) :: HUSH MONEY : SILENCE

    (**c**) Head money is used as payment for capture. Hush money is used as payment for silence.
    General Information—Description

85. SUSTAIN : OVERRULE :: IN CAMERA : (*a.* in trouble, ***b.* in public**, *c.* in court, *d.* out of court)

    (**b**) *Sustain* and *overrule* are opposites, as are *in camera* and *in public*.
    Social Science—Similarity/Contrast

86. CRONUS : SATURN :: (*a.* Poseidon, ***b.* Ares**, *c.* Zeus, *d.* Hermes) : MARS

    (**b**) Cronus was the Greek name, and Saturn the Roman name, of the Titan who overthrew his father to become ruler of the universe, only to be overthrown by his own son (named Zeus by the Greeks, Jupiter by the Romans). Ares is the Greek name and Mars is the Roman name for the god of war.
    Humanities—Similarity/Contrast

87. D MINOR : F MAJOR :: (*a.* E minor, *b.* F minor, *c.* **F# minor**, *d.* G# minor) : A MAJOR

   (**c**) The musical keys of D minor and F major both have one flat, while the keys of F# minor and A major both have three sharps.
   Humanities—Description

88. TAME : MATE :: LAME : (*a.* female, *b.* injured, *c.* **male**, *d.* excuse)

   (**c**) *Mate* can be obtained from *tame* by reversing the initial three letters. *Male* can be obtained from *lame*, also by reversing the initial three letters.
   Nonsemantic

89. (*a.* spinal, *b.* neutral, *c.* **temporal**, *d.* spatial) : PARIETAL :: OCCIPITAL : FRONTAL

   (**c**) The four lobes of the brain are the temporal, parietal, occipital, and frontal.
   Natural Science—Class

90. PARADISE : LOST :: JERUSALEM : (*a.* Sanctified, *b.* Discovered, *c.* **Delivered**, *d.* Vanquished)

   (**c**) *Paradise Lost* and *Jerusalem Delivered* are both epics, the former by Milton and the latter by Tasso.
   Humanities—Completion

91. PENN : PENNSYLVANIA :: CALVERT : (*a.* South Carolina, *b.* Vermont, *c.* **Maryland**, *d.* Rhode Island)

   (**c**) Penn founded Pennsylvania, while Calvert founded Maryland. South Carolina was named by King Charles II of England. Vermont was created by Ethan Allen and his brothers as well as Seth Warner whom they recruited for an informal militia, the Green Mountain Boys. Roger Williams was the founder of Rhode Island.
   Humanities—Description

92. ETEOCLES : (*a.* Theseus, *b.* Laius, *c.* Oedipus, *d.* **Polynices**) :: ANTIGONE : ISMENE

   (**d**) Eteocles and Polynices were siblings, as were Antigone and Ismene. Theseus was a king of Athens and son of either Aegeus and Aethra or of Poseidon and Aethra. Laius was a king of Thebes who was killed by his son Oedipus.
   Humanities—Class

93. DECIMAL : 10 :: DUODECIMAL : (*a.* 2, *b.* 8, *c.* **12**, *d.* 16)

   (**c**) The decimal system has 10 as its base. The duodecimal system has 12 as its base.
   Mathematics—Description

Answer Explanations

94. RATIONALIST : EMPIRICIST :: (*a*. Berkeley, *b*. Hume, *c*. Mill, **d. Leibniz**) : LOCKE

(**d**) Leibniz was a famous rationalist philosopher. Locke was a famous empiricist. Hume and Berkeley were empiricists. John Stuart Mill was a utilitarianist.
Humanities—Description

95. (**a. Ivan Karamazov**, *b*. Anna Karenina, *c*. Nicolai Gogol, *d*. Grigory Smirnov) : DOSTOYEVSKY :: THÉRÈSE : MAURIAC

(**a**) Ivan Karamazov is a literary character created by Dostoyevsky. Thérèse is a literary character created by Mauriac. *Anna Karenina* is a novel by Leo Tolstoy. Nicolai Gogol was a Russian writer. Grigory Smirnov is a distracter term.
Humanities—Description

96. PALESTRINA : 16th :: (*a*. Beethoven, *b*. Bach, *c*. Tchaikovsky, **d. Stravinsky**) : 20th

(**d**) Palestrina (ca. 1525–1594) was a 16th century composer; Stravinsky (1882–1971) was a 20th century composer. Beethoven lived from 1770 to 1827. Johann Sebastian Bach lived from 1685 to 1750. Tchaikovsky lived from 1840 to 1893.
Humanities—Description

97. NICHOLAS II : RUSSIAN REVOLUTION :: (*a*. Louis XIV, *b*. Louis XV, **c. Louis XVI**, *d*. Louis XVII) : FRENCH REVOLUTION

(**c**) The Russian Revolution overthrew Nicholas II in 1905. The French Revolution (1789–1799) overthrew Louis XVI.
Humanities—Description

98. GLENN GOULD : PIANO :: YO-YO MA : (*a*. piano, *b*. violin, **c. cello**, *d*. clarinet)

(**c**) Glenn Gould was a famous pianist; Yo-Yo Ma is a famous cellist.
Humanities—Description

99. (**a. Versailles**, *b*. Xanadu, *c*. St. Malo, *d*. Rouen) : LOUIS XIV :: AMBOISE : FRANCIS II

(**a**) Amboise is the location of the palace of Francis II. Versailles is the location of the palace of Louis XIV.
Humanities—Description

100. ISHMAEL : (***a. Hagar***, *b*. Rebeccah, *c*. Esther, *d*. Sophia) :: ISAAC : SARAH

   (**a**) According to the Bible, Ishmael was the son of Hagar and Abraham, while Isaac was the son of Sarah and Abraham. Rebeccah was the wife of Isaac. Esther was a queen of Persia; a book in the Old Testament is named after her. Sophia is a Greek name meaning "wisdom."
   Humanities—Description

101. COLITIS : COLON :: ENCEPHALITIS : (***a. brain***, *b*. duodenum, *c*. pancreas, *d*. liver)

   (**a**) Colitis refers to a swelling of the colon and encephalitis describes a swelling of the brain.
   General Information—Description

102. GOLDA MEIR : (*a*. Poland, ***b. Israel***, *c*. United States, *d*. Czech Republic) :: MARGARET THATCHER : GREAT BRITAIN

   (**b**) Golda Meir was the first female prime minister of Israel (1969–1973). Margaret Thatcher was the first female prime minister of Great Britain (1979–1990).
   General Information—Description

103. PICCOLO : FLUTE :: EUPHONIUM : (*a*. phonograph, ***b. tuba***, *c*. organ, *d*. homonym)

   (**b**) A piccolo is an instrument much like a flute, but smaller. A euphonium is an instrument much like a tuba, but smaller.
   Humanities—Description

104. FORCE : DISTANCE :: (***a. mass × acceleration***, *b*. friction × momentum, *c*. volume / temperature, *d*. mass / energy) : RATE × TIME

   (**a**) Force is equal to mass times acceleration just as distance is equal to rate times time.
   Natural Science—Equality/Negation

105. (*a*. spear, *b*. cupid, ***c. arrow***, *d*. wing) : LOVE :: SCYTHE : DEATH

   (**c**) An arrow is the classical symbol of impending love, and the scythe is the classical symbol of impending death.
   Humanities—Description

106. CEILING : GLASS :: (*a*. heart, *b*. wall, *c*. side, ***d. curtain***) : IRON

   (**d**) One metaphorical barrier is a glass ceiling. Another is the iron curtain.
   General Information—Completion

107. LEGS : EGGS :: FROG : (*a.* chicken, *b.* dolphin, **c. sturgeon**, *d.* goose)

(**c**) Frog legs are considered a delicacy, while eggs from a sturgeon, also known as caviar, are also a delicacy.
General Information—Description

108. GOAT : (*a.* pan, **b. faun**, *c.* pegasus, *d.* minotaur) :: HORSE : CENTAUR

(**b**) The mythical creature of a man combined with a goat is called a faun. A man combined with a horse is called a centaur. Minotaur is a creature with the head of a bull and the body of a man. Pegasus was a winged horse that sprang from Medusa's body when she was killed. Pan is the Greek god of sheperds, woods, and mountains.
Humanities—Description

109. ORCZY : PIMPERNEL :: HAWTHORNE : (**a. letter**, *b.* rose, *c.* wind, *d.* tide)

(**a**) Orczy wrote the novel *The Scarlet Pimpernel*. Hawthorne wrote the novel *The Scarlet Letter*.
Humanities—Description

110. GUSTAV : (*a.* Wolfgang, *b.* Friedrich, *c.* Johann, **d. Ludwig**) :: MAHLER : BEETHOVEN

(**d**) Gustav is the first name of composer Mahler. Ludwig is the first name of composer Beethoven.
Humanities—Completion

111. RESTIVE : TRANQUIL :: VERBOSE : (*a.* loquacious, *b.* timorous, *c.* talkative, **d. taciturn**)

(**d**) Restive, which describes someone who is active or restless, means the opposite of tranquil. Verbose, which describes someone who is very talkative, means the opposite of taciturn.
Vocabulary—Similarity/Contrast

112. HOLY SEE : (*a.* Rome, *b.* Hungary, **c. Italy**, *d.* Chad) :: LESOTHO : SOUTH AFRICA

(**c**) Holy See is a country completely landlocked within Italy. Lesotho is a country completely landlocked within South Africa.
General Information—Description

113. LEAGUE OF NATIONS : UNITED NATIONS :: THE ARTICLES OF CONFEDERATION : (**a. U.S. Constitution**, *b.* The Bill of Rights, *c.* Human Rights Treaty, *d.* The Constitution of the Confederate States)

(**a**) The League of Nations was the failed predecessor of the United Nations, just as The Articles of Confederation were the failed predecessor of the U.S. Constitution.
General Information—Description

114. AM : AMPLITUDE :: FM : (*a.* force, ***b.* frequency**, *c.* Fahrenheit, *d.* friction)

(**b**) The radio term AM stands for Amplitude Modulation just as the term FM stands for Frequency Modulation.
Natural Science—Equality/Negation

115. (*a.* England, ***b.* Waterloo**, *c.* Russia, *d.* Elba) : NAPOLEON :: LITTLE BIG HORN RIVER : CUSTER

(**b**) Waterloo was where Napoleon was defeated. The Little Big Horn River was where Custer was defeated.
General Information—Description

116. ROMEO : JULIET :: PYRAMUS : (***a.* Thisbe**, *b.* Titania, *c.* Helen, *d.* Athena)

(**a**) Romeo died while in love with Juliet just as Pyramus died while in love with Thisbe. *Romeo and Juliet* was written by Shakespeare. The story of Pyramus and Thisbe was told by Ovid. Titania is the name of a character in Shakespeare's *A Midsummer Night's Dream*. Helen was the daughter of Zeus and Leda and was abducted by Paris, which led to the Trojan War. Athena was the goddess of wisdom, useful arts, and prudent warfare.
Humanities—Description

117. GOAT : WORM :: (*a.* wool, *b.* felt, ***c.* cashmere**, *d.* chinchilla) : SILK

(**c**) The goat produces the hair that is used to make the fabric cashmere. A worm produces the thread used to make the fabric silk.
General Information—Description

118. XXIX : 29 :: MDVI : (*a.* 1551, *b.* 1056, *c.* 1061, ***d.* 1506**)

(**d**) XXIX is the Roman numeral expression of the value 29. MDVI is the Roman numeral expression of the value 1,506. In Roman numerals, I = 1, V = 5, X = 10, L = 50, C = 100, D = 500, M = 1,000.
Mathematics—Equality/Negation

Answer Explanations

119. GUANINE : (***a*. cytosine**, *b*. purine, *c*. uracil, *d*. pyrimidine) ::
ADENINE : THYMINE

(**a**) In human DNA, guanine is the purine that pairs with the pyrimidine cytosine. Likewise, adenine is the purine that pairs with the pyrimidine thymine. Pyrimidine is a base that is a component of DNA.
Natural Science—Description

120. ESOPHAGUS : SARCOPHAGUS :: GULLET : (*a*. trachea, *b*. monument, ***c*. stone coffin**, *d*. crystal chandelier)

(**c**) Esophagus is another name for the gullet. Sarcophagus is the name for a stone coffin.
Vocabulary—Similarity/Contrast

PRACTICE TEST 2

Item Classification Chart

	RELATIONSHIP						
	Similarity/ Contrast	Description	Class	Completion	Part/ Whole	Equality/ Negation	Nonsemantic
Vocabulary	5, 14, 23, 26, 39, 41, 54, 55, 59, 65, 69, 71, 81, 111, 120	2, 3, 9, 24, 25, 52, 56		28, 37			
General Information	12, 18, 33, 60, 64	1, 8, 10, 13, 15, 16, 19, 20, 21, 22, 27, 32, 34, 35, 48, 62, 83, 84, 101, 102, 107, 112, 113, 115, 117	17, 38, 40, 43, 45, 47, 49	11, 106	61		
Humanities	30, 86	7, 31, 42, 46, 50, 57, 63, 70, 77, 87, 91, 94, 95, 96, 97, 98, 99, 100, 103, 105, 108, 109, 116	68, 80, 92	74, 90, 110			
Social Science	85	73					
Natural Science	53	6, 36, 44, 58, 66, 67, 72, 76, 79, 119	89			104, 114	
Mathematics		51, 78, 93				4, 75, 82, 118	
Nonsemantic							29, 88

CONTENT

Item Classification

Answer Sheet

PRACTICE TEST 3

1 Ⓐ Ⓑ Ⓒ Ⓓ	31 Ⓐ Ⓑ Ⓒ Ⓓ	61 Ⓐ Ⓑ Ⓒ Ⓓ	91 Ⓐ Ⓑ Ⓒ Ⓓ
2 Ⓐ Ⓑ Ⓒ Ⓓ	32 Ⓐ Ⓑ Ⓒ Ⓓ	62 Ⓐ Ⓑ Ⓒ Ⓓ	92 Ⓐ Ⓑ Ⓒ Ⓓ
3 Ⓐ Ⓑ Ⓒ Ⓓ	33 Ⓐ Ⓑ Ⓒ Ⓓ	63 Ⓐ Ⓑ Ⓒ Ⓓ	93 Ⓐ Ⓑ Ⓒ Ⓓ
4 Ⓐ Ⓑ Ⓒ Ⓓ	34 Ⓐ Ⓑ Ⓒ Ⓓ	64 Ⓐ Ⓑ Ⓒ Ⓓ	94 Ⓐ Ⓑ Ⓒ Ⓓ
5 Ⓐ Ⓑ Ⓒ Ⓓ	35 Ⓐ Ⓑ Ⓒ Ⓓ	65 Ⓐ Ⓑ Ⓒ Ⓓ	95 Ⓐ Ⓑ Ⓒ Ⓓ
6 Ⓐ Ⓑ Ⓒ Ⓓ	36 Ⓐ Ⓑ Ⓒ Ⓓ	66 Ⓐ Ⓑ Ⓒ Ⓓ	96 Ⓐ Ⓑ Ⓒ Ⓓ
7 Ⓐ Ⓑ Ⓒ Ⓓ	37 Ⓐ Ⓑ Ⓒ Ⓓ	67 Ⓐ Ⓑ Ⓒ Ⓓ	97 Ⓐ Ⓑ Ⓒ Ⓓ
8 Ⓐ Ⓑ Ⓒ Ⓓ	38 Ⓐ Ⓑ Ⓒ Ⓓ	68 Ⓐ Ⓑ Ⓒ Ⓓ	98 Ⓐ Ⓑ Ⓒ Ⓓ
9 Ⓐ Ⓑ Ⓒ Ⓓ	39 Ⓐ Ⓑ Ⓒ Ⓓ	69 Ⓐ Ⓑ Ⓒ Ⓓ	99 Ⓐ Ⓑ Ⓒ Ⓓ
10 Ⓐ Ⓑ Ⓒ Ⓓ	40 Ⓐ Ⓑ Ⓒ Ⓓ	70 Ⓐ Ⓑ Ⓒ Ⓓ	100 Ⓐ Ⓑ Ⓒ Ⓓ
11 Ⓐ Ⓑ Ⓒ Ⓓ	41 Ⓐ Ⓑ Ⓒ Ⓓ	71 Ⓐ Ⓑ Ⓒ Ⓓ	101 Ⓐ Ⓑ Ⓒ Ⓓ
12 Ⓐ Ⓑ Ⓒ Ⓓ	42 Ⓐ Ⓑ Ⓒ Ⓓ	72 Ⓐ Ⓑ Ⓒ Ⓓ	102 Ⓐ Ⓑ Ⓒ Ⓓ
13 Ⓐ Ⓑ Ⓒ Ⓓ	43 Ⓐ Ⓑ Ⓒ Ⓓ	73 Ⓐ Ⓑ Ⓒ Ⓓ	103 Ⓐ Ⓑ Ⓒ Ⓓ
14 Ⓐ Ⓑ Ⓒ Ⓓ	44 Ⓐ Ⓑ Ⓒ Ⓓ	74 Ⓐ Ⓑ Ⓒ Ⓓ	104 Ⓐ Ⓑ Ⓒ Ⓓ
15 Ⓐ Ⓑ Ⓒ Ⓓ	45 Ⓐ Ⓑ Ⓒ Ⓓ	75 Ⓐ Ⓑ Ⓒ Ⓓ	105 Ⓐ Ⓑ Ⓒ Ⓓ
16 Ⓐ Ⓑ Ⓒ Ⓓ	46 Ⓐ Ⓑ Ⓒ Ⓓ	76 Ⓐ Ⓑ Ⓒ Ⓓ	106 Ⓐ Ⓑ Ⓒ Ⓓ
17 Ⓐ Ⓑ Ⓒ Ⓓ	47 Ⓐ Ⓑ Ⓒ Ⓓ	77 Ⓐ Ⓑ Ⓒ Ⓓ	107 Ⓐ Ⓑ Ⓒ Ⓓ
18 Ⓐ Ⓑ Ⓒ Ⓓ	48 Ⓐ Ⓑ Ⓒ Ⓓ	78 Ⓐ Ⓑ Ⓒ Ⓓ	108 Ⓐ Ⓑ Ⓒ Ⓓ
19 Ⓐ Ⓑ Ⓒ Ⓓ	49 Ⓐ Ⓑ Ⓒ Ⓓ	79 Ⓐ Ⓑ Ⓒ Ⓓ	109 Ⓐ Ⓑ Ⓒ Ⓓ
20 Ⓐ Ⓑ Ⓒ Ⓓ	50 Ⓐ Ⓑ Ⓒ Ⓓ	80 Ⓐ Ⓑ Ⓒ Ⓓ	110 Ⓐ Ⓑ Ⓒ Ⓓ
21 Ⓐ Ⓑ Ⓒ Ⓓ	51 Ⓐ Ⓑ Ⓒ Ⓓ	81 Ⓐ Ⓑ Ⓒ Ⓓ	111 Ⓐ Ⓑ Ⓒ Ⓓ
22 Ⓐ Ⓑ Ⓒ Ⓓ	52 Ⓐ Ⓑ Ⓒ Ⓓ	82 Ⓐ Ⓑ Ⓒ Ⓓ	112 Ⓐ Ⓑ Ⓒ Ⓓ
23 Ⓐ Ⓑ Ⓒ Ⓓ	53 Ⓐ Ⓑ Ⓒ Ⓓ	83 Ⓐ Ⓑ Ⓒ Ⓓ	113 Ⓐ Ⓑ Ⓒ Ⓓ
24 Ⓐ Ⓑ Ⓒ Ⓓ	54 Ⓐ Ⓑ Ⓒ Ⓓ	84 Ⓐ Ⓑ Ⓒ Ⓓ	114 Ⓐ Ⓑ Ⓒ Ⓓ
25 Ⓐ Ⓑ Ⓒ Ⓓ	55 Ⓐ Ⓑ Ⓒ Ⓓ	85 Ⓐ Ⓑ Ⓒ Ⓓ	115 Ⓐ Ⓑ Ⓒ Ⓓ
26 Ⓐ Ⓑ Ⓒ Ⓓ	56 Ⓐ Ⓑ Ⓒ Ⓓ	86 Ⓐ Ⓑ Ⓒ Ⓓ	116 Ⓐ Ⓑ Ⓒ Ⓓ
27 Ⓐ Ⓑ Ⓒ Ⓓ	57 Ⓐ Ⓑ Ⓒ Ⓓ	87 Ⓐ Ⓑ Ⓒ Ⓓ	117 Ⓐ Ⓑ Ⓒ Ⓓ
28 Ⓐ Ⓑ Ⓒ Ⓓ	58 Ⓐ Ⓑ Ⓒ Ⓓ	88 Ⓐ Ⓑ Ⓒ Ⓓ	118 Ⓐ Ⓑ Ⓒ Ⓓ
29 Ⓐ Ⓑ Ⓒ Ⓓ	59 Ⓐ Ⓑ Ⓒ Ⓓ	89 Ⓐ Ⓑ Ⓒ Ⓓ	119 Ⓐ Ⓑ Ⓒ Ⓓ
30 Ⓐ Ⓑ Ⓒ Ⓓ	60 Ⓐ Ⓑ Ⓒ Ⓓ	90 Ⓐ Ⓑ Ⓒ Ⓓ	120 Ⓐ Ⓑ Ⓒ Ⓓ

Answer Sheet

Practice Test 3

Directions: In each of the following questions, you will find three initial terms and, in parentheses, four answer options designated *a*, *b*, *c*, and *d*. You are to select from the four answer options the one that best completes the analogy with the three initial terms. To record your answers, use the answer sheet provided.

Time: 60 minutes

1. LAMB : (*a*. goat, *b*. sheep, *c*. mule, *d*. cow) :: COLT : HORSE

2. DOCTOR : ACCOUNTANT :: PATIENT : (*a*. judge, *b*. client, *c*. jury, *d*. district attorney)

3. IRELAND : EIRE :: (*a*. Holland, *b*. Switzerland, *c*. Denmark, *d*. Germany) : DEUTSCHLAND

4. DEFICIT : RED :: SURPLUS : (*a*. black, *b*. green, *c*. brown, *d*. white)

5. LEMON : SOUR :: TOBACCO : (*a*. tasty, *b*. sour, *c*. bitter, *d*. salty)

6. YELLOW : (*a*. blue, *b*. white, *c*. green, *d*. red) :: COWARDLY : GLOOMY

7. HOUDINI : (*a*. magician, *b*. surgeon, *c*. lawyer, *d*. detective) :: FRANKLIN : STATESMAN

8. CURRIER : (*a*. Loewe, *b*. Ives, *c*. Cowe, *d*. Best) :: GILBERT : SULLIVAN

9. DE FACTO : IN FACT :: (*a*. de jure, *b*. de legibus, *c*. ex facto, *d*. ex legato) : IN LAW

10. SQUARE : CUBE :: CIRCLE : (*a*. rectangle, *b*. solid, *c*. ellipse, *d*. sphere)

11. FIDDLER : PRAYING :: (*a*. bow, *b*. bear, *c*. violinist, *d*. crab) : MANTIS

12. WINCHESTER : SHOOT :: CAT-O'-NINE-TAILS : (*a*. stab, *b*. whip, *c*. poison, *d*. drown)

13. FULTON : (*a*. locomotive, *b*. steamboat, *c*. incandescent lamp, *d*. crystal radio) :: WHITNEY : COTTON GIN

14. (*a*. jugular, *b*. carotid, *c*. thorax, *d*. sclerotic) : VEIN :: AORTA : ARTERY

15. HISTRIONICS : (*a.* geriatrics, *b.* hysterics, *c.* theatrics, *d.* pediatrics) :: PATRONYMICS : SURNAMES

16. NUN : HABIT :: (*a.* postal carrier, *b.* surgeon, *c.* knight, *d.* solicitor) : COAT OF MAIL

17. (*a.* people, *b.* automobiles, *c.* horses, *d.* bicycles) : INDIANAPOLIS 500 :: HORSES : KENTUCKY DERBY

18. LOBBYIST : LEGISLATOR :: (*a.* lawyer, *b.* judge, *c.* court stenographer, *d.* foreman) : JURY

19. CONGRESSIONAL MEDAL OF HONOR : SOLDIER :: PULITZER PRIZE : (*a.* lawyer, *b.* journalist, *c.* chemist, *d.* doctor)

20. PART : TRAP :: (*a.* good-bye, *b.* whole, *c.* bait, *d.* tar) : RAT

21. BARTON : (*a.* Candy, *b.* Helen, *c.* Clara, *d.* Elsa) :: NIGHTINGALE : FLORENCE

22. EMERALD : MINE :: PEARL : (*a.* oyster, *b.* clam, *c.* mine, *d.* river)

23. BIOGRAPHY : AUTOBIOGRAPHY :: (*a.* first, *b.* third, *c.* fourth, *d.* fifth) : FIRST

24. DUET : PAIR :: DIALOGUE : (*a.* monologue, *b.* quandary, *c.* bipolar, *d.* quartet)

25. (*a.* foot, *b.* ball, *c.* skate, *d.* stick) : HOCKEY :: BAT : BASEBALL

26. (*a.* chroma, *b.* violet, *c.* rainbow, *d.* black) : COLOR :: VACUUM : AIR

27. FLORIDA : PENINSULA :: CUBA : (*a.* state, *b.* gulf, *c.* nation, *d.* island)

28. URBAN : RURAL :: URBANE : (*a.* lazy, *b.* suburban, *c.* boorish, *d.* effete)

29. (*a.* air, *b.* earth, *c.* fire, *d.* plastic) : PYRO :: WATER : HYDRO

30. (*a.* sailor, *b.* mountebank, *c.* salesman, *d.* villain) : CHARLATAN :: FRAUD : QUACK

31. RULER : LINE SEGMENT :: PROTRACTOR : (*a.* distance, *b.* angle, *c.* perimeter, *d.* velocity)

32. WILLIAMS : (*a.* Massachusetts, *b.* Vermont, *c.* New Hampshire, *d.* Rhode Island) :: PENN : PENNSYLVANIA

33. OLD : (*a.* Two, *b.* Twenty, *c.* Forty, *d.* Sixty) :: MAID : ONE

34. (*a.* princess, *b.* worker, *c.* drone, *d.* servant) : QUEEN :: GANDER :
GOOSE

35. XL : LX :: CC : (*a.* CCC, *b.* CD, *c.* DC, *d.* CM)

36. CASTOR : (*a.* Pisces, *b.* Orion, *c.* Pollux, *d.* Andromeda) :: JACOB : ESAU

37. KEYNES : (*a.* psychology, *b.* economics, *c.* anthropology, *d.* ecology) ::
EINSTEIN : PHYSICS

38. (*a.* New Jersey, *b.* Missouri, *c.* Indian, *d.* Byrd) : ANTARCTIC ::
HUDSON : MISSISSIPPI

39. SPRINGS : PALM :: (*a.* Old, *b.* Mineral, *c.* York, *d.* Tree) : NEW

40. MEGAPHONE : CONE :: (*a.* funnel, *b.* cloud, *c.* hurricane,
d. dictaphone) : TORNADO

41. HARVARD : CAMBRIDGE :: CAMBRIDGE : (*a.* Oxford, *b.* Yale,
c. Cambridge, *d.* Gloucester)

42. ACTUAL : VIRTUAL :: IN FACT : (*a.* in cause, *b.* in time, *c.* in truth,
d. in effect)

43. BRAVE NEW WORLD : (*a.* Winston, *b.* Huxley, *c.* O'Brian, *d.* Wells) ::
1984: ORWELL

44. CANINE : DOG :: EQUINE : (*a.* cow, *b.* goat, *c.* horse, *d.* pig)

45. CENSURE : (*a.* expurgate, *b.* condemn, *c.* praise, *d.* oppose) :: OBTUSE :
DULL

46. USHER : POE :: (*a.* ill Repute, *b.* Seven Gables, *c.* Tara, *d.* No Return) :
HAWTHORNE

47. NUMISMATIST : PHILATELIST :: (*a.* coins, *b.* numbers, *c.* rocks,
d. trinkets) : STAMPS

48. CASTLE : BISHOP :: HORIZONTAL : (*a.* vertical, *b.* diagonal,
c. cathedral, *d.* abbey)

49. (*a.* endemic, *b.* mercurial, *c.* unabating, *d.* retrogressive) : CONSTANT ::
CHANGEABLE : IMMUTABLE

50. TRAGEDY : MELODRAMA :: PATHOS : (*a.* bathos, *b.* ethos, *c.* comedy, *d.* catharsis)

51. PERVADE : PERMEATE :: (*a.* trusting, *b.* mistrustful, *c.* favorable, *d.* unfavorable) : AUSPICIOUS

52. GOOSE : GEESE :: MOOSE : (*a.* moosen, *b.* meese, *c.* mooses, *d.* moose)

53. (*a.* passenger pigeon, *b.* sphinx, *c.* phoenix, *d.* hummingbird) : DODO :: RAVEN : SPARROW

54. EASTERN STANDARD : 8 A.M. :: PACIFIC STANDARD : (*a.* 5 A.M., *b.* 6 A.M., *c.* 10 A.M., *d.* 11 A.M.)

55. CENTIGRADE : 100 :: CELSIUS : (*a.* −173, *b.* 0, *c.* 100, *d.* 212)

56. SURFEIT : EXCESS :: EVANESCENT : (*a.* silent, *b.* eternal, *c.* ephemeral, *d.* celestial)

57. PLUTARCH : (*a.* drama, *b.* biography, *c.* epic, *d.* oration) :: AESOP : FABLE

58. HYDRO : AQUA :: (*a.* air, *b.* gas, *c.* liquid, *d.* water) : WATER

59. REMISS : (*a.* negligent, *b.* careful, *c.* auspicious, *d.* remote) :: DARK : LIGHT

60. FUSTIAN : GALATEA :: MUSLIN : (*a.* grandam, *b.* lydgate, *c.* gabardine, *d.* rhodium)

61. BLUE : STRAW :: RASP : (*a.* yellow, *b.* hay, *c.* black, *d.* shriek)

62. BUFFALO BILL : (*a.* Cody, *b.* James, *c.* Bowman, *d.* Broderick) :: WILD BILL : HICKOK

63. MOURNER : TEARS :: (*a.* hypochondriac, *b.* lover, *c.* troglodyte, *d.* hypocrite) : CROCODILE TEARS

64. CEDE : SEED :: (*a.* run, *b.* win, *c.* yield, *d.* go) : PLANT

65. INGENUOUS : (*a.* clever, *b.* innocent, *c.* pastoral, *d.* hopeful) :: INFRACTION : VIOLATION

66. SECULAR : (*a.* sacred, *b.* ecclesiastical, *c.* lay, *d.* regular) :: BISHOP : MONK

67. EXTIRPATE : (*a.* evade, *b.* examine, *c.* exude, *d.* eradicate) :: BUOY : ENCOURAGE

68. THREE : (*a.* Two, *b.* Five, *c.* Seven, *d.* Ten) :: MUSKETEERS : LITTLE PEPPERS

69. WEND : END :: (*a.* food, *b.* wait, *c.* tend, *d.* beginning) : ATE

70. VOLT : POTENTIAL DIFFERENCE :: WATT : (*a.* resistance, *b.* brightness, *c.* power, *d.* actual difference)

71. POINT : 0 :: HEXAGON : (*a.* 1, *b.* 2, *c.* 3, *d.* 4)

72. (*a.* Troy, *b.* Athens, *c.* Carthage, *d.* Milan) : PUNIC :: SPARTA : PELOPONNESIAN

73. WINDY CITY : CHICAGO :: GOTHAM : (*a.* San Francisco, *b.* Paris, *c.* New York City, *d.* London)

74. INCANDESCENT : FILAMENT :: FLUORESCENT : (*a.* air, *b.* vacuum, *c.* energy, *d.* phosphor)

75. CABAL : (*a.* trivia, *b.* plot, *c.* wire, *d.* quibble) :: CAPABLE : COMPETENT

76. ORDER : (*a.* human, *b.* primates, *c.* erectus, *d.* mammalia) :: SPECIES : SAPIENS

77. GRENDEL : BEOWULF :: HYDRA : (*a.* Achilles, *b.* Vulcan, *c.* Atlas, *d.* Hercules)

78. 2^{-2} : 2^{-1} :: 2^2 : (*a.* 2^0, *b.* 2^1, *c.* 2^2, *d.* 2^3)

79. DEARTH : SHORTAGE :: PLETHORA : (*a.* abundance, *b.* scarcity, *c.* excess, *d.* necessity)

80. WANDERING JEW : EARTH :: FLYING DUTCHMAN : (*a.* seas, *b.* stars, *c.* heaven, *d.* hell)

81. ASTROLABE : SEXTANT :: SUNDIAL : (*a.* time, *b.* electric clock, *c.* ruler, *d.* light rays)

82. VENAL : (*a.* rigid, *b.* cold, *c.* humorless, *d.* mercenary) :: VENIAL : EXCUSABLE

83. E# : F♭ :: B : (*a.* C♭, *b.* B♭, *c.* C, *d.* B)

84. MELIORATE : AMELIORATE :: HASTEN : (*a.* speed up, *b.* slow down, *c.* better, *d.* worsen)

85. MACHIAVELLI : PRINCE :: CASTIGLIONE : (*a.* Knight, *b.* Courtier, *c.* King, *d.* Yeoman)

86. NOSTRUM : (*a.* pedestal, *b.* disease, *c.* panacea, *d.* pabulum) :: VERACIOUS : HONEST

87. DWARF : PITUITARY :: CRETIN : (*a.* endocrine, *b.* thyroid, *c.* thalamus, *d.* hypothalamus)

88. (*a.* barometer, *b.* tachometer, *c.* hydrometer, *d.* voltmeter) : THERMOMETER :: SPEED : TEMPERATURE

89. FROWARD : BACKWARD :: (*a.* dilatory, *b.* upside down, *c.* refractory, *d.* right side up) : REVERSED

90. LEWIN : (*a.* attribution theory, *b.* dissonance theory, *c.* field theory, *d.* psychoanalytic theory) :: JUNG : ANALYTIC THEORY

91. BUNSEN BURNER : GAS :: AUTOCLAVE : (*a.* oil, *b.* electricity, *c.* steam, *d.* solar energy)

92. BACH : (*a.* invention, *b.* symphony, *c.* waltz, *d.* polyphony) :: CHOPIN : MAZURKA

93. BANISHMENT : COUNTRY :: DEFENESTRATION : (*a.* ceiling, *b.* floor, *c.* city, *d.* window)

94. CADMEAN : (*a.* Caesarian, *b.* Augustan, *c.* Napoleonic, *d.* Pyrrhic) :: EXPENSIVE : COSTLY

95. MOSES : (*a.* Abraham, *b.* Joseph, *c.* Joshua, *d.* Gideon) :: ROOSEVELT : TRUMAN

96. PARASYMPATHETIC : (*a.* sympathetic, *b.* protosympathetic, *c.* asympathetic, *d.* prosympathetic) :: SLOW DOWN : SPEED UP

97. (*a.* Galileo, *b.* Newton, *c.* Galen, *d.* Ptolemy) : COPERNICUS :: GEOCENTRIC : HELIOCENTRIC

98. TOSCANINI : (*a.* Fournier, *b.* Ormandy, *c.* Goodman, *d.* Heifetz) :: VAN CLIBURN : RUBENSTEIN

99. RICHELIEU : CARDINAL :: (*a.* Henry IV, *b.* Louis XIII, *c.* Francis I, *d.* Napoleon III) : KING

100. JAMES : FUNCTIONALISM :: (*a.* Dewey, *b.* Levi-Strauss, *c.* Watson, *d.* Klineberg) : STRUCTURALISM

101. FAUST : DR. FAUSTUS :: (*a.* Goethe, *b.* Mr. Marlowe, *c.* Hyde, *d.* Kafka) : MARLOWE

102. RHODESIA : (*a.* Indonesia, *b.* Zimbabwe, *c.* Namibia, *d.* Israel) :: BURMA : MYANMAR

103. SALT : WATER :: (*a.* desalinate, *b.* desaltify, *c.* purify, *d.* reduce) : DEHYDRATE

104. HART : DEER :: COLT : (*a.* stallion, *b.* horse, *c.* filly, *d.* foal)

105. (*a.* liver, *b.* brain, *c.* ear, *d.* pancreas) : HEART :: LOBE : CHAMBER

106. NADIR : (*a.* penultimate, *b.* depth, *c.* zenith, *d.* low) :: STYGIAN : BRIGHT

107. 32 : FAHRENHEIT :: (*a.* –32, *b.* 100, *c.* 10, *d.* 0) : CELSIUS

108. GRAPE : RAISIN :: PLUM : (*a.* date, *b.* fig, *c.* prune, *d.* currant)

109. NORTH : CANCER :: SOUTH : (*a.* Virgo, *b.* Capricorn, *c.* Sagittarius, *d.* Equator)

110. EVELYN : DACTYL :: (*a.* Michelle, *b.* Holly, *c.* Erica, *d.* Emily) : IAMB

111. MOZART : (*a.* Violin, *b.* Flute, *c.* Viola, *d.* Cello) :: BACH : ORGAN

112. (*a.* pizzicato, *b.* staccato, *c.* diminuendo, *d.* piano) : FORTE :: SOFT : LOUD

113. INDIA : HINDUISM :: INDONESIA : (*a.* Buddhism, *b.* Confucianism, *c.* Christianity, *d.* Islam)

114. OBOE : REED :: (*a.* viola, *b.* bassoon, *c.* timpani, *d.* french horn) : STRING

115. MORE : (*a.* Utopia, *b.* Paradise Lost, *c.* 1984, *d.* On the Beach) :: HUXLEY : BRAVE NEW WORLD

116. BASEBALL : BAT :: TABLE TENNIS : (*a.* mallet, *b.* paddle, *c.* stick, *d.* racquet)

117. ETYMOLOGY : ENTOMOLOGY :: (*a.* letters, *b.* arachnids, *c.* disease, *d.* words) : INSECTS

118. ADAM : (*a.* Eden, *b.* Israel, *c.* heaven, *d.* hell) :: ROMEO : VERONA

119. $8^{1/3} : 25^{1/2} ::$ (*a.* 25^2, *b.* $100^{1/3}$, *c.* $100^{1/2}$, *d.* $16^{1/2}$) $: 625^{1/2}$

120. AUGMENTED THIRD : DIMINISHED THIRD :: FOUR : (*a.* two and a half, *b.* three, *c.* two, *d.* three and a half)

Answer Key
PRACTICE TEST 3

1.	B	31.	B	61.	C	91.	C
2.	B	32.	D	62.	A	92.	A
3.	D	33.	B	63.	D	93.	D
4.	A	34.	C	64.	C	94.	D
5.	C	35.	A	65.	B	95.	C
6.	A	36.	C	66.	D	96.	A
7.	A	37.	B	67.	D	97.	D
8.	B	38.	C	68.	B	98.	B
9.	A	39.	C	69.	B	99.	B
10.	D	40.	A	70.	C	100.	B
11.	D	41.	C	71.	B	101.	A
12.	B	42.	D	72.	C	102.	B
13.	B	43.	B	73.	C	103.	A
14.	A	44.	C	74.	D	104.	D
15.	C	45.	B	75.	B	105.	B
16.	C	46.	B	76.	B	106.	C
17.	B	47.	A	77.	D	107.	D
18.	A	48.	B	78.	D	108.	C
19.	B	49.	B	79.	C	109.	B
20.	D	50.	A	80.	A	110.	A
21.	C	51.	C	81.	B	111.	A
22.	A	52.	D	82.	D	112.	D
23.	B	53.	A	83.	B	113.	D
24.	C	54.	A	84.	A	114.	A
25.	D	55.	C	85.	B	115.	A
26.	D	56.	C	86.	C	116.	B
27.	D	57.	B	87.	B	117.	D
28.	C	58.	D	88.	B	118.	A
29.	C	59.	B	89.	C	119.	C
30.	B	60.	C	90.	C	120.	A

ANSWER EXPLANATIONS FOR PRACTICE TEST 3

In the following, explanations concerning the correct response are in a large font. Explanations regarding distracters (incorrect responses) that are not self-explaining or could be misinterpreted are in a smaller font in order to highlight the explanations of the answers that are correct.

1. LAMB : (*a.* goat, *b.* **sheep**, *c.* mule, *d.* cow) :: COLT : HORSE
   (**b**) A lamb is a young sheep; a colt is a young horse.
   General Information—Description

2. DOCTOR : ACCOUNTANT :: PATIENT : (*a.* judge, *b.* **client**, *c.* jury, *d.* district attorney)

   (**b**) A doctor serves patients; an accountant serves clients.
   General Information—Description

3. IRELAND : EIRE :: (*a.* Holland, *b.* Switzerland, *c.* Denmark, *d.* **Germany**) : DEUTSCHLAND

   (**d**) Ireland and Eire are the same country, as are Germany and Deutschland.
   General Information—Similarity/Contrast

4. DEFICIT : RED :: SURPLUS : (*a.* **black**, *b.* green, *c.* brown, *d.* white)

   (**a**) To be in the red is to show a deficit, while to be in the black is to show a surplus.
   General Information—Similarity/Contrast

5. LEMON : SOUR :: TOBACCO : (*a.* tasty, *b.* sour, *c.* **bitter**, *d.* salty)

   (**c**) A lemon is sour; tobacco is bitter.
   General Information—Description

6. YELLOW : (*a.* **blue**, *b.* white, *c.* green, *d.* red) :: COWARDLY : GLOOMY

   (**a**) A cowardly person is sometimes referred to as "yellow." A gloomy person is sometimes referred to as feeling "blue."
   General Information—Similarity/Contrast

7. HOUDINI : (*a.* **magician**, *b.* surgeon, *c.* lawyer, *d.* detective) :: FRANKLIN : STATESMAN

   (**a**) Harry Houdini was a magician; Benjamin Franklin, a statesman.
   General Information—Description

8. CURRIER : (*a.* Loewe, *b.* **Ives**, *c.* Cowe, *d.* Best) :: GILBERT : SULLIVAN

(**b**) Currier and Ives were a team of artists, while Gilbert and Sullivan were a team who wrote operettas, including "The Mikado." Currier and Ives had a printmaking firm that produced some of the most popular art of the 19th century.
Humanities—Class

9. DE FACTO : IN FACT :: (*a.* **de jure**, *b.* de legibus, *c.* ex facto, *d.* ex legato) : IN LAW

(**a**) *De facto* means "in fact." *De jure* means "in law." *De legibus* is a dialogue written by Cicero. *Ex facto* means "after the fact."
Vocabulary—Similarity/Contrast

10. SQUARE : CUBE :: CIRCLE : (*a.* rectangle, *b.* solid, *c.* ellipse, *d.* **sphere**)

(**d**) A two-dimensional "slice" through a cube yields a square. A two-dimensional "slice" through a sphere yields a circle.
Mathematics—Description

11. FIDDLER : PRAYING :: (*a.* bow, *b.* bear, *c.* violinist, *d.* **crab**) : MANTIS

(**d**) The fiddler crab and praying mantis are both types of animal.
Natural Science—Completion

12. WINCHESTER : SHOOT :: CAT-O'-NINE-TAILS : (*a.* stab, *b.* **whip**, *c.* poison, *d.* drown)

(**b**) A Winchester can be used to shoot someone. A cat-o'-nine-tails can be used to whip someone. A Winchester is a shoulder rifle. A cat-o'-nine-tails is a whip with nine separate woven tails.
General Information—Description

13. FULTON : (*a.* locomotive, *b.* **steamboat**, *c.* incandescent lamp, *d.* crystal radio) :: WHITNEY : COTTON GIN

(**b**) Robert Fulton invented the steamboat. Eli Whitney invented the cotton gin.
Social Science—Description

14. (*a.* **jugular**, *b.* carotid, *c.* thorax, *d.* sclerotic) : VEIN :: AORTA : ARTERY

(**a**) The jugular is a vein; the aorta is an artery. *Carotid* relates to the chief arteries that pass up the neck. The thorax is the part of the body between the neck and abdomen. *Sclerotic* relates to the dense fibrous outer coat of the eyeball.
Natural Science—Class

15. HISTRIONICS : (*a.* geriatrics, *b.* hysterics, ***c.* theatrics**, *d.* pediatrics) :: PATRONYMICS : SURNAMES

(**c**) Histrionics are theatrics; patronymics are surnames.
Vocabulary—Similarity/Contrast

16. NUN : HABIT :: (*a.* postal carrier, *b.* surgeon, ***c.* knight**, *d.* solicitor) : COAT OF MAIL

(**c**) A nun sometimes wears a habit. A knight wore a coat of mail.
General Information—Similarity/Contrast

17. (*a.* people, ***b.* automobiles**, *c.* horses, *d.* bicycles) : INDIANAPOLIS 500 :: HORSES : KENTUCKY DERBY

(**b**) The Indianapolis 500 is an automobile race. The Kentucky Derby is a horse race.
General Information—Description

18. LOBBYIST : LEGISLATOR :: (***a.* lawyer**, *b.* judge, *c.* court stenographer, *d.* foreman) : JURY

(**a**) The job of a lobbyist is to persuade a legislator. The job of a lawyer is to persuade a jury.
General Information—Description

19. CONGRESSIONAL MEDAL OF HONOR : SOLDIER :: PULITZER PRIZE : (*a.* lawyer, ***b.* journalist**, *c.* chemist, *d.* doctor)

(**b**) The Congressional Medal of Honor is given to outstanding soldiers. The Pulitzer Prize is given to outstanding journalists.
General Information—Description

20. PART : TRAP :: (*a.* good-bye, *b.* whole, *c.* bait, ***d.* tar**) : RAT

(**d**) *Part* is *trap* spelled backwards. *Tar* is *rat* spelled backwards.
Nonsemantic

21. BARTON : (*a.* Candy, *b.* Helen, ***c.* Clara**, *d.* Elsa) :: NIGHTINGALE : FLORENCE

(**c**) Clara Barton (1821–1912) and Florence Nightingale (1821–1910) are both famous for their work in nursing.
General Information—Completion

22. EMERALD : MINE :: PEARL : (***a.* oyster**, *b.* clam, *c.* mine, *d.* river)

(**a**) Emeralds are found in mines. Pearls are found in oysters.
Natural Science—Description

23. BIOGRAPHY : AUTOBIOGRAPHY :: (*a.* first, *b.* **third**, *c.* fourth, *d.* fifth) : FIRST

(**b**) A biography is written in third person. An autobiography is written in first person.
Humanities—Description

24. DUET : PAIR :: DIALOGUE : (*a.* monologue, *b.* quandary, *c.* **bipolar**, *d.* quartet)

(**c**) *Duet*, *pair*, *dialogue*, and *bipolar* all refer to two of something. A *monologue* refers to one; a *quartet* to four; a *quandary* refers to a state of perplexity or doubt.
General Information—Similarity/Contrast

25. (*a.* foot, *b.* ball, *c.* skate, *d.* **stick**) : HOCKEY :: BAT : BASEBALL

(**d**) In hockey, players hit a puck with a stick. In baseball, players hit a ball with a bat.
General Information—Description

26. (*a.* chroma, *b.* violet, *c.* rainbow, *d.* **black**) : COLOR :: VACUUM : AIR

(**d**) Black is an absence of color. A vacuum is an absence of air.
Natural Science—Description

27. FLORIDA : PENINSULA :: CUBA : (*a.* state, *b.* gulf, *c.* nation, *d.* **island**)

(**d**) Florida is a peninsula. Cuba is an island.
General Information—Description

28. URBAN : RURAL :: URBANE : (*a.* lazy, *b.* suburban, *c.* **boorish**, *d.* effete)

(**c**) *Urban* and *rural* are antonyms, as are *urbane* and *boorish*.
Vocabulary—Similarity/Contrast

29. (*a.* air, *b.* earth, *c.* **fire**, *d.* plastic) : PYRO :: WATER : HYDRO

(**c**) *Pyro-* is a prefix meaning *fire*, while *hydro-* is a prefix meaning *water*.
Vocabulary—Similarity/Contrast

30. (*a.* sailor, *b.* **mountebank**, *c.* salesman, *d.* villain) : CHARLATAN :: FRAUD : QUACK

(**b**) A mountebank is a charlatan, and a fraud is a quack.
Vocabulary—Similarity/Contrast

31. RULER : LINE SEGMENT :: PROTRACTOR : (*a.* distance, **b. angle**, *c.* perimeter, *d.* velocity)

    (**b**) A ruler is used to measure a line segment, while a protractor is used to measure an angle.
    Mathematics—Description

32. WILLIAMS : (*a.* Massachusetts, *b.* Vermont, *c.* New Hampshire, **d. Rhode Island**) :: PENN : PENNSYLVANIA

    (**d**) Roger Williams founded the state of Rhode Island; William Penn founded the state of Pennsylvania. The colony of Massachusetts Bay was founded by John Winthrop. Vermont was founded by Ethan Allen and his brothers as well as Seth Warner, whom they recruited for an informal militia, the Green Mountain Boys. John Mason was the founder of New Hampshire.
    Humanities—Description

33. OLD : (*a.* Two, **b. Twenty**, *c.* Forty, *d.* Sixty) :: MAID : ONE

    (**b**) Old Maid and Twenty-One are both card games.
    General Information—Completion

34. (*a.* princess, *b.* worker, **c. drone**, *d.* servant) : QUEEN :: GANDER : GOOSE

    (**c**) A drone bee is male, and a queen bee is female. A gander is a male, and a goose is a female.
    Natural Science—Class

35. XL : LX :: CC : (**a. CCC**, *b.* CD, *c.* DC, *d.* CM)

    (**a**) 40 is to 60 as 200 is to 300. In Roman numerals, I = 1, V = 5, X = 10, L = 50, C = 100, D = 500, M = 1,000.
    Mathematics—Equality/Negation

36. CASTOR : (*a.* Pisces, *b.* Orion, **c. Pollux**, *d.* Andromeda) :: JACOB : ESAU

    (**c**) Castor and Pollux were twins, as were Jacob and Esau. Pisces, Orion, and Andromeda are all constellations. Orion was a hunter in Greek mythology. Andromeda was the wife of Perseus.
    Humanities—Class

37. KEYNES : (*a.* psychology, **b. economics**, *c.* anthropology, *d.* ecology) :: EINSTEIN : PHYSICS

    (**b**) John Maynard Keynes revolutionized economic theory, while Albert Einstein revolutionized theory in physics.
    Social Science—Description

Answer Explanations

38. (*a.* New Jersey, *b.* Missouri, **c. Indian**, *d.* Byrd) : ANTARCTIC :: HUDSON : MISSISSIPPI

(**c**) The Indian and the Antarctic are both oceans. The Hudson and the Mississippi are both rivers.
General Information—Class

39. SPRINGS : PALM :: (*a.* Old, *b.* Mineral, **c. York**, *d.* Tree) : NEW

(**c**) Palm Springs and New York are both major cities.
General Information—Completion

40. MEGAPHONE : CONE :: (**a. funnel**, *b.* cloud, *c.* hurricane, *d.* dictaphone) : TORNADO

(**a**) A megaphone, a funnel, a cone, and a tornado all have approximately the same shape.
General Information—Class

41. HARVARD : CAMBRIDGE :: CAMBRIDGE : (*a.* Oxford, *b.* Yale, **c. Cambridge**, *d.* Gloucester)

(**c**) Harvard University is in Cambridge, Massachusetts, and Cambridge University is in Cambridge, England.
General Information—Description

42. ACTUAL : VIRTUAL :: IN FACT : (*a.* in cause, *b.* in time, *c.* in truth, **d. in effect**)

(**d**) *Actual* means *in fact. Virtual* means *in effect.*
Vocabulary—Similarity/Contrast

43. BRAVE NEW WORLD : (*a.* Winston, **b. Huxley**, *c.* O'Brian, *d.* Wells) :: 1984 : ORWELL

(**b**) *Brave New World* is a novel by Huxley; *1984* is a novel by Orwell. (Both describe nightmarish societies of the future.)
Humanities—Description

44. CANINE : DOG :: EQUINE : (*a.* cow, *b.* goat, **c. horse**, *d.* pig)

(**c**) *Canine* means *doglike. Equine* means *horselike.* Cowlike is *bovine,* goatlike is *hircine,* and piglike is *porcine.*
General Information—Description

45. CENSURE : (*a.* expurgate, **b. condemn**, *c.* praise, *d.* oppose) :: OBTUSE : DULL

(**b**) To censure is to condemn. To be obtuse is to be dull.
Vocabulary—Similarity/Contrast

Answer Explanations

46. USHER : POE :: (*a.* ill Repute, ***b.* Seven Gables**, *c.* Tara, *d.* No Return) : HAWTHORNE

(**b**) Poe wrote about the House of Usher; Hawthorne wrote about the House of the Seven Gables.
Humanities—Description

47. NUMISMATIST : PHILATELIST :: (***a.* coins**, *b.* numbers, *c.* rocks, *d.* trinkets) : STAMPS

(**a**) A numismatist collects coins; a philatelist collects stamps.
General Information—Description

48. CASTLE : BISHOP :: HORIZONTAL : (*a.* vertical, ***b.* diagonal**, *c.* cathedral, *d.* abbey)

(**b**) In the game of chess, a castle is capable of horizontal movement, while a bishop is capable of diagonal movement.
General Information—Description

49. (*a.* endemic, ***b.* mercurial**, *c.* unabating, *d.* retrogressive) : CONSTANT :: CHANGEABLE : IMMUTABLE

(**b**) *Mercurial* and *constant* are antonyms, as are *changeable* and *immutable*.
Vocabulary—Similarity/Contrast

50. TRAGEDY : MELODRAMA :: PATHOS : (***a.* bathos**, *b.* ethos, *c.* comedy, *d.* catharsis)

(**a**) Tragedy expresses pathos, while melodrama expresses bathos.
Humanities—Description

51. PERVADE : PERMEATE :: (*a.* trusting, *b.* mistrustful, ***c.* favorable**, *d.* unfavorable) : AUSPICIOUS

(**c**) *Pervade* and *permeate* are synonyms, as are *favorable* and *auspicious*.
Vocabulary—Similarity/Contrast

52. GOOSE : GEESE :: MOOSE : (*a.* moosen, *b.* meese, *c.* mooses, ***d.* moose**)

(**d**) The plural of *goose* is *geese*. The plural of *moose* is *moose*.
Nonsemantic

53. (***a*. passenger pigeon**, *b*. sphinx, *c*. phoenix, *d*. hummingbird) : DODO :: RAVEN : SPARROW

(**a**) The passenger pigeon and the dodo are both extinct species of birds. The raven and the sparrow are not extinct. The hummingbird is also not extinct; a phoenix is a mythical bird that burned itself and arose from the ashes to live again; the sphinx is a mythical Egyptian creature that has the body of a lion and the head of a man.
Natural Science—Class

54. EASTERN STANDARD : 8 A.M. :: PACIFIC STANDARD : (***a*. 5 A.M.**, *b*. 6 A.M., *c*. 10 A.M., *d*. 11 A.M.)

(**a**) When it is 8 A.M. Eastern Standard Time, it is 5 A.M. Pacific Standard Time.
General Information—Similarity/Contrast

55. CENTIGRADE : 100 :: CELSIUS : (*a*. –173, *b*. 0, ***c*. 100**, *d*. 212)

(**c**) The centigrade and Celsius temperature scales are identical, so 100 degrees centigrade equals 100 degrees Celsius.
Natural Science—Equality/Negation

56. SURFEIT : EXCESS :: EVANESCENT : (*a*. silent, *b*. eternal, ***c*. ephemeral**, *d*. celestial)

(**c**) *Surfeit* and *excess* are synonyms, as are *evanescent* and *ephemeral*.
Vocabulary—Similarity/Contrast

57. PLUTARCH : (*a*. drama, ***b*. biography**, *c*. epic, *d*. oration) :: AESOP : FABLE

(**b**) Plutarch is famous as a writer of biography. Aesop is famous as a writer of fables. Plutarch wrote *Parallel Lives*; famous fables of Aesop are, for example, *The Fox and the Grapes* and *The Tortoise and the Hare*.
Humanities—Description

58. HYDRO : AQUA :: (*a*. air, *b*. gas, *c*. liquid, ***d*. water**) : WATER

(**d**) *Hydro-* and *aqua-* are both prefixes meaning *water*.
Vocabulary—Similarity/Contrast

59. REMISS : (*a*. negligent, ***b*. careful**, *c*. auspicious, *d*. remote) :: DARK : LIGHT

(**b**) *Remiss* is the opposite of *careful*; *dark* is the opposite of *light*.
Vocabulary—Similarity/Contrast

Answer Explanations

60. FUSTIAN : GALATEA :: MUSLIN : (*a*. grandam, *b*. lydgate, **c. gabardine**, *d*. rhodium)

(**c**) Fustian, galatea, muslin, and gabardine are all types of cloth.
Grandam refers to an old woman. John Lydgate was an English poet (ca. 1370–1450).
Rhodium is a rare metallic element.
General Information—Class

61. BLUE : STRAW :: RASP : (*a*. yellow, *b*. hay, **c. black**, *d*. shriek)

(**c**) A blueberry, a strawberry, a raspberry, and a blackberry are all types of berries.
General Information—Class

62. BUFFALO BILL : (**a. Cody**, *b*. James, *c*. Bowman, *d*. Broderick) :: WILD BILL : HICKOK

(**a**) Buffalo Bill Cody and Wild Bill Hickok were both famous cowboys.
General Information—Completion

63. MOURNER : TEARS :: (*a*. hypochondriac, *b*. lover, *c*. troglodyte, **d. hypocrite**) : CROCODILE TEARS

(**d**) A mourner sheds tears. A hypocrite sheds crocodile tears.
Vocabulary—Description

64. CEDE : SEED :: (*a*. run, *b*. win, **c. yield**, *d*. go) : PLANT

(**c**) To cede is to yield. To seed is to plant.
Vocabulary—Similarity/Contrast

65. INGENUOUS : (*a*. clever, **b. innocent**, *c*. pastoral, *d*. hopeful) :: INFRACTION : VIOLATION

(**b**) *Ingenuous* and *innocent* are synonyms, as are *infraction* and *violation*.
Vocabulary—Similarity/Contrast

66. SECULAR : (*a*. sacred, *b*. ecclesiastical, *c*. lay, **d. regular**) :: BISHOP : MONK

(**d**) A bishop is a member of the secular clergy. A monk is a member of the regular clergy. Secular and regular clergy are terms from the Catholic Church. Secular clergy are priests and deacons, for example, who are not bound by the vows of a monastic order. Regular clergy, to the contrary, take vows of a monastic order, such as poverty and obedience.
Humanities—Class

67. EXTIRPATE : (*a.* evade, *b.* examine, *c.* exude, ***d.* eradicate**) :: BUOY :
ENCOURAGE

(**d**) To extirpate is to eradicate. To buoy is to encourage.
Vocabulary—Similarity/Contrast

68. THREE : (*a.* Two, ***b.* Five**, *c.* Seven, *d.* Ten) :: MUSKETEERS :
LITTLE PEPPERS

(**b**) There were, so the stories go, Three Musketeers, but five little peppers.
Humanities—Completion

69. WEND : END :: (*a.* food, ***b.* wait**, *c.* tend, *d.* beginning) : ATE

(**b**) *Wend* is pronounced like end, except for the added initial *w* consonant
sound. *Wait* is pronounced like *ate*, also except for the initial *w* consonant
sound.
Nonsemantic

70. VOLT : POTENTIAL DIFFERENCE :: WATT : (*a.* resistance,
b. brightness, ***c.* power**, *d.* actual difference)

(**c**) The volt is a measure of potential difference. The watt is a measure
of power.
Natural Science—Description

71. POINT : 0 :: HEXAGON : (*a.* 1, ***b.* 2**, *c.* 3, *d.* 4)

(**b**) A point occupies 0 dimension, while a hexagon occupies 2 dimensions.
Mathematics—Description

72. (*a.* Troy, *b.* Athens, ***c.* Carthage**, *d.* Milan) : PUNIC :: SPARTA :
PELOPONNESIAN

(**c**) Carthage was one of the opposing sides in the Punic Wars (264–241
B.C., 218–201 B.C., 149–146 B.C.); the other side was Rome. Sparta was
one of the opposing sides in the Peloponnesian Wars (431–404 B.C.);
the other side was Athens and its allies. Rome and Sparta eventually won
their respective wars.
Humanities—Description

73. WINDY CITY : CHICAGO :: GOTHAM : (*a.* San Francisco, *b.* Paris,
***c.* New York City**, *d.* London)

(**c**) Windy City is another name for Chicago. Gotham is another name for
New York City.
General Information—Similarity/Contrast

74. INCANDESCENT : FILAMENT :: FLUORESCENT : (*a.* air, *b.* vacuum, *c.* energy, ***d.* phosphor**)

(**d**) The filament glows in an incandescent lamp. The phosphor glows in a fluorescent lamp.
Natural Science—Description

75. CABAL : (*a.* trivia, ***b.* plot**, *c.* wire, *d.* quibble) :: CAPABLE : COMPETENT

(**b**) *Cabal* and *plot* are synonyms, as are *capable* and *competent*.
Vocabulary—Similarity/Contrast

76. ORDER : (*a.* human, ***b.* primates**, *c.* erectus, *d.* mammalia) :: SPECIES : SAPIENS

(**b**) Human beings are of order Primates and species *sapiens*.
Natural Science—Class

77. GRENDEL : BEOWULF :: HYDRA : (*a.* Achilles, *b.* Vulcan, *c.* Atlas, ***d.* Hercules**)

(**d**) Beowulf slew Grendel; Hercules slew Hydra. Achilles was the greatest warrior of the Greeks in the Trojan War. Vulcan was the god of fire and metalworking in Roman mythology. Atlas was a titan who was forced by Zeus to carry the heavens on his shoulders.
Humanities—Description

78. $2^{-2} : 2^{-1} :: 2^2 : (a.\ 2^0,\ b.\ 2^1,\ c.\ 2^2,\ \boldsymbol{d.\ 2^3})$

(**d**) $\frac{1}{4}$ is to $\frac{1}{2}$ as 4 is to 8.
Mathematics—Class

79. DEARTH : SHORTAGE :: PLETHORA : (*a.* abundance, *b.* scarcity, ***c.* excess**, *d.* necessity)

(**c**) A dearth is a shortage. A plethora is an excess.
Vocabulary—Similarity/Contrast

80. WANDERING JEW : EARTH :: FLYING DUTCHMAN : (***a.* seas**, *b.* stars, *c.* heaven, *d.* hell)

(**a**) The Wandering Jew was doomed to wander the earth. The Flying Dutchman was doomed to wander the seas.
Humanities—Description

81. ASTROLABE : SEXTANT :: SUNDIAL : (*a.* time, ***b.* electric clock**, *c.* ruler, *d.* light rays)

    (**b**) The sextant replaced the astrolabe; the electric clock replaced the sundial.
    Natural Science—Description

82. VENAL : (*a.* rigid, *b.* cold, *c.* humorless, ***d.* mercenary**) :: VENIAL : EXCUSABLE

    (**d**) *Venal* and *mercenary* are synonyms, as are *venial* and *excusable*.
    Vocabulary—Similarity/Contrast

83. E# : F_b :: B : (*a.* Cb, ***b.* B_b**, *c.* C, *d.* B)

    (**b**) E# is a half-tone higher than F_b. B is a half-tone higher than B_b.
    Humanities—Description

84. MELIORATE : AMELIORATE :: HASTEN : (***a.* speed up**, *b.* slow down, *c.* better, *d.* worsen)

    (**a**) *Meliorate* and *ameliorate* mean the same thing, as do *hasten* and *speed up*.
    Vocabulary—Similarity/Contrast

85. MACHIAVELLI : PRINCE :: CASTIGLIONE : (*a.* Knight, ***b.* Courtier**, *c.* King, *d.* Yeoman)

    (**b**) Machiavelli is the author of *The Prince*. Castiglione is the author of *The Courtier*.
    Humanities—Description

86. NOSTRUM : (*a.* pedestal, *b.* disease, ***c.* panacea**, *d.* pabulum) :: VERACIOUS : HONEST

    (**c**) A nostrum is a panacea (remedy for all ills). A veracious person is an honest person.
    Vocabulary—Similarity/Contrast

87. DWARF : PITUITARY :: CRETIN : (*a.* endocrine, ***b.* thyroid**, *c.* thalamus, *d.* hypothalamus)

    (**b**) A dwarf has a malfunctioning pituitary gland. A cretin has a malfunctioning thyroid gland.
    Natural Science—Description

88. (*a.* barometer, ***b.* tachometer**, *c.* hydrometer, *d.* voltmeter) :: THERMOMETER :: SPEED : TEMPERATURE

    (**b**) A tachometer measures speed. A thermometer measures temperature.
    Natural Science—Description

89. FROWARD : BACKWARD :: (*a.* dilatory, *b.* upside down, **c. refractory**, *d.* right side up) : REVERSED

(**c**) *Froward* means *refractory*. *Backward* means *reversed*.
Vocabulary—Similarity/Contrast

90. LEWIN : (*a.* attribution theory, *b.* dissonance theory, **c. field theory**, *d.* psychoanalytic theory) :: JUNG : ANALYTIC THEORY

(**c**) Lewin's theory of personality is classified as a field theory. Jung's theory of personality is called analytic theory.
Social Science—Description

91. BUNSEN BURNER : GAS :: AUTOCLAVE : (*a.* oil, *b.* electricity, **c. steam**, *d.* solar energy)

(**c**) A Bunsen burner produces heat through gas. An autoclave produces heat through steam.
Natural Science—Description

92. BACH : (***a.* invention**, *b.* symphony, *c.* waltz, *d.* polyphony) :: CHOPIN : MAZURKA

(**a**) Bach was a composer of inventions. Chopin was a composer of mazurkas. Mazurkas are Polish folk dances; inventions are short pieces developing a single theme contrapuntally.
Humanities—Description

93. BANISHMENT : COUNTRY :: DEFENESTRATION : (*a.* ceiling, *b.* floor, *c.* city, ***d.* window**)

(**d**) Banishment occurs when someone is thrown out of a country. Defenestration occurs when someone is thrown out of a window.
Vocabulary—Description

94. CADMEAN : (*a.* Caesarian, *b.* Augustan, *c.* Napoleonic, ***d.* Pyrrhic**) :: EXPENSIVE : COSTLY

(**d**) Both a Cadmean and a Pyrrhic victory are excessively (costly) types of victory. The armed men who sprang from the teeth of the dragon sown by Cadmus killed each other. A Pyrrhic victory is so called because the army of King Pyrrhus of Epirus suffered enormous losses during the Pyrrhic War in which the Romans were eventually defeated at Heraclea (280 B.C.) and Asculum (279 B.C.).
Humanities—Similarity/Contrast

95. MOSES : (*a.* Abraham, *b.* Joseph, ***c.* Joshua**, *d.* Gideon) :: ROOSEVELT : TRUMAN

(**c**) Joshua succeeded Moses as leader of the Israelites. Truman succeeded Roosevelt as president of the United States. Abraham is regarded by Jews as the founder of the Hebrew people (via his son Isaac) and by Muslims as the founder of the Muslim people (via his son Ishmael). Joseph was one of Jacob's sons who was sold into slavery by his brothers; Joseph was also the name of Mary's husband. Gideon appears in the Book of Judges and defeated the Midianites.
Humanities—Description

96. PARASYMPATHETIC : (***a.* sympathetic**, *b.* protosympathetic, *c.* asympathetic, *d.* prosympathetic) :: SLOW DOWN : SPEED UP

(**a**) The parasympathetic nervous system slows down the heartbeat, while the sympathetic nervous system speeds it up.
Natural Science—Description

97. (*a.* Galileo, *b.* Newton, *c.* Galen, ***d.* Ptolemy**) : COPERNICUS :: GEOCENTRIC : HELIOCENTRIC

(**d**) Ptolemy is known for his geocentric theory of the solar system, while Copernicus is known for his heliocentric theory. Newton is known for describing universal gravitation; Galen was a Greek physician and one of the first experimental physiologists. Galileo was an Italian physicist and astronomer who improved the telescope and is called the "father of modern observational astronomy." He was a supporter of Copernicanism.
Natural Science—Description

98. TOSCANINI : (*a.* Fournier, ***b.* Ormandy**, *c.* Goodman, *d.* Heifetz) :: VAN CLIBURN : RUBENSTEIN

(**b**) Toscanini and Ormandy attained fame as conductors; Van Cliburn and Rubenstein became famous as pianists.
Humanities—Class

99. RICHELIEU : CARDINAL :: (*a.* Henry IV, ***b.* Louis XIII**, *c.* Francis I, *d.* Napoleon III) : KING

(**b**) Richelieu (1585–1642) was cardinal when Louis XIII (1601–1643) was king.
Humanities—Description

100. JAMES : FUNCTIONALISM :: (*a.* Dewey, ***b.* Levi-Strauss**, *c.* Watson, *d.* Klineberg) : STRUCTURALISM

    (**b**) James was a functionalist; Levi-Strauss, a structuralist. Dewey was a pragmatist and functionalist. John B. Watson was a behaviorist. Klineberg was an anthropologist.
    Social Science—Description

101. FAUST : DR. FAUSTUS :: (***a.* Goethe**, *b.* Mr. Marlowe, *c.* Hyde, *d.* Kafka) : MARLOWE

    (**a**) *Faust* was written by Goethe just as *Dr. Faustus* was written by Marlowe.
    Humanities—Description

102. RHODESIA : (*a.* Indonesia, ***b.* Zimbabwe**, *c.* Namibia, *d.* Israel) :: BURMA : MYANMAR

    (**b**) Rhodesia is the former name of the country today known as Zimbabwe. Burma is the former name of present-day Myanmar. Indonesia was previously known as Dutch East Indies. Namibia was formerly known as German Southwest Africa.
    General Information—Similarity/Contrast

103. SALT : WATER :: (***a.* desalinate**, *b.* desaltify, *c.* purify, *d.* reduce) : DEHYDRATE

    (**a**) To reduce salt content is to desalinate. To reduce water content is to dehydrate.
    Vocabulary—Description

104. HART : DEER :: COLT : (*a.* stallion, *b.* horse, *c.* filly, ***d.* foal**)

    (**d**) A hart is a male deer, and a colt is a male foal.
    Vocabulary—Class

105. (*a.* liver, ***b.* brain**, *c.* ear, *d.* pancreas) : HEART :: LOBE : CHAMBER

    (**b**) The brain is made up of separate lobes, while the heart is made up of separate chambers.
    General Information—Part/Whole

106. NADIR : (*a.* penultimate, *b.* depth, ***c.* zenith**, *d.* low) :: STYGIAN : BRIGHT

    (**c**) The nadir, or lowest point, is the opposite of the zenith. Likewise, stygian, meaning dark and dismal, is the opposite of bright.
    Vocabulary—Similarity/Contrast

107. 32 : FAHRENHEIT :: (*a.* –32, *b.* 100, *c.* 10, ***d.* 0**) : CELSIUS

(**d**) 32 degrees Fahrenheit is the point at which water freezes just as 0 degrees Celsius is the point at which water freezes.
Natural Science—Equality/Negation

108. GRAPE : RAISIN :: PLUM : (*a.* date, *b.* fig, ***c.* prune**, *d.* currant)

(**c**) A dried grape is called a raisin and a dried plum is called a prune.
General Information—Class

109. NORTH : CANCER :: SOUTH : (*a.* Virgo, ***b.* Capricorn**, *c.* Sagittarius, *d.* Equator)

(**b**) North of the equator lies the Tropic of Cancer and south of it lies the Tropic of Capricorn (lines of altitude about 23° north and south of the equator).
General Information—Description

110. EVELYN : DACTYL :: (***a.* Michelle**, *b.* Holly, *c.* Erica, *d.* Emily) : IAMB

(**a**) Evelyn is a name whose metric foot is a dactyl. Michelle is a name whose metric foot is an iamb. A dactyl is a metrical foot consisting of one stressed and two unstressed syllables. An iamb is a metrical foot that consists of one unstressed and one stressed syllable.
Humanities—Description

111. MOZART : (***a.* Violin**, *b.* Flute, *c.* Viola, *d.* Cello) :: BACH : ORGAN

(**a**) Mozart was most accomplished instrumentally on the violin. Bach was most accomplished on the organ.
Humanities—Description

112. (*a.* pizzicato, *b.* staccato, *c.* diminuendo, ***d.* piano**) : FORTE :: SOFT : LOUD

(**d**) The musical term *piano* indicates that one should play softly, whereas *forte* directs one to play loudly. A *pizzicato* is a passage played by plucking strings. *Staccato* means that notes are being played in a detached manner that separates them from each other. *Diminuendo* means decreasing the volume of a played passage.
Humanities—Similarity/Contrast

113. INDIA : HINDUISM :: INDONESIA : (*a.* Buddhism, *b.* Confucianism, *c.* Christianity, ***d.* Islam**)

(**d**) India is the country with the greatest population of people practicing Hinduism, whereas Indonesia is the country with the greatest population of people practicing Islam.
General Information—Description

114. OBOE : REED :: (***a. viola***, *b.* bassoon, *c.* timpani, *d.* french horn) : STRING

    (**a**) The vibration of a reed produces the sound of an oboe, just as the vibration of a string produces the sound of a viola.
    Humanities—Part/Whole

115. MORE : (***a. Utopia***, *b.* Paradise Lost, *c.* 1984, *d.* On the Beach) :: HUXLEY : BRAVE NEW WORLD

    (**a**) Aldous Huxley wrote a futuristic novel entitled *Brave New World*. Thomas More wrote about a ficticious island in a book entitled *Utopia*.
    Humanities—Description

116. BASEBALL : BAT :: TABLE TENNIS : (*a.* mallet, ***b. paddle***, *c.* stick, *d.* racquet)

    (**b**) In baseball, the ball is hit with a bat. In table tennis, the ball is hit with a paddle.
    General Information—Description

117. ETYMOLOGY : ENTOMOLOGY :: (*a.* letters, *b.* arachnids, *c.* disease, ***d. words***) : INSECTS

    (**d**) Etymology is the study of words just as entomology is the study of insects.
    Vocabulary—Description

118. ADAM : (***a. Eden***, *b.* Israel, *c.* heaven, *d.* hell) :: ROMEO : VERONA

    (**a**) Adam was banished from Eden and Romeo was banished from Verona.
    Humanities—Description

119. $8^{1/3} : 25^{1/2}$ :: (*a.* 25^2, *b.* $100^{1/3}$, ***c.*** $\mathbf{100^{1/2}}$, *d.* $16^{1/2}$) : $625^{1/2}$

    (**c**) The cube root of eight is 2, and the square root of 25 is 5, creating a ratio of 2 to 5. Similarly, the square root of 100 is 10 and the square root of 625 is 25, creating a ratio of 2 to 5.
    Mathematics—Equality/Negation

120. AUGMENTED THIRD : DIMINISHED THIRD :: FOUR : (***a. two-and-a-half***, *b.* three, *c.* two, *d.* three-and-a-half)

    (**a**) An augmented third and a diminished third are one-and-a-half units apart, as are the numbers four and two-and-a-half.
    Humanities—Equality/Negation

PRACTICE TEST 3

Item Classification Chart

		RELATIONSHIP					
C O N T E N T		Similarity/ Contrast	Description	Class	Completion	Part/ Whole	Equality/ Negation	Nonsemantic
	Vocabulary	9, 15, 28, 29, 30, 42, 45, 49, 51, 56, 58, 59, 64, 65, 67, 75, 79, 82, 84, 86, 89, 106	63, 93, 103, 117	104				
	General Information	3, 4, 6, 16, 24, 54, 73, 102	1, 2, 5, 7, 12, 17, 18, 19, 25, 27, 41, 44, 47, 48, 109, 113, 116	38, 40, 60, 61, 108	21, 33, 39, 62	105		
	Humanities	94, 112	23, 32, 43, 46, 50, 57, 72, 77, 80, 83, 85, 92, 95, 99, 101, 110, 111, 115, 118	8, 36, 66, 98	68	114	120	
	Social Science		13, 37, 90, 100					
	Natural Science		22, 26, 70, 74, 81, 87, 88, 91, 96, 97	14, 34, 53, 76	11		55, 107	
	Mathematics		10, 31, 71	78			35, 119	
	Nonsemantic							20, 52, 69

Answer Sheet
PRACTICE TEST 4

1 Ⓐ Ⓑ Ⓒ Ⓓ   31 Ⓐ Ⓑ Ⓒ Ⓓ   61 Ⓐ Ⓑ Ⓒ Ⓓ   91 Ⓐ Ⓑ Ⓒ Ⓓ
2 Ⓐ Ⓑ Ⓒ Ⓓ   32 Ⓐ Ⓑ Ⓒ Ⓓ   62 Ⓐ Ⓑ Ⓒ Ⓓ   92 Ⓐ Ⓑ Ⓒ Ⓓ
3 Ⓐ Ⓑ Ⓒ Ⓓ   33 Ⓐ Ⓑ Ⓒ Ⓓ   63 Ⓐ Ⓑ Ⓒ Ⓓ   93 Ⓐ Ⓑ Ⓒ Ⓓ
4 Ⓐ Ⓑ Ⓒ Ⓓ   34 Ⓐ Ⓑ Ⓒ Ⓓ   64 Ⓐ Ⓑ Ⓒ Ⓓ   94 Ⓐ Ⓑ Ⓒ Ⓓ
5 Ⓐ Ⓑ Ⓒ Ⓓ   35 Ⓐ Ⓑ Ⓒ Ⓓ   65 Ⓐ Ⓑ Ⓒ Ⓓ   95 Ⓐ Ⓑ Ⓒ Ⓓ
6 Ⓐ Ⓑ Ⓒ Ⓓ   36 Ⓐ Ⓑ Ⓒ Ⓓ   66 Ⓐ Ⓑ Ⓒ Ⓓ   96 Ⓐ Ⓑ Ⓒ Ⓓ
7 Ⓐ Ⓑ Ⓒ Ⓓ   37 Ⓐ Ⓑ Ⓒ Ⓓ   67 Ⓐ Ⓑ Ⓒ Ⓓ   97 Ⓐ Ⓑ Ⓒ Ⓓ
8 Ⓐ Ⓑ Ⓒ Ⓓ   38 Ⓐ Ⓑ Ⓒ Ⓓ   68 Ⓐ Ⓑ Ⓒ Ⓓ   98 Ⓐ Ⓑ Ⓒ Ⓓ
9 Ⓐ Ⓑ Ⓒ Ⓓ   39 Ⓐ Ⓑ Ⓒ Ⓓ   69 Ⓐ Ⓑ Ⓒ Ⓓ   99 Ⓐ Ⓑ Ⓒ Ⓓ
10 Ⓐ Ⓑ Ⓒ Ⓓ   40 Ⓐ Ⓑ Ⓒ Ⓓ   70 Ⓐ Ⓑ Ⓒ Ⓓ   100 Ⓐ Ⓑ Ⓒ Ⓓ
11 Ⓐ Ⓑ Ⓒ Ⓓ   41 Ⓐ Ⓑ Ⓒ Ⓓ   71 Ⓐ Ⓑ Ⓒ Ⓓ   101 Ⓐ Ⓑ Ⓒ Ⓓ
12 Ⓐ Ⓑ Ⓒ Ⓓ   42 Ⓐ Ⓑ Ⓒ Ⓓ   72 Ⓐ Ⓑ Ⓒ Ⓓ   102 Ⓐ Ⓑ Ⓒ Ⓓ
13 Ⓐ Ⓑ Ⓒ Ⓓ   43 Ⓐ Ⓑ Ⓒ Ⓓ   73 Ⓐ Ⓑ Ⓒ Ⓓ   103 Ⓐ Ⓑ Ⓒ Ⓓ
14 Ⓐ Ⓑ Ⓒ Ⓓ   44 Ⓐ Ⓑ Ⓒ Ⓓ   74 Ⓐ Ⓑ Ⓒ Ⓓ   104 Ⓐ Ⓑ Ⓒ Ⓓ
15 Ⓐ Ⓑ Ⓒ Ⓓ   45 Ⓐ Ⓑ Ⓒ Ⓓ   75 Ⓐ Ⓑ Ⓒ Ⓓ   105 Ⓐ Ⓑ Ⓒ Ⓓ
16 Ⓐ Ⓑ Ⓒ Ⓓ   46 Ⓐ Ⓑ Ⓒ Ⓓ   76 Ⓐ Ⓑ Ⓒ Ⓓ   106 Ⓐ Ⓑ Ⓒ Ⓓ
17 Ⓐ Ⓑ Ⓒ Ⓓ   47 Ⓐ Ⓑ Ⓒ Ⓓ   77 Ⓐ Ⓑ Ⓒ Ⓓ   107 Ⓐ Ⓑ Ⓒ Ⓓ
18 Ⓐ Ⓑ Ⓒ Ⓓ   48 Ⓐ Ⓑ Ⓒ Ⓓ   78 Ⓐ Ⓑ Ⓒ Ⓓ   108 Ⓐ Ⓑ Ⓒ Ⓓ
19 Ⓐ Ⓑ Ⓒ Ⓓ   49 Ⓐ Ⓑ Ⓒ Ⓓ   79 Ⓐ Ⓑ Ⓒ Ⓓ   109 Ⓐ Ⓑ Ⓒ Ⓓ
20 Ⓐ Ⓑ Ⓒ Ⓓ   50 Ⓐ Ⓑ Ⓒ Ⓓ   80 Ⓐ Ⓑ Ⓒ Ⓓ   110 Ⓐ Ⓑ Ⓒ Ⓓ
21 Ⓐ Ⓑ Ⓒ Ⓓ   51 Ⓐ Ⓑ Ⓒ Ⓓ   81 Ⓐ Ⓑ Ⓒ Ⓓ   111 Ⓐ Ⓑ Ⓒ Ⓓ
22 Ⓐ Ⓑ Ⓒ Ⓓ   52 Ⓐ Ⓑ Ⓒ Ⓓ   82 Ⓐ Ⓑ Ⓒ Ⓓ   112 Ⓐ Ⓑ Ⓒ Ⓓ
23 Ⓐ Ⓑ Ⓒ Ⓓ   53 Ⓐ Ⓑ Ⓒ Ⓓ   83 Ⓐ Ⓑ Ⓒ Ⓓ   113 Ⓐ Ⓑ Ⓒ Ⓓ
24 Ⓐ Ⓑ Ⓒ Ⓓ   54 Ⓐ Ⓑ Ⓒ Ⓓ   84 Ⓐ Ⓑ Ⓒ Ⓓ   114 Ⓐ Ⓑ Ⓒ Ⓓ
25 Ⓐ Ⓑ Ⓒ Ⓓ   55 Ⓐ Ⓑ Ⓒ Ⓓ   85 Ⓐ Ⓑ Ⓒ Ⓓ   115 Ⓐ Ⓑ Ⓒ Ⓓ
26 Ⓐ Ⓑ Ⓒ Ⓓ   56 Ⓐ Ⓑ Ⓒ Ⓓ   86 Ⓐ Ⓑ Ⓒ Ⓓ   116 Ⓐ Ⓑ Ⓒ Ⓓ
27 Ⓐ Ⓑ Ⓒ Ⓓ   57 Ⓐ Ⓑ Ⓒ Ⓓ   87 Ⓐ Ⓑ Ⓒ Ⓓ   117 Ⓐ Ⓑ Ⓒ Ⓓ
28 Ⓐ Ⓑ Ⓒ Ⓓ   58 Ⓐ Ⓑ Ⓒ Ⓓ   88 Ⓐ Ⓑ Ⓒ Ⓓ   118 Ⓐ Ⓑ Ⓒ Ⓓ
29 Ⓐ Ⓑ Ⓒ Ⓓ   59 Ⓐ Ⓑ Ⓒ Ⓓ   89 Ⓐ Ⓑ Ⓒ Ⓓ   119 Ⓐ Ⓑ Ⓒ Ⓓ
30 Ⓐ Ⓑ Ⓒ Ⓓ   60 Ⓐ Ⓑ Ⓒ Ⓓ   90 Ⓐ Ⓑ Ⓒ Ⓓ   120 Ⓐ Ⓑ Ⓒ Ⓓ

Practice Test 4

Directions: In each of the following questions, you will find three initial terms and, in parentheses, four answer options designated *a*, *b*, *c*, and *d*. You are to select from the four answer options the one that best completes the analogy with the three initial terms. To record your answers, use the answer sheet provided.

Time: 60 minutes

1. POLAND : POLISH :: (*a.* Holland, *b.* Dublin, *c.* Denmark, *d.* Dansk) : DANISH

2. UNION : (*a.* green, *b.* brown, *c.* blue, *d.* white) :: CONFEDERACY : GRAY

3. ARTICLE : (*a.* preposition, *b.* conjunction, *c.* adjective, *d.* verb) :: THE : AND

4. SAFETY : 2 :: TOUCHDOWN : (*a.* 2, *b.* 4, *c.* 6, *d.* 8)

5. CIRCLE : ELLIPSE :: SQUARE : (*a.* triangle, *b.* rectangle, *c.* pentagon, *d.* hexagon)

6. BIRD : (*a.* nest, *b.* worm, *c.* wings, *d.* fly) :: GENIE : MAGIC CARPET

7. FOXHOLE : (*a.* foxes, *b.* gunfire, *c.* discovery, *d.* earthquakes) :: RAINCOAT : RAIN

8. FOOLISH : OWL :: (*a.* timid, *b.* large, *c.* wise, *d.* temperamental) : LION

9. SINBAD : (*a.* sailor, *b.* squire, *c.* sinner, *d.* poet) :: ARTHUR : KING

10. SOLOMON : WISE :: NERO : (*a.* stupid, *b.* bold, *c.* just, *d.* cruel)

11. GRAPE : VINE :: RUBBER : (*a.* tree, *b.* conifer, *c.* root, *d.* leaf)

12. (*a.* Georgia, *b.* Massachusetts, *c.* New Jersey, *d.* Ohio) : MIDDLE ATLANTIC : VERMONT : NEW ENGLAND

13. BALD : HAIR :: ALBINO : (*a.* height, *b.* pain, *c.* sight, *d.* pigment)

14. BOW : (*a.* arrow, *b.* curtsey, *c.* stern, *d.* fore) :: FRONT : REAR

15. MONOGYNY : POLYGYNY :: ONE : (*a.* none, *b.* two, *c.* eight, *d.* many)

16. ATTA : AL-SHEHHI :: JARRAH : (*a.* Mohammed, *b.* bin Laden, *c.* Binalshibh, *d.* Atef)

17. (*a.* secret codes, *b.* inscriptions on church vaults, *c.* science fiction, *d.* religious rituals) : CRYPTOGRAPHY :: DICTIONARIES : LEXICOGRAPHY

18. $E = mc^2$: EINSTEIN :: $C^2 = A^2 + B^2$: (*a.* Bernoulli, *b.* Cauchy, *c.* Descartes, *d.* Pythagoras)

19. GREEK : GREEK :: ROMAN : (*a.* Indo-European, *b.* Latin, *c.* Mediterranean, *d.* Romanish)

20. (*a.* Jesus, *b.* hell, *c.* heaven, *d.* Satan) : CHRISTIANITY :: NIRVANA : BUDDHISM

21. U.S. CALENDAR : U.S. FISCAL CALENDAR :: JANUARY : (*a.* December, *b.* March, *c.* July, *d.* September)

22. PHOTOMETER : (*a.* light, *b.* distance, *c.* magnetism, *d.* velocity) :: AUDIOMETER : SOUND

23. (*a.* believable, *b.* wrong, *c.* fanciful, *d.* humorous) : INCREDIBLE :: AUGMENT : DIMINISH

24. INFINITIVE : (*a.* having eaten, *b.* to sleep, *c.* has tried, *d.* to the store) :: PARTICIPLE : WALKING

25. MARX : COMMUNISM :: (*a.* Hamilton, *b.* Lenin, *c.* Smith, *d.* Davis) : CAPITALISM

26. (*a.* Iambic, *b.* Doric, *c.* Spartan, *d.* Grecian) : CORINTHIAN :: SONATA : CONCERTO

27. SOCCER : BALL :: (*a.* cricket, *b.* rugby, *c.* hockey, *d.* lacrosse) : PUCK

28. (*a.* sheep, *b.* plasma, *c.* vulture, *d.* harass) : BLOOD :: DOG : HOUND

29. (*a.* hawk, *b.* owl, *c.* bluejay, *d.* ostrich) : NOCTURNAL :: ROBIN : DIURNAL

30. PHLEGM : PHLEGMATIC :: BILE : (*a.* bilious, *b.* billiard, *c.* binding, *d.* bilabial)

31. HEAVY-HANDED : (*a.* uncoordinated, *b.* tactless, *c.* strong, *d.* coordinated) :: HEAVY-FOOTED : PLODDING

32. PALEFACE : WHITE :: BLUENOSE : (*a.* frigid, *b.* tough, *c.* unkind, *d.* puritanical)

33. PROTON : NEUTRON :: POSITIVE : (*a.* negative, *b.* uncharged, *c.* positive, *d.* nucleonic)

34. SPHINX : (*a.* pterodactyl, *b.* dodo, *c.* vulture, *d.* phoenix) :: LION : EAGLE

35. ANDAMAN : ACEH :: SRI LANKA : (*a.* Bali, *b.* Phuket, *c.* Fiji, *d.* Guam)

36. RADIUS : 4 :: DIAMETER : (*a.* 16, *b.* 8, *c.* 87π, *d.* 167π)

37. PIKE : (*a.* sturgeon, *b.* lion, *c.* whale, *d.* buffalo) :: COW : PIG

38. WASSERMANN : (*a.* heart disease, *b.* diabetes, *c.* syphilis, *d.* lung cancer) :: PAP : CERVICAL CANCER

39. COMPLEMENTARY : SUPPLEMENTARY :: (*a.* 0, *b.* 45, *c.* 90, *d.* 360) : 180

40. E.G. : FOR EXAMPLE :: VIZ. : (*a.* namely, *b.* except for, *c.* according to, *d.* generally)

41. GRAPE : WINE :: (*a.* apple, *b.* potato, *c.* pomegranate, *d.* malt) : VODKA

42. RISING : FALLING :: (*a.* bull, *b.* bird, *c.* sparrow, *d.* antelope) : BEAR

43. XX : FEMALE :: (*a.* XY, *b.* YY, *c.* XZ, *d.* ZZ) : MALE

44. RESPECT : (*a.* love, *b.* protect, *c.* revere, *d.* obey) :: DISLIKE : HATE

45. PARLIAMENT : LORDS :: (*a.* House of Representatives, *b.* Congress, *c.* White House, *d.* Supreme Court) : SENATE

46. (*a.* parsing, *b.* gender, *c.* case, *d.* declension) : NOUN :: CONJUGATION : VERB

47. MC : MD :: MMCC : (*a.* MCM, *b.* MGM, *c.* MDM, *d.* MMM)

48. (*a.* dour, *b.* caustic, *c.* sweet, *d.* mild) : ACRID :: BITTER : ACRIMONIOUS

49. PORCINE : (*a.* porcupine, *b.* goat, *c.* dog, *d.* pig) :: FELINE : CAT

50. TIPPECANOE : AND TYLER TOO :: FIFTY-FOUR FORTY : (*a.* forever, *b.* or fight, *c.* and forward, *d.* to fortune)

51. IMPEACH : (*a.* prove the guilt of, *b.* overturn, *c.* acquit, *d.* accuse) :: CONVICT : FIND GUILTY

52. CITY OF SEVEN HILLS : ROME :: CITY OF GOD : (*a.* heaven, *b.* Jerusalem, *c.* Bethlehem, *d.* Jericho)

53. WOOD : PAPER :: LATEX : (*a.* cotton, *b.* plastic, *c.* rayon, *d.* rubber)

54. TEXTILE : RAYON :: GEM : (*a.* sapphire, *b.* diamond, *c.* spinel, *d.* quartz)

55. SIAM : (*a.* Mongolia, *b.* China, *c.* Thailand, *d.* Nepal) :: PERSIA : IRAN

56. HABEAS CORPUS : LAW :: EXEUNT OMNES : (*a.* medicine, *b.* drama, *c.* law, *d.* political theory)

57. PENTHOUSE APARTMENT : TOP FLOOR :: DUPLEX APARTMENT : (*a.* two rooms, *b.* two floors, *c.* two bedrooms, *d.* two persons)

58. XENOPHOBIA : (*a.* foreigners, *b.* death, *c.* insanity, *d.* live burial) :: CLAUSTROPHOBIA : CONFINED PLACES

59. LOCKJAW : TETANUS :: HYDROPHOBIA : (*a.* encephalitis, *b.* malaria, *c.* syphilis, *d.* rabies)

60. ENGLISH : CANADA :: (*a.* Italian, *b.* Portuguese, *c.* Brazilian, *d.* French) : BRAZIL

61. MITIGATE : ASSUAGE :: MODERATE : (*a.* lessen, *b.* make worse, *c.* disprove, *d.* approve)

62. $1^0 : 1^{10}$ :: 10^0 : (*a.* 10^0, *b.* 10^1, *c.* 10^2, *d.* 10^{10})

63. PUSILLANIMOUS : AUDACIOUS :: (*a.* brave, *b.* purposive, *c.* cowardly, *d.* evanescent) : BOLD

64. HANNIBAL : (*a.* Theseus, *b.* Scipio, *c.* Cicero, *d.* Marcion) :: NAPOLEON : WELLINGTON

65. EPITOME : (*a.* monologue, *b.* prevarication, *c.* summary, *d.* diatribe) :: PREFACE : PROLOGUE

66. (*a.* wave, *b.* radian, *c.* alpha, *d.* roentgen) : RADIATION :: MINUTE : TIME

67. VERACIOUS : (*a.* repeated, *b.* horizontal, *c.* diagonal, *d.* truthful) :: CONTINUAL : INCESSANT

68. SOLAR : SUN :: (*a.* lunar, *b.* diurnal, *c.* stellar, *d.* nocturnal) : MOON

69. LINCOLN STEFFENS : POLITICAL MACHINES :: UPTON SINCLAIR : (*a.* meat-packing industry, *b.* financial speculators, *c.* railroad magnates, *d.* patent medicine quacks)

70. FAMILY : HOMINIDAE :: (*a.* sapiens, *b.* species, *c.* genus, *d.* class) : HOMO

71. OVERWEENING : (*a.* conceited, *b.* modest, *c.* spoiled, *d.* underprotected) :: BLUNT : SHARP

72. HEARSAY : GOSSIP :: GAINSAY : (*a.* oppose, *b.* protect, *c.* lose, *d.* take)

73. (*a.* thin, *b.* analogy, *c.* happy, *d.* fat) : FIAT :: SMILE : SIMILE

74. ROUNDHEAD : SHORT HAIR :: (*a.* Tory, *b.* Whig, *c.* Royalist, *d.* Cavalier) : LONG HAIR

75. EUGENICS : HEREDITY :: (*a.* euthanasia, *b.* euthenics, *c.* mnemonics, *d.* dialectics) : ENVIRONMENT

76. THERMO : (*a.* cryo, *b.* iso, *c.* crypto, *d.* paleo) :: HOT : COLD

77. (*a.* North Carolina, *b.* South Carolina, *c.* Georgia, *d.* Florida) : OGLETHORPE :: PENNSYLVANIA : PENN

78. BANEFUL : (*a.* baleful, *b.* salutary, *c.* promiscuous, *d.* remorseful) :: PERSONABLE : HANDSOME

79. WERTHEIMER : GESTALT :: (*a.* Watson, *b.* Köhler, *c.* Koffka, *d.* Piaget) : BEHAVIORIST

80. (*a.* depilate, *b.* dampen, *c.* derogate, *d.* desiccate) : DRY :: MOISTEN : WET

81. GLUCOSE : (*a.* comatose, *b.* malactose, *c.* lactose, *d.* adipose) :: SUCROSE : FRUCTOSE

82. ABLE : MELBA :: (*a*. colt, *b*. peach, *c*. era, *d*. willing) : MARE

83. (*a*. Mars, *b*. Jupiter, *c*. Venus, *d*. Pluto) : PROSERPINA :: ZEUS : HERA

84. FLEET STREET : (*a*. press, *b*. police, *c*. amusement, *d*. high fashion) :: DOWNING STREET : GOVERNMENT

85. ARTUR RUBINSTEIN : PIANO :: ISAAC STERN : (*a*. piano, *b*. violin, *c*. trumpet, *d*. oboe)

86. DURKHEIM : (*a*. Homocide, *b*. Matricide, *c*. Suicide, *d*. Genocide) :: BECKER : OUTSIDERS

87. JOHN WESLEY : METHODIST :: MARY BAKER EDDY : (*a*. Presbyterian, *b*. Baha'i, *c*. Jehovah's Witness, *d*. Christian Science)

88. BACH : BAROQUE :: GRIEG : (*a*. classical, *b*. modern, *c*. romantic, *d*. medieval)

89. (*a*. Husserl, *b*. Heidegger, *c*. Comte, *d*. Camus) : POSITIVISM :: SARTRE : EXISTENTIALISM

90. F# : Gb :: B : (*a*. C_b, *b*. A_b, *c*. G#, *d*. G_b)

91. SECOND : THIRD :: (*a*. clergy, *b*. king, *c*. commoners, *d*. nobility) : BOURGEOISIE

92. ALEXANDER : GREAT :: JULIAN : (*a*. Ingenious, *b*. Meek, *c*. Bold, *d*. Apostate)

93. (*a*. Helen, *b*. Jezebel, *c*. Una, *d*. Archimago) : DUESSA :: GOOD : EVIL

94. D : R × T :: (*a*. A, *b*. C, *c*. F, *d*. H) : M × A

95. PURLOINED : (*a*. Melville, *b*. Doyle, *c*. Poe, *d*. Conrad) :: SCARLET : HAWTHORNE

96. PROPHASE : METAPHASE :: ANAPHASE : (*a*. meiophase, *b*. telophase, *c*. mitophase, *d*. protophase)

97. NEWBERY : (*a*. Wohlenberg, *b*. Caldecott, *c*. Pulitzer, *d*. Thompsen) :: STORY : ARTWORK

98. COUNTESS AURELIA : THE MADWOMAN OF CHAILLOT :: (*a*. Lear, *b*. Othello, *c*. Antonio, *d*. Iago) : THE MERCHANT OF VENICE

99. PICASSO : GUERNICA :: (*a.* Manet, *b.* Raphael, *c.* David, *d.* Leger) : LUNCHEON ON THE GRASS

100. RACINE : MOLIÈRE :: SOPHOCLES : (*a.* Zeno, *b.* Aristophanes, *c.* Plato, *d.* Aristotle)

101. (*a.* Queen Victoria, *b.* Queen Virginia, *c.* Queen Elizabeth, *d.* Queen Mary) : VIRGINIA :: KING GEORGE : GEORGIA

102. MITOSIS : MEIOSIS :: (*a.* 1, *b.* 2, *c.* 4, *d.* 8) : 4

103. DAGGER : STAR :: (*a.* rune, *b.* allograph, *c.* knife, *d.* obelisk) : ASTERISK

104. MISER : (*a.* chary, *b.* mercurial, *c.* acquisitive, *d.* munificent) :: GLUTTON : ABSTEMIOUS

105. (*a.* pork, *b.* sweet, *c.* appetizer, *d.* vegetable) : SWEETMEAT :: FRUIT : BREADFRUIT

106. $2\pi r^2$: $\pi(2r)^2$ :: LW : (*a.* (1/2)LW, *b.* LW, *c.* 2LW, *d.* 4LW)

107. (*a.* hatred, *b.* naiveté, *c.* envy, *d.* sickness) : SORROW :: GREEN : BLUE

108. MOHS : HARDNESS :: RICHTER : (*a.* magnitude, *b.* earthquake, *c.* quality, *d.* extremity)

109. FROGS : SEAGULL :: (*a.* Shakespeare, *b.* Marlowe, *c.* Wilde, *d.* Aristophanes) : CHEKHOV

110. INDIA : PAKISTAN :: PAKISTAN : (*a.* Kashmir, *b.* Bangladesh, *c.* Nepal, *d.* Sri Lanka)

111. ORGAN : ORGANELLE :: LIVER : (*a.* vacuole, *b.* pancreas, *c.* kidney, *d.* cell)

112. MASS AND ENERGY : (*a.* Bernoulli, *b.* Newton, *c.* Gauss, *d.* Einstein) :: VOLUME AND DISPLACEMENT : ARCHIMEDES

113. DOGS : PEAS :: PAVLOV : (*a.* Darwin, *b.* Gauss, *c.* Curie, *d.* Mendel)

114. (*a.* King, *b.* Martha, *c.* Reverend, *d.* Priest) : CARVER :: MARTIN LUTHER : GEORGE WASHINGTON

115. SESAME SEEDS : TAHINI :: PEANUTS : (*a.* roots, *b.* shell, *c.* peanut butter, *d.* oil)

116. BASS : (*a.* clarinet, *b.* viola, *c.* cello, *d.* trumpet) :: TREBLE : FLUTE

117. MAL : BEN :: ANTI : (*a.* un, *b.* inter, *c.* pro, *d.* pre)

118. (*a.* meat packing, *b.* clear cutting, *c.* poaching, *d.* iron mining) : PESTICIDES :: THE JUNGLE : SILENT SPRING

119. HANUKKAH : DIVALI :: JUDAISM : (*a.* Buddhism, *b.* Hinduism, *c.* Zoroastrianism, *d.* Islam)

120. SQUARE ROOT : SQUARE :: (*a.* dividend, *b.* root, *c.* log, *d.* integral) : DERIVATIVE

Answer Key
PRACTICE TEST 4

1.	C	31.	B	61.	A	91.	D
2.	C	32.	D	62.	A	92.	D
3.	B	33.	B	63.	C	93.	C
4.	C	34.	D	64.	B	94.	C
5.	B	35.	B	65.	C	95.	C
6.	C	36.	B	66.	D	96.	B
7.	B	37.	A	67.	D	97.	B
8.	A	38.	C	68.	A	98.	C
9.	A	39.	C	69.	A	99.	A
10.	D	40.	A	70.	C	100.	B
11.	A	41.	B	71.	B	101.	C
12.	C	42.	A	72.	A	102.	B
13.	D	43.	A	73.	D	103.	D
14.	C	44.	C	74.	D	104.	D
15.	D	45.	B	75.	B	105.	B
16.	C	46.	D	76.	A	106.	C
17.	A	47.	D	77.	C	107.	C
18.	D	48.	B	78.	A	108.	A
19.	B	49.	D	79.	A	109.	D
20.	C	50.	B	80.	D	110.	B
21.	C	51.	D	81.	C	111.	A
22.	A	52.	A	82.	C	112.	D
23.	A	53.	D	83.	D	113.	D
24.	B	54.	C	84.	A	114.	A
25.	C	55.	C	85.	B	115.	C
26.	B	56.	B	86.	C	116.	C
27.	C	57.	B	87.	D	117.	C
28.	A	58.	A	88.	C	118.	A
29.	B	59.	D	89.	C	119.	B
30.	A	60.	B	90.	A	120.	D

ANSWER EXPLANATIONS FOR PRACTICE TEST 4

In the following, explanations concerning the correct response are in a large font. Explanations regarding distracters (incorrect responses) that are not self-explaining or could be misinterpreted are in a smaller font in order to highlight the explanations of the answers that are correct.

1. POLAND : POLISH :: (*a.* Holland, *b.* Dublin, **c. Denmark**, *d.* Dansk) : DANISH

    (**c**) A Polish person is from Poland; a Danish person is from Denmark.
    General Information—Description

2. UNION : (*a.* green, *b.* brown, **c. blue**, *d.* white) :: CONFEDERACY : GRAY

    (**c**) During the Civil War, Union soldiers wore blue uniforms and soldiers of the Confederacy wore gray uniforms.
    Humanities—Description

3. ARTICLE : (*a.* preposition, **b. conjunction**, *c.* adjective, *d.* verb) :: THE : AND

    (**b**) *The* is an article; *and* is a conjunction. A conjunction is a linguistic form that connects two complete clauses.
    Humanities—Description

4. SAFETY : 2 :: TOUCHDOWN : (*a.* 2, *b.* 4, **c. 6**, *d.* 8)

    (**c**) In football, a safety is worth 2 points and a touchdown is worth 6 points.
    General Information—Description

5. CIRCLE : ELLIPSE :: SQUARE : (*a.* triangle, **b. rectangle**, *c.* pentagon, *d.* hexagon)

    (**b**) Both a circle and an ellipse are closed curves. Both a square and a rectangle are polygons with four sides.
    Mathematics—Class

6. BIRD : (*a.* nest, *b.* worm, **c. wings**, *d.* fly) :: GENIE : MAGIC CARPET

    (**c**) A bird flies by means of its wings. A genie flies by means of a magic carpet.
    General Information—Description

7. FOXHOLE : (*a.* foxes, ***b.* gunfire**, *c.* discovery, *d.* earthquakes) ::
RAINCOAT : RAIN

(**b**) A foxhole provides protection from gunfire. A raincoat provides
protection from rain.
General Information—Description

8. FOOLISH : OWL :: (***a.* timid**, *b.* large, *c.* wise, *d.* temperamental) : LION

(**a**) An owl is reputed to be wise, which is the opposite of foolish.
A lion is reputed to be bold, which is the opposite of timid.
General Information—Description

9. SINBAD : (***a.* sailor**, *b.* squire, *c.* sinner, *d.* poet) :: ARTHUR : KING

(**a**) Sinbad was a sailor, Arthur a king. Sinbad was a sailor whose stories
are told in *The Book of One Thousand and One Nights*; King Arthur was
a legendary king of the Britons.
Humanities—Description

10. SOLOMON : WISE :: NERO : (*a.* stupid, *b.* bold, *c.* just, ***d.* cruel**)

(**d**) Solomon was wise; Nero was cruel.
Humanities—Description

11. GRAPE : VINE :: RUBBER : (***a.* tree**, *b.* conifer, *c.* root, *d.* leaf)
(**a**) Grapes come from a vine; rubber comes from a tree.
General Information—Description

12. (*a.* Georgia, *b.* Massachusetts, ***c.* New Jersey**, *d.* Ohio) : MIDDLE
ATLANTIC :: VERMONT : NEW ENGLAND

(**c**) New Jersey is a Middle Atlantic state. Vermont is a New England state.
Massachusetts is a New England state, Georgia a Southern state, and Ohio is a Midwestern
state.
General Information—Description

13. BALD : HAIR :: ALBINO : (*a.* height, *b.* pain, *c.* sight, ***d.* pigment**)

(**d**) A bald person lacks hair. An albino lacks pigment.
General Information—Description

14. BOW : (*a.* arrow, *b.* curtsey, ***c.* stern**, *d.* fore) :: FRONT : REAR

(**c**) The bow is the front of a ship; the stern is the rear.
General Information—Similarity/Contrast

15. MONOGYNY : POLYGYNY :: ONE : (*a.* none, *b.* two, *c.* eight, **d. many**)

    (**d**) Monogyny is marriage to one spouse. Polygyny is marriage to many spouses.
    Social Science—Description

16. ATTA : AL-SHEHHI :: JARRAH : (*a.* Mohammed, *b.* bin Laden, **c. Binalshibh**, *d.* Atef)

    (**c**) Mohamed Atta, Marwan al-Shehhi, Ziad Jarrah, and Ramzi Binalshibh were hijackers in the September 11 attacks. Osama bin Laden, Khalid Sheikh Mohammed, and Mohammed Atef were involved in the planning of the September 11 attacks.
    General Information—Description

17. (**a. secret codes**, *b.* inscriptions on church vaults, *c.* science fiction, *d.* religious rituals) : CRYPTOGRAPHY :: DICTIONARIES : LEXICOGRAPHY

    (**a**) Cryptography is the art of writing secret codes. Lexicography is the art of writing dictionaries.
    General Information—Description

18. $E = mc^2$: EINSTEIN :: $C^2 = A^2 + B^2$: (*a.* Bernoulli, *b.* Cauchy, *c.* Descartes, **d. Pythagoras**)

    (**d**) The equation $E = mc^2$ is attributable to Einstein. The equation $C^2 = A^2 + B^2$ is attributable to Pythagoras. Bernoulli applied mathematics to mechanics and is especially known for the Bernoulli principle. Descartes introduced the use of coordinates to locate a point in one or two dimensions (Cartesian coordinate system). Cauchy (a French mathematician) was a pioneer in analysis and the theory of substitution of groups.
    Mathematics—Description

19. GREEK : GREEK :: ROMAN : (*a.* Indo-European, **b. Latin**, *c.* Mediterranean, *d.* Romansh)

    (**b**) The ancient Greeks spoke Greek. The ancient Romans spoke Latin.
    Humanities—Description

20. (*a.* Jesus, *b.* Hell, **c. Heaven**, *d.* Satan) : CHRISTIANITY :: NIRVANA : BUDDHISM

    (**c**) The concept of heaven in Christianity serves a function similar to that of nirvana in Buddhism.
    Humanities—Description

21. U.S. CALENDAR : U.S. FISCAL CALENDAR :: JANUARY :
(*a.* December, *b.* March, **c. July**, *d.* September)

(**c**) The first month of the U.S. calendar is January. The first month of the
U.S. fiscal calendar is July.
General Information—Description

22. PHOTOMETER : (***a.* light**, *b.* distance, *c.* magnetism, *d.* velocity) ::
AUDIOMETER : SOUND

(**a**) A photometer is used to measure light; an audiometer is used to measure
sound.
Natural Science—Description

23. (***a.* believable**, *b.* wrong, *c.* fanciful, *d.* humorous) : INCREDIBLE ::
AUGMENT : DIMINISH

(**a**) *Incredible* and *believable* are antonyms, as are *augment* and *diminish*.
Vocabulary—Similarity/Contrast

24. INFINITIVE : (*a.* having eaten, ***b.* to sleep**, *c.* has tried, *d.* to the store) ::
PARTICIPLE : WALKING

(**b**) *To sleep* is an infinitive. *Walking* is a participle.
Humanities—Class

25. MARX : COMMUNISM :: (*a.* Hamilton, *b.* Lenin, **c. Smith**, *d.* Davis) :
CAPITALISM

(**c**) Karl Marx is famous for his writing on communism. Adam Smith is
famous for his writing on capitalism. Hamilton was the first Secretary of Treasury in
the United States as well as an economist and philosopher. Lenin was the first head of the
Soviet Socialist Republic. Davis is a distracter term.
Social Science—Description

26. (*a.* Iambic, ***b.* Doric**, *c.* Spartan, *d.* Grecian) : CORINTHIAN :: SONATA :
CONCERTO

(**b**) Doric and Corinthian are both types of columns. A sonata and a
concerto are both types of musical compositions. Doric refers to the Ancient
Greeks of Doris or to a dialect of Ancient Greek that is spoken in the
Peloponnesus. Corinthian refers to somebody from the city of Corinth or
to somebody who likes to seek pleasure. A sonata is a composition for one
or two instruments that typically has three or four movements. A concerto
is a composition for an entire orchestra and one or more soloists. Iamb is
a metrical foot that consists of one unstressed and one stressed syllable. Grecian refers to
something from Greece. Spartan refers to something from the Greek city of Sparta.
Humanities—Class

27. SOCCER : BALL :: (*a.* cricket, *b.* rugby, *c.* **hockey**, *d.* lacrosse) : PUCK

    (**c**) Soccer is played with a ball, hockey with a puck.
    General Information—Description

28. (*a.* **sheep**, *b.* plasma, *c.* vulture, *d.* harass) : BLOOD :: DOG : HOUND

    (**a**) A sheep dog and a bloodhound are both types of dogs.
    General Information—Completion

29. (*a.* hawk, *b.* **owl**, *c.* bluejay, *d.* ostrich) : NOCTURNAL :: ROBIN : DIURNAL

    (**b**) An owl is a nocturnal bird; a robin is a diurnal bird.
    Natural Science—Description

30. PHLEGM : PHLEGMATIC :: BILE : (*a.* **bilious**, *b.* billiard, *c.* binding, *d.* bilabial)

    (**a**) The word *phlegmatic* derives from *phlegm*. The word *bilious* derives from *bile*.
    Vocabulary—Description

31. HEAVY-HANDED : (*a.* uncoordinated, *b.* **tactless**, *c.* strong, *d.* coordinated) :: HEAVY-FOOTED : PLODDING

    (**b**) Someone who is heavy-handed is tactless. Someone who is heavy-footed is plodding.
    Vocabulary—Similarity/Contrast

32. PALEFACE : WHITE :: BLUENOSE : (*a.* frigid, *b.* tough, *c.* unkind, *d.* **puritanical**)

    (**d**) A paleface is a white person. A bluenose is puritanical.
    General Information—Description

33. PROTON : NEUTRON :: POSITIVE : (*a.* negative, *b.* **uncharged**, *c.* positive, *d.* nucleonic)

    (**b**) A proton has a positive electrical charge. A neutron is uncharged.
    Natural Science—Description

34. SPHINX : (*a*. pterodactyl, *b*. dodo, *c*. vulture, ***d*. phoenix**) :: LION : EAGLE

(**d**) A sphinx and a phoenix are both mythological animals. A lion and an eagle are both real animals. The sphinx is a mythical Egyptian creature that has a lion's body and a man's head. A phoenix is a mythical bird that burned itself and arose from the ashes to live again. A pterodactyl is a winged flying reptile that is extinct. A dodo is an extinct flightless bird from Mauritius.
Humanities—Class

35. ANDAMAN : ACEH :: SRI LANKA : (*a*. Bali, ***b*. Phuket**, *c*. Fiji, *d*. Guam)

(**b**) The Andaman Islands, Aceh, Sri Lanka, and Phuket were regions that were affected by the Indian Ocean Tsunami on December 26, 2004.
General Information—Description

36. RADIUS : 4 :: DIAMETER : (*a*. 16, ***b*. 8**, *c*. 87π, *d*. 167π)

(**b**) If the radius of a circle is 4, the circle's diameter is 8.
Mathematics—Description

37. PIKE : (***a*. sturgeon**, *b*. lion, *c*. whale, *d*. buffalo) :: COW : PIG

(**a**) A pike and a sturgeon are both fishes. A cow and a pig are both mammals.
Natural Science—Class

38. WASSERMANN : (*a*. heart disease, *b*. diabetes, ***c*. syphilis**, *d*. lung cancer) :: PAP : CERVICAL CANCER

(**c**) The Wassermann test is for syphilis. The Pap test is for cervical cancer.
Natural Science—Description

39. COMPLEMENTARY : SUPPLEMENTARY :: (*a*. 0, *b*. 45, ***c*. 90**, *d*. 360) : 180

(**c**) Complementary angles sum to 90 degrees. Supplementary angles sum to 180 degrees.
Mathematics—Description

40. e.g. : FOR EXAMPLE :: viz. : (***a*. namely**, *b*. except for, *c*. according to, *d*. generally)

(**a**) The abbreviation *e.g.* means "for example"; *viz.* means "namely." *e.g.* is the abbreviation for *exempli gratia* (for example); *viz.* is the abbreviation for *videlicet* (namely).
General Information—Similarity/Contrast

41. GRAPE : WINE :: (*a.* apple, ***b.* potato**, *c.* pomegranate, *d.* malt) : VODKA

    (**b**) Grapes are used to make wine, potatoes to make vodka.
    General Information—Description

42. RISING : FALLING :: (***a.* bull**, *b.* bird, *c.* sparrow, *d.* antelope) : BEAR

    (**a**) A rising market is a bull market. A falling market is a bear market.
    Social Science—Similarity/Contrast

43. XX : FEMALE :: (***a.* XY**, *b.* YY, *c.* XZ, *d.* ZZ) : MALE

    (**a**) A female is distinguished by an XX chromosome. A male is distinguished by an XY chromosome.
    Natural Science—Description

44. RESPECT : (*a.* love, *b.* protect, ***c.* revere**, *d.* obey) :: DISLIKE : HATE

    (**c**) To revere is to respect a great deal. To hate is to dislike a great deal.
    Vocabulary—Description

45. PARLIAMENT : LORDS :: (*a.* House of Representatives, ***b.* Congress**, *c.* White House, *d.* Supreme Court) : SENATE

    (**b**) The House of Lords is the upper chamber of the British Parliament. The Senate is the upper chamber of the U.S. Congress.
    Social Science—Description

46. (*a.* parsing, *b.* gender, *c.* case, ***d.* declension**) : NOUN :: CONJUGATION : VERB

    (**d**) Nouns may belong to a declension, verbs to a conjugation.
    Humanities—Description

47. MC : MD :: MMCC : (*a.* MCM, *b.* MGM, *c.* MDM, ***d.* MMM**)

    (**d**) 1,100 is to 1,500 as 2,200 is to 3,000. In Roman numerals, I = 1, V = 5, X = 10, L = 50, C = 100, D = 500, M = 1,000.
    Mathematics—Equality/Negation

48. (*a.* dour, ***b.* caustic**, *c.* sweet, *d.* mild) : ACRID :: BITTER : ACRIMONIOUS

    (**b**) *Caustic, acrid, bitter,* and *acrimonious* all mean the same thing.
    Vocabulary—Similarity/Contrast

49. PORCINE : (*a.* porcupine, *b.* goat, *c.* dog, ***d.* pig**) :: FELINE : CAT

    (**d**) *Porcine* means *piglike. Feline* means *catlike.* Goatlike is hircine. Doglike is canine. A porcupine is a rodent.
    Vocabulary—Description

50. TIPPECANOE : AND TYLER TOO :: FIFTY-FOUR FORTY : (*a.* forever, ***b.* or fight**, *c.* and forward, *d.* to fortune)

(**b**) "Tippecanoe and Tyler too" and "Fifty-four forty or fight" were both slogans in the American past.
Humanities—Completion

51. IMPEACH : (*a.* prove the guilt of, *b.* overturn, *c.* acquit, ***d.* accuse**) :: CONVICT : FIND GUILTY

(**d**) To impeach is to accuse. To convict is to find guilty. In the United States, the House of Representatives can impeach a person; the Senate tries the accused.
Vocabulary—Similarity/Contrast

52. CITY OF SEVEN HILLS : ROME :: CITY OF GOD : (***a.* heaven**, *b.* Jerusalem, *c.* Bethlehem, *d.* Jericho)

(**a**) Rome is the City of Seven Hills. Heaven is the City of God. The seven hills of Rome are called Palatine, Capitoline, Quirinal, Viminal, Esquiline, Caelian, and Aventine.
Humanities—Similarity/Contrast

53. WOOD : PAPER :: LATEX : (*a.* cotton, *b.* plastic, *c.* rayon, ***d.* rubber**)

(**d**) Wood is used to make paper. Latex is used to make rubber.
Natural Science—Description

54. TEXTILE : RAYON :: GEM : (*a.* sapphire, *b.* diamond, ***c.* spinel**, *d.* quartz)

(**c**) Rayon is a synthetic textile. Spinel is a synthetic gem.
Natural Science—Class

55. SIAM : (*a.* Mongolia, *b.* China, ***c.* Thailand**, *d.* Nepal) :: PERSIA : IRAN

(**c**) Siam is the former name of Thailand. Persia is the former name of Iran. Nepal was once the Kingdom of Mustang.
General Information—Similarity/Contrast

56. HABEAS CORPUS : LAW :: EXEUNT OMNES : (*a.* medicine, ***b.* drama**, *c.* law, *d.* political theory)

(**b**) *Habeas corpus* is an expression used in law. *Exeunt omnes* is an expression used in drama. *Habeas corpus* refers to a writ needed to bring a party before court. *Exeunt omnes* means that all characters exit the stage.
Humanities—Description

57. PENTHOUSE APARTMENT : TOP FLOOR :: DUPLEX APARTMENT : (*a.* two rooms, ***b.* two floors**, *c.* two bedrooms, *d.* two persons)

(**b**) A penthouse apartment is on the top floor. A duplex apartment has two floors.
General Information—Description

58. XENOPHOBIA : (***a.* foreigners**, *b.* death, *c.* insanity, *d.* live burial) :: CLAUSTROPHOBIA : CONFINED PLACES

(**a**) Xenophobia is a fear of foreigners. Claustrophobia is a fear of confined places.
Vocabulary—Description

59. LOCKJAW : TETANUS :: HYDROPHOBIA : (*a.* encephalitis, *b.* malaria, *c.* syphilis, ***d.* rabies**)

(**d**) Tetanus is sometimes called lockjaw. Rabies is sometimes called hydrophobia.
Natural Science—Similarity/Contrast

60. ENGLISH : CANADA :: (*a.* Italian, ***b.* Portuguese**, *c.* Brazilian, *d.* French) : BRAZIL

(**b**) English is the most widely spoken language in Canada. Portuguese is the most widely spoken language in Brazil.
General Information—Description

61. MITIGATE : ASSUAGE :: MODERATE : (***a.* lessen**, *b.* make worse, *c.* disprove, *d.* approve)

(**a**) *Mitigate*, *assuage*, *moderate*, and *lessen* can all be used interchangeably.
Vocabulary—Similarity/Contrast

62. $1^0 : 1^{10} :: 10^0 : ($***a.* 10^0**, *b.* 10^1, *c.* 10^2, *d.* 10^{10})

(**a**) 1 is to 1 as 1 is to 1.
Mathematics—Equality/Negation

63. PUSILLANIMOUS : AUDACIOUS :: (*a.* brave, *b.* purposive, ***c.* cowardly**, *d.* evanescent) : BOLD

(**c**) *Pusillanimous* and *cowardly* are synonyms, as are *audacious* and *bold*.
Vocabulary—Similarity/Contrast

64. HANNIBAL : (*a.* Theseus, ***b.* Scipio**, *c.* Cicero, *d.* Marcion) :: NAPOLEON : WELLINGTON

    (**b**) Hannibal was defeated by Scipio in the Punic Wars. Napoleon was defeated by Wellington at the Battle of Waterloo. Theseus was a king of Athens. Cicero was a Roman statesman and philosopher. Marcion was an early Christian theologian who was excommunicated by the Church at Rome.
    Humanities—Description

65. EPITOME : (*a.* monologue, *b.* prevarication, ***c.* summary**, *d.* diatribe) :: PREFACE : PROLOGUE

    (**c**) An epitome is a summary. A preface is a prologue. To prevaricate means to deviate from the truth. A monologue is a long speech by one person. A diatribe is a sharp denunciation.
    Vocabulary—Similarity/Contrast

66. (*a.* wave, *b.* radian, *c.* alpha, ***d.* roentgen**) : RADIATION :: MINUTE : TIME

    (**d**) A roentgen is a unit of radiation. A minute is a unit of time.
    Natural Science—Description

67. VERACIOUS : (*a.* repeated, *b.* horizontal, *c.* diagonal, ***d.* truthful**) :: CONTINUAL : INCESSANT

    (**d**) *Veracious* means *truthful*. *Continual* means *incessant*.
    Vocabulary—Similarity/Contrast

68. SOLAR : SUN :: (***a.* lunar**, *b.* diurnal, *c.* stellar, *d.* nocturnal) : MOON

    (**a**) The word *solar* derives from Sol, the Roman god of the sun. The word *lunar* derives from Luna, the Roman goddess of the moon.
    Humanities—Description

69. LINCOLN STEFFENS : POLITICAL MACHINES :: UPTON SINCLAIR :
    (***a.* meat-packing industry**, *b.* financial speculators, *c.* railroad magnates, *d.* patent medicine quacks)

    (**a**) Lincoln Steffens was a muckraker who exposed political machines. Upton Sinclair was a muckraker who exposed the sordid conditions in the meat-packing industry.
    Humanities—Description

70. FAMILY : HOMINIDAE :: (*a.* sapiens, *b.* species, ***c.* genus**, *d.* class) : HOMO

    (**c**) Human beings are of family Hominidae and genus *Homo*.
    Natural Science—Class

71. OVERWEENING : (*a.* conceited, ***b.* modest**, *c.* spoiled, *d.* underprotected) :: BLUNT : SHARP

    (**b**) *Overweening* is the opposite of *modest*. *Blunt* is the opposite of *sharp*.
    Vocabulary—Similarity/Contrast

72. HEARSAY : GOSSIP :: GAINSAY : (***a.* oppose**, *b.* protect, *c.* lose, *d.* take)

    (**a**) Hearsay is gossip. To gainsay is to oppose.
    Vocabulary—Similarity/Contrast

73. (*a.* thin, *b.* analogy, *c.* happy, ***d.* fat**) : FIAT :: SMILE : SIMILE

    (**d**) *Simile* is *smile* with an *i* added to the interior of the word. *Fiat* is *fat* with an *i* added to the interior of the word.
    Nonsemantic

74. ROUNDHEAD : SHORT HAIR :: (*a.* Tory, *b.* Whig, *c.* Royalist, ***d.* Cavalier**) : LONG HAIR

    (**d**) The Roundheads were known for their short hair. The Cavaliers were known for their long hair. Roundheads was a nickname for the supporters of the English Parliament during the English Civil War. Cavaliers were Royalist supporters during that war.
    Humanities—Description

75. EUGENICS : HEREDITY :: (*a.* euthanasia, ***b.* euthenics**, *c.* mnemonics, *d.* dialectics) : ENVIRONMENT

    (**b**) Eugenics studies how to "improve" the human "race" through the manipulation of heredity. Euthenics studies how to do the same through the manipulation of the environment. *Euthanasia* means "to kill someone painlessly." *Mnemonics* are techniques to improve memory. *Dialectics* involve reasoning by dialogue.
    Vocabulary—Description

76. THERMO : (***a.* cryo**, *b.* iso, *c.* crypto, *d.* paleo) :: HOT : COLD

    (**a**) *Thermo-* is a prefix meaning *heat*. *Cryo-* is a prefix meaning *cold*.
    Vocabulary—Similarity/Contrast

77. (*a.* North Carolina, *b.* South Carolina, **c. Georgia**, *d.* Florida) :
OGLETHORPE :: PENNSYLVANIA : PENN

    (**c**) Oglethorpe founded Georgia. Penn founded Pennsylvania. Ponce de Leon
    discovered Florida and gave it its name. South Carolina was named by King Charles II
    of England. North Carolina is not associated with a single founder.
    Humanities—Description

78. BANEFUL : (**a. baleful**, *b.* salutary, *c.* promiscuous, *d.* remorseful) ::
PERSONABLE : HANDSOME

    (**a**) *Baneful* means *baleful*. *Personable* means *handsome*.
    Vocabulary—Similarity/Contrast

79. WERTHEIMER : GESTALT :: (**a. Watson**, *b.* Köhler, *c.* Koffka, *d.* Piaget) :
BEHAVIORIST

    (**a**) Wertheimer was a leading psychologist in the Gestalt movement.
    Watson was a leading psychologist in the behaviorist movement. Kurt Koffka
    was a Gestalt psychologist, as was Wolfgang Köhler. Jean Piaget was a famous
    developmental psychologist and genetic epistemologist.
    Social Science—Description

80. (*a.* depilate, *b.* dampen, *c.* derogate, **d. desiccate**) : DRY :: MOISTEN :
WET

    (**d**) To desiccate is to dry. To moisten is to wet.
    Vocabulary—Similarity/Contrast

81. GLUCOSE : (*a.* comatose, *b.* malactose, **c. lactose**, *d.* adipose) ::
SUCROSE : FRUCTOSE

    (**c**) Glucose, lactose, sucrose, and fructose are all sugars.
    Natural Science—Class

82. ABLE : MELBA :: (*a.* colt, *b.* peach, **c. era**, *d.* willing) : MARE

    (**c**) *Melba* is *able* spelled backwards, with an added initial *m*. *Mare* is *era*
    spelled backwards, with an added initial *m*.
    Nonsemantic

83. (*a.* Mars, *b.* Jupiter, *c.* Venus, **d. Pluto**) : PROSERPINA :: ZEUS : HERA

    (**d**) In Roman mythology, Proserpina was the wife of Pluto. In Greek
    mythology, Hera was the wife of Zeus. Mars was the god of war in Roman
    mythology. Jupiter was the god of sky and thunder. Venus was the Roman goddess of love
    and beauty.
    Humanities—Class

84. FLEET STREET : (***a. press***, *b.* police, *c.* amusement, *d.* high fashion) :: DOWNING STREET : GOVERNMENT

    (**a**) In London, Fleet Street has many of the offices of the press, while Downing Street has many of the offices of the government.
    General Information—Description

85. ARTUR RUBINSTEIN : PIANO :: ISAAC STERN : (*a.* piano, ***b. violin***, *c.* trumpet, *d.* oboe)

    (**b**) Artur Rubenstein was a pianist. Isaac Stern is a violinist.
    Humanities—Description

86. DURKHEIM : (*a.* Homocide, *b.* Matricide, ***c. Suicide***, *d.* Genocide) :: BECKER : OUTSIDERS

    (**c**) Durkheim is the author of the sociological work *Suicide*. Becker is the author of the sociological study *Outsiders*.
    Social Science—Description

87. JOHN WESLEY : METHODIST :: MARY BAKER EDDY : (*a.* Presbyterian, *b.* Baha'i, *c.* Jehovah's Witness, ***d. Christian Science***)

    (**d**) John Wesley was the founder of the Methodist church. Mary Baker Eddy was the founder of the Christian Science church. The founder of the Presbyterian church was John Calvin; the founder of the Baha'i faith was the Baha'u'llah; the founder of Jehovah's Witnesses was Charles Russell.
    Humanities—Description

88. BACH : BAROQUE :: GRIEG : (*a.* classical, *b.* modern, ***c. romantic***, *d.* medieval)

    (**c**) Bach was a composer in the baroque period of music. Grieg was a romantic composer.
    Humanities—Description

89. (*a.* Husserl, *b.* Heidegger, ***c. Comte***, *d.* Camus) : POSITIVISM :: SARTRE : EXISTENTIALISM

    (**c**) Comte helped shape the movement in philosophy now known as positivism. Sartre was a major shaper of existentialism. Edmund Husserl was the founder of phenomenology. Martin Heidegger was a philosopher; his most popular book is *Being and Time*. Albert Camus was a French writer who wrote *The Plague*.
    Humanities—Description

90. F# : G♭ :: B : (***a*. C♭**, *b.* A♭, *c.* G#, *d.* G♭)

    (**a**) F# is the same as G♭. B is the same as C♭.
    Humanities—Similarity/Contrast

91. SECOND : THIRD :: (*a.* clergy, *b.* king, *c.* commoners, ***d*. nobility**) : BOURGEOISIE

    (**d**) The nobility comprised the Second Estate of the French Estates-General. The bourgeoisie comprised the Third Estate.
    Humanities—Description

92. ALEXANDER : GREAT :: JULIAN : (*a.* Ingenious, *b.* Meek, *c.* Bold, ***d*. Apostate**)

    (**d**) Alexander was called the Great and was an ancient Greek king of Macedon. Julian was called the Apostate and was a Roman Emperor.
    Humanities—Description

93. (*a.* Helen, *b.* Jezebel, ***c*. Una**, *d.* Archimago) : DUESSA :: GOOD : EVIL

    (**c**) In Spenser's poem, *The Faerie Queene*, Una represents the forces of good and Duessa the forces of evil. Archimago is a sorcerer in Spenser's *Faerie Queene*. Helen was the daughter of Zeus and Leda, and was abducted by Paris, which led to the Trojan War. Jezebel was a queen of Ancient Israel, married to King Ahab.
    Humanities—Description

94. D : R × T :: (*a.* A, *b.* C, ***c*. F**, *d.* H) : M × A

    (**c**) In physics, Distance = Rate × Time and Force = Mass × Acceleration.
    Natural Science—Equality/Negation

95. PURLOINED : (*a.* Melville, *b.* Doyle, ***c*. Poe**, *d.* Conrad) :: SCARLET : HAWTHORNE

    (**c**) *The Purloined Letter* is a story by Poe. *The Scarlet Letter* is a story by Hawthorne.
    Humanities—Description

96. PROPHASE : METAPHASE :: ANAPHASE : (*a.* meiophase, ***b*. telophase**, *c.* mitophase, *d.* protophase)

    (**b**) Prophase, metaphase, anaphase, and telophase are all stages in mitosis (a form of cell division).
    Natural Science—Class

97. NEWBERY : (*a.* Wohlenberg, *b.* **Caldecott**, *c.* Pulitzer, *d.* Thompsen) :: STORY : ARTWORK

(**b**) The Newbery Medal is awarded annually to a distinguished children's story book. The Caldecott Medal is also awarded annually for distinguished artwork in a children's book. The Wohlenberg Prize is a prize for seniors of the physical sciences or engineering at Berkeley College of Yale. The Pulitzer Prize is a prize in journalism and literature. Thompson is a distracter term.
General Information—Description

98. COUNTESS AURELIA : THE MADWOMAN OF CHAILLOT :: (*a.* Lear, *b.* Othello, *c.* **Antonio**, *d.* Iago) : THE MERCHANT OF VENICE

(**c**) Countess Aurelia is the Madwoman of Chaillot in the play by the same name. Antonio is the Merchant of Venice in the play by the same name. Iago tricked Othello into murdering his wife in Shakespeare's tragedy *Othello*. *King Lear* is another tragedy written by Shakespeare.
Humanities—Similarity/Contrast

99. PICASSO : GUERNICA :: (*a.* **Manet**, *b.* Raphael, *c.* David, *d.* Leger) : LUNCHEON ON THE GRASS

(**a**) Picasso is the artist who painted *Guernica*. Manet is the artist who painted *Luncheon on the Grass*. A famous work of Raphael is the *Sistine Madonna*. A famous painting of Fernand Leger is *Nudes in the Forest*. A well-known painting of Jacques-Louis David is the *Oath of the Horatii*.
Humanities—Description

100. RACINE : MOLIÈRE :: SOPHOCLES : (*a.* Zeno, *b.* **Aristophanes**, *c.* Plato, *d.* Aristotle)

(**b**) Racine was a French playwright who wrote tragedies, while Molière was a French playwright who wrote comedies. Sophocles was a Greek playwright who wrote tragedies, while Aristophanes was a Greek playwright who wrote comedies. Zeno, Plato, and Aristotle were ancient Greek philosophers.
Humanities—Class

101. (*a.* Queen Victoria, *b.* Queen Virginia, *c.* **Queen Elizabeth**, *d.* Queen Mary) : VIRGINIA :: KING GEORGE : GEORGIA

(**c**) Queen Elizabeth, known as "the virgin queen," had the state of Virginia named for her. King George inspired the naming of the state of Georgia.
General Information—Description

102. MITOSIS : MEIOSIS :: (*a.* 1, *b.* **2**, *c.* 4, *d.* 8) : 4

(**b**) Mitosis is the process of cell division that results in two discrete cells. Meiosis results in four.
Natural Science—Description

103. DAGGER : STAR :: (*a.* rune, *b.* allograph, *c.* knife, *d.* **obelisk**) : ASTERISK

(**d**) The name of the written symbol that looks like a dagger is an obelisk just as the star-shaped symbol is called an asterisk. Rune is the name for any letter belonging to the ancient Germanic alphabet. An allograph is a signature that is made by one person for another.
General Information—Similarity/Contrast

104. MISER : (*a.* chary, *b.* mercurial, *c.* acquisitive, *d.* **munificent**) :: GLUTTON : ABSTEMIOUS

(**d**) A miser is the opposite of munificent, meaning giving, and a glutton is the opposite of abstemious, meaning abstaining from excess food and drink.
Vocabulary—Description

105. (*a.* pork, *b.* **sweet**, *c.* appetizer, *d.* vegetable) : SWEETMEAT :: FRUIT : BREADFRUIT

(**b**) A sweetmeat is a type of sweet food, and a breadfruit is a type of fruit.
General Information—Class

106. $2\pi r^2$: $\pi(2r)^2$ :: LW : (*a.* (1/2)LW, *b.* LW, *c.* **2LW**, *d.* 4LW)

(**c**) $2\pi r^2$ is half of $\pi(2r)^2$, which is to say the area of two circles of the same radius is half the size of the area of one circle with twice that radius. Similarly, LW, the area of a rectangle, is half of 2LW.
Mathematics—Equality/Negation

107. (*a.* hatred, *b.* naiveté, *c.* **envy**, *d.* sickness) : SORROW :: GREEN : BLUE

(**c**) Envy is the emotion that is evoked by the color green just as sorrow is the emotion evoked by the color blue.
General Information—Description

108. MOHS : HARDNESS :: RICHTER : (*a.* **magnitude**, *b.* earthquake, *c.* quality, *d.* extremity)

(**a**) The Mohs Scale measures hardness (of solid objects). The Richter Scale measures magnitude (of earthquakes).
Natural Science—Description

109. FROGS : SEAGULL :: (*a.* Shakespeare, *b.* Marlowe, *c.* Wilde, *d.* **Aristophanes**) : CHEKHOV

(**d**) *The Frogs* was a play written by Aristophanes, and *The Seagull* was a play written by Chekhov. Shakespeare is known, among others, for his tragedies *Hamlet*, *King Lear*, and *Macbeth*. Marlowe is known for his plays which include *Doctor Faustus* and *The Massacre at Paris*. Oscar Wilde is known, for example, for his play *The Importance of Being Earnest*.
Humanities—Description

110. INDIA : PAKISTAN :: PAKISTAN : (*a.* Kashmir, *b.* **Bangladesh**, *c.* Nepal, *d.* Sri Lanka)

(**b**) Pakistan was part of India until it seceded and became sovereign. Bangladesh was part of Pakistan until it seceded and became sovereign.
General Information—Description

111. ORGAN : ORGANELLE :: LIVER : (*a.* **vacuole**, *b.* pancreas, *c.* kidney, *d.* cell)

(**a**) The liver is an example of an organ, and a vacuole is an example of an organelle, or intracellular structure.
Natural Science—Class

112. MASS AND ENERGY : (*a.* Bernoulli, *b.* Newton, *c.* Gauss, *d.* **Einstein**) :: VOLUME AND DISPLACEMENT : ARCHIMEDES

(**d**) Einstein was the first to directly relate mass and energy and Archimedes was the first to relate volume and displacement. Bernoulli applied mathematics to mechanics and is especially known for the Bernoulli principle. Newton is known for describing universal gravitation. Gauss is associated with the normal distribution, also called Gaussian distribution.
Natural Science—Description

113. DOGS : PEAS :: PAVLOV : (*a.* Darwin, *b.* Gauss, *c.* Curie, *d.* **Mendel**)

(**d**) Pavlov is famous for his groundbreaking scientific work with dogs in classical conditioning. Mendel is famous for his scientific discoveries made with peas in the area of genetics and inheritance. Darwin developed the Theory of Evolution. Gauss is associated with the normal distribution, also called Gaussian distribution. Curie won the Nobel Prize in chemistry in 1911 for her discovery of the elements radium and polonium.
Social Science—Description

114. (*a.* **King**, *b.* Martha, *c.* Reverend, *d.* Priest) : CARVER :: MARTIN LUTHER : GEORGE WASHINGTON

(**a**) Both Martin Luther King (Jr.) and George Washington Carver went on to become famous, as were those men for whom they were named at birth.
General Information—Description

115. SESAME SEEDS : TAHINI :: PEANUTS : (*a*. roots, *b*. shell,
c. peanut butter, *d*. oil)

(**c**) Sesame seeds are ground to make the spread known as tahini just as
peanuts are ground to make peanut butter.
General Information—Description

116. BASS : (*a*. clarinet, *b*. viola, **c. cello**, *d*. trumpet) :: TREBLE : FLUTE

(**c**) Most written music for the cello is presented in the bass cleft. Most flute
music is written in the treble cleft.
Humanities—Description

117. MAL : BEN :: ANTI : (*a*. un, *b*. inter, **c. pro**, *d*. pre)

(**c**) Mal- and ben- are prefixes with opposite connotations (negative and
positive, respectively). Likewise, anti- and pro- are prefixes with opposite
meanings (negating and supporting, respectively). The prefix *un-* means "not, or
lack of"; *inter-* means "in between"; *pre-* means "before."
Vocabulary—Similarity/Contrast

118. (**a. meat packing**, *b*. clear cutting, *c*. poaching, *d*. iron mining) :
PESTICIDES :: THE JUNGLE : SILENT SPRING

(**a**) Upton Sinclair's book *The Jungle* exposed abuses in the meat-packing
industry just as Rachel Carson's *Silent Spring* exposed abuses of pesticides.
Humanities—Description

119. HANUKKAH : DIVALI :: JUDAISM : (*a*. Buddhism, **b. Hinduism**,
c. Zoroastrianism, *d*. Islam)

(**b**) The holidays Hanukkah and Divali are also known in their respective
religions, Judaism and Hinduism, as the Festival of Lights.
Humanities—Description

120. SQUARE ROOT : SQUARE :: (*a*. dividend, *b*. root, *c*. log, **d. integral**) :
DERIVATIVE

(**d**) Finding the square root requires the opposite action as finding the
square of a number. Likewise, finding the integral is the opposite of
finding the derivative of a number.
Mathematics—Equality/Negation

PRACTICE TEST 4

Item Classification Chart

	RELATIONSHIP						
CONTENT	Similarity/ Contrast	Description	Class	Completion	Part/ Whole	Equality/ Negation	Nonsemantic
Vocabulary	23, 31, 48, 51, 61, 63, 65, 67, 71, 72, 76, 78, 80, 117	30, 44, 49, 58, 75, 104					
General Information	14, 40, 55, 103	1, 4, 6, 7, 8, 11, 12, 13, 16, 17, 21, 27, 32, 35, 41, 57, 60, 84, 97, 101, 107, 110, 114, 115	105	28			
Humanities	52, 90, 98	2, 3, 9, 10, 19, 20, 46, 56, 64, 68, 69, 74, 77, 85, 87, 88, 89, 91, 92, 93, 95, 99, 109, 116, 118, 119	24, 26, 34, 83, 100	50			
Social Science	42	15, 25, 45, 79, 86, 113					
Natural Science	59	22, 29, 33, 38, 43, 53, 66, 102, 108, 112	37, 54, 70, 81, 96, 111			94	
Mathematics		18, 36, 39	5			47, 62, 106, 120	
Nonsemantic							73, 82

Answer Sheet
PRACTICE TEST 5

1 Ⓐ Ⓑ Ⓒ Ⓓ	31 Ⓐ Ⓑ Ⓒ Ⓓ	61 Ⓐ Ⓑ Ⓒ Ⓓ	91 Ⓐ Ⓑ Ⓒ Ⓓ
2 Ⓐ Ⓑ Ⓒ Ⓓ	32 Ⓐ Ⓑ Ⓒ Ⓓ	62 Ⓐ Ⓑ Ⓒ Ⓓ	92 Ⓐ Ⓑ Ⓒ Ⓓ
3 Ⓐ Ⓑ Ⓒ Ⓓ	33 Ⓐ Ⓑ Ⓒ Ⓓ	63 Ⓐ Ⓑ Ⓒ Ⓓ	93 Ⓐ Ⓑ Ⓒ Ⓓ
4 Ⓐ Ⓑ Ⓒ Ⓓ	34 Ⓐ Ⓑ Ⓒ Ⓓ	64 Ⓐ Ⓑ Ⓒ Ⓓ	94 Ⓐ Ⓑ Ⓒ Ⓓ
5 Ⓐ Ⓑ Ⓒ Ⓓ	35 Ⓐ Ⓑ Ⓒ Ⓓ	65 Ⓐ Ⓑ Ⓒ Ⓓ	95 Ⓐ Ⓑ Ⓒ Ⓓ
6 Ⓐ Ⓑ Ⓒ Ⓓ	36 Ⓐ Ⓑ Ⓒ Ⓓ	66 Ⓐ Ⓑ Ⓒ Ⓓ	96 Ⓐ Ⓑ Ⓒ Ⓓ
7 Ⓐ Ⓑ Ⓒ Ⓓ	37 Ⓐ Ⓑ Ⓒ Ⓓ	67 Ⓐ Ⓑ Ⓒ Ⓓ	97 Ⓐ Ⓑ Ⓒ Ⓓ
8 Ⓐ Ⓑ Ⓒ Ⓓ	38 Ⓐ Ⓑ Ⓒ Ⓓ	68 Ⓐ Ⓑ Ⓒ Ⓓ	98 Ⓐ Ⓑ Ⓒ Ⓓ
9 Ⓐ Ⓑ Ⓒ Ⓓ	39 Ⓐ Ⓑ Ⓒ Ⓓ	69 Ⓐ Ⓑ Ⓒ Ⓓ	99 Ⓐ Ⓑ Ⓒ Ⓓ
10 Ⓐ Ⓑ Ⓒ Ⓓ	40 Ⓐ Ⓑ Ⓒ Ⓓ	70 Ⓐ Ⓑ Ⓒ Ⓓ	100 Ⓐ Ⓑ Ⓒ Ⓓ
11 Ⓐ Ⓑ Ⓒ Ⓓ	41 Ⓐ Ⓑ Ⓒ Ⓓ	71 Ⓐ Ⓑ Ⓒ Ⓓ	101 Ⓐ Ⓑ Ⓒ Ⓓ
12 Ⓐ Ⓑ Ⓒ Ⓓ	42 Ⓐ Ⓑ Ⓒ Ⓓ	72 Ⓐ Ⓑ Ⓒ Ⓓ	102 Ⓐ Ⓑ Ⓒ Ⓓ
13 Ⓐ Ⓑ Ⓒ Ⓓ	43 Ⓐ Ⓑ Ⓒ Ⓓ	73 Ⓐ Ⓑ Ⓒ Ⓓ	103 Ⓐ Ⓑ Ⓒ Ⓓ
14 Ⓐ Ⓑ Ⓒ Ⓓ	44 Ⓐ Ⓑ Ⓒ Ⓓ	74 Ⓐ Ⓑ Ⓒ Ⓓ	104 Ⓐ Ⓑ Ⓒ Ⓓ
15 Ⓐ Ⓑ Ⓒ Ⓓ	45 Ⓐ Ⓑ Ⓒ Ⓓ	75 Ⓐ Ⓑ Ⓒ Ⓓ	105 Ⓐ Ⓑ Ⓒ Ⓓ
16 Ⓐ Ⓑ Ⓒ Ⓓ	46 Ⓐ Ⓑ Ⓒ Ⓓ	76 Ⓐ Ⓑ Ⓒ Ⓓ	106 Ⓐ Ⓑ Ⓒ Ⓓ
17 Ⓐ Ⓑ Ⓒ Ⓓ	47 Ⓐ Ⓑ Ⓒ Ⓓ	77 Ⓐ Ⓑ Ⓒ Ⓓ	107 Ⓐ Ⓑ Ⓒ Ⓓ
18 Ⓐ Ⓑ Ⓒ Ⓓ	48 Ⓐ Ⓑ Ⓒ Ⓓ	78 Ⓐ Ⓑ Ⓒ Ⓓ	108 Ⓐ Ⓑ Ⓒ Ⓓ
19 Ⓐ Ⓑ Ⓒ Ⓓ	49 Ⓐ Ⓑ Ⓒ Ⓓ	79 Ⓐ Ⓑ Ⓒ Ⓓ	109 Ⓐ Ⓑ Ⓒ Ⓓ
20 Ⓐ Ⓑ Ⓒ Ⓓ	50 Ⓐ Ⓑ Ⓒ Ⓓ	80 Ⓐ Ⓑ Ⓒ Ⓓ	110 Ⓐ Ⓑ Ⓒ Ⓓ
21 Ⓐ Ⓑ Ⓒ Ⓓ	51 Ⓐ Ⓑ Ⓒ Ⓓ	81 Ⓐ Ⓑ Ⓒ Ⓓ	111 Ⓐ Ⓑ Ⓒ Ⓓ
22 Ⓐ Ⓑ Ⓒ Ⓓ	52 Ⓐ Ⓑ Ⓒ Ⓓ	82 Ⓐ Ⓑ Ⓒ Ⓓ	112 Ⓐ Ⓑ Ⓒ Ⓓ
23 Ⓐ Ⓑ Ⓒ Ⓓ	53 Ⓐ Ⓑ Ⓒ Ⓓ	83 Ⓐ Ⓑ Ⓒ Ⓓ	113 Ⓐ Ⓑ Ⓒ Ⓓ
24 Ⓐ Ⓑ Ⓒ Ⓓ	54 Ⓐ Ⓑ Ⓒ Ⓓ	84 Ⓐ Ⓑ Ⓒ Ⓓ	114 Ⓐ Ⓑ Ⓒ Ⓓ
25 Ⓐ Ⓑ Ⓒ Ⓓ	55 Ⓐ Ⓑ Ⓒ Ⓓ	85 Ⓐ Ⓑ Ⓒ Ⓓ	115 Ⓐ Ⓑ Ⓒ Ⓓ
26 Ⓐ Ⓑ Ⓒ Ⓓ	56 Ⓐ Ⓑ Ⓒ Ⓓ	86 Ⓐ Ⓑ Ⓒ Ⓓ	116 Ⓐ Ⓑ Ⓒ Ⓓ
27 Ⓐ Ⓑ Ⓒ Ⓓ	57 Ⓐ Ⓑ Ⓒ Ⓓ	87 Ⓐ Ⓑ Ⓒ Ⓓ	117 Ⓐ Ⓑ Ⓒ Ⓓ
28 Ⓐ Ⓑ Ⓒ Ⓓ	58 Ⓐ Ⓑ Ⓒ Ⓓ	88 Ⓐ Ⓑ Ⓒ Ⓓ	118 Ⓐ Ⓑ Ⓒ Ⓓ
29 Ⓐ Ⓑ Ⓒ Ⓓ	59 Ⓐ Ⓑ Ⓒ Ⓓ	89 Ⓐ Ⓑ Ⓒ Ⓓ	119 Ⓐ Ⓑ Ⓒ Ⓓ
30 Ⓐ Ⓑ Ⓒ Ⓓ	60 Ⓐ Ⓑ Ⓒ Ⓓ	90 Ⓐ Ⓑ Ⓒ Ⓓ	120 Ⓐ Ⓑ Ⓒ Ⓓ

Answer Sheet

Practice Test 5

Directions: In each of the following questions, you will find three initial terms and, in parentheses, four answer options designated *a*, *b*, *c*, and *d*. You are to select from the four answer options the one that best completes the analogy with the three initial terms. To record your answers, use the answer sheet provided.

Time: 60 minutes

1. BOW : (*a.* arrow, *b.* grenade, *c.* quiver, *d.* target) :: RIFLE : BULLET

2. MARK TWAIN : HANNIBAL :: (*a.* Ernest Hemingway, *b.* Stephen Crane, *c.* William Shakespeare, *d.* Victor Hugo) : STRATFORD-UPON-AVON

3. UNITED : STAND :: DIVIDED : (*a.* fall, *b.* sit, *c.* lie, *d.* rise)

4. (*a.* Asia, *b.* South America, *c.* Africa, *d.* North America) : SAHARA :: NORTH AMERICA : PAINTED

5. TARANTULA : (*a.* spider, *b.* rabbit, *c.* cat, *d.* cockroach) :: COBRA : SNAKE

6. (*a.* 6, *b.* 9, *c.* 12, *d.* 15) : BASEBALL :: 5 : BASKETBALL

7. SEINE : (*a.* Canada, *b.* Holland, *c.* Germany, *d.* France) :: THAMES : ENGLAND

8. PLIABLE : BEND :: (*a.* brittle, *b.* transparent, *c.* opaque, *d.* flexible) : BREAK

9. ADVERB : HAPPILY :: PREPOSITION : (*a.* the, *b.* or, *c.* on, *d.* none)

10. RIGHT ANGLE : (*a.* 0, *b.* 45, *c.* 90, *d.* 360) :: STRAIGHT ANGLE : 180

11. AUTHOR : PEN :: PAINTER : (*a.* brush, *b.* paint, *c.* canvas, *d.* picture)

12. ASTRONAUT : ROCKET SHIP :: WITCH : (*a.* cauldron, *b.* vulture, *c.* black cat, *d.* broomstick)

13. (*a.* achievement, *b.* permission, *c.* month, *d.* desire) : ABILITY :: MAY : CAN

14. IBM : (*a.* Industrial Business Machines, *b.* Innovative Business Machines, *c.* International Business Machines, *d.* Intelligent Business Machines) :: GOP : REPUBLICAN PARTY

15. (*a.* earthling, *b.* earthian, *c.* earthing, *d.* earthan) : EARTH :: MARTIAN : MARS

16. ASBESTOS : FIRE :: (*a.* vinyl, *b.* air, *c.* cotton, *d.* faucet) : WATER

17. DAVY JONES : (*a.* Great Britain, *b.* Planet Earth, *c.* the sun, *d.* the sea) :: LAND OF THE RISING SUN : JAPAN

18. PAIR : PARE :: COUPLE : (*a.* several, *b.* one, *c.* pear, *d.* prune)

19. ASCETIC : (*a.* businessman, *b.* monk, *c.* carpenter, *d.* policeman) :: CRAFTY : CONFIDENCE MAN

20. GUILLOTINE : ROBESPIERRE :: (*a.* noose, *b.* poison, *c.* knife, *d.* illness) : SOCRATES

21. GIN : BLACK :: (*a.* apple, *b.* whiskey, *c.* cotton, *d.* rummy) : JACK

22. PESO : MEXICO :: (*a.* ounce, *b.* pound, *c.* ruble, *d.* mark) : ENGLAND

23. SILVER : GOLD :: (*a.* Si, *b.* Sl, *c.* Ag, *d.* Hg) : Au

24. VALEDICTORIAN : SALUTATORIAN :: PRIME : (*a.* excellent, *b.* good, *c.* choice, *d.* alternative)

25. CHEROKEE : (*a.* Indian, *b.* aborigine, *c.* Seminole, *d.* pariah) :: APACHE : NAVAHO

26. (*a.* musical instruments, *b.* books, *c.* weather systems, *d.* diseases) : DEWEY :: LIVING THINGS : LINNAEUS

27. IVAN : TERRIBLE :: PETER : (*a.* Hairy, *b.* Reformer, *c.* Great, *d.* Awful)

28. SQUARE : 360 :: RECTANGLE : (*a.* 90, *b.* 180, *c.* 270, *d.* 360)

29. WHALE : (*a.* mammal, *b.* reptile, *c.* amphibian, *d.* fish) :: LIZARD : REPTILE

30. LINCOLN : (*a.* 1, *b.* 5, *c.* 10, *d.* 16) :: JACKSON : 20

31. CONJUNCTION : DISJUNCTION :: AND : (*a.* but, *b.* if . . . then, *c.* or, *d.* because)

32. AENEAS : (*a.* Virgil, *b.* Plutarch, *c.* Caesar, *d.* Demosthenes) :: ODYSSEUS: HOMER

33. AGORAPHOBIA : ARACHNOPHOBIA :: OPEN SPACES : (*a.* lizards, *b.* snakes, *c.* spiders, *d.* dragons)

34. GRIMM : (*a.* Donne, *b.* Petrarch, *c.* Nash, *d.* Andersen) :: CHAUCER : BOCCACCIO

35. CYCLONE : TORNADO :: HURRICANE : (*a.* storm, *b.* typhoon, *c.* rain, *d.* miasma)

36. GREENHOUSE : PLANTS :: AVIARY : (*a.* birds, *b.* bees, *c.* rodents, *d.* fish)

37. (*a.* $A \cap B$, *b.* $B \cap A$, *c.* $A \cup B$, *d.* $B \cup A$) : $B \cup A$ :: $X \wedge Y$: $Y \vee X$

38. OFFER : JOB :: TENDER : (*a.* resignation, *b.* retirement, *c.* delicate, *d.* rough)

39. HICCUP : HICCOUGH :: EYE : (*a.* light, *b.* ice, *c.* I, *d.* iris)

40. (*a.* black, *b.* white, *c.* orange, *d.* brown) : BLUE :: RED : GREEN

41. ASPIRIN : (*a.* anaphoric, *b.* mycin, *c.* antibiotic, *d.* analgesic) :: PENICILLIN : ANTIBIOTIC

42. (*a.* Istanbul, *b.* Dar es Salaam, *c.* Jerusalem, *d.* Mecca) : MOHAMMED :: BETHLEHEM : JESUS

43. CETANE : DIESEL FUEL OIL :: (*a.* octane, *b.* heptane, *c.* methane, *d.* propane) : GASOLINE

44. DEAD DUCK : GONER :: LAME DUCK : (*a.* one who finishes a term after failing re-election, *b.* one who gives up easily, *c.* one who invests cautiously, *d.* one who complains incessantly)

45. ARGONAUTS : (*a.* Francis Marion, *b.* Jason, *c.* Achilles, *d.* George Washington) :: GREEN MOUNTAIN BOYS : ETHAN ALLEN

46. LYNX : CAT :: BOAR : (*a.* hog, *b.* dog, *c.* goat, *d.* ram)

47. LENIN : BOLSHEVIK :: (*a.* Stalin, *b.* Kerensky, *c.* Trotsky, *d.* Marx) : MENSHEVIK

48. (*a.* oak, *b.* walnut, *c.* balsa, *d.* corundum) : HICKORY :: TIN : STEEL

49. ROCK : ROCKET :: (*a.* coat, *b.* cloth, *c.* jack, *d.* wasp) : JACKET

50. MALARIA : CHILLS :: GOITER : (*a.* pockmarks, *b.* swelling, *c.* fever, *d.* hypertension)

51. PIZARRO : INCA :: (*a.* Ponce de Leon, *b.* Hudson, *c.* Velásquez, *d.* Cortez) : AZTEC

52. ASTROLOGY : (*a.* astronomy, *b.* physics, *c.* pharmacology, *d.* phrenology) :: ASTRONOMY : ANATOMY

53. DUET : SEXTET :: SOLO : (*a.* quartet, *b.* quintet, *c.* chorus, *d.* trio)

54. ANDES : (*a.* Asia, *b.* Africa, *c.* South America, *d.* Europe) :: ALPS : EUROPE

55. MYOPIA : (*a.* hyperopia, *b.* scotopia, *c.* photopia, *d.* metropia) :: NEARSIGHTED : FARSIGHTED

56. PASTORAL : (*a.* religious, *b.* rustic, *c.* metropolitan, *d.* worldly) :: URBAN : CITIFIED

57. SEA : TIGER :: LION : (*a.* land, *b.* fauna, *c.* lily, *d.* heart)

58. ASTRONAUT : SPACESUIT :: (*a.* judge, *b.* baker, *c.* ballerina, *d.* monk) : HABIT

59. MONOGAMY : BIGAMY :: BIPED : (*a.* unipod, *b.* pedate, *c.* millipede, *d.* quadruped)

60. POPE : ROMAN :: (*a.* Metropolitan, *b.* Patriarch, *c.* Cardinal, *d.* Bishop) : GREEK ORTHODOX

61. SEXTANT : (*a.* navigator, *b.* architect, *c.* archeologist, *d.* priest) :: SCALPEL : SURGEON

62. PRIDE : PREJUDICE :: SENSE : (*a.* Folly, *b.* Prentense, *c.* Sensibility, *d.* Sanity)

63. PACIFIST : PEACE :: (*a.* revolutionary, *b.* diplomat, *c.* charlatan, *d.* traitor) : WAR

64. (*a.* brown, *b.* gray, *c.* purple, *d.* blue) : UMBER :: GREEN : CHARTREUSE

65. INCREASE : LESSEN :: (*a.* fair, *b.* final, *c.* incipient, *d.* unfair) : INCHOATE

66. EXCALIBUR : (*a.* sword, *b.* pony, *c.* lioness, *d.* cannon) :: LASSIE : DOG

67. (*a.* Bern, *b.* Geneva, *c.* Zurich, *d.* Lucerne) : SWITZERLAND ::
NEW DELHI : INDIA

68. SILVER-TONGUED : ELOQUENT :: JANUS-FACED : (*a.* duplicitous,
b. versatile, *c.* incredibly ugly, *d.* honest)

69. PRESENT : FUTURE PERFECT :: GO : (*a.* would go, *b.* will go,
c. will have gone, *d.* would have gone)

70. AMPLITUDE : FREQUENCY :: RATE : (*a.* distance, *b.* velocity,
c. acceleration, *d.* time)

71. GREENHORN : NOVICE :: NEOPHYTE : (*a.* expert, *b.* priest,
c. beginner, *d.* novelist)

72. PANEGYRIC : (*a.* prayer, *b.* joke, *c.* threat, *d.* eulogy) :: TEMPEST :
STORM

73. CARMEN : (*a.* Verdi, *b.* Bizet, *c.* Gounod, *d.* Wagner) ::
BARBER OF SEVILLE : ROSSINI

74. PALPITATE : QUIVER :: MASTICATE : (*a.* abuse, *b.* remove, *c.* stomp,
d. chew)

75. BOLÍVAR : (*a.* Venezuela, *b.* Spain, *c.* United States, *d.* Mexico) ::
WASHINGTON : ENGLAND

76. CORNUCOPIA : (*a.* horn of plenty, *b.* horn of Roland, *c.* hornpipe,
d. hornstone) :: TENET : PRECEPT

77. SHRIMP : CRUSTACEAN :: (*a.* snail, *b.* lobster, *c.* goldfish, *d.* brine) :
MOLLUSK

78. NEW AMSTERDAM : NEW YORK :: SIAM : (*a.* Thailand, *b.* Cambodia,
c. Laos, *d.* China)

79. HIRSUTE : (*a.* pleasantly plump, *b.* well-dressed, *c.* handsome, *d.* hairy) ::
EXTROVERTED : OUTGOING

80. EYE : LIP :: ELBOW : (*a.* forehead, *b.* nose, *c.* foot, *d.* chest)

81. (*a.* feldspar, *b.* talc, *c.* quartz, *d.* topaz) : 1 :: DIAMOND : 10

82. TORTUOUS : (*a.* painless, *b.* painful, *c.* straight, *d.* winding) :: SOBER :
INEBRIATED

83. NONPLUS : (*a.* perplexity, *b.* disappointment, *c.* deletion, *d.* elation) :: NONPAREIL : UNEQUALED

84. CROCKETT : ALAMO :: BONAPARTE : (*a.* Madrid, *b.* St. Helena, *c.* Rome, *d.* London)

85. EL GRECO : (*a.* impressionist, *b.* mannerist, *c.* expressionist, *d.* realist) :: DAVID : NEOCLASSICIST

86. GRAY : COUNTRY CHURCHYARD :: (*a.* Keats, *b.* Poe, *c.* Byron, *d.* Longfellow) : GRECIAN URN

87. MITER : (*a.* dancer, *b.* cartoonist, *c.* queen, *d.* bishop) :: CROWN : KING

88. $2^0 : 2^{-2} :: 2^2 :$ (*a.* $2^{1/4}$, *b.* 2^0, *c.* 2^1, *d.* 2^{-1})

89. FLOWER : GARDEN :: (*a.* pinnacle, *b.* stalagmite, *c.* cavern, *d.* explorer) : CAVE

90. LEVITICUS : OLD :: (*a.* Deuteronomy, *b.* Isaiah, *c.* Numbers, *d.* Ephesians) : NEW

91. LOUVRE : PARIS :: PRADO : (*a.* Madrid, *b.* Seville, *c.* Florence, *d.* Chartres)

92. CUL-DE-SAC : BLIND ALLEY :: SANGFROID : (*a.* carelessness, *b.* timidity, *c.* courage, *d.* imperturbability)

93. ENCOMIUM : TRIBUTE :: (*a.* admonition, *b.* excoriation, *c.* benison, *d.* exegesis) : CRITICAL ANALYSIS

94. CARPETBAGGER : NORTH :: (*a.* Granger, *b.* Scalawag, *c.* Bull Moose, *d.* Tweety Pie) : SOUTH

95. MERCURIAL : (*a.* pretty, *b.* plutonic, *c.* hateful, *d.* hermetic) :: MARTIAL : AREOLOGY

96. LEGATO : BOW :: PIZZICATO : (*a.* fingers, *b.* bow, *c.* reed, *d.* feet)

97. NICK ADAMS : (*a.* Fitzgerald, *b.* Faulkner, *c.* Hemingway, *d.* Joyce) :: ARROWSMITH : LEWIS

98. (*a.* Burgundian, *b.* Prussian, *c.* Turkish, *d.* Bulgarian) : OTTOMAN :: FRENCH : BOURBON

99. ORPHEUS : EURYDICE :: DAPHNIS : (*a.* Pyramus, *b.* Thisbe, *c.* Chloe, *d.* Helen)

100. (*a.* darling, *b.* wench, *c.* harridan, *d.* myrmidon) : SHREW ::
MOLLYCODDLE : SISSY

101. PULLEY : (*a.* screw, *b.* saw, *c.* pliers, *d.* nail) :: WEDGE :
INCLINED PLANE

102. LIVE WIRE : LOOSE CANNON :: ENERGETIC : (*a.* powerful,
b. threatening, *c.* reckless, *d.* peaceable)

103. ARM : LEG :: (*a.* radius, *b.* ulna, *c.* humerus, *d.* scapula) : FEMUR

104. VENUSIAN : (*a.* Venus, *b.* Earth, *c.* Moon, *d.* Mercury) :: MARTIAN :
JUPITER

105. (*a.* oil, *b.* air, *c.* nitrates, *d.* blood) : TOURNIQUET :: WATER : DAM

106. OBJURGATE : (*a.* vituperate, *b.* venerate, *c.* abrogate, *d.* enervate) ::
RECANT : RETRACT

107. PERFIDIOUS : BENEFICENT :: (*a.* obvious, *b.* capricious, *c.* intractable,
d. renitent) : STEADFAST

108. MAN : LAZARUS :: BIRD : (*a.* dragon, *b.* albatross, *c.* phoenix, *d.* dodo)

109. FIREWORKS : (*a.* Japan, *b.* Korea, *c.* Indonesia, *d.* China) ::
LIGHTBULB : THE UNITED STATES

110. GI TRACT : GI JOE :: GASTROINTESTINAL : (*a.* General Infantry,
b. Galvanized Iron, *c.* Government Issue, *d.* General Information)

111. WET SUIT : (*a.* spandex, *b.* neoprene, *c.* nylon, *d.* Lycra) ::
BULLETPROOF VEST : KEVLAR

112. (*a.* yellow, *b.* pink, *c.* white, *d.* green) : BLUE :: JAUNDICED :
CYANOTIC

113. MONET : WATER LILIES :: DEGAS : (*a.* windmills, *b.* sailboats,
c. polo players, *d.* ballet dancers)

114. WAR : (*a.* birth, *b.* flood, *c.* death, *d.* fall) :: ANTEBELLUM :
ANTEDILUVIAN

115. DILETTANTE : DEBUTANTE :: (*a.* amateur, *b.* professional, *c.* actor,
d. student) : YOUNG WOMAN

116. DOG : CAT :: (*a.* loud, *b.* skinny, *c.* under, *d.* hound) : FAT

117. RIDE : (*a.* U.S. senator, *b.* doctor, *c.* pilot, *d.* astronaut) :: O'CONNOR : SUPREME COURT JUSTICE

118. (*a.* panda, *b.* opossum, *c.* mouse, *d.* anteater) : WALLABY :: KANGAROO : WOMBAT

119. ANDREW : ABRAHAM :: LYNDON : (*a.* John, *b.* Robert, *c.* Joseph, *d.* Edward)

120. MYOPIA: CONCAVE :: (*a.* mytopia, *b.* astigmatism, *c.* hyperopia, *d.* diopia) : CONVEX

Answer Key
PRACTICE TEST 5

1. **A**	31. **C**	61. **A**	91. **A**
2. **C**	32. **A**	62. **C**	92. **D**
3. **A**	33. **C**	63. **A**	93. **D**
4. **C**	34. **D**	64. **A**	94. **B**
5. **A**	35. **B**	65. **B**	95. **D**
6. **B**	36. **A**	66. **A**	96. **A**
7. **D**	37. **A**	67. **A**	97. **C**
8. **A**	38. **A**	68. **A**	98. **C**
9. **C**	39. **C**	69. **C**	99. **C**
10. **C**	40. **C**	70. **D**	100. **C**
11. **A**	41. **D**	71. **C**	101. **A**
12. **D**	42. **D**	72. **D**	102. **C**
13. **B**	43. **A**	73. **B**	103. **C**
14. **C**	44. **A**	74. **D**	104. **B**
15. **A**	45. **B**	75. **B**	105. **D**
16. **A**	46. **A**	76. **A**	106. **A**
17. **D**	47. **B**	77. **A**	107. **B**
18. **D**	48. **C**	78. **A**	108. **C**
19. **B**	49. **C**	79. **D**	109. **D**
20. **B**	50. **B**	80. **C**	110. **C**
21. **D**	51. **D**	81. **B**	111. **B**
22. **B**	52. **D**	82. **C**	112. **A**
23. **C**	53. **D**	83. **A**	113. **D**
24. **C**	54. **C**	84. **B**	114. **B**
25. **C**	55. **A**	85. **B**	115. **A**
26. **B**	56. **B**	86. **A**	116. **C**
27. **C**	57. **C**	87. **D**	117. **D**
28. **D**	58. **D**	88. **B**	118. **B**
29. **A**	59. **D**	89. **B**	119. **A**
30. **B**	60. **B**	90. **D**	120. **C**

Answer Key

ANSWER EXPLANATIONS FOR PRACTICE TEST 5

> In the following, explanations concerning the correct response are in a large font. Explanations regarding distracters (incorrect responses) that are not self-explaining or could be misinterpreted are in a smaller font in order to highlight the explanations of the answers that are correct.

1. BOW : (*a. arrow*, *b.* grenade, *c.* quiver, *d.* target) :: RIFLE : BULLET

   (**a**) An arrow is shot from a bow; a bullet is shot from a rifle.
   General Information—Description

2. MARK TWAIN : HANNIBAL :: (*a.* Ernest Hemingway, *b.* Stephen Crane, **c. William Shakespeare**, *d.* Victor Hugo) : STRATFORD-UPON-AVON

   (**c**) Mark Twain was born in Hannibal, Missouri. William Shakespeare was born in Stratford-upon-Avon, England. Ernest Hemingway was born in Oak Park, Illinois; Stephen Crane was born in Newark, New Jersey; Victor Hugo was born in Besancon, France.
   Humanities—Description

3. UNITED : STAND :: DIVIDED : (*a. fall*, *b.* sit, *c.* lie, *d.* rise)

   (**a**) "United we stand, divided we fall" is a familiar saying.
   General Information—Completion

4. (*a.* Asia, *b.* South America, **c. Africa**, *d.* North America) : SAHARA :: NORTH AMERICA : PAINTED

   (**c**) The Sahara Desert is in Africa. The Painted Desert is in North America.
   General Information—Description

5. TARANTULA : (*a. spider*, *b.* rabbit, *c.* cat, *d.* cockroach) :: COBRA : SNAKE

   (**a**) A tarantula is a type of spider; a cobra is a type of snake.
   Natural Science—Class

6. (*a.* 6, *b. 9*, *c.* 12, *d.* 15) : BASEBALL :: 5 : BASKETBALL

   (**b**) There are 9 players on a baseball team, and 5 on a basketball team.
   General Information—Description

7. SEINE : (*a.* Canada, *b.* Holland, *c.* Germany, *d. France*) :: THAMES : ENGLAND

   (**d**) The Seine River is in France, while the Thames River is in England.
   General Information—Description

8. PLIABLE : BEND :: (***a*. brittle**, *b*. transparent, *c*. opaque, *d*. flexible) : BREAK

   (**a**) A pliable object will easily bend, while a brittle substance will easily break.
   General Information—Description

9. ADVERB : HAPPILY :: PREPOSITION : (*a*. the, *b*. or, ***c*. on**, *d*. none)

   (**c**) *Happily* is an adverb. *On* is a preposition.
   Humanities—Description

10. RIGHT ANGLE : (*a*. 0, *b*. 45, ***c*. 90**, *d*. 360) :: STRAIGHT ANGLE : 180

    (**c**) A right angle is 90 degrees; a straight angle is 180 degrees.
    Mathematics—Description

11. AUTHOR : PEN :: PAINTER : (***a*. brush**, *b*. paint, *c*. canvas, *d*. picture)

    (**a**) An author does his or her writing with a pen; a painter does his or her painting with a brush.
    General Information—Description

12. ASTRONAUT : ROCKET SHIP :: WITCH : (*a*. cauldron, *b*. vulture, *c*. black cat, ***d*. broomstick**)

    (**d**) An astronaut flies by rocket ship. A witch "flies" by broomstick.
    General Information—Description

13. (*a*. achievement, ***b*. permission**, *c*. month, *d*. desire) : ABILITY :: MAY : CAN

    (**b**) Someone who can do something is able to do it. Someone who may do something has permission to do it.
    General Information—Description

14. IBM : (*a*. Industrial Business Machines, *b*. Innovative Business Machines, ***c*. International Business Machines**, *d*. Intelligent Business Machines) :: GOP : Republican Party

    (**c**) IBM is a common abbreviation for International Business Machines. GOP is an abbreviation for the Grand Old Party, which is the Republican Party.
    General Information—Similarity/Contrast

15. (***a*. earthling**, *b*. earthian, *c*. earthing, *d*. earthan) : EARTH :: MARTIAN : MARS

    (**a**) An earthling is an inhabitant of the Earth. A Martian is an inhabitant of Mars.
    General Information—Description

Answer Explanations

16. ASBESTOS : FIRE :: (***a. vinyl***, *b.* air, *c.* cotton, *d.* faucet) : WATER

    (**a**) Asbestos is fireproof. Vinyl is waterproof.
    General Information—Description

17. DAVY JONES : (*a.* Great Britain, *b.* Planet Earth, *c.* the sun, ***d. the sea***) ::
    LAND OF THE RISING SUN : JAPAN

    (**d**) Davy Jones refers to the bottom of the sea; the origins of this term are
    unclear. The Land of the Rising Sun is Japan.
    General Information—Similarity/Contrast

18. PAIR : PARE :: COUPLE : (*a.* several, *b.* one, *c.* pear, ***d. prune***)

    (**d**) A pair is a couple. To pare is to prune.
    Vocabulary—Similarity/Contrast

19. ASCETIC : (*a.* businessman, ***b. monk***, *c.* carpenter, *d.* policeman) ::
    CRAFTY : CONFIDENCE MAN

    (**b**) A monk is ascetic. A confidence man is crafty.
    General Information—Description

20. GUILLOTINE : ROBESPIERRE :: (*a.* noose, ***b. poison***, *c.* knife,
    d. illness) : SOCRATES

    (**b**) Robespierre was killed by the guillotine. Socrates was killed by poison.
    Humanities—Description

21. GIN : BLACK :: (*a.* apple, *b.* whiskey, *c.* cotton, ***d. rummy***) : JACK

    (**d**) Gin rummy and blackjack are both card games.
    General Information—Completion

22. PESO : MEXICO :: (*a.* ounce, ***b. pound***, *c.* ruble, *d.* mark) : ENGLAND

    (**b**) The peso is the unit of currency in Mexico. The pound is the unit of
    currency in England. An ounce is a unit of weight. The ruble is the unit of currency in
    Russia. The mark was formerly the unit of currency in Germany.
    General Information—Description

23. SILVER : GOLD :: (*a.* Si, *b.* Sl, ***c. Ag***, *d.* Hg) : Au

    (**c**) The chemical symbol for silver is Ag; that for gold is Au. Si stands for
    silicon; Hg stands for mercury.
    Natural Science—Similarity/Contrast

24. VALEDICTORIAN : SALUTATORIAN :: PRIME : (*a.* excellent, *b.* good, *c.* **choice**, *d.* alternative)

   (**c**) A valedictorian is the highest-ranking student in a class, while a salutatorian is the second highest. Prime meat is the highest-ranked type of meat, while choice meat is the second highest-ranked.
   General Information—Class

25. CHEROKEE : (*a.* Indian, *b.* aborigine, *c.* **Seminole**, *d.* pariah) :: APACHE : NAVAJO

   (**c**) The Cherokee, Seminole, Apache, and Navajo are all tribes of American Indians. Aborigines are members of the original population of a place, as opposed to the colonizing people. Pariahs are members of a traditionally low caste in India.
   Social Science—Class

26. (*a.* musical instruments, *b.* **books**, *c.* weather systems, *d.* diseases) : DEWEY :: LIVING THINGS : LINNAEUS

   (**b**) Dewey devised a system for classifying books (Dewey Decimal Classification, DDC). Linnaeus devised a system for classifying living things (biological classification).
   Humanities—Description

27. IVAN : TERRIBLE :: PETER : (*a.* Hairy, *b.* Reformer, *c.* **Great**, *d.* Awful)

   (**c**) Ivan the Terrible (1530–1584) and Peter the Great (1672–1725) were both rulers of Russia.
   Humanities—Completion

28. SQUARE : 360 :: RECTANGLE : (*a.* 90, *b.* 180, *c.* 270, *d.* **360**)

   (**d**) Both a square and a rectangle have interior angles summing to 360 degrees.
   Mathematics—Description

29. WHALE : (*a.* **mammal**, *b.* reptile, *c.* amphibian, *d.* fish) :: LIZARD : REPTILE

   (**a**) A whale is a mammal; a lizard is a reptile.
   Natural Science—Class

30. LINCOLN : (*a.* 1, *b.* **5**, *c.* 10, *d.* 16) :: JACKSON : 20

   (**b**) President Lincoln's portrait appears on a $5 bill; President Jackson's portrait appears on a $20 bill. George Washington appears on the $1 bill. Alexander Hamilton appears on the $10 bill. Ulysses Grant appears on the $50 bill. Benjamin Franklin appears on the $100 bill.
   General Information—Description

Answer Explanations

31. CONJUNCTION : DISJUNCTION :: AND : (*a.* but, *b.* if . . . then, *c.* **or**, *d.* because)

    (**c**) In logic, *and* expresses conjunction and *or* expresses disjunction.
    Mathematics—Class

32. AENEAS : (*a.* **Virgil**, *b.* Plutarch, *c.* Caesar, *d.* Demosthenes) :: ODYSSEUS : HOMER

    (**a**) Virgil wrote about the travels of Aeneas; Homer wrote about the travels of Odysseus. Plutarch wrote *Parallel Lives*; famous fables of Aesop are, for example, *The Fox and the Grapes* and *The Tortoise and the Hare*. Caesar was a dictator of the Roman Republic and wrote *Commentarii de Bello Gallico*, among other works. Demosthenes was a Greek orator who published many of his orations.
    Humanities—Description

33. AGORAPHOBIA : ARACHNOPHOBIA :: OPEN SPACES : (*a.* lizards, *b.* snakes, *c.* **spiders**, *d.* dragons)

    (**c**) Agoraphobia is a fear of open spaces. Arachnophobia is a fear of spiders.
    Vocabulary—Description

34. GRIMM : (*a.* Donne, *b.* Petrarch, *c.* Nash, *d.* **Andersen**) :: CHAUCER : BOCCACCIO

    (**d**) Grimm and Andersen both wrote fairy tales. Chaucer and Boccaccio both wrote collections of tales told by groups of people.
    Humanities—Class

35. CYCLONE : TORNADO :: HURRICANE : (*a.* storm, *b.* **typhoon**, *c.* rain, *d.* miasma)

    (**b**) Cyclone, tornado, hurricane, and typhoon are all types of major storms. Cyclones are storms that rotate around a center and often come with rain. Hurricanes are tropical cyclones that are faster than 73 miles per hour; they mostly appear in the western Atlantic. Typhoons are a kind of hurricane that mostly appears in the China Sea or the Philippines. Tornadoes occur over land.
    Natural Science—Class

36. GREENHOUSE : PLANTS :: AVIARY : (*a.* **birds**, *b.* bees, *c.* rodents, *d.* fish)

    (**a**) A greenhouse houses plants. An aviary houses birds.
    Natural Science—Description

37. (*a. **A** ∩ **B***, *b. B ∩ A*, *c. A ∪ B*, *d. B ∪ A*) : *B ∪ A* :: *X ∧ Y* : *Y ∨ X*

    (**a**) *A ∩ B* and *X ∧ Y* are equivalent, as are *B ∪ A* and *Y ∨ X*.
    Mathematics—Equality/Negation

38. OFFER : JOB :: TENDER : (***a. resignation***, *b.* retirement, *c.* delicate, *d.* rough)

    (**a**) One offers a job, but tenders a resignation.
    General Information—Description

39. HICCUP : HICCOUGH :: EYE : (*a.* light, *b.* ice, ***c. I***, *d.* iris)

    (**c**) *Hiccup* and *hiccough* are pronounced identically, as are *eye* and *I*.
    Nonsemantic

40. (*a.* black, *b.* white, ***c. orange***, *d.* brown) : BLUE :: RED : GREEN

    (**c**) Orange and blue are complementary colors, as are red and green.
    Complementary colors are colors that produce white light when combined.
    Natural Science—Similarity/Contrast

41. ASPIRIN : (*a.* anaphoric, *b.* mycin, *c.* antibiotic, ***d. analgesic***) ::
    PENICILLIN : ANTIBIOTIC

    (**d**) Aspirin is an analgesic, while penicillin is an antibiotic. Analgesic
    medication alleviates pain. An antibiotic kills or inhibits the growth of
    microorganisms. Anaphoric refers to the repetition of a word or phrase at the beginning
    of a clause; mycin is a suffix that refers to a substance gained from a fungus-like bacterium.
    Natural Science—Class

42. (*a.* Istanbul, *b.* Dar es Salaam, *c.* Jerusalem, ***d. Mecca***) : MOHAMMED ::
    BETHLEHEM : JESUS

    (**d**) Mecca was the birthplace of Mohammed, while Bethlehem was the
    birthplace of Jesus.
    Humanities—Description

43. CETANE : DIESEL FUEL OIL :: (***a. octane***, *b.* heptane, *c.* methane,
    d. propane) : GASOLINE

    (**a**) Diesel fuel oil is given a cetane rating as an index of quality, while
    gasoline is given an octane rating for the same purpose.
    Natural Science—Description

44. DEAD DUCK : GONER :: LAME DUCK : (**a. one who finishes a term after failing re-election**, *b.* one who gives up easily, *c.* one who invests cautiously, *d.* one who complains incessantly)

    (**a**) A dead duck is a goner; a lame duck is an elected official who finishes his or her term after failing re-election.
    General Information—Similarity/Contrast

45. ARGONAUTS : (*a.* Francis Marion, **b. Jason**, *c.* Achilles, *d.* George Washington) :: GREEN MOUNTAIN BOYS : ETHAN ALLEN

    (**b**) The Argonauts accompanied Jason in his exploits; the Green Mountain Boys accompanied Ethan Allen in his exploits. *Argonautica* is an Ancient Greek poem. The Green Mountain Boys were an informal militia of the Vermont Republic.
    Humanities—Description

46. LYNX : CAT :: BOAR : (**a. hog**, *b.* dog, *c.* goat, *d.* ram)

    (**a**) A lynx is a type of wild cat. A boar is a type of wild hog.
    Natural Science—Class

47. LENIN : BOLSHEVIK :: (*a.* Stalin, **b. Kerensky**, *c.* Trotsky, *d.* Marx) : MENSHEVIK

    (**b**) After the Russian Revolution, Lenin led the Bolsheviks and Kerensky led the Mensheviks.
    Humanities—Description

48. (*a.* oak, *b.* walnut, **c. balsa**, *d.* corundum) : HICKORY :: TIN : STEEL

    (**c**) Balsa is a soft wood; hickory a hard wood. Tin is a soft metal; steel a hard metal. Oak is a hard wood, as is walnut. Corundum is a very hard mineral.
    Natural Science—Class

49. ROCK : ROCKET :: (*a.* coat, *b.* cloth, **c. jack**, *d.* wasp) : JACKET

    (**c**) Rocket is rock with -*et* at the end. *Jacket* is *jack* with -*et* at the end.
    Nonsemantic

50. MALARIA : CHILLS :: GOITER : (*a.* pockmarks, **b. swelling**, *c.* fever, *d.* hypertension)

    (**b**) Malaria results in chills. Goiter results in swelling.
    Natural Science—Description

51. PIZARRO : INCA :: (*a.* Ponce de Leon, *b.* Hudson, *c.* Velásquez, *d.* **Cortez**) : AZTEC

   (**d**) Pizarro (ca. 1475–1541) conquered the Inca Indians. Cortez (1485–1547) conquered the Aztecs.
   Humanities—Description

52. ASTROLOGY : (*a.* astronomy, *b.* physics, *c.* pharmacology, *d.* **phrenology**) :: ASTRONOMY : ANATOMY

   (**d**) Astrology and phrenology (drawing conclusions from the shape of skull to character traits) are commonly considered pseudosciences, while astronomy and anatomy are accepted as natural sciences.
   Natural Science—Class

53. DUET : SEXTET :: SOLO : (*a.* quartet, *b.* quintet, *c.* chorus, *d.* **trio**)

   (**d**) Two is to six as one is to three.
   Mathematics—Equality/Negation

54. ANDES : (*a.* Asia, *b.* Africa, *c.* **South America**, *d.* Europe) :: ALPS : EUROPE

   (**c**) The Andes mountain range is in South America; the Alps are in Europe.
   General Information—Description

55. MYOPIA : (*a.* **hyperopia**, *b.* scotopia, *c.* photopia, *d.* metropia) :: NEARSIGHTED : FARSIGHTED

   (**a**) A nearsighted person has myopia, while a farsighted person has hyperopia. Scotopia is the ability to see in darkness. Photopia is vision in bright light.
   Natural Science—Description

56. PASTORAL : (*a.* religious, *b.* **rustic**, *c.* metropolitan, *d.* worldly) :: URBAN : CITIFIED

   (**b**) *Pastoral* and *rustic* are synonyms, as are *urban* and *citified*.
   Vocabulary—Similarity/Contrast

57. SEA : TIGER :: LION : (*a.* land, *b.* fauna, *c.* **lily**, *d.* heart)

   (**c**) A sea lion and a tiger lily are both living things.
   General Information—Class

58. ASTRONAUT : SPACESUIT :: (*a.* judge, *b.* baker, *c.* ballerina, *d.* **monk**) : HABIT

   (**d**) An astronaut wears a spacesuit; a monk wears a habit.
   General Information—Description

Answer Explanations

59. MONOGAMY : BIGAMY :: BIPED : (*a.* unipod, *b.* pedate, *c.* millipede, **d. quadruped**)

(**d**) One is to two as two is to four. A biped is a two-footed animal.
A millipede is an invertebrate with many legs. *Pedate* means "having or resembling a foot."
A unipod is a pole to support cameras (similar to a tripod).
Mathematics—Class

60. POPE : ROMAN :: (*a.* Metropolitan, **b. Patriarch**, *c.* Cardinal, *d.* Bishop) : GREEK ORTHODOX

(**b**) The Pope is the spiritual leader of the Roman Catholic Church, while the Patriarch is the spiritual leader of the Greek Orthodox Catholic Church.
A cardinal is a member of the Sacred College in the Roman Catholic Church. Cardinals elect the Pope and serve as his advisors. A bishop is a clergyman overseeing a diocese.
Humanities—Description

61. SEXTANT : (**a. navigator**, *b.* architect, *c.* archeologist, *d.* priest) :: SCALPEL : SURGEON

(**a**) A sextant is used by a navigator, while a scalpel is used by a surgeon.
Natural Science—Description

62. PRIDE : PREJUDICE :: SENSE : (*a.* Folly, *b.* Pretense, **c. Sensibility**, *d.* Sanity)

(**c**) *Pride and Prejudice* and *Sense and Sensibility* are both novels by Jane Austen.
Humanities—Completion

63. PACIFIST : PEACE :: (**a. revolutionary**, *b.* diplomat, *c.* charlatan, *d.* traitor) : WAR

(**a**) A pacifist seeks peace; a revolutionary seeks war.
Vocabulary—Description

64. (**a. brown**, *b.* gray, *c.* purple, *d.* blue) : UMBER :: GREEN : CHARTREUSE

(**a**) Umber is a shade of brown; chartreuse is a shade of green.
Vocabulary—Class

65. INCREASE : LESSEN :: (*a.* fair, **b. final**, *c.* incipient, *d.* unfair) : INCHOATE

(**b**) *Increase* and *lessen* are antonyms, as are *final* and *inchoate*.
Vocabulary—Similarity/Contrast

66. EXCALIBUR : (*a.* **sword**, *b.* pony, *c.* lioness, *d.* cannon) :: LASSIE : DOG

    (**a**) Excalibur was the name of a sword (King Arthur's). Lassie was the name of a dog (Jeff Miller's).
    Humanities—Description

67. (*a.* **Bern**, *b.* Geneva, *c.* Zurich, *d.* Lucerne) : SWITZERLAND ::
    NEW DELHI : INDIA

    (**a**) Bern is the capital of Switzerland; New Delhi is the capital of India.
    General Information—Description

68. SILVER-TONGUED : ELOQUENT :: JANUS-FACED : (*a.* **duplicitous**,
    b. versatile, *c.* incredibly ugly, *d.* honest)

    (**a**) A silver-tongued person is eloquent. A Janus-faced person is duplicitous—literally, two-faced.
    Vocabulary—Similarity/Contrast

69. PRESENT : FUTURE PERFECT :: GO : (*a.* would go, *b.* will go,
    c. **will have gone**, *d.* would have gone)

    (**c**) *Go* is the present tense, and *will have gone* the future perfect tense, of the same verb.
    Humanities—Description

70. AMPLITUDE : FREQUENCY :: RATE : (*a.* distance, *b.* velocity,
    c. acceleration, *d.* **time**)

    (**d**) Amplitude and frequency of a wave are inversely related, as are rate and time traveled by an object.
    Natural Science—Equality/Negation

71. GREENHORN : NOVICE :: NEOPHYTE : (*a.* expert, *b.* priest,
    c. **beginner**, *d.* novelist)

    (**c**) *Greenhorn, novice, neophyte,* and *beginner* are all synonymous.
    Vocabulary—Similarity/Contrast

72. PANEGYRIC : (*a.* prayer, *b.* joke, *c.* threat, *d.* **eulogy**) :: TEMPEST :
    STORM

    (**d**) A panegyric is a eulogy. A tempest is a storm.
    Vocabulary—Similarity/Contrast

73. CARMEN : (*a.* Verdi, ***b.* Bizet**, *c.* Gounod, *d.* Wagner) ::
BARBER OF SEVILLE : ROSSINI

    (**b**) *Carmen* is an opera by Bizet. *The Barber of Seville* is an opera by Rossini.
    Rigoletto and *Nabucco* were composed by Verdi. The opera *Faust* is by Gounod. Wagner
    wrote *The Ring of the Nibelung*.
    Humanities—Description

74. PALPITATE : QUIVER :: MASTICATE : (*a.* abuse, *b.* remove, *c.* stomp,
***d.* chew**)

    (**d**) To palpitate is to quiver. To masticate is to chew.
    Vocabulary—Similarity/Contrast

75. BOLÍVAR : (*a.* Venezuela, ***b.* Spain**, *c.* United States, *d.* Mexico) ::
WASHINGTON : ENGLAND

    (**b**) Simon Bolívar fought against Spain for the liberation of South American
    countries. George Washington fought against England for the liberation of
    the newly formed United States.
    Humanities—Description

76. CORNUCOPIA : (***a.* horn of plenty**, *b.* horn of Roland, *c.* hornpipe,
d. hornstone) :: TENET : PRECEPT

    (**a**) A cornucopia is a horn of plenty. A tenet is a precept.
    Vocabulary—Similarity/Contrast

77. SHRIMP : CRUSTACEAN :: (***a.* snail**, *b.* lobster, *c.* goldfish, *d.* brine) :
MOLLUSK

    (**a**) A shrimp is a form of crustacean. A snail is a form of mollusk. A lobster is
    a crustacean; a goldfish is a freshwater fish; brine is water containing salts.
    Natural Science—Class

78. NEW AMSTERDAM : NEW YORK :: SIAM : (***a.* Thailand**, *b.* Cambodia,
c. Laos, *d.* China)

    (**a**) New York was formerly called New Amsterdam. Thailand was formerly
    called Siam. Cambodia was formerly named the Khmer Republic and Kampuchea.
    General Information—Similarity/Contrast

79. HIRSUTE : (*a.* pleasantly plump, *b.* well-dressed, *c.* handsome, ***d.* hairy**) ::
EXTROVERTED : OUTGOING

    (**d**) A hirsute person is hairy. An extroverted person is outgoing.
    Vocabulary—Similarity/Contrast

80. EYE : LIP :: ELBOW : (*a.* forehead, *b.* nose, ***c.* foot**, *d.* chest)

   (**c**) A normal human being has two eyes, lips, elbows, and feet.
   General Information—Class

81. (*a.* feldspar, ***b.* talc**, *c.* quartz, *d.* topaz) : 1 :: DIAMOND : 10

   (**b**) On the Mohs scale of hardness, talc is rated 1 (softest) and diamond is
   rated 10 (hardest). Quartz is rated 7; feldspar is rated 6; topaz is rated 8.
   Natural Science—Description

82. TORTUOUS : (*a.* painless, *b.* painful, ***c.* straight**, *d.* winding) :: SOBER :
   INEBRIATED

   (**c**) *Tortuous* and *straight* are opposites, as are *sober* and *inebriated*.
   Vocabulary—Similarity/Contrast

83. NONPLUS : (***a.* perplexity**, *b.* disappointment, *c.* deletion, *d.* elation) ::
   NONPAREIL : UNEQUALED

   (**a**) Nonplus is perplexity. Something that is nonpareil is unequaled.
   Vocabulary—Similarity/Contrast

84. CROCKETT : ALAMO :: BONAPARTE : (*a.* Madrid, ***b.* St. Helena**,
   c. Rome, *d.* London)

   (**b**) Davy Crockett died at the Alamo. Napoleon Bonaparte died on
   St. Helena.
   Humanities—Description

85. EL GRECO : (*a.* impressionist, ***b.* mannerist**, *c.* expressionist, *d.* realist) ::
   DAVID : NEOCLASSICIST

   (**b**) El Greco was a mannerist painter. David was a neoclassicist painter.
   Humanities—Description

86. GRAY : COUNTRY CHURCHYARD :: (***a.* Keats**, *b.* Poe, *c.* Byron,
   d. Longfellow) : GRECIAN URN

   (**a**) Thomas Gray is famous for his "Elegy in a Country Churchyard,"
   while John Keats is famous for his "Ode on a Grecian Urn." Edgar Allan Poe
   is famous as a mystery writer; one of his works is *The Pit and the Pendulum*. Henry
   Wadsworth Longfellow was an American poet whose works include *Paul Revere's Ride*.
   George Byron was a British poet and wrote *When We Two Parted*.
   Humanities—Description

87. MITER : (*a.* dancer, *b.* cartoonist, *c.* queen, ***d.* bishop**) :: CROWN : KING

   (**d**) A miter is a headpiece worn by a bishop. A crown is a headpiece worn
   by a king.
   General Information—Description

Answer Explanations

88. $2^0 : 2^{-2} :: 2^2 : (a.\ 2^{1/4},\ \boldsymbol{b.\ 2^0},\ c.\ 2^1,\ d.\ 2^{-1})$

   (**b**) 1 is to $^1/_4$ as 4 is to 1.
   Mathematics—Equality/Negation

89. FLOWER : GARDEN :: (*a.* pinnacle, ***b.* stalagmite**, *c.* cavern, *d.* explorer) : CAVE

   (**b**) Flowers grow up from a garden; stalagmites "grow" up from the floor of a cave.
   Natural Science—Description

90. LEVITICUS : OLD :: (*a.* Deuteronomy, *b.* Isaiah, *c.* Numbers, ***d.* Ephesians**) : NEW

   (**d**) Leviticus is a book in the Old Testament, while Ephesians is a book in the New Testament. Deuteronomy, Numbers, and Isaiah are books in the Old Testament of the Bible.
   Humanities—Description

91. LOUVRE : PARIS :: PRADO : (***a.* Madrid**, *b.* Seville, *c.* Florence, *d.* Chartres)

   (**a**) The Louvre is an art museum in Paris; the Prado is an art museum in Madrid.
   Humanities—Description

92. CUL-DE-SAC : BLIND ALLEY :: SANGFROID : (*a.* carelessness, *b.* timidity, *c.* courage, ***d.* imperturbability**)

   (**d**) A cul-de-sac is a blind alley. Sangfroid is imperturbability.
   Vocabulary—Similarity/Contrast

93. ENCOMIUM : TRIBUTE :: (*a.* admonition, *b.* excoriation, *c.* benison, ***d.* exegesis**) : CRITICAL ANALYSIS

   (**d**) An encomium is a tribute. An exegesis is a critical analysis.
   Vocabulary—Similarity/Contrast

94. CARPETBAGGER : NORTH :: (*a.* Granger, ***b.* Scalawag**, *c.* Bull Moose, *d.* Tweety Pie) : SOUTH

   (**b**) After the Civil War, intruders from the North were called carpetbaggers, and Northern sympathizers (usually Republicans) from the South were called scalawags. The Bull Moose Party is a former political party in the United States founded by Theodore Roosevelt. Tweety Pie is a cartoon character. A granger is a farmer.
   Humanities—Description

95. MERCURIAL : (*a.* pretty, *b.* plutonic, *c.* hateful, ***d.* hermetic**) :: MARTIAL : AREOLOGY

   (**d**) The word *mercurial* is derived from the Roman name and the word *hermetic* from the Greek name, for the messenger of the gods (Mercury or Hermes, respectively). The word *martial* is derived from the Roman name, and the word *areology* from the Greek name, for the god of war (Mars or Ares, respectively).
   Humanities—Description

96. LEGATO : BOW :: PIZZICATO : (***a.* fingers**, *b.* bow, *c.* reed, *d.* feet)

   (**a**) On a string instrument, legato notes are played with a bow, while pizzicato notes are played with the fingers.
   Humanities—Description

97. NICK ADAMS : (*a.* Fitzgerald, *b.* Faulkner, ***c.* Hemingway**, *d.* Joyce) :: ARROWSMITH : LEWIS

   (**c**) Nick Adams was a character in stories by Ernest Hemingway. Arrowsmith was a character in a novel (entitled *Arrowsmith*) by Sinclair Lewis.
   Humanities—Description

98. (*a.* Burgundian, *b.* Prussian, ***c.* Turkish**, *d.* Bulgarian) : OTTOMAN :: FRENCH : BOURBON

   (**c**) The Ottomans were Turkish; the Bourbons were French. The Burgundians were French; the Prussians were German.
   Humanities—Description

99. ORPHEUS : EURYDICE :: DAPHNIS : (*a.* Pyramus, *b.* Thisbe, ***c.* Chloe**, *d.* Helen)

   (**c**) Orpheus and Eurydice were lovers, as were Daphnis and Chloe. The story of Pyramus and Thisbe was told by Ovid; they were lovers as well. Helen was the daughter of Zeus and Leda and was abducted by Paris, which led to the Trojan War.
   Humanities—Class

100. (*a.* darling, *b.* wench, ***c.* harridan**, *d.* myrmidon) : SHREW :: MOLLYCODDLE : SISSY

   (**c**) A harridan is a shrew. A mollycoddle is a sissy.
   Vocabulary—Similarity/Contrast

Answer Explanations

101. PULLEY : (*a.* **screw**, *b.* saw, *c.* pliers, *d.* nail) :: WEDGE : INCLINED PLANE

    (**a**) Among the six basic simple machines are a pulley, screw, wedge, and inclined plane (as well as the lever and the wheel and axle).
    Natural Science—Class

102. LIVE WIRE : LOOSE CANNON :: ENERGETIC : (*a.* powerful, *b.* threatening, ***c.* reckless**, *d.* peaceable)

    (**c**) A person who is very energetic can be described as a live wire, whereas a reckless person can be described as a loose cannon.
    General Information—Similarity/Contrast

103. ARM : LEG :: (*a.* radius, *b.* ulna, ***c.* humerus**, *d.* scapula) : FEMUR

    (**c**) The humerus is the upper armbone just as the femur is the upper legbone. The ulna is the elbow bone. The radius is the bone on the side of the thumb of a forearm. The scapulae are a pair of large triangular bones that form the posterior part of the shoulder.
    Natural Science—Description

104. VENUSIAN : (*a.* Venus, ***b.* Earth**, *c.* Moon, *d.* Mercury) :: MARTIAN : JUPITER

    (**b**) A Venusian is a hypothetical inhabitant of the planet whose orbit around the Sun is just inside that of the planet Earth. A Martian is a hypothetical inhabitant of the planet whose orbit is just inside that of Jupiter. The order of the planets orbiting the Sun is (in order from the Sun): Mercury, Venus, Earth, Mars, Jupiter, Saturn, Uranus, Neptune.
    General Information—Description

105. (*a.* oil, *b.* air, *c.* nitrates, ***d.* blood**) : TOURNIQUET :: WATER : DAM

    (**d**) The function of a tourniquet is to stop the flow of blood beyond a certain point just as the function of a dam is to stop the flow of water beyond a certain point.
    Vocabulary—Description

106. OBJURGATE : (***a.* vituperate**, *b.* venerate, *c.* abrogate, *d.* enervate) :: RECANT : RETRACT

    (**a**) To objurgate is to harshly criticize, as is to vituperate. Likewise, recant and retract share the same meaning, to withdraw in a way.
    Vocabulary—Similarity/Contrast

107. PERFIDIOUS : BENEFICENT :: (*a.* obvious, ***b.* capricious**, *c.* intractable, *d.* renitent) : STEADFAST

(**b**) Perfidious and beneficent are antonyms, as are capricious, meaning changing quickly, and steadfast, meaning dependable and constant.
Vocabulary—Similarity/Contrast

108. MAN : LAZARUS :: BIRD : (*a.* dragon, *b.* albatross, ***c.* phoenix**, *d.* dodo)

(**c**) Lazarus was a man said to rise from the dead. The phoenix was a bird said to rise from the dead.
Humanities—Description

109. FIREWORKS : (*a.* Japan, *b.* Korea, *c.* Indonesia, ***d.* China**) :: LIGHTBULB : THE UNITED STATES

(**d**) Fireworks were first invented in China just as the lightbulb was first known in the United States.
General Information—Description

110. GI TRACT : GI JOE :: GASTROINTESTINAL : (*a.* General Infantry, *b.* Galvanized Iron, ***c.* Government Issue**, *d.* General Information)

(**c**) GI Tract is short for Gastrointestinal Tract. GI Joe is short for Government Issue Joe (which is also an action figure).
General Information—Equality/Negation

111. WET SUIT : (*a.* spandex, ***b.* neoprene**, *c.* nylon, *d.* Lycra) :: BULLETPROOF VEST : KEVLAR

(**b**) The artificial material used to make wet suits is neoprene just as the artificial material used to make bulletproof vests is Kevlar. Spandex is an elastic synthetic fiber; the most famous brand name associated with Spandex is Lycra. Nylon is a strong elastic polyamide material.
General Information—Part/Whole

112. (***a.* yellow**, *b.* pink, *c.* white, *d.* green) : BLUE :: JAUNDICED : CYANOTIC

(**a**) Someone who is jaundiced has a skin color that is tinted yellow. Likewise, a cyanotic person has blue-tinted skin.
Natural Science—Description

113. MONET : WATER LILIES :: DEGAS : (*a.* windmills, *b.* sailboats, *c.* polo players, ***d.* ballet dancers**)

(**d**) Just as Monet had water lilies as a favorite subject for his art, so did Degas often feature ballet dancers in his paintings and sculptures.
Humanities—Description

114. WAR : (*a.* birth, ***b.* flood**, *c.* death, *d.* fall) :: ANTEBELLUM : ANTEDILUVIAN

    (**b**) Antebellum refers to a time before a war and antediluvian refers to a time before the flood. *Prenatal* means "before birth"; *antemortem* refers to the time before death.
    Vocabulary—Description

115. DILETTANTE : DEBUTANTE :: (***a.* amateur**, *b.* professional, *c.* actor, *d.* student) : YOUNG WOMAN

    (**a**) Dilettantes are amateurs and debutantes are young women.
    Vocabulary—Class

116. DOG : CAT :: (*a.* loud, *b.* skinny, ***c.* under**, *d.* hound) : FAT

    (**c**) "Underdog" and "fat cat" are both terms used to describe types of people.
    General Information—Completion

117. RIDE : (*a.* U.S. senator, *b.* doctor, *c.* pilot, ***d.* astronaut**) :: O'CONNOR : SUPREME COURT JUSTICE

    (**d**) Sally Ride was the first female astronaut. Sandra Day O'Connor was the first female Supreme Court Justice.
    General Information—Description

118. (*a.* panda, ***b.* opossum**, *c.* mouse, *d.* anteater) : WALLABY :: KANGAROO : WOMBAT

    (**b**) Opossums, wallabies, kangaroos, and wombats are all marsupial mammals.
    General Information—Class

119. ANDREW : ABRAHAM :: LYNDON : (***a.* John**, *b.* Robert, *c.* Joseph, *d.* Edward)

    (**a**) Andrew Johnson succeeded Abraham Lincoln as president. Lyndon Johnson succeeded John Kennedy as president.
    General Information—Description

120. MYOPIA: CONCAVE :: (*a.* mytopia, *b.* astigmatism, ***c.* hyperopia**, *d.* diopia) : CONVEX

    (**c**) A concave lens is typically used to correct for myopia, or nearsightedness. A convex lens corrects for hyperopia (farsightedness).
    Natural Science—Description

PRACTICE TEST 5

Item Classification Chart

	RELATIONSHIP						
	Similarity/ Contrast	Description	Class	Completion	Part/ Whole	Equality/ Negation	Nonsemantic
Vocabulary	18, 56, 65, 68, 71, 72, 74, 76, 79, 82, 83, 92, 93, 100, 106, 107	33, 63, 105, 114	64, 115				
General Information	14, 17, 44, 78, 102	1, 4, 6, 7, 8, 11, 12, 13, 15, 16, 19, 22, 30, 38, 54, 58, 67, 87, 104, 109, 117, 119	24, 57, 80, 118	3, 21, 116	111	110	
Humanities		2, 9, 20, 26, 32, 42, 45, 47, 51, 60, 66, 69, 73, 75, 84, 85, 86, 90, 91, 94, 95, 96, 97, 98, 108, 113	34, 99	27, 62			
Social Science			25				
Natural Science	23, 40	36, 43, 50, 55, 61, 81, 89, 103, 112, 120	5, 29, 35, 41, 46, 48, 52, 77,101			70	
Mathematics		10, 28	31, 59			37, 53, 88	
Nonsemantic							39, 49

Content (vertical label on left side)

Item Classification (vertical label on right side)

Answer Sheet

PRACTICE TEST 6

1 Ⓐ Ⓑ Ⓒ Ⓓ	31 Ⓐ Ⓑ Ⓒ Ⓓ	61 Ⓐ Ⓑ Ⓒ Ⓓ	91 Ⓐ Ⓑ Ⓒ Ⓓ
2 Ⓐ Ⓑ Ⓒ Ⓓ	32 Ⓐ Ⓑ Ⓒ Ⓓ	62 Ⓐ Ⓑ Ⓒ Ⓓ	92 Ⓐ Ⓑ Ⓒ Ⓓ
3 Ⓐ Ⓑ Ⓒ Ⓓ	33 Ⓐ Ⓑ Ⓒ Ⓓ	63 Ⓐ Ⓑ Ⓒ Ⓓ	93 Ⓐ Ⓑ Ⓒ Ⓓ
4 Ⓐ Ⓑ Ⓒ Ⓓ	34 Ⓐ Ⓑ Ⓒ Ⓓ	64 Ⓐ Ⓑ Ⓒ Ⓓ	94 Ⓐ Ⓑ Ⓒ Ⓓ
5 Ⓐ Ⓑ Ⓒ Ⓓ	35 Ⓐ Ⓑ Ⓒ Ⓓ	65 Ⓐ Ⓑ Ⓒ Ⓓ	95 Ⓐ Ⓑ Ⓒ Ⓓ
6 Ⓐ Ⓑ Ⓒ Ⓓ	36 Ⓐ Ⓑ Ⓒ Ⓓ	66 Ⓐ Ⓑ Ⓒ Ⓓ	96 Ⓐ Ⓑ Ⓒ Ⓓ
7 Ⓐ Ⓑ Ⓒ Ⓓ	37 Ⓐ Ⓑ Ⓒ Ⓓ	67 Ⓐ Ⓑ Ⓒ Ⓓ	97 Ⓐ Ⓑ Ⓒ Ⓓ
8 Ⓐ Ⓑ Ⓒ Ⓓ	38 Ⓐ Ⓑ Ⓒ Ⓓ	68 Ⓐ Ⓑ Ⓒ Ⓓ	98 Ⓐ Ⓑ Ⓒ Ⓓ
9 Ⓐ Ⓑ Ⓒ Ⓓ	39 Ⓐ Ⓑ Ⓒ Ⓓ	69 Ⓐ Ⓑ Ⓒ Ⓓ	99 Ⓐ Ⓑ Ⓒ Ⓓ
10 Ⓐ Ⓑ Ⓒ Ⓓ	40 Ⓐ Ⓑ Ⓒ Ⓓ	70 Ⓐ Ⓑ Ⓒ Ⓓ	100 Ⓐ Ⓑ Ⓒ Ⓓ
11 Ⓐ Ⓑ Ⓒ Ⓓ	41 Ⓐ Ⓑ Ⓒ Ⓓ	71 Ⓐ Ⓑ Ⓒ Ⓓ	101 Ⓐ Ⓑ Ⓒ Ⓓ
12 Ⓐ Ⓑ Ⓒ Ⓓ	42 Ⓐ Ⓑ Ⓒ Ⓓ	72 Ⓐ Ⓑ Ⓒ Ⓓ	102 Ⓐ Ⓑ Ⓒ Ⓓ
13 Ⓐ Ⓑ Ⓒ Ⓓ	43 Ⓐ Ⓑ Ⓒ Ⓓ	73 Ⓐ Ⓑ Ⓒ Ⓓ	103 Ⓐ Ⓑ Ⓒ Ⓓ
14 Ⓐ Ⓑ Ⓒ Ⓓ	44 Ⓐ Ⓑ Ⓒ Ⓓ	74 Ⓐ Ⓑ Ⓒ Ⓓ	104 Ⓐ Ⓑ Ⓒ Ⓓ
15 Ⓐ Ⓑ Ⓒ Ⓓ	45 Ⓐ Ⓑ Ⓒ Ⓓ	75 Ⓐ Ⓑ Ⓒ Ⓓ	105 Ⓐ Ⓑ Ⓒ Ⓓ
16 Ⓐ Ⓑ Ⓒ Ⓓ	46 Ⓐ Ⓑ Ⓒ Ⓓ	76 Ⓐ Ⓑ Ⓒ Ⓓ	106 Ⓐ Ⓑ Ⓒ Ⓓ
17 Ⓐ Ⓑ Ⓒ Ⓓ	47 Ⓐ Ⓑ Ⓒ Ⓓ	77 Ⓐ Ⓑ Ⓒ Ⓓ	107 Ⓐ Ⓑ Ⓒ Ⓓ
18 Ⓐ Ⓑ Ⓒ Ⓓ	48 Ⓐ Ⓑ Ⓒ Ⓓ	78 Ⓐ Ⓑ Ⓒ Ⓓ	108 Ⓐ Ⓑ Ⓒ Ⓓ
19 Ⓐ Ⓑ Ⓒ Ⓓ	49 Ⓐ Ⓑ Ⓒ Ⓓ	79 Ⓐ Ⓑ Ⓒ Ⓓ	109 Ⓐ Ⓑ Ⓒ Ⓓ
20 Ⓐ Ⓑ Ⓒ Ⓓ	50 Ⓐ Ⓑ Ⓒ Ⓓ	80 Ⓐ Ⓑ Ⓒ Ⓓ	110 Ⓐ Ⓑ Ⓒ Ⓓ
21 Ⓐ Ⓑ Ⓒ Ⓓ	51 Ⓐ Ⓑ Ⓒ Ⓓ	81 Ⓐ Ⓑ Ⓒ Ⓓ	111 Ⓐ Ⓑ Ⓒ Ⓓ
22 Ⓐ Ⓑ Ⓒ Ⓓ	52 Ⓐ Ⓑ Ⓒ Ⓓ	82 Ⓐ Ⓑ Ⓒ Ⓓ	112 Ⓐ Ⓑ Ⓒ Ⓓ
23 Ⓐ Ⓑ Ⓒ Ⓓ	53 Ⓐ Ⓑ Ⓒ Ⓓ	83 Ⓐ Ⓑ Ⓒ Ⓓ	113 Ⓐ Ⓑ Ⓒ Ⓓ
24 Ⓐ Ⓑ Ⓒ Ⓓ	54 Ⓐ Ⓑ Ⓒ Ⓓ	84 Ⓐ Ⓑ Ⓒ Ⓓ	114 Ⓐ Ⓑ Ⓒ Ⓓ
25 Ⓐ Ⓑ Ⓒ Ⓓ	55 Ⓐ Ⓑ Ⓒ Ⓓ	85 Ⓐ Ⓑ Ⓒ Ⓓ	115 Ⓐ Ⓑ Ⓒ Ⓓ
26 Ⓐ Ⓑ Ⓒ Ⓓ	56 Ⓐ Ⓑ Ⓒ Ⓓ	86 Ⓐ Ⓑ Ⓒ Ⓓ	116 Ⓐ Ⓑ Ⓒ Ⓓ
27 Ⓐ Ⓑ Ⓒ Ⓓ	57 Ⓐ Ⓑ Ⓒ Ⓓ	87 Ⓐ Ⓑ Ⓒ Ⓓ	117 Ⓐ Ⓑ Ⓒ Ⓓ
28 Ⓐ Ⓑ Ⓒ Ⓓ	58 Ⓐ Ⓑ Ⓒ Ⓓ	88 Ⓐ Ⓑ Ⓒ Ⓓ	118 Ⓐ Ⓑ Ⓒ Ⓓ
29 Ⓐ Ⓑ Ⓒ Ⓓ	59 Ⓐ Ⓑ Ⓒ Ⓓ	89 Ⓐ Ⓑ Ⓒ Ⓓ	119 Ⓐ Ⓑ Ⓒ Ⓓ
30 Ⓐ Ⓑ Ⓒ Ⓓ	60 Ⓐ Ⓑ Ⓒ Ⓓ	90 Ⓐ Ⓑ Ⓒ Ⓓ	120 Ⓐ Ⓑ Ⓒ Ⓓ

Answer Sheet

Practice Test 6

Directions: In each of the following questions, you will find three initial terms and, in parentheses, four answer options designated *a*, *b*, *c*, and *d*. You are to select from the four answer options the one that best completes the analogy with the three initial terms. To record your answers, use the answer sheet provided.

Time: 60 minutes

1. LETTER : WORD :: (*a.* paragraph, *b.* word, *c.* period, *d.* meaning) : SENTENCE

2. GIVEN NAME : FIRST :: (*a.* Christian name, *b.* real name, *c.* nickname, *d.* surname) : LAST

3. JUDICIARY : (*a.* Circuit Court, *b.* Supreme Court, *c.* District Court, *d.* Court of Appeals) :: LEGISLATIVE : CONGRESS

4. (*a.* magna cum laude, *b.* optima cum laude, *c.* puella cum laude, *d.* summa cum laude) : HIGHEST HONOR :: CUM LAUDE : HONOR

5. WILLIAM JAMES : PHILOSOPHER :: HENRY JAMES : (*a.* chemist, *b.* novelist, *c.* lawyer, *d.* politician)

6. OUNCE : PREVENTION :: POUND : (*a.* remedy, *b.* prophylaxis, *c.* medicine, *d.* cure)

7. (*a.* decline, *b.* recline, *c.* acclaim, *d.* reclaim) : ASCEND :: INCLINE : DESCEND

8. CARNIVORE : ANIMALS :: (*a.* omnivore, *b.* herbivore, *c.* carnivore, *d.* vegetivore) : VEGETABLES

9. COLD : (*a.* caress, *b.* shiver, *c.* legs, *d.* shoulder) :: OPEN : ARMS

10. DROUGHT : (*a.* desert, *b.* thirst, *c.* rain, *d.* crops) :: FAMINE : FOOD

11. WESTMINSTER ABBEY : ENGLAND :: TAJ MAHAL : (*a.* Iran, *b.* India, *c.* Pakistan, *d.* China)

12. LEGISLATOR : MAKES :: POLICE OFFICER : (*a.* interprets, *b.* enforces, *c.* breaks, *d.* enacts)

13. DIRECT : INDIRECT :: HIM : (*a.* him, *b.* his, *c.* he, *d.* he'd)

14. ZIP : LETTER :: AREA : (*a.* volume, *b.* πr^2, *c.* post box, *d.* telephone call)

15. COURSE : COARSE :: (*a.* ruffle, *b.* direction, *c.* jagged, *d.* golf) : ROUGH

16. DIRIGIBLE : (*a.* air, *b.* sea, *c.* land, *d.* underground) :: AUTOMOBILE : LAND

17. MENDEL : (*a.* inequality, *b.* dominance, *c.* depression, *d.* orbits) :: MENDELEEV : PERIODICITY

18. LIVID : ASHEN :: JAUNDICED : (*a.* white, *b.* black, *c.* red, *d.* yellow)

19. AMIABLE : UNFRIENDLY :: AFFABLE : (*a.* unpleasant, *b.* ugly, *c.* beautiful, *d.* kindly)

20. JUNEAU : ALASKA :: (*a.* Waikiki, *b.* Honolulu, *c.* Oahu, *d.* Hawaii) : HAWAII

21. EAT : DRINK :: EDIBLE : (*a.* palpable, *b.* potable, *c.* lacteal, *d.* labile)

22. WHITE LIE : LIE :: (*a.* hurricane, *b.* drizzle, *c.* storm, *d.* humidity) : RAINFALL

23. (*a.* net, *b.* ten, *c.* met, *d.* end) : TEND :: MEN : MEND

24. FLAPJACK : (*a.* pumpkin pie, *b.* pancake, *c.* sponge cake, *d.* paddycake) :: GRIDDLECAKE : HOTCAKE

25. BINOMIAL : POLYNOMIAL :: TWO : (*a.* four, *b.* eight, *c.* all, *d.* many)

26. SAUDI ARABIA : OIL :: (*a.* Iran, *b.* Brazil, *c.* Hungary, *d.* Guatemala) : COFFEE

27. MONARCHY : ONE :: OLIGARCHY : (*a.* two, *b.* three, *c.* several, *d.* multitudes)

28. PASADENA : FOOTBALL :: WIMBLEDON : (*a.* tennis, *b.* boxing, *c.* golf, *d.* basketball)

29. MOLEHILL : EARTH :: DUNE : (*a.* rock, *b.* desert, *c.* mud, *d.* sand)

30. (*a.* plankton, *b.* gizzard, *c.* oyster, *d.* dinosaur) : REPTILE :: FROG : AMPHIBIAN

31. (*a.* Andersen, *b.* Grimm, *c.* Milne, *d.* Alcott) : WINNIE :: DISNEY : MICKEY

32. PATRICIAN : PLEBEIAN :: NOBILITY : (*a.* clergy, *b.* lordship, *c.* proletariat, *d.* bourgeoisie)

33. (*a.* fungi, *b.* water, *c.* gases, *d.* algae) : HYDROLOGY :: LIFE : BIOLOGY

34. GOTHIC : POINTED :: ROMANESQUE : (*a.* rounded, *b.* scalloped, *c.* squared, *d.* buttressed)

35. (*a.* 7, *b.* 9, *c.* 10, *d.* 12) : PLAGUES :: 7 : DEADLY SINS

36. STEP : PETS :: REEL : (*a.* fishes, *b.* rod, *c.* leer, *d.* real)

37. HAWK : PREY :: SWINDLER : (*a.* dupe, *b.* dodge, *c.* doll, *d.* dolt)

38. SOPORIFIC : (*a.* pain, *b.* sleepiness, *c.* hunger, *d.* thirst) :: APHRODISIAC : SEXUAL DESIRE

39. PASTEURIZE : (*a.* chemically treat, *b.* strain, *c.* chill, *d.* partially sterilize) :: HOMOGENIZE : MAKE UNIFORM

40. DECLARATIVE : . :: INTERROGATIVE : (*a.* !, *b.* :, *c.* –, *d.* ?)

41. ALLEGRO : (*a.* largo, *b.* presto, *c.* crescendo, *d.* cantabile) :: FAST : SLOW

42. PENCE : POUND :: CENTS : (*a.* nickel, *b.* dime, *c.* quarter, *d.* dollar)

43. CLANDESTINE : (*a.* surreptitious, *b.* tacit, *c.* sanguine, *d.* outgoing) :: SHY : DIFFIDENT

44. INCOGNITO : (*a.* ignorant, *b.* uninterested, *c.* unofficial, *d.* disguised) :: SATISFACTORY : ADEQUATE

45. ANTIDOTE : POISON :: (*a.* mycin, *b.* antibiotic, *c.* analgesic, *d.* antigen) : BACTERIA

46. DIRTY : LINEN :: FILTHY : (*a.* flax, *b.* burlap, *c.* lummox, *d.* lucre)

47. POLAR : (*a.* equatorial, *b.* mammoth, *c.* coordinate, *d.* grizzly) :: FORD : CHEVROLET

48. ONTOLOGY : BEING :: EPISTEMOLOGY : (*a.* spirit, *b.* knowledge, *c.* metaphysics, *d.* causality)

49. RECORDER : (*a.* flute, *b.* magnetic tape, *c.* player piano, *d.* trombone) :: LUTE : GUITAR

50. MILLIMETER : METER :: METER : (*a*. centimeter, *b*. decimeter, *c*. decameter, *d*. kilometer)

51. GENDARMES : FRANCE :: CARABINIERI : (*a*. Spain, *b*. Italy, *c*. Switzerland, *d*. Turkey)

52. RENOIR : IMPRESSIONIST :: (*a*. Braque, *b*. Matisse, *c*. Monet, *d*. Stella) : CUBIST

53. SCOTLAND YARD : CRIME :: EXCHEQUER : (*a*. agriculture, *b*. industry, *c*. defense, *d*. money)

54. (*a*. magician, *b*. tycoon, *c*. adventurer, *d*. usurer) : GENTLEMAN OF FORTUNE :: ATTENDANT : GENTLEMAN IN WAITING

55. HALCYON : (*a*. tranquil, *b*. agitated, *c*. bounteous, *d*. impoverished) :: FORTUITOUS : PLANNED

56. UTOPIA : (*a*. More, *b*. Plato, *c*. Becket, *d*. Aquinas) :: LILLIPUT : SWIFT

57. MERIDIAN : LONGITUDE :: (*a*. meridian, *b*. prime, *c*. parallel, *d*. perpendicular) : LATITUDE

58. CENTURY : HUNDRED :: MILLENNIUM : (*a*. A.D. 1, *b*. eternity, *c*. thousand, *d*. million)

59. COLD-BLOODED : HARD-HEARTED :: HOT-BLOODED : (*a*. cruel, *b*. listless, *c*. cold-hearted, *d*. excitable)

60. ASSIDUOUS : (*a*. ambitious, *b*. favorable, *c*. diligent, *d*. evergreen) :: ASSIMILATE : ABSORB

61. NETREBKO : SOPRANO :: DOMINGO : (*a*. soprano, *b*. contralto, *c*. tenor, *d*. bass)

62. CARDINAL : ORDINAL :: 8 : (*a*. −2, *b*. 60%, *c*. 5th, *d*. 9)

63. VALJEAN : (*a*. Mauriac, *b*. Balzac, *c*. Hugo, *d*. Molière) :: GORIOT : BALZAC

64. MAUVE : (*a*. brown, *b*. red, *c*. purple, *d*. green) :: TAN : BROWN

65. RANGERS : (*a*. basketball, *b*. polo, *c*. football, *d*. hockey) :: CARDINALS : BASEBALL

66. CARTIER : (*a.* Hudson, *b.* Missouri, *c.* St. Lawrence, *d.* Cartesian) :: MARQUETTE : MISSISSIPPI

67. BUCOLIC : (*a.* rural, *b.* urban, *c.* spicy, *d.* mild) :: TIMID : SHY

68. MERSEAULT : (*a.* Linda, *b.* Suzanne, *c.* Jacqueline, *d.* Marie) :: TOM : BECKY

69. (*a.* scrupulous, *b.* shrewd, *c.* ingenuous, *d.* indigenous) : WILY :: NAIVE : SOPHISTICATED

70. MAXIM : (*a.* chisel, *b.* saw, *c.* palindrome, *d.* deed) :: ADAGE : PROVERB

71. BUCKINGHAM PALACE : MONARCH OF ENGLAND :: PANDEMONIUM : (*a.* Neptune, *b.* Genghis Khan, *c.* Satan, *d.* Citizen Kane)

72. TAXONOMY : LIFE FORMS :: NOSOLOGY : (*a.* noses, *b.* laws, *c.* coins, *d.* diseases)

73. PENOLOGY : OENOLOGY :: PEAL : (*a.* wine, *b.* oil, *c.* poll, *d.* eel)

74. FATHERS : SONS :: SONS (*a.* Daughters, *b.* Lovers, *c.* Strangers, *d.* Mothers)

75. CATATONIC : HEBEPHRENIC :: ANAL : (*a.* genital, *b.* phallic, *c.* oral, *d.* Oedipal)

76. (*a.* Joyce, *b.* Wilde, *c.* James, *d.* O'Henry) : DORIAN GRAY :: JOYCE : ARTIST AS A YOUNG MAN

77. EISENHOWER : REPUBLICAN :: (*a.* T. Roosevelt, *b.* Harrison, *c.* Fillmore, *d.* Wilson) : BULL MOOSE

78. TANGENT X : COTANGENT X :: X : (*a.* X^2, *b.* $1/X$, *c.* $X - 1$, *d.* $\tan X - \sin X$)

79. (*a.* mammals, *b.* life, *c.* fish, *d.* humans) : PALEOZOIC :: DINOSAURS : MESOZOIC

80. CITY OF SEVEN HILLS : ROME :: CITY OF LIGHT : (*a.* New York, *b.* Paris, *c.* London, *d.* Venice)

81. SLEEP : SOMNAMBULIST :: (*a.* pimp, *b.* crime, *c.* street, *d.* bed) : PROSTITUTE

82. CELSIUS : 0 :: KELVIN : (*a.* 32, *b.* 0, *c.* −100, *d.* 273)

83. DIONYSUS : DAMOCLES :: (*a.* Zeus, *b.* Pandora, *c.* Ares, *d.* Cronus) : PROMETHEUS

84. PENCIL LEAD : GRAPHITE :: CHALK : (*a.* limestone, *b.* sandstone, *c.* talc, *d.* gypsum)

85. MAUDLIN : (*a.* immature, *b.* humorous, *c.* munificent, *d.* mawkish) :: MODERATE : TEMPERATE

86. RHEOSTAT : ELECTRICITY :: (*a.* automobile, *b.* traffic light, *c.* car-counter, *d.* bottleneck) : TRAFFIC

87. CHAUCER : SWEET SHOWERS :: ELIOT : (*a.* stinging rain, *b.* sweet breath, *c.* swich licour, *d.* cruellest month)

88. 8^{-1} : 8^1 :: −1 : (*a.* −64, *b.* −8, *c.* 8, *d.* 64)

89. BIGOT : ZEALOT :: TROGLODYTE : (*a.* cave dweller, *b.* hero, *c.* traitor, *d.* reformer)

90. TEMPER : (*a.* piano, *b.* moisture, *c.* docility, *d.* tape recorder) :: FOCUS : CAMERA

91. ZEUS : HERA :: (*a.* Ulysses, *b.* Orestes, *c.* Agamemnon, *d.* Paris) : CLYTEMNESTRA

92. TRITIUM : HYDROGEN :: OZONE : (*a.* oxygen, *b.* nitrogen, *c.* carbon dioxide, *d.* cesium)

93. METROPOLITAN MUSEUM : NEW YORK :: RIJKSMUSEUM : (*a.* Utrecht, *b.* Munich, *c.* Paris, *d.* Amsterdam)

94. POSEIDON : (*a.* Uranus, *b.* Mars, *c.* Saturn, *d.* Neptune) :: ZEUS : JUPITER

95. (*a.* zz, *b.* Zuider, *c.* zero, *d.* zee) : ZED :: BAR : PUB

96. (*a.* hot, *b.* bacterium, *c.* virus, *d.* lungs) : TUBERCULOSIS :: VIRUS : COLD

97. MOLLY : (*a.* Madison, *b.* Monroe, *c.* Maguire, *d.* Malone) :: KNOW : NOTHING

98. ANEMOMETER : WIND SPEED :: MANOMETER : (*a.* blood pressure, *b.* heart rate, *c.* visual acuity, *d.* auditory acuity)

99. HERODOTUS : (*a.* history, *b.* medicine, *c.* his city, *d.* Greece) :: WASHINGTON : HIS COUNTRY

100. (*a.* Washington, *b.* Jackson, *c.* Eisenhower, *d.* Polk) : CORNWALLIS :: GRANT : LEE

101. $Y = X^2$: PARABOLA :: $Y = X + 1$: (*a.* cube, *b.* slope, *c.* circle, *d.* line)

102. NOM DE PLUME : (*a.* maiden name, *b.* middle name, *c.* pen name, *d.* married name) :: JE NE SAIS QUOI : INDEFINABLE QUALITY

103. (*a.* sheep, *b.* mutton, *c.* offal, *d.* venison) : LAMB :: BEEF : VEAL

104. RADIOACTIVE FALLOUT : CHERNOBYL :: (*a.* oil, *b.* propane, *c.* carbon monoxide, *d.* benzene) : VALDEZ

105. HELIUM : NEON :: ARGON : (*a.* cryon, *b.* iodine, *c.* xenon, *d.* hydrogen)

106. BATHYSPHERE : (*a.* rain forest, *b.* ice field, *c.* ocean, *d.* cave) :: SHUTTLE : SPACE

107. DEBUT : GURU :: FRENCH : (*a.* Greek, *b.* Spanish, *c.* Zulu, *d.* Hindi)

108. SHEPHERD : (*a.* sheep, *b.* human, *c.* goat, *d.* dog) :: MAHOUT : ELEPHANT

109. HMS : GREAT BRITAIN :: (*a.* SSS, *b.* SOS, *c.* USAS, *d.* USS) : UNITED STATES

110. (*a.* Ethiopia, *b.* Somalia, *c.* Djibouti, *d.* Eritrea) : MOGADISHU :: KENYA : NAIROBI

111. ALLUSION : ALLEGORY :: REFERENCE : (*a.* summary, *b.* parable, *c.* idiom, *d.* anecdote)

112. HORUS : (*a.* horse, *b.* dog, *c.* hawk, *d.* hare) :: ANUBIS : JACKAL

113. GOERING : NUREMBERG :: (*a.* Hitler, *b.* Hussein, *c.* Mussolini, *d.* Milosevic) : THE HAGUE

114. FOUR SCORE : (*a.* 40, *b.* 4, *c.* 28, *d.* 80) :: BAKER'S DOZEN : 13

115. KHOI SAN : SOUTH AFRICA :: MAORI : (*a.* New Zealand, *b.* Papua New Guinea, *c.* Fiji, *d.* Australia)

116. BEMUSE : AMUSE :: (*a.* humor, *b.* confuse, *c.* irritate, *d.* inspire) :: ENTERTAIN

117. PLESSY : FERGUSON :: BROWN : (*a.* The State, *b.* Topeka, *c.* Board of Education, *d.* Wade)

118. HONG KONG : (*a.* Hang Seng, *b.* NASDAQ, *c.* HKSE, *d.* Nikkei) :: UNITED STATES : DOW JONES

119. LAKERS : DODGERS :: (*a.* Orlando, *b.* Minneapolis, *c.* Albany, *d.* New Orleans) : BROOKLYN

120. (*a.* juniper, *b.* hickory, *c.* aspen, *d.* beech) : CEDAR :: TAMARAC : PINE

Answer Key
PRACTICE TEST 6

1. **B**	31. **C**	61. **C**	91. **C**
2. **D**	32. **C**	62. **C**	92. **A**
3. **B**	33. **B**	63. **C**	93. **D**
4. **D**	34. **A**	64. **C**	94. **D**
5. **B**	35. **C**	65. **D**	95. **D**
6. **D**	36. **C**	66. **C**	96. **B**
7. **A**	37. **A**	67. **A**	97. **C**
8. **B**	38. **B**	68. **D**	98. **A**
9. **D**	39. **D**	69. **C**	99. **A**
10. **C**	40. **D**	70. **B**	100. **A**
11. **B**	41. **A**	71. **C**	101. **D**
12. **B**	42. **D**	72. **D**	102. **C**
13. **A**	43. **A**	73. **D**	103. **B**
14. **D**	44. **D**	74. **B**	104. **A**
15. **B**	45. **B**	75. **C**	105. **C**
16. **A**	46. **D**	76. **B**	106. **C**
17. **B**	47. **D**	77. **A**	107. **D**
18. **D**	48. **B**	78. **B**	108. **A**
19. **A**	49. **A**	79. **C**	109. **D**
20. **B**	50. **D**	80. **B**	110. **B**
21. **B**	51. **B**	81. **C**	111. **B**
22. **B**	52. **A**	82. **D**	112. **C**
23. **B**	53. **D**	83. **A**	113. **D**
24. **B**	54. **C**	84. **A**	114. **D**
25. **D**	55. **B**	85. **D**	115. **A**
26. **B**	56. **A**	86. **B**	116. **B**
27. **C**	57. **C**	87. **D**	117. **C**
28. **A**	58. **C**	88. **A**	118. **A**
29. **D**	59. **D**	89. **A**	119. **B**
30. **D**	60. **C**	90. **A**	120. **A**

Answer Key

ANSWER EXPLANATIONS FOR PRACTICE TEST 6

In the following, explanations concerning the correct response are in a large font. Explanations regarding distracters (incorrect responses) that are not self-explaining or could be misinterpreted are in a smaller font in order to highlight the explanations of the answers that are correct.

1. LETTER : WORD :: (*a.* paragraph, *b.* **word**, *c.* period, *d.* meaning) : SENTENCE

   (**b**) A word is composed of letters. A sentence is composed of words.
   General Information—Part/Whole

2. GIVEN NAME : FIRST :: (*a.* Christian name, *b.* real name, *c.* nickname, ***d.* surname**) : LAST

   (**d**) A given name is a first name. A surname is a last name.
   Vocabulary—Similarity/Contrast

3. JUDICIARY : (*a.* Circuit Court, *b.* **Supreme Court**, *c.* District Court, *d.* Court of Appeals) :: LEGISLATIVE : CONGRESS

   (**b**) The Supreme Court is the highest judiciary body in the United States. The Congress is the highest legislative body in the United States.
   Social Science—Description

4. (*a.* magna cum laude, *b.* optima cum laude, *c.* puella cum laude, ***d.* summa cum laude**) :: HIGHEST HONOR :: CUM LAUDE : HONOR

   (**d**) *Summa cum laude* denotes highest honor; *cum laude*, honor. *Magna cum laude* means "with great honor."
   General Information—Similarity/Contrast

5. WILLIAM JAMES : PHILOSOPHER :: HENRY JAMES : (*a.* chemist, ***b.* novelist**, *c.* lawyer, *d.* politician)

   (**b**) William James was a philosopher; his brother Henry was a novelist.
   Humanities—Description

6. OUNCE : PREVENTION :: POUND : (*a.* remedy, *b.* prophylaxis, *c.* medicine, ***d.* cure**)

   (**d**) "An ounce of prevention is worth a pound of cure," or so the saying goes.
   General Information—Completion

7. (***a*. decline**, *b*. recline, *c*. acclaim, *d*. reclaim) : ASCEND :: INCLINE : DESCEND

   (**a**) *Decline* and *incline* are antonyms, as are *ascend* and *descend*.
   Vocabulary—Similarity/Contrast

8. CARNIVORE : ANIMALS :: (*a*. omnivore, ***b*. herbivore**, *c*. carnivore, *d*. vegetivore) : VEGETABLES

   (**b**) A carnivore eats (the flesh of) animals; an herbivore eats vegetables.
   An omnivore eats both plants and animals.
   Vocabulary—Description

9. COLD : (*a*. caress, *b*. shiver, *c*. legs, ***d*. shoulder**) :: OPEN : ARMS

   (**d**) A person may be greeted either with a cold shoulder or with open arms.
   General Information—Completion

10. DROUGHT : (*a*. desert, *b*. thirst, ***c*. rain**, *d*. crops) :: FAMINE : FOOD

    (**c**) A drought is caused by lack of rain; a famine is caused by lack of food.
    Vocabulary—Description

11. WESTMINSTER ABBEY : ENGLAND :: TAJ MAHAL : (*a*. Iran, ***b*. India**, *c*. Pakistan, *d*. China)

    (**b**) Westminster Abbey is in England. The Taj Mahal is in India.
    General Information—Description

12. LEGISLATOR : MAKES :: POLICE OFFICER : (*a*. interprets, ***b*. enforces**, *c*. breaks, *d*. enacts)

    (**b**) A legislator makes laws; a police officer enforces them.
    General Information—Description

13. DIRECT : INDIRECT :: HIM : (***a*. him**, *b*. his, *c*. he, *d*. he'd)

    (**a**) *Him* is the correct form of the personal pronoun for use as either a direct or an indirect object.
    Humanities—Description

14. ZIP : LETTER :: AREA : (*a*. volume, *b*. πr^2, *c*. post box, ***d*. telephone call**)

    (**d**) A zip code is used for a letter, while an area code is used for a telephone call.
    General Information—Description

15. COURSE : COARSE :: (*a*. ruffle, ***b*. direction**, *c*. jagged, *d*. golf) : ROUGH

    (**b**) *Course* and *direction* are synonyms, as are *coarse* and *rough*.
    Vocabulary—Similarity/Contrast

16. DIRIGIBLE : (***a. air***, *b.* sea, *c.* land, *d.* underground) :: AUTOMOBILE : LAND

    (**a**) A dirigible travels by air, while an automobile travels by land.
    General Information—Description

17. MENDEL : (*a.* inequality, ***b. dominance***, *c.* depression, *d.* orbits) :: MENDELEEV : PERIODICITY

    (**b**) Mendel formulated the law of dominance (in the field of inheritance); Mendeleev formulated the law of periodicity (in the field of chemistry).
    Natural Science—Description

18. LIVID : ASHEN :: JAUNDICED : (*a.* white, *b.* black, *c.* red, ***d. yellow***)

    (**d**) Something that is livid is ashen. Something that is jaundiced is yellow.
    Vocabulary—Similarity/Contrast

19. AMIABLE : UNFRIENDLY :: AFFABLE : (***a. unpleasant***, *b.* ugly, *c.* beautiful, *d.* kindly)

    (**a**) *Amiable* and *unfriendly* are opposites, as are *affable* and *unpleasant*.
    Vocabulary—Similarity/Contrast

20. JUNEAU : ALASKA :: (*a.* Waikiki, ***b. Honolulu***, *c.* Oahu, *d.* Hawaii) : HAWAII

    (**b**) Juneau is the capital of Alaska; Honolulu is the capital of Hawaii.
    Hawaii and Oahu are islands that are part of Hawaii. Waikiki is a neighborhood of Honolulu.
    General Information—Description

21. EAT : DRINK :: EDIBLE : (*a.* palpable, ***b. potable***, *c.* lacteal, *d.* labile)

    (**b**) One can eat what is edible and drink what is potable.
    Vocabulary—Description

22. WHITE LIE : LIE :: (*a.* hurricane, ***b. drizzle***, *c.* storm, *d.* humidity) : RAINFALL

    (**b**) A white lie is a minor lie; a drizzle is a minor rainfall.
    Vocabulary—Description

23. (*a.* net, ***b. ten***, *c.* met, *d.* end) : TEND :: MEN : MEND

    (**b**) *Tend* is pronounced as *ten*, but with an added *d* consonant sound at the end. *Mend* is pronounced as *men*, but again with an added *d* consonant sound at the end.
    Nonsemantic

24. FLAPJACK : (*a.* pumpkin pie, ***b.* pancake**, *c.* sponge cake, *d.* paddycake) :: GRIDDLECAKE : HOTCAKE

    (**b**) Flapjack, pancake, griddlecake, and hotcake are all names for the same food.
    General Information—Similarity/Contrast

25. BINOMIAL : POLYNOMIAL :: TWO : (*a.* four, *b.* eight, *c.* all, ***d.* many**)

    (**d**) A binomial is an equation with two terms. A polynomial is an equation with many terms.
    Mathematics—Description

26. SAUDI ARABIA : OIL :: (*a.* Iran, ***b.* Brazil**, *c.* Hungary, *d.* Guatemala) : COFFEE

    (**b**) Saudi Arabia is a major source of oil. Brazil is a major source of coffee.
    General Information—Description

27. MONARCHY : ONE :: OLIGARCHY : (*a.* two, *b.* three, ***c.* several**, *d.* multitudes)

    (**c**) A monarchy is a government of one ruler; an oligarchy is a government several individuals rule jointly.
    Social Science—Description

28. PASADENA : FOOTBALL :: WIMBLEDON : (***a.* tennis**, *b.* boxing, *c.* golf, *d.* basketball)

    (**a**) Pasadena is the location of a major football game (the Rose Bowl). Wimbledon is the location of a major tennis tournament.
    General Information—Description

29. MOLEHILL : EARTH :: DUNE : (*a.* rock, *b.* desert, *c.* mud, ***d.* sand**)

    (**d**) A molehill is composed of earth. A dune is composed of sand.
    General Information—Description

30. (*a.* plankton, *b.* gizzard, *c.* oyster, ***d.* dinosaur**) : REPTILE :: FROG : AMPHIBIAN

    (**d**) A dinosaur is a form of reptile. A frog is a form of amphibian. Amphibians are cold-blooded vertebrates that have gilled aquatic larvae and air-breathing adults. Reptiles are cold-blooded vertebrates that are different from amphibians in that they have scales and lay hard-shelled amniotic eggs.
    Natural Science—Class

Answer Explanations

31. (*a.* Andersen, *b.* Grimm, *c.* **Milne**, *d.* Alcott) : WINNIE :: DISNEY : MICKEY

(**c**) A. A. Milne created the character Winnie (the Pooh). Walt Disney created the character Mickey (Mouse). Anderson wrote *The Princess and the Pea*. The Brothers Grimm wrote *Hansel and Gretel*, among other fairy tales. Alcott wrote *Little Women*.
Humanities—Description

32. PATRICIAN : PLEBEIAN :: NOBILITY : (*a.* clergy, *b.* lordship, *c.* **proletariat**, *d.* bourgeoisie)

(**c**) In ancient Rome, the patricians were members of the nobility and the plebeians were members of the proletariat.
Humanities—Similarity/Contrast

33. (*a.* fungi, *b.* **water**, *c.* gases, *d.* algae) : HYDROLOGY :: LIFE : BIOLOGY

(**b**) Hydrology is the study of water; biology is the study of life.
Natural Science—Description

34. GOTHIC : POINTED :: ROMANESQUE : (*a.* **rounded**, *b.* scalloped, *c.* squared, *d.* buttressed)

(**a**) Gothic arches are pointed, while Romanesque arches are rounded.
Humanities—Description

35. (*a.* 7, *b.* 9, *c.* **10**, *d.* 12) : PLAGUES :: 7 : DEADLY SINS

(**c**) There were 10 plagues in Egypt, and there are 7 deadly sins.
The 7 deadly sins are pride, avarice, envy, wrath, lust, gluttony, and sloth.
The 10 plagues were water to blood, frogs, lice, flies, livestock disease, boils, thunder and hail, locusts, darkness, and the death of the firstborns.
Humanities—Description

36. STEP : PETS :: REEL : (*a.* fishes, *b.* rod, *c.* **leer**, *d.* real)

(**c**) *Pets* is *step* spelled backwards. *Leer* is *reel* spelled backwards.
Nonsemantic

37. HAWK : PREY :: SWINDLER : (*a.* **dupe**, *b.* dodge, *c.* doll, *d.* dolt)

(**a**) A hawk victimizes prey. A swindler victimizes dupes.
General Information—Description

38. SOPORIFIC : (*a.* pain, *b.* **sleepiness**, *c.* hunger, *d.* thirst) :: APHRODISIAC : SEXUAL DESIRE

(**b**) A soporific induces sleepiness. An aphrodisiac induces sexual desire.
Vocabulary—Description

39. PASTEURIZE : (*a.* chemically treat, *b.* strain, *c.* chill, ***d.* partially sterilize**) :: HOMOGENIZE : MAKE UNIFORM

   (**d**) To pasteurize milk is to partially sterilize it. To homogenize milk is to make it uniform.
   General Information—Similarity/Contrast

40. DECLARATIVE : . :: INTERROGATIVE : (*a.* !, *b.* :, *c.* –, ***d.* ?**)

   (**d**) A declarative sentence ends with a period (.). An interrogative sentence ends with a question mark (?).
   Humanities—Description

41. ALLEGRO : (***a.* largo**, *b.* presto, *c.* crescendo, *d.* cantabile) :: FAST : SLOW

   (**a**) In music, an allegro tempo is a fast one, while a largo tempo is a slow one. *Presto* means "fast," *crescendo* means "increasing loudness," and *cantabile* means "singing."
   Humanities—Similarity/Contrast

42. PENCE : POUND :: CENTS : (*a.* nickel, *b.* dime, *c.* quarter, ***d.* dollar**)

   (**d**) There are 100 pence in a pound (in English currency) and 100 cents in a dollar (in American currency).
   General Information—Part/Whole

43. CLANDESTINE : (***a.* surreptitious**, *b.* tacit, *c.* sanguine, *d.* outgoing) :: SHY : DIFFIDENT

   (**a**) *Clandestine* means *surreptitious*. *Shy* means *diffident*.
   Vocabulary—Similarity/Contrast

44. INCOGNITO : (*a.* ignorant, *b.* uninterested, *c.* unofficial, ***d.* disguised**) :: SATISFACTORY : ADEQUATE

   (**d**) *Incognito* means *disguised*. *Satisfactory* means *adequate*.
   Vocabulary—Similarity/Contrast

45. ANTIDOTE : POISON :: (*a.* mycin, ***b.* antibiotic**, *c.* analgesic, *d.* antigen) : BACTERIA

   (**b**) An antidote is a cure for the effects of poison; an antibiotic is a remedy for the effects of bacteria. Mycin is a suffix that refers to a substance gained from a fungus-like bacterium. Analgesic medication alleviates pain. An antigen is a substance capable of triggering a response from the immune system.
   Natural Science—Description

46. DIRTY : LINEN :: FILTHY : (*a.* flax, *b.* burlap, *c.* lummox, ***d.* lucre**)

    (**d**) *Dirty linen* and *filthy lucre* are two common English expressions.
    General Information—Completion

47. POLAR : (*a.* equatorial, *b.* mammoth, *c.* coordinate, ***d.* grizzly**) :: FORD : CHEVROLET

    (**d**) A polar bear and a grizzly bear are two types of bears. A Ford and a Chevrolet are two types of cars.
    General Information—Class

48. ONTOLOGY : BEING :: EPISTEMOLOGY : (*a.* spirit, ***b.* knowledge**, *c.* metaphysics, *d.* causality)

    (**b**) Ontology is the study of being; epistemology, the study of knowledge.
    Humanities—Description

49. RECORDER : (***a.* flute**, *b.* magnetic tape, *c.* player piano, *d.* trombone) :: LUTE : GUITAR

    (**a**) A recorder is an early form of flute; a lute is an early form of guitar.
    Humanities—Class

50. MILLIMETER : METER :: METER : (*a.* centimeter, *b.* decimeter, *c.* decameter, ***d.* kilometer**)

    (**d**) There are 1000 millimeters in a meter, and 1000 meters in a kilometer.
    Mathematics—Part/Whole

51. GENDARMES : FRANCE :: CARABINIERI : (*a.* Spain, ***b.* Italy**, *c.* Switzerland, *d.* Turkey)

    (**b**) Police officers in France are called gendarmes; in Italy, they are called carabinieri.
    General Information—Description

52. RENOIR : IMPRESSIONIST :: (***a.* Braque**, *b.* Matisse, *c.* Monet, *d.* Stella) : CUBIST

    (**a**) Renoir was an impressionist painter; Braque was a cubist. Matisse was a leading figure in modern art. Monet was an impressionist. Stella was a minimalist.
    Humanities—Description

53. SCOTLAND YARD : CRIME :: EXCHEQUER : (*a.* agriculture, *b.* industry, *c.* defense, ***d.* money**)

    (**d**) In England, Scotland Yard is charged with the control of crime, the Exchequer with the control of money.
    General Information—Description

54. (*a.* magician, *b.* tycoon, ***c.* adventurer**, *d.* usurer) : GENTLEMAN OF FORTUNE :: ATTENDANT : GENTLEMAN IN WAITING

    (**c**) A gentleman of fortune is an adventurer. A gentleman in waiting is an attendant.
    General Information—Similarity/Contrast

55. HALCYON : (*a.* tranquil, ***b.* agitated**, *c.* bounteous, *d.* impoverished) :: FORTUITOUS : PLANNED

    (**b**) *Halcyon* in an antonym of *agitated*. *Fortuitous* is an antonym of *planned*.
    Vocabulary—Similarity/Contrast

56. UTOPIA : (***a.* More**, *b.* Plato, *c.* Becket, *d.* Aquinas) :: LILLIPUT : SWIFT

    (**a**) Utopia is a land invented by More; Lilliput is a land invented by Swift.
    Plato wrote the *Socratic Dialogues*. Becket was Archbishop of Canterbury from 1162 to 1170. Aquinas wrote *Summa Theologica* and the *Summa Contra Gentiles*.
    Humanities—Description

57. MERIDIAN : LONGITUDE :: (*a.* meridian, *b.* prime, ***c.* parallel**, *d.* perpendicular) : LATITUDE

    (**c**) A meridian is a line of longitude; a parallel is a line of latitude.
    General Information—Description

58. CENTURY : HUNDRED :: MILLENNIUM : (*a.* A.D. 1, *b.* eternity, ***c.* thousand**, *d.* million)

    (**c**) A century is one hundred years; a millennium is one thousand years.
    General Information—Description

59. COLD-BLOODED : HARD-HEARTED :: HOT-BLOODED : (*a.* cruel, *b.* listless, *c.* cold-hearted, ***d.* excitable**)

    (**d**) *Cold-blooded* means *hard-hearted*. *Hot-blooded* means *excitable*.
    Vocabulary—Similarity/Contrast

60. ASSIDUOUS : (*a.* ambitious, *b.* favorable, ***c.* diligent**, *d.* evergreen) :: ASSIMILATE : ABSORB

    (**c**) *Assiduous* is a synonym of *diligent*. *Assimilate* is a synonym of *absorb*.
    Vocabulary—Similarity/Contrast

61. NETREBKO : SOPRANO :: DOMINGO : (*a.* soprano, *b.* contralto, ***c.* tenor**, *d.* bass)

    (**c**) Anna Netrebko is a renowned soprano; Placido Domingo is a renowned tenor.
    Humanities—Description

Answer Explanations

62. CARDINAL : ORDINAL :: 8 : (*a.* −2, *b.* 60%, *c.* **5th**, *d.* 9)

(**c**) 8 is a cardinal number, and 5th is an ordinal number.
Mathematics—Class

63. VALJEAN : (*a.* Mauriac, *b.* Balzac, *c.* **Hugo**, *d.* Molière) :: GORIOT : BALZAC

(**c**) Jean Valjean is a character created by the French novelist Victor Hugo. Père Goriot is a character created by the French novelist Honoré de Balzac. Francois Mauriac wrote *Le Desert de l'Amour*. Honore de Balzac wrote *La Comedie Humaine*, which contains about 100 novels and plays that describe French life after the fall of Napoleon. Moliere (Jean-Baptiste Poquelin) is known for the drama *Le Misanthrope*, among other plays.
Humanities—Description

64. MAUVE : (*a.* brown, *b.* red, *c.* **purple**, *d.* green) :: TAN : BROWN

(**c**) Mauve is a shade of purple; tan is a shade of brown.
General Information—Class

65. RANGERS : (*a.* basketball, *b.* polo, *c.* football, *d.* **hockey**) :: CARDINALS : BASEBALL

(**d**) The Rangers are a hockey team. The Cardinals are a baseball team.
General Information—Description

66. CARTIER : (*a.* Hudson, *b.* Missouri, *c.* **St. Lawrence**, *d.* Cartesian) :: MARQUETTE : MISSISSIPPI

(**c**) Cartier explored the St. Lawrence River; Marquette explored the Mississippi River. Henry Hudson was the first European who sailed up the Hudson River. The Missouri was first explored by the French: Louis Jolliet and Jacques Marquette. Cartesian means that something is related to the French philosopher Rene Descartes.
Humanities—Description

67. BUCOLIC : (*a.* **rural**, *b.* urban, *c.* spicy, *d.* mild) :: TIMID : SHY

(**a**) *Bucolic* means *rural*; *timid* means *shy*.
Vocabulary—Similarity/Contrast

68. MERSEAULT : (*a.* Linda, *b.* Suzanne, *c.* Jacqueline, *d.* **Marie**) :: TOM : BECKY

(**d**) In *The Stranger* (by Albert Camus), Marie is the girlfriend of Merseault. In *Tom Sawyer* (by Mark Twain), Becky is the girlfriend to Tom.
Humanities—Class

Answer Explanations

69. (*a.* scrupulous, *b.* shrewd, **c. ingenuous**, *d.* indigenous) : WILY :: NAIVE : SOPHISTICATED

    (**c**) *Ingenuous* and *wily* are opposites, as are *naive* and *sophisticated.*
    Vocabulary—Similarity/Contrast

70. MAXIM : (*a.* chisel, **b. saw**, *c.* palindrome, *d.* deed) :: ADAGE : PROVERB

    (**b**) *Maxim, saw, adage,* and *proverb* are all synonymous. A palindrome is a word or number that can be read the same way in any direction (e.g., "mom" or "101").
    Vocabulary—Similarity/Contrast

71. BUCKINGHAM PALACE : MONARCH OF ENGLAND :: PANDEMONIUM : (*a.* Neptune, *b.* Genghis Khan, **c. Satan**, *d.* Citizen Kane)

    (**c**) Buckingham Palace is the palace of the monarch of England. Pandemonium, in *Paradise Lost* (by John Milton), is the palace of Satan.
    Humanities—Description

72. TAXONOMY : LIFE FORMS :: NOSOLOGY : (*a.* noses, *b.* laws, *c.* coins, **d. diseases**)

    (**d**) Taxonomy is classification of life forms. Nosology is classification of diseases.
    Natural Science—Description

73. PENOLOGY : OENOLOGY :: PEAL : (*a.* wine, *b.* oil, *c.* poll, **d. eel**)

    (**d**) *Penology* and *oenology* have the same initial vowel sound, as do *peal* and *eel.*
    Nonsemantic

74. FATHERS : SONS :: SONS (*a.* Daughters, **b. Lovers**, *c.* Strangers, *d.* Mothers)

    (**b**) *Fathers and Sons* is a novel by Ivan Turgenev. *Sons and Lovers* is a novel by D. H. Lawrence.
    Humanities—Completion

75. CATATONIC : HEBEPHRENIC :: ANAL : (*a.* genital, *b.* phallic, **c. oral**, *d.* Oedipal)

    (**c**) A catatonic shows anal symptomatology. A hebephrenic shows oral symptomatology.
    Social Science—Description

Answer Explanations

76. (*a.* Joyce, ***b.* Wilde**, *c.* James, *d.* O'Henry) : DORIAN GRAY :: JOYCE : ARTIST AS A YOUNG MAN

   (**b**) Oscar Wilde wrote *The Picture of Dorian Gray*. James Joyce wrote *A Portrait of the Artist as a Young Man*.
   Humanities—Description

77. EISENHOWER : REPUBLICAN :: (***a.* T. Roosevelt**, *b.* Harrison, *c.* Fillmore, *d.* Wilson) : BULL MOOSE

   (**a**) President Eisenhower was a member of the Republican Party. President T. (Theodore) Roosevelt was a member of the Bull Moose Party. Harrison was a Republican; Fillmore was a member of the Whig Party; Wilson was a Democrat.
   Social Science—Description

78. TANGENT X : COTANGENT X :: X : (*a.* X^2, ***b.* $1/X$**, *c.* $X-1$, *d.* $\tan X - \sin X$)

   (**b**) The cotangent of X is equal to 1 divided by the tangent of X.
   Mathematics—Description

79. (*a.* mammals, *b.* life, ***c.* fish**, *d.* humans) : PALEOZOIC :: DINOSAURS : MESOZOIC

   (**c**) Fish first appeared in the Paleozoic Era (542–751 million years ago). Dinosaurs first appeared in the Mesozoic Era (251–65 million years ago).
   Natural Science—Description

80. CITY OF SEVEN HILLS : ROME :: CITY OF LIGHT : (*a.* New York, ***b.* Paris**, *c.* London, *d.* Venice)

   (**b**) Rome is the City of Seven Hills; Paris is the City of Light. The seven hills of Rome are called Palatine, Capitoline, Quirinal, Viminal, Esquiline, Caelian, and Aventine.
   Humanities—Similarity/Contrast

81. SLEEP : SOMNAMBULIST :: (*a.* pimp, *b.* crime, ***c.* street**, *d.* bed) : PROSTITUTE

   (**c**) A somnambulist walks in his or her sleep. A prostitute walks in the streets.
   General Information—Description

82. CELSIUS : 0 :: KELVIN : (*a.* 32, *b.* 0, *c.* −100, ***d.* 273**)

   (**d**) Zero degrees Celsius is equal to 273 Kelvin (to the nearest unit).
   Natural Science—Equality/Negation

83. DIONYSUS : DAMOCLES :: (***a. Zeus***, *b.* Pandora, *c.* Ares, *d.* Cronus) : PROMETHEUS

    (**a**) Dionysus punished Damocles (by hanging a sword over his head). Zeus punished Prometheus (by chaining him to a rock). Pandora was the first woman in Greek mythology. Ares was the Greek god of war. Cronus was the Greek god of agriculture and harvest.
    Humanities—Description

84. PENCIL LEAD : GRAPHITE :: CHALK : (***a. limestone***, *b.* sandstone, *c.* talc, *d.* gypsum)

    (**a**) Pencil lead is made of graphite. Chalk is made of limestone.
    General Information—Description

85. MAUDLIN : (*a.* immature, *b.* humorous, *c.* munificent, ***d. mawkish***) :: MODERATE : TEMPERATE

    (**d**) *Maudlin* means *mawkish*. *Moderate* means *temperate*.
    Vocabulary—Similarity/Contrast

86. RHEOSTAT : ELECTRICITY :: (*a.* automobile, ***b. traffic light***, *c.* car-counter, *d.* bottleneck) : TRAFFIC

    (**b**) A rheostat regulates the flow of electricity. A traffic light regulates the flow of traffic.
    Natural Science—Description

87. CHAUCER : SWEET SHOWERS :: ELIOT : (*a.* stinging rain, *b.* sweet breath, *c.* swich licour, ***d. cruellest month***)

    (**d**) In the opening line of *The Canterbury Tales*, Chaucer mentions April in the context of its sweet showers. In the opening line of *The Wasteland*, Eliot alludes to Chaucer, but changes things by mentioning April as the cruellest month.
    Humanities—Description

88. 8^{-1} : 8^1 :: -1 : (***a.* -64**, *b.* -8, *c.* 8, *d.* 64)

    (**a**) $^1/_8$ is to 8 as -1 is to -64.
    Mathematics—Equality/Negation

89. BIGOT : ZEALOT :: TROGLODYTE : (***a. cave dweller***, *b.* hero, *c.* traitor, *d.* reformer)

    (**a**) A bigot is a zealot; a troglodyte was a cave dweller.
    Vocabulary—Similarity/Contrast

90. TEMPER : (*a.* **piano**, *b.* moisture, *c.* docility, *d.* tape recorder) :: FOCUS : CAMERA

(**a**) One tempers a piano; one focuses a camera.
General Information—Description

91. ZEUS : HERA :: (*a.* Ulysses, *b.* Orestes, *c.* **Agamemnon**, *d.* Paris) : CLYTEMNESTRA

(**c**) In Greek mythology, Zeus was the husband of Hera. In Greek literature, Agamemnon was the husband of Clytemnestra. Ulysses is the Latin name for Odysseus. Orestes and Electra were the son and daughter of Agamemnon. Paris was the son of Priam, who in turn was the youngest son of Laomedon and king of Troy during the Trojan War.
Humanities—Class

92. TRITIUM : HYDROGEN :: OZONE : (*a.* **oxygen**, *b.* nitrogen, *c.* carbon dioxide, *d.* cesium)

(**a**) Tritium is a form of hydrogen, H_3. Ozone is a form of oxygen, O_3. Nitrogen is a chemical element (N). Cesium is a chemical element as well (Cs). Carbon dioxide (CO_2) is a chemical compound comprising two atoms of oxygen and one atom of carbon.
Natural Science—Class

93. METROPOLITAN MUSEUM : NEW YORK :: RIJKSMUSEUM : (*a.* Utrecht, *b.* Munich, *c.* Paris, *d.* **Amsterdam**)

(**d**) The Metropolitan Museum is in New York. The Rijksmuseum is in Amsterdam.
General Information—Description

94. POSEIDON : (*a.* Uranus, *b.* Mars, *c.* Saturn, *d.* **Neptune**) :: ZEUS : JUPITER

(**d**) Poseidon was the Greek name, and Neptune the Roman name, for the god of the sea. Zeus was the Greek name, and Jupiter the Roman name, for the king of the gods. Uranus was the god of the sky and had the same name in Greek and Latin. Mars was the god of war, his Greek name was Ares. Saturn is the Latin name of the Greek god Cronus (god of agriculture and harvest).
Humanities—Similarity/Contrast

95. (*a.* zz, *b.* Zuider, *c.* zero, *d.* **zee**) : ZED :: BAR : PUB

(**d**) The British call zed what Americans call zee (the letter Z). The British call a pub what Americans call a bar.
General Information—Similarity/Contrast

96. (*a.* hot, ***b.* bacterium**, *c.* virus, *d.* lungs) : TUBERCULOSIS :: VIRUS : COLD

    (**b**) Tuberculosis is caused by a bacterium; a cold is caused by a virus.
    Natural Science—Description

97. MOLLY : (*a.* Madison, *b.* Monroe, ***c.* Maguire**, *d.* Malone) :: KNOW : NOTHING

    (**c**) The Molly Maguires and the Know-Nothings were both secret political action groups. The Molly Maguires were an Irish rebel group who fought for better working conditions in the coal mines of Pennsylvania (ca. 1860s–1870s). The Know-Nothings were a nativistic movement to combat foreign influences in the United States (ca. 1850s).
    Social Science—Completion

98. ANEMOMETER : WIND SPEED :: MANOMETER : (***a.* blood pressure**, *b.* heart rate, *c.* visual acuity, *d.* auditory acuity)

    (**a**) An anemometer measures wind speed; a manometer measures blood pressure.
    Natural Science—Description

99. HERODOTUS : (***a.* history**, *b.* medicine, *c.* his city, *d.* Greece) :: WASHINGTON : HIS COUNTRY

    (**a**) Herodotus is sometimes called the Father of History (and was the first to have a scientific approach to history). George Washington is sometimes called the Father of His Country.
    Social Science—Description

100. (***a.* Washington**, *b.* Jackson, *c.* Eisenhower, *d.* Polk) : CORNWALLIS :: GRANT : LEE

    (**a**) General Cornwallis surrendered to George Washington. General Lee surrendered to Ulysses S. Grant.
    Humanities—Description

101. $Y = X^2$: PARABOLA :: $Y = X + 1$: (*a.* cube, *b.* slope, *c.* circle, ***d.* line**)

    (**d**) When graphed, the equation $y = x^2$ produces a parabola just as when graphed, the equation $y = x + 1$ produces a line.
    Mathematics—Description

102. NOM DE PLUME : (*a.* maiden name, *b.* middle name, ***c.* pen name**, *d.* married name) :: JE NE SAIS QUOI : INDEFINABLE QUALITY

    (**c**) A *nom de plume* is the commonly used French term for a pen name, just as *je ne sais quoi* is the commonly used French term for an indefinable quality.
    Vocabulary—Similarity/Contrast

Answer Explanations

103. (*a.* sheep, ***b.* mutton**, *c.* offal, *d.* venison) : LAMB :: BEEF : VEAL

    (**b**) Meat eaten from a full-grown sheep is called mutton, whereas meat from a young sheep is called lamb. Likewise, meat from full-grown cattle is called beef and from young cattle is called veal.
    General Information—Similarity/Contrast

104. RADIOACTIVE FALLOUT : CHERNOBYL :: (***a.* oil**, *b.* propane, *c.* carbon monoxide, *d.* benzene) : VALDEZ

    (**a**) Just as the Ukrainian city of Chernobyl was poisoned by radioactive fallout from a nuclear plant (1986), so was Valdez, Alaska, polluted by a massive oil spill (1989).
    General Information—Description

105. HELIUM : NEON :: ARGON : (*a.* cryon, *b.* iodine, ***c.* xenon**, *d.* hydrogen)

    (**c**) Helium, neon, argon, and xenon are all noble gasses.
    Natural Science—Class

106. BATHYSPHERE : (*a.* rain forest, *b.* ice field, ***c.* ocean**, *d.* cave) :: SHUTTLE : SPACE

    (**c**) A bathysphere transports people into the ocean just as a shuttle transports people into space.
    Vocabulary—Description

107. DEBUT : GURU :: FRENCH : (*a.* Greek, *b.* Spanish, *c.* Zulu, ***d.* Hindi**)

    (**d**) Just as the English language has borrowed the word *debut* from French, so has it also borrowed the word *guru* from Hindi.
    Nonsemantic—Nonsemantic

108. SHEPHERD : (***a.* sheep**, *b.* human, *c.* goat, *d.* dog) :: MAHOUT : ELEPHANT

    (**a**) A mahout cares for and leads elephants just as a shepherd cares for and leads sheep.
    Vocabulary—Description

109. HMS : GREAT BRITAIN :: (*a.* SSS, *b.* SOS, *c.* USAS, ***d.* USS**) : UNITED STATES

    (**d**) In Great Britain, state ships are prefixed with "HMS," for "Her Majesty's ship" and in the United States, state ships are prefixed with "USS," for "United States ship." SSS may refer to Server Side Scripting, among other things; SOS stands for Save Our Ship/Souls; USAS stands for the United States Antarctic Service, among other things.
    General Information—Description

110. (*a.* Ethiopia, ***b.* Somalia**, *c.* Djibouti, *d.* Eritrea) : MOGADISHU :: KENYA : NAIROBI

    (**b**) Somalia's capital city is Mogadishu just as Kenya's is Nairobi. The capital of Ethiopia is Addis Ababa. The capital of Djibouti is Djibouti. The capital of Eritrea is Asmara.
    General Information—Description

111. ALLUSION : ALLEGORY :: REFERENCE : (*a.* summary, ***b.* parable**, *c.* idiom, *d.* anecdote)

    (**b**) Allusion is reference (either direct or indirect) to something. Allegory is a sort of parable.
    Vocabulary—Similarity/Contrast

112. HORUS : (*a.* horse, *b.* dog, ***c.* hawk**, *d.* hare) :: ANUBIS : JACKAL

    (**c**) The sons of Egyptian god Osiris, Horus, and Anubis had the heads of a hawk and a jackal respectively.
    Humanities—Description

113. GOERING : NUREMBERG :: (*a.* Hitler, *b.* Hussein, *c.* Mussolini, ***d.* Milosevic**) : THE HAGUE

    (**d**) Goering was prosecuted at an international war crimes tribunal in Nuremberg, Germany. Milosevic was prosecuted in The Hague, Netherlands.
    General Information—Description

114. FOUR SCORE : (*a.* 40, *b.* 4, *c.* 28, ***d.* 80**) :: BAKER'S DOZEN : 13

    (**d**) Four score is the equivalent of 80 (a score is 20), just as a baker's dozen is 13. The expression of a baker's dozen comes from 13th century England where bakers could be severely punished if found to cheat their customers. Therefore, they preferred to bake more items to make sure they would not betray their customers.
    General Information—Equality/Negation

115. KHOI SAN : SOUTH AFRICA :: MAORI : (***a.* New Zealand**, *b.* Papua New Guinea, *c.* Fiji, *d.* Australia)

    (**a**) The Khoi San are native peoples of South Africa and the Maori are native peoples of New Zealand.
    General Information—Description

116. BEMUSE : AMUSE :: (*a.* humor, ***b.* confuse**, *c.* irritate, *d.* inspire) :: ENTERTAIN

    (**b**) To bemuse is to confuse, whereas to amuse is to entertain.
    Vocabulary—Similarity/Contrast

117. PLESSY : FERGUSON :: BROWN : (*a.* The State, *b.* Topeka, *c.* **Board of Education**, *d.* Wade)

(**c**) *Plessy vs. Ferguson* was a historic Supreme Court Case (1886; it upheld the constitutionality of racial segregation) as was *Brown vs. Board of Education* (1954; it overturned rulings from the *Plessy vs. Ferguson* case). *General Information—Completion*

118. HONG KONG : (***a.* Hang Seng**, *b.* NASDAQ, *c.* HKSE, *d.* Nikkei) :: UNITED STATES : DOW JONES

(**a**) Hong Kong's primary stock index is the Hang Seng. The primary stock index of the United States is the Dow Jones. The Nikkei is the primary stock index of Japan. HKSE stands for Hong Kong Stock Exchange. NASDAQ (National Association of Securities Dealers Automated Quotations) is an electronic securities market in the United States. *General Information—Description*

119. LAKERS : DODGERS :: (*a.* Orlando, ***b.* Minneapolis**, *c.* Albany, *d.* New Orleans) : BROOKLYN

(**b**) The Los Angeles Lakers were originally called the Minneapolis Lakers just as the Los Angeles Dodgers were originally called the Brooklyn Dodgers. *General Information—Description*

120. (***a.* juniper**, *b.* hickory, *c.* aspen, *d.* beech) : CEDAR :: TAMARAC : PINE

(**a**) Juniper, cedar, tamarac, and pine trees are all coniferous evergreen trees. *Natural Science—Class*

PRACTICE TEST 6

Item Classification Chart

		RELATIONSHIP						
		Similarity/ Contrast	Description	Class	Completion	Part/ Whole	Equality/ Negation	Nonsemantic
C O N T E N T	**Vocabulary**	2, 7, 15, 18, 19, 43, 44, 55, 59, 60, 67, 69, 70, 85, 89, 102, 111, 116	8, 10, 21, 22, 38, 106, 108					
	General Information	4, 24, 39, 54, 95, 103	11, 12, 14, 16, 20, 26, 28, 29, 37, 51, 53, 57, 58, 65, 81, 84, 90, 93, 104, 109, 110, 113, 115, 118, 119	47, 64	6, 9, 46, 117	1, 42	114	
	Humanities	32, 41, 80, 94	5, 13, 31, 34, 35, 40, 48, 52, 56, 61, 63, 66, 71, 76, 83, 87, 100, 112	49, 68, 91	74			
	Social Science		3, 27, 75, 77, 97, 99					
	Natural Science		17, 33, 45, 72, 79, 86, 96, 98	30, 92, 105, 120			82	
	Mathematics		25, 78, 101	62		50	88	
	Nonsemantic							23, 36, 73, 107

Answer Sheet
PRACTICE TEST 7

1 Ⓐ Ⓑ Ⓒ Ⓓ	31 Ⓐ Ⓑ Ⓒ Ⓓ	61 Ⓐ Ⓑ Ⓒ Ⓓ	91 Ⓐ Ⓑ Ⓒ Ⓓ
2 Ⓐ Ⓑ Ⓒ Ⓓ	32 Ⓐ Ⓑ Ⓒ Ⓓ	62 Ⓐ Ⓑ Ⓒ Ⓓ	92 Ⓐ Ⓑ Ⓒ Ⓓ
3 Ⓐ Ⓑ Ⓒ Ⓓ	33 Ⓐ Ⓑ Ⓒ Ⓓ	63 Ⓐ Ⓑ Ⓒ Ⓓ	93 Ⓐ Ⓑ Ⓒ Ⓓ
4 Ⓐ Ⓑ Ⓒ Ⓓ	34 Ⓐ Ⓑ Ⓒ Ⓓ	64 Ⓐ Ⓑ Ⓒ Ⓓ	94 Ⓐ Ⓑ Ⓒ Ⓓ
5 Ⓐ Ⓑ Ⓒ Ⓓ	35 Ⓐ Ⓑ Ⓒ Ⓓ	65 Ⓐ Ⓑ Ⓒ Ⓓ	95 Ⓐ Ⓑ Ⓒ Ⓓ
6 Ⓐ Ⓑ Ⓒ Ⓓ	36 Ⓐ Ⓑ Ⓒ Ⓓ	66 Ⓐ Ⓑ Ⓒ Ⓓ	96 Ⓐ Ⓑ Ⓒ Ⓓ
7 Ⓐ Ⓑ Ⓒ Ⓓ	37 Ⓐ Ⓑ Ⓒ Ⓓ	67 Ⓐ Ⓑ Ⓒ Ⓓ	97 Ⓐ Ⓑ Ⓒ Ⓓ
8 Ⓐ Ⓑ Ⓒ Ⓓ	38 Ⓐ Ⓑ Ⓒ Ⓓ	68 Ⓐ Ⓑ Ⓒ Ⓓ	98 Ⓐ Ⓑ Ⓒ Ⓓ
9 Ⓐ Ⓑ Ⓒ Ⓓ	39 Ⓐ Ⓑ Ⓒ Ⓓ	69 Ⓐ Ⓑ Ⓒ Ⓓ	99 Ⓐ Ⓑ Ⓒ Ⓓ
10 Ⓐ Ⓑ Ⓒ Ⓓ	40 Ⓐ Ⓑ Ⓒ Ⓓ	70 Ⓐ Ⓑ Ⓒ Ⓓ	100 Ⓐ Ⓑ Ⓒ Ⓓ
11 Ⓐ Ⓑ Ⓒ Ⓓ	41 Ⓐ Ⓑ Ⓒ Ⓓ	71 Ⓐ Ⓑ Ⓒ Ⓓ	101 Ⓐ Ⓑ Ⓒ Ⓓ
12 Ⓐ Ⓑ Ⓒ Ⓓ	42 Ⓐ Ⓑ Ⓒ Ⓓ	72 Ⓐ Ⓑ Ⓒ Ⓓ	102 Ⓐ Ⓑ Ⓒ Ⓓ
13 Ⓐ Ⓑ Ⓒ Ⓓ	43 Ⓐ Ⓑ Ⓒ Ⓓ	73 Ⓐ Ⓑ Ⓒ Ⓓ	103 Ⓐ Ⓑ Ⓒ Ⓓ
14 Ⓐ Ⓑ Ⓒ Ⓓ	44 Ⓐ Ⓑ Ⓒ Ⓓ	74 Ⓐ Ⓑ Ⓒ Ⓓ	104 Ⓐ Ⓑ Ⓒ Ⓓ
15 Ⓐ Ⓑ Ⓒ Ⓓ	45 Ⓐ Ⓑ Ⓒ Ⓓ	75 Ⓐ Ⓑ Ⓒ Ⓓ	105 Ⓐ Ⓑ Ⓒ Ⓓ
16 Ⓐ Ⓑ Ⓒ Ⓓ	46 Ⓐ Ⓑ Ⓒ Ⓓ	76 Ⓐ Ⓑ Ⓒ Ⓓ	106 Ⓐ Ⓑ Ⓒ Ⓓ
17 Ⓐ Ⓑ Ⓒ Ⓓ	47 Ⓐ Ⓑ Ⓒ Ⓓ	77 Ⓐ Ⓑ Ⓒ Ⓓ	107 Ⓐ Ⓑ Ⓒ Ⓓ
18 Ⓐ Ⓑ Ⓒ Ⓓ	48 Ⓐ Ⓑ Ⓒ Ⓓ	78 Ⓐ Ⓑ Ⓒ Ⓓ	108 Ⓐ Ⓑ Ⓒ Ⓓ
19 Ⓐ Ⓑ Ⓒ Ⓓ	49 Ⓐ Ⓑ Ⓒ Ⓓ	79 Ⓐ Ⓑ Ⓒ Ⓓ	109 Ⓐ Ⓑ Ⓒ Ⓓ
20 Ⓐ Ⓑ Ⓒ Ⓓ	50 Ⓐ Ⓑ Ⓒ Ⓓ	80 Ⓐ Ⓑ Ⓒ Ⓓ	110 Ⓐ Ⓑ Ⓒ Ⓓ
21 Ⓐ Ⓑ Ⓒ Ⓓ	51 Ⓐ Ⓑ Ⓒ Ⓓ	81 Ⓐ Ⓑ Ⓒ Ⓓ	111 Ⓐ Ⓑ Ⓒ Ⓓ
22 Ⓐ Ⓑ Ⓒ Ⓓ	52 Ⓐ Ⓑ Ⓒ Ⓓ	82 Ⓐ Ⓑ Ⓒ Ⓓ	112 Ⓐ Ⓑ Ⓒ Ⓓ
23 Ⓐ Ⓑ Ⓒ Ⓓ	53 Ⓐ Ⓑ Ⓒ Ⓓ	83 Ⓐ Ⓑ Ⓒ Ⓓ	113 Ⓐ Ⓑ Ⓒ Ⓓ
24 Ⓐ Ⓑ Ⓒ Ⓓ	54 Ⓐ Ⓑ Ⓒ Ⓓ	84 Ⓐ Ⓑ Ⓒ Ⓓ	114 Ⓐ Ⓑ Ⓒ Ⓓ
25 Ⓐ Ⓑ Ⓒ Ⓓ	55 Ⓐ Ⓑ Ⓒ Ⓓ	85 Ⓐ Ⓑ Ⓒ Ⓓ	115 Ⓐ Ⓑ Ⓒ Ⓓ
26 Ⓐ Ⓑ Ⓒ Ⓓ	56 Ⓐ Ⓑ Ⓒ Ⓓ	86 Ⓐ Ⓑ Ⓒ Ⓓ	116 Ⓐ Ⓑ Ⓒ Ⓓ
27 Ⓐ Ⓑ Ⓒ Ⓓ	57 Ⓐ Ⓑ Ⓒ Ⓓ	87 Ⓐ Ⓑ Ⓒ Ⓓ	117 Ⓐ Ⓑ Ⓒ Ⓓ
28 Ⓐ Ⓑ Ⓒ Ⓓ	58 Ⓐ Ⓑ Ⓒ Ⓓ	88 Ⓐ Ⓑ Ⓒ Ⓓ	118 Ⓐ Ⓑ Ⓒ Ⓓ
29 Ⓐ Ⓑ Ⓒ Ⓓ	59 Ⓐ Ⓑ Ⓒ Ⓓ	89 Ⓐ Ⓑ Ⓒ Ⓓ	119 Ⓐ Ⓑ Ⓒ Ⓓ
30 Ⓐ Ⓑ Ⓒ Ⓓ	60 Ⓐ Ⓑ Ⓒ Ⓓ	90 Ⓐ Ⓑ Ⓒ Ⓓ	120 Ⓐ Ⓑ Ⓒ Ⓓ

Practice Test 7

Directions: In each of the following questions, you will find three initial terms and, in parentheses, four answer options designated *a*, *b*, *c*, and *d*. You are to select from the four answer options the one that best completes the analogy with the three initial terms. To record your answers, use the answer sheet provided.

Time: 60 minutes

1. SUFFOCATION : AIR :: DEHYDRATION : (*a.* food, *b.* shelter, *c.* water, *d.* sunlight)

2. RISE : (*a.* set, *b.* raise, *c.* sit, *d.* decrease) :: EAST : WEST

3. (*a.* greedy, *b.* pleasure-seeking, *c.* lazy, *d.* warlike) : SPARTA :: CULTURED : ATHENS

4. CUBE : SQUARE :: (*a.* ellipsis, *b.* ellipsoid, *c.* oblong, *d.* tetrahedron) : ELLIPSE

5. INFRARED : BELOW :: (*a.* maroon, *b.* aquamarine, *c.* chartreuse, *d.* ultraviolet) : ABOVE

6. (*a.* NW, *b.* SW, *c.* NE, *d.* SE) : SE :: S : N

7. DIASTOLIC : DILATATION :: (*a.* anatolic, *b.* controlic, *c.* catatolic, *d.* systolic) : CONTRACTION

8. CAVALRY : HORSE :: INFANTRY : (*a.* platoon, *b.* stallion, *c.* tank, *d.* foot)

9. MADISON : (*a.* American Revolution, *b.* French-Indian War, *c.* War of 1812, *d.* Spanish-American War) :: LINCOLN : CIVIL WAR

10. SHEEP : (*a.* sheeps, *b.* sheep, *c.* sheepes, *d.* sheepses) :: LIFE : LIVES

11. MICKEY : MOUSE :: POLYPHEMOUS : (*a.* Scylla, *b.* Cyclops, *c.* daemon, *d.* satyr)

12. LABOUR : (*a.* Conservative, *b.* Federalist, *c.* Socialist, *d.* Progressive) :: DEMOCRAT : REPUBLICAN

13. A.M. : (*a.* ab, *b.* ante, *c.* amon, *d.* annuo) :: P.M. : post

14. JUDAISM : TORAH :: (*a.* Hinduism, *b.* Buddhism, *c.* Islam, *d.* Confucianism) : KORAN

15. (*a.* gin, *b.* rummy, *c.* check, *d.* mate) : GIN RUMMY :: CHECKMATE : CHESS

16. SAWYER : THATCHER :: TOM : (*a.* Susie, *b.* Becky, *c.* Janey, *d.* Judy)

17. PRAIRIE SCHOONER : (*a.* covered wagon, *b.* horse, *c.* mule, *d.* railroad train) :: PRAIRIE WOLF : COYOTE

18. YEN : JAPAN :: MARK : (*a.* Germany, *b.* Sweden, *c.* Holland, *d.* France)

19. GENOTYPE : PHENOTYPE :: (*a.* expected, *b.* ontogeny, *c.* philogeny, *d.* environmental) : OBSERVED

20. HOLLAND : NETHERLANDS :: FORMOSA : (*a.* Kemoy, *b.* Matsu, *c.* Taiwan, *d.* Oahu)

21. TABLE : ABLE :: TRACK : (*a.* field, *b.* willing, *c.* rack, *d.* truck)

22. MIDWIFE : (*a.* marriage, *b.* birth, *c.* disease, *d.* death) :: SHERIFF : LAW ENFORCEMENT

23. PRISONER : RELEASE :: SOLDIER : (*a.* draft, *b.* fight, *c.* enlist, *d.* discharge)

24. YELLOW : (*a.* coat, *b.* chicken, *c.* hornet, *d.* jacket) :: BUMBLE : BEE

25. AMERICAN : (*a.* British, *b.* Swiss, *c.* Colombian, *d.* Belgian) :: PARMESAN : CAMEMBERT

26. (*a.* hawk, *b.* dove, *c.* eagle, *d.* robin) : U.S.A. :: MAPLE LEAF : CANADA

27. CIRCE : SWINE :: MEDUSA : (*a.* jackal, *b.* stone, *c.* gold, *d.* snake)

28. (*a.* bones, *b.* skin, *c.* muscles, *d.* blood) : DERMATOLOGY :: IMMUNITY : IMMUNOLOGY

29. TWIDDLE : TWADDLE :: (*a.* jambo, *b.* jimbo, *c.* mumbo, *d.* rumbo) : JUMBO

30. OLFACTORY : (*a.* mouth, *b.* ears, *c.* nose, *d.* fingers) :: VISUAL : EYES

31. ECUADOR : SOUTH AMERICA :: EGYPT : (*a.* Africa, *b.* Asia, *c.* Europe, *d.* India)

32. RED CROSS : RELIEF FROM DISASTERS :: BLUE CROSS :
(*a*. health insurance, *b*. relief from tyranny, *c*. relief from mental illness,
d. medical supplies)

33. EEG : BRAIN :: EKG : (*a*. heart, *b*. brain, *c*. gall bladder, *d*. vagus nerve)

34. ABRAHAM : SARAH :: PUNCH : (*a*. Judy, *b*. Paula, *c*. Pat, *d*. Joanie)

35. MPH : RPM :: MILES : (*a*. rotations, *b*. revolutions, *c*. minutes, *d*. hours)

36. ORDAIN : MINISTER :: (*a*. approve, *b*. obey, *c*. admit, *d*. certify) :
TEACHER

37. WATER : HYDROGEN :: TABLE SALT : (*a*. chlorine, *b*. potassium,
c. nitrogen, *d*. oxygen)

38. ELBOW : ARM :: (*a*. shin, *b*. thigh, *c*. calf, *d*. knee) : LEG

39. NUMBER : GENDER :: SINGULAR : (*a*. plural, *b*. feminine,
c. nominative, *d*. present)

40. PATRICIDE : FATHER :: GENOCIDE : (*a*. enemy, *b*. group, *c*. mother,
d. brother)

41. INCA : (*a*. Mexico, *b*. Panama, *c*. Honduras, *d*. Peru) :: AZTEC : MEXICO

42. ODIOUS : (*a*. burdensome, *b*. easy, *c*. pleasing, *d*. disgusting) ::
HONORABLE : DISGRACEFUL

43. SITTING BULL : CUSTER :: (*a*. Eddington, *b*. Howe, *c*. Sheridan,
d. Wellington) : NAPOLEON BONAPARTE

44. LOG 10 : 1 :: LOG 100 : (*a*. 2, *b*. 5, *c*. 10, *d*. 90)

45. HOMING PIGEON : CARRIER PIGEON :: STOOL PIGEON :
(*a*. fool, *b*. informer, *c*. loser, *d*. passenger pigeon)

46. STOP : POTS :: NOON : (*a*. morning, *b*. noon, *c*. night, *d*. never)

47. EBENEEZER SCROOGE : MISERLY :: SIMON LEGREE :
(*a*. humane, *b*. generous, *c*. stingy, *d*. cruel)

48. PALEONTOLOGIST : (*a*. vertebrates, *b*. rocks, *c*. earthquakes, *d*. fossils) ::
ZOOLOGIST : ANIMALS

49. (*a*. emperor, *b*. pharaoh, *c*. shah, *d*. diet) : CONGRESS ::
PRIME MINISTER : PRESIDENT

50. B$_1$: THIAMINE :: (*a.* B$_2$, *b.* B$_6$, *c.* C, *d.* D) : RIBOFLAVIN

51. GUERNSEY : (*a.* York, *b.* Jersey, *c.* British, *d.* French) :: CHESHIRE : SIAMESE

52. TOURNEY : TOURNAMENT :: TEMPORARY : (*a.* permanent, *b.* sudden, *c.* transitory, *d.* temptation)

53. STOMACH : DIGESTION :: ANATOMY : (*a.* cartography, *b.* biology, *c.* physiology, *d.* proctology)

54. PRE : PRIOR :: PRETER : (*a.* beyond, *b.* as if, *c.* therefore, *d.* only)

55. LINCOLN : KENNEDY :: (*a.* Tyler, *b.* Johnson, *c.* Eisenhower, *d.* Garfield) : McKINLEY

56. FORTE : LOUD :: (*a.* largo, *b.* rubato, *c.* violin, *d.* piano) : SOFT

57. LATIN ALPHABET : FRENCH :: CYRILLIC ALPHABET : (*a.* Russian, *b.* Sanskrit, *c.* Greek, *d.* Chinese)

58. CENTRIFUGAL : (*a.* centripetal, *b.* centrigonal, *c.* centrobaric, *d.* centrosomal) :: AWAY FROM : TOWARD

59. ICHTHYOLOGY : (*a.* insects, *b.* reptiles, *c.* arthropods, *d.* fish) :: ORNITHOLOGY : BIRDS

60. (*a.* wool, *b.* synthetic, *c.* dinosaur, *d.* gasoline) : PETROL :: U.S.A. : BRITAIN

61. (*a.* overindulge, *b.* persevere, *c.* quit, *d.* deprive) : SURFEIT :: CLOY : SATIATE

62. (*a.* Hesse, *b.* Joyce, *c.* Mann, *d.* Proust) : DEATH IN VENICE :: SHAKESPEARE : MERCHANT OF VENICE

63. ROOK : CASTLE :: HORSE : (*a.* knight, *b.* track, *c.* chess, *d.* winner)

64. (*a.* Greuze, *b.* Utrillo, *c.* Seurat, *d.* Manet) : POINTILLISM :: DAVID : NEOCLASSICISM

65. BILL : BEAK :: (*a.* finger, *b.* leg, *c.* hand, *d.* kneecap) : DIGIT

66. GEWGAW : (*a.* trinket, *b.* bottle, *c.* rhinestone, *d.* candy) :: TACITURN : QUIET

67. (*a.* fortunate, *b.* entreat, *c.* unfortunate, *d.* order) : IMPORTUNE ::
    IMPREGNABLE : UNSHAKABLE

68. CULPABLE : GUILTY :: (*a.* preculpable, *b.* exculpable, *c.* multiculpable,
    d. malculpable) : ACQUITTED

69. FOX : (*a.* bovine, *b.* vulpine, *c.* porcine, *d.* equine) :: CAT : FELINE

70. AGONY : ECSTASY :: SOUND : (*a.* Light, *b.* Trumpet, *c.* Signpost,
    d. Fury)

71. LANG SYNE : (*a.* bygone days, *b.* future days, *c.* here and now,
    d. nonexistent times) :: IMMEDIATELY : AT ONCE

72. (*a.* India, *b.* Brazil, *c.* Mexico, *d.* Spain) : GUANAJUATO :: CANADA :
    MANITOBA

73. VERDI : AIDA :: (*a.* Bach, *b.* Mozart, *c.* Beethoven, *d.* Brahms) : FIDELIO

74. TORTUOUS : (*a.* winding, *b.* barbaric, *c.* long, *d.* incomprehensible) ::
    HAPPY : FELICITOUS

75. (*a.* present, *b.* past, *c.* recent, *d.* never) : CURRENT :: ERSTWHILE :
    FORMER

76. DAVID : GOLIATH :: HOLMES : (*a.* Moriarty, *b.* Watson, *c.* Doyle,
    d. Devlin)

77. LUGUBRIOUS : (*a.* shallow, *b.* cheerful, *c.* expensive, *d.* fatuous) ::
    PONDEROUS : LIGHT

78. EXPLETIVE : (*a.* interrogative, *b.* factotum, *c.* oath, *d.* lie) :: EXPOSÉ :
    DISCLOSURE

79. 11 : BINARY :: (*a.* 2, *b.* 3, *c.* 4, *d.* 10) : DECIMAL

80. CHALICE : GOBLET :: LEAF : (*a.* plant, *b.* tree, *c.* sheet, *d.* gold)

81. (*a.* nut, *b.* fruit, *c.* root, *d.* berry) : TURNIP :: STEM : CELERY

82. ABRAM : ABRAHAM :: (*a.* Sarabelle, *b.* Sarai, *c.* Salome, *d.* Sharon) :
    SARAH

83. VELÁSQUEZ : MAIDS OF HONOR :: (*a.* Botticelli, *b.* Bellini, *c.* Bosch,
    d. Uccello) : THE BIRTH OF VENUS

84. CIVIL : (*a.* misdemeanor, *b.* larceny, *c.* tort, *d.* perjury) :: CRIMINAL : FELONY

85. GREGORIAN : NOVEMBER :: FRENCH REVOLUTIONARY : (*a.* Novembre, *b.* February, *c.* Julian, *d.* Thermidor)

86. GOLDEN RULE : LUKE :: CATEGORICAL IMPERATIVE : (*a.* Hegel, *b.* Kant, *c.* Ardrey, *d.* Lorenz)

87. EQUIVOCATION : (*a.* perversity, *b.* exultation, *c.* veracity, *d.* perjury) :: UNCERTAINTY : CERTAINTY

88. TIMBREL : (*a.* cymbals, *b.* zither, *c.* flute, *d.* tambourine) :: LUTE : GUITAR

89. (*a.* Apollo, *b.* Phaeton, *c.* Furies, *d.* Sirens) : EUMENIDES :: PLUTO : HADES

90. JOSEPH K. : TRIAL :: GREGOR SAMSA : (*a.* Hunger Artist, *b.* Death in Venice, *c.* The Flies, *d.* Metamorphosis)

91. $\sqrt{2}$: $\sqrt{18}$ :: 1 : (*a.* 2, *b.* 3, *c.* 6, *d.* 9)

92. TRANSUBSTANTIATION : ACTUAL :: (*a.* insubstantiation, *b.* absubstantiation, *c.* consubstantiation, *d.* desubstantiation) : COEXISTING

93. ABACUS : COMPUTER :: DAGUERROTYPE : (*a.* stereo, *b.* photograph, *c.* tape recorder, *d.* telephone)

94. DECLARATION OF INDEPENDENCE : PHILADELPHIA :: MAGNA CARTA : (*a.* Gloucester, *b.* Runnymede, *c.* Canterbury, *d.* Norwalk)

95. MINTON : ROYAL DOULTON :: MIKASA (*a.* Sony, *b.* Rosenthal, *c.* Lenox, *d.* Noritake)

96. SHYLOCK : SCROOGE :: DON JUAN : (*a.* Antonio, *b.* Don Giovanni, *c.* Lothario, *d.* Don Quixote)

97. SKINNER : EMPIRICIST :: (*a.* Watson, *b.* Aristotle, *c.* Chomsky, *d.* Locke) : RATIONALIST

98. MOHAWK : IROQUOIS :: (*a.* Apache, *b.* Zuni, *c.* Seminole, *d.* Creek) : PUEBLO

99. (*a.* half-life, *b.* radioactivity, *c.* atomic mass, *d.* atomic number) : ISOTOPE :: ATOMIC WEIGHT : ISOBAR

100. SARACEN : (*a.* Hindu, *b.* Muslim, *c.* Shintoist, *d.* Taoist) ::
     EPISCOPALIAN : ANGLICAN

101. WATERGATE : NIXON :: IRAN CONTRA : (*a.* Ford, *b.* Carter,
     c. Reagan, *d.* Bush)

102. GALAPAGOS : SAMOA :: (*a.* Linnaeus, *b.* Magellan, *c.* Rhodes,
     d. Darwin) : MEAD

103. BIGGER THOMAS : (*a.* New York, *b.* Chicago, *c.* St. Louis,
     d. Montgomery) :: RODION RASKOLNIKOV : ST. PETERSBURG

104. TAXONOMY : CLASSIFY :: NOMENCLATURE : (*a.* order, *b.* color,
     c. name, *d.* number)

105. PHYSIOGNOMY : (*a.* face, *b.* stature, *c.* physiology, *d.* gate) ::
     CHIROMANCY : PALM

106. MUTINY : SHIP CAPTAIN :: COUP D'ÉTAT : (*a.* college dean,
     b. military commander, *c.* government, *d.* CEO)

107. (*a.* exaggerated, *b.* understated, *c.* metaphorical, *d.* literal) : HYPERBOLIC ::
     DRAMATIC : HISTRIONIC

108. APPLE : EVE :: (*a.* pear, *b.* pomegranate, *c.* peach, *d.* papaya) :
     PERSEPHONE

109. CEMENTUM : ROOT :: (*a.* bone, *b.* fluoride, *c.* keratin, *d.* enamel) :
     CROWN

110. (*a.* acorn, *b.* cornmeal, *c.* millet, *d.* filbert) : BULGUR :: QUINOA :
     BARLEY

111. MOBY DICK : LEVIATHAN :: MELVILLE : (*a.* Rousseau, *b.* Hobbes,
     c. Kant, *d.* Smith)

112. (*a.* Locke, *b.* Galileo, *c.* Bacon, *d.* Calvin) : ENLIGHTENMENT ::
     DESCARTES : RENAISSANCE

113. STEINWAY : (*a.* piano, *b.* cello, *c.* flute, *d.* organ) :: STRADIVARIUS :
     VIOLIN

114. TERKEL : (*a.* manuscripts, *b.* photographs, *c.* oral histories, *d.* maps) ::
     LOMAX : FOLK MUSIC

115. 6×10^{23} : (*a.* e, *b.* Avogadro's number, *c.* i, *d.* Planck's constant) :: 3.14 : PI

116. CIRRUS : NIMBUS :: CUMULUS : (*a.* bilious, *b.* birrus, *c.* mobius, *d.* stratus)

117. SOCIALISM : (*a.* state, *b.* family, *c.* town, *d.* universal) :: CAPITALISM : PRIVATE

118. (*a.* Pikes Peak, *b.* Mt. Kilimanjaro, *c.* Mt. Vesuvius, *d.* K2) : MT. ST. HELENS :: EXTINCT : ACTIVE

119. IMPERIOUS : IMPERVIOUS :: (*a.* grandiose, *b.* disbelieving, *c.* judgmental, *d.* domineering) : IMMUNE

120. NEUTRAL : NEUTRON :: NEGATIVE : (*a.* atom, *b.* electron, *c.* positron, *d.* negatron)

Answer Key
PRACTICE TEST 7

1. **C**	31. **A**	61. **A**	91. **B**
2. **A**	32. **A**	62. **C**	92. **C**
3. **D**	33. **A**	63. **A**	93. **B**
4. **B**	34. **A**	64. **C**	94. **B**
5. **D**	35. **B**	65. **A**	95. **D**
6. **A**	36. **D**	66. **A**	96. **C**
7. **D**	37. **A**	67. **B**	97. **C**
8. **D**	38. **D**	68. **B**	98. **B**
9. **C**	39. **B**	69. **B**	99. **D**
10. **B**	40. **B**	70. **D**	100. **B**
11. **B**	41. **D**	71. **A**	101. **C**
12. **A**	42. **C**	72. **C**	102. **D**
13. **B**	43. **D**	73. **C**	103. **B**
14. **C**	44. **A**	74. **A**	104. **C**
15. **A**	45. **B**	75. **A**	105. **A**
16. **B**	46. **B**	76. **A**	106. **C**
17. **A**	47. **D**	77. **B**	107. **A**
18. **A**	48. **D**	78. **C**	108. **B**
19. **A**	49. **D**	79. **B**	109. **D**
20. **C**	50. **A**	80. **C**	110. **C**
21. **C**	51. **B**	81. **C**	111. **B**
22. **B**	52. **C**	82. **B**	112. **A**
23. **D**	53. **C**	83. **A**	113. **A**
24. **D**	54. **A**	84. **C**	114. **C**
25. **B**	55. **D**	85. **D**	115. **B**
26. **C**	56. **D**	86. **B**	116. **D**
27. **B**	57. **A**	87. **C**	117. **A**
28. **B**	58. **A**	88. **D**	118. **C**
29. **C**	59. **D**	89. **C**	119. **D**
30. **C**	60. **D**	90. **D**	120. **B**

ANSWER EXPLANATIONS FOR PRACTICE TEST 7

In the following, explanations concerning the correct response are in a large font. Explanations regarding distracters (incorrect responses) that are not self-explaining or could be misinterpreted are in a smaller font in order to highlight the explanations of the answers that are correct.

1. SUFFOCATION : AIR :: DEHYDRATION : (*a.* food, *b.* shelter, **c. water**, *d.* sunlight)

   (**c**) Suffocation is caused by lack of air. Dehydration is caused by lack of water.
   Natural Science—Description

2. RISE : (**a. set**, *b.* raise, *c.* sit, *d.* decrease) :: EAST : WEST

   (**a**) The sun rises in the east and sets in the west.
   General Information—Description

3. (*a.* greedy, *b.* pleasure-seeking, *c.* lazy, **d. warlike**) : SPARTA :: CULTURED : ATHENS

   (**d**) In ancient Greece, the people of Sparta were known to be warlike, while the people of Athens were known to be cultured.
   Humanities—Description

4. CUBE : SQUARE :: (*a.* ellipsis, **b. ellipsoid**, *c.* oblong, *d.* tetrahedron) : ELLIPSE

   (**b**) When a plane is passed through a cube at a right angle, the intersection is a square. When a plane is passed through an ellipsoid at a right angle, the intersection is an ellipse.
   Mathematics—Part/Whole

5. INFRARED : BELOW :: (*a.* maroon, *b.* aquamarine, *c.* chartreuse, **d. ultraviolet**) : ABOVE

   (**d**) Infrared light is below the visible spectrum for human beings; ultraviolet light is above the visible spectrum. The human eye can perceive wavelengths between 380 and 750 nm.
   Natural Science—Description

6. (**a. NW**, *b.* SW, *c.* NE, *d.* SE) : SE :: S : N

   (**a**) NW (northwest) and SE (southeast) are opposing directions, as are S (south) and N (north).
   General Information—Similarity/Contrast

7. DIASTOLIC : DILATATION :: (*a.* anatolic, *b.* controlic, *c.* catatolic, **d. systolic**) : CONTRACTION

   (**d**) Diastolic blood pressure refers to the dilatation of the heart, while systolic blood pressure refers to the contraction of the heart.
   Natural Science—Description

8. CAVALRY : HORSE :: INFANTRY : (*a.* platoon, *b.* stallion, *c.* tank, **d. foot**)

   (**d**) In an army, the cavalry travels by horse, the infantry by foot.
   General Information—Description

9. MADISON : (*a.* American Revolution, *b.* French-Indian War, **c. War of 1812**, *d.* Spanish-American War) :: LINCOLN : CIVIL WAR

   (**c**) Madison (1751–1836) was president during the War of 1812; Lincoln (1809–1865) was president during the Civil War.
   Social Science—Description

10. SHEEP : (*a.* sheeps, **d. sheep**, *c.* sheepes, *d.* sheepses) :: LIFE : LIVES

    (**b**) The plural of *sheep* is *sheep*. The plural of *life* is *lives*.
    Nonsemantic

11. MICKEY : MOUSE :: POLYPHEMOUS : (*a.* Scylla, **b. Cyclops**, *c.* daemon, *d.* satyr)

    (**b**) Mickey is the name of a fictional mouse; Polyphemous is the name of a fictional Cyclops (in Homer's *Odyssey*). In Greek mythology, Scylla was one of two monsters that lived on either side of a very narrow river. Daemons are supernatural beings between humans and gods in ancient Greek religion. They could be bad or good. Satyrs are woodland deities.
    Humanities—Description

12. LABOUR : (**a. Conservative**, *b.* Federalist, *c.* Socialist, *d.* Progressive) :: DEMOCRAT : REPUBLICAN

    (**a**) In British politics, the Labour party has generally been a left of center political party opposing the right of center Conservative party. In U.S. politics, the more left-leaning Democrats have traditionally opposed the more right-leaning Republicans.
    Social Science—Class

13. A.M. : (*a.* ab, **b. ante**, *c.* amon, *d.* annuo) :: P.M. : post

    (**b**) the *A* in *A.M.* is an abbreviation for *ante*; the *P* in *P.M.* is an abbreviation for *post*. The *m* stands for *meridiem*.
    General Information—Description

14. JUDAISM : TORAH :: (*a.* Hinduism, *b.* Buddhism, **c. Islam**, *d.* Confucianism) : KORAN

(**c**) The Torah is a holy book of Judaism, while the Koran is a holy book of Islam. The holy scriptures of Hinduism are the Vedas. A holy text in Confucianism is the Analects. A holy text in Buddhism is the Tipitaka.
Humanities—Description

15. (***a.* gin**, *b.* rummy, *c.* check, *d.* mate) : GIN RUMMY :: CHECKMATE : CHESS

(**a**) The state of gin ends a gin rummy game, just as the state of checkmate ends a chess game.
General Information—Description

16. SAWYER : THATCHER :: TOM : (*a.* Susie, ***b.* Becky**, *c.* Janey, *d.* Judy)

(**b**) Tom Sawyer and Becky Thatcher are both characters in Mark Twain's novel *Tom Sawyer*.
Humanities—Completion

17. PRAIRIE SCHOONER : (***a.* covered wagon**, *b.* horse, *c.* mule, *d.* railroad train) :: PRAIRIE WOLF : COYOTE

(**a**) A prairie schooner is a covered wagon; a prairie wolf is a coyote.
General Information—Similarity/Contrast

18. YEN : JAPAN :: MARK : (***a.* Germany**, *b.* Sweden, *c.* Holland, *d.* France)

(**a**) The yen is the unit of currency in Japan, while the mark was the unit of currency in Germany. The crown is the unit of currency in Sweden; in Holland it was the guilder; and in France, the franc. It is now the euro in Holland, France, and Germany.
General Information—Description

19. GENOTYPE : PHENOTYPE :: (***a.* expected**, *b.* ontogeny, *c.* philogeny, *d.* environmental) : OBSERVED

(**a**) A genotype is what is expected on the basis of heredity, while a phenotype is what is observed on the basis of heredity, environment, and the interaction between them. Ontogeny is the process of an organism growing organically.
Natural Science—Description

20. HOLLAND : NETHERLANDS :: FORMOSA : (*a.* Kemoy, *b.* Matsu, **c. Taiwan**, *d.* Oahu)

(**c**) Holland and Netherlands refer to the same country, as do Formosa and Taiwan.
General Information—Similarity/Contrast

21. TABLE : ABLE :: TRACK : (*a.* field, *b.* willing, **c. rack**, *d.* truck)

    (**c**) *Able* is *table* without the initial *t*; *rack* is *track* without the initial *t*.
    Nonsemantic

22. MIDWIFE : (*a.* marriage, **b. birth**, *c.* disease, *d.* death) :: SHERIFF : LAW ENFORCEMENT

    (**b**) The job of a midwife is to help in birth; the job of a sheriff is to help in law enforcement.
    General Information—Description

23. PRISONER : RELEASE :: SOLDIER : (*a.* draft, *b.* fight, *c.* enlist, **d. discharge**)

    (**d**) A prisoner receives a release from prison; a soldier receives a discharge from the army.
    General Information—Description

24. YELLOW : (*a.* coat, *b.* chicken, *c.* hornet, **d. jacket**) :: BUMBLE : BEE

    (**d**) A yellow jacket and a bumblebee are both types of insect.
    General Information—Description

25. AMERICAN : (*a.* British, **b. Swiss**, *c.* Colombian, *d.* Belgian) :: PARMESAN : CAMEMBERT

    (**b**) American, Swiss, Parmesan, and Camembert are all types of cheese.
    General Information—Class

26. (*a.* hawk, *b.* dove, **c. eagle**, *d.* robin) : U.S.A. :: MAPLE LEAF : CANADA

    (**c**) The eagle is an emblem of the United States, while the maple leaf is an emblem of Canada.
    Social Science—Description

27. CIRCE : SWINE :: MEDUSA : (*a.* jackal, **b. stone**, *c.* gold, *d.* snake)

    (**b**) Circe transformed men into swine; Medusa transformed them into stone.
    Humanities—Description

28. (*a.* bones, **b. skin**, *c.* muscles, *d.* blood) : DERMATOLOGY :: IMMUNITY : IMMUNOLOGY

    (**b**) Dermatology is the branch of medicine dealing with the skin; immunology is the branch of medicine dealing with immunity.
    Natural Science—Description

29. TWIDDLE : TWADDLE :: (*a.* jambo, *b.* jimbo, ***c.* mumbo**, *d.* rumbo) :
JUMBO

    (**c**) Twiddle twaddle and mumbo jumbo both refer to gibberish.
    Vocabulary—Completion

30. OLFACTORY : (*a.* mouth, *b.* ears, ***c.* nose**, *d.* fingers) :: VISUAL : EYES

    (**c**) The olfactory sense (smell) receives sensation through the nose; the visual
    sense (seeing) receives sensation through the eyes.
    Natural Science—Description

31. ECUADOR : SOUTH AMERICA :: EGYPT : (***a.* Africa**, *b.* Asia,
    c. Europe, *d.* India)

    (**a**) Ecuador is a country in South America. Egypt is a country in Africa.
    General Information—Description

32. RED CROSS : RELIEF FROM DISASTERS :: BLUE CROSS :
    (***a.* health insurance**, *b.* relief from tyranny, *c.* relief from mental illness,
    d. medical supplies)

    (**a**) The Red Cross organization provides relief from disasters; the Blue Cross
    organization provides health insurance.
    General Information—Description

33. EEG : BRAIN :: EKG : (***a.* heart**, *b.* brain, *c.* gall bladder, *d.* vagus nerve)

    (**a**) An EEG is a tracing of the changes in electric potential produced by
    the brain, while an EKG is a tracing of the changes in electric potential
    produced by the heart. EEG stands for "electroencephalogram." EKG stands
    for "electrocardiogram."
    Natural Science—Description

34. ABRAHAM : SARAH :: PUNCH : (***a.* Judy**, *b.* Paula, *c.* Pat, *d.* Joanie)

    (**a**) In the Bible, Abraham was the husband of Sarah. In a Punch-and-Judy
    puppet show, Punch is the husband of Judy.
    Humanities—Class

35. MPH : RPM :: MILES : (*a.* rotations, ***b.* revolutions**, *c.* minutes, *d.* hours)

    (**b**) The *m* in *mph* is an abbreviation for *miles* (per hour). The *r* in *rpm* is an
    abbreviation for *revolutions* (per minute).
    Natural Science—Description

36. ORDAIN : MINISTER :: (*a.* approve, *b.* obey, *c.* admit, ***d.* certify**) : TEACHER

    (**d**) A minister is ordained before beginning to preach. A teacher is certified before beginning to teach.
    General Information—Description

37. WATER : HYDROGEN :: TABLE SALT : (***a.* chlorine**, *b.* potassium, *c.* nitrogen, *d.* oxygen)

    (**a**) Water is a chemical compound containing hydrogen, while table salt is a chemical compound containing chlorine. Potassium, nitrogen, and oxygen are chemical elements.
    Natural Science—Part/Whole

38. ELBOW : ARM :: (*a.* shin, *b.* thigh, *c.* calf, ***d.* knee**) : LEG

    (**d**) The elbow is the joint separating the upper and lower arms. The knee is the joint separating the upper and lower legs.
    Natural Science—Part/Whole

39. NUMBER : GENDER :: SINGULAR : (*a.* plural, ***b.* feminine**, *c.* nominative, *d.* present)

    (**b**) In grammar, singular is an example of number, and feminine is an example of gender.
    Humanities—Class

40. PATRICIDE : FATHER :: GENOCIDE : (*a.* enemy, ***b.* group**, *c.* mother, *d.* brother)

    (**b**) Patricide is the murder of a father; genocide is the murder of a group. Matricide is the murder of a mother; fratricide is the murder of a brother.
    Vocabulary—Description

41. INCA : (*a.* Mexico, *b.* Panama, *c.* Honduras, ***d.* Peru**) :: AZTEC : MEXICO

    (**d**) The Inca Indians resided in Peru; the Aztecs resided in Mexico.
    Social Science—Description

42. ODIOUS : (*a.* burdensome, *b.* easy, ***c.* pleasing**, *d.* disgusting) :: HONORABLE : DISGRACEFUL

    (**c**) *Odious* and *pleasing* are antonyms, as are *honorable* and *disgraceful*.
    Vocabulary—Similarity/Contrast

43. SITTING BULL : CUSTER :: (*a.* Eddington, *b.* Howe, *c.* Sheridan, *d.* **Wellington**) : NAPOLEON BONAPARTE

    (**d**) Sitting Bull defeated General Custer at Little Big Horn in 1876. Wellington defeated Napoleon Bonaparte at the Battle of Waterloo in 1815. *Humanities—Description*

44. LOG 10 : 1 :: LOG 100 : (*a.* **2**, *b.* 5, *c.* 10, *d.* 90)

    (**a**) Log 10 is equal to 1. Log 100 is equal to 2. *Mathematics—Equality/Negation*

45. HOMING PIGEON : CARRIER PIGEON :: STOOL PIGEON : (*a.* fool, *b.* **informer**, *c.* loser, *d.* passenger pigeon)

    (**b**) A homing pigeon is a carrier pigeon. A stool pigeon is an informer. *Vocabulary—Similarity/Contrast*

46. STOP : POTS :: NOON : (*a.* morning, *b.* **noon**, *c.* night, *d.* never)

    (**b**) *Stop* spelled backwards is *pots*. *Noon* spelled backwards is *noon*. *Nonsemantic*

47. EBENEEZER SCROOGE : MISERLY :: SIMON LEGREE : (*a.* humane, *b.* generous, *c.* stingy, *d.* **cruel**)

    (**d**) The literary character Ebeneezer Scrooge was miserly (*A Christmas Carol*), while the character Simon Legree was cruel in *Uncle Tom's Cabin*. *Humanities—Description*

48. PALEONTOLOGIST : (*a.* vertebrates, *b.* rocks, *c.* earthquakes, *d.* **fossils**) :: ZOOLOGIST : ANIMALS

    (**d**) A paleontologist studies fossils; a zoologist studies animals. *Natural Science—Description*

49. (*a.* emperor, *b.* pharaoh, *c.* shah, *d.* **diet**) : CONGRESS :: PRIME MINISTER : PRESIDENT

    (**d**) A diet and a congress are both legislative bodies of government. A prime minister and a president are both executive officers of government. *Social Science—Class*

50. B_1 : THIAMINE :: (*a.* **B_2**, *b.* B_6, *c.* C, *d.* D) : RIBOFLAVIN

    (**a**) Thiamine is vitamin B_1. Riboflavin is vitamin B_2. Vitamin C is also called L-ascorbate. Vitamin B_6 can consist of different compounds: pyridoxine, pyridoxal, and pyridoxamine. Vitamin D comes in several different forms like D_2 (or ergocalciferol) and vitamin D_3 (or cholecalciferol). *Natural Science—Similarity/Contrast*

51. GUERNSEY : (*a.* York, ***b.* Jersey**, *c.* British, *d.* French) :: CHESHIRE : SIAMESE

    (**b**) Guernsey and Jersey are both types of cow. Cheshire and Siamese are both types of cat.
    General Information—Class

52. TOURNEY : TOURNAMENT :: TEMPORARY : (*a.* permanent, *b.* sudden, ***c.* transitory**, *d.* temptation)

    (**c**) *Tourney* and *tournament* are synonyms, as are *temporary* and *transitory*.
    Vocabulary—Similarity/Contrast

53. STOMACH : DIGESTION :: ANATOMY : (*a.* cartography, *b.* biology, ***c.* physiology**, *d.* proctology)

    (**c**) Anatomy is the study of body structures, such as the stomach. Physiology is the study of body functions, such as digestion.
    Natural Science—Description

54. PRE : PRIOR :: PRETER : (***a.* beyond**, *b.* as if, *c.* therefore, *d.* only)

    (**a**) *Pre-* is a prefix meaning *prior*. *Preter-* is a prefix meaning *beyond*.
    Vocabulary—Similarity/Contrast

55. LINCOLN : KENNEDY :: (*a.* Tyler, *b.* Johnson, *c.* Eisenhower, ***d.* Garfield**) : McKINLEY

    (**d**) Presidents Lincoln (1865), Garfield (1881), McKinley (1901), and Kennedy (1963) were all assassinated while in office.
    Humanities—Class

56. FORTE : LOUD :: (*a.* largo, *b.* rubato, *c.* violin, ***d.* piano**) : SOFT

    (**d**) In musical contexts, *forte* means loud and *piano* means soft. *Largo* means "slow"; *rubato* means that the tempo can slightly be varied at the discretion of the player.
    Humanities—Similarity/Contrast

57. LATIN ALPHABET : FRENCH :: CYRILLIC ALPHABET : (***a.* Russian**, *b.* Sanskrit, *c.* Greek, *d.* Chinese)

    (**a**) The Latin alphabet is used for writing French, while the Cyrillic alphabet is used for writing Russian.
    Humanities—Description

58. CENTRIFUGAL : (***a*. centripetal**, *b*. centrigonal, *c*. centrobaric, *d*. centrosomal) :: AWAY FROM : TOWARD

    (**a**) *Centrifugal* means "away from center," while *centripetal* means "toward center." *Centrobaric refers to a center of gravity.*
    Natural Science—Description

59. ICHTHYOLOGY : (*a*. insects, *b*. reptiles, *c*. arthropods, ***d*. fish**) :: ORNITHOLOGY : BIRDS

    (**d**) Ichthyology is the study of fish; ornithology is the study of birds.
    Natural Science—Description

60. (*a*. wool, *b*. synthetic, *c*. dinosaur, ***d*. gasoline**) : PETROL :: U.S.A. : BRITAIN

    (**d**) The fuel called gasoline in the United States is called petrol in Britain.
    General Information—Similarity/Contrast

61. (***a*. overindulge**, *b*. persevere, *c*. quit, *d*. deprive) : SURFEIT :: CLOY : SATIATE

    (**a**) *Overindulge*, *surfeit*, *cloy*, and *satiate* are synonyms.
    Vocabulary—Similarity/Contrast

62. (*a*. Hesse, *b*. Joyce, ***c*. Mann**, *d*. Proust) : DEATH IN VENICE :: SHAKESPEARE : MERCHANT OF VENICE

    (**c**) Mann is the author of *Death in Venice*; Shakespeare is the author of *The Merchant of Venice*. *Hesse is the author of Steppenwolf. Joyce is the author of Ulysses. Proust is the author of Remembrances of Times Past.*
    Humanities—Description

63. ROOK : CASTLE :: HORSE : (***a*. knight**, *b*. track, *c*. chess, *d*. winner)

    (**a**) In the game of chess, *rook* and *castle* refer to the same piece, as do *knight* and *horse*.
    General Information—Similarity/Contrast

64. (*a*. Greuze, *b*. Utrillo, ***c*. Seurat**, *d*. Manet) : POINTILLISM :: DAVID : NEOCLASSICISM

    (**c**) Seurat was a leading member in the French school of pointillism. David was a leading member in the French school of neoclassicism. *Greuze was a Rococo era painter. Utrillo specialized in painting cityscapes. Manet was a realist/impressionist painter.*
    Humanities—Description

65. BILL : BEAK :: (**a. finger**, *b.* leg, *c.* hand, *d.* kneecap) : DIGIT

   (**a**) A bill is a beak. A finger is a digit.
   Vocabulary—Similarity/Contrast

66. GEWGAW : (**a. trinket**, *b.* bottle, *c.* rhinestone, *d.* candy) ::
   TACITURN : QUIET

   (**a**) A gewgaw is a trinket. A taciturn person is quiet.
   Vocabulary—Similarity/Contrast

67. (*a.* fortunate, ***b.* entreat**, *c.* unfortunate, *d.* order) : IMPORTUNE ::
   IMPREGNABLE : UNSHAKABLE

   (**b**) *Entreat* and *importune* are synonyms, as are *impregnable* and *unshakable*.
   Vocabulary—Similarity/Contrast

68. CULPABLE : GUILTY :: (*a.* preculpable, ***b.* exculpable**, *c.* multiculpable,
   d. malculpable) : ACQUITTED

   (**b**) Someone who is culpable is guilty; someone who is exculpable
   is acquitted.
   Vocabulary—Similarity/Contrast

69. FOX : (*a.* bovine, ***b.* vulpine**, *c.* porcine, *d.* equine) :: CAT : FELINE

   (**b**) *Vulpine* means foxlike, while *feline* means catlike. *Bovine* means cowlike;
   porcine means piglike; *equine* means horselike.
   Vocabulary—Description

70. AGONY : ECSTASY :: SOUND : (*a.* Light, *b.* Trumpet, *c.* Signpost,
   ***d.* Fury**)

   (**d**) *The Agony and the Ecstasy* (by Irving Stone) and *The Sound and the Fury*
   (by William Faulkner) are both book titles.
   Humanities—Completion

71. LANG SYNE : (**a. bygone days**, *b.* future days, *c.* here and now,
   d. nonexistent times) :: IMMEDIATELY : AT ONCE

   (**a**) *Lang syne* means *bygone days*; *immediately* means *at once*.
   Vocabulary—Similarity/Contrast

72. (*a.* India, *b.* Brazil, **c. Mexico**, *d.* Spain) : GUANAJUATO :: CANADA :
   MANITOBA

   (**c**) Guanajuato is a political subdivision of Mexico. Manitoba is a political
   subdivision of Canada.
   Social Science—Part/Whole

73. VERDI : AIDA :: (*a.* Bach, *b.* Mozart, ***d.* Beethoven**, *d.* Brahms) : FIDELIO

    (c) Verdi composed the opera *Aida*. Beethoven composed the opera *Fidelio*. Bach composed *The Well-Tempered Clavier*; Mozart composed *The Magic Flute*; Brahms composed *A German Requiem*.
    Humanities—Description

74. TORTUOUS : (***a.* winding**, *b.* barbaric, *c.* long, *d.* incomprehensible) :: HAPPY : FELICITOUS

    (a) *Tortuous* and *winding* are synonyms, as are *happy* and *felicitous*.
    Vocabulary—Similarity/Contrast

75. (***a.* present**, *b.* past, *c.* recent, *d.* never) : CURRENT :: ERSTWHILE : FORMER

    (a) A present event is current; a former event is erstwhile.
    Vocabulary—Similarity/Contrast

76. DAVID : GOLIATH :: HOLMES : (***a.* Moriarty**, *b.* Watson, *c.* Doyle, *d.* Devlin)

    (a) Goliath was the mortal enemy of David; Moriarty was the mortal enemy of Holmes. Arthur Conan Doyle was the author of Sherlock Holmes. Watson was Sherlock Holmes's assistant. Devlin is a distracter term.
    Humanities—Description

77. LUGUBRIOUS : (*a.* shallow, ***b.* cheerful**, *c.* expensive, *d.* fatuous) :: PONDEROUS : LIGHT

    (b) *Lugubrious* and *cheerful* are antonyms, as are *ponderous* and *light*.
    Vocabulary—Similarity/Contrast

78. EXPLETIVE : (*a.* interrogative, *b.* factotum, ***c.* oath**, *d.* lie) :: EXPOSÉ : DISCLOSURE

    (c) An expletive is an oath. An exposé is a disclosure.
    Vocabulary—Similarity/Contrast

79. 11 : BINARY :: (*a.* 2, ***b.* 3**, *c.* 4, *d.* 10) : DECIMAL

    (b) The number 11 in binary notation is equal to the number 3 in decimal notation.
    Mathematics—Equality/Negation

80. CHALICE : GOBLET :: LEAF : (*a.* plant, *b.* tree, ***c.* sheet**, *d.* gold)

    (c) A chalice is a goblet. A leaf is a sheet (of paper).
    Vocabulary—Similarity/Contrast

81. (*a.* nut, *b.* fruit, ***c.* root**, *d.* berry) : TURNIP :: STEM : CELERY

    (**c**) The stem of celery is edible, as is the root of turnip.
    General Information—Class

82. ABRAM : ABRAHAM :: (*a.* Sarabelle, ***b.* Sarai**, *c.* Salome, *d.* Sharon) :
    SARAH

    (**b**) After the Covenant with God, Abram's name was changed to Abraham,
    and Sarai's name was changed to Sarah.
    Humanities—Description

83. VELÁSQUEZ : MAIDS OF HONOR :: (***a.* Botticelli**, *b.* Bellini, *c.* Bosch,
    d. Uccello) : THE BIRTH OF VENUS

    (**a**) *Maids of Honor* is a famous painting by Velásquez; *The Birth of Venus*
    is a famous painting by Botticelli. Bellini painted many Christian scenes, like
    St. Francis in Ecstasy. *The Garden of Earthly Delights* is one of Bosch's famous paintings.
    Uccello painted the *Battle of San Romano* in a series of three paintings.
    Humanities—Description

84. CIVIL : (*a.* misdemeanor, *b.* larceny, ***c.* tort**, *d.* perjury) :: CRIMINAL :
    FELONY

    (**c**) A tort is a civil offense, while a felony is a criminal offense.
    Social Science—Class

85. GREGORIAN : NOVEMBER :: FRENCH REVOLUTIONARY :
    (*a.* Novembre, *b.* February, *c.* Julian, ***d.* Thermidor**)

    (**d**) Thermidor in the French Revolutionary calendar corresponded to
    November in the conventional Gregorian calendar in their both being the
    11th month. The months of the French Revolutionary calendar (starting
    in September) were Vendémiaire, Brumaire, Frimaire, Nivôse, Pluviôse,
    Ventôse, Germinal, Floréal, Prairial, Messidor, Thermidor, Fructidor.
    Humanities—Similarity/Contrast

86. GOLDEN RULE : LUKE :: CATEGORICAL IMPERATIVE : (*a.* Hegel,
    ***b.* Kant**, *c.* Ardrey, *d.* Lorenz)

    (**b**) The golden rule—"Do unto others as you would have them do unto
    you"—is found in the Gospel of Luke. The categorical imperative—"One's
    behavior should be governed by the same principles that one would have
    govern other people's behavior"—is found in the philosophy of Kant.
    Humanities—Description

87. EQUIVOCATION : (*a.* perversity, *b.* exultation, *c.* **veracity**, *d.* perjury) :: UNCERTAINTY : CERTAINTY

    (**c**) *Equivocation* is the opposite of *veracity*. *Uncertainty* is the opposite of *certainty*.
    Vocabulary—Similarity/Contrast

88. TIMBREL : (*a.* cymbals, *b.* zither, *c.* flute, *d.* **tambourine**) :: LUTE : GUITAR

    (**d**) A timbrel is an early form of tambourine; a lute is an early form of guitar.
    Humanities—Class

89. (*a.* Apollo, *b.* Phaeton, *c.* **Furies**, *d.* Sirens) : EUMENIDES :: PLUTO : HADES

    (**c**) The Furies and the Eumenides were one and the same; similarly, Pluto and Hades were one and the same. Apollo was the legendary son of Zeus and Leto; he is the Greek and Roman god of light, prophesy, poetry, and music. Phaeton was the son of Helios; he tried to drive his father's chariot and was killed when he came too close to Earth. A siren is a sea nymph that lures sailors into their demise.
    Humanities—Similarity/Contrast

90. JOSEPH K. : TRIAL :: GREGOR SAMSA : (*a.* Hunger Artist, *b.* Death in Venice, *c.* The Flies, *d.* **Metamorphosis**)

    (**d**) Joseph K. is the main character in Kafka's *The Trial*. Gregor Samsa is the main character in Kafka's *The Metamorphosis*. *Death in Venice* is by Thomas Mann; *The Flies* is by Jean-Paul Sartre; *A Hunger Artist* is by Franz Kafka.
    Humanities—Description

91. $\sqrt{2}$: $\sqrt{18}$ :: 1 : (*a.* 2, *b.* **3**, *c.* 6, *d.* 9)
    (**b**) The ratio of $\sqrt{2}$ to $\sqrt{18}$ is equal to the ratio of 1 to 3.
    Mathematics—Equality/Negation

92. TRANSUBSTANTIATION : ACTUAL :: (*a.* insubstantiation, *b.* absubstantiation, *c.* **consubstantiation**, *d.* desubstantiation) : COEXISTING

    (**c**) According to the doctrine of transubstantiation, the actual substances of the bread and of the wine in the Eucharist are changed into the body and blood of Christ; according to the doctrine of consubstantiation, the bread and wine are merely coexisting.
    Humanities—Description

93. ABACUS : COMPUTER :: DAGUERROTYPE : (*a.* stereo, ***b.* photograph**, *c.* tape recorder, *d.* telephone)

(**b**) The abacus is a primitive computer; the daguerrotype is a primitive photograph.
Humanities—Description

94. DECLARATION OF INDEPENDENCE : PHILADELPHIA :: MAGNA CARTA : (*a.* Gloucester, ***b.* Runnymede**, *c.* Canterbury, *d.* Norwalk)

(**b**) The Declaration of Independence (1776) was signed in Philadelphia; the Magna Carta was signed at Runnymede (1215). The Magna Carta was a charter given to the English barons by King John to recognize their rights and privileges.
Humanities—Description

95. MINTON : ROYAL DOULTON :: MIKASA (*a.* Sony, *b.* Rosenthal, *c.* Lenox, ***d.* Noritake**)

(**d**) Minton and Royal Doulton are both English makers of fine china, while Mikasa and Noritake are both Japanese makers of fine china. Rosenthal is a German brand of china. Lenox is an American brand of china.
General Information—Class

96. SHYLOCK : SCROOGE :: DON JUAN : (*a.* Antonio, *b.* Don Giovanni, ***c.* Lothario**, *d.* Don Quixote)

(**c**) In literature, Shylock (of *The Merchant of Venice by Shakespeare*) and Scrooge (of *A Christmas Carol* by Charles Dickens) are both miserly characters, while Don Juan (many authors, e.g., Moliere and Byron) and Lothario (of *The Fair Penitent* by Nicholas Rowe) are both great lovers.
Humanities—Class

97. SKINNER : EMPIRICIST :: (*a.* Watson, *b.* Aristotle, ***c.* Chomsky**, *d.* Locke) : RATIONALIST

(**c**) Skinner was a philosophical empiricist, while Chomsky is a philosophical rationalist. Watson was a behaviorist; Locke was an empiricist; Aristotle was a Greek empiricist philosopher.
Social Science—Description

98. MOHAWK : IROQUOIS :: (*a.* Apache, ***b.* Zuni**, *c.* Seminole, *d.* Creek) : PUEBLO

(**b**) The Mohawks were one of the Iroquois Indian tribes; the Zuni were one of the Pueblo Indian tribes. The Seminoles are a Native American people from the American southeast who now reside primarily in Florida. The Creek are closely related to the Seminoles and call themselves Muscogee today. Apache is a term that refers to several groups of Native Americans who lived in the Great Plains and the southwest of the United States.
Social Science—Class

99. (*a.* half-life, *b.* radioactivity, *c.* atomic mass, ***d.* atomic number**) : ISOTOPE :: ATOMIC WEIGHT : ISOBAR

    (**d**) Chemical isotopes have the same atomic number; chemical isobars have the same atomic weight.
    Natural Science—Description

100. SARACEN : (*a.* Hindu, ***b.* Muslim**, *c.* Shintoist, *d.* Taoist) :: EPISCOPALIAN : ANGLICAN

    (**b**) A Saracen is a Muslim. An Episcopalian is an Anglican.
    Humanities—Similarity/Contrast

101. WATERGATE : NIXON :: IRAN CONTRA : (*a.* Ford, *b.* Carter, ***c.* Reagan**, *d.* Bush)

    (**c**) The Watergate and Iran Contra scandals respectively marred the presidential administrations of Nixon and Reagan. Watergate is a term for a series of scandals that resulted in President Nixon's resignation in 1974. The Iran Contra affair was a series of scandals under Ronald Reagan that involved arms sales to Iran and funding of Contra militants in Nicaragua.
    General Information—Description

102. GALAPAGOS : SAMOA :: (*a.* Linnaeus, *b.* Magellan, *c.* Rhodes, ***d.* Darwin**) : MEAD

    (**d**) Charles Darwin began some of his most prominent scientific work in the South Pacific Galapagos Islands. Likewise, Margaret Mead began some of her most prominent scientific work in the South Pacific, in Samoa.
    Natural Science—Description

103. BIGGER THOMAS : (*a.* New York, ***b.* Chicago**, *c.* St. Louis, *d.* Montgomery) :: RODION RASKOLNIKOV : ST. PETERSBURG

    (**b**) Fictional characters Bigger Thomas (in *Native Son* by Richard Wright) and Rodion Raskolnikov (in *Crime and Punishment* by Fyodor Dostoyevsky) despair after committing murders in their respective homes of Chicago and St. Petersburg.
    Humanities—Description

104. TAXONOMY : CLASSIFY :: NOMENCLATURE : (*a.* order, *b.* color, ***c.* name**, *d.* number)

    (**c**) A taxonomy is the principled system by which things are classified. Nomenclature is the principled system by which things are named.
    Vocabulary—Description

105. PHYSIOGNOMY : (*a. face*, *b.* stature, *c.* physiology, *d.* gate) ::
CHIROMANCY : PALM

    (**a**) Physiognomy is the art of determining something about a person from
    his/her face. Chiromancy is the art of determining something about a person
    from his/her palm.
    General Information—Description

106. MUTINY : SHIP CAPTAIN :: COUP D'ÉTAT : (*a.* college dean,
    b. military commander, *c.* **government**, *d.* CEO)

    (**c**) Just as a mutiny typically refers to the overthrow of a ship's captain,
    so a *coup d'état* traditionally refers to the overthrow of a government.
    Vocabulary—Description

107. (*a.* **exaggerated**, *b.* understated, *c.* metaphorical, *d.* literal) :
    HYPERBOLIC :: DRAMATIC : HISTRIONIC

    (**a**) An exaggerated statement may be described as hyperbolic just as
    a dramatic display may be described as histrionic.
    Vocabulary—Similarity/Contrast

108. APPLE : EVE :: (*a.* pear, *b.* **pomegranate**, *c.* peach, *d.* papaya) :
    PERSEPHONE

    (**b**) Eve was punished for eating the forbidden fruit that tradition in the
    Bible holds was an apple, and Persephone was punished in Greek mythology
    for eating the forbidden fruit pomegranate.
    Humanities—Description

109. CEMENTUM : ROOT :: (*a.* bone, *b.* fluoride, *c.* keratin, *d.* **enamel**) :
    CROWN

    (**d**) Cementum makes up the outer surface of a tooth's root just as enamel
    makes up the outer surface of a tooth's crown.
    Natural Science—Part/Whole

110. (*a.* acorn, *b.* cornmeal, *c.* **millet**, *d.* filbert) : BULGUR :: QUINOA :
    BARLEY

    (**c**) Millet, bulgur, quinoa, and barley are all whole grains.
    General Information—Class

111. MOBY DICK : LEVIATHAN :: MELVILLE : (*a.* Rousseau, *b.* **Hobbes**, *c.* Kant, *d.* Smith)

(**b**) Melville is famous for his book *Moby Dick*, and Hobbes is famous for his book *Leviathan*. Rousseau is known for *Pygmalion* and the *Confessions of a Solitary Walker*. Kant is famous for his *Critique of Pure Reason*. Smith is the author of *The Theory of Moral Sentiments*.
Humanities—Description

112. (*a.* **Locke**, *b.* Galileo, *c.* Bacon, *d.* Calvin) : ENLIGHTENMENT :: DESCARTES : RENAISSANCE

(**a**) Locke was a philosopher of the Enlightenment, as Descartes was a philosopher of the Renaissance. Galileo was an Italian physicist and astronomer who improved the telescope and is called the "father of modern observational astronomy." He was a supporter of Copernicanism. Bacon was an English philosopher and statesman. Calvin was the founder of the Presbyterian church.
Social Science—Description

113. STEINWAY : (*a.* **piano**, *b.* cello, *c.* flute, *d.* organ) :: STRADIVARIUS : VIOLIN

(**a**) Steinway is a maker of highly prized pianos, as Stradivarius is a maker of highly prized violins.
Humanities—Description

114. TERKEL : (*a.* manuscripts, *b.* photographs, *c.* **oral histories**, *d.* maps) :: LOMAX : FOLK MUSIC

(**c**) Terkel was a pioneering anthologist of oral histories and Lomax was a pioneering anthologist of folk music.
Humanities—Description

115. 6×10^{23} : (*a.* e, *b.* **Avogadro's number**, *c.* i, *d.* Planck's constant) :: 3.14 : PI

(**b**) 6×10^{23} (rounded) is also known as Avogadro's number. Likewise, 3.14 (rounded) is known as pi, or the symbol π.
Natural Science—Equality/Negation

116. CIRRUS : NIMBUS :: CUMULUS : (*a.* bilious, *b.* birrus, *c.* mobius, *d.* **stratus**)

(**d**) Cirrus, nimbus, cumulus, and stratus are all types of clouds. Bilious refers to the bile; a birrus is a coarse kind of cloth worn by poor people in the Middle Ages. Mobius was a German mathematician who developed the Mobius strip.
Natural Science—Class

117. SOCIALISM : (***a.* state**, *b.* family, *c.* town, *d.* universal) :: CAPITALISM : PRIVATE

(**a**) Socialism is an economic system based on state ownership of capital. Capitalism is an economic system based on private ownership of capital.
Social Science—Description

118. (*a.* Pikes Peak, *b.* Mt. Kilimanjaro, ***c.* Mt. Vesuvius**, *d.* K2) : MT. ST. HELENS :: EXTINCT : ACTIVE

(**c**) Mt. Vesuvius is an extinct volcano whereas Mt. St. Helens is an active volcano.
Natural Science—Description

119. IMPERIOUS : IMPERVIOUS :: (*a.* grandiose, *b.* disbelieving, *c.* judgmental, ***d.* domineering**) : IMMUNE

(**d**) Imperious means domineering just as impervious means immune.
Vocabulary—Similarity/Contrast

120. NEUTRAL : NEUTRON :: NEGATIVE : (*a.* atom, ***b.* electron**, *c.* positron, *d.* negatron)

(**b**) Neutrons are subatomic particles with a neutral charge. Electrons are subatomic particles with a negative charge.
Natural Science—Description

PRACTICE TEST 7

Item Classification Chart

		RELATIONSHIP					
	Similarity/ Contrast	Description	Class	Completion	Part/ Whole	Equality/ Negation	Nonsemantic
Vocabulary	42, 45, 52, 54, 61, 65, 66, 67, 68, 71, 74, 75, 77, 78, 80, 87, 107, 119	40, 69, 104, 106		29			
General Information	6, 17, 20, 60, 63	2, 8, 13, 15, 18, 22, 23, 31, 32, 36, 101, 105	25, 51, 81, 95, 110	24			
Humanities	56, 85, 89, 100	3, 11, 14, 27, 43, 47, 57, 62, 64, 73, 76, 82, 83, 86, 90, 92, 93, 94, 103, 108, 111, 113, 114	34, 39, 55, 88, 96	16, 70			
Social Science		9, 26, 41, 97, 112, 117	12, 49, 84, 98		72		
Natural Science	50	1, 5, 7, 19, 28, 30, 33, 35, 48, 53, 58, 59, 99, 102, 118, 120	116		37, 38, 109	115	
Mathematics					4	44, 79, 91	
Nonsemantic							10, 21, 46

Answer Sheet
PRACTICE TEST 8

1 Ⓐ Ⓑ Ⓒ Ⓓ	31 Ⓐ Ⓑ Ⓒ Ⓓ	61 Ⓐ Ⓑ Ⓒ Ⓓ	91 Ⓐ Ⓑ Ⓒ Ⓓ
2 Ⓐ Ⓑ Ⓒ Ⓓ	32 Ⓐ Ⓑ Ⓒ Ⓓ	62 Ⓐ Ⓑ Ⓒ Ⓓ	92 Ⓐ Ⓑ Ⓒ Ⓓ
3 Ⓐ Ⓑ Ⓒ Ⓓ	33 Ⓐ Ⓑ Ⓒ Ⓓ	63 Ⓐ Ⓑ Ⓒ Ⓓ	93 Ⓐ Ⓑ Ⓒ Ⓓ
4 Ⓐ Ⓑ Ⓒ Ⓓ	34 Ⓐ Ⓑ Ⓒ Ⓓ	64 Ⓐ Ⓑ Ⓒ Ⓓ	94 Ⓐ Ⓑ Ⓒ Ⓓ
5 Ⓐ Ⓑ Ⓒ Ⓓ	35 Ⓐ Ⓑ Ⓒ Ⓓ	65 Ⓐ Ⓑ Ⓒ Ⓓ	95 Ⓐ Ⓑ Ⓒ Ⓓ
6 Ⓐ Ⓑ Ⓒ Ⓓ	36 Ⓐ Ⓑ Ⓒ Ⓓ	66 Ⓐ Ⓑ Ⓒ Ⓓ	96 Ⓐ Ⓑ Ⓒ Ⓓ
7 Ⓐ Ⓑ Ⓒ Ⓓ	37 Ⓐ Ⓑ Ⓒ Ⓓ	67 Ⓐ Ⓑ Ⓒ Ⓓ	97 Ⓐ Ⓑ Ⓒ Ⓓ
8 Ⓐ Ⓑ Ⓒ Ⓓ	38 Ⓐ Ⓑ Ⓒ Ⓓ	68 Ⓐ Ⓑ Ⓒ Ⓓ	98 Ⓐ Ⓑ Ⓒ Ⓓ
9 Ⓐ Ⓑ Ⓒ Ⓓ	39 Ⓐ Ⓑ Ⓒ Ⓓ	69 Ⓐ Ⓑ Ⓒ Ⓓ	99 Ⓐ Ⓑ Ⓒ Ⓓ
10 Ⓐ Ⓑ Ⓒ Ⓓ	40 Ⓐ Ⓑ Ⓒ Ⓓ	70 Ⓐ Ⓑ Ⓒ Ⓓ	100 Ⓐ Ⓑ Ⓒ Ⓓ
11 Ⓐ Ⓑ Ⓒ Ⓓ	41 Ⓐ Ⓑ Ⓒ Ⓓ	71 Ⓐ Ⓑ Ⓒ Ⓓ	101 Ⓐ Ⓑ Ⓒ Ⓓ
12 Ⓐ Ⓑ Ⓒ Ⓓ	42 Ⓐ Ⓑ Ⓒ Ⓓ	72 Ⓐ Ⓑ Ⓒ Ⓓ	102 Ⓐ Ⓑ Ⓒ Ⓓ
13 Ⓐ Ⓑ Ⓒ Ⓓ	43 Ⓐ Ⓑ Ⓒ Ⓓ	73 Ⓐ Ⓑ Ⓒ Ⓓ	103 Ⓐ Ⓑ Ⓒ Ⓓ
14 Ⓐ Ⓑ Ⓒ Ⓓ	44 Ⓐ Ⓑ Ⓒ Ⓓ	74 Ⓐ Ⓑ Ⓒ Ⓓ	104 Ⓐ Ⓑ Ⓒ Ⓓ
15 Ⓐ Ⓑ Ⓒ Ⓓ	45 Ⓐ Ⓑ Ⓒ Ⓓ	75 Ⓐ Ⓑ Ⓒ Ⓓ	105 Ⓐ Ⓑ Ⓒ Ⓓ
16 Ⓐ Ⓑ Ⓒ Ⓓ	46 Ⓐ Ⓑ Ⓒ Ⓓ	76 Ⓐ Ⓑ Ⓒ Ⓓ	106 Ⓐ Ⓑ Ⓒ Ⓓ
17 Ⓐ Ⓑ Ⓒ Ⓓ	47 Ⓐ Ⓑ Ⓒ Ⓓ	77 Ⓐ Ⓑ Ⓒ Ⓓ	107 Ⓐ Ⓑ Ⓒ Ⓓ
18 Ⓐ Ⓑ Ⓒ Ⓓ	48 Ⓐ Ⓑ Ⓒ Ⓓ	78 Ⓐ Ⓑ Ⓒ Ⓓ	108 Ⓐ Ⓑ Ⓒ Ⓓ
19 Ⓐ Ⓑ Ⓒ Ⓓ	49 Ⓐ Ⓑ Ⓒ Ⓓ	79 Ⓐ Ⓑ Ⓒ Ⓓ	109 Ⓐ Ⓑ Ⓒ Ⓓ
20 Ⓐ Ⓑ Ⓒ Ⓓ	50 Ⓐ Ⓑ Ⓒ Ⓓ	80 Ⓐ Ⓑ Ⓒ Ⓓ	110 Ⓐ Ⓑ Ⓒ Ⓓ
21 Ⓐ Ⓑ Ⓒ Ⓓ	51 Ⓐ Ⓑ Ⓒ Ⓓ	81 Ⓐ Ⓑ Ⓒ Ⓓ	111 Ⓐ Ⓑ Ⓒ Ⓓ
22 Ⓐ Ⓑ Ⓒ Ⓓ	52 Ⓐ Ⓑ Ⓒ Ⓓ	82 Ⓐ Ⓑ Ⓒ Ⓓ	112 Ⓐ Ⓑ Ⓒ Ⓓ
23 Ⓐ Ⓑ Ⓒ Ⓓ	53 Ⓐ Ⓑ Ⓒ Ⓓ	83 Ⓐ Ⓑ Ⓒ Ⓓ	113 Ⓐ Ⓑ Ⓒ Ⓓ
24 Ⓐ Ⓑ Ⓒ Ⓓ	54 Ⓐ Ⓑ Ⓒ Ⓓ	84 Ⓐ Ⓑ Ⓒ Ⓓ	114 Ⓐ Ⓑ Ⓒ Ⓓ
25 Ⓐ Ⓑ Ⓒ Ⓓ	55 Ⓐ Ⓑ Ⓒ Ⓓ	85 Ⓐ Ⓑ Ⓒ Ⓓ	115 Ⓐ Ⓑ Ⓒ Ⓓ
26 Ⓐ Ⓑ Ⓒ Ⓓ	56 Ⓐ Ⓑ Ⓒ Ⓓ	86 Ⓐ Ⓑ Ⓒ Ⓓ	116 Ⓐ Ⓑ Ⓒ Ⓓ
27 Ⓐ Ⓑ Ⓒ Ⓓ	57 Ⓐ Ⓑ Ⓒ Ⓓ	87 Ⓐ Ⓑ Ⓒ Ⓓ	117 Ⓐ Ⓑ Ⓒ Ⓓ
28 Ⓐ Ⓑ Ⓒ Ⓓ	58 Ⓐ Ⓑ Ⓒ Ⓓ	88 Ⓐ Ⓑ Ⓒ Ⓓ	118 Ⓐ Ⓑ Ⓒ Ⓓ
29 Ⓐ Ⓑ Ⓒ Ⓓ	59 Ⓐ Ⓑ Ⓒ Ⓓ	89 Ⓐ Ⓑ Ⓒ Ⓓ	119 Ⓐ Ⓑ Ⓒ Ⓓ
30 Ⓐ Ⓑ Ⓒ Ⓓ	60 Ⓐ Ⓑ Ⓒ Ⓓ	90 Ⓐ Ⓑ Ⓒ Ⓓ	120 Ⓐ Ⓑ Ⓒ Ⓓ

Practice Test 8

Directions: In each of the following questions, you will find three initial terms and, in parentheses, four answer options designated *a*, *b*, *c*, and *d*. You are to select from the four answer options the one that best completes the analogy with the three initial terms. To record your answers, use the answer sheet provided.

Time: 60 minutes

1. STOCKHOLM : (*a.* Switzerland, *b.* Austria, *c.* Finland, *d.* Sweden) ::
   PARIS : FRANCE

2. ESCARGOTS : FRENCH :: SUKIYAKI : (*a.* Japanese, *b.* German,
   c. Hungarian, *d.* Mexican)

3. COBBLER : SHOES :: TAILOR : (*a.* needles, *b.* clothes, *c.* threads,
   d. thimbles)

4. (*a.* black, *b.* yellow, *c.* red, *d.* blue) : SULFUR :: WHITE : GYPSUM

5. TRANSITIVE : HIT :: (*a.* expletive, *b.* intransitive, *c.* nominative,
   d. subjunctive) : IS

6. COMPOSITE : 8 :: PRIME : (*a.* 4, *b.* 6, *c.* 7, *d.* 9)

7. FRESCO : PLASTER :: TAPESTRY : (*a.* stone, *b.* metal, *c.* cloth, *d.* wood)

8. VEGETARIAN : MEAT :: TEETOTALER : (*a.* fruit, *b.* alcoholic beverages,
   c. cooked food, *d.* tobacco)

9. TRAFALGAR SQUARE : (*a.* London, *b.* Florence, *c.* Moscow, *d.* Paris) ::
   TIMES SQUARE : NEW YORK

10. (*a.* appliance, *b.* food, *c.* explosive, *d.* automobile) :: TNT :: COUNTRY :
    U.S.A.

11. YELLOW : COWARDLY :: (*a.* blue, *b.* black, *c.* red, *d.* green) :
    INEXPERIENCED

12. 2 : QUART :: (*a.* 1, *b.* 4, *c.* 8, *d.* 16) : GALLON

13. RED FLAG : REVOLUTION :: WHITE FLAG : (*a.* victory, *b.* surrender,
    c. established order, *d.* purity)

14. ZEBRA : STRIPES :: LEOPARD : (*a.* spots, *b.* stripes, *c.* diagonals, *d.* zigzags)

15. (*a.* tyrant, *b.* wealthy merchant, *c.* explorer, *d.* pirate) : BUCCANEER :: SETTLER : PIONEER

16. CENTIGRADE : 100 :: FAHRENHEIT : (*a.* 0, *b.* 32, *c.* 100, *d.* 212)

17. (*a.* 1, *b.* 5, *c.* 20, *d.* 25) : SILVER :: 50 : GOLD

18. BEEF : STEER :: MUTTON : (*a.* ox, *b.* sheep, *c.* deer, *d.* goat)

19. ATOM : (*a.* molecule, *b.* electron, *c.* nucleus, *d.* gamma ray) :: TREE : FOREST

20. IGNORANCE : (*a.* intelligence, *b.* knowledge, *c.* foresight, *d.* attention) :: STUPIDITY : INTELLIGENCE

21. NONAGENARIAN : 90 :: OCTOGENARIAN : (*a.* 60, *b.* 70, *c.* 80, *d.* 100)

22. LISBON : (*a.* Spain, *b.* Portugal, *c.* Hungary, *d.* Denmark) :: THE HAGUE : NETHERLANDS

23. WAMPUM : (*a.* Dutchman, *b.* Portuguese, *c.* Pakistani, *d.* American Indian) :: DOUBLOON : SPANIARD

24. GREEK ALPHABET : GREEK :: LATIN ALPHABET : (*a.* Russian, *b.* Cyrillic, *c.* Sanskrit, *d.* English)

25. (*a.* 90, *b.* 180, *c.* 270, *d.* 360) : TRIANGLE :: 360 : SQUARE

26. COLUMBIA : (*a.* South America, *b.* North America, *c.* United States, *d.* Brazil) :: BRITANNIA : BRITAIN

27. FINALE : MUSICAL COMPOSITION :: (*a.* check, *b.* checkmate, *c.* rook, *d.* jeopardy) : CHESS

28. YAHWEH : JUDAISM :: ALLAH : (*a.* Islam, *b.* Judaism, *c.* Taoism, *d.* Confucianism)

29. (*a.* nominative, *b.* dative, *c.* accusative, *d.* ablative) : OBJECTIVE :: SHE : HIM

30. RECTANGLE : OCTAGON :: (*a.* triangle, *b.* square, *c.* pentagon, *d.* rhombus) : HEXAGON

31. (*a.* prize, *b.* damn, *c.* reflect, *d.* complete) : PRAISE :: COMPLEMENT : COMPLIMENT

32. SUB : BUS :: TAR : (*a.* car, *b.* road, *c.* vehicle, *d.* rat)

33. MANDATORY : (*a.* laudatory, *b.* damning, *c.* optional, *d.* compulsory) :: DEFINITE : UNCERTAIN

34. ONE : LAND :: TWO : (*a.* air, *b.* sea, *c.* ground, *d.* island)

35. (*a.* eat, *b.* drink, *c.* sever, *d.* mend) : CHALICE :: DIG : SHOVEL

36. CONSONANT : (*a.* syncopated, *b.* rhythmic, *c.* euphemistic, *d.* euphonious) :: DISSONANT : DISCORDANT

37. (*a.* Montague, *b.* Scali, *c.* Dunlop, *d.* Mineo) : ROMEO :: CAPULET : JULIET

38. EMANCIPATE : (*a.* emaciate, *b.* free, *c.* enslave, *d.* deliver) :: EMPTY : FULL

39. PALMISTRY : PALM :: PHRENOLOGY : (*a.* handwriting, *b.* EEG, *c.* eyes, *d.* skull)

40. (*a.* Columbia Gem, *b.* Union Jack, *c.* Royal Ensign, *d.* Fleur-de-Lis) : GREAT BRITAIN :: STARS AND STRIPES : U.S.A.

41. COMMON LOG : 10 :: NATURAL LOG : (*a.* π, *b.* e, *c.* i, *d.* 1)

42. MAE WEST : LIFE JACKET :: MICKEY FINN : (*a.* blackjack, *b.* Molotov cocktail, *c.* drugged liquor, *d.* time bomb)

43. EARTH : AIR :: (*a.* bile, *b.* carbon, *c.* phlogiston, *d.* fire) : WATER

44. CAMUS : STRANGER :: (*a.* Sartre, *b.* Camus, *c.* Mauriac, *d.* Ionesco) : PLAGUE

45. DOG : PIE :: HOT : (*a.* cold, *b.* cat, *c.* pizza, *d.* cake)

46. PIETÀ : MICHELANGELO :: THE KISS : (*a.* Rodin, *b.* Pisano, *c.* Ghiberti, *d.* da Vinci)

47. (*a.* Congress of Vienna, *b.* League of Nations, *c.* Warsaw Pact, *d.* NATO) : UNITED NATIONS :: GASLIGHT : ELECTRIC LIGHT

48. CARAT : (*a.* size, *b.* weight, *c.* brilliance, *d.* value) :: ACRE : AREA

49. $a + b : b + a :: a(b + a)b :$ (*a.* $2a^2b^2$, *b.* $(a + b)^2$, *c.* $a^2b + ab^2$, *d.* $a^2b^2 + ab$)

50. FRANCIS CRICK : STRUCTURE OF DNA MOLECULE :: MARIE CURIE : (*a.* nobelium, *b.* uranium, *c.* radium, *d.* plutonium)

51. ANALOG : SLIDE RULE :: DIGITAL : (*a.* odometer, *b.* ruler, *c.* compass, *d.* protractor)

52. CHARLOTTE'S : PILGRIM'S :: WEB : (*a.* Follies, *b.* Progress, *c.* Pretense, *d.* Journey)

53. VOID : VACUUM :: FULL : (*a.* replete, *b.* deplete, *c.* compact, *d.* empty)

54. HIGH : DIE :: (*a.* gregarious, *b.* reticent, *c.* low, *d.* buy) : SHY

55. (*a.* retina, *b.* iris, *c.* lens, *d.* cone) : ROD :: CHROMATIC : ACHROMATIC

56. BOVINE : (*a.* jackal, *b.* monkey, *c.* ox, *d.* rabbit) :: URSINE : BEAR

57. (*a.* Plato, *b.* Aristotle, *c.* Leibniz, *d.* Locke) : REPUBLIC :: DESCARTES : MEDITATIONS

58. DEER : DEER :: CORPUS : (*a.* corpi, *b.* corpuses, *c.* corpora, *d.* corpes)

59. BUDAPEST : HANOI :: HUNGARY : (*a.* Cambodia, *b.* Laos, *c.* Thailand, *d.* Vietnam)

60. PROMISED LAND : CANAAN :: LAND OF NOD : (*a.* wakefulness, *b.* hell, *c.* sleep, *d.* heaven)

61. MISOGYNIST : WOMEN :: MISOGAMIST : (*a.* men, *b.* people, *c.* marriage, *d.* religion)

62. (*a.* Achilles, *b.* Hector, *c.* Paris, *d.* Troilus) : HELEN :: PLUTO : PROSERPINA

63. BENIGN : BENEVOLENT :: (*a.* beneficent, *b.* nefarious, *c.* tortuous, *d.* voracious) : MALEVOLENT

64. BLOCKHEAD : LUNKHEAD :: MUTTONHEAD : (*a.* fathead, *b.* sleepyhead, *c.* bighead, *d.* egghead)

65. UNCLE TOM : SERVILE :: DUTCH UNCLE : (*a.* hoary, *b.* kind, *c.* stern, *d.* stingy)

66. ALPHA : (*a.* gamma, *b.* zed, *c.* epsilon, *d.* omega) :: A : Z

67. THIAMINE : ASCORBIC ACID :: B_1 : (*a.* B_6, *b.* B_{12}, *c.* C, *d.* E)

68. BRAZIL : (*a.* Portuguese, *b.* Spanish, *c.* French, *d.* Brazilian) :: AUSTRIA : GERMAN

69. CENTURY : EON :: DOZEN : (*a.* one hundred, *b.* gross, *c.* zero, *d.* myriad)

70. SITTING BULL : SIOUX :: GERONIMO : (*a.* Apache, *b.* Pueblo, *c.* Mohawk, *d.* Seminole)

71. AUTOCRACY : AUTARCHY :: MONARCHY : (*a.* democracy, *b.* anarchy, *c.* oligarchy, *d.* kingdom)

72. GOGGLE-EYED : BULGING :: HOOK-NOSED : (*a.* opercular, *b.* oviparous, *c.* ovine, *d.* aquiline)

73. NEPTUNE : DIANA :: SEA : (*a.* hearth, *b.* sun, *c.* moon, *d.* home)

74. EXPEL : DRIVE AWAY :: EXPIATE : (*a.* atone for, *b.* talk at length, *c.* forgive, *d.* speak briefly)

75. LARGO : SLOW :: (*a.* moderato, *b.* allegro, *c.* piano, *d.* fortissimo) : FAST

76. (*a.* with faith, *b.* with truth, *c.* with passion, *d.* with authority) : EX CATHEDRA :: ON THE FACE : EX FACIE

77. FIFE : CLARINET :: TROMBONE : (*a.* lute, *b.* bagpipe, *c.* piano, *d.* violin)

78. PARASITE : LIVING :: (*a.* saprophyte, *b.* neophyte, *c.* pteridophyte, *d.* bryophyte) : DEAD

79. PRINCE : MACHIAVELLI :: PETIT PRINCE : (*a.* Saint-Exupéry, *b.* Mauriac, *c.* Camus, *d.* Lescaut)

80. INDIA : RUPEE :: (*a.* Mexico, *b.* Switzerland, *c.* Great Britain, *d.* Sweden) : FRANC

81. DEMOSTHENES : (*a.* Cicero, *b.* Socrates, *c.* Pericles, *d.* Ovid) :: HOMER : VIRGIL

82. (*a.* mg, *b.* gg, *c.* kg, *d.* cg) : g :: m : mm

83. CIPANGO : JAPAN :: CATHAY : (*a.* China, *b.* Tibet, *c.* Polynesia, *d.* Mongolia)

84. IMPROMPTU : EXTEMPORE :: PROBITY : (*a.* open-mindedness, *b.* dishonesty, *c.* narrow-mindedness, *d.* honesty)

85. FERMI : NUCLEAR PHYSICS :: JANE ADDAMS : (*a.* nursing, *b.* physics, *c.* social work, *d.* drama)

86. (*a.* Inferno, *b.* Decameron, *c.* The Wasteland, *d.* No Exit) : CANTERBURY TALES :: ANTHOLOGY : COLLECTION

87. RICHELIEU : (*a.* Cushing, *b.* Mazarin, *c.* Metternich, *d.* Marat) :: KENNEDY : JOHNSON

88. (*a.* uncertainty, *b.* luck, *c.* sample, *d.* variance) : POPULATION :: STATISTIC : PARAMETER

89. REGAN : GONERIL :: LEAH : (*a.* Jacob, *b.* Rebeccah, *c.* Isaac, *d.* Rachel)

90. TEMPUS : CARPE :: FUGIT : (*a.* cibus, *b.* mater, *c.* diem, *d.* tempum)

91. ERSATZ : (*a.* genuine, *b.* superior, *c.* inferior, *d.* fake) :: FRESH : RANCID

92. EVE : DEED :: MADAM : (*a.* cuckoo, *b.* swoon, *c.* noon, *d.* pool)

93. SLEEPY : SOMNOLENT :: GROGGY : (*a.* asleep, *b.* unsteady, *c.* awake, *d.* dead)

94. AXON : DEPART :: (*a.* neuron, *b.* ganglion, *c.* dendrites, *d.* plasma) : APPROACH

95. BUDGE : TENNIS :: LOUIS : (*a.* hockey, *b.* football, *c.* baseball, *d.* boxing)

96. BLOOD : MELANCHOLY :: CHOLER : (*a.* plasma, *b.* lymph, *c.* phlegm, *d.* saliva)

97. MEXICO : YORK :: CAROLINA : (*a.* Virginia, *b.* Oregon, *c.* Washington, *d.* Dakota)

98. ARGON : NEON :: XENON : (*a.* helium, *b.* oxygen, *c.* mercury, *d.* carbon)

99. HORN : ROLAND :: HARP : (*a.* Gideon, *b.* David, *c.* Moses, *d.* Samuel)

100. GLUTTON : FOOD :: SATYR : (*a.* punishment, *b.* glory, *c.* alcoholic beverages, *d.* sex)

101. ACUTE : (*a.* small, *b.* obtuse, *c.* intense, *d.* right) :: APOGEE : PERIGEE

102. (*a.* berate, *b.* refine, *c.* attenuate, *d.* foreshadow) : ADUMBRATE ::
INTIMATE : HINT

103. PNEUMONECTOMY : LUNG :: (*a.* tonsillectomy, *b.* meningectomy,
c. lobotomy, *d.* encephalotomy) : BRAIN

104. EMPATHY : (*a.* lungs, *b.* soul, *c.* pancreas, *d.* heart) :: BRAVERY : LIVER

105. CIRCUMSPECT : CIRCUMSCRIBE :: (*a.* prudent, *b.* navigate,
c. rounded, *d.* investigate) : ENCIRCLE

106. DEARTH : (*a.* poverty, *b.* abundance, *c.* warmth, *d.* nothing) :: PAUCITY :
PLENTY

107. CAP : LID :: KNEE : (*a.* leg, *b.* patella, *c.* heel, *d.* eye)

108. (*a.* bitterness, *b.* wittiness, *c.* frivolity, *d.* accusation) : ACRIMONIOUS ::
FRUGALITY : PARSIMONIOUS

109. CAESAR : DELIVERY :: ACHILLES : (*a.* surgery, *b.* ligament, *c.* tendon,
d. bone)

110. PROMETHEUS : BOUND :: ATLAS : (*a.* carried, *b.* tied, *c.* shrugged,
d. grew)

111. GENGHIS KHAN : (*a.* China, *b.* Mongolia, *c.* Persia, *d.* Prussia) ::
SHAKA : SOUTH AFRICA

112. (*a.* right to bear arms, *b.* prohibition of alcohol, *c.* right to remain silent,
d. freedom of religion) : 18th AMENDMENT :: WOMEN'S SUFFRAGE :
19th AMENDMENT

113. KID : (*a.* wolf, *b.* goat, *c.* moose, *d.* kangaroo) :: CALF : WHALE

114. HOPI : (*a.* southwest, *b.* southeast, *c.* northwest, *d.* great plains) ::
TLINGIT : NORTHWEST

115. PTOLEMY : EARTH :: COPERNICUS : (*a.* Mars, *b.* Venus, *c.* Moon,
d. Sun)

116. ADAM SMITH : 18th CENTURY :: JOHN MAYNARD KEYNES :
(*a.* 20th century, *b.* 19th century, *c.* 17th century, *d.* 16th century)

117. (*a.* Laos, *b.* Japan, *c.* Taiwan, *d.* China) : JUDO :: KOREA :
TAE KWON DO

118. KHMER ROUGE : POL POT :: COMMUNIST PARTY OF CHINA :
(*a.* Kuomintang, *b.* Confucius, *c.* Mao Zedong, *d.* Chiang Kai-shek)

119. SUEZ CANAL : (*a.* Turkey, *b.* Morocco, *c.* Egypt, *d.* Israel) :: PANAMA
CANAL : PANAMA

120. SOVIET UNION : (*a.* Portugal, *b.* Brazil, *c.* Cuba, *d.* Spain) ::
CHAGALL : DALI

Answer Key
PRACTICE TEST 8

1.	D	31.	D	61.	C	91.	A
2.	A	32.	D	62.	C	92.	C
3.	B	33.	C	63.	B	93.	B
4.	B	34.	B	64.	A	94.	C
5.	B	35.	B	65.	C	95.	D
6.	C	36.	D	66.	D	96.	C
7.	C	37.	A	67.	C	97.	D
8.	B	38.	C	68.	A	98.	A
9.	A	39.	D	69.	D	99.	B
10.	C	40.	B	70.	A	100.	D
11.	D	41.	B	71.	D	101.	B
12.	C	42.	C	72.	D	102.	D
13.	B	43.	D	73.	C	103.	C
14.	A	44.	B	74.	A	104.	D
15.	D	45.	C	75.	B	105.	A
16.	D	46.	A	76.	D	106.	B
17.	D	47.	B	77.	B	107.	D
18.	B	48.	B	78.	A	108.	A
19.	A	49.	C	79.	A	109.	C
20.	B	50.	C	80.	B	110.	C
21.	C	51.	A	81.	A	111.	B
22.	B	52.	B	82.	C	112.	B
23.	D	53.	A	83.	A	113.	B
24.	D	54.	D	84.	D	114.	A
25.	B	55.	D	85.	C	115.	D
26.	C	56.	C	86.	B	116.	A
27.	B	57.	A	87.	B	117.	B
28.	A	58.	C	88.	C	118.	C
29.	A	59.	D	89.	D	119.	C
30.	A	60.	C	90.	C	120.	D

Answer Key

ANSWER EXPLANATIONS FOR PRACTICE TEST 8

In the following, explanations concerning the correct response are in a large font. Explanations regarding distracters (incorrect responses) that are not self-explaining or could be misinterpreted are in a smaller font in order to highlight the explanations of the answers that are correct.

1. STOCKHOLM : (*a.* Switzerland, *b.* Austria, *c.* Finland, ***d.* Sweden**) :: PARIS : FRANCE

   (**d**) Stockholm is the capital of Sweden. Paris is the capital of France. The capital of Switzerland is Bern, the capital of Austria is Vienna, and the capital of Finland is Helsinki.
   General Information—Description

2. ESCARGOTS : FRENCH :: SUKIYAKI : (***a.* Japanese**, *b.* German, *c.* Hungarian, *d.* Mexican)

   (**a**) Escargots are a French food (snails). Sukiyaki is a Japanese food dish (beef hot pot).
   General Information—Description

3. COBBLER : SHOES :: TAILOR : (*a.* needles, ***b.* clothes**, *c.* threads, *d.* thimbles)

   (**b**) A cobbler mends shoes; a tailor mends clothes.
   General Information—Description

4. (*a.* black, ***b.* yellow**, *c.* red, *d.* blue) : SULFUR :: WHITE : GYPSUM

   (**b**) Sulfur is usually yellow; gypsum is usually white.
   Natural Science—Description

5. TRANSITIVE : HIT :: (*a.* expletive, ***b.* intransitive**, *c.* nominative, *d.* subjunctive) : IS

   (**b**) *Hit* is a transitive verb. *Is* is an intransitive verb.
   Humanities—Description

6. COMPOSITE : 8 :: PRIME : (*a.* 4, *b.* 6, ***c.* 7**, *d.* 9)

   (**c**) 8 is a composite number. 7 is a prime number. A composite number can be divided into two or more integers (whole numbers). A prime number is a number that is evenly divisible only by itself and 1.
   Mathematics—Description

7. FRESCO : PLASTER :: TAPESTRY : (*a.* stone, *b.* metal, ***c.* cloth**, *d.* wood)

(**c**) A fresco is made of plaster. A tapestry is made of cloth.
Humanities—Description

8. VEGETARIAN : MEAT :: TEETOTALER : (*a.* fruit,
***b.* alcoholic beverages**, *c.* cooked food, *d.* tobacco)

(**b**) A vegetarian will not eat meat. A teetotaler will not drink alcoholic beverages.
General Information—Description

9. TRAFALGAR SQUARE : (***a.* London**, *b.* Florence, *c.* Moscow, *d.* Paris) ::
TIMES SQUARE : NEW YORK

(**a**) Trafalgar Square is in London. Times Square is in New York.
General Information—Description

10. (*a.* appliance, *b.* food, ***c.* explosive**, *d.* automobile) :: TNT :: COUNTRY :
U.S.A.

(**c**) TNT is an explosive. The United States is a country.
General Information—Class

11. YELLOW : COWARDLY :: (*a.* blue, *b.* black, *c.* red, ***d.* green**) :
INEXPERIENCED

(**d**) A cowardly person is sometimes referred to as yellow. An inexperienced person is sometimes referred to as green. The color blue stands for sadness. The color black stands for death. The color red stands for heat.
General Information—Similarity/Contrast

12. 2 : QUART :: (*a.* 1, *b.* 4, ***c.* 8**, *d.* 16) : GALLON

(**c**) There are 2 pints in a quart, and 8 pints in a gallon.
Mathematics—Class

13. RED FLAG : REVOLUTION :: WHITE FLAG : (*a.* victory, ***b.* surrender**,
c. established order, *d.* purity)

(**b**) A red flag is often used to signify revolution, while a white flag is often used to signify surrender.
General Information—Description

14. ZEBRA : STRIPES :: LEOPARD : (***a.* spots**, *b.* stripes, *c.* diagonals,
d. zigzags)

(**a**) A zebra has stripes; a leopard spots.
General Information—Description

15. (*a.* tyrant, *b.* wealthy merchant, *c.* explorer, ***d.* pirate**) : BUCCANEER :: SETTLER : PIONEER

    (**d**) A buccaneer is a pirate; a pioneer is a settler.
    General Information—Similarity/Contrast

16. CENTIGRADE : 100 :: FAHRENHEIT : (*a.* 0, *b.* 32, *c.* 100, ***d.* 212**)

    (**d**) One hundred degrees centigrade (the boiling point of water) is equal to 212 degrees Fahrenheit. Zero degree centigrade (the freezing point of water) is equal to 32 degrees Fahrenheit.
    Natural Science—Equality/Negation

17. (*a.* 1, *b.* 5, *c.* 20, ***d.* 25**) : SILVER :: 50 : GOLD

    (**d**) A 25th anniversary is often referred to as a silver anniversary, while a 50th anniversary is gold. The 1st anniversary is often referred to as a paper anniversary; the 5th anniversary as a wood anniversary, and the 20th anniversary as a china anniversary.
    General Information—Description

18. BEEF : STEER :: MUTTON : (*a.* ox, ***b.* sheep**, *c.* deer, *d.* goat)

    (**b**) Beef comes from a steer; mutton comes from a sheep.
    General Information—Description

19. ATOM : (***a.* molecule**, *b.* electron, *c.* nucleus, *d.* gamma ray) :: TREE : FOREST

    (**a**) Atoms combine to form a molecule; trees combine to form a forest.
    Natural Science—Part/Whole

20. IGNORANCE : (*a.* intelligence, ***b.* knowledge**, *c.* foresight, *d.* attention) :: STUPIDITY : INTELLIGENCE

    (**b**) Ignorance is the absence of knowledge. Stupidity is the absence of intelligence.
    Vocabulary—Similarity/Contrast

21. NONAGENARIAN : 90 :: OCTOGENARIAN : (*a.* 60, *b.* 70, ***c.* 80**, *d.* 100)

    (**c**) A nonagenarian has lived to the age of 90; an octogenarian has lived to the age of 80. Somebody who has lived to the age of 70 is a septuagenarian.
    Vocabulary—Description

22. LISBON : (*a.* Spain, ***b.* Portugal**, *c.* Hungary, *d.* Denmark) ::
THE HAGUE : NETHERLANDS

    (**b**) Lisbon is the capital of Portugal; The Hague is the capital of the
    Netherlands. Madrid is the capital of Spain; Budapest is the capital of Hungary;
    Copenhagen is the capital of Denmark.
    General Information—Description

23. WAMPUM : (*a.* Dutchman, *b.* Portuguese, *c.* Pakistani,
***d.* American Indian**) :: DOUBLOON : SPANIARD

    (**d**) Wampum was used as a coin by certain American Indian tribes;
    the doubloon was formerly a Spanish coin.
    Humanities—Description

24. GREEK ALPHABET : GREEK :: LATIN ALPHABET : (*a.* Russian,
b. Cyrillic, *c.* Sanskrit, ***d.* English**)

    (**d**) The Greek language uses the Greek alphabet. The English language uses
    the Latin alphabet.
    Humanities—Description

25. (*a.* 90, ***b.* 180**, *c.* 270, *d.* 360) : TRIANGLE :: 360 : SQUARE

    (**b**) A triangle has 180 degrees; a square has 360 degrees.
    Mathematics—Description

26. COLUMBIA : (*a.* South America, *b.* North America, ***c.* U.S.A.**, *d.* Brazil) ::
BRITANNIA : BRITAIN

    (**c**) Columbia is a poetic name for the United States (from Columbus);
    Britannia is a poetic name for Britain.
    General Information—Similarity/Contrast

27. FINALE : MUSICAL COMPOSITION :: (*a.* check, ***b.* checkmate**, *c.* rook,
d. jeopardy) : CHESS

    (**b**) A finale ends a musical composition. Checkmate ends a game of chess.
    General Information—Description

28. YAHWEH : JUDAISM :: ALLAH : (***a.* Islam**, *b.* Judaism, *c.* Taoism,
d. Confucianism)

    (**a**) The concept of Yahweh in Judaism is analogous to the concept of
    Allah in Islam.
    Humanities—Description

Answer Explanations

29. (*a.* **nominative**, *b.* dative, *c.* accusative, *d.* ablative) : OBJECTIVE :: SHE : HIM

    (**a**) The word *she* is in the nominative case; the word *him* is in the objective case.
    General Information—Description

30. RECTANGLE : OCTAGON :: (*a.* **triangle**, *b.* square, *c.* pentagon, *d.* rhombus) : HEXAGON

    (**a**) An octagon has twice as many sides as a rectangle; a hexagon has twice as many sides as a triangle.
    Mathematics—Equality/Negation

31. (*a.* prize, *b.* damn, *c.* reflect, *d.* **complete**) : PRAISE :: COMPLEMENT : COMPLIMENT

    (**d**) A complement completes something; a compliment praises something.
    Vocabulary—Similarity/Contrast

32. SUB : BUS :: TAR : (*a.* car, *b.* road, *c.* vehicle, *d.* **rat**)

    (**d**) *Bus* is *sub* spelled backwards; *rat* is *tar* spelled backwards.
    Nonsemantic

33. MANDATORY : (*a.* laudatory, *b.* damning, *c.* **optional**, *d.* compulsory) :: DEFINITE : UNCERTAIN

    (**c**) *Mandatory* and *optional* are antonyms; *definite* and *uncertain* are antonyms.
    Vocabulary—Similarity/Contrast

34. ONE : LAND :: TWO : (*a.* air, *b.* **sea**, *c.* ground, *d.* island)

    (**b**) Paul Revere was to be informed of the means by which British troops were coming through a system of shining lanterns. One lantern meant the British were coming by land; two meant they were coming by sea.
    Humanities—Description

35. (*a.* eat, *b.* **drink**, *c.* sever, *d.* mend) : CHALICE :: DIG : SHOVEL

    (**b**) One uses a chalice to drink from and a shovel to dig with.
    Vocabulary—Description

36. CONSONANT : (*a.* syncopated, *b.* rhythmic, *c.* euphemistic, *d.* **euphonious**) :: DISSONANT : DISCORDANT

(**d**) Consonant sounds are euphonious; dissonant sounds are discordant. *Euphonious* means "pleasing to the ear." *Discordant* means "not harmonious, displeasing." *Syncopated* means that a usually weak beat is stressed. *Rhythmic* means that something occurs with regularity. *Euphemistic* means that something is softened in expression.
Vocabulary—Similarity/Contrast

37. (*a.* **Montague**, *b.* Scali, *c.* Dunlop, *d.* Mineo) : ROMEO :: CAPULET : JULIET

(**a**) In Shakespeare's play, Montague is the surname of Romeo, Capulet the surname of Juliet.
Humanities—Description

38. EMANCIPATE : (*a.* emaciate, *b.* free, *c.* **enslave**, *d.* deliver) :: EMPTY : FULL

(**c**) *Emancipate* and *enslave* are antonyms, as are *empty* and *full*.
Vocabulary—Similarity/Contrast

39. PALMISTRY : PALM :: PHRENOLOGY : (*a.* handwriting, *b.* EEG, *c.* eyes, *d.* **skull**)

(**d**) Palmistry makes use of the palm in telling about a person; phrenology makes use of the skull.
General Information—Description

40. (*a.* Columbia Gem, *b.* **Union Jack**, *c.* Royal Ensign, *d.* Fleur-de-Lis) : GREAT BRITAIN :: STARS AND STRIPES : U.S.A.

(**b**) The Union Jack is the flag of Great Britain; the Stars and Stripes is the flag of the United States. The fleur-de-lis is associated with the Spanish monarchy and the Grand Duchy of Luxembourg. "Columbia, Gem of the Ocean" is a song.
Social Science—Description

41. COMMON LOG : 10 :: NATURAL LOG : (*a.* π, *b.* **e**, *c.* i, *d.* 1)

(**b**) Common logs are to base 10. Natural logs are to base *e*.
Mathematics—Description

42. MAE WEST : LIFE JACKET :: MICKEY FINN : (*a.* blackjack, *b.* Molotov cocktail, ***c.* drugged liquor**, *d.* time bomb)

   (**c**) A Mae West is a type of life jacket. A Mickey Finn is a form of drugged liquor. Blackjack is a popular Casino game, and a Molotov cocktail is a name for a variety of incendiary weapons.
   General Information—Similarity/Contrast

43. EARTH : AIR :: (*a.* bile, *b.* carbon, *c.* phlogiston, ***d.* fire**) : WATER

   (**d**) Earth, air, fire, and water were once believed to be the four basic elements from which every other substance is composed.
   Humanities—Class

44. CAMUS : STRANGER :: (*a.* Sartre, ***b.* Camus**, *c.* Mauriac, *d.* Ionesco) : PLAGUE

   (**b**) Camus is the author of both *The Stranger* and *The Plague*. Sartre wrote *No Exit* and *The Flies*, among other plays. Mauriac wrote *Le Desert de l'Amour*. Ionesco wrote the play *Rhinoceros*.
   Humanities—Description

45. DOG : PIE :: HOT : (*a.* cold, *b.* cat, ***c.* pizza**, *d.* cake)

   (**c**) A hotdog and a pizza pie are both forms of food.
   General Information—Completion

46. PIETÀ : MICHELANGELO :: THE KISS : (***a.* Rodin**, *b.* Pisano, *c.* Ghiberti, *d.* da Vinci)

   (**a**) *The Pietà* is a sculpture by Michelangelo. *The Kiss* is a sculpture by Rodin. Pisano was an Italian artist who was wrongly credited for the creation of the *Leaning Tower of Pisa*. Ghiberti is known for a set of metal panels called *Gates of Paradise*. Da Vinci painted the *Mona Lisa* and *The Last Supper*, among others.
   Humanities—Description

47. (*a.* Congress of Vienna, ***b.* League of Nations**, *c.* Warsaw Pact, *d.* NATO) : UNITED NATIONS :: GASLIGHT : ELECTRIC LIGHT

   (**b**) The United Nations replaced the League of Nations. The electric light replaced the gaslight. The League of Nations was a supranational organization that was created in the aftermath of World War I; its goals were the prevention of war, settlement of disputes, etc. The Congress of Vienna was a conference to reorganize Europe after the downfall of Napoleon I (1814–1815). The Warsaw Pact (1955) was an organization of Eastern European Communist states that was created in response to the creation of NATO.
   General Information—Description

48. CARAT : (*a.* size, ***b.* weight**, *c.* brilliance, *d.* value) :: ACRE : AREA

    (b) A carat is a measure of weight. An acre is a measure of area.
    Natural Science—Description

49. $a + b : b + a :: a(b + a)b : ($*a.* $2a^2b^2,$ *b.* $(a + b)^2,$ ***c.*** $a^2b + ab^2,$ *d.* $a^2b^2 + ab)$

    (c) $a + b$ is equal to $b + a$. $a(b + a)b$ is equal to $a^2b + ab^2$.
    Mathematics—Equality/Negation

50. FRANCIS CRICK : STRUCTURE OF DNA MOLECULE :: MARIE
    CURIE : (*a.* nobelium, *b.* uranium, ***c.* radium**, *d.* plutonium)

    (c) Francis Crick was a codiscoverer of the structure of the DNA molecule.
    Marie Curie was a codiscoverer of the element radium.
    Natural Science—Description

51. ANALOG : SLIDE RULE :: DIGITAL : (***a.* odometer**, *b.* ruler, *c.* compass,
    d. protractor)

    (a) A slide rule is an analog device. An odometer is a digital device.
    Natural Science—Description

52. CHARLOTTE'S : PILGRIM'S :: WEB : (*a.* Follies, ***b.* Progress**,
    c. Pretense, *d.* Journey)

    (b) *Charlotte's Web* (by E. B. White) and *Pilgrim's Progress* (by John Bunyan)
    are both titles of books.
    Humanities—Description

53. VOID : VACUUM :: FULL : (***a.* replete**, *b.* deplete, *c.* compact, *d.* empty)

    (a) *Void* and *vacuum* are synonyms, as are *full* and *replete*.
    Vocabulary—Similarity/Contrast

54. HIGH : DIE :: (*a.* gregarious, *b.* reticent, *c.* low, ***d.* buy**) : SHY

    (d) *High*, *die*, *buy*, and *shy* all rhyme.
    Nonsemantic

55. (*a.* retina, *b.* iris, *c.* lens, ***d.* cone**) : ROD :: CHROMATIC :
    ACHROMATIC

    (d) In the visual system, the cones are responsible for chromatic vision,
    and the rods for achromatic vision.
    Natural Science—Description

56. BOVINE : (*a.* jackal, *b.* monkey, ***c.* ox**, *d.* rabbit) :: URSINE : BEAR

    (c) A bovine creature is oxlike. An ursine creature is bearlike.
    General Information—Similarity/Contrast

57. (*a.* **Plato**, *b.* Aristotle, *c.* Leibniz, *d.* Locke) : REPUBLIC :: DESCARTES : MEDITATIONS

    (**a**) Plato is the author of the *Republic*. Descartes is the author of *Meditations*. Aristotle's works are collected in the *Corpus Aristotelicum*. Leibniz wrote the *Theodicee*. Locke is the author of *An Essay Concerning Human Understanding* and *Some Thoughts Concerning Education*, among others.
    Humanities—Description

58. DEER : DEER :: CORPUS : (*a.* corpi, *b.* corpuses, *c.* **corpora**, *d.* corpes)

    (**c**) *Deer* is the plural form of *deer*. *Corpora* is the plural form of *corpus*.
    Nonsemantic

59. BUDAPEST : HANOI :: HUNGARY : (*a.* Cambodia, *b.* Laos, *c.* Thailand, *d.* **Vietnam**)

    (**d**) Budapest is the capital of Hungary. Hanoi is the capital of Vietnam. The capital of Thailand is Bangkok. The capital of Cambodia is Phnom Penh. The capital of Laos is Vientiane.
    General Information—Description

60. PROMISED LAND : CANAAN :: LAND OF NOD : (*a.* wakefulness, *b.* hell, *c.* **sleep**, *d.* heaven)

    (**c**) Canaan was the Promised Land for the Israelites. The Land of Nod is sleep. The Land of Nod has been mentioned in the Bible but has more recently been associated with sleep, as in Stevenson's poem "The Land of Nod."
    Humanities—Similarity/Contrast

61. MISOGYNIST : WOMEN :: MISOGAMIST : (*a.* men, *b.* people, *c.* **marriage**, *d.* religion)

    (**c**) A misogynist detests women. A misogamist detests marriage.
    Vocabulary—Description

62. (*a.* Achilles, *b.* Hector, *c.* **Paris**, *d.* Troilus) : HELEN :: PLUTO : PROSERPINA

    (**c**) Paris abducted Helen. Pluto abducted Proserpina. Achilles was the greatest warrior of the Greeks in the Trojan War. Hector was a Trojan prince and warrior in the Trojan War. Troilus was a Trojan prince murdered by Achilles.
    Humanities—Description

63. BENIGN : BENEVOLENT :: (*a.* beneficent, *b.* **nefarious**, *c.* tortuous, *d.* voracious) : MALEVOLENT

    (**b**) *Benign* and *benevolent* are synonyms, as are *nefarious* and *malevolent*.
    Vocabulary—Similarity/Contrast

64. BLOCKHEAD : LUNKHEAD :: MUTTONHEAD : (*a.* **fathead**, *b.* sleepyhead, *c.* bighead, *d.* egghead)

(**a**) A blockhead is a lunkhead is a muttonhead is a fathead.
Vocabulary—Similarity/Contrast

65. UNCLE TOM : SERVILE :: DUTCH UNCLE : (*a.* hoary, *b.* kind, ***c.* stern**, *d.* stingy)

(**c**) An Uncle Tom is servile. A Dutch uncle is stern.
Vocabulary—Description

66. ALPHA : (*a.* gamma, *b.* zed, *c.* epsilon, ***d.* omega**) :: A : Z

(**d**) *Alpha* is the first letter of the Greek alphabet, and *omega* is the last. *A* is the first letter of the English alphabet, and *Z* is the last.
Humanities—Similarity/Contrast

67. THIAMINE : ASCORBIC ACID :: B_1 : (*a.* B_6, *b.* B_{12}, ***c.* C**, *d.* E)

(**c**) Thiamine is vitamin B_1. Ascorbic acid is vitamin C. Vitamin B_6 can consist of different compounds: pyridoxine, pyridoxal, and pyridoxamine. B_{12} can be commonly found as cyanocobalamin. E refers to a group of tocopherols and tocotrienols.
Natural Science—Similarity/Contrast

68. BRAZIL : (*a.* **Portuguese**, *b.* Spanish, *c.* French, *d.* Brazilian) :: AUSTRIA : GERMAN

(**a**) Portuguese is the principal language spoken in Brazil. German is the principal language spoken in Austria.
Social Science—Description

69. CENTURY : EON :: DOZEN : (*a.* one hundred, *b.* gross, *c.* zero, ***d.* myriad**)

(**d**) A century is a specified period of time, and an eon is a long, unspecified period of time. A dozen is a specified amount, and a myriad is a large, unspecified amount.
Vocabulary—Description

70. SITTING BULL : SIOUX :: GERONIMO : (*a.* **Apache**, *b.* Pueblo, *c.* Mohawk, *d.* Seminole)

(**a**) Sitting Bull was a Sioux Indian chief; Geronimo was an Apache Indian chief.
Social Science—Description

Answer Explanations

71. AUTOCRACY : AUTARCHY :: MONARCHY : (*a.* democracy, *b.* anarchy, *c.* oligarchy, **_d._ kingdom**)

    (**d**) An autocracy is an autarchy. A monarchy is a kingdom. Anarchy is the absence of government. Oligarchy is a form of government where power is placed in the hands of a small group of people.
    Social Science—Similarity/Contrast

72. GOGGLE-EYED : BULGING :: HOOK-NOSED : (*a.* opercular, *b.* oviparous, *c.* ovine, **_d._ aquiline**)

    (**d**) Someone who is goggle-eyed has bulging eyes. Someone who is hook-nosed has an aquiline nose.
    Vocabulary—Similarity/Contrast

73. NEPTUNE : DIANA :: SEA : (*a.* hearth, *b.* sun, **_c._ moon**, *d.* home)

    (**c**) In Roman mythology, Neptune was the god of the sea and Diana the goddess of the moon.
    Humanities—Description

74. EXPEL : DRIVE AWAY :: EXPIATE : (**_a._ atone for**, *b.* talk at length, *c.* forgive, *d.* speak briefly)

    (**a**) To expel is to drive away. To expiate is to atone for.
    Vocabulary—Similarity/Contrast

75. LARGO : SLOW :: (*a.* moderato, **_b._ allegro**, *c.* piano, *d.* fortissimo) : FAST

    (**b**) In music, largo signifies a slow tempo; allegro, a fast tempo. *Moderato* means "moderately fast." *Piano* means "soft." *Fortissimo* means "very loud."
    Humanities—Similarity/Contrast

76. (*a.* with faith, *b.* with truth, *c.* with passion, **_d._ with authority**) : EX CATHEDRA :: ON THE FACE : EX FACIE

    (**d**) *Ex cathedra* means *with authority*. *Ex facie* means *on the face*.
    Vocabulary—Similarity/Contrast

77. FIFE : CLARINET :: TROMBONE : (*a.* lute, **_b._ bagpipe**, *c.* piano, *d.* violin)

    (**b**) A fife, a clarinet, a trombone, and a bagpipe are all wind instruments.
    Humanities—Class

78. PARASITE : LIVING :: (**_a._ saprophyte**, *b.* neophyte, *c.* pteridophyte, *d.* bryophyte) : DEAD

    (**a**) A parasite lives off a living organism. A saprophyte lives off a dead organism.
    Natural Science—Description

79. PRINCE : MACHIAVELLI :: PETIT PRINCE : (*a.* **Saint-Exupéry**, *b.* Mauriac, *c.* Camus, *d.* Lescaut)

(**a**) *The Prince* was written by Machiavelli. *Le Petit Prince* was written by Saint-Exupéry. Francois Mauriac wrote *Le Desert de l'Amour*, for example. Albert Camus was a French writer who wrote *The Plague. Manon Lescaut* is an opera by Puccini. *Humanities—Description*

80. INDIA : RUPEE :: (*a.* Mexico, *b.* **Switzerland**, *c.* Great Britain, *d.* Sweden) : FRANC

(**b**) The rupee is the currency of India. The currency of Switzerland is the franc. The currency of Mexico is the peso. The currency of Great Britain is the pound and the currency of Sweden is the crown. *General Information—Description*

81. DEMOSTHENES : (*a.* **Cicero**, *b.* Socrates, *c.* Pericles, *d.* Ovid) :: HOMER : VIRGIL

(**a**) Demosthenes was a Greek orator, and Cicero a Roman orator. Homer was a Greek poet, and Virgil a Roman poet. Socrates was a Greek philosopher. Ovid was a Roman poet. Pericles was a Greek statesman and orator. *Humanities—Class*

82. (*a.* mg, *b.* gg, *c.* **kg**, *d.* cg) : g :: m : mm

(**c**) There are 1,000 grams (g) in a kilogram (kg). There are 1,000 millimeters (mm) in a meter (m). There are 1,000 milligrams (mg) in a gram (g). *Mathematics—Part/Whole*

83. CIPANGO : JAPAN :: CATHAY : (*a.* **China**, *b.* Tibet, *c.* Polynesia, *d.* Mongolia)

(**a**) Cipango is a poetic name for Japan. Cathay is a poetic name for China. *Humanities—Similarity/Contrast*

84. IMPROMPTU : EXTEMPORE :: PROBITY : (*a.* open-mindedness, *b.* dishonesty, *c.* narrow-mindedness, *d.* **honesty**)

(**d**) *Impromptu* and *extempore* are synonyms, as are *probity* and *honesty*. *Vocabulary—Similarity/Contrast*

85. FERMI : NUCLEAR PHYSICS :: JANE ADDAMS : (*a.* nursing, *b.* physics, **c. social work**, *d.* drama)

(**c**) Fermi is famous for his work in nuclear physics. Jane Addams is famous for her social work.
Humanities—Description

86. (*a.* Inferno, ***b.* Decameron**, *c.* The Wasteland, *d.* No Exit) : CANTERBURY TALES :: ANTHOLOGY : COLLECTION

(**b**) *The Decameron* (by Giovanni Boccacio) and *The Canterbury Tales* (by Geoffrey Chaucer) are both anthologies (collections) of stories. *Inferno* is the first canticle of Dante's *Divine Comedy*. *The Wasteland* is a poem by Eliot. *No Exit* is a play by Sartre.
Humanities—Class

87. RICHELIEU : (*a.* Cushing, ***b.* Mazarin**, *c.* Metternich, *d.* Marat) :: KENNEDY : JOHNSON

(**b**) Cardinal Mazarin succeeded Cardinal Richelieu in his French diplomatic role. Johnson succeeded Kennedy as president of the United States.
Social Science—Description

88. (*a.* uncertainty, *b.* luck, ***c.* sample**, *d.* variance) : POPULATION :: STATISTIC : PARAMETER

(**c**) A statistic is a sample value, while a parameter is a population value.
Mathematics—Description

89. REGAN : GONERIL :: LEAH : (*a.* Jacob, *b.* Rebeccah, *c.* Isaac, ***d.* Rachel**)

(**d**) Regan and Goneril were sisters (in *King Lear*), as were Leah and Rachel (in the Bible). Rebeccah was the wife of Isaac. Jacob was their son.
Humanities—Class

90. TEMPUS : CARPE :: FUGIT : (*a.* cibus, *b.* mater, ***c.* diem**, *d.* tempum)

(**c**) *Tempus fugit* and *carpe diem* are both Latinisms used in English. *Tempus fugit* means "time flies," while *carpe diem* means "seize the opportunity"— literally, *the day*.
Vocabulary—Completion

91. ERSATZ : (***a.* genuine**, *b.* superior, *c.* inferior, *d.* fake) :: FRESH : RANCID

(**a**) *Ersatz* and *genuine* are antonyms, as are *fresh* and *rancid*.
Vocabulary—Similarity/Contrast

92. EVE : DEED :: MADAM : (*a.* cuckoo, *b.* swoon, ***c.* noon**, *d.* pool)

    (**c**) *Eve, deed, madam,* and *noon* are all palindromes—they read the same whether spelled forward or backward.
    Nonsemantic

93. SLEEPY : SOMNOLENT :: GROGGY : (*a.* asleep, ***b.* unsteady**, *c.* awake, *d.* dead)

    (**b**) A sleepy person is somnolent; a groggy person is unsteady.
    Vocabulary—Similarity/Contrast

94. AXON : DEPART :: (*a.* neuron, *b.* ganglion, ***c.* dendrites**, *d.* plasma) : APPROACH

    (**c**) Nerve impulses depart from a cell body via the axon; they approach the cell body via the dendrites.
    Natural Science—Description

95. BUDGE : TENNIS :: LOUIS : (*a.* hockey, *b.* football, *c.* baseball, ***d.* boxing**)

    (**d**) Joe Louis was a famous boxer. Don Budge was a famous tennis player.
    General Information—Description

96. BLOOD : MELANCHOLY :: CHOLER : (*a.* plasma, *b.* lymph, ***c.* phlegm**, *d.* saliva)

    (**c**) Blood, phlegm, choler, and melancholy were once believed to be the four body humors (fluids). The idea of body humors is an old one dating back to ancient Egypt, but Hippocrates was the one who applied the concept to medicine.
    Humanities—Class

97. MEXICO : YORK :: CAROLINA : (*a.* Virginia, *b.* Oregon, *c.* Washington, ***d.* Dakota**)

    (**d**) Both (New) Mexico and (New) York are states. Both (North or South) Carolina and (North or South) Dakota are states.
    General Information—Description

98. ARGON : NEON :: XENON : (***a.* helium**, *b.* oxygen, *c.* mercury, *d.* carbon)

    (**a**) Argon, neon, xenon, and helium are all inert (noble) gases.
    The six noble gases are helium, neon, argon, xenon, krypton, and radon.
    Natural Science—Class

99. HORN : ROLAND :: HARP : (*a.* Gideon, ***b.* David**, *c.* Moses, *d.* Samuel)

    (**b**) Roland was famous for his horn; David, for his harp.
    Humanities—Description

100. GLUTTON : FOOD :: SATYR : (*a.* punishment, *b.* glory,
     c. alcoholic beverages, ***d.* sex**)

     (**d**) A glutton overindulges in food; a satyr, in sex.
     General Information—Description

101. ACUTE : (*a.* small, ***b.* obtuse**, *c.* intense, *d.* right) :: APOGEE : PERIGEE

     (**b**) When speaking either of angles or the ability to comprehend something,
     acute means the opposite of obtuse, just as the apogee is the opposite of
     the perigee.
     Vocabulary—Similarity/Contrast

102. (*a.* berate, *b.* refine, *c.* attenuate, ***d.* foreshadow**) : ADUMBRATE ::
     INTIMATE : HINT

     (**d**) To adumbrate is to foreshadow just as to intimate is to hint.
     Vocabulary—Similarity/Contrast

103. PNEUMONECTOMY : LUNG :: (*a.* tonsillectomy, *b.* meningectomy,
     ***c.* lobotomy**, *d.* encephalotomy) : BRAIN

     (**c**) Pneumonectomy is the removal of part of the lung and lobotomy is the
     removal of part of the brain.
     Natural Science—Description

104. EMPATHY : (*a.* lungs, *b.* soul, *c.* pancreas, ***d.* heart**) :: BRAVERY : LIVER

     (**d**) Tradition ascribes empathy and bravery to be seated in the organs of the
     heart and liver respectively.
     General Information—Description

105. CIRCUMSPECT : CIRCUMSCRIBE :: (***a.* prudent**, *b.* navigate,
     c. rounded, *d.* investigate) : ENCIRCLE

     (**a**) To be circumspect is to be prudent, and to circumscribe is to encircle.
     Vocabulary—Similarity/Contrast

106. DEARTH : (*a.* poverty, ***b.* abundance**, *c.* warmth, *d.* nothing) :: PAUCITY :
     PLENTY

     (**b**) Dearth and paucity both describe an insufficiency, whereas abundance
     and plenty describe something bountiful.
     Vocabulary—Similarity/Contrast

107. CAP : LID :: KNEE : (*a.* leg, *b.* patella, *c.* heel, ***d.* eye**)

(**d**) The kneecap and eyelid are both parts of the body.
General Information—Completion

108. (***a.* bitterness**, *b.* wittiness, *c.* frivolity, *d.* accusation) : ACRIMONIOUS ::
FRUGALITY : PARSIMONIOUS

(**a**) *Acrimonious* describes someone who acts with bitterness just as
parsimonious describes someone who acts with frugality.
Vocabulary—Description

109. CAESAR : DELIVERY :: ACHILLES : (*a.* surgery, *b.* ligament, ***c.* tendon**,
d. bone)

(**c**) The cesarean section, the name of a delivery, is named for Caesar.
The Achilles tendon, the name of a tendon, is named for Achilles.
General Information—Description

110. PROMETHEUS : BOUND :: ATLAS : (*a.* carried, *b.* tied, ***c.* shrugged**,
d. grew)

(**c**) *Prometheus Bound* (by Aeschylus) and *Atlas Shrugged* (by Ayn Rand)
are both prominent works of literature.
Humanities—Completion

111. GENGHIS KHAN : (*a.* China, ***b.* Mongolia**, *c.* Persia, *d.* Prussia) ::
SHAKA : SOUTH AFRICA

(**b**) Genghis Khan was a great conqueror born in present-day Mongolia.
Shaka was a great conqueror born in present-day South Africa.
General Information—Description

112. (*a.* right to bear arms, ***b.* prohibition of alcohol**, *c.* right to remain silent,
d. freedom of religion) : 18th AMENDMENT :: WOMEN'S SUFFRAGE :
19th AMENDMENT

(**b**) The 18th Amendment prohibited the consumption of alcohol. The
19th Amendment granted women's suffrage.
General Information—Similarity/Contrast

113. KID : (*a.* wolf, ***b.* goat**, *c.* moose, *d.* kangaroo) :: CALF : WHALE

(**b**) A young goat is called a kid just as a young whale is called a calf.
General Information—Class

Answer Explanations

114. HOPI : (***a. Southwest***, *b.* Southeast, *c.* Northwest, *d.* Great Plains) ::
TLINGIT : NORTHWEST

(**a**) The Hopi tribe is native to the Southwest of what is now the United States. The Tlingit tribe is native to the Northwest of what is now the United States.
General Information—Description

115. PTOLEMY : EARTH :: COPERNICUS : (*a.* Mars, *b.* Venus, *c.* Moon,
d. Sun)

(**d**) Ptolemy proposed a geocentric system in which the Earth was the center of the solar system. Copernicus proposed a heliocentric system, in which the sun was the center.
Natural Science—Description

116. ADAM SMITH : 18th CENTURY :: JOHN MAYNARD KEYNES :
(***a. 20th century***, *b.* 19th century, *c.* 17th century, *d.* 16th century)

(**a**) Smith and Keynes were famous economists of the 18th and 20th centuries, respectively. Smith is well-known as the author of *The Wealth of Nations*. Keynes is the founder of Keynesian economics, which deals with total spending in the economy and its effects on output and inflation.
Social Science—Description

117. (*a.* Laos, ***b. Japan***, *c.* Taiwan, *d.* China) : JUDO :: KOREA :
TAE KWON DO

(**b**) The martial art of Judo originated in Japan just as the martial art Tae Kwon Do originated in Korea.
General Information—Description

118. KHMER ROUGE : POL POT :: COMMUNIST PARTY OF CHINA :
(*a.* Kuomintang, *b.* Confucius ***c. Mao Zedong***, *d.* Chiang Kai-shek)

(**c**) Pol Pot was a leader of the Cambodian Communist Party, commonly known as the Khmer Rouge. Mao Zedong was a leader of the Communist Party of China. Kuomintang is the founding party of Taiwan. Confucius was a Chinese thinker and philosopher in the 5th century B.C. Chiang Kai-shek was a Chinese political leader who served as head of state of the National Government of the Republic of China from 1928 to 1949.
General Information—Description

119. SUEZ CANAL : (*a.* Turkey, *b.* Morocco, ***c. Egypt***, *d.* Israel) ::
PANAMA CANAL : PANAMA

(**c**) The Suez Canal cuts through Egypt just as the Panama Canal cuts through Panama.
General Information—Description

120. SOVIET UNION : (*a.* Portugal, *b.* Brazil, *c.* Cuba, *d.* **Spain**) :: CHAGALL : DALI

(**d**) Chagall and Dali were artists known for their surrealistic paintings; they were from the Soviet Union and Spain respectively.
Humanities—Description

PRACTICE TEST 8

Item Classification Chart

Item Classification

		RELATIONSHIP						
		Similarity/ Contrast	Description	Class	Completion	Part/ Whole	Equality/ Negation	Nonsemantic
C O N T E N T	**Vocabulary**	20, 31, 33, 36, 38, 53, 63, 64, 72, 74, 76, 84, 91, 93, 101, 102, 105, 106	21, 35, 61, 65, 69, 108		90			
	General Information	11, 15, 26, 42, 56, 112	1, 2, 3, 8, 9, 13, 14, 17, 18, 22, 27, 29, 39, 47, 59, 80, 95, 97, 100, 104, 109, 111, 114, 117, 118, 119	10, 113	45, 107			
	Humanities	60, 66, 75, 83	5, 7, 23, 24, 28, 34, 37, 44, 46, 52, 57, 62, 73, 79, 85, 99, 110, 120	43, 77, 81, 86, 89, 96				
	Social Science	71	40, 68, 70, 87, 116					
	Natural Science	67	4, 48, 50, 51, 55, 78, 94, 103, 115	98		19	16	
	Mathematics		6, 25, 41, 88	12		82	30, 49	
	Nonsemantic							32, 54, 58, 92

Answer Sheet
PRACTICE TEST 9

1 Ⓐ Ⓑ Ⓒ Ⓓ	31 Ⓐ Ⓑ Ⓒ Ⓓ	61 Ⓐ Ⓑ Ⓒ Ⓓ	91 Ⓐ Ⓑ Ⓒ Ⓓ
2 Ⓐ Ⓑ Ⓒ Ⓓ	32 Ⓐ Ⓑ Ⓒ Ⓓ	62 Ⓐ Ⓑ Ⓒ Ⓓ	92 Ⓐ Ⓑ Ⓒ Ⓓ
3 Ⓐ Ⓑ Ⓒ Ⓓ	33 Ⓐ Ⓑ Ⓒ Ⓓ	63 Ⓐ Ⓑ Ⓒ Ⓓ	93 Ⓐ Ⓑ Ⓒ Ⓓ
4 Ⓐ Ⓑ Ⓒ Ⓓ	34 Ⓐ Ⓑ Ⓒ Ⓓ	64 Ⓐ Ⓑ Ⓒ Ⓓ	94 Ⓐ Ⓑ Ⓒ Ⓓ
5 Ⓐ Ⓑ Ⓒ Ⓓ	35 Ⓐ Ⓑ Ⓒ Ⓓ	65 Ⓐ Ⓑ Ⓒ Ⓓ	95 Ⓐ Ⓑ Ⓒ Ⓓ
6 Ⓐ Ⓑ Ⓒ Ⓓ	36 Ⓐ Ⓑ Ⓒ Ⓓ	66 Ⓐ Ⓑ Ⓒ Ⓓ	96 Ⓐ Ⓑ Ⓒ Ⓓ
7 Ⓐ Ⓑ Ⓒ Ⓓ	37 Ⓐ Ⓑ Ⓒ Ⓓ	67 Ⓐ Ⓑ Ⓒ Ⓓ	97 Ⓐ Ⓑ Ⓒ Ⓓ
8 Ⓐ Ⓑ Ⓒ Ⓓ	38 Ⓐ Ⓑ Ⓒ Ⓓ	68 Ⓐ Ⓑ Ⓒ Ⓓ	98 Ⓐ Ⓑ Ⓒ Ⓓ
9 Ⓐ Ⓑ Ⓒ Ⓓ	39 Ⓐ Ⓑ Ⓒ Ⓓ	69 Ⓐ Ⓑ Ⓒ Ⓓ	99 Ⓐ Ⓑ Ⓒ Ⓓ
10 Ⓐ Ⓑ Ⓒ Ⓓ	40 Ⓐ Ⓑ Ⓒ Ⓓ	70 Ⓐ Ⓑ Ⓒ Ⓓ	100 Ⓐ Ⓑ Ⓒ Ⓓ
11 Ⓐ Ⓑ Ⓒ Ⓓ	41 Ⓐ Ⓑ Ⓒ Ⓓ	71 Ⓐ Ⓑ Ⓒ Ⓓ	101 Ⓐ Ⓑ Ⓒ Ⓓ
12 Ⓐ Ⓑ Ⓒ Ⓓ	42 Ⓐ Ⓑ Ⓒ Ⓓ	72 Ⓐ Ⓑ Ⓒ Ⓓ	102 Ⓐ Ⓑ Ⓒ Ⓓ
13 Ⓐ Ⓑ Ⓒ Ⓓ	43 Ⓐ Ⓑ Ⓒ Ⓓ	73 Ⓐ Ⓑ Ⓒ Ⓓ	103 Ⓐ Ⓑ Ⓒ Ⓓ
14 Ⓐ Ⓑ Ⓒ Ⓓ	44 Ⓐ Ⓑ Ⓒ Ⓓ	74 Ⓐ Ⓑ Ⓒ Ⓓ	104 Ⓐ Ⓑ Ⓒ Ⓓ
15 Ⓐ Ⓑ Ⓒ Ⓓ	45 Ⓐ Ⓑ Ⓒ Ⓓ	75 Ⓐ Ⓑ Ⓒ Ⓓ	105 Ⓐ Ⓑ Ⓒ Ⓓ
16 Ⓐ Ⓑ Ⓒ Ⓓ	46 Ⓐ Ⓑ Ⓒ Ⓓ	76 Ⓐ Ⓑ Ⓒ Ⓓ	106 Ⓐ Ⓑ Ⓒ Ⓓ
17 Ⓐ Ⓑ Ⓒ Ⓓ	47 Ⓐ Ⓑ Ⓒ Ⓓ	77 Ⓐ Ⓑ Ⓒ Ⓓ	107 Ⓐ Ⓑ Ⓒ Ⓓ
18 Ⓐ Ⓑ Ⓒ Ⓓ	48 Ⓐ Ⓑ Ⓒ Ⓓ	78 Ⓐ Ⓑ Ⓒ Ⓓ	108 Ⓐ Ⓑ Ⓒ Ⓓ
19 Ⓐ Ⓑ Ⓒ Ⓓ	49 Ⓐ Ⓑ Ⓒ Ⓓ	79 Ⓐ Ⓑ Ⓒ Ⓓ	109 Ⓐ Ⓑ Ⓒ Ⓓ
20 Ⓐ Ⓑ Ⓒ Ⓓ	50 Ⓐ Ⓑ Ⓒ Ⓓ	80 Ⓐ Ⓑ Ⓒ Ⓓ	110 Ⓐ Ⓑ Ⓒ Ⓓ
21 Ⓐ Ⓑ Ⓒ Ⓓ	51 Ⓐ Ⓑ Ⓒ Ⓓ	81 Ⓐ Ⓑ Ⓒ Ⓓ	111 Ⓐ Ⓑ Ⓒ Ⓓ
22 Ⓐ Ⓑ Ⓒ Ⓓ	52 Ⓐ Ⓑ Ⓒ Ⓓ	82 Ⓐ Ⓑ Ⓒ Ⓓ	112 Ⓐ Ⓑ Ⓒ Ⓓ
23 Ⓐ Ⓑ Ⓒ Ⓓ	53 Ⓐ Ⓑ Ⓒ Ⓓ	83 Ⓐ Ⓑ Ⓒ Ⓓ	113 Ⓐ Ⓑ Ⓒ Ⓓ
24 Ⓐ Ⓑ Ⓒ Ⓓ	54 Ⓐ Ⓑ Ⓒ Ⓓ	84 Ⓐ Ⓑ Ⓒ Ⓓ	114 Ⓐ Ⓑ Ⓒ Ⓓ
25 Ⓐ Ⓑ Ⓒ Ⓓ	55 Ⓐ Ⓑ Ⓒ Ⓓ	85 Ⓐ Ⓑ Ⓒ Ⓓ	115 Ⓐ Ⓑ Ⓒ Ⓓ
26 Ⓐ Ⓑ Ⓒ Ⓓ	56 Ⓐ Ⓑ Ⓒ Ⓓ	86 Ⓐ Ⓑ Ⓒ Ⓓ	116 Ⓐ Ⓑ Ⓒ Ⓓ
27 Ⓐ Ⓑ Ⓒ Ⓓ	57 Ⓐ Ⓑ Ⓒ Ⓓ	87 Ⓐ Ⓑ Ⓒ Ⓓ	117 Ⓐ Ⓑ Ⓒ Ⓓ
28 Ⓐ Ⓑ Ⓒ Ⓓ	58 Ⓐ Ⓑ Ⓒ Ⓓ	88 Ⓐ Ⓑ Ⓒ Ⓓ	118 Ⓐ Ⓑ Ⓒ Ⓓ
29 Ⓐ Ⓑ Ⓒ Ⓓ	59 Ⓐ Ⓑ Ⓒ Ⓓ	89 Ⓐ Ⓑ Ⓒ Ⓓ	119 Ⓐ Ⓑ Ⓒ Ⓓ
30 Ⓐ Ⓑ Ⓒ Ⓓ	60 Ⓐ Ⓑ Ⓒ Ⓓ	90 Ⓐ Ⓑ Ⓒ Ⓓ	120 Ⓐ Ⓑ Ⓒ Ⓓ

Answer Sheet

Practice Test 9

Directions: In each of the following questions, you will find three initial terms and, in parentheses, four answer options designated *a*, *b*, *c*, and *d*. You are to select from the four answer options the one that best completes the analogy with the three initial terms. To record your answers, use the answer sheet provided.

Time: 60 minutes

1. POSTMAN : LETTER :: (*a.* surgeon, *b.* orthopedist, *c.* obstetrician, *d.* podiatrist) : BABY

2. CHLOROPHYLL : GREEN :: HEMOGLOBIN : (*a.* red, *b.* black, *c.* green, *d.* blue)

3. HAPPY : (*a.* sad, *b.* gay, *c.* indifferent, *d.* ecstatic) :: BRIGHT : BRILLIANT

4. PENCIL : PEN :: (*a.* wood, *b.* ballpoint, *c.* graphite, *d.* boron) : INK

5. ONE BIRD : HAND :: TWO BIRDS : (*a.* bush, *b.* foot, *c.* nest, *d.* head)

6. SILVER : TARNISH :: IRON : (*a.* oxidation, *b.* rust, *c.* magnet, *d.* tin)

7. BUTTERFLY : CATERPILLAR :: (*a.* amphibian, *b.* frog, *c.* salamander, *d.* larva) : TADPOLE

8. GREEN : (*a.* cowardice, *b.* viciousness, *c.* envy, *d.* delight) :: PURPLE : RAGE

9. JUDAS : JESUS :: (*a.* Augustus, *b.* Brutus, *c.* Lucius, *d.* Antony) : JULIUS CAESAR

10. JOLLY ROGER : (*a.* communists, *b.* fascists, *c.* pirates, *d.* anarchists) :: UNION JACK : UNITED KINGDOM

11. DIALECTIC : HEGEL :: DIALECTICAL MATERIALISM : (*a.* Marx, *b.* Fichte, *c.* Schelling, *d.* Kant)

12. (*a.* screen, *b.* camera, *c.* projector, *d.* frame) : MOVIE FILM :: LINK : CHAIN

13. PROLOGUE : (*a.* decalogue, *b.* epilogue, *c.* preface, *d.* forward) :: APPETIZER : DESSERT

14. HAMMERSTEIN : (*a.* Sondheim, *b.* Rodgers, *c.* Gilbert, *d.* Herman) :: LERNER : LOEWE

15. (*a.* dumb, *b.* stupid, *c.* loquacious, *d.* brilliant) : MUTE :: SMART : INTELLIGENT

16. ARCHIVES : (*a.* munitions, *b.* tombs, *c.* documents, *d.* animals) :: PANTRY : KITCHEN UTENSILS

17. DUNCAN : MACBETH :: MACBETH : (*a.* Lady Macbeth, *b.* Macduff, *c.* Polonius, *d.* Claudius)

18. V : X :: D : (*a.* I, *b.* M, *c.* D, *d.* C)

19. JACK SPRAT'S WIFE : LEAN :: VEGETARIAN : (*a.* meat, *b.* fat, *c.* vegetables, *d.* roots)

20. (*a.* politics, *b.* law, *c.* music, *d.* medicine) : HIPPOCRATES :: HISTORY : HERODOTUS

21. (*a.* Russia, *b.* China, *c.* Japan, *d.* Hungary) : BALALAIKA :: SCOTLAND : BAGPIPES

22. TAILPIPE : EXHAUST :: RADIUM : (*a.* beta rays, *b.* strontium, *c.* cosmic rays, *d.* lead)

23. ARGUS : 100 :: CYCLOPS : (*a.* 1000, *b.* 10, *c.* 5, *d.* 1)

24. CANNON : BIG BERTHA :: (*a.* battleship, *b.* bazooka, *c.* bell, *d.* church steeple) : BIG BEN

25. (*a.* pretty, *b.* pretentious, *c.* proud, *d.* portly) : PEACOCK :: SILLY : GOOSE

26. HYPOCRITICAL : INSINCERE :: HYPERCRITICAL : (*a.* overcritical, *b.* sincere, *c.* oversincere, *d.* critical)

27. (*a.* cross, *b.* aisle, *c.* refectory, *d.* nave) : TRANSEPT :: VERTICAL : HORIZONTAL

28. MNEMONIC : (*a.* nymph, *b.* elf, *c.* anger, *d.* knock) :: PNEUMATIC : GNOME

29. FAITH : JOB :: (*a.* wisdom, *b.* age, *c.* wickedness, *d.* courage) : METHUSELAH

30. MRS. GRUNDY : NARROW-MINDED :: POLLYANNA : (*a.* witty, *b.* dull, *c.* pessimistic, *d.* optimistic)

31. MIDNIGHT SUN : (*a.* Russia, *b.* Norway, *c.* China, *d.* South Pole) :: RISING SUN : JAPAN

32. RED-BLOODED : VIGOROUS :: BLUE-BLOODED : (*a.* cowardly, *b.* sickly, *c.* prudish, *d.* aristocratic)

33. (*a.* battle, *b.* artillery, *c.* ammunition, *d.* armory) : WEAPONS :: CLOSET : CLOTHING

34. CHARACTERISTIC : DEFINING :: USUALLY : (*a.* never, *b.* sometimes, *c.* rarely, *d.* always)

35. OBVIATE : (*a.* make unnecessary, *b.* make necessary, *c.* make obvious, *d.* make obscure) :: EXPUNGE : DELETE

36. BROBDINGNAGIAN : GIGANTIC :: (*a.* Lilliputian, *b.* Houyhnhnm, *c.* Vespasian, *d.* Yahoo) :: TINY

37. RUSSIA : (*a.* tsar, *b.* king, *c.* emperor, *d.* autarch) :: FRANCE : KING

38. MINOTAUR : BULL :: CENTAUR : (*a.* cow, *b.* horse, *c.* pig, *d.* goat)

39. INTEGRAL : (*a.* acceleration, *b.* length, *c.* area, *d.* velocity) :: DERIVATIVE : SLOPE

40. GUSTATORY : (*a.* taste, *b.* touch, *c.* sight, *d.* smell) :: AUDITORY : HEARING

41. OCTOPI : OCTOPUSES :: (*a.* cannona, *b.* cannon, *c.* cannones, *d.* cannonade) : CANNONS

42. CRIME : WAR :: PUNISHMENT : (*a.* Destruction, *b.* Treaty, *c.* Peace, *d.* Retribution)

43. SUPPLY : DEMAND :: RATE : (*a.* distance, *b.* time, *c.* velocity, *d.* price)

44. ICONOCLAST : (*a.* religious images, *b.* autocracy, *c.* democratic ideals, *d.* anarchy) :: NIHILIST : SOCIAL ORDER

45. QUIXOTIC : CERVANTES :: FAUSTIAN : (*a.* Hegel, *b.* Faust, *c.* Schiller, *d.* Goethe)

46. EXPEL : STUDENT :: (*a.* expire, *b.* expunge, *c.* expropriate, *d.* exorcise) : SPIRIT

47. (*a.* Julian, *b.* Augustan, *c.* Caesarian, *d.* Publican) : GREGORIAN :: NEWTONIAN : EINSTEINIAN

48. (*a.* Koch, *b.* Pasteur, *c.* Lister, *d.* Sabin) : RABIES :: SALK : POLIO

49. MINNEAPOLIS : ST. PAUL :: (*a.* Uncle, *b.* Rabbit, *c.* Abelard, *d.* Romulus) : REMUS

50. POSSE : SHERIFF :: SQUIRE : (*a.* queen, *b.* bourgeoisie, *c.* knight, *d.* vassal)

51. UNTOUCHABLE : (*a.* Hindu, *b.* Vishnu, *c.* Brahman, *d.* Krishna) :: FLOOR : CEILING

52. PENTAGON : DECAGON :: RECTANGLE : (*a.* square, *b.* pentagon, *c.* heptagon, *d.* octagon)

53. TOWARD : IN THE DIRECTION OF :: UNTOWARD : (*a.* at the location of, *b.* away from, *c.* unseemly, *d.* unsafe)

54. EXOGAMY : OUTBREEDING :: (*a.* endogamy, *b.* inogamy, *c.* anogamy, *d.* onogamy) : INBREEDING

55. GRAND : (*a.* pauvre, *b.* petit, *c.* standard, *d.* legal) :: INDICT : CONVICT

56. CHROMATIC : PASTEL :: ACHROMATIC : (*a.* oil, *b.* tempera, *c.* chiasma, *d.* chiaroscuro)

57. EQUATOR : LATITUDE :: (*a.* North Pole, *b.* apogee, *c.* Greenwich, *d.* meridian) : LONGITUDE

58. ROMEO : JULIET :: PYRAMUS : (*a.* Chloe, *b.* Thisbe, *c.* Helen, *d.* Daphne)

59. PETROLEUM : GASOLINE :: BAUXITE : (*a.* aluminum, *b.* tin, *c.* lead, *d.* fool's gold)

60. 0 : ADDITION :: (*a.* 0, *b.* 1, *c.* −1, *d.* ∞) : MULTIPLICATION

61. GALAHAD : (*a.* Beatrice, *b.* Round Table, *c.* Holy Grail, *d.* True Cross) :: JASON : GOLDEN FLEECE

62. RED HERRING : (*a.* lie, *b.* peccadillo, *c.* diversion, *d.* secret plot) :: BLUE RIBBON : FIRST PRIZE

63. WATERMARK : EARMARK :: (*a.* crops, *b.* tide, *c.* silver, *d.* paper) : ANIMAL

64. ETHER : STARS :: PHLOGISTON : (*a.* earth, *b.* metal, *c.* fire, *d.* water)

65. PARTY : (*a.* revel, *b.* fight, *c.* meeting, *d.* dance) :: SWINE : BOAR

66. RHODE ISLAND : ALASKA :: MERCURY : (*a.* Earth, *b.* Jupiter, *c.* Saturn, *d.* Uranus)

67. MERETRICIOUS : (*a.* egregious, *b.* excellent, *c.* gaudy, *d.* plain) :: APEX : SUMMIT

68. ANTONY : CLEOPATRA :: (*a.* Lancelot, *b.* Arthur, *c.* Merlin, *d.* Gawain) : GUINEVERE

69. MERITOCRACY : MERIT :: PLUTOCRACY : (*a.* wisdom, *b.* money, *c.* power, *d.* physical prowess)

70. INTREPID : (*a.* cowardly, *b.* bold, *c.* voluble, *d.* taciturn) :: AGILE : CLUMSY

71. (*a.* Mars, *b.* Saturn, *c.* Jupiter, *d.* Mercury) : HERMES :: VENUS : APHRODITE

72. COMPLEMENTARY ANGLES : 90° :: COMPLEMENTARY COLORS : (*a.* white, *b.* black, *c.* violet, *d.* red)

73. (*a.* Jefferson, *b.* Adams, *c.* Hamilton, *d.* Madison) : BURR :: LINCOLN : BOOTH

74. PUFFIN : (*a.* bird, *b.* reptile, *c.* mammal, *d.* amphibian) :: STURGEON : FISH

75. BRONZE : (*a.* aluminum, *b.* tin, *c.* gold, *d.* silver) :: BRASS : ZINC

76. G MAJOR : (*a.* B minor, *b.* C minor, *c.* D minor, *d.* E minor) :: C MAJOR : A MINOR

77. (*a.* cow, *b.* jackal, *c.* wolf, *d.* rabbit) : LUPINE :: DOG : CANINE

78. (*a.* one, *b.* few, *c.* ten, *d.* all) : ISOCRACY :: ONE : AUTOCRACY

79. LOG 10 : LOG 100 :: LOG 100 : (*a.* log 1,000, *b.* log 10,000, *c.* log 100,000, *d.* log 1,000,000)

80. HAPPINESS : SHANGRI-LA :: (*a.* wealth, *b.* happiness, *c.* gods, *d.* freedom) : EL DORADO

81. DRACONIAN : (*a.* cowardly, *b.* bold, *c.* cruel, *d.* kindly) :: STENTORIAN : LOUD

82. MANSION : HOUSE :: TOME : (*a.* boat, *b.* book, *c.* desk, *d.* church)

83. NEUTRAL : 7 :: (*a.* alkaline, *b.* acidic, *c.* hydrated, *d.* oxidized) : 1

84. PERUSE : SKIM :: REPEL : (*a.* gloss, *b.* bowdlerize, *c.* drive back, *d.* attract)

85. NUCLEOLUS : NUCLEUS :: SET : (*a.* superset, *b.* set, *c.* subset, *d.* disjoint set)

86. HORSEBACK RIDING : EQUITATION :: (*a.* giving birth, *b.* skydiving, *c.* swimming, *d.* dancing) : NATATION

87. WHIGS : TORIES :: JACOBINS : (*a.* Fascists, *b.* Laborites, *c.* Roundheads, *d.* Girondists)

88. PRIME : (*a.* God, *b.* destiny, *c.* factum, *d.* mover) :: FIRST : CAUSE

89. FRANC : FRANCE :: (*a.* lira, *b.* mark, *c.* guilder, *d.* franc) : SWITZERLAND

90. (*a.* Jungfrau, *b.* Blanc, *c.* Matterhorn, *d.* Olympus) : ALPS :: EVEREST : HIMALAYAS

91. MELANCHOLY : (*a.* blue bile, *b.* green bile, *c.* red bile, *d.* black bile) :: CHOLER : YELLOW BILE

92. ORAL : ANAL :: DEPENDENCY : (*a.* lazy, *b.* thermometer, *c.* stinginess, *d.* independent)

93. (*a.* hit, *b.* die, *c.* invest, *d.* sprout) : BURGEON :: ENTREAT : IMPLORE

94. DEARTH : PAUCITY :: SCARCITY : (*a.* plethora, *b.* shortage, *c.* necessity, *d.* commodity)

95. DELFT : (*a.* glass, *b.* pottery, *c.* stoneware, *d.* silver) :: LIMOGES : CHINA

96. IAMB : RETURN :: TROCHEE : (*a.* stable, *b.* arrive, *c.* defend, *d.* eternal)

97. AUTOCHTHONOUS : (*a.* foreign, *b.* native, *c.* self-governing, *d.* dependent) :: LETTER : EPISTLE

98. (*a.* bells, *b.* horn, *c.* magpies, *d.* toads) : TINTINNABULATION :: GEESE : HONK

99. ELF : FLEE :: TON : (*a.* note, *b.* pound, *c.* dwarf, *d.* find)

100. CODA : (*a.* novel, *b.* musical composition, *c.* sculpture, *d.* ceramic jar) :: LANDING : FLIGHT

101. (*a.* months, *b.* tides, *c.* days, *d.* climates) : SEASONS :: MOON : SUN

102. TARANTELLA : ITALY :: CANCAN : (*a.* Argentina, *b.* Spain, *c.* Colombia, *d.* France)

103. AUDITORY : (*a.* olfactory, *b.* sensory, *c.* occipital, *d.* nasal) :: EAR : NOSE

104. TAILFEATHERS : PEACOCK :: (*a.* coat, *b.* tail, *c.* face, *d.* feet) : MANDRILL

105. BUFFALO : WHEAT :: NICKEL : (*a.* dollar, *b.* quarter, *c.* dime, *d.* penny)

106. ACIDIC : (*a.* 3, *b.* 7, *c.* 10, *d.* 14) :: ALKALINE : 12

107. (*a.* Romania, *b.* Croatia, *c.* Greece, *d.* Hungary) : YUGOSLAVIA :: CZECH REPUBLIC : CZECHOSLOVAKIA

108. ROCKY : SMOKY :: COLORADO : (*a.* West Virginia, *b.* New York, *c.* New Hampshire, *d.* Tennessee)

109. BADGER : DOG :: PESTER : (*a.* track, *b.* avoid, *c.* exhaust, *d.* behave)

110. ACCORDION : (*a.* bagpipe, *b.* flute, *c.* organ, *d.* clarinet) :: HARMONIUM : PIANO

111. RACECAR : RADAR :: (*a.* abbreviation, *b.* homonym, *c.* palindrome, *d.* gerund) : ACRONYM

112. (*a.* 82, *b.* 99, *c.* 22, *d.* 15) : 451 :: CATCH : FAHRENHEIT

113. A : Z :: Alpha : (*a.* Omega, *b.* Beta, *c.* Zed, *d.* Phi)

114. AMETHYST : (*a.* amber, *b.* purple, *c.* crimson, *d.* yellow) :: SAPPHIRE : BLUE

115. SYCOPHANT : TOADY :: MISCREANT : (*a.* artist, *b.* recluse, *c.* follower, *d.* criminal)

116. EKG : (*a.* heart, *b.* pancreas, *c.* bladder, *d.* lungs) :: EEG : brain

117. TONY : OSCAR :: (*a.* music, *b.* theater, *c.* literature, *d.* television) : FILM

118. (*a.* Colorado, *b.* Wyoming, *c.* Idaho, *d.* Alaska) : MCKINLEY :: NEPAL : EVEREST

119. I, CLAUDIUS : GRAVES :: (*a.* I, Julius, *b.* I, Criminal, *c.* I, Nixon, *d.* I, Robot) : ASIMOV

120. VIRGINIA : TENNESSEE :: WOOLF : (*a.* Faulkner, *b.* Percy, *c.* Williams, *d.* O'Connor)

Answer Key
PRACTICE TEST 9

1. **C**	31. **B**	61. **C**	91. **D**
2. **A**	32. **D**	62. **C**	92. **C**
3. **D**	33. **D**	63. **D**	93. **D**
4. **C**	34. **D**	64. **C**	94. **B**
5. **A**	35. **A**	65. **A**	95. **B**
6. **B**	36. **A**	66. **B**	96. **A**
7. **B**	37. **A**	67. **C**	97. **B**
8. **C**	38. **B**	68. **A**	98. **A**
9. **B**	39. **C**	69. **B**	99. **A**
10. **C**	40. **A**	70. **A**	100. **B**
11. **A**	41. **B**	71. **D**	101. **B**
12. **D**	42. **C**	72. **A**	102. **D**
13. **B**	43. **B**	73. **C**	103. **A**
14. **B**	44. **A**	74. **A**	104. **C**
15. **A**	45. **D**	75. **B**	105. **D**
16. **C**	46. **D**	76. **D**	106. **A**
17. **B**	47. **A**	77. **C**	107. **B**
18. **B**	48. **B**	78. **D**	108. **D**
19. **A**	49. **D**	79. **B**	109. **A**
20. **D**	50. **C**	80. **A**	110. **C**
21. **A**	51. **C**	81. **C**	111. **C**
22. **A**	52. **D**	82. **B**	112. **C**
23. **D**	53. **C**	83. **B**	113. **A**
24. **C**	54. **A**	84. **D**	114. **B**
25. **C**	55. **B**	85. **A**	115. **D**
26. **A**	56. **D**	86. **C**	116. **A**
27. **D**	57. **C**	87. **D**	117. **B**
28. **D**	58. **B**	88. **D**	118. **D**
29. **B**	59. **A**	89. **D**	119. **D**
30. **D**	60. **B**	90. **B**	120. **C**

Answer Key

ANSWER EXPLANATIONS FOR PRACTICE TEST 9

In the following, explanations concerning the correct response are in a large font. Explanations regarding distracters (incorrect responses) that are not self-explaining or could be misinterpreted are in a smaller font in order to highlight the explanations of the answers that are correct.

1. POSTMAN : LETTER :: (*a.* surgeon, *b.* orthopedist, *c.* **obstetrician**, *d.* podiatrist) : BABY

   (**c**) A postman delivers a letter; an obstetrician delivers a baby.
   General Information—Description

2. CHLOROPHYLL : GREEN :: HEMOGLOBIN : (*a.* **red**, *b.* black, *c.* green, *d.* blue)

   (**a**) Chlorophyll is a green substance that gives leaves their green color; hemoglobin is a red substance that gives blood its red color.
   Natural Science—Description

3. HAPPY : (*a.* sad, *b.* gay, *c.* indifferent, *d.* **ecstatic**) :: BRIGHT : BRILLIANT

   (**d**) A person who is extremely happy is ecstatic; a person who is extremely bright is brilliant.
   Vocabulary—Description

4. PENCIL : PEN :: (*a.* wood, *b.* ballpoint, *c.* **graphite**, *d.* boron) : INK

   (**c**) The writing substance in a pencil is usually graphite; the writing substance in a pen is usually ink.
   General Information—Description

5. ONE BIRD : HAND :: TWO BIRDS : (*a.* **bush**, *b.* foot, *c.* nest, *d.* head)

   (**a**) A familiar proverb states, "A bird in the hand is worth two in the bush."
   General Information—Completion

6. SILVER : TARNISH :: IRON : (*a.* oxidation, *b.* **rust**, *c.* magnet, *d.* tin)

   (**b**) When silver oxidizes, the result is called tarnish; when iron oxidizes, the result is called rust.
   General Information—Description

7. BUTTERFLY : CATERPILLAR :: (*a.* amphibian, ***b.* frog**, *c.* salamander, *d.* larva) : TADPOLE

   (**b**) A caterpillar is the larval form of a butterfly; a tadpole is the larval form of a frog.
   Natural Science—Description

8. GREEN : (*a.* cowardice, *b.* viciousness, ***c.* envy**, *d.* delight) :: PURPLE : RAGE

   (**c**) Green and purple are colors commonly used to denote emotional states. A person is said to be green with envy or purple with rage.
   General Information—Completion

9. JUDAS : JESUS :: (*a.* Augustus, ***b.* Brutus**, *c.* Lucius, *d.* Antony) : JULIUS CAESAR

   (**b**) Judas betrayed Jesus; Brutus betrayed Julius Caesar.
   Humanities—Description

10. JOLLY ROGER : (*a.* communists, *b.* fascists, ***c.* pirates**, *d.* anarchists) :: UNION JACK : UNITED KINGDOM

    (**c**) The Jolly Roger was the emblem of pirates, while the Union Jack is the emblem of the United Kingdom.
    General Information—Description

11. DIALECTIC : HEGEL :: DIALECTICAL MATERIALISM : (***a.* Marx**, *b.* Fichte, *c.* Schelling, *d.* Kant)

    (**a**) Hegel developed the philosophical notion of the dialectic, while Marx developed the philosophical notion of dialectical materialism. Fichte was one of the founders of German Idealism, which developed on the basis of Kant's thoughts. He investigated self-consciousness. Schelling was involved in German Idealism and investigated conceptions of nature in his *Naturphilosophie*. Kant is famous for his *Critique of Pure Reason*, which investigates reason itself.
    Humanities—Description

12. (*a.* screen, *b.* camera, *c.* projector, ***d.* frame**) : MOVIE FILM :: LINK : CHAIN

    (**d**) A movie film is composed of successive frames, while a chain is composed of successive links.
    General Information—Part/Whole

13. PROLOGUE : (*a.* decalogue, ***b.* epilogue**, *c.* preface, *d.* forward) :: APPETIZER : DESSERT

(**b**) A prologue introduces a book, and an epilogue closes it; an appetizer introduces a meal, and a dessert closes it.
Humanities—Class

14. HAMMERSTEIN : (*a.* Sondheim, ***b.* Rodgers**, *c.* Gilbert, *d.* Herman) :: LERNER : LOEWE

(**b**) Hammerstein and Rodgers created Broadway musicals, with Hammerstein writing the lyrics and Rodgers composing the music; Lerner and Loewe also created Broadway musicals, with Lerner writing the lyrics and Loewe composing the music.
Humanities—Class

15. (***a.* dumb**, *b.* stupid, *c.* loquacious, *d.* brilliant) : MUTE :: SMART : INTELLIGENT

(**a**) *Dumb* and *mute* are synonyms, as are *smart* and *intelligent*.
Vocabulary—Similarity/Contrast

16. ARCHIVES : (*a.* munitions, *b.* tombs, ***c.* documents**, *d.* animals) :: PANTRY : KITCHEN UTENSILS

(**c**) Documents are stored in archives, while kitchen utensils are stored in a pantry.
General Information—Description

17. DUNCAN : MACBETH :: MACBETH : (*a.* Lady Macbeth, ***b.* Macduff**, *c.* Polonius, *d.* Claudius)

(**b**) In Shakespeare's play *Macbeth*, Macbeth kills Duncan and Macduff kills Macbeth. Polonius was Chamberlain to King Claudius in Shakespeare's *Hamlet*. Lady Macbeth is the wife of Macbeth in Shakespeare's *Macbeth*.
Humanities—Description

18. V : X :: D : (*a.* I, ***b.* M**, *c.* D, *d.* C)

(**b**) The terms of the analogy are Roman numerals; 10 is equal to twice 5, and 1,000 is equal to twice 500. In Roman numerals, I = 1, V = 5, X = 10, L = 50, C = 100, D = 500, M = 1,000.
Mathematics—Equality/Negation

19. JACK SPRAT'S WIFE : LEAN :: VEGETARIAN : (***a.* meat**, *b.* fat, *c.* vegetables, *d.* roots)

(**a**) Jack Sprat's wife would eat no lean, according to the nursery rhyme; a vegetarian will eat no meat.
General Information—Description

20. (*a.* politics, *b.* law, *c.* music, ***d.* medicine**) : HIPPOCRATES :: HISTORY : HERODOTUS

    (**d**) Hippocrates is often referred to as the Father of Medicine, while Herodotus is known as the Father of History.
    Humanities—Description

21. (***a.* Russia**, *b.* China, *c.* Japan, *d.* Hungary) : BALALAIKA :: SCOTLAND : BAGPIPES

    (**a**) The balalaika is a Russian musical instrument; the bagpipes are a Scottish musical instrument.
    Humanities—Description

22. TAILPIPE : EXHAUST :: RADIUM : (***a.* beta rays**, *b.* strontium, *c.* cosmic rays, *d.* lead)

    (**a**) A tailpipe emits exhaust; radium emits beta rays.
    Natural Science—Description

23. ARGUS : 100 :: CYCLOPS : (*a.* 1000, *b.* 10, *c.* 5, ***d.* 1**)

    (**d**) According to legend, Argus had 100 eyes, while Cyclops had just 1.
    Humanities—Description

24. CANNON : BIG BERTHA :: (*a.* battleship, *b.* bazooka, ***c.* bell**, *d.* church steeple) : BIG BEN

    (**c**) Big Bertha is the name of a cannon; Big Ben is the name of a bell.
    General Information—Class

25. (*a.* pretty, *b.* pretentious, ***c.* proud**, *d.* portly) : PEACOCK :: SILLY : GOOSE

    (**c**) People are often likened either to a peacock or to a goose. One may be proud as a peacock or silly as a goose.
    General Information—Completion

26. HYPOCRITICAL : INSINCERE :: HYPERCRITICAL : (***a.* overcritical**, *b.* sincere, *c.* oversincere, *d.* critical)

    (**a**) *Hypocritical* and *insincere* are synonyms, as are *hypercritical* and *overcritical*.
    Vocabulary—Similarity/Contrast

27. (*a.* cross, *b.* aisle, *c.* refectory, ***d.* nave**) : TRANSEPT :: VERTICAL : HORIZONTAL

(**d**) In a cross-shaped church, the nave and the transept are perpendicular to each other, as are any objects that are vertical and horizontal with respect to each other.
Humanities—Similarity/Contrast

28. MNEMONIC : (*a.* nymph, *b.* elf, *c.* anger, ***d.* knock**) :: PNEUMATIC : GNOME

(**d**) *Mnemonic*, *pneumatic*, *gnome*, and *knock* each has a silent consonant preceding the initial voiced consonant, *n*.
Nonsemantic

29. FAITH : JOB :: (*a.* wisdom, ***b.* age**, *c.* wickedness, *d.* courage) : METHUSELAH

(**b**) In the Bible, Job distinguished himself by his great faith in God, while Methuselah distinguished himself by the great age to which he lived (969 years).
Humanities—Description

30. MRS. GRUNDY : NARROW-MINDED :: POLLYANNA : (*a.* witty, *b.* dull, *c.* pessimistic, ***d.* optimistic**)

(**d**) Mrs. Grundy is a literary character in Thomas Morton's play *Speed the Plow*, known for her narrow-mindedness. Pollyanna is a literary character in *Pollyanna* by Eleanor Porter, known for her optimism.
Humanities—Description

31. MIDNIGHT SUN : (*a.* Russia, ***b.* Norway**, *c.* China, *d.* South Pole) :: RISING SUN : JAPAN

(**b**) Norway is the Land of the Midnight Sun, while Japan is the Land of the Rising Sun.
General Information—Description

32. RED-BLOODED : VIGOROUS :: BLUE-BLOODED : (*a.* cowardly, *b.* sickly, *c.* prudish, ***d.* aristocratic**)

(**d**) A vigorous person is sometimes referred to as red-blooded, while an aristocratic person is sometimes referred to as blue-blooded.
Vocabulary—Similarity/Contrast

33. (*a.* battle, *b.* artillery, *c.* ammunition, ***d.* armory**) : WEAPONS :: CLOSET : CLOTHING

(**d**) An armory is used to store weapons; a closet is used to store clothing.
General Information—Description

34. CHARACTERISTIC : DEFINING :: USUALLY : (*a.* never, *b.* sometimes, *c.* rarely, ***d.* always**)

(**d**) A characteristic feature is one usually possessed by an object, while a defining feature is one always possessed by an object.
General Information—Description

35. OBVIATE : (***a.* make unnecessary**, *b.* make necessary, *c.* make obvious, *d.* make obscure) :: EXPUNGE : DELETE

(**a**) To obviate is to make unnecessary; to expunge is to delete.
Vocabulary—Similarity/Contrast

36. BROBDINGNAGIAN : GIGANTIC :: (***a.* Lilliputian**, *b.* Houyhnhnm, *c.* Vespasian, *d.* Yahoo) :: TINY

(**a**) In the novel *Gulliver's Travels* (by Jonathan Swift), the Brobdingnagians are gigantic people, while the Lilliputians are tiny ones.
Humanities—Description

37. RUSSIA : (***a.* tsar**, *b.* king, *c.* emperor, *d.* autarch) :: FRANCE : KING

(**a**) Russia was formerly ruled by a tsar, France by a king.
Social Science—Description

38. MINOTAUR : BULL :: CENTAUR : (*a.* cow, ***b.* horse**, *c.* pig, *d.* goat)

(**b**) The minotaur, according to mythology, was part bull and part man; the centaur was part horse and part man.
Humanities—Description

39. INTEGRAL : (*a.* acceleration, *b.* length, ***c.* area**, *d.* velocity) :: DERIVATIVE : SLOPE

(**c**) In calculus, an integral can be computed to determine area, while a derivative can be calculated to determine slope.
Mathematics—Description

40. GUSTATORY : (***a.* taste**, *b.* touch, *c.* sight, *d.* smell) :: AUDITORY : HEARING

(**a**) *Gustatory* refers to taste; *auditory*, to hearing. *Kinesthetic* refers to touch, *visual* refers to sight, and *olfactory* refers to smell.
Natural Science—Description

41. OCTOPI : OCTOPUSES :: (*a.* cannona, ***b.* cannon**, *c.* cannones, *d.* cannonade) : CANNONS

(**b**) *Octopi* and *octopuses* are both plural forms of the word *octopus*; *cannon* and *cannons* are both plural forms of the word *cannon*.
Humanities—Similarity/Contrast

42. CRIME : WAR :: PUNISHMENT : (*a.* Destruction, *b.* Treaty, **c. Peace**, *d.* Retribution)

(**c**) *Crime and Punishment* is a novel by the Russian author Dostoevski. *War and Peace* is a novel by the Russian author Tolstoy.
Humanities—Completion

43. SUPPLY : DEMAND :: RATE : (*a.* distance, ***b.* time**, *c.* velocity, *d.* price)

(**b**) Supply and demand are inversely related, as are rate and time.
Mathematics—Equality/Negation

44. ICONOCLAST : (***a.* religious images**, *b.* autocracy, *c.* democratic ideals, *d.* anarchy) :: NIHILIST : SOCIAL ORDER

(**a**) The goal of an iconoclast is to destroy religious images; the goal of a nihilist is to destroy social order.
Vocabulary—Description

45. QUIXOTIC : CERVANTES :: FAUSTIAN : (*a.* Hegel, *b.* Faust, *c.* Schiller, ***d.* Goethe**)

(**d**) The word *quixotic* is derived from the name of a literary character, Don Quixote, who is the subject of a work by Cervantes; the word *faustian* is derived from the name of a character, Faust, who is the subject of a work by Goethe.
Humanities—Description

46. EXPEL : STUDENT :: (*a.* expire, *b.* expunge, *c.* expropriate, ***d.* exorcise**) : SPIRIT

(**d**) A student is expelled from school; a spirit is exorcised from the body.
Vocabulary—Description

47. (***a.* Julian**, *b.* Augustan, *c.* Caesarian, *d.* Publican) : GREGORIAN :: NEWTONIAN : EINSTEINIAN

(**a**) The Julian calendar was replaced by the Gregorian calendar; Newtonian physics was replaced by Einsteinian physics.
Humanities—Description

48. (*a.* Koch, ***b.* Pasteur**, *c.* Lister, *d.* Sabin) : RABIES :: SALK : POLIO

(**b**) Pasteur developed an antirabies vaccine; Salk developed an antipolio vaccine. Lister promoted the idea of sterile surgery. Sabin developed the oral vaccine for polio. Koch is well known for isolating the tuberculosis bacillus, *Bacillus anthracis*.
Natural Science—Description

49. MINNEAPOLIS : ST. PAUL :: (*a.* Uncle, *b.* Rabbit, *c.* Abelard, *d.* **Romulus**) : REMUS

    (**d**) Minneapolis and St. Paul are twin cities. Romulus and Remus, according to legend, were twin brothers.
    Humanities—Class

50. POSSE : SHERIFF :: SQUIRE : (*a.* queen, *b.* bourgeoisie, *c.* **knight**, *d.* vassal)

    (**c**) A posse assists a sheriff; a squire assisted a knight.
    General Information—Description

51. UNTOUCHABLE : (*a.* Hindu, *b.* Vishnu, *c.* **Brahman**, *d.* Krishna) :: FLOOR : CEILING

    (**c**) In former times, an untouchable was a member of the lowest Indian caste, while a Brahman was a member of the highest one. A floor is the lowest part of a room, while a ceiling is the highest part.
    General Information—Similarity/Contrast

52. PENTAGON : DECAGON :: RECTANGLE : (*a.* square, *b.* pentagon, *c.* heptagon, *d.* **octagon**)

    (**d**) A decagon has twice as many sides as a pentagon; an octagon has twice as many sides as a rectangle.
    Mathematics—Equality/Negation

53. TOWARD : IN THE DIRECTION OF :: UNTOWARD : (*a.* at the location of, *b.* away from, *c.* **unseemly**, *d.* unsafe)

    (**c**) *Toward* means in the direction of. *Untoward* means unseemly.
    Vocabulary Similarity/Contrast

54. EXOGAMY : OUTBREEDING :: (*a.* **endogamy**, *b.* inogamy, *c.* anogamy, *d.* onogamy) : INBREEDING

    (**a**) *Exogamy* refers to outbreeding, while *endogamy* refers to inbreeding.
    Natural Science—Description

55. GRAND : (*a.* pauvre, *b.* **petit**, *c.* standard, *d.* legal) :: INDICT : CONVICT

    (**b**) A grand jury has the power to indict an individual for a crime, while a petit jury has the power to convict him or her of it.
    Social Science—Description

56. CHROMATIC : PASTEL :: ACHROMATIC : (*a.* oil, *b.* tempera, *c.* chiasma, ***d.* chiaroscuro**)

(**d**) Pastel is a chromatic form of artwork (with colors), while chiaroscuro is an achromatic form (black and white).
Humanities—Description

57. EQUATOR : LATITUDE :: (*a.* North Pole, *b.* apogee, ***c.* Greenwich**, *d.* meridian) : LONGITUDE

(**c**) The equator is at 0° latitude; Greenwich is at 0° longitude.
General Information—Description

58. ROMEO : JULIET :: PYRAMUS : (*a.* Chloe, ***b.* Thisbe**, *c.* Helen, *d.* Daphne)

(**b**) Romeo and Juliet were lovers, as were Pyramus and Thisbe. Chloe is another name for Demeter, who was the goddess of harvest and fertility in Greek mythology. Helen was the daughter of Zeus and Leda, wife of King Menelaus of Sparta, and was abducted by Paris, which led to the Trojan War. Daphne was a nymph in Greek mythology.
Humanities—Class

59. PETROLEUM : GASOLINE :: BAUXITE : (***a.* aluminum**, *b.* tin, *c.* lead, *d.* fool's gold)

(**a**) Petroleum is the raw material used to make gasoline, while bauxite is the raw material from which aluminum is obtained. Pewter is an alloy that contains tin. Lead is a heavy metal that may be added in smaller amounts to pewter as well.
Natural Science—Description

60. 0 : ADDITION :: (*a.* 0, ***b.* 1**, *c.* −1, *d.* ∞) : MULTIPLICATION

(**b**) Zero is the identity element for addition—any number plus 0 equals that number. One is the identity element for multiplication—any number times 1 equals that number.
Mathematics—Description

61. GALAHAD : (*a.* Beatrice, *b.* Round Table, ***c.* Holy Grail**, *d.* True Cross) :: JASON : GOLDEN FLEECE

(**c**) According to legend, Galahad succeeded in his quest for the Holy Grail, while Jason succeeded in his quest for the Golden Fleece.
Humanities—Description

62. RED HERRING : (*a*. lie, *b*. peccadillo, ***c*. diversion**, *d*. secret plot) ::
BLUE RIBBON : FIRST PRIZE

(**c**) A red herring is a diversion. A blue ribbon is a first prize.
Vocabulary—Description

63. WATERMARK : EARMARK :: (*a*. crops, *b*. tide, *c*. silver, ***d*. paper**) :
ANIMAL

(**d**) Paper is sometimes identified by a watermark; an animal is sometimes
identified by an earmark.
General Information—Description

64. ETHER : STARS :: PHLOGISTON : (*a*. earth, *b*. metal, ***c*. fire**, *d*. water)

(**c**) In medieval times, it was believed that the stars were composed of a
substance called ether, and that fire was composed of a substance called
phlogiston.
Natural Science—Description

65. PARTY : (***a*. revel**, *b*. fight, *c*. meeting, *d*. dance) :: SWINE : BOAR

(**a**) A revel is a wild party. A boar is a form of wild swine.
General Information—Description

66. RHODE ISLAND : ALASKA :: MERCURY : (*a*. Earth, ***b*. Jupiter**,
c. Saturn, *d*. Uranus)

(**b**) Rhode Island is the smallest state; Alaska, the largest. Mercury is the
smallest planet (in our solar system); Jupiter, the largest. The size of the
planets (starting with the smallest): Mercury, Mars, Venus, Earth, Neptune,
Uranus, Saturn, Jupiter.
Natural Science—Class

67. MERETRICIOUS : (*a*. egregious, *b*. excellent, ***c*. gaudy**, *d*. plain) :: APEX :
SUMMIT

(**c**) *Meretricious* and *gaudy* are synonyms, as are *apex* and *summit*.
Vocabulary—Similarity/Contrast

68. ANTONY : CLEOPATRA :: (***a*. Lancelot**, *b*. Arthur, *c*. Merlin, *d*. Gawain) :
GUINEVERE

(**a**) Cleopatra was the mistress of Antony; Guinevere was the mistress of
Lancelot. King Arthur was a British king in the 6th century who defended Britain against
invaders from Saxony. Merlin was a wizard from the Arthurian legend. Gawain was King
Arthur's nephew and a member of the Round Table.
Humanities—Class

69. MERITOCRACY : MERIT :: PLUTOCRACY : (*a.* wisdom, **b. money**, *c.* power, *d.* physical prowess)

    (**b**) A meritocracy is rule by those demonstrating merit; a plutocracy is rule by the wealthy.
    Social Science—Description

70. INTREPID : (**a. cowardly**, *b.* bold, *c.* voluble, *d.* taciturn) :: AGILE : CLUMSY

    (**a**) *Intrepid* and *cowardly* are antonyms, as are *agile* and *clumsy*.
    Vocabulary—Similarity/Contrast

71. (*a.* Mars, *b.* Saturn, *c.* Jupiter, **d. Mercury**) : HERMES :: VENUS : APHRODITE

    (**d**) Mercury is the Roman name, and Hermes the Greek name, for the messenger of the gods. Venus is the Roman name, and Aphrodite the Greek name, for the goddess of beauty. Mars was the god of war in Roman mythology. Jupiter was the god of sky and thunder. Saturn was the god of agriculture and harvest.
    Humanities—Similarity/Contrast

72. COMPLEMENTARY ANGLES : 90° :: COMPLEMENTARY COLORS : (**a. white**, *b.* black, *c.* violet, *d.* red)

    (**a**) Complementary angles sum to 90°; complementary colors sum to white.
    Natural Science—Description

73. (*a.* Jefferson, *b.* Adams, **c. Hamilton**, *d.* Madison) : BURR :: LINCOLN : BOOTH

    (**c**) Aaron Burr killed Alexander Hamilton, while John Wilkes Booth killed Abraham Lincoln.
    Humanities—Description

74. PUFFIN : (**a. bird**, *b.* reptile, *c.* mammal, *d.* amphibian) :: STURGEON : FISH

    (**a**) A puffin is a kind of bird; a sturgeon is a kind of fish.
    General Information—Description

75. BRONZE : (*a.* aluminum, **b. tin**, *c.* gold, *d.* silver) :: BRASS : ZINC

    (**b**) Bronze is a combination of copper and tin, while brass is a combination of copper and zinc.
    Natural Science—Description

Answer Explanations

76. G MAJOR : (*a.* B minor, *b.* C minor, *c.* D minor, ***d.* E minor**) :: C MAJOR : A MINOR

    (**d**) The keys of G major and E minor both have one sharp, while the keys of C major and A minor have none.
    Humanities—Description

77. (*a.* cow, *b.* jackal, ***c.* wolf**, *d.* rabbit) : LUPINE :: DOG : CANINE

    (**c**) To be lupine is to be wolflike; to be canine is to be doglike.
    Vocabulary—Description

78. (*a.* one, *b.* few, *c.* ten, ***d.* all**) : ISOCRACY :: ONE : AUTOCRACY

    (**d**) An isocracy is rule by all; an autocracy is rule by one.
    Social Science—Description

79. LOG 10 : LOG 100 :: LOG 100 : (*a.* log 1,000, ***b.* log 10,000**, *c.* log 100,000, *d.* log 1,000,000)

    (**b**) Log 100 is twice as great as log 10 (2 : 1). Log 10,000 is twice as great as log 100 (4 : 2).
    Mathematics—Class

80. HAPPINESS : SHANGRI-LA :: (***a.* wealth**, *b.* happiness, *c.* gods, *d.* freedom) : EL DORADO

    (**a**) Shangri-La is an imaginary land of great happiness; El Dorado is an imaginary land of great wealth.
    General Information—Description

81. DRACONIAN : (*a.* cowardly, *b.* bold, ***c.* cruel**, *d.* kindly) :: STENTORIAN : LOUD

    (**c**) A draconian person is cruel; a stentorian person is loud.
    Vocabulary—Description

82. MANSION : HOUSE :: TOME : (*a.* boat, ***b.* book**, *c.* desk, *d.* church)

    (**b**) A mansion is a large house. A tome is a large book.
    Vocabulary—Description

83. NEUTRAL : 7 :: (*a.* alkaline, ***b.* acidic**, *c.* hydrated, *d.* oxidized) : 1

    (**b**) On the pH scale, 7 is neutral and 1 is acidic. Numbers greater than 7 indicate alkalinity.
    Natural Science—Description

84. PERUSE : SKIM :: REPEL : (*a.* gloss, *b.* bowdlerize, *c.* drive back, **d. attract**)

   (**d**) *Peruse* and *skim* are antonyms, as are *repel* and *attract*.
   Vocabulary—Similarity/Contrast

85. NUCLEOLUS : NUCLEUS :: SET : (**a. superset**, *b.* set, *c.* subset, *d.* disjoint set)

   (**a**) In a cell, the nucleolus is contained in the nucleus. Similarly, a set is contained in a superset.
   Natural Science—Part/Whole

86. HORSEBACK RIDING : EQUITATION :: (*a.* giving birth, *b.* skydiving, **c. swimming**, *d.* dancing) : NATATION

   (**c**) Equitation is the art of horseback riding; natation is the art of swimming.
   General Information—Description

87. WHIGS : TORIES :: JACOBINS : (*a.* Fascists, *b.* Laborites, *c.* Roundheads, **d. Girondists**)

   (**d**) During the American Revolution, the Whigs represented a radical faction and the Tories a more conservative one. During the French Revolution, the Jacobins represented a radical faction and the Girondists a more conservative one.
   Humanities—Class

88. PRIME : (*a.* God, *b.* destiny, *c.* factum, **d. mover**) :: FIRST : CAUSE

   (**d**) In Aristotelian philosophy, the prime mover was a first cause (of all movement).
   Humanities—Completion

89. FRANC : FRANCE :: (*a.* lira, *b.* mark, *c.* guilder, **d. franc**) : SWITZERLAND

   (**d**) The franc was the unit of currency in both France and Switzerland (although the two francs are not equivalent). The lira was the currency of Italy, the mark was the currency of Germany, and the guilder was the currency of the Netherlands (before the euro).
   General Information—Description

90. (*a.* Jungfrau, **b. Blanc**, *c.* Matterhorn, *d.* Olympus) : ALPS :: EVEREST : HIMALAYAS

   (**b**) Mont Blanc is the highest peak in the Alps; Mount Everest is the highest peak in the Himalayas. Jungfrau and Matterhorn are mountains of the Swiss Alps; Mount Olympus is the highest mountain of Greece.
   General Information—Description

91. MELANCHOLY : (*a.* blue bile, *b.* green bile, *c.* red bile, ***d.* black bile**) :: CHOLER : YELLOW BILE

    (**d**) According to the physiology of days gone by, melancholy is black bile, while choler is yellow bile.
    Natural Science—Similarity/Contrast

92. ORAL : ANAL :: DEPENDENCY : (*a.* lazinesss, *b.* thermometer, ***c.* stinginess**, *d.* independence)

    (**c**) In psychodynamic theory, dependency is an oral trait and stinginess an anal trait.
    Social Science—Description

93. (*a.* hit, *b.* die, *c.* invest, ***d.* sprout**) : BURGEON :: ENTREAT : IMPLORE

    (**d**) *Sprout* and *burgeon* are synonyms, as are *entreat* and *implore*.
    Vocabulary—Similarity/Contrast

94. DEARTH : PAUCITY :: SCARCITY : (*a.* plethora, ***b.* shortage**, *c.* necessity, *d.* commodity)

    (**b**) *Dearth* and *paucity* are synonyms, as are *scarcity* and *shortage*. (All four words are synonymous.)
    Vocabulary—Similarity/Contrast

95. DELFT : (*a.* glass, ***b.* pottery**, *c.* stoneware, *d.* silver) :: LIMOGES : CHINA

    (**b**) Delft is known for its beautiful painted pottery; Limoges is known for its beautiful painted china.
    General Information—Description

96. IAMB : RETURN :: TROCHEE : (***a.* stable**, *b.* arrive, *c.* defend, *d.* eternal)

    (**a**) *Return* is pronounced as an iamb; *stable* is pronounced as a trochee. An iamb is a metrical foot that consists of one unstressed and one stressed syllable; a trochee consists of one long (stressed) syllable that is followed by a short (unstressed) one.
    Humanities—Class

97. AUTOCHTHONOUS : (*a.* foreign, ***b.* native**, *c.* self-governing, *d.* dependent) :: LETTER : EPISTLE

    (**b**) *Autochthonous* and *native* are synonyms, as are *letter* and *epistle*.
    Vocabulary—Similarity/Contrast

98. (***a.* bells**, *b.* horn, *c.* magpies, *d.* toads) : TINTINNABULATION :: GEESE : HONK

    (**a**) Tintinnabulation is a sound made by bells; honk is a sound made by geese.
    Vocabulary—Description

Answer Explanations

99. ELF : FLEE :: TON : (***a. note***, *b.* pound, *c.* dwarf, *d.* find)

(**a**) *Flee* is *elf* spelled backwards, but with an added *e* at the end. *Note* is *ton* spelled backwards, also with an added *e* at the end.
Nonsemantic

100. CODA : (*a.* novel, ***b. musical composition***, *c.* sculpture, *d.* ceramic jar) :: LANDING : FLIGHT

(**b**) A coda concludes a musical composition; a landing concludes a flight.
Humanities—Description

101. (*a.* months, ***b. tides***, *c.* days, *d.* climates) : SEASONS :: MOON : SUN

(**b**) The tides change as the earth's positional relationship to the moon changes. The seasons change as the earth's positional relationship to the sun changes.
Natural Science—Description

102. TARANTELLA : ITALY :: CANCAN : (*a.* Argentina, *b.* Spain, *c.* Colombia, ***d. France***)

(**d**) The tarantella and cancan are dances that originated in Italy and France, respectively. Flamenco is a dance from Spain, tango is from Argentina, and bambuco is from Colombia.
Humanities—Description

103. AUDITORY : (***a. olfactory***, *b.* sensory, *c.* occipital, *d.* nasal) :: EAR : NOSE

(**a**) The ear is responsible for auditory sensation, or hearing. The nose is responsible for olfactory sensation, or smelling.
Vocabulary—Description

104. TAILFEATHERS : PEACOCK :: (*a.* coat, *b.* tail, ***c. face***, *d.* feet) : MANDRILL

(**c**) A peacock is known for its brightly colored tailfeathers just as a mandrill is known for its brightly colored face.
General Information—Description

105. BUFFALO : WHEAT :: NICKEL : (*a.* dollar, *b.* quarter, *c.* dime, ***d. penny***)

(**d**) A buffalo was formerly placed on one side of the nickel, and these coins were known as buffalo nickels. A shaft of wheat was formerly placed on one side of the penny, and these coins were known as wheat pennies.
General Information—Completion

106. ACIDIC : (**a. 3**, *b.* 7, *c.* 10, *d.* 14) :: ALKALINE : 12

(**a**) A solution with a pH level of 3 is acidic, just as a solution with a pH level of 12 is alkaline.
Natural Science—Description

107. (*a.* Romania, **b. Croatia**, *c.* Greece, *d.* Hungary) : YUGOSLAVIA :: CZECH REPUBLIC : CZECHOSLOVAKIA

(**b**) Croatia is part of the country once known as Yugoslavia. The Czech Republic is part of the country once known as Czechoslovakia.
General Information—Description

108. ROCKY : SMOKY :: COLORADO : (*a.* West Virginia, *b.* New York, *c.* New Hampshire, **d. Tennessee**)

(**d**) The Rocky Mountains can be found in the state of Colorado just as the Smoky Mountains can be found in Tennessee.
General Information—Description

109. BADGER : DOG :: PESTER : (**a. track**, *b.* avoid, *c.* exhaust, *d.* behave)

(**a**) To badger is to pester someone persistently. To dog is to track someone or something persistently.
General Information—Similarity/Contrast

110. ACCORDION : (*a.* bagpipe, *b.* flute, **c. organ**, *d.* clarinet) :: HARMONIUM : PIANO

(**c**) The accordion, organ, harmonium, and piano are all instruments with black and white keyboards.
Humanities—Class

111. RACECAR : RADAR :: (*a.* abbreviation, *b.* homonym, **c. palindrome**, *d.* gerund) : ACRONYM

(**c**) The word racecar is a palindrome: it reads the same forward and backward. The word radar is an acronym: it stands for RAdio Detection And Ranging.
Nonsemantic—Nonsemantic

112. (*a.* 82, *b.* 99, **c. 22**, *d.* 15) : 451 :: CATCH : FAHRENHEIT

(**c**) *Catch 22* and *Fahrenheit 451* are both popular novels, by Joseph Heller and Ray Bradbury respectively.
Humanities—Description

113. A : Z :: Alpha : (*a.* **Omega**, *b.* Beta, *c.* Zed, *d.* Phi)

(**a**) A is the first and Z (Zed) the last letter of the English alphabet. Alpha is the first and Omega the last letter of the Greek alphabet.
General Information—Description

114. AMETHYST : (*a.* amber, ***b.* purple**, *c.* crimson, *d.* yellow) :: SAPPHIRE : BLUE

(**b**) Amethyst is a gemstone that is typically purple in color. Sapphire is a gemstone that is typically blue in color.
Natural Science—Description

115. SYCOPHANT : TOADY :: MISCREANT : (*a.* artist, *b.* recluse, *c.* follower, ***d.* criminal**)

(**d**) A *sycophant* is a *toady*, just as a *miscreant* is a *criminal*.
Vocabulary—Similarity/Contrast

116. EKG : (*a.* **heart**, *b.* pancreas, *c.* bladder, *d.* lungs) :: EEG : brain

(**a**) An EKG machine measures activity in the heart just as an EEG machine measures activity in the brain. EEG stands for electroencephalogram. EKG stands for electrocardiogram.
Natural Science—Description

117. TONY : OSCAR :: (*a.* music, ***b.* theater**, *c.* literature, *d.* television) : FILM

(**b**) The Tony Award is given for accomplishments in theater just as the Oscar is given for accomplishments in film.
General Information—Description

118. (*a.* Colorado, *b.* Wyoming, *c.* Idaho, ***d.* Alaska**) : MCKINLEY :: NEPAL : EVEREST

(**d**) Mount McKinley is in Alaska and Mount Everest is in Nepal.
General Information—Description

119. I, CLAUDIUS : GRAVES :: (*a.* I, Julius, *b.* I, Criminal, *c.* I, Nixon, ***d.* I, Robot**) : ASIMOV

(**d**) Graves wrote the novel *I, Claudius* and Asimov wrote the novel *I, Robot.*
Humanities—Description

120. VIRGINIA : TENNESSEE :: WOOLF : (*a.* Faulkner, *b.* Percy, ***c.* Williams**, *d.* O'Connor)

(**c**) Virginia Woolf and Tennessee Williams were both writers. Woolf wrote *Mrs. Dalloway* and *Orlando*, for example. Williams' works include *Cat on a Hot Tin Roof* and *A Streetcar Named Desire.*
Humanities—Description

PRACTICE TEST 9

Item Classification Chart

		RELATIONSHIP						
		Similarity/ Contrast	Description	Class	Completion	Part/ Whole	Equality/ Negation	Nonsemantic
C O N T E N T	**Vocabulary**	15, 26, 32, 35, 53, 67, 70, 84, 93, 94, 97, 115	3, 44, 46, 62, 77, 81, 82, 98, 103					
	General Information	51, 109	1, 4, 6, 10, 16, 19, 31, 33, 34, 50, 57, 63, 65, 74, 80, 86, 89, 90, 95, 104, 107, 108, 113, 117, 118	24	5, 8, 25, 105	12		
	Humanities	27, 41, 71	9, 11, 17, 20, 21, 23, 29, 30, 36, 38, 45, 47, 56, 61, 73, 76, 100, 102, 112, 119, 120	13, 14, 49, 58, 68, 87, 96, 110	42, 88			
	Social Science		37, 55, 69, 78, 92					
	Natural Science	91	2, 7, 22, 40, 48, 54, 59, 64, 72, 75, 83, 101, 106, 114, 116	66		85		
	Mathematics		39, 60	79			18, 43, 52	
	Nonsemantic							28, 99, 111

Answer Sheet
PRACTICE TEST 10

1 Ⓐ Ⓑ Ⓒ Ⓓ	31 Ⓐ Ⓑ Ⓒ Ⓓ	61 Ⓐ Ⓑ Ⓒ Ⓓ	91 Ⓐ Ⓑ Ⓒ Ⓓ
2 Ⓐ Ⓑ Ⓒ Ⓓ	32 Ⓐ Ⓑ Ⓒ Ⓓ	62 Ⓐ Ⓑ Ⓒ Ⓓ	92 Ⓐ Ⓑ Ⓒ Ⓓ
3 Ⓐ Ⓑ Ⓒ Ⓓ	33 Ⓐ Ⓑ Ⓒ Ⓓ	63 Ⓐ Ⓑ Ⓒ Ⓓ	93 Ⓐ Ⓑ Ⓒ Ⓓ
4 Ⓐ Ⓑ Ⓒ Ⓓ	34 Ⓐ Ⓑ Ⓒ Ⓓ	64 Ⓐ Ⓑ Ⓒ Ⓓ	94 Ⓐ Ⓑ Ⓒ Ⓓ
5 Ⓐ Ⓑ Ⓒ Ⓓ	35 Ⓐ Ⓑ Ⓒ Ⓓ	65 Ⓐ Ⓑ Ⓒ Ⓓ	95 Ⓐ Ⓑ Ⓒ Ⓓ
6 Ⓐ Ⓑ Ⓒ Ⓓ	36 Ⓐ Ⓑ Ⓒ Ⓓ	66 Ⓐ Ⓑ Ⓒ Ⓓ	96 Ⓐ Ⓑ Ⓒ Ⓓ
7 Ⓐ Ⓑ Ⓒ Ⓓ	37 Ⓐ Ⓑ Ⓒ Ⓓ	67 Ⓐ Ⓑ Ⓒ Ⓓ	97 Ⓐ Ⓑ Ⓒ Ⓓ
8 Ⓐ Ⓑ Ⓒ Ⓓ	38 Ⓐ Ⓑ Ⓒ Ⓓ	68 Ⓐ Ⓑ Ⓒ Ⓓ	98 Ⓐ Ⓑ Ⓒ Ⓓ
9 Ⓐ Ⓑ Ⓒ Ⓓ	39 Ⓐ Ⓑ Ⓒ Ⓓ	69 Ⓐ Ⓑ Ⓒ Ⓓ	99 Ⓐ Ⓑ Ⓒ Ⓓ
10 Ⓐ Ⓑ Ⓒ Ⓓ	40 Ⓐ Ⓑ Ⓒ Ⓓ	70 Ⓐ Ⓑ Ⓒ Ⓓ	100 Ⓐ Ⓑ Ⓒ Ⓓ
11 Ⓐ Ⓑ Ⓒ Ⓓ	41 Ⓐ Ⓑ Ⓒ Ⓓ	71 Ⓐ Ⓑ Ⓒ Ⓓ	101 Ⓐ Ⓑ Ⓒ Ⓓ
12 Ⓐ Ⓑ Ⓒ Ⓓ	42 Ⓐ Ⓑ Ⓒ Ⓓ	72 Ⓐ Ⓑ Ⓒ Ⓓ	102 Ⓐ Ⓑ Ⓒ Ⓓ
13 Ⓐ Ⓑ Ⓒ Ⓓ	43 Ⓐ Ⓑ Ⓒ Ⓓ	73 Ⓐ Ⓑ Ⓒ Ⓓ	103 Ⓐ Ⓑ Ⓒ Ⓓ
14 Ⓐ Ⓑ Ⓒ Ⓓ	44 Ⓐ Ⓑ Ⓒ Ⓓ	74 Ⓐ Ⓑ Ⓒ Ⓓ	104 Ⓐ Ⓑ Ⓒ Ⓓ
15 Ⓐ Ⓑ Ⓒ Ⓓ	45 Ⓐ Ⓑ Ⓒ Ⓓ	75 Ⓐ Ⓑ Ⓒ Ⓓ	105 Ⓐ Ⓑ Ⓒ Ⓓ
16 Ⓐ Ⓑ Ⓒ Ⓓ	46 Ⓐ Ⓑ Ⓒ Ⓓ	76 Ⓐ Ⓑ Ⓒ Ⓓ	106 Ⓐ Ⓑ Ⓒ Ⓓ
17 Ⓐ Ⓑ Ⓒ Ⓓ	47 Ⓐ Ⓑ Ⓒ Ⓓ	77 Ⓐ Ⓑ Ⓒ Ⓓ	107 Ⓐ Ⓑ Ⓒ Ⓓ
18 Ⓐ Ⓑ Ⓒ Ⓓ	48 Ⓐ Ⓑ Ⓒ Ⓓ	78 Ⓐ Ⓑ Ⓒ Ⓓ	108 Ⓐ Ⓑ Ⓒ Ⓓ
19 Ⓐ Ⓑ Ⓒ Ⓓ	49 Ⓐ Ⓑ Ⓒ Ⓓ	79 Ⓐ Ⓑ Ⓒ Ⓓ	109 Ⓐ Ⓑ Ⓒ Ⓓ
20 Ⓐ Ⓑ Ⓒ Ⓓ	50 Ⓐ Ⓑ Ⓒ Ⓓ	80 Ⓐ Ⓑ Ⓒ Ⓓ	110 Ⓐ Ⓑ Ⓒ Ⓓ
21 Ⓐ Ⓑ Ⓒ Ⓓ	51 Ⓐ Ⓑ Ⓒ Ⓓ	81 Ⓐ Ⓑ Ⓒ Ⓓ	111 Ⓐ Ⓑ Ⓒ Ⓓ
22 Ⓐ Ⓑ Ⓒ Ⓓ	52 Ⓐ Ⓑ Ⓒ Ⓓ	82 Ⓐ Ⓑ Ⓒ Ⓓ	112 Ⓐ Ⓑ Ⓒ Ⓓ
23 Ⓐ Ⓑ Ⓒ Ⓓ	53 Ⓐ Ⓑ Ⓒ Ⓓ	83 Ⓐ Ⓑ Ⓒ Ⓓ	113 Ⓐ Ⓑ Ⓒ Ⓓ
24 Ⓐ Ⓑ Ⓒ Ⓓ	54 Ⓐ Ⓑ Ⓒ Ⓓ	84 Ⓐ Ⓑ Ⓒ Ⓓ	114 Ⓐ Ⓑ Ⓒ Ⓓ
25 Ⓐ Ⓑ Ⓒ Ⓓ	55 Ⓐ Ⓑ Ⓒ Ⓓ	85 Ⓐ Ⓑ Ⓒ Ⓓ	115 Ⓐ Ⓑ Ⓒ Ⓓ
26 Ⓐ Ⓑ Ⓒ Ⓓ	56 Ⓐ Ⓑ Ⓒ Ⓓ	86 Ⓐ Ⓑ Ⓒ Ⓓ	116 Ⓐ Ⓑ Ⓒ Ⓓ
27 Ⓐ Ⓑ Ⓒ Ⓓ	57 Ⓐ Ⓑ Ⓒ Ⓓ	87 Ⓐ Ⓑ Ⓒ Ⓓ	117 Ⓐ Ⓑ Ⓒ Ⓓ
28 Ⓐ Ⓑ Ⓒ Ⓓ	58 Ⓐ Ⓑ Ⓒ Ⓓ	88 Ⓐ Ⓑ Ⓒ Ⓓ	118 Ⓐ Ⓑ Ⓒ Ⓓ
29 Ⓐ Ⓑ Ⓒ Ⓓ	59 Ⓐ Ⓑ Ⓒ Ⓓ	89 Ⓐ Ⓑ Ⓒ Ⓓ	119 Ⓐ Ⓑ Ⓒ Ⓓ
30 Ⓐ Ⓑ Ⓒ Ⓓ	60 Ⓐ Ⓑ Ⓒ Ⓓ	90 Ⓐ Ⓑ Ⓒ Ⓓ	120 Ⓐ Ⓑ Ⓒ Ⓓ

Practice Test 10

Directions: In each of the following questions, you will find three initial terms and, in parentheses, four answer options designated *a*, *b*, *c*, and *d*. You are to select from the four answer options the one that best completes the analogy with the three initial terms. To record your answers, use the answer sheet provided.

Time: 60 minutes

1. PEN : INK :: PENCIL : (*a.* limestone, *b.* graphite, *c.* talc, *d.* gypsum)

2. (*a.* probably, *b.* possibly, *c.* virtually, *d.* certainly) : 1 :: MAYBE : .5

3. HORRIFIC : HORROR :: SOPORIFIC : (*a.* joy, *b.* boredom, *c.* sleep, *d.* stupidity)

4. A/B : B/A :: (*a.* 1/15, *b.* 1/3, *c.* 2/3, *d.* 3/2) : 1.5

5. UNINTERRUPTED : (*a.* discrete, *b.* repeated, *c.* endless, *d.* likely) :: CONTINUOUS : CONTINUAL

6. PTOLEMY : EARTH :: COPERNICUS : (*a.* moon, *b.* sun, *c.* Jupiter, *d.* universe)

7. (*a.* sculptor, *b.* painter, *c.* poet, *d.* architect) : VENUS DE MILO :: AUTHOR : THE SCARLET LETTER

8. QUICK : RABBIT :: (*a.* sleepy, *b.* wise, *c.* hungry, *d.* angry) : OWL

9. PATRICIDE : (*a.* brother, *b.* sister, *c.* king, *d.* father) :: MATRICIDE : MOTHER

10. AMA : DOCTORS :: ABA : (*a.* athletes, *b.* miners, *c.* lawyers, *d.* historians)

11. WOODHULL : PELOSI :: ALBRIGHT : (*a.* Day O'Connor, *b.* Bush, *c.* Sebelius, *d.* Ginsburg)

12. MADISON : WAR OF 1812 :: (*a.* Reagan, *b.* G. H. Bush, *c.* Clinton, *d.* G. W. Bush) : GULF WAR

13. BULLET : (*a.* noose, *b.* head, *c.* force, *d.* blade) :: GUN : GUILLOTINE

14. (*a.* ·, *b.* ÷, *c.* **, *d.* undefined) : MULTIPLICATION :: + : ADDITION

15. PSYCHOLOGY : MIND :: PHYCOLOGY : (*a.* herbivores, *b.* carnivores, *c.* algae, *d.* cacti)

16. (*a.* Third Estate, *b.* House, *c.* Parliament, *d.* Commons) : LOWER :: LORDS : UPPER

17. BACTERIA : (*a.* bacteria, *b.* bacterium, *c.* bacterius, *d.* bacterion) :: MANY : ONE

18. SCURVY : VITAMIN C :: KWASHIORKOR : (*a.* vitamin A, *b.* vitamin B$_{12}$, *c.* protein, *d.* niacin)

19. CONVERSE : CONTRAPOSITIVE :: (*a.* B → A, *b.* A → B, *c.* not B → A, *d.* not A → B) : NOT B → NOT A

20. (*a.* New York, *b.* New Mexico, *c.* Missouri, *d.* Michigan) : LAKE :: MISSISSIPPI : RIVER

21. 0 PERCENT : (*a.* pressure, *b.* wind chill, *c.* THI, *d.* humidity) :: ABSOLUTE 0 : TEMPERATURE

22. OBTUSE : ACUTE :: (*a.* 0, *b.* 100, *c.* 180, *d.* 270) : 45

23. AB : AWAY :: (*a.* a, *b.* contra, *c.* ex, *d.* ad) : WITHOUT

24. UNCLE : (*a.* paternal, *b.* avuncular, *c.* uncial, *d.* uncinate) :: BROTHER : FRATERNAL

25. (*a.* women, *b.* marriage, *c.* falsehood, *d.* enlightenment) : MISOLOGY :: NOVELTY : MISONEISM

26. LIE : (*a.* lie, *b.* lay, *c.* laid, *d.* lain) :: LAY : LAID

27. HELTER : SKELTER :: HIGGLEDY : (*a.* niggledy, *b.* piggledy, *c.* spiggledy, *d.* wiggledy)

28. SPOOL : LOOPS :: (*a.* water, *b.* pools, *c.* dinghy, *d.* tools) : SLOOP

29. RILL : (*a.* stream, *b.* lake, *c.* ocean, *d.* lagoon) : NOVELLA : NOVEL

30. SONATA : SONATINA :: CONCERTO : (*a.* concertino, *b.* concertina, *c.* concert, *d.* concerto grosso)

31. NEW JERSEY : 8:00 :: OREGON : (*a.* 5:00, *b.* 6:00, *c.* 9:00, *d.* 10:00)

32. LINCOLN : 1 :: JEFFERSON : (*a.* 3, *b.* 5, *c.* 10, *d.* 25)

33. PLINY THE ELDER : (*a.* Carthaginian, *b.* Athenian, *c.* Milanese, *d.* Roman) :: THUCYDIDES : GREEK

34. (*a.* Uruguay, *b.* Argentina, *c.* Paraguay, *d.* Guatemala) : CENTRAL :: BRAZIL : SOUTH

35. ETHER : GENERAL :: NOVOCAINE : (*a.* specific, *b.* particulate, *c.* local, *d.* toxic)

36. D'ARTAGNAN : (*a.* Hugo, *b.* Mauriac, *c.* Dumas, *d.* Balzac) :: GATSBY : FITZGERALD

37. ARMY : LAND :: (*a.* Marines, *b.* Navy, *c.* CIA, *d.* Secret Service) : AMPHIBIOUS

38. TWO : (*a.* hydrogen, *b.* uranium, *c.* americium, *d.* deuterium) :: THREE : TRITIUM

39. YORK : N.Y. :: ORLEANS : (*a.* O.R., *b.* La., *c.* Fr., *d.* Miss.)

40. (*a.* Copland, *b.* Mendelssohn, *c.* Shostakovich, *d.* Bach) : 19th :: MOZART : 18th

41. MENELAUS : (*a.* Agamemnon, *b.* Priam, *c.* Achilles, *d.* Spartacus) :: HECTOR : PARIS

42. MAJORITY : MINORITY :: (*a.* Bolshevik, *b.* Maoist, *c.* Marxist, *d.* Trotskyite) : MENSHEVIK

43. FEIGN : FINE :: (*a.* right, *b.* writ, *c.* rate, *d.* rat) : WRITE

44. FATUOUS : (*a.* bright, *b.* prodigal, *c.* contemptuous, *d.* foolish) :: FASTIDIOUS : HARD TO PLEASE

45. (*a.* Ayer, *b.* Peirce, *c.* Santayana, *d.* Russell) : PRAGMATIST :: SARTRE : EXISTENTIALIST

46. ADDITIVE : (*a.* blue, *b.* red, *c.* green, *d.* white) :: SUBTRACTIVE : YELLOW

47. PROTON : NUCLEON :: MUON : (*a.* meson, *b.* electron, *c.* pion, *d.* positron)

48. BOARD : (*a.* fifteen, *b.* checkers, *c.* bridge, *d.* thirty-six) :: DECK : TWENTY-ONE

49. C# : Db :: B# : (*a.* Cb, *b.* Bb, *c.* C, *d.* Db)

50. SEVER : PERSEVERANCE :: CUT : (*a.* perseveration, *b.* perspective, *c.* pertinence, *d.* persistence)

51. FREUD : (*a.* Skinner, *b.* Allport, *c.* Murray, *d.* Erikson) :: KOHLBERG : PIAGET

52. (*a.* ellipsoid, *b.* semicircle, *c.* rhombus, *d.* angle) : PROTRACTOR :: RECTANGLE : RULER

53. BIPOLARITY : MONOLOGUE :: (*a.* dicotyledon, *b.* stamen, *c.* deciduous, *d.* pistil) : UNION

54. (*a.* patent medicine, *b.* adage, *c.* theory, *d.* heretic) : APOTHEGM :: DEXTERITY : ADROITNESS

55. FROM : TO :: (*a.* artery, *b.* ventricle, *c.* atrium, *d.* carotid) : JUGULAR

56. SOUSA : (*a.* waltzes, *b.* symphonies, *c.* marches, *d.* hymns) :: VERDI : OPERAS

57. INVOCATION : (*a.* benediction, *b.* recessional, *c.* prayer, *d.* vesper) :: START : FINISH

58. SASKATCHEWAN : REGINA :: (*a.* Quebec, *b.* Alberta, *c.* Ontario, *d.* Manitoba) : TORONTO

59. (*a.* obvious, *b.* latent, *c.* proximate, *d.* apposite) : MANIFEST :: COVERT : OVERT

60. DIRGE : REQUIEM :: GRIEF : (*a.* thanksgiving, *b.* mourning, *c.* penitence, *d.* joy)

61. (*a.* metropolitan, *b.* synod, *c.* district, *d.* diocese) : BISHOP :: PARISH : PRIEST

62. CONSONANT : VOWEL :: COMPOSITE : (*a.* prime, *b.* irrational, *c.* integer, *d.* zero)

63. IMPLODE : (*a.* explode, *b.* beseech, *c.* implicate, *d.* burst inward) :: IMPLY : HINT AT

64. EARTH : SUN :: PLANET : (*a.* heavenly body, *b.* sol, *c.* star, *d.* nova)

65. OCTOPUS : (*a.* six, *b.* eight, *c.* ten, *d.* twelve) :: PERSON : TWO

66. QUARTER : DOLLAR :: (*a.* season, *b.* day, *c.* month, *d.* decade) : YEAR

67. CAPTAIN : (*a.* admiral, *b.* ensign, *c.* commodore, *d.* midshipman) ::
CORPORAL : SERGEANT

68. DAVID : VAN DYCK :: FRENCH : (*a.* Italian, *b.* German, *c.* Flemish,
d. British)

69. (*a.* poulet, *b.* glacé, *c.* citron, *d.* entrecote) : SWEET :: CAFÉ : BITTER

70. WAIVE : WAVE :: (*a.* relinquish, *b.* relegate, *c.* remand, *d.* redress) :
UNDULATE

71. WORK : (*a.* joule, *b.* ohm, *c.* ampere, *d.* coulomb) :: POTENTIAL
DIFFERENCE : VOLT

72. PHILOLOGY : LANGUAGES :: MYCOLOGY : (*a.* flowering plants,
b. ferns, *c.* weeds, *d.* fungi)

73. DEPENDENT : INDEPENDENT :: (*a.* autochthonous, *b.* canonical,
c. anaclitic, *d.* irrecusable) : SELF-RELIANT

74. CX : (*a.* CXV, *b.* CL, *c.* CLX, *d.* CC) :: LV : LXXV

75. CAMEL : RHINOCEROS :: HUMP : (*a.* armor, *b.* snout, *c.* horn, *d.* hide)

76. ONTOLOGY : (*a.* being, *b.* metaphysics, *c.* growth, *d.* knowledge) ::
DEONTOLOGY : ETHICS

77. (*a.* leukocytes, *b.* platelets, *c.* hormones, *d.* erythrocytes) : ANEMIA ::
INSULIN : DIABETES

78. CALVIN : COOLIDGE :: (*a.* Alexander, *b.* Franklin, *c.* William, *d.* Robert) :
PIERCE

79. PONTIUS PILATE : JESUS :: CREON : (*a.* Orestes, *b.* Oedipus,
c. Antigone, *d.* Electra)

80. (*a.* bellicose, *b.* periphrastic, *c.* altruistic, *d.* nihilistic) : AGGRESSION ::
IRENIC : PEACE

81. FIRST : LAST :: GENESIS : (*a.* Exodus, *b.* Deuteronomy, *c.* Leviticus,
d. Numbers)

82. πr^2 : $2\pi r$ :: AREA : (*a.* diameter, *b.* circumference, *c.* perimeter, *d.* volume)

83. BUCKINGHAM PALACE : XANADU :: ELIZABETH II :
(*a.* Genghis Khan, *b.* Charles V, *c.* Citizen Kane, *d.* Donald Trump)

84. MONOGYNY : (*a.* life, *b.* religion, *c.* child, *d.* wife) :: MONOTHEISM : GOD

85. ESPRESSO : BLACK :: ORANGE PEKOE : (*a.* green, *b.* white, *c.* black, *d.* red)

86. DIANA : (*a.* Artemis, *b.* Minerva, *c.* Aphrodite, *d.* Hera) :: JUPITER : ZEUS

87. (*a.* B♭ major, *b.* E♭ major, *c.* F major, *d.* A major) : C MINOR :: G MAJOR : E MINOR

88. MAN : NAME :: (*a.* rig, *b.* appellation, *c.* maiden, *d.* woman) : GIRL

89. MANON LESCAUT : (*a.* wise, *b.* arrogant, *c.* promiscuous, *d.* wicked) :: TOM SAWYER : ADVENTUROUS

90. (*a.* Bull Moose, *b.* Whig, *c.* Socialist, *d.* Know-Nothing) : DEBS :: DEMOCRAT : STEVENSON

91. FIRST : CLERGY :: FOURTH : (*a.* nobles, *b.* commoners, *c.* children, *d.* journalists)

92. AMETHYST : GARNET :: PURPLE : (*a.* red, *b.* green, *c.* transparent, *d.* blue)

93. (*a.* loquacious, *b.* refractory, *c.* ostentatious, *d.* timid) : GARRULOUS :: AUDACIOUS : BOLD

94. FOUR : APRIL FOOL'S DAY :: (*a.* one, *b.* two, *c.* five, *d.* ten) : MAY DAY

95. STEEPLE : CHURCH :: (*a.* minaret, *b.* muezzin, *c.* imam, *d.* arch) : MOSQUE

96. VANILLA : (*a.* bean, *b.* Sussex, *c.* hasty, *d.* Brazil) :: RICE : YORKSHIRE

97. (*a.* Saint-Saëns, *b.* Strindberg, *c.* Bernstein, *d.* Rubinstein) : PLAYS :: FROST : POEMS

98. THERMO : HEAT :: ISO : (*a.* cold, *b.* pressure, *c.* humidity, *d.* same)

99. (*a.* Scotch, *b.* vermouth, *c.* gin, *d.* bourbon) : TOM COLLINS :: VODKA : BLOODY MARY

100. BELLEEK : (*a.* Scotland, *b.* Ireland, *c.* Holland, *d.* Belgium) :: LIMOGES : FRANCE

101. AMPERE : (*a.* current, *b.* magnetism, *c.* speed, *d.* gravity) :: WATT : POWER

102. BAIKAL : RUSSIA :: (*a.* Michigan, *b.* Superior, *c.* Ontario, *d.* Placid) : UNITED STATES

103. (*a.* Lady's Man, *b.* Black Beauty, *c.* Secretariat, *d.* Fortune's Fool) : MAN O' WAR :: SEABISCUIT : WAR ADMIRAL

104. GAVRILO PRINCIP : ARCHDUKE FERDINAND :: (*a.* Robert E. Lee, *b.* Lee Harvey Oswald, *c.* John Hinckley, *d.* John Wilkes Booth) : PRESIDENT LINCOLN

105. KILOGRAM : POUND :: 1 : (*a.* 2.2, *b.* 5, *c.* 0.2, *d.* 7.3)

106. ROSEMARY : (*a.* oregano, *b.* cumin, *c.* nutmeg, *d.* cinnamon) :: BASIL : SAGE

107. COBBLER : SHOES :: (*a.* tanner, *b.* smith, *c.* cooper, *d.* miller) : BARRELS

108. EXPECTORATE : (*a.* bite, *b.* spit, *c.* deliver, *d.* swallow) :: MASTICATE : CHEW

109. (*a.* net, *b.* hat trick, *c.* goalie, *d.* puck) : ICE HOCKEY :: SHUTTLECOCK : BADMINTON

110. ARMSTRONG : TRUMPET :: COLTRANE : (*a.* piano, *b.* saxophone, *c.* clarinet, *d.* trombone)

111. MOHAMMED : JESUS :: (*a.* Judea, *b.* Constantinople, *c.* Mecca, *d.* Jerusalem) : BETHLEHEM

112. RHOMBUS : HEXAGON :: 4 : (*a.* 8, *b.* 7, *c.* 6, *d.* 5)

113. RECORD PLAYER : (*a.* loudest, *b.* loud, *c.* quiet, *d.* quieter) :: SUPERANNUATED : SUPERLATIVE

114. (*a.* feet, *b.* obedience, *c.* thought, *d.* memory) : ELEPHANT :: STRENGTH : ANT

115. DIAMOND : SAPPHIRE :: (*a.* Hope, *b.* Diana's, *c.* Indian, *d.* Pharoah's) : LOGAN

116. HEAVEN : ST. PETER :: HADES : (*a.* Lucifer, *b.* Scylla, *c.* Charybdis, *d.* Cerberus)

117. r-p-o-p-h-e-s-s-a-g-r : JABBERWOCKY :: CUMMINGS : (*a.* Milne, *b.* Cleary, *c.* Carroll, *d.* Eliot)

118. X : (*a.* w, *b.* y, *c.* u, *d.* a) :: VERTICAL : HORIZONTAL

119. (*a.* nostalgia, *b.* kindness, *c.* loyalty, *d.* naiveté) :: POLLYANNA :: DOUBT : THOMAS

120. MAASAI : EAST AFRICA :: LAPP : (*a.* Australia, *b.* Middle East, *c.* South Asia, *d.* Scandinavia)

Answer Key
PRACTICE TEST 10

1. **B**	31. **A**	61. **D**	91. **D**
2. **D**	32. **B**	62. **A**	92. **A**
3. **C**	33. **D**	63. **D**	93. **A**
4. **C**	34. **D**	64. **C**	94. **C**
5. **B**	35. **C**	65. **B**	95. **A**
6. **B**	36. **C**	66. **A**	96. **C**
7. **A**	37. **A**	67. **C**	97. **B**
8. **B**	38. **D**	68. **C**	98. **D**
9. **D**	39. **B**	69. **B**	99. **C**
10. **C**	40. **B**	70. **A**	100. **B**
11. **A**	41. **A**	71. **A**	101. **A**
12. **B**	42. **A**	72. **D**	102. **B**
13. **D**	43. **C**	73. **C**	103. **C**
14. **A**	44. **D**	74. **B**	104. **D**
15. **C**	45. **B**	75. **C**	105. **A**
16. **D**	46. **C**	76. **A**	106. **A**
17. **B**	47. **A**	77. **D**	107. **C**
18. **C**	48. **B**	78. **B**	108. **B**
19. **A**	49. **C**	79. **C**	109. **D**
20. **D**	50. **D**	80. **A**	110. **B**
21. **D**	51. **D**	81. **B**	111. **C**
22. **B**	52. **B**	82. **B**	112. **C**
23. **A**	53. **A**	83. **C**	113. **A**
24. **B**	54. **B**	84. **D**	114. **D**
25. **D**	55. **D**	85. **C**	115. **A**
26. **B**	56. **C**	86. **A**	116. **D**
27. **B**	57. **A**	87. **B**	117. **C**
28. **B**	58. **C**	88. **A**	118. **B**
29. **A**	59. **B**	89. **C**	119. **D**
30. **A**	60. **B**	90. **C**	120. **D**

ANSWER EXPLANATIONS FOR PRACTICE TEST 10

In the following, explanations concerning the correct response are in a large font. Explanations regarding distracters (incorrect responses) that are not self-explaining or could be misinterpreted are in a smaller font in order to highlight the explanations of the answers that are correct.

1. PEN : INK :: PENCIL : (*a.* limestone, ***b.* graphite**, *c.* talc, *d.* gypsum)

   (**b**) A pen writes with ink; a pencil writes with graphite.
   General Information—Description

2. (*a.* probably, *b.* possibly, *c.* virtually, ***d.* certainly**) : 1 :: MAYBE : .5

   (**d**) Something that is certainly true has probability 1 of occurrence; something that is maybe true can have probability .5 of occurrence.
   General Information—Description

3. HORRIFIC : HORROR :: SOPORIFIC : (*a.* joy, *b.* boredom, ***c.* sleep**, *d.* stupidity)

   (**c**) Something horrific causes horror; something soporific causes sleep.
   Vocabulary—Description

4. A/B : B/A :: (*a.* 1/15, *b.* 1/3, ***c.* 2/3**, *d.* 3/2) : 1.5

   (**c**) $B/A = 1/(A/B)$; $1.5 = 1/(2/3)$.
   Mathematics—Equality/Negation

5. UNINTERRUPTED : (*a.* discrete, ***b.* repeated**, *c.* endless, *d.* likely) :: CONTINUOUS : CONTINUAL

   (**b**) Something that is uninterrupted is continuous; something that is repeated is continual.
   Vocabulary—Similarity/Contrast

6. PTOLEMY : EARTH :: COPERNICUS : (*a.* moon, ***b.* sun**, *c.* Jupiter, *d.* universe)

   (**b**) Ptolemy believed that the earth is at the center of the planetary system; Copernicus believed that the sun is at the center.
   Natural Science—Description

7. (***a.* sculptor**, *b.* painter, *c.* poet, *d.* architect) : VENUS DE MILO :: AUTHOR : THE SCARLET LETTER

   (**a**) Venus de Milo was created by a sculptor (unknown); *The Scarlet Letter*, by an author (Nathaniel Hawthorne).
   Humanities—Description

8. QUICK : RABBIT :: (*a.* sleepy, ***b.* wise**, *c.* hungry, *d.* angry) : OWL

(**b**) A rabbit is reputed to be quick; an owl is reputed to be wise.
General Information—Description

9. PATRICIDE : (*a.* brother, *b.* sister, *c.* king, ***d.* father**) :: MATRICIDE :
MOTHER

(**d**) Patricide is the murder of one's father; matricide is the murder of one's
mother. Fratricide stands for the murder of a brother; regicide refers to the murder of a
monarch; sororicide stands for the murder of a sister.
Vocabulary—Description

10. AMA : DOCTORS :: ABA : (*a.* athletes, *b.* miners, ***c.* lawyers**, *d.* historians)

(**c**) The AMA (American Medical Association) is an association of doctors;
the ABA (American Bar Association) is an association of lawyers.
General Information—Description

11. WOODHULL : PELOSI :: ALBRIGHT : (***a.* Day O'Connor**, *b.* Bush,
c. Sebelius, *d.* Ginsburg)

(**a**) Victoria Claflin Woodhull was the first woman to run for President;
Nancy Pelosi was the first female Speaker of the U.S. House of
Representatives; Madeleine Albright was the first woman to become U.S.
Secretary of State; Sandra Day O'Connor was the first woman justice
of the Supreme Court.
General Information—Description

12. MADISON : WAR OF 1812 :: (*a.* Reagan, ***b.* G. H. W. Bush**, *c.* Clinton,
d. G. W. Bush) : GULF WAR

(**b**) Madison was president during the War of 1812. G. H. W. Bush was
president during the Gulf War.
Humanities—Description

13. BULLET : (*a.* noose, *b.* head, *c.* force, ***d.* blade**) : GUN : GUILLOTINE

(**d**) A gun kills by a bullet; a guillotine kills by a blade.
General Information—Description

14. (***a.*** ·, *b.* ÷, *c.* **, *d.* undefined) : MULTIPLICATION :: + : ADDITION

(**a**) A raised dot (·) can be used to signify multiplication; a plus sign (+)
can be used to signify addition.
Mathematics—Description

15. PSYCHOLOGY : MIND :: PHYCOLOGY : (*a.* herbivores, *b.* carnivores, *c.* **algae**, *d.* cacti)

    (**c**) Psychology is the science of the mind; phycology is the science of algae.
    Natural Science—Description

16. (*a.* Third Estate, *b.* House, *c.* Parliament, *d.* **Commons**) : LOWER ::
    LORDS : UPPER

    (**d**) The House of Commons is the lower house, and the House of Lords
    the upper house, of the British Parliament.
    General Information—Description

17. BACTERIA : (*a.* bacteria, *b.* **bacterium**, *c.* bacterius, *d.* bacterion) ::
    MANY : ONE

    (**b**) One refers to many bacteria (plural) or one bacterium (singular).
    Vocabulary—Description

18. SCURVY : VITAMIN C :: KWASHIORKOR : (*a.* vitamin A,
    b. vitamin B_{12}, *c.* **protein**, *d.* niacin)

    (**c**) Scurvy is caused by a deficiency of vitamin C; kwashiorkor is caused by
    a deficiency of protein. Pellagra is caused by lack of niacin. One of the results of
    vitamin A deficiency is impaired vision. A lack of vitamin B_{12} causes macrocytic anemia
    and cognitive deficits like memory loss.
    Natural Science—Description

19. CONVERSE : CONTRAPOSITIVE :: (*a.* **B → A**, *b.* A → B, *c.* not B →
    A, *d.* not A → B) : (NOT B → NOT A)

    (**a**) The converse of $A \rightarrow B$ is $B \rightarrow A$; the contrapositive of $A \rightarrow B$ is (not B
    → not A).
    Humanities—Description

20. (*a.* New York, *b.* New Mexico, *c.* Missouri, *d.* **Michigan**) : LAKE ::
    MISSISSIPPI : RIVER

    (**d**) Lake Michigan and the Mississippi River are bodies of water.
    General Information—Completion

21. 0 PERCENT : (*a.* pressure, *b.* wind chill, *c.* THI, *d.* **humidity**) ::
    ABSOLUTE 0 : TEMPERATURE

    (**d**) 0 percent is the minimum possible humidity; absolute 0 is the
    minimum possible temperature.
    General Information—Description

22. OBTUSE : ACUTE :: (*a.* 0, ***b.* 100**, *c.* 180, *d.* 270) : 45

    (**b**) A 100° angle is obtuse; a 45° angle is acute.
    Mathematics—Description

23. AB : AWAY :: (***a.* a**, *b.* contra, *c.* ex, *d.* ad) : WITHOUT

    (**a**) The prefix *ab-* means "away"; the prefix *a-* means "without." The prefix *contra-* means "against." The prefix *ex-* means "excluding/without." The prefix *ad-* means "to/towards."
    Vocabulary—Similarity/Contrast

24. UNCLE : (*a.* paternal, ***b.* avuncular**, *c.* uncial, *d.* uncinate) :: BROTHER : FRATERNAL

    (**b**) Someone who is avuncular is like an uncle; someone who is fraternal is like a brother. Someone who is paternal is like a father; uncial means written in capital letters; uncinate means that a tip is bent like a hook.
    Vocabulary—Description

25. (*a.* women, *b.* marriage, *c.* falsehood, ***d.* enlightenment**) : MISOLOGY :: NOVELTY : MISONEISM

    (**d**) Misology is hatred of enlightenment; misoneism is hatred of novelty.
    Vocabulary—Description

26. LIE : (*a.* lie, ***b.* lay**, *c.* laid, *d.* lain) :: LAY : LAID

    (**b**) The past tense of *lie* is *lay* (or, in another meaning of *lie*, *lied*, but this is not an option); the past tense of *lay* is *laid*.
    General Information—Class

27. HELTER : SKELTER :: HIGGLEDY : (*a.* niggledy, ***b.* piggledy**, *c.* spiggledy, *d.* wiggledy)

    (**b**) *Helter-skelter* and *higgledy-piggledy* are synonyms.
    Vocabulary—Completion

28. SPOOL : LOOPS :: (*a.* water, ***b.* pools**, *c.* dinghy, *d.* tools) : SLOOP

    (**b**) *Spool* spelled backward is *loops*; *pools* spelled backward is *sloop*.
    Nonsemantic

29. RILL : (***a.* stream**, *b.* lake, *c.* ocean, *d.* lagoon) : NOVELLA : NOVEL

    (**a**) A rill is a small stream; a novella is a small novel.
    Vocabulary—Description

30. SONATA : SONATINA :: CONCERTO : (**a. concertino**, *b*. concertina, *c*. concert, *d*. concerto grosso)

(**a**) A sonatina is a small sonata; a concertino is a small concerto. A concerto grosso is a baroque composition in which a small group of solo instruments play with an orchestra.
Humanities—Description

31. NEW JERSEY : 8:00 :: OREGON : (**a. 5:00**, *b*. 6:00, *c*. 9:00, *d*. 10:00)

(**a**) When it is 8:00 in New Jersey, it is 5:00 in Oregon.
General Information—Description

32. LINCOLN : 1 :: JEFFERSON : (*a*. 3, **b. 5**, *c*. 10, *d*. 25)

(**b**) The head of Lincoln appears on a 1-cent piece; the head of Jefferson appears on a 5-cent piece. Franklin Roosevelt is featured on a 10-cent piece. The regular 25-cent coin features George Washington.
General Information—Description

33. PLINY THE ELDER : (*a*. Carthaginian, *b*. Athenian, *c*. Milanese, **d. Roman**) :: THUCYDIDES : GREEK

(**d**) Pliny the Elder was a Roman writer who wrote *Naturalis Historia*. Thucydides was a Greek historian who wrote *History of the Peloponnesian War*.
Humanities—Description

34. (*a*. Uruguay, *b*. Argentina, *c*. Paraguay, **d. Guatemala**) : CENTRAL :: BRAZIL : SOUTH

(**d**) Guatemala is in Central America, Brazil in South America. Argentina, Uruguay, and Paraguay are in South America.
General Information—Part/Whole

35. ETHER : GENERAL :: NOVOCAINE : (*a*. specific, *b*. particulate, **d. local**, *d*. toxic

(**c**) Ether is a general anesthetic; novocaine is a local anesthetic.
General Information—Description

36. D'ARTAGNAN : (*a*. Hugo, *b*. Mauriac, **c. Dumas**, *d*. Balzac) :: GATSBY : FITZGERALD

(**c**) D'Artagnan was a character created by Dumas in *The Three Musketeers*; Gatsby was a character created by Fitzgerald in *The Great Gatsby*. Francois Mauriac wrote *Le Desert de l'Amour*. Honore Balzac wrote *La Comedie Humaine*, which contains about 100 novels and plays that describe French life after the fall of Napoleon. Victor Hugo wrote *Les Miserables*.
Humanities—Description

37. ARMY : LAND :: (***a.* Marines**, *b.* Navy, *c.* CIA, *d.* Secret Service) : AMPHIBIOUS

(**a**) The Army is intended to engage primarily in land warfare; the Marines are intended to engage primarily in amphibious warfare. The Navy is intended to engage primarily in sea warfare. The CIA is the intelligence agency of the United States that collects information about foreign governments and persons. The Secret Service protects leaders of the United States and visiting leaders from other countries. It also safeguards the payment and financial systems of the United States.
General Information—Description

38. TWO : (*a.* hydrogen, *b.* uranium, *c.* americium, ***d.* deuterium**) :: THREE : TRITIUM

(**d**) Deuterium is an isotope of hydrogen with an atomic weight of 2; tritium is an isotope of hydrogen with an atomic weight of 3.
Natural Science—Description

39. YORK : N.Y. :: ORLEANS : (*a.* O.R., ***b.* La.**, *c.* Fr., *d.* Miss.)

(**b**) (New) York (the city) is in the state of New York (N.Y.): (New) Orleans is in the state of Louisiana (La.).
General Information—Part/Whole

40. (*a.* Copland, ***b.* Mendelssohn**, *c.* Shostakovich, *d.* Bach) : 19th :: MOZART : 18th

(**b**) Mendelssohn was a 19th century composer (1809–1847); Mozart was an 18th century composer (1756–1791). Copland (1900–1990) was a 20th century composer. Shostakovich (1906–1975) was a 20th century composer. J. S. Bach (1685–1750) is an 18th century composer.
Humanities—Completion

41. MENELAUS : (***a.* Agamemnon**, *b.* Priam, *c.* Achilles, *d.* Spartacus) :: HECTOR : PARIS

(**a**) Menelaus and Agamemnon were brothers, as were Hector and Paris. Priam was the youngest son of Laomedon and king of Troy during the Trojan War. Achilles was the greatest warrior of the Greeks in the Trojan War. Spartacus was a Roman slave who led an unsuccessful slave uprising (the Third Servile War).
Humanities—Class

42. MAJORITY : MINORITY :: (***a.* Bolshevik**, *b.* Maoist, *c.* Marxist, *d.* Trotskyite) : MENSHEVIK

    (**a**) In Revolutionary Russia, the Bolsheviks were the majority, or greater (*bolshe*), party, and the Mensheviks were the minority, or smaller, (*mensche*) party.
    Humanities—Description

43. FEIGN : FINE :: (*a.* right, *b.* writ, ***c.* rate**, *d.* rat) : WRITE

    (**c**) The pronounced vowel sounds are the same in *feign* and *rate*, and in *fine* and *write*.
    Nonsemantic

44. FATUOUS : (*a.* bright, *b.* prodigal, *c.* contemptuous, ***d.* foolish**) :: FASTIDIOUS : HARD TO PLEASE

    (**d**) *Fatuous* and *foolish* are synonyms, as are *fastidious* and *hard to please*.
    Vocabulary—Similarity/Contrast

45. (*a.* Ayer, ***b.* Peirce**, *c.* Santayana, *d.* Russell) : PRAGMATIST :: SARTRE : EXISTENTIALIST

    (**b**) Peirce was a major philosopher in the pragmatist movement; Sartre was a major philosopher in the existentialist movement. Ayer was a logical positivist; Santayana was an aphorist; Russell was one of the founders of analytic philosophy.
    Humanities—Description

46. ADDITIVE : (*a.* blue, *b.* red, ***c.* green**, *d.* white) :: SUBTRACTIVE : YELLOW

    (**c**) Green is an additive (but not a subtractive) primary color in light; yellow is a subtractive (but not an additive) primary color. The subtractive color model involves pigments with colors that add up to black. The additive color model involves light with colors that add up to white.
    General Information—Description

47. PROTON : NUCLEON :: MUON : (***a.* meson**, *b.* electron, *c.* pion, *d.* positron)

    (**a**) A proton is a nucleon; a muon is a meson (a fundamental particle responsible for the forces in the atomic nucleus).
    Natural Science—Class

48. BOARD : (*a.* fifteen, ***b.* checkers**, *c.* bridge, *d.* thirty-six) :: DECK : TWENTY-ONE

    (**b**) Checkers is played with a board; twenty-one is played with a deck.
    General Information—Description

49. C# : Db :: B# : (*a.* Cb, *b.* Bb, ***c.* C**, *d.* Db)

(**c**) C# and Db are played instrumentally as the same note, as are B# and C.
Humanities—Similarity/Contrast

50. SEVER : PERSEVERANCE :: CUT : (*a.* perseveration, *b.* perspective, *c.* pertinence, ***d.* persistence**)

(**d**) *Sever* and *cut* are synonyms, as are *perseverance* and *persistence*.
Vocabulary—Similarity/Contrast

51. FREUD : (*a.* Skinner, *b.* Allport, *c.* Murray, ***d.* Erikson**) :: KOHLBERG : PIAGET

(**d**) Freud, Erikson, Kohlberg, and Piaget were all prominent psychological theorists postulating stages of development. Burrhus F. Skinner was a psychologist who is known for his work on operant conditioning. Gordon Allport is considered one of the founding fathers of personality psychology. Charles Murray is a political scientist and well known for writing *The Bell Curve* (with Richard Herrnstein) about the role of IQ in American society.
Social Science—Class

52. (*a.* ellipsoid, ***b.* semicircle**, *c.* rhombus, *d.* angle) : PROTRACTOR :: RECTANGLE : RULER

(**b**) A protractor is usually in the shape of a semicircle. A ruler is usually in the shape of a rectangle.
Mathematics—Description

53. BIPOLARITY : MONOLOGUE :: (***a.* dicotyledon**, *b.* stamen, *c.* deciduous, *d.* pistil) : UNION

(**a**) *Bipolarity* and *dicotyledon* refer to two of something; *monologue* and *union* refer to one of something.
Vocabulary—Equality/Negation

54. (*a.* patent medicine, ***a.* adage**, *c.* theory, *d.* heretic) : APOTHEGM :: DEXTERITY : ADROITNESS

(**b**) *Adage* and *apothegm* are synonyms, as are *dexterity* and *adroitness*.
Vocabulary—Similarity/Contrast

55. FROM : TO :: (*a.* artery, *b.* ventricle, *c.* atrium, ***d.* carotid**) : JUGULAR

(**d**) The carotid is an artery carrying blood away from the heart; the jugular is a vein carrying blood to the heart.
Natural Science—Description

56. SOUSA : (*a.* waltzes, *b.* symphonies, **c. marches**, *d.* hymns) :: VERDI : OPERAS

    (**c**) Sousa (1854–1932) composed primarily marches; Verdi (1813–1901) composed primarily operas.
    Humanities—Description

57. INVOCATION : (**a. benediction**, *b.* recessional, *c.* prayer, *d.* vesper) :: START : FINISH

    (**a**) An invocation starts a religious service; a benediction finishes it.
    General Information—Description

58. SASKATCHEWAN : REGINA :: (*a.* Quebec, *b.* Alberta, **c. Ontario**, *d.* Manitoba) :: TORONTO

    (**c**) The capital of the Canadian province of Saskatchewan is Regina; the capital of Ontario is Toronto. Quebec City is the capital of Quebec. Edmonton is the capital of Alberta. Winnipeg is the capital of Manitoba.
    General Information—Description

59. (*a.* obvious, **b. latent**, *c.* proximate, *d.* apposite) : MANIFEST :: COVERT : OVERT

    (**b**) *Latent* and *manifest* are antonyms, as are *covert* and *overt*.
    Vocabulary—Similarity/Contrast

60. DIRGE : REQUIEM :: GRIEF : (*a.* thanksgiving, ***b.* mourning**, *c.* penitence, *d.* joy)

    (**b**) A dirge and a requiem both express grief and mourning.
    Vocabulary—Description

61. (*a.* metropolitan, *b.* synod, *c.* district, ***d.* diocese**) : BISHOP :: PARISH : PRIEST

    (**d**) A diocese is under the jurisdiction of a bishop; a parish is under the jurisdiction of a priest.
    General Information—Description

62. CONSONANT : VOWEL :: COMPOSITE : (**a. prime**, *b.* irrational, *c.* integer, *d.* zero)

    (**a**) All letters are either consonants or vowels; all numbers are either composite or prime.
    Mathematics—Class

63. IMPLODE : (*a.* explode, *b.* beseech, *c.* implicate, ***d.* burst inward**) ::
IMPLY : HINT AT

(**d**) To implode is to burst inward; to imply is to hint at.
Vocabulary—Similarity/Contrast

64. EARTH : SUN :: PLANET : (*a.* heavenly body, *b.* sol, *c.* **star**, *d.* nova)

(**c**) The earth is a planet; the sun is a star. A nova is a star that abruptly increases
its light output and later on fades back to its normal state.
General Information—Class

65. OCTOPUS : (*a.* six, ***b.* eight**, *c.* ten, *d.* twelve) :: PERSON : TWO

(**b**) An octopus has eight arms; a person has two arms.
General Information—Description

66. QUARTER : DOLLAR :: (***a.* season**, *b.* day, *c.* month, *d.* decade) : YEAR

(**a**) There are four quarters in a dollar and four seasons in a year.
General Information—Equality/Negation

67. CAPTAIN : (*a.* admiral, *b.* ensign, ***c.* commodore**, *d.* midshipman) ::
CORPORAL : SERGEANT

(**c**) In the Navy, a captain is immediately below a commodore in rank;
in the Army, a corporal is immediately below a sergeant in rank.
General Information—Description

68. DAVID : VAN DYCK :: FRENCH : (*a.* Italian, *b.* German, ***c.* Flemish**,
d. British)

(**c**) David was a French painter; Van Dyck was a Flemish painter (Flanders
is part of Belgium).
Humanities—Description

69. (*a.* poulet, ***b.* glacé**, *c.* citron, *d.* entrecote) : SWEET :: CAFÉ : BITTER

(**b**) Glacé (ice cream) is sweet; café (coffee) is bitter.
General Information—Description

70. WAIVE : WAVE :: (***a.* relinquish**, *b.* relegate, *c.* remand, *d.* redress) :
UNDULATE

(**a**) To waive is to relinquish; to wave is to undulate.
Vocabulary—Similarity/Contrast

71. WORK : (***a*. joule**, *b*. ohm, *c*. ampere, *d*. coulomb) :: POTENTIAL DIFFERENCE : VOLT

    (**a**) A joule is a unit of work; a volt is a measure of potential difference. Ohm is the unit of electrical resistance. Ampere is a unit of electric current. Coulomb is the unit of electric charge.
    Natural Science—Description

72. PHILOLOGY : LANGUAGES :: MYCOLOGY : (*a*. flowering plants, *b*. ferns, *c*. weeds, ***d*. fungi**)

    (**d**) Philology is the study of languages; mycology is the study of fungi.
    Natural Science—Description

73. DEPENDENT : INDEPENDENT :: (*a*. autochthonous, *b*. canonical, ***c*. anaclitic**, *d*. irrecusable) : SELF-RELIANT

    (**c**) *Dependent* and *anaclitic* are synonyms, as are *independent* and *self-reliant*.
    Vocabulary—Similarity/Contrast

74. CX : (*a*. CXV, ***b*. CL**, *c*. CLX, *d*. CC) :: LV : LXXV

    (**b**) The terms of the analogy are Roman numerals expressing the ratio 110 : 150 :: 55 : 75. In Roman numerals, I = 1, V = 5, X = 10, L = 50, C = 100, D = 500, M = 1,000.
    Mathematics—Equality/Negation

75. CAMEL : RHINOCEROS :: HUMP : (*a*. armor, *b*. snout, ***c*. horn**, *d*. hide)

    (**c**) A camel may have one hump or two; a rhinoceros may have one horn or two.
    General Information—Description

76. ONTOLOGY : (***a*. being**, *b*. metaphysics, *c*. growth, *d*. knowledge) :: DEONTOLOGY : ETHICS

    (**a**) Ontology is the study of being; deontology is the study of ethics.
    Humanities—Description

77. (*a*. leukocytes, *b*. platelets, *c*. hormones, ***d*. erythrocytes**) : ANEMIA :: INSULIN : DIABETES

    (**d**) Anemia is characterized by a shortage of erythrocytes (red blood cells), diabetes by a shortage of insulin.
    Natural Science—Description

78. CALVIN : COOLIDGE :: (*a*. Alexander, **b. Franklin**, *c*. William, *d*. Robert) : PIERCE

    (**b**) Calvin Coolidge and Franklin Pierce were both presidents of the United States.
    General Information—Completion

79. PONTIUS PILATE : JESUS :: CREON : (*a*. Orestes, *b*. Oedipus, **c. Antigone**, *d*. Electra)

    (**c**) Pontius Pilate sentenced Jesus to death; Creon sentenced Antigone to death. Orestes and Electra were the son and daughter, respectively, of Agamemnon. Oedipus was a king of Thebes in Greek mythology who killed his father and married his mother.
    Humanities—Description

80. (**a. bellicose**, *b*. periphrastic, *c*. altruistic, *d*. nihilistic) : AGGRESSION :: IRENIC : PEACE

    (**a**) Someone who is bellicose fosters aggression; someone who is irenic fosters peace.
    Vocabulary—Description

81. FIRST : LAST :: GENESIS : (*a*. Exodus, **b. Deuteronomy**, *c*. Leviticus, *d*. Numbers)

    (**b**) Genesis is the first book of the Torah; Deuteronomy, the last book.
    Humanities—Description

82. πr^2 : $2\pi r$ :: AREA : (*a*. diameter, **b. circumference**, *c*. perimeter, *d*. volume)

    (**b**) πr^2 is the formula for the area of a circle; $2\pi r$ is the formula for the circumference of a circle.
    Mathematics—Equality/Negation

83. BUCKINGHAM PALACE : XANADU :: ELIZABETH II : (*a*. Genghis Khan, *b*. Charles V, **c. Citizen Kane**, *d*. Donald Trump)

    (**c**) Buckingham Palace is the abode of Elizabeth II; Xanadu was the abode of Citizen Kane (a fictitious character fashioned after William Randolph Hearst).
    General Information—Description

84. MONOGYNY : (*a*. life, *b*. religion, *c*. child, **d. wife**) :: MONOTHEISM : GOD

    (**d**) Monogyny is belief in one wife; monotheism is belief in one God.
    Vocabulary—Description

85. ESPRESSO : BLACK :: ORANGE PEKOE : (*a.* green, *b.* white, **c. black**, *d.* red)

    (**c**) Espresso (coffee) is black in color; orange pekoe (tea) is also black in color.
    General Information—Description

86. DIANA : (**a. Artemis**, *b.* Minerva, *c.* Aphrodite, *d.* Hera) :: JUPITER : ZEUS

    (**a**) Diana and Artemis are the Roman and Greek names, respectively, for the goddess of the moon and of hunting; Jupiter and Zeus are the Roman and Greek names, respectively, for the king of the gods. Minerva was the Roman goddess of warriors, poetry, and medicine. Her Greek name was Athena. Aphrodite was the Greek goddess of love and beauty. Hera was the Greek goddess of women and marriage.
    Humanities—Similarity/Contrast

87. (*a.* B♭ major, **b. E♭ major**, *c.* F major, *d.* A major) : C MINOR :: G MAJOR : E MINOR

    (**b**) The keys of E♭ major and C minor both have three flats; the keys of G major and E minor both have one sharp.
    Humanities—Similarity/Contrast

88. MAN : NAME :: (**a. rig**, *b.* appellation, *c.* maiden, *d.* woman) : GIRL

    (**a**) The letters in *man* form the first three letters in *name* reversed; the letters in *rig* form the first three letters in *girl* reversed.
    Nonsemantic

89. MANON LESCAUT : (*a.* wise, *b.* arrogant, **c. promiscuous**, *d.* wicked) :: TOM SAWYER : ADVENTUROUS

    (**c**) Manon Lescaut is a promiscuous literary character (by Francois Prévost); Tom Sawyer is an adventurous one (by Mark Twain).
    Humanities—Description

90. (*a.* Bull Moose, *b.* Whig, **c. Socialist**, *d.* Know-Nothing) : DEBS :: DEMOCRAT : STEVENSON

    (**c**) Eugene Debs was an unsuccessful Socialist candidate for president; Adlai Stevenson was an unsuccessful Democratic candidate for president.
    Humanities—Description

91. FIRST : CLERGY :: FOURTH : (*a.* nobles, *b.* commoners, *c.* children, **_d._ journalists**)

    (**d**) The clergy formed the First Estate; journalists form what is sometimes called the Fourth Estate.
    Vocabulary—Description

92. AMETHYST : GARNET :: PURPLE : (**_a._ red**, *b.* green, *c.* transparent, *d.* blue)

    (**a**) An amethyst is purple; a garnet is red.
    General Information—Description

93. (**_a._ loquacious**, *b.* refractory, *c.* ostentatious, *d.* timid) : GARRULOUS :: AUDACIOUS : BOLD

    (**a**) *Loquacious* and *garrulous* have similar meanings, as do *audacious* and *bold*.
    Vocabulary—Similarity/Contrast

94. FOUR : APRIL FOOL'S DAY :: (*a.* one, *b.* two, **_c._ five**, *d.* ten) : MAY DAY

    (**c**) April Fool's Day is the first day of the fourth month; May Day is the first day of the fifth month.
    General Information—Description

95. STEEPLE : CHURCH :: (**_a._ minaret**, *b.* muezzin, *c.* imam, *d.* arch) : MOSQUE

    (**a**) A steeple protrudes from the top of a church; a minaret protrudes from the top of a mosque.
    General Information—Description

96. VANILLA : (*a.* bean, *b.* Sussex, **_c._ hasty**, *d.* Brazil) :: RICE : YORKSHIRE

    (**c**) Four types of pudding are vanilla pudding, hasty pudding, rice pudding, and Yorkshire pudding.
    General Information—Class

97. (*a.* Saint-Saëns, **_b._ Strindberg**, *c.* Bernstein, *d.* Rubinstein) : PLAYS :: FROST : POEMS

    (**b**) Strindberg wrote plays; Frost wrote poems. Leonard Bernstein was a conductor. Arthur Rubinstein was a pianist.
    Humanities—Description

98. THERMO : HEAT :: ISO : (*a.* cold, *b.* pressure, *c.* humidity, **_d._ same**)

    (**d**) *Thermo-* is a prefix meaning *heat*; *iso-* is a prefix meaning *same*.
    Vocabulary—Similarity/Contrast

99. (*a.* Scotch, *b.* vermouth, *c.* **gin**, *d.* bourbon) : TOM COLLINS :: VODKA : BLOODY MARY

(**c**) A Tom Collins is a mixed drink containing gin; a Bloody Mary is a mixed drink containing vodka.
General Information—Description

100. BELLEEK : (*a.* Scotland, *b.* **Ireland**, *c.* Holland, *d.* Belgium) :: LIMOGES : FRANCE

(**b**) Belleek is a town in Ireland (and also a generic name for a type of porcelain). Limoges is a town in France (and also a generic name for a type of china).
General Information—Description

101. AMPERE : (*a.* **current**, *b.* magnetism, *c.* speed, *d.* gravity) :: WATT : POWER

(**a**) An ampere is a unit used to measure current just as a watt is a unit used to measure power.
Natural Science—Description

102. BAIKAL : RUSSIA :: (*a.* Michigan, *b.* **Superior**, *c.* Ontario, *d.* Placid) : UNITED STATES

(**b**) Lake Baikal is the largest lake in Russia just as Lake Superior is the largest lake in the United States.
General Information—Description

103. (*a.* Lady's Man, *b.* Black Beauty, *c.* **Secretariat**, *d.* Fortune's Fool) : MAN O' WAR :: SEABISCUIT : WAR ADMIRAL

(**c**) Secretariat, Man o' War, Seabiscuit, and War Admiral are all famous race horses.
General Information—Class

104. GAVRILO PRINCIP : ARCHDUKE FERDINAND :: (*a.* Robert E. Lee, *b.* Lee Harvey Oswald, *c.* John Hinckley, *d.* **John Wilkes Booth**) : PRESIDENT LINCOLN

(**d**) Gavrilo Princip assassinated Archduke Ferdinand in 1914 just as John Wilkes Booth assassinated President Lincoln (1865).
General Information—Description

105. KILOGRAM : POUND :: 1 : (*a.* **2.2**, *b.* 5, *c.* 0.2, *d.* 7.3)

(**a**) There are 2.2 pounds in 1 kilogram.
General Information—Equality/Negation

106. ROSEMARY : (***a.* oregano**, *b.* cumin, *c.* nutmeg, *d.* cinnamon) :: BASIL : SAGE

(**a**) Rosemary, oregano, basil, and sage are all leafy herbs used to season food.
General Information—Class

107. COBBLER : SHOES :: (*a.* tanner, *b.* smith, ***c.* cooper**, *d.* miller) : BARRELS

(**c**) The 18th century occupations cobbler and cooper worked on shoes and barrels respectively.
General Information—Description

108. EXPECTORATE : (*a.* bite, ***b.* spit**, *c.* deliver, *d.* swallow) :: MASTICATE : CHEW

(**b**) To expectorate is to spit just as to masticate is to chew.
Vocabulary—Similarity/Contrast

109. (*a.* net, *b.* hat trick, *c.* goalie, ***d.* puck**) : ICE HOCKEY :: SHUTTLECOCK : BADMINTON

(**d**) In the sports of ice hockey and badminton, the objects whose possession is passed between players and teams are the puck and shuttlecock respectively.
General Information—Description

110. ARMSTRONG : TRUMPET :: COLTRANE : (*a.* piano, ***b.* saxophone**, *c.* clarinet, *d.* trombone)

(**b**) Louis Armstrong and John Coltrane are jazz musicians who played the trumpet and saxophone respectively.
Humanities—Description

111. MOHAMMED : JESUS :: (*a.* Judea, *b.* Constantinople, ***c.* Mecca**, *d.* Jerusalem) : BETHLEHEM

(**c**) Religious tradition holds that Mohammed was born in Mecca and that Jesus was born in Bethlehem.
Humanities—Description

112. RHOMBUS : HEXAGON :: 4 : (*a.* 8, *b.* 7, ***c.* 6**, *d.* 5)

(**c**) A rhombus has four sides just as a hexagon has six sides.
Mathematics—Description

113. RECORD PLAYER : (*a. loudest*, *b.* loud, *c.* quiet, *d.* quieter) ::
SUPERANNUATED : SUPERLATIVE

    (**a**) The record player, used for playing music, is superannuated, or obsolete.
    The word loudest is superlative, the most extreme degree of the adjective.
    Vocabulary—Class

114. (*a.* feet, *b.* obedience, *c.* thought, *d. memory*) : ELEPHANT ::
STRENGTH : ANT

    (**d**) Elephants are known for their powers of memory just as ants are known
    for their feats of strength.
    General Information—Description

115. DIAMOND : SAPPHIRE :: (*a. Hope*, *b.* Diana's, *c.* Indian, *d.* Pharoah's) :
LOGAN

    (**a**) The Hope Diamond and Logan Sapphire are famous examples of
    these gemstones.
    General Information—Description

116. HEAVEN : ST. PETER :: HADES : (*a.* Lucifer, *b.* Scylla, *c.* Charybdis,
d. Cerberus)

    (**d**) Various traditions hold that St. Peter guards the gates to heaven just as
    Cerberus, the three-headed dog, guards the gates to Hades. Lucifer is the devil.
    In Greek mythology, Scylla and Charybdis were two monsters that lived on either side of
    a very narrow river. When sailors wanted to pass by, they got into reach of one monster
    when trying to avoid the other.
    Humanities—Description

117. r-p-o-p-h-e-s-s-a-g-r : JABBERWOCKY :: CUMMINGS : (*a.* Milne,
b. Cleary, *c. Carroll*, *d.* Eliot)

    (**c**) e. e. cummings and Lewis Carroll wrote the somewhat nonsensical
    poems *r-p-o-p-h-e-s-s-a-g-r* and *Jabberwocky* respectively.
    Humanities—Description

118. X : (*a.* w, *b. y*, *c.* u, *d.* a) :: VERTICAL : HORIZONTAL

    (**b**) On two-dimensional graphs, the x-axis is vertical and the y-axis is
    horizontal.
    Mathematics—Description

119. (*a.* nostalgia, *b.* kindness, *c.* loyalty, ***d.* naiveté**) :: POLLYANNA :: DOUBT : THOMAS

    (**d**) To call someone Pollyanna calls attention to his/her naiveté, and to call someone Thomas calls attention to his/her doubt. These allusions are literary ones.
    General Information—Similarity/Contrast

120. MAASAI : EAST AFRICA :: LAPP : (*a.* Australia, *b.* Middle East, *c.* South Asia, ***d.* Scandinavia**)

    (**d**) The Maasai people are native to East Africa just as the Lapp people are native to Scandinavia.
    General Information—Description

Item Classification

PRACTICE TEST 10

Item Classification Chart

CONTENT	RELATIONSHIP						
	Similarity/ Contrast	Description	Class	Completion	Part/ Whole	Equality/ Negation	Nonsemantic
Vocabulary	5, 23, 44, 50, 54, 59, 63, 70, 73, 93, 98, 108	3, 9, 17, 24, 25, 29, 60, 80, 84, 91	113	27		53	
General Information	119	1, 2, 8, 10, 11, 13, 16, 21, 31, 32, 35, 37, 46, 48, 57, 58, 61, 65, 67, 69, 75, 83, 85, 92, 94, 95, 99, 100, 102, 104, 107, 109, 114, 115, 120	26, 64, 96, 103, 106	20, 78	34, 39	66, 105	
Humanities	49, 86, 87	7, 12, 19, 30, 33, 36, 42, 45, 56, 68, 76, 79, 81, 89, 90, 97, 110, 111, 116, 117	41	40			
Social Science			51				
Natural Science		6, 15, 18, 38, 55, 71, 72, 77, 101	47				
Mathematics		14, 22, 52, 112, 118	62			4, 74, 82	
Nonsemantic							28, 43, 88